CROSSCURRENTS

INTERNATIONAL

RELATIONS

FOURTH EDITION

MARK CHARLTON
Trinity Western University

THOMSON

NELSON

Australia   Canada   Mexico   Singapore   Spain   United Kingdom   United Sta

THOMSON
∗
NELSON ™

Crosscurrents: International Relations

Fourth Edition

by Mark Charlton

Associate Vice-President, Editorial Director:
Evelyn Veitch

Publisher:
Chris Carson

Senior Marketing Manager:
Murray Moman

Developmental Editor:
Katherine Goodes

Permissions Coordinator:
Nicola Winstanley

Production Editors:
Wendy Yano
Julie van Veen

Copy Editor:
Eliza Marciniak

Proofreader:
Shannon McDunnough

Senior Production Coordinator:
Helen Locsin

Creative Director:
Angela Cluer

Interior Design Modifications:
Katherine Strain

Cover Design:
Angela Cluer

Cover Image:
Andersen/Carsten A. Scanpix

Compositor:
Integra

Printer:
Thomson/West

COPYRIGHT © 2005 by Nelson, a division of Thomson Canada Limited.

3 4 07 06

For more information contact Nelson, 1120 Birchmount Road, Toronto, Ontario, M1K 5G4. Or you can visit our Internet site at http://www.nelson.com

ALL RIGHTS RESERVED. No part of this work covered by the copyright herein may be reproduced, transcribed, or used in any form or by any means—graphic, electronic, or mechanical, including photocopying, recording,

ISBN-13: 978-0-17-641502-0
ISBN-10: 0-17-641502-5

taping, Web distribution, or information storage and retrieval systems—without the written permission of the publisher.

For permission to use material from this text or product, submit a request online at www.thomsonrights.com

Every effort has been made to trace ownership of all copyrighted material and to secure permission from copyright holders. In the event of any question arising as to the use of any material, we will be pleased to make the necessary corrections in future printings.

Library and Archives Canada Cataloguing in Publication

Crosscurrents: international relations/edited by Mark Charlton. — 4th ed.

Includes bibliographical references.
ISBN 0-17-641502-5

1. International relations.
I. Charlton, Mark William, 1948–

D860.C76 2004 327
C2004-904787-6

Contents

Contents

Contributors

Lloyd Axworthy is a senior associate of the Liu Institute for Global Issues at the University of British Columbia and a former minister of foreign affairs of Canada.

William W. Bain is a lecturer in international relations theory at the University of Wales at Aberystwyth.

Frank Biermann is the leader of the Global Governance Project at the Potsdam Institute for Climate Impact Research.

Jutta Brunnee is a professor at the Faculty of Law, University of Toronto.

George W. Bush is the 43rd President of the United States.

Douglas Cassel is the director of the Center for International Human Rights at Northwestern University School of Law in Chicago.

Lucille Charlton is an instructor at Kwantlen University College.

Michel Chossudovsky is a professor of economics and international development at the University of Ottawa.

Thomas J. Courchene is a professor of economic and financial policy at Queen's University and a senior scholar at the Institute for Research on Public Policy in Montreal.

Andrew Coyne is a journalist who writes for the *National Post*.

Neta C. Crawford is a professor of political science at the University of Massachusetts at Amherst.

G.E. Dirks recently retired as a professor of political science at Brock University.

Richard Falk is a visiting professor of global studies at the University of California in Santa Barbara and professor emeritus of international law at Princeton University.

Denise Froning is a policy analyst with the Center for International Trade and Economics at the Heritage Foundation in Washington, D.C.

Francis Fukuyama is a consultant with the Rand Corporation.

Stephen Gill is a professor of political science at York University.

Kenneth Green is a chief scientist at the Fraser Institute in Vancouver.

Romilly Greenhill in an economist with Jubilee Research.

Frank P. Harvey is the director of the Centre for Foreign Policy Studies at Dalhousie University.

Samuel Huntington is a professor of political science at Harvard University.

Andrew Jackson is a senior economist with the Canadian Labour Association.

Rebecca Johnson is a research fellow at the Brookings Institution.

Robert Kagan is a senior associate at the Carnegie Endowment for International Peace.

Désirée McGraw is a consultant in international negotiations and communications.

Steven Meyer is a professor of political science at the Industrial College of the Armed Forces at the National Defense University in Washington, D.C.

Adil Najam teaches international environmental policy at the Fletcher School of Law and Diplomacy at Tufts University.

Joanna R. Quinn is a professor of political science at the University of Western Ontario.

Ernie Regehr is the executive director for Project Ploughshares.

Douglas Alan Ross is a professor of political science at Simon Fraser University.

Alfred P. Rubin is a professor of international law at the Fletcher School of Law and Diplomacy at Tufts University.

Gautam Sen is a lecturer in the Department of International Relations at the London School of Economics and Political Science.

Jan Aart Scholte is a professor of politics and international studies at the University of Warwick.

Susan Strange, until her death in 1998, was a professor of international political economics at the University of Warwick.

J. Ann Tickner teaches in the School of International Relations at the University of Southern California.

Richard Ashby Wilson is the director of the Human Rights Institute at the University of Connecticut.

David Wingfield is a lawyer with the Toronto firm Weir Foulds.

Martin Wolf is an associate editor and chief economics commentator at the *Financial Times*.

Micah Zenko is a research associate with the Belfer Center for Science and International Affairs.

Introduction

When the first edition of *Crosscurrents: International Relations* was published in 1993, the introduction began with the following words from Charles Dickens: "It was the best of times, it was the worst of times." Dickens wrote those words in response to the tumult of revolutionary France in the eighteenth century. His words seem even more apt for the current situation than when I cited them eleven years ago. For many, the past decade has been one of growing prosperity, expanding human rights, and progress toward democratization. The emergence of a global civil society and the "democratization" of foreign policy have enabled new actors on the global scene to achieve successes in promoting issues – such as a global ban on landmines and international debt relief – that were unheard of decades ago.

At the same time, others experienced the 1990s as a period of increased impoverishment and alienation. Resistance to the forces of globalization intensified and took more violent forms. Genocidal warfare in Rwanda and the former Yugoslavia challenged the ability of the international community to respond. Our entry into the new millennium has also brought new hopes and disappointments. As part of its Millennium Development Goals, the United Nations has planned to cut the amount of global poverty and hunger in half by the year 2015. In its 2004 annual review, the World Bank claimed that we are well on our way to meeting these targets. At the same time, the attacks on the United States on September 11, 2001, and the subsequent military interventions in Afghanistan and Iraq have heightened international tensions and fears. The conflicts and hatreds in the Middle East are more entrenched than ever. Terrorist attacks in countries that had not experienced them before have given new credence to talk of a "new world disorder." Indeed, "the best of times, the worst of times" continues to be an apt description of our entry into the new millennium.

As we reach the halfway point in the first decade of a new century, we continue to be faced with a number of complex questions: Will American military predominance contribute to a more stable and peaceful world, or will it trigger a backlash that leads to greater conflict and instability? Will cultural, religious, and ethnic differences be the major fault lines for future international conflicts? Do the forces associated with globalization threaten to undermine a more equitable distribution of resources and progress toward human rights? Have old institutions such as the NATO alliance become irrelevant in a new age of global terrorism? Will new institutions such as the International Criminal Court provide the basis for building a more stable global society? Are new forms of international governance needed to address issues of international debt, migration, and the environment?

THE DEBATE FORMAT

In preparing the fourth edition of *Crosscurrents: International Relations*, it is my hope that students will be challenged to wrestle with many of these questions. Students enrolling in introductory international relations courses generally do so in the hopes of gaining a better understanding of contemporary world issues and events. In contrast, many international relations texts focus on structures, abstract concepts, and theories that, while vital to the discipline, when taken alone fail to address students' interest in current world developments. The debate format in the *Crosscurrents* series, I believe, provides a structured way of relating topical information about current affairs to the broader concepts and theories of the discipline. By evaluating contending arguments concerning various global issues, students will be encouraged to analyze for themselves the relevance of different theories and concepts for explaining contemporary international developments.

While the debate format has its advantages, it sometimes limits the choice of readings. Thus, some of the more seminal pieces on particular topics were not included because they were not suitable to the debate format, or adequate companion pieces could not be found for them. In these cases, I have added them to the suggested reading list in the postscripts.

USAGE IN THE CLASSROOM

Crosscurrents: International Relations is designed as a flexible pedagogical tool that can be incorporated into courses in several ways.

i. Perhaps the most effective use of *Crosscurrents: International Relations* is to utilize the readings as a means of organizing weekly discussion sessions in a debate format. On each topic, two students may be asked to argue the case for the opposing sides, and these arguments could be followed by a group discussion. This format requires students to adopt a particular point of view and defend that position. Because the necessary background material is provided in the readings, this format is very easily adapted to large courses in which teaching assistants are responsible for weekly tutorial sessions.

ii. Some may wish to assign the chapters simply as supplementary readings reinforcing material covered in the lectures, and to use them as points of illustration in classroom lectures or discussions. In this way, the text can be used as a more traditional course reader, with the instructor having the option of assigning only one of the readings under each topic.

iii. Others may wish to use the readings as a point of departure for essay assignments in the course. In some cases, the readings and the postscript, with its suggestion of further readings, could simply serve as a starting point for researching the topic under discussion. In other cases, the instructor might want to encourage students to develop their critical skills by having them write an assessment of the arguments and evidence presented by the writers in a particular debate. Alternatively, students could select one side of the debate and write a persuasive essay developing their own arguments in favour of that point of view. I have included, as an appendix, instructions on writing an argumentative essay that should serve as a useful guide to students.

OTHER FEATURES

The availability of Internet resources and electronic journals has significantly expanded the range of materials at the disposal of students. To enhance the students' ability to find additional resources for both their participation in class discussions and for writing papers, I provide two useful features in addition to the list of suggested readings:

- Web resources: At the end of each postscript, I provide an annotated list of suggested website resources. The list is also available on the Thomson Nelson website for this book, at www.crosscurrents.nelson.com, where students can connect directly to the recommended sites. Instructors may also wish to have their students purchase Grant Heckman, *Nelson Guide to Web Research 2005–2006* (Scarborough: Thomson Nelson, 2005). This manual not only provides useful tips on conducting web research, but also includes information on citing web resources in both MLA and APA formats.

- InfoTrac®: Students purchasing this edition of *Crosscurrents: International Relations* will receive a free four-month subscription to InfoTrac® College Edition. This is an online library containing full-text articles from a large number of scholarly journals and popular news magazines. In each postscript, I have suggested useful keywords that students may wish to use when doing research. A separate *User Guide for Instructors* is available from Nelson.

ACKNOWLEDGMENTS

I would like to express appreciation to the reviewers who provided many valuable suggestions and comments: Aurélie Dépelteau-Lacassagne, Algoma University College; Leonard Friesen, Wilfrid Laurier University; Malcolm Grieve, Acadia University; and David Winchester, Capilano College. Appreciation is also expressed to the authors and publishers who have given permission to include their work in this volume. At Nelson, I would like to acknowledge the excellent and patient support of Chris Carson, Katherine Goodes, and other members of the staff. Finally, a word of thanks to Lucille, Daniel, and David for the sacrifices that they have made while I was completing this project.

Mark Charlton
Trinity Western University
Langley, B.C.

About the Editor

Mark Charlton is a professor of political science at Trinity Western University. He has written *The Making of Canadian Food Aid Policy* (1992) and has co-edited, with Paul Barker, *Crosscurrents: Contemporary Political Issues*, 4th edition (2002). He has also published a number of articles in *International Journal*, *Études Internationales*, and *The Canadian Journal of Development Studies*.

About the Editor

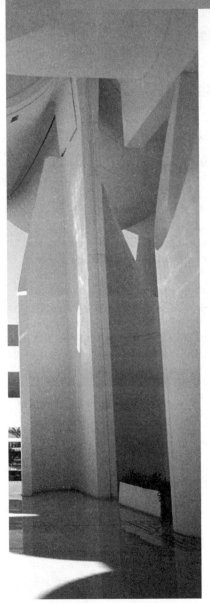

PART ONE

UNDERSTANDING OUR CHANGING WORLD

Will American hegemony produce
a better world for everyone?

Is globalization undermining the power
of the nation-state?

Is the world fragmenting into
antagonistic cultures?

Will American Hegemony Produce a Better World for Everyone?

✔ **YES**
ROBERT KAGAN, "The Benevolent Empire," *Foreign Policy* 111 (Summer 1998): 24–35.

✘ **NO**
RICHARD FALK, "Will the Empire Be Fascist?" The Transnational Foundation for Peace and Future Research, online publications at www.transnational.org (March 2003)

Shortly after the collapse of the Soviet Union and the end of the Cold War, international relations analysts, especially in the United States, sought to predict the changing global order. For the previous forty-five years, international politics had been defined by the ideological struggle between the two major superpowers, the United States and the Soviet Union.

In looking at what would replace the bipolar structure of the Cold War era, analysts presented quite different visions of the future. John Mueller predicted that war between the major powers was becoming obsolete and that war as an "institution" would disappear in much the same way that duelling and slavery had in the past. Francis Fukuyama suggested that the collapse of Soviet communism signalled the triumph of liberal democratic capitalist states. Given that democratic states rarely, if ever, go to war with each other, Fukuyama optimistically predicted that history, in the sense of being a record of conflict and ideological struggle, had come to an end. Thus, he predicted that the global acceptance of democratic governments and market economics would lead to an increasingly peaceful and prosperous era.

Not everyone was so optimistic. In contrast, Samuel Huntington described a world of increasingly hostile, religiously defined civilizations. Instead of a more peaceful, stable world, Huntington foresaw a growing "clash of civilizations," particularly along the geographic fault lines that divided these cultural groupings. Benjamin Barber, in his bestselling book *MacWorld vs. Jihad*, talked about the paradoxical nature of the spread of globalization. On the one hand, globalization is leading to an increasingly homogenous and integrated world. On the other, religious and ethnic fundamentalism is on the rise as a backlash to the forces of globalization. Both trends, Barber noted, pose a threat to the future of democracy in the world.

Other scholars focused on the implications of the passing of the Cold War bipolar structure of power. John Mearsheimer argued that the nuclear standoff between the two superpowers had actually played a positive role in maintaining order and stability in the international system. In an article in the *Atlantic Monthly* (August 1990) entitled "Why We Will Soon Miss the Cold War," Mearsheimer warned that a shift to a multipolar system could increasingly lead to conflict and uncertainty. Charles Krauthammer noted that we were entering a transitional period between a bipolar and a multipolar system. Believing that the conditions were not yet ripe for the emergence of a nineteenth-century – type balance-of-power multipolar system, he argued that a strong hegemonic power was needed to maintain international order and stability — to play the role of a "global cop" during this "unipolar moment." He fretted that the tendency of the American public to drift toward isolationist attitudes would lead the American government to retreat from a stronger role in international affairs.

In the decade since these authors made their prognostications, two developments have become significant. First, it has become clear that the "unipolar" era is unlikely to be a short-lived transitional period. If anything, American dominance in military, economic, and cultural terms has become increasingly pronounced. Second, the attacks of September 11, 2001, and the subsequent declaration of an ongoing war against terrorism have ensured that the Americans can no longer see isolationism as an option. The increasing sense of insecurity and vulnerability has reinforced the determination of the American government to maintain and even expand its current military predominance.

Thus, the image of the international system that has come to monopolize discussion is of a world dominated by a single hegemonic power — an American empire. For Americans, discussion of "empire" has not come easily. Throughout American history, the notion of empire has had largely negative connotations. The American War of Independence was seen as a struggle against the British Empire. American presidents had consistently tried to avoid entanglement in conflicts fought between competing European empires. It is not surprising that when a reporter used the term in reference to American foreign policy, Donald Rumsfeld, the American secretary of defense, replied testily, "We don't do empire."

Nevertheless, the word "empire" has progressively entered debates over the nature of the present international system. Mainstream academic journals and think tanks in the United States have suggested that it is now time to come to terms with the reality of the "new American Empire." While many critics continue to use the term with derision, a growing number of intellectuals in the United States have embraced it, suggesting that the new era of American hegemony will in fact bestow many benefits on the world. These intellectuals have sought to reassure the world that there is little to fear from American hegemony. What characterizes the American empire and makes it different from all previous empires is its "exceptional nature." Unlike previous empires, the United States is committed to democracy, human rights, and economic freedom. If there is any danger, it is that the United States will not live up to its responsibilities as an "imperial power." In his provocative book, *Empire Lite*, Michael Ignatieff, a Canadian, worries that while the United States has intervened abroad to promote democracy and human rights, it will not have the strength of will to stay the course for the long haul.

Robert Kagan represents the group of intellectuals who see the United States as a "benevolent empire." Kagan's writings, including his book *Of Paradise and Power: America and Europe in the New World Order* (Atlantic Books, 2003), have had a significant influence on the policymakers in the Bush administration. In the first reading included here, Kagan expresses skepticism regarding the hope that a more multipolar international system would provide security and prosperity for the world. Instead, he argues that only a strong American empire will ensure that not only the United States but also the rest of the world is prosperous and safe.

Needless to say, not everyone is as welcoming of the notion of American empire. For many, the term still remains synonymous with exploitation and domination. In the second article, Richard Falk, a specialist in international law, sees the American empire as much more malevolent.

✔ YES
The Benevolent Empire
ROBERT KAGAN

Not so long ago, when the Monica Lewinsky scandal first broke in the global media, an involuntary and therefore unusually revealing gasp of concern could be heard in the capitals of many of the world's most prominent nations. Ever so briefly, prime ministers and pundits watched to see if the drive wheel of the international economic, security, and political systems was about to misalign or lose its power, with all that this breakdown would imply for the rest of the world. Would the Middle East peace process stall? Would Asia's financial crisis spiral out of control? Would the Korean peninsula become unsettled? Would pressing issues of European security go unresolved? "In all the world's trouble spots," the *Times* of London noted, leaders were "calculating what will happen when Washington's gaze is distracted."

Temporarily interrupting their steady grumbling about American arrogance and hegemonic pretensions, Asian, European, and Middle Eastern editorial pages paused to contemplate the consequences of a crippled American presidency. The liberal German newspaper *Frankfurter Rundschau*, which a few months earlier had been accusing Americans of arrogant zealotry and a "camouflaged neocolonialism," suddenly fretted that the "problems in the Middle East, in the Balkans or in Asia" will not be solved "without U.S. assistance and a president who enjoys respect" and demanded that, in the interests of the entire world, the president's accusers quickly produce the goods or shut up. In Hong Kong, the *South China Morning Post* warned that the "humbling" of an American president had "implications of great gravity" for international affairs; in Saudi Arabia, the *Arab News* declared that this was "not the time that America or the world needs an inward-looking or wounded president. It needs one unencumbered by private concerns who can make tough decisions."

The irony of these pleas for vigorous American leadership did not escape notice, even in Paris, the intellectual and spiritual capital of antihegemony and "multipolarity." As one pundit (Jacques Amalric) noted wickedly in the left-leaning *Liberation*, "Those who accused the United States of being overbearing are today praying for a quick end to the storm." Indeed, they were and with good reason. As Aldo Rizzo observed, part in lament and part in tribute, in Italy's powerful *La Stampa*: "It is in times like these that we feel the absence of a power, certainly not [an] alternative, but at least complementary, to America, something which Europe could be. Could be, but is not. Therefore, good luck to Clinton and, most of all, to America."

This brief moment of international concern passed, of course, as did the flash of candor about the true state of world affairs and America's essential role in preserving a semblance of global order. The president appeared to regain his balance, the drivewheel kept spinning, and in the world's great capitals talk resumed of American arrogance and bullying and the need for a more genuinely multipolar system to manage international affairs. But the almost universally expressed fear of a weakened U.S. presidency provides a useful antidote to the pervasive hand-wringing, in Washington as well as in foreign capitals, over the "problem" of American hegemony. There is much less to this problem than meets the eye.

The commingled feelings of reliance on and resentment toward America's international dominance these days are neither strange nor new. The resentment of power, even when it is in the hands of one's friends, is a normal, indeed, timeless human emotion – no less so than the arrogance of power. And perhaps only Americans, with their rather short memory, could imagine that the current resentment is the unique product of the expansion of American dominance in the post–Cold War era. During the confrontation with the Soviet Union, now recalled in the United States as a time of Edenic harmony among the Western allies, not just French but also British leaders chafed under the leadership of a sometimes overbearing America. As political scientist A.W. DePorte noted some 20 years ago, the schemes of European unity advanced by French financial planner Jean Monnet and French foreign minister Robert Schuman in 1950 aimed "not only to strengthen Western Europe in the face of the Russian threat but also – though this was less talked about – to strengthen it vis-à-vis its indispensable but overpowering American ally." Today's call for "multipolarity" in international affairs, in short, has a history, as do European yearnings for unity as a counterweight to American power. Neither of these professed desires is a new response to the particular American hegemony of the last nine years.

And neither of them, one suspects, is very seriously intended. For the truth about America's dominant role in the world is known to most clear-eyed international observers. And the truth is that the benevolent hegemony exercised by the United States is good for a vast portion of the world's population. It is certainly a better international arrangement than all realistic alternatives. To undermine it would cost many others around the world far more than it would cost Americans – and far sooner. As Samuel Huntington wrote five years ago, before he joined the plethora of scholars disturbed by the "arrogance" of American hegemony: "A world without U.S. primacy will be a world with more violence and disorder and less democracy and economic growth than a world where the United States continues to have more influence than any other country shaping global affairs."

The unique qualities of American global dominance have never been a mystery, but these days they are more and more forgotten or, for convenience' sake, ignored. There was a time when the world clearly saw how different the American superpower was from all the previous aspiring hegemons. The difference lay in the exercise of power. The strength acquired by the United States in the aftermath of World War II was far greater than any single nation had ever possessed, at least since the Roman Empire. America's share of the world economy, the over-whelming superiority of its military capacity – augmented for a time by a monopoly of nuclear weapons and the capacity to deliver them – gave it the choice of pursuing any number of global ambitions. That the American people "might have set the crown of world empire on their brows," as one British statesman put it in 1951, but chose not to, was a decision of singular importance in world history and recognized as such. America's self-abnegation was unusual, and its uniqueness was not lost on peoples who had just suffered the horrors of wars brought on by powerful nations with overweening ambitions to empire of the most coercive type. Nor was it lost on those who saw what the Soviet Union planned to do with its newfound power after World War II.

The uniqueness persisted. During the Cold War, America's style of hegemony reflected its democratic form of government as much as Soviet hegemony reflected Stalin's approach to governance. The "habits of democracy," as Cold War historian John Lewis Gaddis has noted, made compromise and mutual accommo-dation the norm in U.S.–Allied relations. This approach to international affairs was not an example of selfless behavior. The Americans had an instinctive sense, based on their own experience growing up in a uniquely open system of democ-ratic capitalism, that their power and influence would be enhanced by allowing subordinate allies a great measure of internal and even external freedom of maneuver. But in practice, as Gaddis points out, "Americans so often deferred to the wishes of allies during the early Cold War that some historians have seen the Europeans – especially the British – as having managed them."

Beyond the style of American hegemony, which, even if unevenly applied, undoubtedly did more to attract than repel other peoples and nations, American grand strategy in the Cold War consistently entailed providing far more to friends and allies than was expected from them in return. Thus, it was American strategy to raise up from the ruins powerful economic competitors in Europe and Asia, a strategy so successful that by the 1980s the United States was thought to be in a state of irreversible "relative" economic decline – relative, that is, to those very nations whose economies it had restored after World War II.

And it was American strategy to risk nuclear annihilation on its otherwise unthreatened homeland in order to deter attack, either nuclear or conventional, on a European or Asian ally. This strategy also came to be taken for granted. But when one considers the absence of similarly reliable guarantees among the var-ious European powers in the past (between, say, Great Britain and France in the 1920s and 1930s), the willingness of the United States, standing in relative safety behind two oceans, to link its survival to that of other nations was extraordinary.

Even more remarkable may be that the United States has attempted not only to preserve these guarantees but to expand them in the post–Cold War era. Much is made these days, not least in Washington, of the American defense budget now being several times higher than that of every other major power. But on what is that defense budget spent? Very little funding goes to protect national territory. Most of it is devoted to making good on what Americans call their international "commitments."

Even in the absence of the Soviet threat, America continues, much to the chagrin of some of its politicians, to define its "national security" broadly, as encompassing the security of friends and allies, and even of abstract principles, far from American shores. In the Gulf War, more than 90 percent of the military forces sent to expel Iraq's army from Kuwait were American. Were 90 percent of the interests threatened American? In almost any imaginable scenario in which the United States might deploy troops abroad, the primary purpose would be the defense of interests of more immediate concern to America's allies — as it has been in Bosnia. This can be said about no other power.

Ever since the United States emerged as a great power, the identification of the interests of others with its own has been the most striking quality of American foreign and defense policy. Americans seem to have internalized and made second nature a conviction held only since World War II: Namely, that their own well-being depends fundamentally on the well-being of others; that American prosperity cannot occur in the absence of global prosperity; that American freedom depends on the survival and spread of freedom elsewhere; that aggression anywhere threatens the danger of aggression everywhere; and that American national security is impossible without a broad measure of international security.

Let us not call this conviction selfless: Americans are as self-interested as any other people. But for at least 50 years they have been guided by the kind of enlightened self-interest that, in practice, comes dangerously close to resembling generosity. If that generosity seems to be fading today (and this is still a premature judgment), it is not because America has grown too fond of power. Quite the opposite. It is because some Americans have grown tired of power, tired of leadership, and, consequently, less inclined to demonstrate the sort of generosity that has long characterized their nation's foreign policy. What many in Europe and elsewhere see as arrogance and bullying may be just irritability born of weariness.

If fatigue is setting in, then those nations and peoples who have long benefited, and still benefit, from the international order created and upheld by American power have a stake in bolstering rather than denigrating American hegemony. After all, what, in truth, are the alternatives?

Whatever America's failings, were any other nation to take its place, the rest of the world would find the situation less congenial. America may be arrogant; Americans may at times be selfish; they may occasionally be ham-handed in their exercise of power. But, excusez-moi, compared with whom? Can anyone believe that were France to possess the power the United States now has, the French would be less arrogant, less selfish, and less prone to making mistakes? Little in France's history as a great power, or even as a medium power, justifies such optimism. Nor can one easily imagine power on an American scale being employed in a more enlightened fashion by China, Germany, Japan, or Russia. And even the leaders of that least benighted of empires, the British, were more arrogant, more bloody-minded, and, in the end, less capable managers of world affairs than the inept Americans have so far proved to be. If there is to be a sole superpower, the world is better off if that power is the United States.

What, then, of a multipolar world? There are those, even in the United States, who believe a semblance of international justice can be achieved only in a world characterized by a balance among relative equals. In such circumstances, national arrogance must theoretically be tempered, national aspirations limited, and attempts at hegemony, either benevolent or malevolent, checked. A more evenly balanced world, they assume, with the United States cut down a peg (or two, or three) would be freer, fairer, and safer.

A distant, though unacknowledged cousin of this realist, balance-of-power theory is the global parliamentarianism, or world federalism, that animates so many Europeans today, particularly the French apostles of European union. (It is little recalled, especially by modern proponents of foreign policy "realism," that Hans Morgenthau's seminal work, *Politics Among Nations*, builds slowly and methodically to the conclusion that what is needed to maintain international peace is a "world state.") In fact, many of today's calls for multipolarity seem to spring from the view, popular in some Washington circles but downright pervasive in European capitals, that traditional measures of national power, and even the nation state itself, are passé. If Europe is erasing borders, what need is there for an overbearing America to keep the peace? America's military power is archaic in a world where finance is transnational and the modem is king.

We need not enter here into the endless and so far unproductive debate among international-relations theorists over the relative merits of multipolar, bipolar, and unipolar international "systems" for keeping the peace. It is sufficient to note that during the supposed heyday of multipolarity — the eighteenth century, when the first "Concert of Europe" operated — war among the great powers was a regular feature, with major and minor, and global and local, conflicts erupting throughout almost every decade.

We should also not forget that utopian fancies about the obsolescence of military power and national governments in a transnational, "economic" era have blossomed before, only to be crushed by the next "war to end all wars." The success of the European Union, such as it is, and, moreover, the whole dream of erasing boundaries, has been made possible only because the more fundamental and enduring issues of European security have been addressed by the United States through its leadership of NATO, that most archaic and least utopian of institutions. Were American hegemony really to disappear, the old European questions — chiefly, what to do about Germany — would quickly rear their hoary heads.

But let's return to the real world. For all the bleating about hegemony, no nation really wants genuine multipolarity. No nation has shown a willingness to take on equal responsibilities for managing global crises. No nation has been willing to make the same kinds of short-term sacrifices that the United States has been willing to make in the long-term interest of preserving the global order. No nation, except China, has been willing to spend the money to acquire the military power necessary for playing a greater role relative to the United States — and China's military buildup has not exactly been viewed by its neighbors as creating a more harmonious environment.

If Europeans genuinely sought multipolarity, they would increase their defense budgets considerably, instead of slashing them. They would take the lead in the Balkans, instead of insisting that their participation depends on America's partici-pation. But neither the French, other Europeans, nor even the Russians are prepared to pay the price for a genuinely multipolar world. Not only do they shy away from the expense of creating and preserving such a world; they rightly fear the geopo-litical consequences of destroying American hegemony. Genuine multipolarity would inevitably mean a return to the complex of strategic issues that plagued the world before World War II: in Asia, the competition for regional preeminence among China, Japan, and Russia; in Europe, the competition among France, Germany, Great Britain, and Russia.

Kenneth Waltz once made the seemingly obvious point that "in interna-tional politics, overwhelming power repels and leads other states to balance against it" — a banal truism, and yet, as it happens, so untrue in this era of American hegemony. What France, Russia, and some others really seek today is not genuine multipolarity but a false multipolarity, an honorary multipolarity. They want the pretense of equal partnership in a multipolar world without the price or responsibility that equal partnership requires. They want equal say on the major decisions in global crises (as with Iraq and Kosovo) without having to pos-sess or wield anything like equal power. They want to increase their own prestige at the expense of American power but without the strain of having to fill the gap left by a diminution of the American role. And at the same time, they want to make short-term, mostly financial, gains, by taking advantage of the continuing U.S. focus on long-term support of the international order.

The problem is not merely that some of these nations are giving themselves a "free ride" on the back of American power, benefiting from the international order that American hegemony undergirds, while at the same time puncturing little holes in it for short-term advantage. The more serious danger is that this behavior will gradually, or perhaps not so gradually, erode the sum total of power that can be applied to protecting the international order altogether. The false multipolarity sought by France, Russia, and others would reduce America's ability to defend common interests without increasing anyone else's ability to do so.

In fact, this erosion may already be happening. In the recent case of Iraq, America's ability to pursue the long-term goal of defending the international order against President Saddam Hussein was undermined by the efforts of France and Russia to attain short-term economic gains and enhanced prestige. Both these powers achieved their goal of a "multipolar" solution: They took a slice out of American hegemony. But they did so at the price of leaving in place a long-term threat to an international system from which they continue to draw immense benefits but which they by themselves have no ability to defend. They did not possess the means to solve the Iraq problem, only the means to prevent the United States from solving it.

This insufficiency is the fatal flaw of multilateralism, as the Clinton administration learned in the case of Bosnia. In a world that is not genuinely multipolar — where there is instead a widely recognized hierarchy of power — multilateralism, if rigorously pursued, guarantees failure in meeting international crises. Those nations that lack the power to solve an international problem cannot be expected to take the lead in demanding the problem be solved. They may even eschew the exercise of power altogether, both because they do not have it and because the effective exercise of it by someone else, such as the United States, only serves to widen the gap between the hegemon and the rest. The lesson President Bill Clinton was supposed to have learned in the case of Bosnia is that to be effective, multilateralism must be preceded by unilateralism. In the toughest situations, the most effective multilateral response comes when the strongest power decides to act, with or without the others, and then asks its partners whether they will join. Giving equal say over international decisions to nations with vastly unequal power often means that the full measure of power that can be deployed in defense of the international community's interests will, in fact, not be deployed.

Those contributing to the growing chorus of antihegemony and multipolarity may know they are playing a dangerous game, one that needs to be conducted with the utmost care, as French leaders did during the Cold War, lest the entire international system come crashing down around them. What they may not have adequately calculated, however, is the possibility that Americans will not respond as wisely as they generally did during the Cold War.

Americans and their leaders should not take all this sophisticated whining about U.S. hegemony too seriously. They certainly should not take it more seriously than the whiners themselves do. But, of course, Americans are taking it seriously. In the United States these days, the lugubrious guilt trip of post-Vietnam liberalism is echoed even by conservatives, with William Buckley, Samuel Huntington, and James Schlesinger all decrying American "hubris," "arrogance," and "imperialism." Clinton administration officials, in between speeches exalting America as the "indispensable" nation, increasingly behave as if what is truly indispensable is the prior approval of China, France, and Russia for every military action. Moreover, at another level, there is a stirring of neo-isolationism in America today, a mood that nicely complements the view among many Europeans that America is meddling too much in everyone else's business and taking too little time to mind its own. The existence of the Soviet Union disciplined Americans and made them see that their enlightened self-interest lay in a relatively generous foreign policy. Today, that discipline is no longer present.

In other words, foreign grumbling about American hegemony would be merely amusing, were it not for the very real possibility that too many Americans will forget — even if most of the rest of the world does not — just how important continued American dominance is to the preservation of a reasonable level of international security and prosperity. World leaders may want to keep this in mind when they pop the champagne corks in celebration of the next American humbling.

✗ NO
Will the Empire Be Fascist?
RICHARD FALK

The United States is by circumstance and design an emergent global empire, the first in the history of the world. Prior empires have had frontiers and boundaries, although occupying large expanses of territory, and exerting control from . . . distant center[s] that due to available technologies of communication and transportation were further away in time than is any part of the globe from Washington. In purely temporal terms, the American Empire is thus smaller than earlier great empires associated with China, the Ottomans, the Persians, the Austro-Hungarian, and the overseas empires of the British, French, Dutch, Spanish, and Portuguese.

It is important to appreciate the consequences of an empire of global scope. Such an empire, to the extent that it is established and sustained without significant resistance, raise[s] a special challenge to world order. Over the course of modern history, in particular, stability in international relations has been maintained primarily by reliance on countervailing power, often interpreted by reference to "the balance of power," and giving rise to various schools of "realist" thinking to explain the central ordering role of power. Such an international equilibrium was complemented in the Westphalia Era by "war," which served as a crude and cruel legislative substitute, introducing periodic changes in maps portraying the boundaries of territorial states. A third ordering instrument was by way of various forms of "hegemony" that established geographic zones of control, known as "spheres of influence," by which powerful states exerted control over the behavior of weaker states, as illustrated by such patterns as the Monroe Doctrine, the Soviet Bloc, and the Atlantic Alliance. The fourth and weakest, yet most promising ordering device in world politics, is associated with international law, especially as institutionalized within the United Nations. Such a framework of international law, the struggle to find an alternative to war in the sett[l]ing of conflict and change has taken on a sense of urgency since the development of weaponry of mass destruction, but lacks the independent capabilities to ensure respect for its constraints by powerful states and by newly formidable non-state actors (the al Qaeda network).

Against this background the shape of the world order crisis becomes more evident. An American Empire that repudiates international law and is unchecked by countervailing power is a political actor that possesses an abundant arsenal of nuclear weapons and is confronted by a non-state enemy that has been pronounced as "evil," justifying an exterminist approach to the conflict. Beyond this, the American approach to global security extends its response to anti-terrorism to encompass states that are perceived as hostile, and possess or may possess weaponry of mass destruction. The Iraq War is an expression of this extension, made particularly disturbing because the alleged casus belli was not endorsed by the United Nations Security Council and cannot be reconciled with international law.

This essay explores the implication of these trends as defining the American Empire, and specifically argues that the prospects associated with such a reality no longer support, if indeed they ever did, the school of benign imperialists who while acknowledging the imperial moment for the United States, insisted that it was a benevolent political configuration as compared to prior imperial projects, and provided the world with the global public good of security without oppression and exploitation. [Prime explicit imperialists of this stripe are Robert Kagan, Michael Ignatieff.] Indeed, I believe that the American Empire is turning toward a system of militarized control that includes a repudiation of the authority of international law and of the United Nations. To underscore my sense of concern about this style of imperial control I treat these trends as posing a threat of "global fascism." It is a threat that has begun to be realized in the context of the American response to the September 11 attacks, but especially by the extension of this response by way of aggressive war making to the "axis of evil" countries. Such a threat is also accentuated by the development of resistance to this American project by the peoples of the world, as evident in the anti-war movement that took shape during the Iraq crisis, including in the United States itself. The response of cynical disregard by the US Government occurred in an atmosphere in which sweeping claims to curtail liberties have been given legislative backing by the Congress and where discriminatory policies have been formally and informally pursued with respect to Muslims resident in the United States, especially young male Arab-Americans and non-citizens. Given this rising tide of resistance that encounters an official mindset that is empowered by a dangerous blend of religious and geopolitical zeal, the moves toward fascist modes of control are plausibly feared and anticipated.

AN IMPERIAL MOMENT

Andrew Bacevich expresses clearly a view that is increasingly encountered in mainstream American commentary, acknowledging for better or worse, a new imperial role for the United States: "the question that Americans can no longer afford to dodge – is not whether the United States has become an imperial power. The question is what sort of empire they intend theirs to be." [Andrew J. Bacevich, *American Empire: The Realities and Consequences of U.S. Diplomacy* (Cambridge, MA: Harvard University Press, 2002): 244] Bacevich ends his book by stressing the importance of this acknowledgement of empire, insisting that concealing such an imperial reality will lead to "not just the demise of the American empire but great danger for what used to be known as the American republic." [also, p. 244]

A similar theme was influentially intoned by Michael Ignatieff who calls for an American understanding of its imperial role as "a burden" that is the consequence of its preeminence in the world. Ignatieff gives empire a potentially favorable gloss, arguing that "[t]he case for empire is that it has become, in a place like Iraq, the last hope of democracy and stability alike." [Michael Ignatieff, "The Burden," *NYTimes Magazine*, Jan. 5, 2003, 22–27, 50–54, at 54] Ignatieff couples his advocacy with the warning that empires decline and fall when they overreach, ignoring limits on their capabilities. As with Bacevich, Ignatieff believes that overcoming the American inhibition to mention the "E-word" is the first requirement for reinterpreting the appropriate US global role given its preeminent power.

Clarifying this American role did not begin with the presidency of George W. Bush. Ever since the collapse of the Soviet Union in 1991 there have been strong statements based on a new American-dominated power structure, including celebrations of a so-called "unipolar moment" (Charles Krauthammer) and assertions that the United States is "the indispensable nation" (Madeleine Albright). [Krauthammer, "The Unipolar Moment," *Foreign Affairs* 70 (No. 1) 1990–91] These sentiments as intoned during the Bush Sr. and Clinton years were mostly understood as leadership challenges to be met by the United States in the aftermath of the cold war. In the wings of American policymaking were still more radical neoconservative voices arguing that the end of the cold war presented the US Government with an extraordinary opportunity to fill the vacuum created by the Soviet collapse with American power for the benefit of the world. Such a vision hatched in the ideologically overheated incubators of such well-financed think tanks as the American Enterprise Institute and the Heritage Foundation. This historic possibility, it was argued, could only be realized if the US Government would consciously pursue a global dominance project by way of an increased investment in military capabilities, that is, going against the flow of mainstream thinking at the time that "a peace dividend" and nuclear disarmament were the best ways to take advantage of the end of the cold war. It was further contended that if the United States failed to rise to the occasion, it would encourage forces of disorder throughout the world, producing a variety of dangers and setbacks for the United States. In a sense, there was no choice but to make use of American power, as enhanced by an expanded global military capability. [These neo-con views were influentially laid out by the contributors to Robert Kagan & William Kristol, eds., *Present Dangers: Crisis and Opportunity in American Foreign and Defense Policy* (San Francisco, CA: Encounter Books, 2002); and again in the report of the project of The New American Century Project entitled "Rebuilding our Defenses," published in 2000.]

In the same period, more centrist figures in the United States were articulating more modest versions of a parallel vision of a reconstituted world order. [For example, under the auspices of the Council of Foreign Relations see Jan Lodel, *The Price of Dominance* (New York: Council of Foreign Relations Press, 2001); also G. John Ikenberry, ed., *America Unrivaled: The Future of the Balance of Power* (Ithaca, NY: Cornell University Press, 2002).] Joseph Nye suggested that American superiority in the increasingly important domains of "soft power" would allow the establishment of a more stable and beneficial world order that was anchored in multilateralism and patterns of cooperative international problem-solving. [Joseph S. Nye, Jr., *Bound to Lead: The Changing Nature of American Power* (New York: Basic Books, 1991); also, Nye, *The Paradox of American Power: Why the World's Only Superpower Can't Go It Alone* (New York: Oxford, 2002).] These centrist leadership models relied on non-military means to sustain American global dominance, and avoided illiberal designations such as "empire" or "imperial" to designate the process. Yet, by so framing the grand strategy debate in this period after the cold war, it provided space for those more neo-conservative perspectives that insisted that these goals could only be reached by "hard power," the ability and willingness to project superior military to the four corners of the planet. [See Frank Carlucci, Robert Hunter, and Zalmay Khalilzad, eds., *Taking Charge: A Bipartisan Report to the President-Elect on Foreign Policy and National Security* (Santa Monica, CA: RAND, 2001).]

This commentary on the global scene was basically overshadowed during the 1990s by the preoccupation with economic globalization as the defining reality of a new era of international relations in which market forces associated with trade and investment assume priority over traditional security concerns, given the absence of serious strategic or ideological conflict among leading states. From this perspective, a principal world order concern was the future of the sovereign state, as well as the struggle of non-Western peoples to sustain their distinctive identities in a consumerist world shaped by the materialist tastes of the American people and their hegemonic popular culture. This challenge mounted by the economic globalizers energized global civil society, giving rise to a global democracy movement designed to make the world economy more equitable in its distribution of benefits, and accountable to the peoples of the world as well as to their corporate boards. It also gave rise to a religious resurgence of global scope, which in certain manifestations, especially in the Islamic world posed a direct challenge to globalization and American global leadership. [For an assessment of this dynamic see Richard Falk, *Religion and Humane Global Governance* (New York: Palgrave, 2001).]

The September 11 attacks occurred against such a background, and almost immediately moved the global security agenda back onto the center stage world politics, and once again removed global economic issues from active public concern. But what became clear almost from the first responses by the US Government was a decision by the White House to frame its response to mega-terrorism in terms that incorporated the radical neo-conservative conception of a future world order. President Bush immediately insisted that other countries have the choice of either being on the side of the United States or "with the terrorists." At the same time, the net was spread much wider than the defensive necessities of the situation, encompassing "terrorism" in general, and not just the "mega-terrorism" of the al Qaeda challenge. [This distinction is a central theme of my book, Falk, *The Great Terror War* (Northhampton, MA: Olive Branch Press, 2003).] This enlarged conception of "the war" allowed the Bush administration to shift the focus of the American response from the al Qaeda presence in Afghanistan to "the axis of evil" countries that had essentially no connection with mega-terrorism, but were definitely standing in the way of the American espousal of global dominance as a goal to be actively pursued. It is this shift that has brought the issue of "empire" into the open, and raised the question of what type of empire, what repercussions it would have for America as a constitutional democracy, and how it would play out in world politics. The international turmoil generated by the White House resolve to wage war against Iraq has placed these issues in the sharpest possible relief, giving rise to a massive popular mobilization of resistance throughout the world and a diplomatic revolt by some of America's closest allies and traditional friends. The Iraq crisis played out in part within the United Nations Security Council posed a dreadful choice for the membership, to go along with aggressive warmaking in violation of the UN Charter or to find itself bypassed by American military unilateralism.

DEPICTING THE RADICAL VISION OF THE BUSH ADMINISTRATION AT HOME AND ABROAD

President Bush has set forth the American commitment to an imperial world order with relative clarity. Elements of this vision were being promoted by the Bush presidency well before September. The priority accorded to the militarization of space, which included the unilateral scrapping of the Anti-Ballistic Missile Treaty, was certainly an expensive, destabilizing step taken in the direction of American global dominance. Beyond this, an imperial approach to the rest of the world was disclosed by the repudiation of the Kyoto Protocol on the emission of greenhouse gasses, by a reject of the treaty setting up the International Criminal Court, and by an overall diplomatic posture that was dismissive of humanitarian undertakings. Also, relevant was the appointment to positions of the greatest influence in the Bush administration the most extreme cold war hawks who were the principal authors of the neo-con worldview in the 1990s, including Paul Wolfowitz and Dick Cheney, the reputed architects of a Pentagon leaked document in 1992 that advocated an American grand strategy that was centered on ensuring that in no region of the world should the United States allow a military power to emerge that might be capable of challenging American dominance. [David Armstrong, "Dick Cheney's Song of America: Drafting a Plan for Global Dominance," *Harper's Magazine*, Oct. 2002, 76–83; Nicholas Lemann, "The Next World Order," *The New Yorker*, April 1, 2002, 42–48; and see Robert Kagan writing in 1998, "The Benevolent Empire," *Foreign Policy*, Summer 1998, 24–35.]

The American response to September 11 has greatly accelerated the drive for global dominance, although it has been masked beneath the banners of anti-terrorism. The rapid military buildup of American forces, their adaptation to the challenges of hostile forces in the non-Western world, the extension of anti-terrorism to "axis of evil" countries, and the general acceptance of this role by mainstream American public opinion have all had the effect of moving the project of American empire into the center of political consciousness. The Bush administration in its formal public presentations has been careful to discuss its goals as premised upon anti-terrorism, but the broader claims, although expressed in an indirect form lent undeniable support to imperial allegations. President Bush has made his most authoritative statement in a June 2002 address at West Point, and more comprehensively in *The National Security Strategy of the United States of America* released by the White House in September 2002.

At West Point Bush repeated the familiar litany about American goals in the world as fully compatible with traditional ideas of world order based on the interaction of sovereign states. The president told the graduating cadets that "America has no empire to extend or utopia to establish." He then went on, after describing the threats posed by weaponry of mass destruction in hostile hands, to articulate precisely American plans for global dominance and a utopia of sorts. The utopian element was the promise to eliminate war among "civilized" states from the international scene, insisting that "civilized nations find themselves on the same side . . . thereby making the destabilizing arms races of other eras pointless, and limiting rivalries to trade and other pursuits of peace." But such a promise was coupled with the dominance theme, indeed, present in the same sentence: "America has, and intends to keep, military strengths beyond challenge." And so the global security system is based on the combination of demilitarization for the rest of the world, while the US relies on its military might to keep the peace. [Quoted passages all from the text of the West Point speech as available from the White House website, at www.whitehouse.gov/news/releases/2002/06/print.html.]

This double emphasis is repeated in a more oblique form, yet unmistakably, in the White House *National Security Strategy* document. In his signed cover letter introducing the document Bush says "[t]oday, the international community has the best chance since the rise of the nation-state in the seventeenth century to build a world where great powers compete in peace instead of continually prepare for war. Today, the world's great powers find ourselves on the same side — united by common dangers of terrorist violence and chaos. The United States will build on these common interests to promote global security." Such expectations are accompanied by an embrace of "the democratic peace theory" so popular among the benign imperialists during the 1990s. In Bush's words, "the United States will use this moment of opportunity to extend the benefits of freedom across the globe. We will actively work to bring the hope of democracy, development, free markets, and free trade to every corner of the world." Such a design combines ideas of American dominance associated with economic globalization, that were prevalent before September 11, with more militarist ideas associated with the anti-terrorist climate of the early 21st century.

There is the further disclosure of a deliberate bid to impose a hierarchical form of world order, in other words, an imperial structure on the rest of the world, by the official approach taken in *NSS* 2002 toward its one plausible geopolitical rival, China. In discussing American plans for Asia-Pacific region China is given some patronizing advice, sure to cause consternation in the policy institutes at work in Beijing and Shanghai. The language is worth quoting: "In pursuing advanced military capabilities that can threaten its neighbors in the Asia-Pacific region, China is following an outdated path that, in the end, will hamper its own pursuit of national greatness. In time, China will find that social and political freedom is the only source of that greatness." [*NSS* 2002, 27] Apparently oblivious to the inconsistency, a few paragraphs later *NSS* 2002 suggests the essential reliance of the US on its military superiority: "It is time to reaffirm the essential role of American military strength. We must build our defenses beyond challenge." [p.29] And further, "[T]he unparalleled strength of the United States armed forces, and their forward presence, have maintained the peace in some of the world's most strategically vital regions." [p.29] To lecture China (and presumably others) about the outdatedness of military power while [. . .] devoting more resources to its [American] military budget than the next fifteen countries combined can only be understood as a message from the imperial capital to a subordinate part of the empire.

It seems safe to conclude the following about the drift of American power in the early 21st century. The basic move is to adopt policies that anchor the imperial project in a military approach to global security. While not abandoning the ideological precepts of neoliberal globalization, the Bush administration places its intense free market advocacy beneath a security blanket that includes suspect advice to other governments to devote their resources to non-military activities. Such advice is coupled with an acknowledgement of the new and acute American vulnerability to mega-terrorist attack by non-state actors, and an accompanying call for unity at home and internationally to help in confronting such a threat. There was a considerable show of such unity in the aftermath of September 11, but it has started to fray when the Bush administration extended its response to Iraq, raising suspicions that it was deliberately confusing the challenge of mega-terrorism with the ambition to establish an American Empire.

There is another quite different line of interpretation suggested by Nelson Mandela that September 11 had a disorienting effect on President Bush and his entourage of advisors. In Mandela's words, "[W]hat I am condemning is that one power, with a president who has no foresight, who cannot think properly, is now wanting to plunge the world into a holocaust." [quoted from a speech at the International Women's Forum in Sandton, South Africa, Feb. 2003] In effect, Mandela is implying that the imperial option to the extent pursued by the Bush approach will produce a massive war, not an era of peace, prosperity, and security.

What is meant by "think properly" can be understood in different ways. If taken to mean in a clear and self-interested way, it is a prediction that aggressive American military moves will provoke forms of resistance that eventuate in a war that is a disaster for America as well as for the rest of the world. But think properly can also be interpreted to mean in accordance with ethical and legal norms in which case the disregard of this framework of restraint will itself lead to an all-encompassing tragedy.

WHY GLOBAL FASCISM?

The benevolent empire school that surfaced in the 1990s, and maintains a subdued voice on the sidelines at present, was based on an acceptance of American claims of "moral exceptionalism." It focused on America as the vehicle for the spread of democracy and the only political actor willing to and capable of managing humanitarian interventions. Its advocates also believed that to the extent that countries could be induced to enter the modern world of industrial development and technological innovation within the setting of a globalizing world economy, the problems of disorder and political extremism would be abated. [For example, Thomas Friedman, *The Lexus and the Olive Tree: Understanding Globalization* (New York: Farrar, Straus, Giroux, 1999).] The Bush approach seemingly repudiated such a path, insisting that the alleged "nation-building" of the 1990s was not serving America's strategic interests, and that much more emphasis should be placed on military capabilities to project American power to the four corners of the earth. This course of action suddenly became national policy, reinforced by support from the entire political spectrum, in the patriotic climate of opinion that has prevailed since the momentous events of September 11.

But to some extent, the idealism of the benevolent school has been incorporated into the refashioning of the imperial project by the Bush leadership. While other countries have interests, the United States has sustained the pretension, that it additionally, unlike other great powers of the past, embodies values of benefit to all, a claim repeated as if a mantra by President Bush and his main advisors. These values are designated as "the nonnegotiable demands of human dignity: the rule of law; limits on the absolute power of the state; free speech; freedom of worship; equal justice; respect for women; religious and ethnic tolerance; and respect for private property." [*NSS*, p. 3] In the *NSS* document: "The U.S. National security strategy will be based on a distinctly American internationalism that reflects the union of our values and our national interests. The aim of this strategy is to help make the world not just safer but better." [p. 1] In relation to both the Afghanistan and Iraq wars the US Government has defended its warmaking by pointing to alleged humanitarian gains associated with its reliance on military power. The US Government also disavowed any self-aggrandizing goals, angrily dismissing widespread accusations of anti-war critics that recourse to war against Iraq was driven by its oil ambitions, and promising to hold oil in trust for the people of Iraq during any period of American occupation.

Given this kind of emphasis is it not misleading to suggest that there has been a shift from the benevolent empire model that was articulated in the 1990s? And further, has not the reliance on military power been justified by the changed global circumstances brought about by the September 11 attacks and their repetition? Is not, in fact, the American advocacy of democracy and human rights both a continuation of the nation-building of the 1990s that it had earlier derided and an expression of an anti-fascist geopolitics? The weight of such questions does suggest that the debate about American Empire is far from over, but it does not undermine the argument of an emergent global fascism.

The analysis offered here is largely structural, although bolstered by the way in which the authority of the UN Security Council was manipulated by the United States, and then disregarded. The structural element arises from the facts of American military, economic, and diplomatic preeminence, and its explicit resolve to keep that edge. The US Government is devoting huge resources to the monopolistic militarization of space, the development of more usable nuclear weapons, and the strengthening of its world-girdling ring of military bases and its global navy, as the most tangible way to discourage any strategic challenges to its preeminence. True[,] the realities of dominance are unlikely to be translated into formal relations of governance and subordination, but non-compliant actors in the world will either be destroyed or replaced with compliant actors. Compliance will be measured by accepting the American approach to global security, including the espousal of a free market ideology and the practice of a nominal constitutionalism. This combination of factors adds up to "empire" according to my assessment.

But why fascist? I would stress three elements. First of all, the combination of unchallengeable military preeminence with a rejection by the US Government of the restraining impact of international law and the United Nations. The Iraq debate brought this global militarist posture into the open. The Bush administration has relied on a novel and extensive doctrine of "preemption" (redescribed as "preventive war" by some critics to emphasize the absence of any show of imminent threat) that claims a right by the United States (but presumably no others) to initiate war against a foreign state without sustaining the burden of demonstrating a defensive necessity. It has further strained credulity, and weakened world order, by applying this doctrine to the circumstances of Iraq without even making a minimally credible showing of justifying evidence of an Iraqi threat. To take advantage of the anti-terrorist mood in the United States to mount this war was widely understood as the practice of vengeful geopolitics against an essentially helpless country.

The fact that this policy was filtered through the United Nations both revealed the imperial structure and the prospect of resistance. The imperial structure was evident in the manner with which the issue of Iraqi inspections was unanimously framed by UNSC Res. 1441, which accepted implicitly the central unsubstantiated claim that Iraq's possession of weaponry of mass destruction posed a war threat, which if not immediately removed by inspection and Iraqi disarmament, would lead to an American-led war outside the United Nations. If the Charter had been the guideline, it would be Iraq that would have received protection against such American provocations as constant military intrusions on its airspace over the course of years, ill-concealed programs of support for armed uprising by the enemies of the Baghdad regime, covert operations designed to destabilize governmental control in Iraq, and a military buildup that was shamelessly threatening a "shock and awe" attack unless the regime of Saddam Hussein capitulated to the demands being made that encroached centrally on Iraqi sovereign rights. Instead, the UN membership tried to reach the proclaimed American goals by reliance on inspection leading to disarmament. But the proclaimed American goals were rather evidently not fully expressive of American objectives, and so even effective inspection was not acceptable to Washington as an alternative to war and "regime change."

It is here that the membership of the Security Council has drawn the line, rejecting an abandonment of inspection despite the increasing evidence that it was accomplishing what the United States contended was the basis of the Iraqi threat and the grounds for the hypocritical claim that it was important to the credibility of the UN that its resolutions be implemented. It did not take observers long to note the US unwillingness to take steps over the years to implement the numerous Security Council resolutions directed at Israel with respect to withdrawal from the territories occupied during the 1967 War and the application of the Geneva Conventions specifying the obligations of Israel as the occupying power in the West Bank and Gaza.

From the moment the United States agreed to seek support for war at the UN, a seemingly multilateralist step that was vigorously opposed by the administration's ultra-hawks who sought to fashion American foreign policy without the bother of collective procedures, the UN was placed in an untenable position. The speech of President Bush on September 12, 2002 to the General Assembly gave the UN the choice of supporting the US position, which seemed from the outset irreconcilable with international law and the UN Charter, or finding its authority bypassed by action undertaken by the United States and whatever coalition partners it could muster. The UNSC struggled hard to avoid an outcome that appeared to make its authority "irrelevant," bending 80% of the way in Washington's direction, but in the end it was not enough.

The major point here is that the US puts its strategic approach above the claims of international law and the procedures of the UN on the most vital matter of the decision to embark on a non-defensive war. Its shaping of the issue at the UN confirms the imperial structure of world politics, but the outcome reveals anti-imperial tensions that threaten to shrink the American Empire from its pretensions of global reach. The Iraq debate can thus be seen as both confirming the existence of an American Empire, but also as expressive of an emerging geopolitical resistance. The American defiance of this resistance, its abandonment of diplomacy and accommodation, is expressive of global fascism. It represents a consolidation of unaccountable military power on a global scale that overrides the constraints of international law and disregards the procedural role of the UNSC in authorizing uses of international force that cannot be encompassed within the right of self-defense enjoyed by all sovereign states.

Secondly, the US Government in moving against terrorism has claimed sweeping powers to deal with the concealed al Qaeda network. Some of these claims are necessary and justifiable to deal with the magnitude and nature of the threats posed by mega-terrorism. But the character of the powers claimed that include secret detentions, the authority to designate American citizens as "enemy combatants" without any rights, the public consideration of torture as a permissible police practice in anti-terrorist work, the scrutiny applied to those of Muslim faith, the reliance on assassination directed at terrorist suspects wherever they are found, and numerous invasions of privacy directed at ordinary people. These mechanisms of state power, given legal backing in the USA Patriots Act, and awaiting expected further strengthening in proposed legislation now called the Domestic Security Enhancement Act prepared by the Justice Department. The slide toward fascism at home is given tangible expression by these practices, but it is also furthered by an uncritical and chauvinistic patriotism, by the release of periodic alarmist warnings of mega-terrorist imminent attacks that fail to materialize, and by an Attorney General, John Ashcroft, who seems to exult in an authoritarian approach to law enforcement.

The third main concern about the onset of fascism arises from an impending collision between Washington's imperial geopolitics and the rising tendencies of grassroots resistance to the American Empire, along with the planetary spread of anti-American resentment. If such a movement from below becomes more aggressive, as is likely, and to the extent the other elements of the American approach continue, there will be felt the need to control and repress this populist resistance. Such an interaction will inflame feelings on both sides, making reliance on a fascist conception of control likely to prevail despite continuing American professions of belief in the ways of democracy and freedom.

For all these reasons, the dangers of global fascism cannot be discounted as imaginary or alarmist. Hopefully, counter-tendencies within the United States and the world will be sufficiently awakened by these dangers to fashion an effective response. America has proved to be resilient in the past as when anti-democratic forces were unleashed by the rabid witch-hunting anti-communism of McCarthyism during the 1950s, but this resilience is now being tested as never before, because the proponents of this extremist American global strategy currently occupy the heights of political influence in and around the White House and Pentagon, and seem to have no intention of giving ground under the increasing pressure of a growing challenge mounted by American grassroots opposition as reinforced by international public opinion.

Along the lines of the overall argument presented here, removing the threat of global fascism would not entirely dispose of the existence of an American Empire. There would still be the advocates of benevolent empire and the structural possibilities of reviving an economistic approach to globalization as existed in the 1990s. [See Falk, *Predatory Globalization: A Critique* (Cambridge: Polity, 2000); also Michael Hardt and Antonio Negri, *Empire* (Cambridge, MA: Harvard University Press, 2000).]

POSTSCRIPT

In an article published in 2002 entitled "The Unipolar Moment Revisited," Charles Krauthammer reflects on his analysis of a decade earlier. He notes that what appeared to be a "moment" in the 1990s had now become a "unipolar era." Krauthammer expresses satisfaction with the emergence of a "new unilateralism," which "argues explicitly and unashamedly . . . for sustaining America's unrivaled dominance for the foreseeable future." Yet, he still fears that the American public may seek to retreat from its responsibility as the lone superpower. He asserts that the real threat to unipolarity comes from inside the United States, not outside. Paraphrasing Benjamin Franklin, Krauthammer states, "States have given you an empire, if you will keep it."

International relations scholars and historians have long noted the tendency for empires to decline or even collapse as a result of imperial overreach or loss of will. Commentators like Krauthammer are anxious for the United States to maintain vigilance against such a decline. However, others have suggested that the United States is already in decline. In an article entitled "The Eagle Has Crash Landed" (*Foreign Policy*, June–July 2002), Immanuel Wallerstein argues that "the economic, political, and military factors that contributed to U.S. hegemony are the same factors that will inexorably produce the coming U.S. decline." Wallerstein points to numerous instances that reflect America's declining influence in world affairs. He concludes, "the real question is not whether U.S. hegemony is waning but whether the United States can devise a way to descend gracefully, with minimum damage to the world, and to itself." Wallerstein's argument raises an important question. Even if one accepts Robert Kagan's contention that the American empire will be benevolent, how is the United States likely to maintain its present dominance? Is there already evidence of its impending decline?

Suggested Additional Readings

Bacevich, Andrew J. *American Empire: The Realities and Consequences of US Diplomacy.* Cambridge, Mass.: Harvard University Press, 2002.

Barkawi, Tarak, and Mark Laffey. "Retrieving the Imperial: Empire and International Relations." *Millennium: Journal of International Studies* 31 (2002): 109–27.

Barry, Tom. "Hegemony to Imperium." *Foreign Policy in Focus* 6, no. 29 (September 26, 2002): 1–2.

Ferguson, Niall. "Hegemony or Empire?" *Foreign Affairs* 82, no. 5 (September–October 2003): 154.

Hardt, Michael, and Toni Negri. *Empire.* Cambridge, Mass.: Harvard University Press, 2001.

Huntington, Samuel P. "The Lonely Superpower." *Foreign Affairs* 78, no. 2 (March–April 1999): 35–49.

Magstadt, Thomas M. *An Empire If You Can Keep It: Power and Principle in American Foreign Policy.* Washington, D.C.: CQ Press, 2004.

Nye, Joseph S. *The Paradox of American Power: Why the World's Only Superpower Can't Go It Alone.* New York: Oxford University Press, 2002.

Prestowitz, Clyde. *Rogue Nation: American Unilateralism and the Failure of Good Intentions.* New York: Basic Books, 2003.

Wallerstein, Immanuel. "U.S. Weakness and the Struggle for Hegemony." *Monthly Review* 55, no. 3 (July–August 2003): 23–29.

InfoTrac® College Edition

Search for the following articles in the InfoTrac® database:

Alsace, Juan A. "In Search of Monsters to Destroy: American Empire in the New Millennium." *Parameters* 33, no. 3 (Autumn 2003): 122–29.

Hendrickson, David. "Toward Universal Empire: Dangerous Quest for Absolute Security?" *World Policy Journal* 19, no. 3 (Fall 2002): 1–9.

Jervis, Robert. "The Compulsive Empire: U.S. Hegemony." *Foreign Policy* 137 (July–August 2003): 82–87.

Wallerstein, Immanuel. "The Eagle Has Crash Landed." *Foreign Policy* 131 (July–August 2002): 60–68.

For more articles, enter:
"American empire," "unilateralism," or "hegemony" in the keyword search.

Web Resources

For current URLs for the following websites, visit www.crosscurrents.nelson.com.

CARNEGIE COUNCIL ON ETHICS AND INTERNATIONAL AFFAIRS: EMPIRE BIBLIOGRAPHY

www.cceia.org/viewMedia.php/prmTemplateID/8/prmID/1065

The CCEIA has produced an extensive bibliography on the subject of empire and recent developments in American foreign policy. Look for additional resources under their Empire and Democracy Project.

OPENDEMOCRACY DEBATE ON AMERICAN POWER AND THE WORLD

www.opendemocracy.net/debates/debate-3-77.jsp

The website of this nonprofit organization based in the United Kingdom features an extensive collection of articles and debates on the implications of American predominance.

SOCIAL SCIENCE RESEARCH COUNCIL ESSAYS

www.ssrc.org/sept11/essays/

This prominent research foundation offers an excellent collection of essays on America's place in the world by leading American and non-American scholars. Look particularly for essays under the subject heading New World Order.

CARNEGIE ENDOWMENT FOR INTERNATIONAL PEACE: U.S. LEADERSHIP PROJECT

www.ceip.org/files/projects/usl/usl_home.ASP

This project by the Carnegie Endowment for International Peace is directed by Robert Kagan. The page contains op-ed articles on the current role of the United States in the world.

Is Globalization Undermining the Power of the Nation-State?

✔ **YES**

SUSAN STRANGE, "The Erosion of the State," *Current History* 96, no. 613 (November 1997): 365–69

✘ **NO**

MARTIN WOLF, "Will the Nation-State Survive Globalization?" *Foreign Affairs* 80, no. 1 (January–February 2001): 178–90

The concept of the state has always been central in thinking about international relations. Scholars date the modern international system of states from the Peace of Westphalia in 1648. This agreement, designed to bring an end to the Thirty Years War, signified both the secularization of politics and the rise of the territorial state as the principal unit of political organization. The peace redrew the map of Europe into a society of legally equal states. Each claimed to exercise sovereignty within fairly well-defined frontiers and acknowledged no authority above itself. Inherent in this notion was the claim that each state has the right to non-interference by others in its domestic affairs.

Since 1648, the territorial state has become the principal vehicle for organizing humankind into political communities. The composition of the international system has grown from a handful of European states in the seventeenth century to over 200 states and territorial entities today. States remain the highest level of political authority. Decisions made by bodies such as the United Nations and the International Court of Justice in the Hague are adhered to by states only on a voluntary basis. There has yet to emerge anything like a global state or world government.

Given the power and importance of sovereign states, it is perhaps not surprising that scholars have traditionally focused on a "state-centric" approach to the study of international politics. According to this view, the focus of the study of international relations is really *interstate* relations. Although there may be many other "actors" on the global scene, states remain the dominant actors because they alone can claim monopoly of legal authority within their territory and of the use of military force within and beyond that territory.

Why have states emerged as the predominant form of political organization? John Herz argues that the strength of states lies in their capacity to perform two major functions: defend those citizens who live within their borders and promote the economic well-being of their citizens. States have been successful to the extent that they have been able to build a "hard shell" of impermeability around themselves while ensuring a degree of self-sufficiency and autonomy.

In the twentieth century, there have been frequent predictions that the notion of the sovereign, territorial state is in demise. Herz himself, in the aftermath of World War II, predicted the imminent end of the territorial state. The development of instruments of total war, especially nuclear weapons, demonstrated that no state could any longer claim to provide a hard shell of security for its citizens. Herz later retracted his gloomy prediction in the wake of postwar decolonization and the birth of dozens of new states. He pointed out the "synthetic" quality of these states and argued for an international role in their "hardening" over time (John Herz, *The Nation-State and the Crisis of World Politics* [New York: David McKay, 1976]).

However, in the past decade, new concerns have been raised by those who believe that the forces of globalization now threaten the future of the nation-state. These analysts argue that since the early 1970s the international political economy has been experiencing a profound transformation. The idea of national economies, enclosed by national borders and controlled by national governments, is being rendered nearly meaningless by a globalized economy. As a result, the modern state is faced with an increasing inability to provide economic prosperity within its borders. In a global marketplace, few states can claim economic autonomy or self-sufficiency. The prosperity of citizens is now to a large extent determined beyond their national borders, rather than by any decisions made by their national governments.

Those who believe that the state is in decline argue that students of international relations need to broaden their focus beyond an analysis of state behaviour, to the growing role played by transnational corporations, non-governmental organizations (NGOs), and international institutions. In addition, they suggest a need to shift the focus away from considerations of military power as the primary determinant in international politics to other forms of power and influence. However, while some see the state in permanent decline, others are not so certain. They suggest that states are resilient and have many resources at their disposal to ensure their role as the principal influence in international relations.

In the following readings, we enter into this debate with two leading analysts of the modern state. In the first reading, Susan Strange, who until her recent death was a professor of international political economy at the University of Warwick, examines the pressures that are leading to a decline in the authority of states. She suggests that international relations analysts need to take these changes into account and shift away from a "state-centric" focus. In the second reading, Martin Wolf, chief economics commentator for the *Financial Times*, argues that globalization, if anything, has strengthened the role of states.

✔ YES
The Erosion of the State
SUSAN STRANGE

I hear two choruses of voices raised against the whole notion of globalization; I have some sympathy with one and none at all with the other. Explaining this requires me to say — briefly — what I understand the term to mean, and forms the first part of this essay. It also helps to make clear what I understand to be the root causes behind the process of globalization. This is the essay's second part. And, for the last part, I explain what I understand to be the main consequences of globalization for the state in the context of consequences for other political institutions and social and economic groups.

THE NAYSAYERS

The chorus of voices with whom I have no sympathy — or very little — is that which denies the reality of globalization and claims that nothing has really changed. According to this chorus it is all "globaloney," a great myth, an illusion, and therefore not to be taken seriously. Globalization, according to them, is an illusion because the state still exists; because enterprises still "belong" to one particular state in the sense that their headquarters are located in the territory of the state from which they sprang; because their directors are almost exclusively of one national origin; and because their corporate culture is markedly different from that of other "national" firms.

They are wrong, however: the fact that states still exist does not prove that globalization is not a part of the reality in which we all live. Nor does the fact that firms are referred to as "American," "British," or "Japanese" mean that the nature and behavior of firms, like that of states, has not been changed by globalization. Although it is hard to measure the process of globalization, it is no myth. It exists, and it changes things, on several levels. As an international political economist, I perceive these changes first of all in what the French historian Fernand Braudel called "material life" — the production structure that determines what material goods and services are produced by human societies for their survival and comfort. Instead of goods and services being predominantly produced by and for people living in the territory of a state, they are now increasingly produced by people in several states, for a world market instead of for a local market.

Second, globalization involves changes in the financial structure — the system by which credit is created to finance production and trade in goods and services. Where once the creation and use of credit mostly took place within the societies of territorial states, it now takes place across territorial frontiers, in global markets electronically linked into a single system. True, within that system there are local banks and markets creating credit for local use. But these are no longer autonomous; they are part of the larger system, more vulnerable to its ups and downs than it is to their ups and downs.

Finally, globalization takes place on a third level: the level of perceptions, beliefs, ideas, and tastes. Here, while cultural differences persist, the sensitivities and susceptibilities of individual human beings are increasingly being modified by the processes of global homogenization. While made easier and faster by the so-called information revolution and the falling costs of international communications, these are only channels, the means by which the processes of globalization take place. Although this third level of globalization is the hardest to quantify or monitor, it may in the long run be the most significant of all the changes brought by globalization.

Yet this level is the one most often overlooked by those economists and others who join the chorus denying the reality of globalization. While some merely question whether the extent of change attributable to globalization is being exaggerated, others call the whole concept of globalization into question, denying that there has been any real change.[1]

Many of these voices belong to my former colleagues in that branch of social science called international relations. It is a branch that did not exist before the First World War, and in America, not until after the Second World War. The terrible destruction and waste in both conflicts prompted intellectuals to ask the question, "Why do states wage war on each other?" The problematic of international relations, therefore, was the causes of interstate conflict and war, and whether, and how, war could be prevented and peace preserved. Always, the state was the primary focus of attention and was often habitually treated also as a unitary actor. Because discussion of globalization introduces other actors – markets and firms, and other forces of change, like technology, the media, and communications – such discussion implies the growing obsolescence of the study of international relations. On top of these longer-term secular changes, moreover, came the end of the cold war, removing one of the main dangers inherent in the international political system.

Like a stag at bay, the professor of international relations is apt to turn and hurl defiance at those who would bring him down. For myself, as an international political economist, I believe study of the world we live in should adapt to change, not resist it; I have little sympathy with those who deny the reality of globalization and cling to an obsolescing paradigm and a problematic superseded by others. As I have argued elsewhere, the danger of major wars between states has paled beside the danger of long-lasting economic depression resulting from flaws in the financial system and of irreversible environmental damage resulting from worldwide industrialization.[2]

THREE DILEMMAS AND AN EXPLANATION

With the other chorus that acknowledges the reality but urges resistance to it, I have more sympathy. Change always creates losers as well as winners. It is never painless for everyone. There are costs, and it can be (and is) argued that the costs are not worth the benefits: that the pace of change is so fast that the risks are greater than the opportunities. If globalization cannot be reversed or even resisted, it should at least be slowed down. For reasons that will be clearer when I come to the consequences of globalization, I think this may be a tenable view. It seems to be especially prevalent in Europe. A recent book, *The Global Trap*, by Harald Schumann and Hans-Peter Martin of *Der Spiegel*, proved an unexpected bestseller in Germany in 1996.[3] Germans generally prefer the deutsche mark to the euro, the national past to the globalized future.

Three dilemmas for the world political economy result from the effects of globalization on the state. One is economic. A market economy, whether global or national, needs a lender of last resort, an authority – call it hegemonic, though the term misleads – able to discipline but also to give confidence to banks and financial markets, and able to apply Keynesian logic in times of slow growth and recession. The dilemma is that neither former hegemons nor international organizations can be relied on for either task.

Another dilemma is environmental. The motivations of corporate players in the world market economy lead most of them to destroy and pollute the planet, while the necessary countervailing power of the states is handicapped by principles of international law, sovereignty, and the like.

The third dilemma is political. The long struggle for liberty and accountability gradually made at least some states accountable to the people, but globalization, by shifting power from states to firms, has allowed international bureaucracies to undermine that accountability. None of the new nonstate authorities are accountable; few are even transparent. There is a democratic deficit, not only in Europe, but in America, Japan – the entire globalized economy.

As to the underlying causes of globalization – and the consequential retreat of the state from its predominant position of authority in the economy and society – I would point first to the accelerating rate of technological change, and second to the accelerated mobility of capital, as the two indispensable factors affecting production in a modern economy.[4] Both are too often overlooked and neglected by social scientists. An appreciation of their importance surely requires a historical perspective. Their origins go back at least 200 years to the late eighteenth century – or in the case of technological change, as far back as Galileo and da Vinci. Both men believed that science held the answers to the great puzzles of life on the planet and had the potential to change the human condition for the better. That belief (reinforced by the competition of states for technical advantage in waging war) has sustained the pursuit of scientific discovery and technological innovation from the Industrial Revolution onward. Yet the application of the discoveries and the innovations beyond the place where they were made would have been impossible if capital had not been mobile enough to move from where credit was created to where it could be profitably invested. The international mobility of capital, in short, which began to be seen in small ways by the late eighteenth century, has been the sine qua non of twentieth-century globalization.

What must be additionally explained is why both technological change and capital mobility began to accelerate around the middle of this century. The two are interrelated but the cause of one was mainly economic, the other mainly political. Technological change has typically involved the substitution of capital for labor. That was the essence of Fordism: by installing a capital-intensive assembly line and the management to go with it at Willow Run, Henry Ford could employ cheap unskilled labor instead of skilled expensive labor. Afterward, even cheaper robots replaced the workers, once again involving higher capital costs as the price of lower running costs. In Marxist terms, technological change altered the organic composition of capital, thus increasing the demand for capital and lowering the demand for labor.

By mid-century, this substitution was fueling the expansion of international trade since newcomers like the Japanese could lower marginal costs by producing for export as well as the home market. In sector after sector, from steel to beer, production for the world market became imperative. Every technological innovation called for more capital investment. And as the pace of technological innovation accelerated under the pressure of competition between firms for market shares, it became less and less possible to survive on the basis of profits in a home market. Firms, in short, did not choose to produce for foreign markets; they were forced to do so or go under. The price of entry, in many cases but especially in developing countries with potentially large markets, was often relocation of manufacturing capacity inside the trade barriers against competitive imports.[5]

THE NEW DIPLOMACY

None of this would have been possible without the greater mobility of capital. For this, the Europeans and especially the British were responsible during the long nineteenth century to 1914, and the Americans thereafter. Mobility slowed almost to a standstill after the crash of 1929, but even then United States firms continued to invest in international production in Europe and Latin America. After 1945, successive American governments pushed for the reduction of exchange controls over capital movements. This, more than the reduction of tariffs and other barriers to trade, created the necessary and sufficient conditions for the internalization of production. Firms found it increasingly easy to borrow in one country or currency − not necessarily their own − and invest it in another. It could be done through banks or through stock markets, and the whole business was greatly aided by the creation of the unregulated, untaxed Eurocurrency markets.

First in the new postwar wave of foreign investment were the American multinationals. They soon overtook the British, Swiss, and Dutch as the major holders of the stock of foreign direct investment. The big enterprises were soon followed by much smaller firms. The American multinationals were soon joined by the Japanese, Koreans, Taiwanese, and others. Their spread into other markets was made easier by the concurrent change in the attitudes of host countries. Where these had initially been hostile to foreign firms, by the 1980s most had realized that the foreign firms held three keys to earning the foreign exchange so necessary for industrialization. These three keys were: command of technology; ready access to mobile capital; and (often the most important) the brand name and distribution network that gave ready access to the rich markets of America and Europe.

The significance of this "new diplomacy" (as John Stopford and I called it) has been largely lost on conventional writers on international relations. For it means that states are joined by firms as the authorities exercising power over the course of national and global economic development. The governments of states may still be the gatekeepers to the territory over which other states recognize their authority. But if no foreign firms want to go through their gate, their countries have a slim chance of keeping up with the competition from other, more welcoming governments for world market shares. Even if firms do seek entry, governments have to negotiate with them over terms. The balance of power between host and foreign firm then becomes an important field of study in comparative political economy, with much depending on the size of the host market and the firm's standing in the kind of business it is in.

Another aspect of the new diplomacy is also of growing importance in world politics and world economics. Corporate takeovers and strategic alliances between firms increasingly determine future trends in economic growth, employment, and trade. Recall the fuss in Europe over Boeing's takeover of McDonnell-Douglas. It created an aircraft manufacturer likely to dominate the world market, a competitor for Europe's Airbus even more formidable than before. Recall the alarm felt in Hong Kong last August when Li Ka-shing bought 3 percent of the shares in Jardine Mathieson, raising doubts over how long Beijing would allow non-Chinese interests to survive the new regime. Such questions — both political and economic in their implications — call for more serious study of firm-firm relations than exists at the moment. It is a new field where experts in international business and management have to work with those in international relations, and to listen carefully, too, to business historians.

Although neglected, the growing importance of state-firm and of firm-firm diplomacy is only one aspect of the rising power of firms and other non-state actors and the corresponding decline in the authority of the state in the world economy and society. But before attempting to demonstrate this decline in a more systemic manner, it should be pointed out that "decline" may have been preceded by "rise," and that it may be dangerous to extrapolate decline into the future. This is to say that the predominance of the nation-state as the foremost authority over society and economy may turn out to have been exceptional, not normal. In a longer historical perspective, multiple sources of authority were perhaps the norm, and the concentration of power in the hands of state governments in this century and the last may have been a deviation. Second, those of us who perceive decline in state authority in the last decade or two are not necessarily predicting that the decline will continue indefinitely into the future. We simply do not know.

ERODING THE STATE'S AUTHORITY

There are three main areas in which state authority has declined. Other aspects of decline are almost all subsidiary to these three. The first is defense: the security of society from violence. The second is finance: the preservation of money as a reliable means of exchange, unit of account, and store of value (this is especially necessary to a market, as opposed to a state-planned, economy). And the third is the provision of welfare: the assurance that some of the benefits of greater wealth go to the poor, the weak, the sick, and the old. This too is particularly necessary in a capitalist market economy, where the system tends to make the rich conspicuously richer and the gap wider between them and the disadvantaged. It can be quickly and easily shown that the power of most states in all three — and therefore the justification for their claims on society — has seriously declined. And it has done so as a result of the forces of globalization already described.

Defense against foreign invasion is no longer necessary if — as is now mostly the case — neighbors show no sign of wanting to invade for the sake of command over territory. There are now only three exceptional cases where neighbors may be so tempted. One is for command over oil or gas fields. Another is for control over water supplies. The third is irredentism, where societies or their governments feel a moral or emotional compulsion to incorporate territory inhabited by ethnic or religious groups into the state to safeguard their interests and security (there are more cases today where this might have happened but has not, than there are where it has).

For the most part, the obsolescence of major interstate war is implicit in state policies, for the very good reason that people recognize that success in gaining world market shares has replaced territorial acquisition as the means of survival. Armies and navies continue to exist — not least because of competition for world market shares in the arms trade — but more because they are needed to preserve civil order rather than to repel invaders. Where there is no risk of civil disorder, they are merely an ornamental anachronism. Where there is such a risk parts of society will regard national armed forces as a threat to their security, not as an impartial guardian of the peace. The decline of support for conscription in many countries is one indicator of this change.

The second justification for state authority — that it maintains the value of the currency — is also fast disappearing. With probably the sole exception of the United States (and possibly the Swiss Confederation), states are no longer able to resist the foreign exchange markets. It is not that speculators have run amok, but that the mobility of capital mentioned earlier means that flows of money in and out of currencies, not trade balances, trigger market responses, which in turn move exchange rates. And only a powerful coalition of major central banks led by the United States (as in the Mexican peso crisis in 1994) can stop a collapsing currency.

With one of the three legs of monetary stability so weak, what of the other two, interest rates and inflation rates? Governments can determine the first, but only within limits set by the markets. Too high an interest rate may keep money flowing in but – as in Germany recently, or Britain under Gordon Brown as finance minister – this will impose excruciating costs on small business and will push the exchange rate too high to make exports competitive.

As for inflation rates, governments pretend to control the money supply, and thus the value of money, mainly by varying interest rates. But technology is about to frustrate their efforts. Credit card spending is rising quickly in the United States and now in Britain. It is purchasing power over which the state has no control. Digital money and digital shopping on the Internet will be even less under state control and potentially even more disruptive. Much depends on the banks as major players in the money markets. Yet the central banks' Bank for International Settlements in Basel confessed just this past year that its concordats on bank regulation cannot be relied on to preserve the global financial system against the dangers besetting it. Rules of thumb on reserve requirements that used to limit growth in the money supply, and therefore the value of money, no longer work. Commercial banks therefore must be trusted (and helped) to regulate themselves. But trusting the bankers to discipline themselves is like asking poachers to see that there is no poaching. So far, so good ...

The state as social safety net, redistributing resources and entitlements to make good the shortcomings of the market, has been a recent but important justification for its authority and one most powerfully appreciated by the Europeans. The superiority of "Rhenish capitalism" in the vocabulary of Michel Albert (over Anglo-Saxon capitalism) was precisely that it ensured a measure of social justice denied by the market.[6]

This justification is still made, but it lacks creditability. Globalization has opened tax-evading doors for multinationals and many individuals. As more tax havens open up and more use is made of them, states' revenues suffer; everywhere, welfare services are cut back (the age at which state pensions are paid will soon be raised in Italy, France, and probably Germany). In desperation, states raise money by selling off state-owned enterprises. The public sector that once – even in the United States in World War II – was an important lever of state power over the economy cannot survive the pressures of global competition. Even the power of the state to use trade protection as an economic weapon against foreign competition and a supplementary safety net for those (such as farmers, fishermen, miners, or steelworkers) in declining occupations is fast disappearing. The global consensus declares protectionism wrong, liberalization right. National experience is that it often protects the inefficient and uncompetitive and is therefore counterproductive.

The "globaloney" school is not only wrong, but by trying to persuade people that nothing has changed, is also encouraging an ostrich-like response to recent changes in the world economy. If, as I have argued, the state's power to provide economic and financial stability, to protect the vulnerable in society, and to preserve the environment has been weakened, society is at the mercy of big business. That is not a prospect I suspect most Europeans and many Americans really want for their children and their grandchildren in the years to come.

NOTES

1. See, for example, Paul Hirst and Grahame Thompson, *Globalization in Question: The International Economy and the Possibilities of Governance* (Cambridge: Polity Press, 1996).

2. See Susan Strange, *Statistics and Markets*, 2nd ed. (London: Pinter, 1994), pp. 60–63; and ibid., *The Retreat of the State: The Diffusion of Power in the World Economy* (Cambridge: Cambridge University Press, 1996), pp. 66–87.

3. Harald Schumann and Hans-Peter Martin, *The Global Trap* (London: Zed Books, 1997).

4. This argument is developed at greater length in *The Retreat of the State*, op cit.

5. See John Stopford and Susan Strange, *Rival States, Rival Firms: Competition for World Market Shares* (Cambridge: Cambridge University Press, 1991), pp. 1–64.

6. See Michel Albert, *Capitalism against Capitalism* (London: Whurr, 1993).

✗ **NO**

Will the Nation-State Survive Globalization?
MARTIN WOLF

DEFINING GLOBALIZATION

A specter is haunting the world's governments — the specter of globalization. Some argue that predatory market forces make it impossible for benevolent governments to shield their populations from the beasts of prey that lurk beyond their borders. Others counter that benign market forces actually prevent predatory governments from fleecing their citizens. Although the two sides see different villains, they draw one common conclusion: omnipotent markets mean impotent politicians. Indeed, this formula has become one of the cliches of our age. But is it true that governments have become weaker and less relevant than ever before? And does globalization, by definition, have to be the nemesis of national government?

Globalization is a journey. But it is a journey toward an unreachable destination — "the globalized world." A "globalized" economy could be defined as one in which neither distance nor national borders impede economic transactions. This would be a world where the costs of transport and communications were zero and the barriers created by differing national jurisdictions had vanished. Needless to say, we do not live in anything even close to such a world. And since many of the things we transport (including ourselves) are physical, we never will.

This globalizing journey is not a new one. Over the past five centuries, technological change has progressively reduced the barriers to international integration. Transatlantic communication, for example, has evolved from sail power to steam, to the telegraph, the telephone, commercial aircraft, and now to the Internet. Yet states have become neither weaker nor less important during this odyssey. On the contrary, in the countries with the most advanced and internationally integrated economies, governments' ability to tax and redistribute incomes, regulate the economy, and monitor the activity of their citizens has increased beyond all recognition. This has been especially true over the past century.

The question that remains, however, is whether today's form of globalization is likely to have a different impact from that of the past. Indeed, it may well, for numerous factors distinguish today's globalizing journey from past ones and could produce a different outcome. These distinctions include more rapid communications, market liberalization, and global integration of the production of goods and services. Yet contrary to one common assumption, the modern form of globalization will not spell the end of the modern nation-state.

THE PAST AS PROLOGUE

Today's growing integration of the world economy is not unprecedented, at least when judged by the flow of goods, capital, and people. Similar trends occurred in the late nineteenth and early twentieth centuries.

First, the proportion of world production that is traded on global markets is not that much higher today than it was in the years leading up to World War I. Commerce was comparably significant in 1910, when ratios of trade (merchandise exports plus imports) to GDP hit record highs in several of the advanced economies. Global commerce then collapsed during the Great Depression and World War II, but since then world trade has grown more rapidly than output. The share of global production traded worldwide grew from about 7 percent in 1950 to more than 20 percent by the mid-1990s; in consequence, trade ratios have risen in almost all of the advanced economies. In the United Kingdom, for example, exports and imports added up to 57 percent of GDP in 1995 compared to 44 percent in 1910; for France the 1995 proportion was 43 percent against 35 percent in 1910; and for Germany it was 46 percent against 38 percent in the same years. But Japan's trade ratio was actually lower in 1995 than it had been in 1910. In fact, among today's five biggest economies, the only one in which trade has a remarkably greater weight in output than it had a century ago is the United States, where the ratio has jumped from 11 percent in 1910 to 24 percent in 1995. That fact may help explain why globalization is more controversial for Americans than for people in many other countries.

Second, by the late nineteenth century many countries had already opened their capital markets to international investments, before investments, too, collapsed during the interwar period. As a share of GDP, British capital investments abroad — averaging 4.6 percent of GDP between 1870 and 1913 — hit levels unparalleled in contemporary major economies. More revealing is that the correlation between domestic investment and savings (a measure of the extent to which savings remain within one country) was lower between 1880 and 1910 than in any subsequent period.

Historical differences exist, however. Although current capital mobility has precedents from the pre-World War I era, the composition of capital flows has changed. Short-term capital today is much more mobile than ever before. Moreover, long-term flows now are somewhat differently constituted than in the earlier period. Investment in the early twentieth century took the form of tangible assets rather than intangible ones. Portfolio flows predominated over direct investment in the earlier period (that trend has been reversed since World War II); within portfolios, stocks have increased in relative importance to roughly equal bonds today. And finally, before 1914, direct investment was undertaken largely by companies investing in mining and transportation, whereas today multinational companies predominate, with a large proportion of their investment in services.

Today's high immigration flows are also not unprecedented. According to economists Paul Hirst and Grahame Thompson, the greatest era for recorded voluntary mass migration was the century after 1815. Around 60 million people left Europe for the Americas, Oceania, and South and East Africa. An estimated 10 million voluntarily migrated from Russia to Central Asia and Siberia. A million went from Southern Europe to North America. About 12 million Chinese and 6 million Japanese left their homelands and emigrated to eastern and southern Asia. One and a half million left India for Southeast Asia and Southwest Africa.

Population movement peaked during the 1890s. In those years, the United States absorbed enough immigrants to increase the U.S. population from the beginning of the decade by 9 percent. In Argentina, the increase in the 1890s was 26 percent; in Australia, it was 17 percent. Europe provided much of the supply: the United Kingdom gave up 5 percent of its initial population, Spain 6 percent, and Sweden 7 percent. In the 1990s, by contrast, the United States was the only country in the world with a high immigration rate, attracting newcomers primarily from the developing world rather than from Europe. These immigrants increased the population by only 4 percent.

As all of this suggests, despite the many economic changes that have occurred over the course of a century, neither the markets for goods and services nor those for factors of production appear much more integrated today than they were a century ago. They seem more integrated for trade, at least in the high-income countries; no more integrated for capital – above all for long-term capital – despite important changes in the composition of capital flows; and much less integrated for labor.

So why do so many people believe that something unique is happening today? The answer lies with the two forces driving contemporary economic change: falling costs of transport and communications on the one hand, and liberalizing economic policies on the other.

THE TECHNOLOGICAL REVOLUTION

Advances in technology and infrastructure substantially and continuously reduced the costs of transport and communications throughout the nineteenth and early twentieth centuries. The first transatlantic telegraph cable was laid in 1866. By the turn of the century, the entire world was connected by telegraph, and communication times fell from months to minutes. The cost of a three-minute telephone call from New York to London in current prices dropped from about $250 in 1930 to a few cents today. In more recent years, the number of voice paths across the Atlantic has skyrocketed from 100,000 in 1986 to more than 2 million today. The number of Internet hosts has risen from 5,000 in 1986 to more than 30 million now.

A revolution has thus occurred in collecting and disseminating information, one that has dramatically reduced the cost of moving physical objects. But these massive improvements in communications, however important, simply continue the trends begun with the first submarine cables laid in the last century. Furthermore, distances still impose transport and communications costs that continue to make geography matter in economic terms. Certain important services still cannot be delivered from afar.

Diminishing costs of communications and transport were nevertheless pointing toward greater integration throughout the last century. But if historical experience demonstrates anything, it is that integration is not technologically determined. If it were, integration would have gone smoothly forward over the past two centuries. On the contrary, despite continued falls in the costs of transport and communications in the first half of the twentieth century, integration actually reversed course.

Policy, not technology, has determined the extent and pace of international economic integration. If transport and communications innovations were moving toward global economic integration throughout the last century and a half, policy was not — and that made all the difference. For this reason, the growth in the potential for economic integration has greatly outpaced the growth of integration itself since the late nineteenth century. Globalization has much further to run, if it is allowed to do so.

CHOOSING GLOBALIZATION

Globalization is not destined, it is chosen. It is a choice made to enhance a nation's economic well-being — indeed, experience suggests that the opening of trade and of most capital flows enriches most citizens in the short run and virtually all citizens in the long run. (Taxation on short-term capital inflows to emerging market economies is desirable, however, particularly during a transition to full financial integration.) But if integration is a deliberate choice, rather than an ineluctable destiny, it cannot render states impotent. Their potency lies in the choices they make.

Between 1846 and 1870, liberalization spread from the United Kingdom to the rest of Europe. Protectionism, which had never waned in the United States, returned to continental Europe after 1878 and reached its peak in the 1930s.

A new era of global economic integration began only in the postwar era, and then only partially: from the end of World War II through the 1970s, only the advanced countries lowered their trade barriers. The past two decades, by contrast, have seen substantial liberalization take root throughout the world. By the late 1990s, no economically significant country still had a government committed to protectionism.

This historical cycle is also apparent in international capital investments. Capital markets stayed open in the nineteenth and early twentieth centuries, partly because governments did not have the means to control capital flows.

They acquired and haltingly solidified this capacity between 1914 and 1945, progressively closing their capital markets. Liberalization of capital flows then began in a few advanced countries during the 1950s and 1960s. But the big wave of liberalization did not start in earnest until the late 1970s, spreading across the high-income countries, much of the developing world, and, by the 1990s, to the former communist countries. Notwithstanding a large number of financial crises over this period, this trend has remained intact.

In monetary policy, the biggest change has been the move from the gold standard of the 1870–1914 era to the floating currencies of today. The long-run exchange-rate stability inherent in the gold standard promoted long-term capital flows, particularly bond financing, more efficiently than does the contemporary currency instability. Today's vast short-term financial flows are not just a consequence of exchange-rate instability, but one of its causes.

Yet governments' control over the movement of people in search of employment tightened virtually everywhere in the early part of the last century. With the exception of the free immigration policy among members of the European Union (EU), immigration controls are generally far tighter now than they were a hundred years ago.

The policy change that has most helped global integration to flourish is the growth of international institutions since World War II. Just as multinational companies now organize private exchange, so global institutions organize and discipline the international face of national policy. Institutions such as the World Trade Organization (WTO), the International Monetary Fund (IMF), the World Bank, the EU, and the North American Free Trade Agreement underpin cooperation among states and consolidate their commitments to liberalize economic policy. The nineteenth century was a world of unilateral and discretionary policy. The late twentieth century, by comparison, was a world of multilateral and institutionalized policy.

TRADEOFFS FACING STATES

Ironically, the technology that is supposed to make globalization inevitable also makes increased surveillance by the state, particularly over people, easier than it would have been a century ago. Indeed, here is the world we now live in: one with fairly free movement of capital, continuing (though declining) restrictions on trade in goods and services, but quite tight control over the movement of people.

Economies are also never entirely open or entirely closed. Opening requires governments to loosen three types of economic controls: on capital flows, goods and services, and people. Liberalizing one of the above neither requires nor always leads to liberalization in the others. Free movement of goods and services makes regulating capital flows more difficult, but not impossible; foreign direct investment can flow across national barriers to trade in goods without knocking them down. It is easier still to trade freely and abolish controls on capital movement, while nevertheless regulating movement of people.

The important questions, then, concern the tradeoffs confronting governments that have chosen a degree of international economic integration. How constrained will governments find themselves once they have chosen openness?

THREE VITAL AREAS

Globalization is often perceived as destroying governments' capacities to do what they want or need, particularly in the key areas of taxation, public spending for income redistribution, and macroeconomic policy. But how true is this perception?

In fact, no evidence supports the conclusion that states can no longer raise taxes. On the contrary: in 1999, EU governments spent or redistributed an average of 47 percent of their GDPs. An important new book by Vito Tanzi of the IMF and Ludger Schuknecht of the European Central Bank underlines this point. Over the course of the twentieth century, the average share of government spending among Organization for Economic Cooperation and Development (OECD) member states jumped from an eighth to almost half of GDP. In some high-income countries such as France and Germany, these ratios were higher than ever before.

Until now, it has been electoral resistance, not globalization, that has most significantly limited the growth in taxation. Tanzi claims that this is about to change. He argues that collecting taxes is becoming harder due to a long list of "fiscal termites" gnawing at the foundations of taxation regimes: more cross-border shopping, the increased mobility of skilled labor, the growth of electronic commerce, the expansion of tax havens, the development of new financial instruments and intermediaries, growing trade within multinational companies, and the possible replacement of bank accounts with electronic money embedded in "smart cards."

The list is impressive. That governments take it seriously is demonstrated by the attention that leaders of the OECD and the EU are devoting to "harmful tax competition," information exchange, and the implications of electronic commerce. Governments, like members of any other industry, are forming a cartel to halt what they see as "ruinous competition" in taxation. This sense of threat has grown out of several fiscal developments produced by globalization: increased mobility of people and money, greater difficulty in collecting information on income and spending, and the impact of the Internet on information flows and collection.

Yet the competitive threat that governments face must not be exaggerated. The fiscal implications of labor, capital, and spending mobility are already evident in local jurisdictions that have the freedom to set their own tax rates. Even local governments can impose higher taxes than their neighbors, provided they contain specific resources or offer location-specific amenities that residents desire and consume. In other words, differential taxation is possible if there are at least some transport costs — and there always are.

These costs grow with a jurisdiction's geographic size, which thus strongly influences a local government's ability to raise taxes. The income of mobile capital is the hardest to tax; the income of land and immobile labor is easiest. Corporate income can be taxed if it is based on resources specific to that location, be they natural or human. Spending can also be taxed more heavily in one jurisdiction than another, but not if transport costs are very low (either because distances are short or items are valuable in relation to costs). Similarly, it is difficult to tax personal incomes if people can live in low-tax jurisdictions while enjoying the amenities of high-tax ones.

Eliminating legal barriers to mobility therefore constrains, but does not eliminate, the ability of some jurisdictions to levy far higher taxes than others. The ceiling on higher local taxes rises when taxable resources or activities remain relatively immobile or the jurisdiction provides valuable specific amenities just for that area.

The international mobility of people and goods is unlikely ever to come close to the kind of mobility that exists between states in the United States. Legal, linguistic, and cultural barriers will keep levels of cross-border migration far lower than levels of movement within any given country. Since taxes on labor income and spending are the predominant source of national revenue, the modern country's income base seems quite safe. Of course, although the somewhat greater mobility resulting from globalization makes it harder for governments to get information about what their residents own and spend abroad, disguising physical movement, consumption, or income remains a formidable task.

The third major aspect of globalization, the Internet, may have an appreciable impact on tax collection. Stephane Buydens of the OECD plausibly argues that the Internet will primarily affect four main areas: taxes on spending, tax treaties, internal pricing of multinational companies, and tax administration.

Purely Internet-based transactions — downloading of films, software, or music — are hard to tax. But when the Internet is used to buy tangible goods, governments can impose taxes, provided that the suppliers cooperate with the fiscal authorities of their corresponding jurisdictions. To the extent that these suppliers are large shareholder-owned companies, which they usually are, this cooperation may not be as hard to obtain as is often supposed.

It is also sometimes difficult to locate an Internet server. If one cannot do so, how are taxes to be levied and tax treaties applied? Similar problems arise with multinational companies' ability to charge submarket prices to their subsidiaries abroad (so-called "transfer pricing" within multinationals), which leaves uncertain the question of how and in which country to levy the tax. This scenario suggests that classic concepts in the taxation of corporations may have to be modified or even radically overhauled.

The overall conclusion, then, is that economic liberalization and technology advances will make taxation significantly more challenging. Taxes on spending may have to be partially recast. Taxation of corporate profits may have to be radically redesigned or even abandoned. Finally, the ability of governments to impose taxes that bear no relation to the benefits provided may be more constrained than before.

Nevertheless, the implications of these changes can easily be exaggerated. Taxation of corporate income is rarely more than ten percent of revenue, whereas taxes on income and spending are the universal pillars of the fiscal system. Yet even lofty Scandinavian taxes are not forcing skilled people to emigrate in droves. People will still happily pay to enjoy high-quality schools or public transport. Indeed, one of the most intriguing phenomena of modern Europe is that the hightax, big-spending Scandinavian countries are leading the "new economy."

Governments will also use the exchange of information and other forms of cooperation to sustain revenue and may even consider international agreements on minimum taxes. They will certainly force the publicly quoted companies that continue to dominate transactions, both on-line and off, to cooperate with fiscal authorities. But competition among governments will not be eliminated, because the powerful countries that provide relatively low-tax, low-spending environments will want to maintain them.

The bottom line is that the opening of economies and the blossoming of new technologies are reinforcing constraints that have already developed within domestic politics. National governments are becoming a little more like local governments. The result will not necessarily be minimal government. But governments, like other institutions, will be forced to provide value to those who pay for their services.

Meanwhile, governments can continue the practice of income redistribution to the extent that the most highly taxed citizens and firms cannot — or do not wish to — evade taxation. In fact, if taxes are used to fund what are believed to be location-specific benefits, such as income redistribution or welfare spending, taxpayers will likely be quite willing to pay, perhaps because they either identify with the beneficiaries, fear that they could become indigent themselves, or treasure the security that comes from living among people who are not destitute. Taxpayers may also feel a sense of moral obligation to the poor, a sentiment that seems stronger in small, homogeneous societies. Alternatively, they may merely be unable to evade or avoid those taxes without relocating physically outside the jurisdiction. For all these reasons, sustaining a high measure of redistributive taxation remains perfectly possible. The constraint is not globalization, but the willingness of the electorate to tolerate high taxation.

Last but not least, some observers argue that globalization limits governments' ability to run fiscal deficits and pursue inflationary monetary policy. But macroeconomic policy is always vulnerable to the reaction of the private sector, regardless of whether the capital market is internationally integrated. If a government pursues a consistently inflationary policy, long-term nominal interest rates will rise, partly to compensate for inflation and partly to insure the bondholders against inflation risk. Similarly, if a government relies on the printing press to finance its activity, a flight from money into goods, services, and assets will ensue – and, in turn, generate inflation.

Within one country, these reactions may be slow. A government can pursue an inflationary policy over a long period and boost the economy; the price may not have to be paid for many years. What difference, then, does it make for the country to be open to international capital flows? The most important change is that the reaction of a government's creditors is likely to be quicker and more brutal because they have more alternatives. This response will often show itself in a collapsing exchange rate, as happened in East Asia in 1997 and 1998.

THE CONTINUING IMPORTANCE OF STATES

A country that chooses international economic integration implicitly accepts constraints on its actions. Nevertheless, the idea that these constraints wither away the state's capacity to tax, regulate, or intervene is wrong. Rather, international economic integration accelerates the market's responses to policy by increasing the range of alternative options available to those affected. There are also powerful reasons for believing that the constraints imposed on (or voluntarily accepted by) governments by globalization are, on balance, desirable.

For example, the assumption that most governments are benevolent welfare-maximizers is naive. International economic integration creates competition among governments – even countries that fiercely resist integration cannot survive with uncompetitive economies, as shown by the fate of the Soviet Union. This competition constrains the ability of governments to act in a predatory manner and increases the incentive to provide services that are valued by those who pay the bulk of the taxes.

Another reason for welcoming the constraints is that self-imposed limits on a government's future actions enhance the credibility of even a benevolent government's commitments to the private sector. An open capital account is one such constraint. Treaties with other governments, as in the WTO, are another, as are agreements with powerful private parties. Even China has come to recognize the economic benefits that it can gain from international commitments of this kind.

The proposition that globalization makes states unnecessary is even less credible than the idea that it makes states impotent. If anything, the exact opposite is true, for at least three reasons. First, the ability of a society to take advantage of the opportunities offered by international economic integration depends on the quality of public goods, such as property rights, an honest civil service, personal security, and basic education. Without an appropriate legal framework, in particular, the web of potentially rewarding contracts is vastly reduced. This point may seem trivial, but many developing economies have failed to achieve these essential preconditions of success.

Second, the state normally defines identity. A sense of belonging is part of the people's sense of security, and one that most people would not want to give up, even in the age of globalization. It is perhaps not surprising that some of the most successfully integrated economies are small, homogeneous countries with a strong sense of collective identity.

Third, international governance rests on the ability of individual states to provide and guarantee stability. The bedrock of international order is the territorial state with its monopoly on coercive power within its jurisdiction. Cyberspace does not change this: economies are ultimately run for and by human beings, who have a physical presence and, therefore, a physical location.

Globalization does not make states unnecessary. On the contrary, for people to be successful in exploiting the opportunities afforded by international integration, they need states at both ends of their transactions. Failed states, disorderly states, weak states, and corrupt states are shunned as the black holes of the global economic system.

What, then, does globalization mean for states? First, policy ultimately determines the pace and depth of international economic integration. For each country, globalization is at least as much a choice as a destiny. Second, in important respects — notably a country's monetary regime, capital account, and above all, labor mobility — the policy underpinnings of integration are less complete than they were a century ago. Third, countries choose integration because they see its benefits. Once chosen, any specific degree of international integration imposes constraints on the ability of governments to tax, redistribute income, and influence macroeconomic conditions. But those constraints must not be exaggerated, and their effects are often beneficial. Fourth, international economic integration magnifies the impact of the difference between good and bad states — between states that provide public goods and those that serve predatory private interests, including those of the rulers.

Finally, as the world economy continues to integrate and cross-border flows become more important, global governance must be improved. Global governance will come not at the expense of the state but rather as an expression of the interests that the state embodies. As the source of order and basis of governance, the state will remain in the future as effective, and will be as essential, as it has ever been.

POSTSCRIPT

The debate over the impact of globalization on the future of the nation-state has led to a growing interest in alternative forms of political community. Since states have little control over global markets and limited influence on decisions made by transnational corporations, some argue that we need to move toward some form of cosmopolitan democracy. Advocates of this view suggest that individuals need to think of themselves as transnational or world citizens and should join together to seek to democratize international institutions. Some have suggested that international institutions such as the United Nations need to be reformed to permit direct popular participation. Perhaps citizens of individual countries could elect representatives to a Popular Assembly of the United Nations much like Europeans elect representatives to the European Parliament today.

Others see a different future. They suggest that we are entering a situation much like that occurring in Europe in the Middle Ages. In this view, individuals would be governed in the future by a number of overlapping authorities. States would transfer some powers to international institutions to deal with global problems. At the same time, they would transfer some powers to more regional units, where the sense of distinctive identities is stronger. States would occupy only one level of government among many. Citizens would divide their loyalty between states, sub-state entities, and transnational political authorities. Some believe that Europe is farthest along this path. Whether one accepts either of these visions of the future, both suggest that the role of the nation-state in global governance will be significantly different than it has been in the past.

Suggested Additional Readings

Cerny, Philip G. "What Next for the State?" In Elenore Kofman and Gillian Youngs, eds., *Globalization: Theory and Practice*. London: Pinter, 1996: 123–37.

Del Rosso, Jr., Stephen J. "The Insecure State (What Future for the State?)." *Daedalus* 124, no. 2 (Spring 1995): 175–207.

Evans, Peter. "The Eclipse of the State? Reflections on Statelessness in the Era of Globalization." *World Politics* 50, no. 1 (October 1997): 62–87.

Held, D., and A. McGrew, eds. *The Global Transformations Reader*. Cambridge: Polity, 2000.

Holton, Robert J. *Globalization and the Nation-State*. London: MacMillan, 1998.

Mann, Michael. "Has Globalization Ended the Rise and Rise of the Nation-State?" *Review of International Political Economy* 4, no. 3 (Autumn 1997): 472–96.

Ohmae, Kenichi. "The Rise of the Region State." *Foreign Affairs* 72, no. 2 (Spring 1993): 78–87.

Opello, Jr., Walter C., and Stephen J. Rosow. *The Nation-State and Global Order: An Historical Introduction to Contemporary Politics.* Boulder, Col.: Lynne Rienner, 1999.

Rosenau, James. "The State in an Era of Cascading Politics." In James Caporaso, ed., *The Elusive State: International and Comparative Perspectives.* London: Sage, 1990: 17–48.

Saul, John Ralston. "The Collapse of Globalism." *Harper's Magazine* 308, no. 1846 (March 2004): 33–43.

Strange, Susan. *Retreat of the State: The Diffusion of Power in the World Economy.* Cambridge: Cambridge University Press, 1996.

InfoTrac® College Edition

Search for the following articles in the InfoTrac® database:

Carnoy, Martin. "The Demise of the Nation-State?" *Theoria* 97 (June 2001): 69–82.

Walby, Sylvia. "The Myth of the Nation-State: Theorizing Society and Polities in a Global Era," *Sociology* 37, no. 3 (August 2003): 529–46.

For more articles, enter:
"globalization and state" in the keyword search.
"globalization" in the subject guide, then go to the subdivision "political aspects."

Web Resources

For current URLs for the following websites, visit www.crosscurrents.nelson.com.

GLOBAL POLICY: NATIONS AND STATES

www.globalpolicy.org/nations/index.htm

Global Policy, a nonprofit site on global issues, provides a series of articles on the concept of nation and state. Explore the sections on the future of states and on statehood and sovereignty for articles touching on the impact of globalization.

JURGEN HABERMAS, "THE EUROPEAN NATION-STATE: ON THE PAST AND FUTURE OF SOVEREIGNTY AND CITIZENSHIP," *PUBLIC CULTURE* 10, no. 2 (Winter 1998)

www.uchicago.edu/research/jnl-pub-cult/backissues/pc25/habermas.html

This article looks at the recent events related to the nation-state from a historical and philosophical perspective.

MURRAY N. ROTHBARD, "NATIONS BY DESCENT: DECOMPOSING THE NATION-STATE," *JOURNAL OF LIBERTARIAN STUDIES* 11, no. 1 (Fall 1984)

www.mises.org/jlsdisplay.asp

Choose "N" under author names and scroll to this item. This paper examines the re-emergence of the nation from a libertarian perspective.

NATIONALISM: A CONCEPTUAL STUDY

www.shef.ac.uk/~surc/politics/Definitions_of_Nationalism.html

This site offers in-depth definitions of the terms "nation," "nation-state," and "nationalism" prepared by students in the politics department of the University of Sheffield.

Is the World Fragmenting into Antagonistic Cultures?

✔ **YES**
SAMUEL HUNTINGTON, "The Clash of Civilizations? The Next Pattern of Conflict," *Foreign Affairs* 72, no. 3 (Summer 1993): 22–28

✘ **NO**
DOUGLAS ALAN ROSS, "Ten Years After: The Inevitable Waning of Huntington's Civilizational Clash Theory?"

As the Cold War drew to an end, international relations scholars began debating what the implications of this development would be for international politics. One of the first to address this issue was Francis Fukuyama in an article entitled "The End of History?" (*The National Interest* 16, 1989). Fukuyama argued that the end of the Cold War signalled the end of humankind's ideological evolution and the triumph of Western liberal democracy. He predicted that international conflict, especially between the major powers, would be significantly diminished — that we were moving to a new era of peace and stability. One of the scholars to respond to Fukuyama's thesis was Samuel Huntington, whose article "No Exit: The Errors of Endism" (*The National Interest* 17, 1989) challenged such an optimist assessment of the end of the Cold War.

Huntington was concerned with the growing preoccupation with "endism" or, as he put it, the view that "bad things are coming to an end." In particular, he feared that Fukuyama's optimistic predictions of a new era of expanding zones of peace and tranquility would tempt American policymakers into pursing a policy of retreat and isolationism. Huntington warned that the world was instead moving into a new era of possibly greater "instability, unpredictability, and violence in international affairs." In his article in *The National Interest*, he said that "endism" is "dangerous and subversive" because it "present[s] an illusion of well-being."

In making his case, Huntington noted that the structure of bipolarity and the presence of nuclear weapons had both defined the nature of and placed constraints on U.S.–Soviet rivalry. The end of the Cold War did not "mean the end of the struggle for power and influence." In fact, the end of the "balance of terror" between the two superpowers presaged a slide into a more chaotic and troubling time.

In 1993, Huntington published an article in which he sought to identify in clearer terms the sources of this increased instability and unpredictability. In this article, reproduced here, Huntington claims to be presenting students of international relations with a new and more comprehensive paradigm for understanding world politics. He stresses that rather than simply thinking about the structure of world politics in terms of polarity and balance of power between nation-states, we should take into account the relevance of civilizations and cultures in shaping international conflict, a dimension that has often been ignored in traditional realist analyses of world politics. This "new paradigm," he argues, is necessitated by the evolution of history. According to Huntington, the modern world has evolved through three phases of conflict, progressing from conflicts between princes to conflicts between nation-states and then to conflicts between ideologies. We are entering a new phase of human history in which conflict between civilizations will supplant ideological conflict as a dominant force in international politics.

In the future, Huntington contends, conflicts are most likely to develop between groups that are part of different civilizations. He argues that the cultural differences between the eight different civilizations he identifies will become more dangerous and entrenched than traditional ideological and economic clashes. Advances in communications technologies, and increased economic and social interaction, rather than creating a globalized culture, will magnify "civilizational conscious-ness" and exacerbate future conflicts. Because questions of identity, culture, and religion are more fundamental to people, future conflicts will be less amenable to negotiation and compromise. As Islamic and Confucian states increasingly chal-lenge Western political, economic, and cultural dominance, the possibility of conflict on a global scale − the "West against the rest" − becomes increasingly likely. Accordingly, Huntington issues a call to the American policymakers to be vigilant and not give into the temptation of retreating into an isolationist stance.

Huntington's "clash of civilizations" has been widely debated in the 1990s. Many rejected his thesis outright, and some criticized its author for offering spurious academic arguments in order to justify increased defence expenditures in a period of growing peace and stability. However, the events of September 11, 2001, led many to take a renewed interest in Huntington's thesis. The bold attacks on the United States by Islamist radicals seem to give new impetus to his argument that we may be facing a new and more dangerous era of civilizational conflict.

Nevertheless, many are still skeptical about Huntington's thesis. In response to Huntington's 1993 article that triggered the whole discussion, Douglas Ross of Simon Fraser University critically examines the usefulness of the "clash of civilizations" thesis in understanding international conflict today.

✔ YES

The Clash of Civilizations? The Next Pattern of Conflict

SAMUEL HUNTINGTON

World politics is entering a new phase, and intellectuals have not hesitated to proliferate visions of what it will be — the end of history, the return of traditional rivalries between nation states, and the decline of the nation state from the conflicting pulls of tribalism and globalism, among others. Each of these visions catches aspects of the emerging reality. Yet they all miss a crucial, indeed a central, aspect of what global politics is likely to be in the coming years.

It is my hypothesis that the fundamental source of conflict in this new world will not be primarily ideological or primarily economic. The great divisions among humankind and the dominating source of conflict will be cultural. Nation states will remain the most powerful actors in world affairs, but the principal conflicts of global politics will occur between nations and groups of different civilizations. The clash of civilizations will dominate global politics. The fault lines between civilizations will be the battle lines of the future.

Conflict between civilizations will be the latest phase in the evolution of conflict in the modern world. For a century and a half after the emergence of the modern international system with the Peace of Westphalia, the conflicts of the Western world were largely among princes — emperors, absolute monarchs, and constitutional monarchs attempting to expand their bureaucracies, their armies, their mercantilist economic strength and, most important, the territory they ruled. In the process they created nation states, and beginning with the French Revolution the principal lines of conflict were between nations rather than princes. In 1793, as R.R. Palmer put it, "The wars of kings were over; the wars of peoples had begun." This nineteenth-century pattern lasted until the end of World War I.

Then, as a result of the Russian Revolution and the reaction against it, the conflict of nations yielded to the conflict of ideologies, first among communism, fascism-Nazism, and liberal democracy, and then between communism and liberal democracy. During the Cold War, this latter conflict became embodied in the struggle between the two superpowers, neither of which was a nation state in the classical European sense and each of which defined its identity in terms of its ideology.

These conflicts between princes, nation states, and ideologies were primarily conflicts within Western civilization, "Western civil wars," as William Lind has labeled them. This was as true of the Cold War as it was of the world wars and the earlier wars of the seventeenth, eighteenth, and nineteenth centuries. With the end of the Cold War, international politics moves out of its Western phase, and its centerpiece becomes the interaction between the West and non-Western civilizations and among non-Western civilizations. In the politics of civilizations, the peoples and governments of non-Western civilizations no longer remain the objects of history as targets of Western colonialism but join the West as movers and shapers of history.

THE NATURE OF CIVILIZATIONS

During the Cold War the world was divided into the First, Second, and Third Worlds. Those divisions are no longer relevant. It is far more meaningful now to group countries not in terms of their political or economic systems or in terms of their level of economic development but rather in terms of their culture and civilization.

What do we mean when we talk of a civilization? A civilization is a cultural entity. Villages, regions, ethnic groups, nationalities, religious groups, all have distinct cultures at different levels of cultural heterogeneity. The culture of a village in southern Italy may be different from that of a village in northern Italy, but both will share in a common Italian culture that distinguishes them from German villages. European communities, in turn, will share cultural features that distinguish them from Arab or Chinese communities. Arabs, Chinese, and Westerners, however, are not part of any broader cultural entity. They constitute civilizations. A civilization is thus the highest cultural grouping of people and the broadest level of cultural identity people have short of that which distinguishes humans from other species. It is defined both by common objective elements, such as language, history, religion, customs, and institutions, and by the subjective self-identification of people. People have levels of identity: a resident of Rome may define himself with varying degrees of intensity as a Roman, an Italian, a Catholic, a Christian, a European, a Westerner. The civilization to which he belongs is the broadest level of identification with which he intensely identifies. People can and do redefine their identities and, as a result, the composition and boundaries of civilizations change.

Civilizations may involve a large number of people, as with China ("a civilization pretending to be a state," as Lucian Pye put it), or a very small number of people, such as the Anglophone Caribbean. A civilization may include several nation states, as is the case with Western, Latin American, and Arab civilizations, or only one, as is the case with Japanese civilization. Civilizations obviously blend and overlap, and may include subcivilizations. Western civilization has two major variants, European and North American, and Islam has its Arab, Turkic, and Malay subdivisions. Civilizations are nonetheless meaningful entities, and while the lines between them are seldom sharp, they are real. Civilizations are dynamic; they rise and fall; they divide and merge. And, as any student of history knows, civilizations disappear and are buried in the sands of time.

Westerners tend to think of nation states as the principal actors in global affairs. They have been that, however, for only a few centuries. The broader reaches of human history have been the history of civilizations. In *A Study of History*, Arnold Toynbee identified 21 major civilizations; only six of them exist in the contemporary world.

WHY CIVILIZATIONS WILL CLASH

Civilization identity will be increasingly important in the future, and the world will be shaped in large measure by the interactions among seven or eight major civilizations. These include Western, Confucian, Japanese, Islamic, Hindu, Slavic-Orthodox, Latin American, and possibly African civilization. The most important conflicts of the future will occur along the cultural fault lines separating these civilizations from one another.

Why will this be the case?

First, differences among civilizations are not only real; they are basic. Civilizations are differentiated from each other by history, language, culture, tradition, and, most important, religion. The people of different civilizations have different views on the relations between God and man, the individual and the group, the citizen and the state, parents and children, husband and wife, as well as differing views of the relative importance of rights and responsibilities, liberty and authority, equality and hierarchy. These differences are the product of centuries. They will not soon disappear. They are far more fundamental than differences among political ideologies and political regimes. Differences do not necessarily mean conflict, and conflict does not necessarily mean violence. Over the centuries, however, differences among civilizations have generated the most prolonged and the most violent conflicts.

Second, the world is becoming a smaller place. The interactions between peoples of different civilizations are increasing; these increasing interactions intensify civilization consciousness and awareness of differences between civilizations and commonalities within civilizations. North African immigration to France generates hostility among Frenchmen and at the same time increased receptivity to immigration by "good" European Catholic Poles. Americans react far more negatively to Japanese investment than to larger investments from Canada and European countries. Similarly, as Donald Horowitz has pointed out, "An Ibo may be . . . an Owerri Ibo or an Onitsha Ibo in what was the Eastern region of Nigeria. In Lagos, he is simply an Ibo. In London, he is a Nigerian. In New York, he is an African." The interactions among peoples of different civilizations enhance the civilization-consciousness of people that, in turn, invigorates differences and animosities stretching or thought to stretch back deep into history.

Third, the processes of economic modernization and social change throughout the world are separating people from longstanding local identities. They also weaken the nation state as a source of identity. In much of the world religion has moved in to fill this gap, often in the form of movements that are labeled "fundamentalist." Such movements are found in Western Christianity, Judaism, Buddhism, and Hinduism, as well as in Islam. In most countries and most religions the people active in fundamentalist movements are young, college-educated, middle-class technicians, professionals, and business persons. The "unsecularization of the world," George Weigel has remarked, "is one of the dominant social facts of life in the late twentieth century." The revival of religion, "la revanche de Dieu," as Gilles Kepel labeled it, provides a basis for identity and commitment that transcends national boundaries and unites civilizations.

Fourth, the growth of civilization-consciousness is enhanced by the dual role of the West. On the one hand, the West is at a peak of power. At the same time, however, and perhaps as a result, a return to the roots phenomenon is occurring among non-Western civilizations. Increasingly one hears references to trends toward a turning inward and "Asianization" in Japan, the end of the Nehru legacy and the "Hinduization" of India, the failure of Western ideas of socialism and nationalism and hence "re-Islamization" of the Middle East, and now a debate over Westernization versus Russianization in Boris Yeltsin's country. A West at the peak of its power confronts non-Wests that increasingly have the desire, the will, and the resources to shape the world in non-Western ways.

In the past, the elites of non-Western societies were usually the people who were most involved with the West, had been educated at Oxford, the Sorbonne or Sandhurst, and had absorbed Western attitudes and values. At the same time, the populace in non-Western countries often remained deeply imbued with the indigenous culture. Now, however, these relationships are being reversed. A de-Westernization and indigenization of elites is occurring in many non-Western countries at the same time that Western, usually American, cultures, styles, and habits become more popular among the mass of the people.

Fifth, cultural characteristics and differences are less mutable and hence less easily compromised and resolved than political and economic ones. In the former Soviet Union, communists can become democrats, the rich can become poor and the poor rich, but Russians cannot become Estonians and Azeris cannot become Armenians. In class and ideological conflicts, the key question was "Which side are you on?" and people could and did choose sides and change sides. In conflicts between civilizations, the question is "What are you?" That is a given that cannot be changed. And as we know, from Bosnia to the Caucasus to the Sudan, the wrong answer to that question can mean a bullet in the head. Even more than ethnicity, religion discriminates sharply and exclusively among people. A person can be half-French and half-Arab and simultaneously even a citizen of two countries. It is more difficult to be half-Catholic and half-Muslim.

Finally, economic regionalism is increasing. The proportions of total trade that were intraregional rose between 1980 and 1989 from 51 percent to 59 percent in Europe, 33 percent to 37 percent in East Asia, and 32 percent to 36 percent in North America. The importance of regional economic blocs is likely to continue to increase in the future. On the one hand, successful economic regionalism will reinforce civilization-consciousness. On the other hand, economic regionalism may succeed only when it is rooted in a common civilization. The European Community rests on the shared foundation of European culture and Western Christianity. The success of the North American Free Trade Area depends on the convergence now underway of Mexican, Canadian, and American cultures. Japan, in contrast, faces difficulties in creating a comparable economic entity in East Asia because Japan is a society and civilization unique to itself. However strong the trade and investment links Japan may develop with other East Asian countries, its cultural differences with those countries inhibit and perhaps preclude its promoting regional economic integration like that in Europe and North America.

Common culture, in contrast, is clearly facilitating the rapid expansion of the economic relations between the People's Republic of China and Hong Kong, Taiwan, Singapore, and the overseas Chinese communities in other Asian countries. With the Cold War over, cultural commonalities increasingly overcome ideological differences, and mainland China and Taiwan move closer together. If cultural commonality is a prerequisite for economic integration, the principal East Asian economic bloc of the future is likely to be centered on China. This bloc is, in fact, already coming into existence. As Murray Weidenbaum has observed,

> Despite the current Japanese dominance of the region, the Chinese-based economy of Asia is rapidly emerging as a new epicenter for industry, commerce and finance. This strategic area contains substantial amounts of technology and manufacturing capability (Taiwan), outstanding entrepreneurial, marketing and services acumen (Hong Kong), a fine communications network (Singapore), a tremendous pool of financial capital (all three), and very large endowments of land, resources and labor (mainland China).... From Guangzhou to Singapore, from Kuala Lumpur to Manila, this influential network — often based on extensions of the traditional clans — has been described as the backbone of the East Asian economy.[1]

Culture and religion also form the basis of the Economic Cooperation Organization, which brings together ten non-Arab Muslim countries: Iran, Pakistan, Turkey, Azerbaijan, Kazakhstan, Kyrgyzstan, Turkmenistan, Tadjikistan, Uzbekistan, and Afghanistan. One impetus to the revival and expansion of this organization, founded originally in the 1960s by Turkey, Pakistan, and Iran, is the realization by the leaders of several of these countries that they had no chance of admission to the European Community. Similarly, Caricom, the Central American Common Market and Mercosur rest on common cultural foundations. Efforts to build a broader Caribbean-American economic entity bridging the Anglo-Latin divide, however, have to date failed.

As people define their identity in ethnic and religious terms, they are likely to see an "us" versus "them" relation existing between themselves and people of different ethnicity or religion. The end of ideologically defined states in Eastern Europe and the former Soviet Union permits traditional ethnic identities and animosities to come to the fore. Differences in culture and religion create differences over policy issues, ranging from human rights to immigration to trade and commerce to the environment. Geographical propinquity gives rise to conflicting territorial claims from Bosnia to Mindanao. Most important, the efforts of the West to promote its values of democracy and liberalism as universal values, to maintain its military predominance, and to advance its economic interests engender countering responses from other civilizations. Decreasingly able to mobilize support and form coalitions on the basis of ideology, governments and groups will increasingly attempt to mobilize support by appealing to common religion and civilization identity.

The clash of civilizations thus occurs at two levels. At the micro-level, adjacent groups along the fault lines between civilizations struggle, often violently, over the control of territory and each other. At the macro-level, states from different civilizations compete for relative military and economic power, struggle over the control of international institutions and third parties, and competitively promote their particular political and religious values.

THE FAULT LINES BETWEEN CIVILIZATIONS

The fault lines between civilizations are replacing the political and ideological boundaries of the Cold War as the flash points for crisis and bloodshed. The Cold War began when the Iron Curtain divided Europe politically and ideologically; The Cold War ended with the end of the Iron Curtain. As the ideological division of Europe has disappeared, the cultural division of Europe between Western Christianity, on the one hand, and Orthodox Christianity and Islam, on the other, has reemerged. The most significant dividing line in Europe, as William Wallace has suggested, may well be the eastern boundary of Western Christianity in the year 1500. This line runs along what are now the boundaries between Finland and Russia and between the Baltic states and Russia, cuts through Belarus and Ukraine separating the more Catholic western Ukraine from Orthodox eastern Ukraine, swings westward separating Transylvania from the rest of Romania, and then goes through Yugoslavia almost exactly along the line now separating Croatia and Slovenia from the rest of Yugoslavia. In the Balkans this line, of course, coincides with the historic boundary between the Hapsburg and Ottoman empires. The peoples to the north and west of this line are Protestant or Catholic; they shared the common experiences of European history – feudalism, the Renaissance, the Reformation, the Enlightenment, the French Revolution, the Industrial Revolution; they are generally economically better off than the peoples to the east; and they may now look forward to increasing involvement in a common European economy and to the consolidation of democratic political systems. The peoples to the east and south of this line are Orthodox or Muslim; they historically belonged to the Ottoman or Tsarist empires and were only lightly touched by the shaping events in the rest of Europe; they are generally less advanced economically; they seem much less likely to develop stable democratic political systems. The Velvet Curtain of culture has replaced the Iron Curtain of ideology as the most significant dividing line in Europe. As the events in Yugoslavia show, it is not only a line of difference; it is also at times a line of bloody conflict.

Conflict along the fault line between Western and Islamic civilizations has been going on for 1,300 years. After the founding of Islam, the Arab and Moorish surge west and north only ended at Tours in 732. From the eleventh to the thirteenth century the Crusaders attempted with temporary success to bring Christianity and Christian rule to the Holy Land. From the fourteenth to the seventeenth century, the Ottoman Turks reversed the balance, extended their sway over the Middle East and the Balkans, captured Constantinople, and twice laid siege to Vienna. In the nineteenth and early twentieth centuries as Ottoman power declined, Britain, France, and Italy established Western control over most of North Africa and the Middle East.

After World War II, the West, in turn, began to retreat; the colonial empires disappeared; first Arab nationalism and then Islamic fundamentalism manifested themselves; the West became heavily dependent on the Persian Gulf countries for its energy; the oil-rich Muslim countries became money-rich and, when they wished to, weapons-rich. Several wars occurred between Arabs and Israel (created by the West). France fought a bloody and ruthless war in Algeria for most of the 1950s; British and French forces invaded Egypt in 1956; American forces went into Lebanon in 1958; subsequently American forces returned to Lebanon, attacked Libya, and engaged in various military encounters with Iran; Arab and Islamic terrorists, supported by at least three Middle Eastern governments, employed the weapon of the weak and bombed Western planes and installations and seized Western hostages. This warfare between Arabs and the West culminated in 1990, when the United States sent a massive army to the Persian Gulf to defend some Arab countries against aggression by another. In its aftermath NATO planning is increasingly directed to potential threats and instability along its "southern tier."

This centuries-old military interaction between the West and Islam is unlikely to decline. It could become more virulent. The Gulf War left some Arabs feeling proud that Saddam Hussein had attacked Israel and stood up to the West. It also left many feeling humiliated and resentful of the West's military presence in the Persian Gulf, the West's overwhelming military dominance, and their apparent inability to shape their own destiny. Many Arab countries, in addition to the oil exporters, are reaching levels of economic and social development where autocratic forms of government become inappropriate and efforts to introduce democracy become stronger. Some openings in Arab political systems have already occurred. The principal beneficiaries of these openings have been Islamist movements. In the Arab world, in short, Western democracy strengthens anti-Western political forces. This may be a passing phenomenon, but it surely complicates relations between Islamic countries and the West.

Those relations are also complicated by demography. The spectacular population growth in Arab countries, particularly in North Africa, has led to increased migration to Western Europe. The movement within Western Europe toward minimizing internal boundaries has sharpened political sensitivities with respect to this development. In Italy, France, and Germany, racism is increasingly open, and political reactions and violence against Arab and Turkish migrants have become more intense and more widespread since 1990. On both sides the interaction between Islam and the West is seen as a clash of civilizations. The West's "next confrontation," observes M.J. Akbar, an Indian Muslim author, "is definitely going to come from the Muslim world. It is in the sweep of the Islamic nations from the Maghreb to Pakistan that the struggle for a new world order will begin." Bernard Lewis comes to a similar conclusion:

> We are facing a mood and a movement far transcending the level of issues and policies and the governments that pursue them. This is no less than a clash of civilizations — the perhaps irrational but surely historic reaction of an ancient rival against our Judeo-Christian heritage, our secular present, and the worldwide expansion of both.[2]

Historically, the other great antagonistic interaction of Arab Islamic civilization has been with the pagan, animist, and now increasingly Christian black peoples to the south. In the past, this antagonism was epitomized in the image of Arab slave dealers and black slaves. It has been reflected in the on-going civil war in the Sudan between Arabs and blacks, the fighting in Chad between Libyan-supported insurgents and the government, the tensions between Orthodox Christians and Muslims in the Horn of Africa, and the political conflicts, recurring riots, and communal violence between Muslims and Christians in Nigeria. The modernization of Africa and the spread of Christianity are likely to enhance the probability of violence along this fault line. Symptomatic of the intensification of this conflict was Pope John Paul II's speech in Khartoum in February 1993 attacking the actions of the Sudan's Islamist government against the Christian minority there.

On the northern border of Islam, conflict has increasingly erupted between Orthodox and Muslim peoples, including the carnage of Bosnia and Sarajevo, the simmering violence between Serb and Albanian, the tenuous relations between Bulgarians and their Turkish minority, the violence between Ossetians and Ingush, the unremitting slaughter of each other by Armenians and Azeris, the tense relations between Russians and Muslims in Central Asia, and the deployment of Russian troops to protect Russian interests in the Caucasus and Central Asia. Religion reinforces the revival of ethnic identities and restimulates Russian fears about the security of their southern borders. This concern is well captured by Archie Roosevelt:

> Much of Russian history concerns the struggle between the Slavs and the Turkic peoples on their borders, which dates back to the foundation of the Russian state more than a thousand years ago. In the Slavs' millennium-long

confrontation with their eastern neighbors lies the key to an understanding not only of Russian history, but Russian character. To understand Russian realities today one has to have a concept of the great Turkic ethnic group that has preoccupied Russians through the centuries.[3]

The conflict of civilizations is deeply rooted elsewhere in Asia. The historic clash between Muslim and Hindu in the subcontinent manifests itself now not only in the rivalry between Pakistan and India but also in intensifying religious strife within India between increasingly militant Hindu groups and India's substantial Muslim minority. The destruction of the Ayodhya mosque in December 1992 brought to the fore the issue of whether India will remain a secular democratic state or become a Hindu one. In East Asia, China has outstanding territorial disputes with most of its neighbors. It has pursued a ruthless policy toward the Buddhist people of Tibet, and it is pursuing an increasingly ruthless policy toward its Turkic-Muslim minority. With the Cold War over, the underlying differences between China and the United States have reasserted themselves in areas such as human rights, trade, and weapons proliferation. These differences are unlikely to moderate. A "new cold war," Deng Xaioping reportedly asserted in 1991, is under way between China and America.

The same phrase has been applied to the increasingly difficult relations between Japan and the United States. Here cultural difference exacerbates economic conflict. People on each side allege racism on the other, but at least on the American side the antipathies are not racial but cultural. The basic values, attitudes, and behavioral patterns of the two societies could hardly be more different. The economic issues between the United States and Europe are no less serious than those between the United States and Japan, but they do not have the same political salience and emotional intensity because the differences between American culture and European culture are so much less than those between American civilization and Japanese civilization.

The interactions between civilizations vary greatly in the extent to which they are likely to be characterized by violence. Economic competition clearly predominates between the American and European subcivilizations of the West and between both of them and Japan. On the Eurasian continent, however, the proliferation of ethnic conflict, epitomized at the extreme in "ethnic cleansing," has not been totally random. It has been most frequent and most violent between groups belonging to different civilizations. In Eurasia the great historic fault lines between civilizations are once more aflame. This is particularly true along the boundaries of the crescent-shaped Islamic bloc of nations from the bulge of Africa to central Asia. Violence also occurs between Muslims, on the one hand, and Orthodox Serbs in the Balkans, Jews in Israel, Hindus in India, Buddhists in Burma, and Catholics in the Philippines. Islam has bloody borders.

CIVILIZATION RALLYING: THE KIN-COUNTRY SYNDROME

Groups or states belonging to one civilization that becomes involved in war with people from a different civilization naturally try to rally support from other members of their own civilization. As the post–Cold War world evolves, civilization commonality, what H.D.S. Greenway has termed the "kin-country" syndrome, is replacing political ideology and traditional balance of power considerations as the principal basis for cooperation and coalitions. It can be seen gradually emerging in the post–Cold War conflicts in the Persian Gulf, the Caucasus, and Bosnia. None of these was a full-scale war between civilizations, but each involved some elements of civilizational rallying, which seemed to become more important as the conflict continued and which may provide a foretaste of the future.

First, in the Gulf War one Arab state invaded another and then fought a coalition of Arab, Western, and other states. While only a few Muslim governments overtly supported Saddam Hussein, many Arab elites privately cheered him on, and he was highly popular among large sections of the Arab publics. Islamic fundamentalist movements universally supported Iraq rather than the Western-backed governments of Kuwait and Saudi Arabia. Forswearing Arab nationalism, Saddam Hussein explicitly invoked an Islamic appeal. He and his supporters attempted to define the war as a war between civilizations. "It is not the world against Iraq," as Safar Al-Hawaii, dean of Islamic Studies at the Umm Al-Qura University in Mecca, put it in a widely circulated tape. "It is the West against Islam." Ignoring the rivalry between Iran and Iraq, the chief Iranian religious leader, Ayatollah Ali Khamenei, called for a holy war against the West: "The struggle against American aggression, greed, plans and policies will be counted as a jihad, and anybody who is killed on that path is a martyr." "This is a war," King Hussein of Jordan argued, "against all Arabs and all Muslims and not against Iraq alone."

The rallying of substantial sections of Arab elites and publics behind Saddam Hussein caused those Arab governments in the anti-Iraq coalition to moderate their activities and temper their public statements. Arab governments opposed or distanced themselves from subsequent Western efforts to apply pressure on Iraq, including enforcement of a no-fly zone in the summer of 1992 and the bombing of Iraq in January 1993. The Western-Soviet-Turkish-Arab anti-Iraq coalition of 1990 had by 1993 become a coalition of almost only the West and Kuwait against Iraq.

Muslims contrasted Western actions against Iraq with the West's failure to protect Bosnians against Serbs and to impose sanctions on Israel for violating U.N. resolutions. The West, they alleged, was using a double standard. A world of clashing civilizations, however, is inevitably a world of double standards: people apply one standard to their kin-countries and a different standard to others.

Second, the kin-country syndrome also appeared in conflicts in the former Soviet Union. Armenian military successes in 1992 and 1993 stimulated Turkey to become increasingly supportive of its religious, ethnic, and linguistic brethren in

Azerbaijan. "We have a Turkish nation feeling the same sentiments as the Azerbaijanis," said one Turkish official in 1992. "We are under pressure. Our newspapers are full of the photos of atrocities and are asking us if we are still serious about pursuing our neutral policy. Maybe we should show Armenia that there's a big Turkey in the region." President Turgut Ozal agreed, remarking that Turkey should at least "scare the Armenians a little bit." Turkey, Ozal threatened again in 1993, would "show its fangs." Turkish Air Force jets flew reconnaissance flights along the Armenian border; Turkey suspended food shipments and air flights to Armenia; and Turkey and Iran announced they would not accept dismemberment of Azerbaijan. In the last years of its existence, the Soviet government supported Azerbaijan because its government was dominated by former communists. With the end of the Soviet Union, however, political considerations gave way to religious ones. Russian troops fought on the side of the Armenians, and Azerbaijan accused the "Russian government of turning 180 degrees" toward support for Christian Armenia.

Third, with respect to the fighting in the former Yugoslavia, Western publics manifested sympathy and support for the Bosnian Muslims and the horrors they suffered at the hands of the Serbs. Relatively little concern was expressed, however, over Croatian attacks on Muslims and participation in the dismemberment of Bosnia-Herzegovina. In the early stages of the Yugoslav breakup, Germany, in an unusual display of diplomatic initiative and muscle, induced the other 11 members of the European Community to follow its lead in recognizing Slovenia and Croatia. As a result of the Pope's determination to provide strong backing to the two Catholic countries, the Vatican extended recognition even before the Community did. The United States followed the European lead. Thus the leading actors in Western civilization rallied behind their coreligionists. Subsequently Croatia was reported to be receiving substantial quantities of arms from Central European and other Western countries. Boris Yeltsin's government, on the other hand, attempted to pursue a middle course that would be sympathetic to the Orthodox Serbs but not alienate Russia from the West. Russian conservative and nationalist groups, however, including many legislators, attacked the government for not being more forthcoming in its support for the Serbs. By early 1993 several hundred Russians apparently were serving with the Serbian forces, and reports circulated of Russian arms being supplied to Serbia.

Islamic governments and groups, on the other hand, castigated the West for not coming to the defense of the Bosnians. Iranian leaders urged Muslims from all countries to provide help to Bosnia; in violation of the U.N. arms embargo, Iran supplied weapons and men for the Bosnians; Iranian-supported Lebanese groups sent guerrillas to train and organize the Bosnian forces. In 1993 up to 4,000 Muslims from over two dozen Islamic countries were reported to be fighting in Bosnia. The governments of Saudi Arabia and other countries felt under increasing pressure from fundamentalist groups in their own societies to provide more vigorous support for the Bosnians. By the end of 1992, Saudi Arabia had reportedly supplied substantial funding for weapons and supplies for the Bosnians, which significantly increased their military capabilities vis-à-vis the Serbs.

In the 1930s the Spanish Civil War provoked intervention from countries that politically were fascist, communist, and democratic. In the 1990s the Yugoslav conflict is provoking intervention from countries that are Muslim, Orthodox, and Western Christian. The parallel has not gone unnoticed. "The war in Bosnia-Herzegovina has become the emotional equivalent of the fight against fascism in the Spanish Civil War," one Saudi editor observed. "Those who died there are regarded as martyrs who tried to save their fellow Muslims."

Conflicts and violence will also occur between states and groups within the same civilization. Such conflicts, however, are likely to be less intense and less likely to expand than conflicts between civilizations. Common membership in a civilization reduces the probability of violence in situations where it might otherwise occur. In 1991 and 1992 many people were alarmed by the possibility of violent conflict between Russia and Ukraine over territory, particularly Crimea, the Black Sea fleet, nuclear weapons, and economic issues. If civilization is what counts, however, the likelihood of violence between Ukrainians and Russians should be low. They are two Slavic, primarily Orthodox peoples who have had close relationships with each other for centuries. As of early 1993, despite all the reasons for conflict, the leaders of the two countries were effectively negotiating and defusing the issues between the two countries. While there has been serious fighting between Muslims and Christians elsewhere in the former Soviet Union and much tension and some fighting between Western and Orthodox Christians in the Baltic states, there has been virtually no violence between Russians and Ukrainians.

Civilization rallying to date has been limited, but it has been growing, and it clearly has the potential to spread much further. As the conflicts in the Persian Gulf, the Caucasus and Bosnia continued, the positions of nations and the cleavages between them increasingly were along civilizational lines. Populist politicians, religious leaders, and the media have found it a potent means of arousing mass support and of pressuring hesitant governments. In the coming years, the local conflicts most likely to escalate into major wars will be those, as in Bosnia and the Caucasus, along the fault lines between civilizations. The next world war, if there is one, will be a war between civilizations.

THE WEST VERSUS THE REST

The West is now at an extraordinary peak of power in relation to other civilizations. Its superpower opponent has disappeared from the map. Military conflict among Western states is unthinkable, and Western military power is unrivaled. Apart from Japan, the West faces no economic challenge. It dominates international political and security institutions and with Japan international economic institutions. Global political and security issues are effectively settled by a directorate of the United States, Britain, and France, world economic issues by a directorate of the United States, Germany, and Japan, all of which maintain extraordinarily close relations with each other to the exclusion of lesser and largely non-Western countries. Decisions made at the U.N. Security Council or in the International Monetary Fund that reflect the interests of the West are presented to the world as reflecting the desires of the world community. The very phrase "the world community" has become the euphemistic collective noun (replacing "the Free World") to give global legitimacy to actions reflecting the interests of the United States and other Western powers.[4] Through the IMF and other international economic institutions, the West promotes its economic interests and imposes on other nations the economic policies it thinks appropriate. In any poll of non-Western peoples, the IMF undoubtedly would win the support of finance ministers and a few others, but get an overwhelmingly unfavorable rating from just about everyone else, who would agree with Georgy Arbatov's characterization of IMF officials as "neo-Bolsheviks who love expropriating other people's money, imposing undemocratic and alien rules of economic and political conduct and stifling economic freedom."

Western domination of the U.N. Security Council and its decisions, tempered only by occasional abstention by China, produced U.N. legitimation of the West's use of force to drive Iraq out of Kuwait and its elimination of Iraq's sophisticated weapons and capacity to produce such weapons. It also produced the quite unprecedented action by the United States, Britain, and France in getting the Security Council to demand that Libya hand over the Pan Am 103 bombing suspects and then to impose sanctions when Libya refused. After defeating the largest Arab army, the West did not hesitate to throw its weight around in the Arab world. The West in effect is using international institutions, military power, and economic resources to run the world in ways that will maintain Western predominance, protect Western interests, and promote Western political and economic values.

That at least is the way in which non-Westerners see the new world, and there is a significant element of truth in their view. Differences in power and struggles for military, economic, and institutional power are thus one source of conflict between the West and other civilizations. Differences in culture, that is basic values and beliefs, are a second source of conflict. V.S. Naipaul has argued that Western civilization is the "universal civilization" that "fits all men." At a superficial level much of Western culture has indeed permeated the rest of the world. At a more basic level, however, Western concepts differ fundamentally from those prevalent in other civilizations. Western ideas of individualism, liberalism, constitutionalism, human rights, equality, liberty, the rule of law, democracy, free markets, the separation of church and state, often have little resonance in Islamic, Confucian, Japanese, Hindu, Buddhist, or Orthodox cultures. Western efforts to propagate such ideas produce instead a reaction against "human rights imperialism" and a reaffirmation of indigenous values, as can be seen in the support for religious fundamentalism by the younger generation in non-Western cultures. The very notion that there could be a "universal civilization" is a Western idea, directly at odds with the particularism of most Asian societies and their emphasis on what distinguishes one people from another. Indeed, the author of a review of 100 comparative studies of values in different societies concluded that "the values that are most important in the West are least important worldwide."[5] In the political realm, of course, these differences are most manifest in the efforts of the United States and other Western powers to induce other peoples to adopt Western ideas concerning democracy and human rights. Modern democratic government originated in the West. When it has developed in non-Western societies it has usually been the product of Western colonialism or imposition.

The central axis of world politics in the future is likely to be, in Kishore Mahbubani's phrase, the conflict between "the West and the Rest" and the responses of non-Western civilizations to Western power and values.[6] Those responses generally take one or a combination of three forms. At one extreme, non-Western states can, like Burma and North Korea, attempt to pursue a course of isolation, to insulate their societies from penetration or "corruption" by the West, and, in effect, to opt out of participation in the Western-dominated global community. The costs of this course, however, are high, and few states have pursued it exclusively. A second alternative, the equivalent of "bandwagoning" in international relations theory, is to attempt to join the West and accept its values and institutions. The third alternative is to attempt to "balance" the West by developing economic and military power and cooperating with other non-Western societies against the West, while preserving indigenous values and institutions; in short, to modernize but not to Westernize.

THE TORN COUNTRIES

In the future, as people differentiate themselves by civilization, countries with large numbers of peoples of different civilizations, such as the Soviet Union and Yugoslavia, are candidates for dismemberment. Some other countries have a fair degree of cultural homogeneity but are divided over whether their society belongs to one civilization or another. These are torn countries. Their leaders typically wish to pursue a bandwagoning strategy and to make their countries members of the West, but the history, culture, and traditions of their countries are non-Western. The most obvious and prototypical torn country is Turkey. The late-twentieth-century leaders of Turkey have followed in the Attaturk tradition and defined Turkey as a modern, secular, Western nation state. They allied Turkey with the West in NATO and in the Gulf War; they applied for membership in the European Community. At the same time, however, elements in Turkish society have supported an Islamic revival and have argued that Turkey is basically a Middle Eastern Muslim society.

In addition, while the elite of Turkey has defined Turkey as a Western society, the elite of the West refuses to accept Turkey as such. Turkey will not become a member of the European Community, and the real reason, as President Ozal said, "is that we are Muslim and they are Christian and they don't say that." Having rejected Mecca, and then being rejected by Brussels, where does Turkey look? Tashkent may be the answer. The end of the Soviet Union gives Turkey the opportunity to become the leader of a revived Turkic civilization involving seven countries from the borders of Greece to those of China. Encouraged by the West, Turkey is making strenuous efforts to carve out this new identity for itself.

During the past decade Mexico has assumed a position somewhat similar to that of Turkey. Just as Turkey abandoned its historic opposition to Europe and attempted to join Europe, Mexico has stopped defining itself by its opposition to the United States and is instead attempting to imitate the United States and to join it in the North American Free Trade Area. Mexican leaders are engaged in the great task of redefining Mexican identity and have introduced fundamental economic reforms that eventually will lead to fundamental political change. In 1991 a top adviser to President Carlos Salinas de Gortari described at length to me all the changes the Salinas government was making. When he finished, I remarked: "That's most impressive. It seems to me that basically you want to change Mexico from a Latin American country into a North American country." He looked at me with surprise and exclaimed: "Exactly! That's precisely what we are trying to do, but of course we could never say so publicly." As his remark indicates, in Mexico as in Turkey, significant elements in society resist the redefinition of their country's identity. In Turkey, European-oriented leaders have to make gestures to Islam (Ozal's pilgrimage to Mecca); so also Mexico's North American–oriented leaders have to make gestures to those who hold Mexico to be a Latin American country (Salinas's Ibero-American Guadalajara summit).

Historically Turkey has been the most profoundly torn country. For the United States, Mexico is the most immediate torn country. Globally the most important torn country is Russia. The question of whether Russia is part of the West or the leader of a distinct Slavic-Orthodox civilization has been a recurring one in Russian history. That issue was obscured by the communist victory in Russia, which imported a Western ideology, adapted it to Russian conditions, and then challenged the West in the name of that ideology. The dominance of communism shut off the historic debate over Westernization versus Russification. With communism discredited, Russians once again face that question.

President Yeltsin is adopting Western principles and goals and seeking to make Russia a "normal" country and a part of the West. Yet both the Russian elite and the Russian public are divided on this issue. Among the more moderate dissenters, Sergei Stankevich argues that Russia should reject the "Atlanticist" course, which would lead it "to become European, to become a part of the world economy in rapid and organized fashion, to become the eighth member of the Seven, and to put particular emphasis on Germany and the United States as the two dominant members of the Atlantic alliance." While also rejecting an exclusively Eurasian policy, Stankevich nonetheless argues that Russia should give priority to the protection of Russians in other countries, emphasize its Turkic and Muslim connections, and promote "an appreciable redistribution of our resources, our options, our ties, and our interests in favor of Asia, of the eastern direction." People of this persuasion criticize Yeltsin for subordinating Russia's interests to those of the West, for reducing Russian military strength, for failing to support traditional friends such as Serbia, and for pushing economic and political reform in ways injurious to the Russian people. Indicative of this trend is the new popularity of the ideas of Petr Savitsky, who in the 1920s argued that Russia was a unique Eurasian civilization.[7] More extreme dissidents voice much more blatantly nationalist, anti-Western, and anti-Semitic views, and urge Russia to redevelop its military strength and to establish closer ties with China and Muslim countries. The people of Russia are as divided as the elite. An opinion survey in European Russia in the spring of 1992 revealed that 40 percent of the public had positive attitudes toward the West and 36 percent had negative attitudes. As it has been for much of its history, Russia in the early 1990s is truly a torn country.

To redefine its civilization identity, a torn country must meet three requirements. First, its political and economic elite has to be generally supportive of and enthusiastic about this move. Second, its public has to be willing to acquiesce in the redefinition. Third, the dominant groups in the recipient civilization have to be willing to embrace the convert. All three requirements in large part exist with respect to Mexico. The first two in large part exist with respect to Turkey. It is not clear that any of them exist with respect to Russia's joining the West. The conflict between liberal democracy and Marxism-Leninism was between ideologies which, despite their major differences, ostensibly shared ultimate goals of freedom, equality, and prosperity. A traditional, authoritarian, nationalist Russia could have quite different goals. A Western democrat could carry on an intellectual debate with a Soviet Marxist. It would be virtually impossible for him to do that with a Russian traditionalist. If, as the Russians stop behaving like Marxists, they reject liberal democracy and begin behaving like Russians but not like Westerners, the relations between Russia and the West could again become distant and conflictual.[8]

THE CONFUCIAN–ISLAMIC CONNECTION

The obstacles to non-Western countries joining the West vary considerably. They are least for Latin American and East European countries. They are greater for the Orthodox countries of the former Soviet Union. They are still greater for Muslim, Confucian, Hindu, and Buddhist societies. Japan has established a unique position for itself as an associate member of the West: it is in the West in some respects but clearly not of the West in important dimensions. Those countries that for reasons of culture and power do not wish to, or cannot, join the West compete with the West by developing their own economic, military, and political power. They do this by promoting their internal development and by cooperating with other non-Western countries. The most prominent form of this cooperation is the Confucian–Islamic connection that has emerged to challenge Western interests, values, and power.

Almost without exception, Western countries are reducing their military power; under Yeltsin's leadership so also is Russia. China, North Korea, and several Middle Eastern states, however, are significantly expanding their military capabilities. They are doing this by the import of arms from Western and non-Western sources and by the development of indigenous arms industries. One result is the emergence of what Charles Krauthammer has called "Weapon States," and the Weapon States are not Western states. Another result is the redefinition of arms control, which is a Western concept and a Western goal. During the Cold War the primary purpose of arms control was to establish a stable military balance between the United States and its allies and the Soviet Union and its allies. In the post–Cold War world the primary objective of arms control is to prevent the development by non-Western societies of military capabilities that could threaten Western interests. The West attempts to do this through international agreements, economic pressure, and controls on the transfer of arms and weapons technologies.

The conflict between the West and the Confucian–Islamic states focuses largely, although not exclusively, on nuclear, chemical, and biological weapons, ballistic missiles and other sophisticated means for delivering them, and the guidance, intelligence, and other electronic capabilities for achieving that goal. The West promotes nonproliferation as a universal norm and nonproliferation treaties and inspections as means of realizing that norm. It also threatens a variety of sanctions against those who promote the spread of sophisticated weapons and proposes some benefits for those who do not. The attention of the West focuses, naturally, on nations that are actually or potentially hostile to the West.

The non-Western nations, on the other hand, assert their right to acquire and to deploy whatever weapons they think necessary for their security. They also have absorbed, to the full, the truth of the response of the Indian defense minister when asked what lesson he learned from the Gulf War: "Don't fight the United States unless you have nuclear weapons." Nuclear weapons, chemical weapons, and missiles are viewed, probably erroneously, as the potential equalizer of superior Western conventional power. China, of course, already has nuclear weapons; Pakistan and India have the capability to deploy them. North Korea, Iran, Iraq, Libya, and Algeria appear to be attempting to acquire them. A top Iranian official has declared that all Muslim states should acquire nuclear weapons, and in 1988 the president of Iran reportedly issued a directive calling for development of "offensive and defensive chemical, biological and radiological weapons."

Centrally important to the development of counter-West military capabilities is the sustained expansion of China's military power and its means to create military power. Buoyed by spectacular economic development, China is rapidly increasing its military spending and vigorously moving forward with the modernization of its armed forces. It is purchasing weapons from the former Soviet states; it is developing long-range missiles; in 1992 it tested a one-megaton nuclear device. It is developing power-projection capabilities, acquiring aerial refueling technology, and trying to purchase an aircraft carrier. Its military buildup and assertion of sovereignty over the South China Sea are provoking a multilateral regional arms race in East Asia. China is also a major exporter of arms and weapons technology. It has exported materials to Libya and Iraq that could be used to manufacture nuclear weapons and nerve gas. It has helped Algeria build a reactor suitable for nuclear weapons research and production. China has sold to Iran nuclear technology that American officials believe could only be used to create weapons and apparently has shipped components of 300 mile-range missiles to Pakistan. North Korea has had a nuclear weapons program under way for some while and has sold advanced missiles and missile technology to Syria and Iran. The flow of weapons and weapons technology is generally from East Asia to the Middle East. There is, however, some movement in the reverse direction; China has received Stinger missiles from Pakistan.

A Confucian–Islamic military connection has thus come into being, designed to promote acquisition by its members of the weapons and weapons technologies needed to counter the military power of the West. It may or may not last. At present, however, it is, as Dave McCurdy has said, "a renegades' mutual support pact, run by the proliferators and their backers." A new form of arms competition is thus occurring between Islamic–Confucian states and the West. In an old-fashioned arms race, each side developed its own arms to balance or to achieve superiority against the other side. In this new form of arms competition, one side is developing its arms and the other side is attempting not to balance but to limit and prevent that arms build-up while at the same time reducing its own military capabilities.

IMPLICATIONS FOR THE WEST

This article does not argue that civilization identities will replace all other identities, that nation states will disappear, that each civilization will become a single coherent political entity, that groups within a civilization will not conflict with and even fight each other. This paper does set forth the hypotheses that differences between civilizations are real and important; civilization-consciousness is increasing; conflict between civilizations will supplant ideological and other forms of conflict as the dominant global form of conflict; international relations, historically a game played out within Western civilization, will increasingly be de-Westernized and become a game in which non-Western civilizations are actors and not simply objects; successful political, security, and economic international institutions are more likely to develop within civilizations than across civilizations; conflicts between groups in different civilizations will be more frequent, more sustained, and more violent than conflicts between groups in the same civilization; violent conflicts between groups in different civilizations are the most likely and most dangerous source of escalation that could lead to global wars; the paramount axis of world politics will be the relations between "the West and the Rest"; the elites in some torn non-Western countries will try to make their countries part of the West, but in most cases face major obstacles to accomplishing this; a central focus of conflict for the immediate future will be between the West and several Islamic–Confucian states.

This is not to advocate the desirability of conflicts between civilizations. It is to set forth descriptive hypotheses as to what the future may be like. If these are plausible hypotheses, however, it is necessary to consider their implications for Western policy. These implications should be divided between short-term advantage and long-term accommodation. In the short term it is clearly in the interest of the West to promote greater cooperation and unity within its own civilization, particularly between its European and North American components; to incorporate into the West societies in Eastern Europe and Latin America whose cultures are close to those of the West; to promote and maintain cooperative relations with Russia and Japan; to prevent escalation of local inter-civilization conflicts into major inter-civilization wars; to limit the expansion of the military strength of Confucian and Islamic states; to moderate the reduction of Western military capabilities and maintain military superiority in East and Southwest Asia; to exploit differences and conflicts among Confucian and Islamic states; to support in other civilizations groups sympathetic to Western values and interests; to strengthen international institutions that reflect and legitimate Western interests and values and to promote the involvement of non-Western states in those institutions.

In the longer term other measures would be called for. Western civilization is both Western and modern. Non-Western civilizations have attempted to become modern without becoming Western. To date only Japan has fully succeeded in this quest. Non-Western civilizations will continue to attempt to acquire the wealth, technology, skills, machines, and weapons that are part of being modern. They will also attempt to reconcile this modernity with their traditional culture and values. Their economic and military strength relative to the West will increase. Hence the West will increasingly have to accommodate these non-Western modern civilizations whose power approaches that of the West but whose values and interests differ significantly from those of the West. This will require the West to maintain the economic and military power necessary to protect its interests in relation to these civilizations. It will also, however, require the West to develop a more profound understanding of the basic religious and philosophical assumptions underlying other civilizations and the ways in which people in those civilizations see their interests. It will require an effort to identify elements of commonality between

Western and other civilizations. For the relevant future, there will be no universal civilization, but instead a world of different civilizations, each of which will have to learn to coexist with the others.

NOTES

1. Murray Weidenbaum, *Greater China: The Next Economic Superpower?* St. Louis: Washington University Center for the Study of American Business, Contemporary Issues, Series 57, February 1993, pp. 2–3.

2. Bernard Lewis, "The Roots of Muslim Rage," *The Atlantic Monthly*, vol. 266, September 1990, p. 60; *Time*, June 15, 1992, pp. 24–28.

3. Archie Roosevelt, *For Lust of Knowing*. Boston: Little, Brown, 1988, pp. 332–33.

4. Almost invariably Western leaders claim they are acting on behalf of "the world community." One minor lapse occurred during the run-up to the Gulf War. In an interview on *Good Morning America*, Dec. 21, 1990, British Prime Minister John Major referred to the actions "the West" was taking against Saddam Hussein. He quickly corrected himself and subsequently referred to "the world community." He was, however, right when he erred.

5. Harry C. Triandis, *The New York Times*, Dec. 25, 1990, p. 41, and "Cross-Cultural Studies of Individualism and Collectivism," *Nebraska Symposium on Motivation*, vol. 37, 1989, pp. 41–133.

6. Kishore Mahbubani, "The West and the Rest," *The National Interest*, Summer 1992, pp. 3–13.

7. Sergei Stankevich, "Russia in Search of Itself," *The National Interest*, Summer 1992, pp. 47–51; Daniel Schneider, "A Russian Movement Rejects Western Tilt," *Christian Science Monitor*, Feb. 5, 1993, pp. 5–7.

8. Owen Harries has pointed out that Australia is trying (unwisely in his view) to become a torn country in reverse. Although it has been a full member not only of the West but also of the ABCA military and intelligence core of the West, its current leaders are in effect proposing that it defect from the West, redefine itself as an Asian country and cultivate close ties with its neighbors. Australia's future, they argue, is with the dynamic economies of East Asia. But, as I have suggested, close economic cooperation normally requires a common cultural base. In addition, none of the three conditions necessary for a torn country to join another civilization is likely to exist in Australia's case.

✗ NO

Ten Years After: The Inevitable Waning of Huntington's Civilizational Clash Theory?
DOUGLAS ALAN ROSS

The publication of Samuel Huntington's "clash of civilizations" hypothesis in 1993[1] generated a spirited debate about the plausibility and accuracy of his strategic "climate forecast" for the globe. Many critics from across the analytical spectrum leapt into the intellectual fray eager to criticize a paradigm that sympathetic observers thought might become the doctrinal successor to George Kennan's containment theory. Just as Kennan's 1947 "X" article had shaped American foreign policy thinking for most of the Cold War,[2] so too, some argued, might Huntington's cautionary warning concerning allegedly impending "fault line wars" – the only conflicts that he believed had the potential to spawn the next "world" war. Huntington's declaration that there was an urgent need to unify the Western countries against what soon might become an implacably hostile world as "the West" duelled with "the rest" was interpreted as a profoundly pessimistic (some said paranoid[3]) basis for the formulation of American foreign policy.

Over the ensuing decade, Huntington rejected such allegations, pointing out that many of his critics had failed to notice the question mark at the end of the title of his 1993 article. Where Kennan at the outset of the Cold War saw no alternative to the firm, patient, and active containment of an unremittingly hostile, authentically paranoid, opportunistically expansionist, and ideologically obsessed Soviet state, Huntington at least decreed that the cultural differences between various civilizations need not inevitably lead to war, nor even hostility and distrust. Major inter-civilizational war was a contingent risk, not a certainty. Cultural differences with the potential for catalyzing global war might possibly be managed, Huntington claimed, by civilizational "core states," who possessed a sensible disposition to compromise, a modicum of geopolitical self-restraint, and a political-diplomatic capacity to manage the bellicose impulses of their respective cultural satellites. So long as the leaders of the major civilizations respect a principle of non-interference in each others' cultural spheres of influence, so long as they act promptly to mediate jointly whenever fault line wars develop, and so long as they follow Lester Pearson's advice to promote mutual cultural understanding and learning, the avoidance of major wars is conceivable.[4] To the extent that such wisdom is absent in the twenty-first century, the risk of major inter-civilizational war will rise accordingly.

The body of this essay reviews the criticism that has been directed at Huntington's clash thesis since it first was published. It also provides some supplementary information about Huntington's views as they developed subsequent to the original article in both his 1996 book, titled *The Clash of Civilizations and the Remaking of World Order*, and several additional articles. Huntington's clash paradigm has evolved over the past eleven years, but the changes have been modest. His thinking has demonstrated remarkable consistency and internal coherence, and his pessimism about both global relations and, even more, the foolhardy risks taken by successive American administrations in trying to project American values onto unreceptive cultures and societies remains unaltered by the passage of time. Following the summary of a decade of critical responses to Huntington's thought, some concluding observations about Huntington's role as a strategic analyst are provided, and some additional criticism directed toward the clash thesis from a "grand strategy" perspective – a vantage point rarely heard in international security debates outside of the United States. In the words of one of his greatest admirers, Robert Kaplan, Samuel Huntington is "someone who combines liberal ideals with a deeply conservative understanding of history and foreign policy." Greatly influenced by Reinhold Niebuhr, Huntington shares a similar "tragic sensibility" that is embodied in all Niebuhr's thought, sensibility that "is the key to Huntington's definition of conservatism."[5]

The clash debate is unlikely to wane any time soon because Huntington is determined to continue to play the role of a responsible public intellectual warning against what he sincerely believes is the triumph of illogic, arrogance, and self-delusion in American foreign policy. Following the events of 11 September 2001, the overthrow of the Taliban regime in Afghanistan by American and NATO forces in 2002, and the invasion and occupation of Iraq by George W. Bush's "coalition of the willing" in March and April of 2003, Huntington's clash theory gained a new lease on life. In all probability, his writings have an even greater readership in 2004 than they did in the mid-1990s. Huntington somewhat coyly stated in 1996 that his clash writings were not meant to be taken as political science – without stating in precisely what category of analysis they should be placed. Clearly that field is strategy and international security studies, a domain that is far more "art" than "science." Notwithstanding this fact, it has generally been only analysts and social scientists in international relations who have taken up the challenge of debating the clash thesis. This is unfortunate.

In the words of one of Britain's foremost strategic thinkers, Colin Gray, strategy is "the use that is made of force and the threat of force for the ends of policy."[6] Huntington's work is at its core an exercise in threat analysis and national security policy planning – albeit in the very long term. As such, his work is most appropriately viewed within the debate on American "grand strategy," which may be defined as the formulation of feasible, long-term, security-enhancing political goals in conjunction with the coordination and management of national and allied resources and capabilities so as to promote the achievement of those goals.[7] Britain's greatest twentieth-century strategic analyst, Basil H. Liddell Hart, observed more than a half a century ago that "the realm of grand strategy is for the most part *terra incognita* – still awaiting exploration, and understanding."[8]

Huntington sallied forth into that unknown country. The product of his threat analysis and strategic "climate" forecast is highly debatable and to be sure "unscientific" (as are all long-term threat forecasts), but to the extent that he has challenged Americans and others to engage in their own informed speculation about our common future, he has done the global academic community an important service. The third part of this essay comments on where his analysis may be correct and where he may be quite mistaken.

HUNTINGTON'S MANY CRITICS

Neoliberals attacked Huntington's pessimism because it implied a need for clear limits to global economic integration, if not a wholesale scaling back of American involvement in the world economy, so as to preserve American and Western scientific, technical, and economic advantages over rising civilizational competitors. A benign world congenial to ever-expanding trade and unimpeded flows of investment under the transcendent guidance of the multinational corporate managerialists was clearly a vision of the future in no way shared by Huntington, who at root is an unabashed American economic nationalist. For defenders of international corporate governance, the steady rise in incomes in many developing countries[9] has invariably produced pressure for some form of liberal democratic governance and enhanced personal freedom. Thus it is no surprise that authoritarian regimes have been everywhere in retreat since the early 1980s. To neoliberals in the business community and government, this suggests that the Western "model" of development may in fact be of near universal appeal − contrary to one of Huntington's central themes. With English spreading worldwide as the preferred language of trade and investment, with American popular culture spreading just as quickly (the twin engines of Barber's McWorld), and with global economic interdependence evolving quickly, assisted by the rapid spread of new information technologies to almost all countries, is it really plausible to suppose that deep antagonisms to the West will be felt in most of the other "civilizations"?[10] While not overtly protectionist in his call for setting national and Western alliance-wide limits to technology transfers to other rival civilizations, Huntington has implied unambiguously that the days of unfettered decisionmaking by the international corporate elite should end soon. For Huntington, the international corporate elite, including the now largely deracinated American corporate managers, has become a *de facto* alien threat to the citizenry of both the United States and other Western countries − in effect, "an emerging global superclass."[11] Most neoliberal analysts who might have detected such thinking in Huntington's various writings would therefore dismiss his increasingly explicit anti-elitist, anti-globalization critique as utterly antediluvian, nostalgic conservatism.

Constructivist writers in international relations were appalled to find that Huntington was claiming that "culture does matter," but that allegedly immutable cultural differences were deepening and setting the stage not for cooperation through a constructivist program founded on the willful rejection of the tenets of statist "realism," but rather for the potential stimulation of both intense intra-state and inter-civilizational conflict not seen since the European religious wars of the early seventeenth century or the crusades of the Middle Ages. For constructivist analysts in international relations, Huntington's clash model is a central challenge to their belief in the steady enhancement of transcultural communication and thus the rosy prospects for multicultural tolerance and growing international cooperation.[12] For postmodernist, postcolonial analysts such as the late Edward Said, Huntington's civilizational categories of analysis are grotesque, cartoon-like caricatures of what in fact are incredibly complex interwoven cultures where most individuals' identities are constantly reshaped.[13]

Early critiques also focused on Huntington's impressionistic but still expansive concept of civilizations and their allegedly new capacities for provoking war. In a comment that would be repeated subsequently by many other realist critics, Fouad Ajami expressed astonishment that any observer with Huntington's years of scholarly analysis of the role of the state could assert that these mysterious civilizational entities would soon displace states as the most important organizing force in the international system. States make wars, not civilizations, said Ajami, and they do so with an "unsentimental and cold-blooded nature."[14] A politically destabilizing "indigenization" or introversion of culture in India, China, and the Islamic world is extremely unlikely to happen, Ajami argued, because these societies already have been penetrated and transformed by "modernity and secularism." The strife of industrialization and modernization in countries such as Turkey, Algeria, Egypt, and Iran will only rarely produce theocratic rule. The forces representing religious repression and extremist anti-Western hysteria across the Islamic world are unlikely to broaden their appeal. The sensational press accounts of televisions being thrown from windows by angry mullahs, or nightclubs being attacked, or women being forced into Taliban-style, burka-bound subjugation will remain the exception. Much of the highly differentiated Islamic world has already undergone dramatic modernization, especially the Gulf states and the Muslim countries of Southeast Asia. While the sensationalist press may give undue attention to religious reactionaries and extremists (what Said saw as the equivalent of the Branch Davidians or Aum Shinrikyo), they are in fact symptomatic of "panic and bewilderment and guilt that the border with 'the other' has been crossed."[15] Ajami added, "it is hard to think of Russia, ravaged as it is by inflation, taking up the grand cause of a 'second Byzantium,' the bearer of the orthodox-Slavic torch."[16] And India's leaders will not jeopardize their country's attainment of great power status by a detour into the past; Bollywood and continued market liberalization and technical modernization, not Hindu drives for political purification along ethnic lines, will surely prevail.

For Ajami there was no credible basis for Huntington to assert that Saddam's Iraq had taken up the banner of Islam successfully. Saddam, a long-time student of Stalin, opportunistically tried to recreate himself as a standard bearer for Islam in 1990–91. The exercise was a transparent sham to everyone across the Middle East, hence the denunciations fired at him from Islamic religious leaders in Egypt and Saudi Arabia, as well as the complete absence of any support from Iran for Saddam in the leadup to the fighting in early 1991. So Iraq was left to confront not only American military might but also American troops from Saudi Arabia, Egypt, Turkey, and Syria. Only the desperate Palestinians rallied to Saddam's call for support, with very negative consequences for them in the aftermath of the war. The Gulf War demonstrated that a Pax Americana had replaced the Pax Britannica, but the rules of state behaviour and imperial interventionary practice had not changed: "The new power standing sentry in the gulf belonged to the civilization of the West, as did the prior one. But the American presence had the anxious consent of the Arab lands of the Persian Gulf. The stranger coming in to check the kinsmen."[17]

Jeane Kirkpatrick, President Reagan's former secretary of state, objected to Huntington's identified list of major civilizations. Why separate Latin American countries from North America and Western Europe, she asked, given the common cultural origins of all these regions? Why was Russia not considered "Western" too for that matter? Slavic Orthodox Christianity is hardly sufficiently different to warrant its own status separate from Europe.[18] And she might have added, on what basis can Japan be said to constitute a "civilization" in isolation? And why has Israel not been included in the West, given the heavy strategic and economic involvement of that country with the United States since its birth in 1948? Over the past four centuries, Kirkpatrick noted, and most especially during the twentieth century, the most violent major wars and genocidal assaults on people all occurred "within" civilizations, not between them: purges by Stalin and Mao, the Nazi and Khmer Rouge holocausts, the "European civil war" of World War I, and certainly the allied war against Nazi Germany were all "internal" to the classificatory divisions that Huntington formulated.[19] On what basis then can Huntington forecast a radically different risk of organized mass violence against human beings during the coming century?

Following the publication of *The Clash of Civilizations and the Remaking of World Order* in 1996, a second wave of criticism concentrated on Huntington's sweeping generalizations and his provocatively realist premises. For Barry Buzan, Huntington's "civilisational realpolitik" was based on a territorialization of civilizational cultures that is quite inappropriate. Historically, great cultural inventions and grand civilizational norms have transcended state boundaries and informed and influenced many societies for decades, centuries, or millennia after they were first formulated.[20] The rule of law is not confined to the states of the West, nor is the practice of democracy once literacy levels surpass fifty percent of national populations and once mass media communications are widely distributed. As Gwynne Dyer put it, when societies can in a practical way "talk things over," there is no need to rule by terror or authoritarian means; the adoption of some form of democracy becomes inevitable.[21]

Huntington's concept of a pivotal role for "core states" in each civilization was also greeted with skepticism by Buzan. The appeal of Islam in recent decades has been growing without any sponsoring "core state" promoting it. Buddhist religion and concepts spread over much of Asia and made inroads into Western states without any political or material territorial base pushing it forward. So too did Protestant Christianity spread to Asia, Africa, and Latin America during the twentieth century, long after the European and American governments ceased to promote it. Western ideas, ideals, and social, economic, and political norms also have spread far beyond their Western European region of origin. State sovereignty, market economics, nationalism, the scientific method, and the idea of progress itself – all the key elements of "modernity," said Buzan, are now the globalized foundations for all other civilizations: "the fact that so many fundamental Western ideas have become universal more than outweighs the fact that some, most notably human rights and individualism, are still hotly contested."[22] The vast scale of the cultural impact of the West on the rest of the world is, he noted, not without precedent:

> Over 2,300 years ago, five centuries of classical Greek civilisation transformed itself into the much wider-ranging Hellenistic period, which lasted for nearly two millennia until Byzantium fell, and profoundly changed its Greek heartland in the process. Now the five-century run of classical Western civilisation is similarly transforming itself into a wider Westernistic world, which will also feed many new forces into the old West. Although Atlanticism is a useful contribution to global stability, the West does not need to retreat into the Atlanticist bunker that Huntington thinks is its last best hope.[23]

G. John Ikenberry criticized what he saw as Huntington's "wildly overstated" warnings of inter-civilizational war. To assume now that international relations will turn out very badly in the twenty-first century and to take precautionary security measures now to try to weaken potential adversaries and build up one's own military capabilities while constraining theirs certainly will risk inducing a self-fulfilling prophecy. Huntington's urgent plea to reunify the countries of the Atlantic alliance would likely prove to be a massive geostrategic blunder, said Ikenberry:

> Declaring civilizational divides would invite counter-groupings and risk triggering precisely the types of antagonisms that Huntington anticipates. This is the civilizational equivalent of the "security dilemma" – Huntington wants the West to defensively guard against the coming clash, but to other powers like China and Japan the circling of the Western wagons will look like a declaration of a new Cold War.[24]

Both Ikenberry and Buzan evinced concern about the inherently policy-oriented character of Huntington's analytical perspective. Concerns about the neo-isolationist pessimism implicit in Huntington's work was developed in other critiques as well.

In a previous commentary on Huntington's paradigm,[25] I noted that his policy prescriptions entailed a number of very troubling and very specific foreign policy recommendations for the United States:

- Withdrawal of the American security guarantee to Japan, the expansion of security ties with the "kin" countries of Western Europe, and the enlargement of NATO to include all European states that are "Western in their history, religion and culture." Countries that have been "primarily Muslim or Orthodox" were to be denied membership. Huntington claimed that over time one should expect Turkish and Greek membership to "weaken . . . come to an end or become meaningless."[26]

- Forging a strategic relationship of convenience with some combination of India, Russia, or Japan, or all three if possible, so as to be able to spread the burden of containing both China and the countries of the Islamic world.[27]

- Termination of American support for international intervention to prevent human-rights abuses ("promiscuous intervention" wastes resources and will generate needless inter-civilizational conflict[28]). By implication, the provision of international development assistance should also be cut back or eliminated because it too would counterproductively strengthen the economies of other civilizations while depleting Western strength.

- Reduction of the American effort to promote international treaties that will effectively regulate or ban nuclear, biological, or chemical weapons. "Universalist" arms control and disarmament treaties aimed at reducing the threat posed by weapons of mass destruction (WMDs) were instruments of the Cold War, said Huntington. Trying to eliminate WMDs in the early twenty-first century would be an error. Now that the United States is involved in a long term struggle to maintain its scientific and military superiority over more populous rivals whose economies may surpass that of the U.S. in a few decades (China, India, and possibly Europe too, if the Franco-German partnership decides to leave the Euro-American, Atlanticist civilizational bloc), agreeing to forego WMDs could well be something that future American governments would greatly regret. Accordingly, treaty instruments like the foundational Russian–American Anti-Ballistic Missile Treaty of 1972 was something that should be jettisoned as soon as possible because it inhibited research and development in an area of American technological strength.[29] Nor should any tears be spilled over the decreasing respect for the Nuclear Non-Proliferation Treaty (NPT). The covert arms trade and weapons technology sharing that occurred among China, North Korea, Pakistan, Iraq, Iran, Libya, and Syria was extensive through the 1990s and was the most tangible proof of "Confucian–Islamic" collusion to spread WMDs. Their successful collusion illustrated the inherent unworkability and unreliability of global disarmament measures.[30] It would only be a matter of time before the West was subject to direct terrorist threats involving mass destruction technologies.[31]

- Relative American disengagement from the Middle East. While the status of Israel apparently was not discussed systematically by Huntington in any of his writings on the clash thesis, again by implication (Israel is not included among the Western states in the maps in his 1996 book) his views can be inferred from indirect comments. Given Huntington's premise of an inherently adversarial character of the Islamic–Western relationship for some time to come, and given its current condition of what Huntington terms "quasi war,"[32] the U.S. should sensibly retrench from its overexposed position in the Middle East as a supporter of Israel. While there might be some value in the U.S. playing a role as an external balancer power to try to shore up the nuclear-biological-chemical (NBC) peace, there would be uncertain political-strategic gain and the certainty of immense costs and unwarranted risks in any attempt to democratize the Islamic world by trying to impose it on Iraq or Iran by force – especially in an era when terrorists may be able to acquire nuclear, radiological, or biological weapons. In 2002, Huntington counselled against American military intervention in Iraq.[33] He thereby anticipated (and possibly influenced) a similar judgment of several other prominent American realist international relations scholars who opposed the attack on Saddam's regime.[34]

- The end of any sort of governmental policies of multicultural accommodation and their replacement by intensely assimilationist measures for all recent immigrants now inside the U.S. Assimilationism would be assisted by a drastic reduction of Hispanic immigration that Huntington felt threatened the integrity of the dominant Protestant Christian ethos of American society. Continued high immigration from Mexico would be very dangerous in the long term, potentially setting the stage for future Mexican "revanchism" with respect to the American southwestern states.[35] What the U.S. had conquered in the nineteenth century might be lost in the twenty-first. In the same vein, Huntington applauded Western European efforts to slow dramatically the entry into the EU of illegal Muslim migrants, who threatened to turn European states into "cleft" societies.[36] The effective management of immigration flows and the fostering of institutions able to acculturate them to existing norms and values was critical, he argued, to the very survival of the West. Its elites should not forget that "the export of people was perhaps the single most important dimension of the rise of the West between the sixteenth and twentieth centuries."[37]

The net effect on American thinking of Huntington's multidimensional inventory of policy prescriptions is unclear. Few American analysts seem inclined to accept his "decline of the West" thesis, although some may privately agree that American strength of character has been badly corroded. Huntington's policy message has been termed nationalist at best and irrationally nativist at worst. No doubt many American academics see him as a national embarrassment — about as politically incorrect as one could be. He would return the favour and likely denounce them in return as "dead soul" traitors to core American values.[38] Attacking people of colour as culturally subversive to American values in general, and Hispanic migrants in particular as a *de facto* fifth column preparing for a demographic takeover of the American southwest, is not something that can be articulated in polite liberal or social democratic discourse.

Huntington's analysis also has prompted quantitatively based criticism by several researchers. Their criticism has been very limited, however, in its impact, largely because of their very narrowly circumscribed analysis. Russett, Oneal, and Cox published a lengthy study in 2000. They looked at patterns of conflict from 1950 to 1992 and concluded that "civilizational differences have no significant effect on the probability that a dyad will become involved in conflict once either realist or liberal theories are taken into account."[39] In this study, countries with democratic governance and high levels of trade were seen to have had a lower incidence of disputes. When allowance was made for these factors and for the variable of geographical contiguity, civilizational difference had no statistically significant impact on the incidence of conflict. The study also indicated that "civilizational conflicts did not increase as the Cold War waned."[40] Overall, the researchers found that "military, political and economic interests measured by our realist and liberal variables provide a substantially better account of interstate violence than does Huntington's theory."[41] They then asserted that "policymakers should focus on what they can do: peacefully extending democracy and economic interdependence to parts of the world still excluded. . . . Strengthening the liberal forces for peace can mitigate what might otherwise appear to be the clash of civilizations."[42]

The persuasiveness of the Russett, Oneal, and Cox study was undercut, however, by their own acknowledgment that "if the clash thesis is simply a prophecy about what may happen in the 21st century, that would immunize it to any current empirical test."[43] Throughout his book, Huntington indeed argued that future conflicts will arise from fundamentally different causes than in the past. He repeatedly claimed that there is an almost organic, evolutionary process at work in social relations worldwide, and that the historical epoch of nation-states is destined to give way to civilizational rivalries and manoeuvring, as people worldwide identify with ever larger socio-political collectivities, continuing a millennia-long process. While one can see hints of future behaviour in some of the conflicts of the 1990s and earlier, the full pattern of conflict causation in the next century is only now in the process of being revealed.[44] What is clear, Huntington believes, is that the two principal threats to the United States and the West will arise from a fully modernized China and a Muslim world experiencing a still more fully developed "Islamic Resurgence." For a Western world in relative demographic and economic decline, not to speak of the internal moral crisis of social decay and disorder that Huntington also laments,[45] the power capabilities of the West will have to be carefully monitored and protected by a governing elite with far more judgment, circumspection, and prudence than has been demonstrated thus far in the post–Cold War era. Thus, the most important specific predictions about future conflict were not and could not have been tested by Russett and his colleagues. Their findings may be quite accurate, but Huntington can with some justification dismiss them as irrelevant.

A second quantitatively based analytical investigation of Huntington's clash theme was produced shortly after the events of 9/11. Pippa Norris and Ronald Inglehart examined data from the World Values Survey, 1995–2001, and found that "when political attitudes are compared (including evaluations of how well democracy works in practice, support for democratic ideals, and disapproval of strong leaders), far from a 'clash of values,' there is minimal difference between the Islamic world and the West." Of the regions assessed only post-Communist Eastern Europe lagged substantially in support of democratic values. Popular attitudes in Islamic countries were much closer to those in Western Europe and North America. The most important finding indicated that the largest cultural cleavage between the West and the Islamic world concerned "social beliefs about gender equality and sexual liberalization." On these issues, the authors noted, "the West is far more egalitarian and liberal than all other societies, particularly Islamic nations. Moreover cohort analysis suggests that this gap has steadily widened and the younger generation in the West has gradually become more liberal in their sexual mores while the younger generation in Islamic countries remains deeply traditional."[46] Sexual liberalization as represented by greater social and economic equality for women, permissiveness toward homosexuality, serial marriage and divorce, abortion, and the sexualization of mass advertising and popular entertainment together constitute the truly great divergence from the values of Islamic societies – not any alleged divergence in levels of popular respect for democratic principles.

The Norris and Inglehart study is significant in that it suggests that democracy may indeed be in the offing for Islamic societies, but that such democracy would not be socially liberal and would probably be characterized by a highly constrained involvement of women. But Norris and Inglehart presume too much in suggesting that their findings throw substantial doubt on Huntington's diagnosis. Indeed, it is highly doubtful that he would find anything in their findings really surprising. Dislike of democracy was not the core of what Huntington identified as the heart of the Islamic opposition to the United States; rather, it was the sense of frustration with what most people in Islamic states saw as American manipulation of their societies and governments and their collective determination to assert their own path and priorities, domestically and internationally.[47] Islamic opposition to human-rights pressure from the U.S. and other Western states may very well be founded on the rejection of social, economic, and political equality for women. Equality for women plus equality for homosexuals is simply too much to bear for highly traditional cultures where the political left has been largely discredited and the liberal centre has had a hopeless task in trying to promote human rights as understood in Western countries, just as Huntington pointed out.[48]

A decade of critical responses to Huntington's thinking has not really dampened his enthusiasm for proclaiming the demise of the West, the arrogance and insensitivity of American foreign policy, and the stupidity of the neoliberal "imperialist" managerialists in Washington, most of whom seem to subscribe implicitly to some version of hegemonic stability theory. In sum, none of the critical reflections on Huntington's clash thesis have inflicted mortal damage on his broader argument and concerns, primarily because the criticisms are very limited in their applicability or, at their worst, they are little more than *ad hominem* attacks on Huntington and his conservative, nationalist values. But does he offer a sensible "grand strategy" for the countries of the West? What alternatives are available?

A WORLD OF WMD-ARMED CIVILIZATIONAL RIVALS OR AN ERA OF "COOPERATIVE SECURITY"?

What has happened on the ground since 1993? In China, both the suppression of Tibetan Buddhism and the tactics of demographic engulfment of the Tibetan people through forced migration was continued. Chinese repression of the Turkic-Muslim minority peoples in the far west of the country apparently intensified in the years after 9/11 as leaders in Beijing came to fear the prospect of an evermore coordinated Islamist terrorist insurgency. The protracted fight for independence in East Timor met unexpectedly with success against a shaky Indonesian elite; an uncompromising secessionist movement in Chechnya against the Russian Federation did not. The Islamic world continued to be involved in a large number of conflicts: Sudan, Pakistan, Turkey, Thailand, Indonesia, and the Philippines all saw substantial fighting and acts of terrorism over the past decade. Al Qaeda–linked terrorism spread to Southeast Asia after 9/11, leading to many victims in Indonesia and the Philippines. Jemaah Islamiya, a regional offshoot of Al Qaeda, proclaimed the goal of creating an Islamic Southeast Asian superstate living under *sharia*. Islamic extremists, after losing their principal training site when the U.S. deposed the Taliban, continued to organize and fight in western Pakistan and eastern Afghanistan to try to prevent the creation of a stable, more or less democratic government in Kabul. Islamic extremists undoubtedly rallied to the anti-American fight inside occupied Iraq in 2003–04 and may have begun a concerted campaign to try to topple the Saudi dynasty and the Jordanian monarchy.

Huntington thus appears to have been correct in forecasting a continuation of ethnically driven or exacerbated wars and intra-state civil strife. But to reiterate, to date there has been no evidence of an *intensification* of such violence. Violence overall does appear to have de-escalated globally, with the number of insurgencies falling gradually but steadily. As Ted Gurr noted, political accommodation techniques for economically and socially disempowered minorities do seem to be improving across the globe.[49] Huntington's prediction of more and more "fault line wars" has yet to be borne out.

On the WMD proliferation front, Huntington's pessimism has received greater validation. But that is due in part to American actions and policies, not merely the drive for WMD "autonomy" by smaller states or would-be rivals to American military hegemony. Despite the reduction in the number of operational nuclear warheads worldwide from roughly 70 000 in the mid-1980s to some 20 000 currently, there have been major setbacks to the cause of global nuclear disarmament. The ability to build weapons of mass destruction continued to proliferate over the decade, with North Korea, Pakistan, and China continuing to engage in the dissemination of ballistic missiles, development of uranium enrichment capacity, and possibly development of biological weapons capacity too. Iran continued covert efforts to acquire nuclear weapons and to extend the range of its ballistic missiles, even though it agreed in principle to accept more intensive IAEA inspections to verify its nuclear weapon-free status. Iraq's covert programs, if they existed by the late 1990s, were either destroyed or driven far underground (or out of the country) by the American invasion and occupation after March 2003. The solitary success of the Bush administration in disarming Libya in early 2004 was an important achievement for its counterproliferation policy. But that success was offset by the North Koreans' formal renunciation of membership in the NPT in 2002 and their declaration of intent to expand their small arsenal of a handful of atomic weapons quickly. The Bush administration has responded with further high-tech reinforcement of its sizeable conventional forces in South Korea, indicating that a military confrontation remains a serious risk.[50]

Although the potential nuclear successor states of Ukraine, Kazakhstan, and Belarus all opted for non-nuclear weapon state status and transferred their nuclear warheads and launchers to Russia in the mid-1990s, both India and Pakistan abandoned policies of "nuclear opacity" and publicly tested over a dozen nuclear devices in the summer of 1998. Tensions over Kashmir nearly flared into major warfare in 1999 and 2000 (including near use of nuclear weapons) between an Indian government composed of Hindu nationalists and a Pakistani Muslim government. Both Russia and China have begun what are likely to be large nuclear modernization programs in response to the Bush administration's decision to press forward with its ABM deployments in 2004 and beyond, to develop new nuclear warhead designs, and to develop "an ability to fight into, through and from space," while at the same time forging ahead relentlessly with its effort to widen American conventional military superiority over all other potential rivals. In view of American, Russian, and Chinese nuclear modernization, the cuts in the British and French nuclear arsenals implemented over the past decade may well be reversed in coming years.

Over the past decade, Russian security fears were heightened by NATO's two rounds of geographic expansion (under unilateral American direction) to include most of the countries to the west of the "Velvet Curtain of culture" — a move that Huntington endorsed in his 1993 article. Poland, the Czech Republic, and Hungary were admitted in March 1999, followed by the Baltic states of Slovakia, Slovenia, and Romania in April 2004.[51] Whether Huntington's strategic advice in this regard influenced Clinton and Bush administration officials is not known. But his analysis and recommendations probably helped smooth the path of domestic public opinion for such expansion.

Huntington's intellectual aid and comfort to those in Washington who have been pressing for permanent military superiority over all potential challengers cannot but be of deep concern to those who still hold to a liberal-internationalist perspective on world affairs. Huntington's grand strategy vision is the very antithesis of working for an evolving, multilateral "cooperative security" approach that would seek to build a broad international coalition of countries who would work jointly to eliminate the threat posed by nuclear and biological weapons of mass destruction. Only "cooperative security" holds out real promise for halting and then reversing the development of WMDs.[52] Huntington's primacist policy recommendations, if they all were to be implemented, would first commit the U.S. to retaining a significant margin of military superiority against all potential peer competitors. This is a formula for a renewed multilateral arms race. American efforts to develop new nuclear weapons and to achieve military control of space would threaten the NPT and likely stimulate still more nuclear proliferation. Second, a primacy-seeking grand strategy would carry the risk, as Ikenberry noted above, of creating an image of "circling the wagons" and awakening foreign fears that time was running out before the big shoot-out. American governments that seek perpetual military and economic "primacy" as recommended by Huntington (and others) — an approach that has been publicly endorsed by the Bush administration[53] — would almost certainly provoke retaliatory "balancing" by the other major powers in the system.

In a Huntingtonian approach to grand strategy, an American retreat from its security guarantees to Japan and South Korea might also catalyze the start of both Japanese and Korean nuclear weapons programs. The Bush administration's 2002 National Security Strategy, with its strong endorsement of preventive war ("preemption" is a polite euphemism) and the "dissuasion" of potential peer competitors militarily,[54] certainly helped provoke the North Koreans into a sprint to build a small but credible nuclear arsenal. That same document and those same policies of military and strategic preeminence will almost certainly drive Chinese and Russian military spending to levels much higher than they would otherwise be while poisoning the well for nuclear and other greatly needed disarmament measures.

Samuel Huntington's "clash" strategic package has a profound potential for destabilizing world politics. Its bleak vision of the future should be rejected. Liddell Hart's short chapter on grand strategy included the observation that "the object in war is to attain a better peace—even if only from your own point of view. Hence it is essential to conduct war with constant regard to the peace you desire."[55] Part of Huntington's vision of the future *does* include the real possibility of an eventual mutually constructive dialogue of civilizations (recall his question mark). Mutually tolerant and cooperative relations do need to be, and can be, established. Huntington's invocation of Lester Pearson's wise words recognize that fact. But one cannot build trust and tolerance or promote mutual learning in the long term by retreating into a heavily armed "Atlanticist bunker" and being ready to rain down destruction from the heavens at the push of button, as Buzan rightly noted. There are far better strategic alternatives than what Huntington has offered. Huntington is not "wrong" about his choice of ends—just seriously misguided in his selection of means.

NOTES

1. Samuel Huntington, "The Clash of Civilizations? The Next Pattern of Conflict," *Foreign Affairs*, v. 72 n. 3 (Summer 1993), 22–49; cited hereafter as Huntington, "Clash."

2. "X" (George F. Kennan), "The Sources of Soviet Conduct," *Foreign Affairs*, v. 26 (July 1947).

3. Kishore Mahbubani, "The Dangers of Decadence: What the Rest Can Teach the West," *Foreign Affairs*, v. 72 n. 4 (September/October 1993), 12. See also the angry denunciation of Huntington by the late Edward W. Said, who termed the clash thesis the work of an ideologist and propagandist—a collection of "vast abstractions that may give momentary satisfaction but little self-knowledge or informed analysis." Said, "The Clash of Ignorance," *The Nation*, 22 October 2001; accessed online 28 April 2004, at www.thenation.com/doc.mhtml?i = 20011022&ts = said; cited hereafter as Said, "Ignorance."

4. Samuel P. Huntington, *The Clash of Civilizations and the Remaking of World Order* (New York: Simon and Schuster, 1996), 320–21; cited hereafter as *Remaking of World Order*.

5. Robert D. Kaplan, "Looking the World in the Eye," *The Atlantic Monthly* (December 2001); from *The Atlantic Online*, accessed 17 October 2002, at www.theatlantic.com.

6. Colin S. Gray, *Modern Strategy* (Oxford: Oxford University Press, 1999), 17.

7. This definition is a modified version of the elements brought together by Basil H. Liddell Hart. See B.H. Liddell Hart, *Strategy*, 2nd rev. ed. (New York: Signet/New American Library, 1974), 322.

8. Ibid.

9. According the chief economist of the World Bank, the proportion of people living on less than $1 per day worldwide declined from 40% to 21% between 1981 and 2001. The number of people living in extreme poverty apparently fell from 1.5 to 1.1 billion,

although in sub-Saharan Africa the number of extremely poor people increased from 164 to 314 million, or rate of 47% of the region's population. Rapid growth in China and India generated most of the good news – a fall in extreme poverty in China from over 60% to under 20% and in India from over 55% to just over 30%. The World Bank analysts attribute these two countries' success to their internal economic reforms diminishing the role of government, far greater reliance on market allocation, and greatly increased openness to foreign trade and competition. See Francois Bourguignon, "A Wealthier World," *National Post*, 24 April 2004; also, Joseph Brean, "Global Poverty in Steep Decline," *National Post*, 24 April 2004.

10. Robert L. Bartley, "The Case for Optimism: The West Should Believe in Itself," *Foreign Affairs*, v. 72 n. 4 (September/October 1993), 16–17. Simon Murden observed that the "biggest omission" in Huntington's model is the lack of a plausible discussion of the pacifying impact of the world market economy. See his concluding comment in Murden, "Review Article: Huntington and His Critics," *Political Geography*, v. 18 (1999), 1022; cited hereafter as Murden, "Huntington and Critics."

11. See his attack on the systemic disengagement of, and loss of patriotic sentiment by, the American corporate "cosmopolitan" class as well as liberal or left-wing academics in Samuel P. Huntington, "Dead Souls: The Denationalization of the American Elite," *The National Interest*, n. 75 (Spring 2004), 8; cited hereafter as Huntington, "Dead Souls."

12. For a discussion of the responses of several constructivists and critical theorists, see Murden, "Huntington and Critics," 1017–20.

13. Said, "Ignorance."

14. Fouad Ajami, "The Summoning," *Foreign Affairs*, v. 72 n. 4 (September/October 1993), 2.

15. Ibid., 3–4.

16. Ibid., 7.

17. Ibid., 8–9.

18. Jeane J. Kirkpatrick, "The Modernizing Imperative," *Foreign Affairs*, v. 72 n. 4 (September/October 1993), 22–23. For Kirkpatrick, "orthodox theology and liturgy, Leninism and Tolstoy are expressions of Western culture."

19. Ibid.

20. Barry Buzan, "Civilisational *Realpolitik* as the New World Order?" *Survival*, v. 39 n. 1 (Spring 1997), 180–81; cited hereafter as Buzan, "Realpolitik."

21. This point is made very effectively in Gwynne Dyer's four-part film production *The Human Race* (Montreal: National Film Board of Canada/Gree Lion Productions, 1994); cited hereafter as Dyer, *Human Race*.

22. Buzan, "Realpolitik," 183.

23. Ibid.

24. G. John Ikenberry, "Just Like the Rest," *Foreign Affairs*, v. 76 n. 2 (March/April 1997), 163.

25. Douglas Ross, "Despair, Defeatism, and Isolationism in American 'Grand Strategy': The Seductive Convenience of Huntington's 'Civilizational Clash' Thesis," in Mark Charlton, ed., *Crosscurrents: International Relations in the Post-Cold War Era*, 2nd ed. (Toronto: ITP Nelson, 1999), 55–72. While this article stressed the exceptionally blunt

implications of Huntington's analysis for American international security policy, one of the senior editors for *Business Week* declared that Huntington's writing "offers virtually no guidance in applied foreign policy." See Bruce Nussbaum, "Capital, Not Culture," *Foreign Affairs*, v. 76 n. 2 (March/April 1997), 165.

26. Samuel P. Huntington, "The West: Unique, Not Universal," *Foreign Affairs*, v. 75 n. 6 (November/December 1996), 45.

27. Huntington, *Remaking of World Order*, 241–45.

28. Ibid., 316.

29. Huntington, "Clash," 46; also Huntington, *Remaking of World Order*, 309.

30. Huntington, *Remaking of World Order*, 188–89.

31. Ibid., 187–88.

32. See his trenchant summation of the state of this "quasi war" in *Remaking of World Order*, 216–18. American moralizing, crusading, and interventionism is as much to blame for the strife as Islamic rage: "The underlying problem for the West is not Islamic fundamentalism. It is Islam, a different civilization whose people are convinced of the superiority of their culture and are obsessed with the inferiority of their power. The problem for Islam is not the CIA, or the U.S. Department of Defense. It is the West, a different civilization whose people are convinced of the universality of their culture and believe that their superior, if declining, power imposes on them the obligation to extend that culture throughout the world. These are the basic ingredients that fuel conflict between Islam and the West."

33. Beth Baker, Huntington's assistant, confirmed to Ann Kooy that Huntington did speak out against U.S. military intervention in Iraq in 2002. My thanks to Ms. Kooy, an M.A. candidate in political science at SFU, for sharing this information. Daniel Pipes noted that Huntington will soon publish another study explaining why the present American government's "imperialist" effort to remake the Middle East through enforced democratization starting with Iraq is unlikely to succeed. See Pipes, "Bringing Democracy to Iraq beyond Reach of U.S.," *Chicago Sun-Times*, 28 April 2004; accessed online 3 May 2004, at www.chicagosuntimes.com/output/otherviews/cst-edt-pipes28.html.

34. See, for example, John J. Mearsheimer and Stephen M. Walt, "An Unnecessary War," *Foreign Policy* (January/February 2003), 50–59; also, Richard K. Betts, "Suicide From Fear of Death?" *Foreign Affairs*, v. 82 n. 1 (January/February 2003), 34–43.

35. Huntington, *Remaking of World Order*, 206.

36. Ibid., 204–6.

37. Ibid., 198.

38. Huntington, "Dead Souls," 9–10.

39. Bruce M. Russett, John R. Oneal, and Michaelene Cox, "Clash of Civilizations, or Realism and Liberalism Déjà Vu? Some Evidence," *Journal of Peace Research*, v. 37 n. 5 (2000), 595.

40. Ibid., 600.

41. Ibid., 602.

42. Ibid.

43. Ibid.

44. For the same reason, Huntington probably would dismiss the findings of Ted Robert Gurr that the incidence of ethnic conflict was declining worldwide throughout the decade of the 1990s. Gurr's study is nevertheless very important. See Gurr, "Ethnic Warfare on the Wane," *Foreign Affairs*, v. 79 n. 3 (May/June 2000), 52–64. Another study attacking the notion of cultural differences inciting conflict challenged the characterization of the breakup of Yugoslavia and the slaughter in Rwanda as "ethnic wars." John Mueller's iconoclastic but still compelling case study treatment of these two conflicts deserves a close reading. See Mueller, "The Banality of 'Ethnic War,'" *International Security*, v. 25 n. 1 (Summer 2000), 42–70.

45. Huntington sees the increased unwillingness of Americans to pay taxes and their declining willingness to have citizens die for national interests as significant indicators of national moral decline. A reluctance to fund public institutions and programs and to fight for the country are, he believes, grave symptoms of social malaise.

46. Pippa Norris and Ronald Inglehart, "Islam & the West: Testing the 'Clash of Civilizations' Thesis," Faculty Research Working Paper Series, April 2002, RWP02-015, Kennedy School of Government, Harvard University; accessed online 3 May 2004, at ksgnotes1. harvard.edu/research/wpaper.nsf/rwp/RWP02-015/$File/rwp02_015_norris_rev1.pdf.

47. This point is central to Huntington's denunciation of the Clinton administration's efforts to impose its own ideas of order on most of the world, leading to virtually all other regional powers viewing the U.S. as a "rogue superpower" that had to be contained. See Samuel P. Huntington, "The Lonely Superpower," *Foreign Affairs*, v. 78 n. 2 (March/April 1999), 40–44.

48. Huntington, *Remaking of World Order*, 111–14.

49. See Gurr, "Ethnic Warfare on the Wane," 63–64.

50. See Robert Wall, "Strategy in Korea: Better Defense, Better Offense," *Aviation Week and Space Technology*, 12 April 2004.

51. The inclusion in the 2004 expansion of eastern Romania and Bulgaria are modest exceptions to the Velvet Curtain boundary Huntington specified, but can be justified, if only on grounds of geographic contiguity and ease of defence.

52. "Cooperative security" as a strategy has been summarized usefully and compared with alternative 'grand strategy' approaches in Barry R. Posen and Andrew L. Ross, "Competing Visions for U.S. Grand Strategy," *International Security*, v. 21 n. 3 (Winter 1996/97), 5–53. For a discussion of its relevance to Canadian international security policy, see Douglas A. Ross, "Canada's International Security Policy in an Era of American Hyperpower and Continental Vulnerability," *International Journal*, v. 58 n. 4 (Autumn 2003), 533–69.

53. See *The National Security Strategy of the United States*, September 2002; available online at the White House website, at www.whitehouse.gov/nsc/nssall.html; accessed 22 August 2003.

54. Ibid., 30.

55. Hart, *Strategy*, 353.

POSTSCRIPT

Interestingly, even though many in President Bush's administration may be sympathetic to Huntington's thesis, the president himself has been reluctant to give it credence in public statements. In the period following September 11, 2001, President Bush repeatedly stated that the United States was not engaged in a war with Islam itself and focused instead on arguing that radical Islamists represented a distortion of Islam, which he called a religion of peace. It appears that the president fears that if the label of civilizational conflict is applied to the "war on terrorism," it might constitute a self-fulfilling prophecy.

Today, it is difficult not to read this debate in the context of the American war on terrorism and the apparent escalating conflict between Islamic and Western forces in many parts of the world. In recent times, we have seen growing conflicts between Muslims and Christians in Nigeria and Indonesia and between Muslims and Buddhists in Thailand. How do we interpret Huntington's civilizational clash in the post–September 11 era? Do these events give greater credence to his theory? Does the theory provide a framework for understanding the major fault lines of conflict today? If not, what alternative explanations may be offered? Huntington argues that civilizational conflict will be more intractable and less easy to resolve by conflict and negotiation. If this is true, what implications does this have for the foreign policy of our governments?

Suggested Additional Readings

Abrahamian, Ervand. "The US Media, Huntington and September 11." *Third World Quarterly* 24, no. 13 (June 2003): 529–44.

Aysha, Emad El-Din. "Huntington's Shift to the Declinist Camp: Conservative Declinism and the 'Historical Function' of the Clash of Civilisations." *International Relations* 17, no. 4 (December 2003): 429–52.

Chiozza, Giacomo. "Is There a Clash of Civilizations? Evidence from Patterns of International Conflict Involvement, 1946–9." *Journal of Peace Research* 39, no. 6 (November 2002): 711–35.

Cox, Robert. "Civilisations: Encounters and Transformations." *Studies in Political Economy* 47 (Summer 1995): 7–31.

Falk, Richard. "False Universalism and the Geopolitics of Exclusion: The Case of Islam." *Third World Quarterly* 18, no. 1 (March 1997): 7–24.

Henderson, Errol A., and R. Tucker. "Clear and Present Strangers: The Clash of Civilizations and International Conflict." *International Studies Quarterly* 45, no. 2 (June 2001): 317–38.

Kurtz, Stanley. "The Future of 'History.'" *Policy Review* 113 (June–July 2002): 43–58. Available at www.policyreview.org/jun02/kurtz.html.

Lewis, Bernard. "I'm Right, You're Wrong, Go to Hell." *Atlantic Monthly* 291, no. 4 (May 2003): 36–42.

Norris, Pipa, and Ronald Inglehart. "Islamic Culture and Democracy: Testing the 'Clash of Civilizations' Thesis." *Comparative Sociology* 1, no. 3–4 (August 2002): 235–64.

Rajendram, Lavina. "Does the Clash of Civilizations Paradigm Provide a Persuasive Explanation of International Politics post September 11th?" *Cambridge Review of International Affairs* 15, no. 2 (July 2002): 217–33.

Vasillopulos, Christopher. "Clash of Civilizations: Prophecy or Contradiction in Terms?" *Arab Studies Quarterly* 25, no. 1–2 (Winter–Spring 2003): 89–100.

InfoTrac® College Edition

Search for the following articles in the InfoTrac® database:

Fox, Jonathan. "Ethnic Minorities and the Clash of Civilizations: A Quantitative Analysis of Huntington's Thesis." *British Journal of Political Science* 32, no. 3 (July 2002): 415–34.

Inglehart, Ronald, and Pippa Norris. "The True Clash of Civilizations." *Foreign Policy* 135 (March–April 2003): 63–70.

Kibble, David G. "The Attacks of 9/11: Evidence of a Clash of Religions?" *Parameters* 32, no. 3 (Autumn 2002): 34–45.

For more articles, enter:
"clash of civilizations" in the keyword search.
"Samuel Huntington" in the author search (under advanced search).

Web Resources

For current URLs for the following websites, visit www.crosscurrents.nelson.com.

CLASH OF CIVILIZATIONS: A READING GUIDE

www.csmonitor.com/specials/sept11/flash_civClash.html

Prepared by *The Christian Science Monitor*, this site contains a good collection of academic articles debating Huntington's thesis, along with links to articles discussing the concept in relation to the war on terrorism.

SEIZABURO SATO, "THE CLASH OF CIVILIZATIONS: A VIEW FROM JAPAN," *ASIA PACIFIC REVIEW* (October 1997)

www.sbpark.com/inn60.html

This article, appearing on the website of the Okamoto International Affairs Research Institute, provides a Japanese perspective on Huntington's thesis.

DAVID SKIDMORE, "HUNTINGTON'S CLASH REVISITED," *JOURNAL OF WORLD-SYSTEMS RESEARCH* 4, no. 2 (Fall 1998)

www.jwsr.ucr.edu/archive/vol4/v4n2r2.php

This book review offers a critical look at Huntington's *The Clash of Civilizations and the Remaking of World Order.*

PART TWO

ENSURING PEACE AND SECURITY

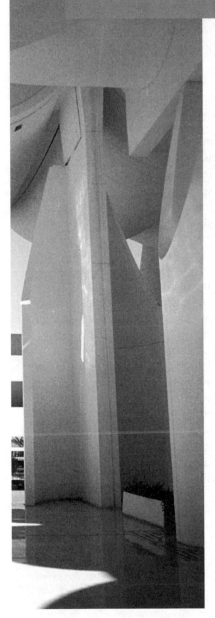

Will the Bush Doctrine of preemptive war promote a more secure world?

Did the war against Iraq violate international law?

Will a ballistic defence system undermine global security?

Has NATO become irrelevant in an age of terrorism?

Do biological differences predispose men to war?

Will the Bush Doctrine of Preemptive War Promote a More Secure World?

✔ **YES**

GEORGE W. BUSH, *The National Security Strategy of the United States of America*

✘ **NO**

NETA C. CRAWFORD, "The Slippery Slope to Preventive War," *Ethics and International Affairs* 17, no. 1 (2003): 30–36

September 11, 2001, marked a significant turning point in American defence strategy. The magnitude and suddenness of the simultaneous attacks on New York City and Washington, D.C., heightened American feelings of vulnerability to new attacks and threats. In the wake of the attack, the American leadership argued that it was time to reassess its traditional foreign policy strategies and map new directions for the future. The following June, in a graduation address at West Point, President George W. Bush noted that the world stood "at the crossroads of radicalism and technology" where "even weak states and small groups could attain a catastrophic power to strike great nations." In a series of speeches by the president and other administration officials, the case for a new approach to foreign policy was laid out, culminating in the publication – just a year after the events of September 11 – of *The National Security Strategy of the United States of America*. This document now forms the cornerstone of American defence policy and provides the foundation for what has become known as the Bush Doctrine.

The basic assumption underlying the strategy is that American foreign policy in the past has largely been reactive in nature. The twin pillars shaping the American response to the Soviet threat during the Cold War were the concepts of deterrence and containment. The theory of deterrence was based on the notion that the ability to annihilate or at least inflict an unacceptable level of damage on an opponent, even after being attacked first, would deter an attack from happening in the first place. The key to defence policy was to ensure that one had sufficient "second strike capability" to launch a retaliatory attack even if one had been attacked by surprise. The theory of containment called for supplying military, economic, and technical assistance to an opponent's neighbours in order to curtail any efforts by the opponent to expand its influence. This policy was deeply rooted in the balance-of-power thinking of the realist tradition. Its defenders suggest that the fact that the U.S. and U.S.S.R. did not confront each other in a direct war (producing the so-called "long peace") was largely the result of a skillful application of the balance-of-power concepts.

The argument put forward in the *National Security Strategy* is that the international environment is now significantly different. During the Cold War, the Soviet Union was largely a risk-averse, status quo power for whom a strategy of deterrence and containment both made sense and was successful. What has changed, as George W. Bush noted in a speech at West Point, is the emergence of the "crossroads of radicalism and technology." The threat facing us today comes from the combination of growing alliance between radical terrorist groups and "rogue" states who are not constrained by traditional laws of war or by rational calculations of cost–benefit. Fuelled by new technologies that permit the development of weapons of mass destruction, which can easily be transported and hidden, the risk of an unprovoked and unexpected attack, threatening death to large numbers of civilians, has greatly increased. Thus, the argument goes, the United States must abandon its largely passive strategy for a more direct one.

The origins of the Bush Doctrine are not rooted in the events of September 11 alone, but appear to have germinated in the immediate aftermath of the end of the Cold War. In March 1992, *The New York Times* published a leaked U.S. Department of Defense document drafted by under secretary of defense, Paul Wolfowitz. The document emphasized the importance of thwarting any attempts in the post–Cold War period of any state, or group of states, to develop a capability to rival American military hegemony. It argued that the United States should be prepared to act independently if necessary to thwart such threats when collective efforts could not be organized. In particular, it insisted that the American government should abandon the strategy of containment as a relic of the past and move toward a more proactive strategy of preemption.

The leaked document provoked a strong reaction in many quarters. The administration of George Bush Senior moved quickly to reject suggestions of a unilateral policy of preemption. Paul Wolfowitz was ordered to redraft the document, removing any references to unilateralism and preemption. The president's success in developing a broad coalition of states and gaining UN Security Council support for military action against Iraq after its invasion of Kuwait, it was argued, demonstrated that multilateralism could still work. When President Bush lost the subsequent election, the new Clinton administration largely ignored the ideas outlined in the document.

However, these ideas did not die out. In 1997, a group calling itself the Project for the New American Century was established. Members of the project included members of the former Bush administration, such as Dick Cheney, Paul Wolfowitz, Donald Rumsfeld, Elliot Abrams, and William Bennet, and prominent intellectuals, such as George Weigel, Norman Prodhoretz, Robert Kagan, and Francis Fukuyama. Through public letters, articles, and books, the Project for the New American Century developed and articulated more fully many of the ideas that Wolfowitz had advocated in 1992. Their work culminated in 2000 in the publication of a document entitled *Rebuilding America's Defenses: Strategy, Forces and Resources for a New Century*.

By January 2001, many founding members of the project were appointed to prominent positions in the new administration of George W. Bush. Dick Cheney became vice president, Donald Rumsfeld was now secretary of defense, and Paul Wolfowitz was deputy secretary of defense. But these more hawkish voices seemed to have a counterweight in the appointment as secretary of state of Colin Powell, who was widely perceived as a dove, advocating continued emphasis on multilateralism and diplomacy. At first it appeared that there would be a prolonged tug of war between these hawkish and dovish factions for influence within the new administration.

The tragic events of September 11, however, dramatically changed the environment in which the new Bush administration was formulating its policies. Suddenly, the 1992 Wolfowitz document appeared to be both prophetic and highly relevant to the new circumstances. The ideas promoted by the Project for a New American Century now seemed to provide a guide to chartering American foreign policy through these uncertain and dangerous waters. It is perhaps not surprising then that these ideas would come to form the basis for the Bush administration's attempts to articulate a new foreign policy strategy.

The first reading consists of excerpts from *The National Security Strategy of the United States*, released a year after the attacks of September 11, 2001. The document sets out the case for what has come to be called the Bush Doctrine, arguing in particular for a strategy of preemption when necessary in order to curtail future attacks on the United States. In the second reading, Neta C. Crawford critiques many of the assumptions of the Bush Doctrine and questions whether it will in fact lead to the increased security for the United States.

✔ YES
The National Security Strategy of the United States of America
GEORGE W. BUSH

The great struggles of the twentieth century between liberty and totalitarianism ended with a decisive victory for the forces of freedom — and a single sustainable model for national success: freedom, democracy, and free enterprise. In the twenty-first century, only nations that share a commitment to protecting basic human rights and guaranteeing political and economic freedom will be able to unleash the potential of their people and assure their future prosperity. People everywhere want to be able to speak freely; choose who will govern them; worship as they please; educate their children — male and female; own property; and enjoy the benefits of their labor. These values of freedom are right and true for every person, in every society — and the duty of protecting these values against their enemies is the common calling of freedom-loving people across the globe and across the ages.

Today, the United States enjoys a position of unparalleled military strength and great economic and political influence. In keeping with our heritage and principles, we do not use our strength to press for unilateral advantage. We seek instead to create a balance of power that favors human freedom: conditions in which all nations and all societies can choose for themselves the rewards and challenges of political and economic liberty. In a world that is safe, people will be able to make their own lives better. We will defend the peace by fighting terrorists and tyrants. We will preserve the peace by building good relations among the great powers. We will extend the peace by encouraging free and open societies on every continent.

Defending our Nation against its enemies is the first and fundamental commitment of the Federal Government. Today, that task has changed dramatically. Enemies in the past needed great armies and great industrial capabilities to endanger America. Now, shadowy networks of individuals can bring great chaos and suffering to our shores for less than it costs to purchase a single tank. Terrorists are organized to penetrate open societies and to turn the power of modern technologies against us.

To defeat this threat we must make use of every tool in our arsenal — military power, better homeland defenses, law enforcement, intelligence, and vigorous efforts to cut off terrorist financing. The war against terrorists of global reach is a global enterprise of uncertain duration. America will help nations that need our assistance in combating terror. And America will hold to account nations that are compromised by terror, including those who harbor terrorists — because the allies of terror are the enemies of civilization. The United States and countries cooperating with us must not allow the terrorists to develop new home bases. Together, we will seek to deny them sanctuary at every turn.

The gravest danger our Nation faces lies at the crossroads of radicalism and technology. Our enemies have openly declared that they are seeking weapons of mass destruction, and evidence indicates that they are doing so with determination. The United States will not allow these efforts to succeed. We will build defenses against ballistic missiles and other means of delivery. We will cooperate with other nations to deny, contain, and curtail our enemies' efforts to acquire dangerous technologies. And, as a matter of common sense and self-defense, America will act against such emerging threats before they are fully formed. We cannot defend America and our friends by hoping for the best. So we must be prepared to defeat our enemies' plans, using the best intelligence and proceeding with deliberation. History will judge harshly those who saw this coming danger but failed to act. In the new world we have entered, the only path to peace and security is the path of action.

As we defend the peace, we will also take advantage of an historic opportunity to preserve the peace. Today, the international community has the best chance since the rise of the nation-state in the seventeenth century to build a world where great powers compete in peace instead of continually prepare for war. Today, the world's great powers find ourselves on the same side — united by common dangers of terrorist violence and chaos. The United States will build on these common interests to promote global security. We are also increasingly united by common values. Russia is in the midst of a hopeful transition, reaching for its democratic future and a partner in the war on terror. Chinese leaders are discovering that economic freedom is the only source of national wealth. In time, they will find that social and political freedom is the only source of national greatness. America will encourage the advancement of democracy and economic openness in both nations, because these are the best foundations for domestic stability and international order. We will strongly resist aggression from other great powers — even as we welcome their peaceful pursuit of prosperity, trade, and cultural advancement.

Finally, the United States will use this moment of opportunity to extend the benefits of freedom across the globe. We will actively work to bring the hope of democracy, development, free markets, and free trade to every corner of the world. The events of September 11, 2001, taught us that weak states, like Afghanistan, can pose as great a danger to our national interests as strong states. Poverty does not make poor people into terrorists and murderers. Yet poverty, weak institutions, and corruption can make weak states vulnerable to terrorist networks and drug cartels within their borders.

The United States will stand beside any nation determined to build a better future by seeking the rewards of liberty for its people. Free trade and free markets have proven their ability to lift whole societies out of poverty — so the United States will work with individual nations, entire regions, and the entire global trading community to build a world that trades in freedom and therefore grows in prosperity. The United States will deliver greater development assistance through the New

Millennium Challenge Account to nations that govern justly, invest in their people, and encourage economic freedom. We will also continue to lead the world in efforts to reduce the terrible toll of HIV/AIDS and other infectious diseases.

In building a balance of power that favors freedom, the United States is guided by the conviction that all nations have important responsibilities. Nations that enjoy freedom must actively fight terror. Nations that depend on international stability must help prevent the spread of weapons of mass destruction. Nations that seek international aid must govern themselves wisely, so that aid is well spent. For freedom to thrive, accountability must be expected and required.

We are also guided by the conviction that no nation can build a safer, better world alone. Alliances and multilateral institutions can multiply the strength of freedom-loving nations. The United States is committed to lasting institutions like the United Nations, the World Trade Organization, the Organization of American States, and NATO as well as other long-standing alliances. Coalitions of the willing can augment these permanent institutions. In all cases, international obligations are to be taken seriously. They are not to be undertaken symbolically to rally support for an ideal without furthering its attainment.

Freedom is the non-negotiable demand of human dignity; the birthright of every person — in every civilization. Throughout history, freedom has been threatened by war and terror; it has been challenged by the clashing wills of powerful states and the evil designs of tyrants; and it has been tested by widespread poverty and disease. Today, humanity holds in its hands the opportunity to further freedom's triumph over all these foes. The United States welcomes our responsibility to lead in this great mission.
George W. Bush
THE WHITE HOUSE,
September 17, 2002

I. OVERVIEW OF AMERICA'S INTERNATIONAL STRATEGY

"Our Nation's cause has always been larger than our Nation's defense. We fight, as we always fight, for a just peace — a peace that favors liberty. We will defend the peace against the threats from terrorists and tyrants. We will preserve the peace by building good relations among the great powers. And we will extend the peace by encouraging free and open societies on every continent."

President Bush
West Point, New York
June 1, 2002

The United States possesses unprecedented — and unequaled — strength and influence in the world. Sustained by faith in the principles of liberty, and the value of a free society, this position comes with unparalleled responsibilities, obligations, and opportunity. The great strength of this nation must be used to promote a balance of power that favors freedom.

For most of the twentieth century, the world was divided by a great struggle over ideas: destructive totalitarian visions versus freedom and equality.

That great struggle is over. The militant visions of class, nation, and race which promised utopia and delivered misery have been defeated and discredited. America is now threatened less by conquering states than we are by failing ones. We are menaced less by fleets and armies than by catastrophic technologies in the hands of the embittered few. We must defeat these threats to our Nation, allies, and friends.

This is also a time of opportunity for America. We will work to translate this moment of influence into decades of peace, prosperity, and liberty. The U.S. national security strategy will be based on a distinctly American internationalism that reflects the union of our values and our national interests. The aim of this strategy is to help make the world not just safer but better. Our goals on the path to progress are clear: political and economic freedom, peaceful relations with other states, and respect for human dignity. [...]

II. CHAMPION ASPIRATIONS FOR HUMAN DIGNITY

"Some worry that it is somehow undiplomatic or impolite to speak the language of right and wrong. I disagree. Different circumstances require different methods, but not different moralities."

President Bush
West Point, New York
June 1, 2002

In pursuit of our goals, our first imperative is to clarify what we stand for: the United States must defend liberty and justice because these principles are right and true for all people everywhere. No nation owns these aspirations, and no nation is exempt from them. Fathers and mothers in all societies want their children to be educated and to live free from poverty and violence. No people on earth yearn to be oppressed, aspire to servitude, or eagerly await the midnight knock of the secret police.

America must stand firmly for the nonnegotiable demands of human dignity: the rule of law; limits on the absolute power of the state; free speech; freedom of worship; equal justice; respect for women; religious and ethnic tolerance; and respect for private property.

These demands can be met in many ways. America's constitution has served us well. Many other nations, with different histories and cultures, facing different circumstances, have successfully incorporated these core principles into their own systems of governance. History has not been kind to those nations which ignored or flouted the rights and aspirations of their people.

America's experience as a great multi-ethnic democracy affirms our conviction that people of many heritages and faiths can live and prosper in peace. Our own history is a long struggle to live up to our ideals. But even in our worst moments, the principles enshrined in the Declaration of Independence were there to guide us. As a result, America is not just a stronger, but is a freer and more just society.

Today, these ideals are a lifeline to lonely defenders of liberty. And when openings arrive, we can encourage change – as we did in central and eastern Europe between 1989 and 1991, or in Belgrade in 2000. When we see democratic processes take hold among our friends in Taiwan or in the Republic of Korea, and see elected leaders replace generals in Latin America and Africa, we see examples of how authoritarian systems can evolve, marrying local history and traditions with the principles we all cherish.

Embodying lessons from our past and using the opportunity we have today, the national security strategy of the United States must start from these core beliefs and look outward for possibilities to expand liberty.

Our principles will guide our government's decisions about international cooperation, the character of our foreign assistance, and the allocation of resources. They will guide our actions and our words in international bodies.

We will:

- speak out honestly about violations of the nonnegotiable demands of human dignity using our voice and vote in international institutions to advance freedom;

- use our foreign aid to promote freedom and support those who struggle nonviolently for it, ensuring that nations moving toward democracy are rewarded for the steps they take;

- make freedom and the development of democratic institutions key themes in our bilateral relations, seeking solidarity and cooperation from other democracies while we press governments that deny human rights to move toward a better future; and

- take special efforts to promote freedom of religion and conscience and defend it from encroachment by repressive governments.

We will champion the cause of human dignity and oppose those who resist it.

III. STRENGTHEN ALLIANCES TO DEFEAT GLOBAL TERRORISM AND WORK TO PREVENT ATTACKS AGAINST US AND OUR FRIENDS

"Just three days removed from these events, Americans do not yet have the distance of history. But our responsibility to history is already clear: to answer these attacks and rid the world of evil. War has been waged against us by stealth and deceit and murder. This nation is peaceful, but fierce when stirred to anger. The conflict was begun on the timing and terms of others. It will end in a way, and at an hour, of our choosing."

President Bush
Washington, D.C. (The National Cathedral)
September 14, 2001

The United States of America is fighting a war against terrorists of global reach. The enemy is not a single political regime or person or religion or ideology. The enemy is terrorism — premeditated, politically motivated violence perpetrated against innocents.

In many regions, legitimate grievances prevent the emergence of a lasting peace. Such grievances deserve to be, and must be, addressed within a political process. But no cause justifies terror. The United States will make no concessions to terrorist demands and strike no deals with them. We make no distinction between terrorists and those who knowingly harbor or provide aid to them.

The struggle against global terrorism is different from any other war in our history. It will be fought on many fronts against a particularly elusive enemy over an extended period of time. Progress will come through the persistent accumulation of successes — some seen, some unseen.

Today our enemies have seen the results of what civilized nations can, and will, do against regimes that harbor, support, and use terrorism to achieve their political goals. Afghanistan has been liberated; coalition forces continue to hunt down the Taliban and al-Qaida. But it is not only this battlefield on which we will engage terrorists. Thousands of trained terrorists remain at large with cells in North America, South America, Europe, Africa, the Middle East, and across Asia.

Our priority will be first to disrupt and destroy terrorist organizations of global reach and attack their leadership; command, control, and communications; material support; and finances. This will have a disabling effect upon the terrorists' ability to plan and operate.

We will continue to encourage our regional partners to take up a coordinated effort that isolates the terrorists. Once the regional campaign localizes the threat to a particular state, we will help ensure the state has the military, law enforcement, political, and financial tools necessary to finish the task.

The United States will continue to work with our allies to disrupt the financing of terrorism. We will identify and block the sources of funding for terrorism, freeze the assets of terrorists and those who support them, deny terrorists access to the international financial system, protect legitimate charities from being abused by terrorists, and prevent the movement of terrorists' assets through alternative financial networks.

However, this campaign need not be sequential to be effective, the cumulative effect across all regions will help achieve the results we seek. We will disrupt and destroy terrorist organizations by:

- direct and continuous action using all the elements of national and international power. Our immediate focus will be those terrorist organizations of global reach and any terrorist or state sponsor of terrorism which attempts to gain or use weapons of mass destruction (WMD) or their precursors;

- defending the United States, the American people, and our interests at home and abroad by identifying and destroying the threat before it reaches our borders. While the United States will constantly strive to enlist the support of the international community, we will not hesitate to act alone, if necessary, to exercise our right of selfdefense by acting preemptively against such terrorists, to prevent them from doing harm against our people and our country; and

- denying further sponsorship, support, and sanctuary to terrorists by convincing or compelling states to accept their sovereign responsibilities. We will also wage a war of ideas to win the battle against international terrorism. This includes:

- using the full influence of the United States, and working closely with allies and friends, to make clear that all acts of terrorism are illegitimate so that terrorism will be viewed in the same light as slavery, piracy, or genocide: behavior that no respectable government can condone or support and all must oppose;

- supporting moderate and modern government, especially in the Muslim world, to ensure that the conditions and ideologies that promote terrorism do not find fertile ground in any nation;

- diminishing the underlying conditions that spawn terrorism by enlisting the international community to focus its efforts and resources on areas most at risk; and

- using effective public diplomacy to promote the free flow of information and ideas to kindle the hopes and aspirations of freedom of those in societies ruled by the sponsors of global terrorism.

While we recognize that our best defense is a good offense, we are also strengthening America's homeland security to protect against and deter attack. This Administration has proposed the largest government reorganization since the Truman Administration created the National Security Council and the Department of Defense. Centered on a new Department of Homeland Security and including a new unified military command and a fundamental reordering of the FBI, our comprehensive plan to secure the homeland encompasses every level of government and the cooperation of the public and the private sector.

This strategy will turn adversity into opportunity. For example, emergency management systems will be better able to cope not just with terrorism but with all hazards. Our medical system will be strengthened to manage not just bioterror, but all infectious diseases and mass-casualty dangers. Our border controls will not just stop terrorists, but improve the efficient movement of legitimate traffic.

While our focus is protecting America, we know that to defeat terrorism in today's globalized world we need support from our allies and friends. Wherever possible, the United States will rely on regional organizations and state powers to meet their obligations to fight terrorism. Where governments find the fight against terrorism beyond their capacities, we will match their willpower and their resources with whatever help we and our allies can provide.

As we pursue the terrorists in Afghanistan, we will continue to work with international organizations such as the United Nations, as well as non-governmental organizations, and other countries to provide the humanitarian, political, economic, and security assistance necessary to rebuild Afghanistan so that it will never again abuse its people, threaten its neighbors, and provide a haven for terrorists.

In the war against global terrorism, we will never forget that we are ultimately fighting for our democratic values and way of life. Freedom and fear are at war, and there will be no quick or easy end to this conflict. In leading the campaign against terrorism, we are forging new, productive international relationships and redefining existing ones in ways that meet the challenges of the twenty-first century.

IV. WORK WITH OTHERS TO DEFUSE REGIONAL CONFLICTS

"We build a world of justice, or we will live in a world of coercion. The magnitude of our shared responsibilities makes our disagreements look so small."

President Bush
Berlin, Germany
May 23, 2002

Concerned nations must remain actively engaged in critical regional disputes to avoid explosive escalation and minimize human suffering. In an increasingly interconnected world, regional crisis can strain our alliances, rekindle rivalries among the major powers, and create horrifying affronts to human dignity. When violence erupts and states falter, the United States will work with friends and partners to alleviate suffering and restore stability.

No doctrine can anticipate every circumstance in which U.S. action – direct or indirect – is warranted. We have finite political, economic, and military resources to meet our global priorities. The United States will approach each case with these strategic principles in mind:

- The United States should invest time and resources into building international relationships and institutions that can help manage local crises when they emerge.

The United States should be realistic about its ability to help those who are unwilling or unready to help themselves. Where and when people are ready to do their part, we will be willing to move decisively. [. . .]

V. PREVENT OUR ENEMIES FROM THREATENING US, OUR ALLIES, AND OUR FRIENDS WITH WEAPONS OF MASS DESTRUCTION

"The gravest danger to freedom lies at the crossroads of radicalism and technology. When the spread of chemical and biological and nuclear weapons, along with ballistic missile technology – when that occurs, even weak states and small groups could attain a catastrophic power to strike great nations. Our enemies have

declared this very intention, and have been caught seeking these terrible weapons. They want the capability to blackmail us, or to harm us, or to harm our friends — and we will oppose them with all our power."

President Bush
West Point, New York
June 1, 2002

The nature of the Cold War threat required the United States — with our allies and friends — to emphasize deterrence of the enemy's use of force, producing a grim strategy of mutual assured destruction. With the collapse of the Soviet Union and the end of the Cold War, our security environment has undergone profound transformation.

Having moved from confrontation to cooperation as the hallmark of our relationship with Russia, the dividends are evident: an end to the balance of terror that divided us; an historic reduction in the nuclear arsenals on both sides; and cooperation in areas such as counterterrorism and missile defense that until recently were inconceivable.

But new deadly challenges have emerged from rogue states and terrorists. None of these contemporary threats rival the sheer destructive power that was arrayed against us by the Soviet Union. However, the nature and motivations of these new adversaries, their determination to obtain destructive powers hitherto available only to the world's strongest states, and the greater likelihood that they will use weapons of mass destruction against us, make today's security environment more complex and dangerous.

In the 1990s we witnessed the emergence of a small number of rogue states that, while different in important ways, share a number of attributes. These states:

- brutalize their own people and squander their national resources for the personal gain of the rulers;

- display no regard for international law, threaten their neighbors, and callously violate international treaties to which they are party;

- are determined to acquire weapons of mass destruction, along with other advanced military technology, to be used as threats or offensively to achieve the aggressive designs of these regimes;

- sponsor terrorism around the globe; and

- reject basic human values and hate the United States and everything for which it stands.

At the time of the Gulf War, we acquired irrefutable proof that Iraq's designs were not limited to the chemical weapons it had used against Iran and its own people, but also extended to the acquisition of nuclear weapons and biological agents. In the past decade North Korea has become the world's principal purveyor of ballistic missiles, and has tested increasingly capable missiles while developing its own WMD arsenal. Other rogue regimes seek nuclear, biological, and chemical weapons as well. These states' pursuit of, and global trade in, such weapons has become a looming threat to all nations.

We must be prepared to stop rogue states and their terrorist clients before they are able to threaten or use weapons of mass destruction against the United States and our allies and friends. Our response must take full advantage of strengthened alliances, the establishment of new partnerships with former adversaries, innovation in the use of military forces, modern technologies, including the development of an effective missile defense system, and increased emphasis on intelligence collection and analysis.

Our comprehensive strategy to combat WMD includes:

- *Proactive counterproliferation efforts.* We must deter and defend against the threat before it is unleashed. We must ensure that key capabilities – detection, active and passive defenses, and counterforce capabilities – are integrated into our defense transformation and our homeland security systems. Counterproliferation must also be integrated into the doctrine, training, and equipping of our forces and those of our allies to ensure that we can prevail in any conflict with WMD-armed adversaries.

- *Strengthened nonproliferation efforts to prevent rogue states and terrorists from acquiring the materials, technologies, and expertise necessary for weapons of mass destruction.* We will enhance diplomacy, arms control, multilateral export controls, and threat reduction assistance that impede states and terrorists seeking WMD, and when necessary, interdict enabling technologies and materials. We will continue to build coalitions to support these efforts, encouraging their increased political and financial support for nonproliferation and threat reduction programs. The recent G-8 agreement to commit up to $20 billion to a global partnership against proliferation marks a major step forward.

- *Effective consequence management to respond to the effects of WMD use, whether by terrorists or hostile states.* Minimizing the effects of WMD use against our people will help deter those who possess such weapons and dissuade those who seek to acquire them by persuading enemies that they cannot attain their desired ends. The United States must also be prepared to respond to the effects of WMD use against our forces abroad, and to help friends and allies if they are attacked.

It has taken almost a decade for us to comprehend the true nature of this new threat. Given the goals of rogue states and terrorists, the United States can no longer solely rely on a reactive posture as we have in the past. The inability to deter a potential attacker, the immediacy of today's threats, and the magnitude of potential harm that could be caused by our adversaries' choice of weapons, do not permit that option. We cannot let our enemies strike first.

In the Cold War, especially following the Cuban missile crisis, we faced a generally status quo, risk-averse adversary. Deterrence was an effective defense. But deterrence based only upon the threat of retaliation is less likely to work against leaders of rogue states more willing to take risks, gambling with the lives of their people, and the wealth of their nations.

- In the Cold War, weapons of mass destruction were considered weapons of last resort whose use risked the destruction of those who used them. Today, our enemies see weapons of mass destruction as weapons of choice. For rogue states these weapons are tools of intimidation and military aggression against their neighbors. These weapons may also allow these states to attempt to blackmail the United States and our allies to prevent us from deterring or repelling the aggressive behavior of rogue states. Such states also see these weapons as their best means of overcoming the conventional superiority of the United States.

- Traditional concepts of deterrence will not work against a terrorist enemy whose avowed tactics are wanton destruction and the targeting of innocents; whose so-called soldiers seek martyrdom in death and whose most potent protection is statelessness. The overlap between states that sponsor terror and those that pursue WMD compels us to action.

For centuries, international law recognized that nations need not suffer an attack before they can lawfully take action to defend themselves against forces that present an imminent danger of attack. Legal scholars and international jurists often conditioned the legitimacy of preemption on the existence of an imminent threat — most often a visible mobilization of armies, navies, and air forces preparing to attack.

We must adapt the concept of imminent threat to the capabilities and objectives of today's adversaries. Rogue states and terrorists do not seek to attack us using conventional means. They know such attacks would fail. Instead, they rely on acts of terror and, potentially, the use of weapons of mass destruction — weapons that can be easily concealed, delivered covertly, and used without warning.

The targets of these attacks are our military forces and our civilian population, in direct violation of one of the principal norms of the law of warfare. As was demonstrated by the losses on September 11, 2001, mass civilian casualties is the specific objective of terrorists and these losses would be exponentially more severe if terrorists acquired and used weapons of mass destruction.

The United States has long maintained the option of preemptive actions to counter a sufficient threat to our national security. The greater the threat, the greater is the risk of inaction — and the more compelling the case for taking anticipatory action to defend ourselves, even if uncertainty remains as to the time and place of the enemy's attack. To forestall or prevent such hostile acts by our adversaries, the United States will, if necessary, act preemptively.

The United States will not use force in all cases to preempt emerging threats, nor should nations use preemption as a pretext for aggression. Yet in an age where the enemies of civilization openly and actively seek the world's most destructive technologies, the United States cannot remain idle while dangers gather. We will always proceed deliberately, weighing the consequences of our actions. To support preemptive options, we will:

- build better, more integrated intelligence capabilities to provide timely, accurate information on threats, wherever they may emerge;

- coordinate closely with allies to form a common assessment of the most dangerous threats; and

- continue to transform our military forces to ensure our ability to conduct rapid and precise operations to achieve decisive results.

The purpose of our actions will always be to eliminate a specific threat to the United States or our allies and friends. The reasons for our actions will be clear, the force measured, and the cause just. [. . .]

IX. TRANSFORM AMERICA'S NATIONAL SECURITY INSTITUTIONS TO MEET THE CHALLENGES AND OPPORTUNITIES OF THE TWENTY-FIRST CENTURY

"Terrorists attacked a symbol of American prosperity. They did not touch its source. America is successful because of the hard work, creativity, and enterprise of our people."

President Bush
Washington, D.C. (Joint Session of Congress)
September 20, 2001

The major institutions of American national security were designed in a different era to meet different requirements. All of them must be transformed.

It is time to reaffirm the essential role of American military strength. We must build and maintain our defenses beyond challenge. Our military's highest priority is to defend the United States. To do so effectively, our military must:

- assure our allies and friends;

- dissuade future military competition;

- deter threats against U.S. interests, allies, and friends; and

- decisively defeat any adversary if deterrence fails.

The unparalleled strength of the United States armed forces, and their forward presence, have maintained the peace in some of the world's most strategically vital regions. However, the threats and enemies we must confront have changed, and so must our forces. A military structured to deter massive Cold War-era armies must be transformed to focus more on how an adversary might fight rather than where and when a war might occur. We will channel our energies to overcome a host of operational challenges.

The presence of American forces overseas is one of the most profound symbols of the U.S. commitments to allies and friends. Through our willingness to use force in our own defense and in defense of others, the United States demonstrates its resolve to maintain a balance of power that favors freedom. To contend with uncertainty and to meet the many security challenges we face, the United States will require bases and stations within and beyond Western Europe and Northeast Asia, as well as temporary access arrangements for the long-distance deployment of U.S. forces. [. . .]

We know from history that deterrence can fail; and we know from experience that some enemies cannot be deterred. The United States must and will maintain the capability to defeat any attempt by an enemy — whether a state or non-state actor — to impose its will on the United States, our allies, or our friends. We will maintain the forces sufficient to support our obligations, and to defend freedom. Our forces will be strong enough to dissuade potential adversaries from pursuing a military build-up in hopes of surpassing, or equaling, the power of the United States.

Intelligence — and how we use it — is our first line of defense against terrorists and the threat posed by hostile states. Designed around the priority of gathering enormous information about a massive, fixed object — the Soviet bloc — the intelligence community is coping with the challenge of following a far more complex and elusive set of targets. [. . .]

We must strengthen intelligence warning and analysis to provide integrated threat assessments for national and homeland security. Since the threats inspired by foreign governments and groups may be conducted inside the United States, we must also ensure the proper fusion of information between intelligence and law enforcement. [. . .]

We will take the actions necessary to ensure that our efforts to meet our global security commitments and protect Americans are not impaired by the potential for investigations, inquiry, or prosecution by the International Criminal Court (ICC), whose jurisdiction does not extend to Americans and which we do not accept. We will work together with other nations to avoid complications in our military operations and cooperation, through such mechanisms as multilateral and bilateral agreements that will protect U.S. nationals from the ICC. We will implement fully the American Servicemembers Protection Act, whose provisions are intended to ensure and enhance the protection of U.S. personnel and officials.

We will make hard choices in the coming year and beyond to ensure the right level and allocation of government spending on national security. The United States Government must strengthen its defenses to win this war. At home, our most important priority is to protect the homeland for the American people.

Today, the distinction between domestic and foreign affairs is diminishing. In a globalized world, events beyond America's borders have a greater impact inside them. Our society must be open to people, ideas, and goods from across the globe. The characteristics we most cherish — our freedom, our cities, our systems of movement, and modern life — are vulnerable to terrorism. This vulnerability will persist long after we bring to justice those responsible for the September 11 attacks. As time passes, individuals may gain access to means of destruction that until now could be wielded only by armies, fleets, and squadrons. This is a new condition of life. We will adjust to it and thrive — in spite of it.

In exercising our leadership, we will respect the values, judgment, and interests of our friends and partners. Still, we will be prepared to act apart when our interests and unique responsibilities require. When we disagree on particulars, we will explain forthrightly the grounds for our concerns and strive to forge viable alternatives. We will not allow such disagreements to obscure our determination to secure together, with our allies and our friends, our shared fundamental interests and values.

Ultimately, the foundation of American strength is at home. It is in the skills of our people, the dynamism of our economy, and the resilience of our institutions. A diverse, modern society has inherent, ambitious, entrepreneurial energy. Our strength comes from what we do with that energy. That is where our national security begins.

✗ NO
The Slippery Slope to Preventive War
NETA C. CRAWFORD

The Bush administration's arguments in favor of a preemptive doctrine rest on the view that warfare has been transformed. As Colin Powell argues, "It's a different world . . . it's a new kind of threat."[1] And in several important respects, war has changed along the lines the administration suggests, although that transformation has been under way for at least the last ten to fifteen years. Unconventional adversaries prepared to wage unconventional war can conceal their movements, weapons, and immediate intentions and conduct devastating surprise attacks.[2] Nuclear, chemical, and biological weapons, though not widely dispersed, are more readily available than they were in the recent past. And the everyday infrastructure of the United States can be turned against it as were the planes the terrorists hijacked on September 11, 2001. Further, the administration argues that we face enemies who "reject basic human values and hate the United States and everything for which it stands."[3] Although vulnerability could certainly be reduced in many ways, it is impossible to achieve complete invulnerability.

Such vulnerability and fear, the argument goes, means the United States must take the offensive. Indeed, soon after the September 11, 2001, attacks, members of the Bush administration began equating self-defense with preemption:

> There is no question but that the United States of America has every right, as every country does, of self-defense, and the problem with terrorism is that there is no way to defend against the terrorists at every place and every time against every conceivable technique. Therefore, the only way to deal with the terrorist network is to take the battle to them. That is in fact what we're doing. That is in effect self-defense of a preemptive nature.[4]

The character of potential threats becomes extremely important in evaluating the legitimacy of the new preemption doctrine, and thus the assertion that the United States faces rogue enemies who oppose everything about the United States must be carefully evaluated. There is certainly robust evidence to believe that alQaeda members desire to harm the United States and American citizens. The National Security Strategy makes a questionable leap, however, when it assumes that "rogue states" also desire to harm the United States and pose an imminent military threat. Further, the administration blurs the distinction between "rogue states" and terrorists, essentially erasing the difference between terrorists and those states in which they reside: "We make no distinction between terrorists and those who knowingly harbor or provide aid to them."[5] But these distinctions do indeed make a difference.

Legitimate preemption could occur if four necessary conditions were met. First, the party contemplating preemption would have a narrow conception of the "self" to be defended in circumstances of self-defense. Preemption is not justified to protect imperial interests or assets taken in a war of aggression. Second, there would have to be strong evidence that war was inevitable and likely in the immediate future. Immediate threats are those which can be made manifest within days or weeks unless action is taken to thwart them. This requires clear intelligence showing that a potential aggressor has both the capability and the intention to do harm in the near future. Capability alone is not a justification. Third, preemption should be likely to succeed in reducing the threat. Specifically, there should be a high likelihood that the source of the military threat can be found and the damage that it was about to do can be greatly reduced or eliminated by a preemptive attack. If preemption is likely to fail, it should not be undertaken. Fourth, military force must be necessary; no other measures can have time to work or be likely to work.

A DEFENSIBLE SELF

On the face of it, the self-defense criteria seem clear. When our lives are threatened, we must be able to defend ourselves using force if necessary. But self-defense may have another meaning, that in which our "self" is expressed not only by mere existence, but also by a free and prosperous life. For example, even if a tyrant would allow us to live, but not under institutions of our own choosing, we may justly fight to free ourselves from political oppression. But how far do the rights of the self extend? If someone threatens our access to food, or fuel, or shelter, can we legitimately use force? Or if they allow us access to the material goods necessary for our existence, but charge such a high price that we must make a terrible choice between food and health care, or between mere existence and growth, are we justified in using force to secure access to a good that would enhance the self? When economic interests and vulnerabilities are understood to be global, and when the moral and political community of democracy and human rights are defined more broadly than ever before, the self-conception of great powers tends to enlarge. But a broad conception of self is not necessarily legitimate and neither are the values to be defended completely obvious.

For example, the U.S. definition of the self to be defended has become very broad. The administration, in its most recent Quadrennial Defense Review, defines "enduring national interests" as including "contributing to economic well-being," which entails maintaining "vitality and productivity of the global economy" and "access to key markets and strategic resources." Further, the goal of U.S. strategy, according to this document, is to maintain "preeminence."[6] The National Security Strategy also fuses ambitious political and economic goals with security: "The U.S. national security strategy will be based on a distinctly American internationalism that reflects the fusion of our values and our national interests. The aim of this strategy is to help make the world not just safer but better." And "today the distinction between domestic and foreign affairs is diminishing."[7]

If the self is defined so broadly and threats to this greater "self" are met with military force, at what point does self-defense begin to look like aggression? As Richard Betts has argued, "When security is defined in terms broader than protecting the near-term integrity of national sovereignty and borders, the distinction between offense and defense blurs hopelessly. . . . Security can be as insatiable an appetite as acquisitiveness — there may never be enough buffers."[8] The large self-conception of the United States could lead to a tendency to intervene everywhere that this greater self might conceivably be at risk of, for example, losing access to markets. Thus, a conception of the self that justifies legitimate preemption in self-defense must be narrowly confined to immediate risks to life and health within borders or to the life and health of citizens abroad.

THRESHOLD AND CONDUCT OF JUSTIFIED PREEMPTION

The Bush administration is correct to emphasize the United States' vulnerability to terrorist attack. The administration also argues that the United States cannot wait for a smoking gun if it comes in the form of a mushroom cloud. There may be little or no evidence in advance of a terrorist attack using nuclear, chemical, or biological weapons. Yet, under this view, the requirement for evidence is reduced to a fear that the other has, or might someday acquire, the means for an assault. But the bar for preemption seems to be set too low in the Bush administration's National Security Strategy. How much and what kind of evidence is necessary to justify preemption? What is a credible fear that justifies preemption?

As Michael Walzer has argued persuasively in *Just and Unjust Wars*, simple fear cannot be the only criterion. Fear is omnipresent in the context of a terrorist campaign. And if fear was once clearly justified, when and how will we know that a threat has been significantly reduced or eliminated? The nature of fear may be that once a group has suffered a terrible surprise attack, a government and people will, justifiably, be vigilant. Indeed they may, out of fear, be aware of threats to the point of hypervigilance — seeing small threats as large, and squashing all potential threats with enormous brutality.

The threshold for credible fear is necessarily lower in the context of contemporary counterterrorism war, but the consequences of lowering the threshold may be increased instability and the premature use of force. If this is the case, if fear justifies assault, then the occasions for attack will potentially be limitless since, according to the Bush administration's own arguments, we cannot always know with certainty what the other side has, where it might be located, or when it might be used. If one attacks on the basis of fear, or suspicion that a potential adversary may someday have the intention and capacity to harm you, then the line between preemptive and preventive war has been crossed. Again, the problem is knowing the capabilities and intentions of potential adversaries.

There is thus a fine balance to be struck. The threshold of evidence and warning cannot be too low, where simple apprehension that a potential adversary might be out there somewhere and may be acquiring the means to do the United States harm triggers the offensive use of force. This is not preemption, but paranoid aggression. We must, as stressful as this is psychologically, accept some vulnerability and uncertainty. We must also avoid the tendency to exaggerate the threat and inadvertently to heighten our own fear. For example, although nuclear weapons are more widely available than in the past, as are delivery vehicles of medium and long range, these forces are not yet in the hands of dozens of terrorists. A policy that assumes such a dangerous world is, at this historical juncture, paranoid. We must, rather than assume this is the present case or will be in the future, work to make this outcome less likely.

On the other hand, the threshold of evidence and warning for justified fear cannot be so high that those who might be about to do harm get so advanced in their preparations that they cannot be stopped or the damage limited. What is required, assuming a substantial investment in intelligence gathering, assessment, and understanding of potential advisories, is a policy that both maximizes our understanding of the capabilities and intentions of potential adversaries and minimizes our physical vulnerability. While uncertainty about intentions, capabilities, and risk can never be eliminated, it can be reduced.

Fear of possible future attack is not enough to justify preemption. Rather, aggressive intent, coupled with a capacity and plans to do immediate harm, is the threshold that may trigger justified preemptive attacks. We may judge aggressive intent if the answer to these two questions is yes: First, have potential aggressors said they want to harm us in the near future or have they harmed us in the recent past? Second, are potential adversaries moving their forces into a position to do significant harm?

While it might be tempting to assume that secrecy on the part of a potential adversary is a sure sign of aggressive intentions, secrecy may simply be a desire to prepare a deterrent force. After all, potential adversaries may feel the need to look after their own defense against their neighbors or even the United States. We cannot assume that all forces in the world are aimed offensively at the United States and that all want to broadcast their defensive preparations – especially if that means they might become the target of a preventive offensive strike by the United States.

The conduct of preemptive actions must be limited in purpose to reducing or eliminating the immediate threat. Preemptive strikes that go beyond this purpose will, reasonably, be considered aggression by the targets of such strikes. Those conducting preemptive strikes should also obey the *jus in bello* limits of just war theory, specifically avoiding injury to noncombatants and avoiding disproportionate damage. For example, in the case of the plans for the September 11, 2001, attacks, on these criteria – and assuming intelligence warning of preparations and clear evidence of aggressive intent – a justifiable preemptive action would have been the arrest of the hijackers of the four aircraft that were to be used as weapons. But, prior to the attacks, taking the war to Afghanistan to attack alQaeda camps or the Taliban could not have been justified preemption.

THE RISKS OF PREVENTIVE WAR

Foreign policies must not only be judged on grounds of legality and morality, but also on grounds of prudence. Preemption is only prudent if it is limited to clear and immediate dangers and if there are limits to its conduct – proportionality, discrimination, and limited aims. If preemption becomes a regular practice or if it becomes the cover for a preventive offensive war doctrine, the strategy then may become self-defeating as it increases instability and insecurity.

Specifically, a legitimate preemptive war requires that states identify that potential aggressors have both the capability and the intention of doing great harm to you in the immediate future. However, while capability may not be in dispute, the motives and intentions of a potential adversary may be misinterpreted. Specifically, states may mobilize in what appear to be aggressive ways because they are fearful or because they are aggressive. A preemptive doctrine which has, because of great fear and a desire to control the international environment, become a preventive war doctrine of eliminating potential threats that may materialize at some point in the future is likely to create more of both fearful and aggressive states. Some states may defensively arm because they are afraid of the preemptive-preventive state; others may arm offensively because they resent the preventive war aggressor who may have killed many innocents in its quest for total security.

In either case, whether states and groups armed because they were afraid or because they have aggressive intentions, instability is likely to grow as a preventive war doctrine creates the mutual fear of surprise attack. In the case of the U.S. preemptive-preventive war doctrine, instability is likely to increase because the doctrine is coupled with the U.S. goal of maintaining global preeminence and a military force "beyond challenge."[9]

Further, a preventive offensive war doctrine undermines international law and diplomacy, both of which can be useful, even to hegemonic powers. Preventive war short-circuits nonmilitary means of solving problems. If all states reacted to potential adversaries as if they faced a clear and present danger of imminent attack, security would be destabilized as tensions escalated along already tense borders and regions. Article 51 of the UN Charter would lose much of its force. In sum, a preemptive-preventive doctrine moves us closer to a state of nature than a state of international law. Moreover, while preventive war doctrines assume that today's potential rival will become tomorrow's adversary, diplomacy or some other factor could work to change the relationship from antagonism to accommodation.

As Otto von Bismarck said to Wilhelm I in 1875, "I would ... never advise Your Majesty to declare war forthwith, simply because it appeared that our opponent would begin hostilities in the near future. One can never anticipate the ways of divine providence securely enough for that."[10]

One can understand why any administration would favor preemption and why some would be attracted to preventive wars if they think a preventive war could guarantee security from future attack. But the psychological reassurance promised by a preventive offensive war doctrine is at best illusory, and at worst, preventive war is a recipe for conflict. Preventive wars are imprudent because they bring wars that might not happen and increase resentment. They are also unjust because they assume perfect knowledge of an adversary's ill intentions when such a presumption of guilt may be premature or unwarranted. Preemption can be justified, on the other hand, if it is undertaken due to an immediate threat, where there is no time for diplomacy to be attempted, and where the action is limited to reducing that threat. There is a great temptation, however, to step over the line from preemptive to preventive war, because that line is vague and because the stress of living under the threat of war is great. But that temptation should be avoided, and the stress of living in fear should be assuaged by true prevention – arms control, disarmament, negotiations, confidence-building measures, and the development of international law.

NOTES

1. Colin Powell, "Perspectives: Powell Defends a First Strike as Iraq Option," interview, *New York Times*, September 8, 2002, sec. 1, p. 18.

2. For more on the nature of this transformation, see Neta C. Crawford, "Just War Theory and the U.S. Counterterror War," *Perspectives on Politics* 1 (March 2003), forthcoming.

3. "The National Security Strategy of the United States of America September 2002," p. 14; available at www.whitehouse.gov/nsc/nss.pdf.

4. Donald H. Rumsfeld, "Remarks at Stakeout Outside ABC TV Studio," October 28, 2001; available at www.defenselink.mil/news/Oct2001/t10292001_t1028sd3.html.

5. "National Security Strategy," p. 5.

6. Department of Defense, "Quadrennial Defense Review" (Washington, D.C.: U.S. Government Printing Office, September 30, 2001), pp. 2, 30, 62.

7. "National Security Strategy," pp. 1, 31.

8. Richard K. Betts, *Surprise Attack: Lessons for Defense Planning* (Washington, D.C.: Brookings Institution, 1982), pp. 14–43.

9. Department of Defense, "Quadrennial Defense Review," pp. 30, 62; and "Remarks by President George W. Bush at Graduation Exercise of the United States Military Academy, West Point, New York," June 1, 2002; available at www.whitehouse.gov/news/releases/2002/06/20020601-3.html.

10. Quoted in Gordon A. Craig, *The Politics of the Prussian Army, 1640–1945* (Oxford: Oxford University Press, 1955), p. 255.

POSTSCRIPT

Needless to say, the publication of the *National Security Strategy* and the new focus on preemptive action provoked a vigorous debate both in the United States and abroad. In addition to the political and media debates, established international relations scholars expressed quite differing views on the merits of the administration's new strategy.

John Lewis Gaddis, a historian of American foreign policy at Yale University, called the new security strategy the "most important reformulation of U.S. grand strategy in over half a century." Gaddis believes that the fundamental ideas expressed in the *NSS*, rather than being a departure from the past, are in continuity with the tradition of liberal internationalism established by President Woodrow Wilson. The *NSS*, he claims, combines power and moral principle in a way that provides a clear guide for exercising great power responsibility. While he agrees with analysts like Robert Kagan that the success of the strategy will depend on the maintenance of U.S. hegemony, Gaddis feels confident that the legal and moral bases for a policy of preemption have been established in a way that will allow the world to reap benefits.

Others argue that the U.S. government needs to return to the tradition of balance-of-power realism and multilateralism. John Inkleberry sees the Bush Doctrine as a radical break with a well-tested and prudent tradition on American foreign policy. He suggests that "a mature world power ... seeks stability and pursues its interests in ways that do not fundamentally threaten the position of other states." He asserts that rather than implementing a "new grand strategy," the U.S. government needs to "reinvigorate its older strategies." Stanley Hoffman of Harvard University shares similar concerns. He notes that traditional realists have always shown a commitment to prudence and moderation. In contrast, he finds the Bush Doctrine to be "breathtakingly unrealistic." Noting that the idea of empire has "invariably gone to the heads of imperialists," Hoffman worries that the Bush Doctrine is the expression of a "new American hubris." These debates raise interesting questions regarding whether the Bush Doctrine stands within the traditional strand of classical realism or represents more of an interventionist, liberal, internationalist view of the world.

Suggested Additional Readings

Dombrowski, Peter, and Rodger A. Payne. "Global Debate and the Limits of the Bush Doctrine." *International Studies Perspectives* 4, no. 4 (November 2003): 395–408.

Gaddis, John Lewis. "A Grand Strategy of Transformation." *Foreign Policy* 133, (November–December 2002): 50–57.

Gray, Christine. "The UN National Security Strategy and the New 'Bush Doctrine' on Preemptive Self-Defense." *Chinese Journal of International Law* 2 (2002): 437–47.

Heisbourg, François. "A Work in Process: The Bush Doctrine and Its Consequences." *The Washington Quarterly* 26, no. 2 (2003): 75–88.

Kellner, Douglas. "Postmodern War in the Age of Bush II." *New Political Science* 24, no. 1 (March 2002): 57–72.

Kissinger, Henry. "Preemption and the End of Westphalia." *NPQ: New Perspectives Quarterly* 19, no. 4 (Fall 2002): 31–36. Available at www.digitalnpq.org/archive/2002_fall/kissinger.html.

Knight, Charles. "Essential Elements Missing in the National Security Strategy of 2002." Commonwealth Institute Project on Defense Alternatives Commentary (November 2002). Available at www.comw.org/qdr/0210knight.html.

LaFeber, Walter. "The Bush Doctrine." *Diplomatic History* 26, no. 4 (Fall 2002): 543–58.

Treverton, Gregory F. "Intelligence: The Achilles' Heel of the Bush Doctrine." *NPQ: New Perspectives Quarterly* 20, no. 4 (Fall 2003): 56–61. Available at www.digitalnpq.org/archive/2003_fall/treverton.html.

InfoTrac® College Edition

Search for the following articles in the InfoTrac® database:

Jervis, Robert. "Understanding the Bush Doctrine." *Political Science Quarterly* 118, no. 3 (Fall 2003): 365–88.

Record, Jeffry. "The Bush Doctrine and War with Iraq." *Parameters* 33, no. 1 (Spring 2003): 4–21.

Podhoretz, Norman. "In Praise of the Bush Doctrine." *Commentary* 114, no. 2 (September 2002): 19–28.

For more articles, enter:
"Bush Doctrine" or "National Security Strategy" in the keyword search.
"George Bush" in the subject guide, then go to the subdivision "foreign policy."

Web Resources

For current URLs for the following websites, visit www.crosscurrents.nelson.com.

OPENDEMOCRACY DEBATE ON BUSH DOCTRINE: RIGHT OR WRONG?

www.opendemocracy.net/debates/debate-3-98.jsp

Check this site for articles debating the Bush Doctrine as well as an online discussion forum on the topic.

PBS Special on the Bush Doctrine

www.pbs.org/wgbh/pages/frontline/shows/iraq/

Watch this PBS special on the politics involved in the development of the Bush Doctrine. Other resources, including a chronology of the development of Bush Doctrine, can also be found here.

Project for the New American Century

www.newamericancentury.org

This site contains many key documents from this group of neoconservative thinkers that has influenced the development of the Bush Doctrine. Of particular interest is "Rebuilding America's Defenses," issued in September 2000.

Ethics and International Affairs Roundtable on Evaluating the Preemptive Use of Force

www.cceia.org/viewMedia.php/prmID/850

This page contains a collection of articles on the concept of preemption, which underlies the Bush Doctrine, from a theme issue of the journal *Ethics and International Affairs*.

Did the War against Iraq Violate International Law?

✔ **YES**

JUTTA BRUNNEE, "The Use of Force against Iraq: A Legal Assessment," *Behind the Headlines* 59, no. 4 (Summer 2002): 1–8

✘ **NO**

DAVID WINGFIELD, "Why the Invasion of Iraq Was Lawful," *Behind the Headlines* 59, no. 4 (Summer 2002): 10–16

On March 19, 2003, the United States launched a cruise missile attack against targets in Baghdad in an attempt to "decapitate" the regime of Saddam Hussein. Failing in its attempt to kill the Iraqi leaders, American and allied armed forces crossed the Iraqi–Kuwait border and began moving toward Baghdad while stealth bombers and cruise missiles pummelled targets throughout the country. Within a few weeks, the United States and its allies succeeded in removing the Hussein regime from power and occupied Iraq.

The war on Iraq was a culmination of a series of events that began with President Bush's speech to Congress in January 2002, in which he identified the "axis of evil" countries of special concern to the United States: Iraq, Iran, and North Korea. The president warned that in the face of the growing threat posed by these states, the United States was willing to take preemptive action if needed. In the following months, he laid the basis for the Bush Doctrine, which was discussed in the previous Issue. Iraq, it turned out, would be the first real test of the doctrine.

As the debate on the Bush Doctrine unfolded, considerable attention was focused on the status of the concept of preemptive war under international law. In order to understand this debate and its implications for the war on Iraq, it is useful to look carefully at the Charter of the United Nations.

When states join the United Nations, they pledge not to use armed force "save in the common interest" (Preamble to the UN Charter). Article 2 of the Charter stipulates that all members renounce the "use of force against the territorial integrity" of other states while pursing peaceful means for the resolution of all disputes.

Under international law, two exceptions to this principle have been recognized. Article 51 states that "nothing in the present Charter shall impair the inherent right of individual or collective self-defence if an armed attack occurs against a Member of the United Nations." But the assumption here is that a state will unilaterally act in self-defence only until the UN Security Council has been able to organize a response. Any subsequent use of force must by authorized by the Security Council.

International law has also allowed an exception for "humanitarian intervention." This type of intervention has traditionally been interpreted in a rather restrictive fashion, limiting military intervention in any country only to cases where the intervening state is acting to rescue its own nationals or acting at the invitation of the local government authorities. Despite the great loss of human life under the genocidal regime of Pol Pot, the international community, including Canada and the United States, widely condemned Vietnam for invading in order to "liberate" the Cambodian population from the Khmer Rouge. Vietnam was punished by having comprehensive economic sanctions imposed against it for this violation of another state's sovereignty. Similarly, the Tanzanian government was condemned for sending in troops to overthrow the brutal regime of Idi Amin, even though it claimed that it was acting for humanitarian reasons. Thus, international law provides a very limited basis for justifying military assaults against another state.

In the months following the Iraq invasion, the Bush administration gave several different legal justifications for a war against Iraq. At times, it argued that the Iraqi government was in "material breach" of previous resolutions passed by the Security Council. Following the 1991 war against Iraq for its invasion of Kuwait, the Security Council called on Saddam Hussein to renounce and dismantle all programs for developing chemical, biological, and nuclear weapons. Although Hussein refused to renounce such efforts, UN weapons inspectors could find no evidence that the regime either possessed or was continuing to develop such weapons. The Bush administration denounced the UN weapons inspection process as a failure while arguing that previous Security Council resolutions (such as resolutions 687 and 1441) gave the United States the legal basis to take military action against Iraq in face of clear evidence that it had not complied.

At other times, the Bush administration evoked the principle of humanitarian intervention, citing the terrible human rights abuses by the Iraqi government and its use of chemical weapons against its own civilians during the Iran–Iraq war. The Bush administration argued that the irrational and egomaniacal nature of Saddam Hussein made him dangerous and untrustworthy. Bush warned that once Hussein had weapons of mass destruction in his hands, the United States was in danger of attack at any time. Thus, the U.S. was justified in launching a preemptive strike against the Iraqi regime.

Finally, the Bush administration argued that Saddam Hussein had ties with al-Qaeda. These ties made Iraq an accomplice to the attacks of September 11 and therefore a legitimate target for a war of self-defence.

In the following readings, the debate over the legality of U.S. actions against Iraq is taken up by two Canadian experts in international law. Jutta Brunnee examines the various options for justifying the war against Iraq under international law. After weighing the evidence, she argues that under current international law the war against Iraq was illegal. David Wingfield carefully examines the wording of the Charter of the United Nations and argues that a clear legal basis for the American actions can be found.

✔ YES
The Use of Force against Iraq: A Legal Assessment
JUTTA BRUNNEE

Against the backdrop of two world wars, one of the overriding objectives in creating the United Nations in 1945 was, as outlined in the preamble to the UN charter, to 'save succeeding generations from the scourge of war.' To that end, article 2(4) provides a general prohibition of the threat or use of armed force against other states. An exception to this prohibition is provided only in article 51: pursuant to their 'inherent right of individual or collective self-defence,' states may use force to respond to an 'armed attack.' Arguably, in limited circumstances involving imminent threats, the right to self-defence also encompasses anticipatory action. In all other cases of threats to international peace and security, resort to force must be collective. That means that, outside the ambit of individual states' rights to self-defence, the use of force must be authorized by the United Nations Security Council.

In September 2002, the government of the United States published the much-quoted 2002 *National Security Strategy*, which promotes the adaptation of the rules on the use of force to permit pre-emptive strikes against 'emerging threats' posed by 'rogue states' with weapons of mass destruction.[1] That same month, President George W. Bush took his case for military action against Iraq to the United Nations. Since then, international law has enjoyed unusual popularity as a topic of discussion and concern. Politicians, pundits, and the proverbial people on the street have debated the rules of self-defence and the merits of a doctrine of pre-emptive strike, discussed the 'material breach' of UN Security Council resolutions, or opined on the need for additional resolutions explicitly authorizing the use of force against Iraq. The war in Iraq has generated many strongly held views and much heated rhetoric. This essay aims to look beyond the rhetoric to shed some light on the legality of the Iraq campaign. It provides a review of the three potential legal justifications for the use of force and explains why none of them ultimately supports the US–British intervention.

First, given the US rhetoric regarding the threat posed by Iraq, one might think that self-defence or pre-emptive self-defence was one of the justifications advanced for the intervention. Yet, while the US government may have deployed the language of self-defence at a political level, it was not invoked for purposes of legal justification. It is worth taking a closer look at this fact.

In situations of self-defence, states can act unilaterally. They must simply notify the Security Council that they are acting in self-defence. For example, in the case of military action in Afghanistan in 2001, the US reported to the Council that it had 'initiated actions in the exercise of its inherent right of individual and collective self-defense following armed attacks that were carried out ... on September 11, 2001.'[2] Given the political differences over intervention in Iraq, a self-defence argument would have had the advantage, from a US standpoint, that action could have been taken without Security Council approval. The fact that the US did not invoke self-defence, then, speaks for itself. A case of self-defence simply could not be made. Iraq had not attacked the US, and an attack by Iraq (or attributable to Iraq) was not imminent.

What is perhaps most noteworthy is that the US government refrained not only from making a self-defence argument, but also from relying on the pre-emptive strike doctrine promoted in its *National Security Strategy*. This doctrine has raised concerns because it would leave virtually no standard capable of providing normative guidance or constraining unilateral assessments. In the 1962 Cuban Missile crisis, the United States refrained from invoking pre-emptive self-defence for this very reason.[3] In 2003, one might have expected the Bush administration to make Iraq, a 'rogue state' alleged to have weapons of mass destruction and ties to global terrorism, the test case for the pre-emptive strike doctrine. It did not. In fact, the State Department's legal adviser took pains to bring pre-emption within the confines of the 'traditional framework,' stressing that 'a preemptive use of proportional force is justified only out of necessity.' He added that 'necessity includes both a credible, imminent threat and the exhaustion of peaceful remedies.' Indeed: 'While the definition of imminent must recognize the threat posed by weapons of mass destruction and the intentions of those who possess them, the decision to undertake any action must meet the test of necessity ... in the face of overwhelming evidence of an imminent threat, a nation may take preemptive action to defend its nationals from unimaginable harm.'[4] Three observations can be made. First, it appears that the US acknowledges that a sweeping right to preemptive military strikes does not exist under current international law. Second, in outlining criteria to reign in the overbroad concept of 'emerging threat' contained in the *National Security Strategy*, the United States appears to acknowledge the need for standards of review. Third, political rhetoric notwithstanding, the US government did not seem to think that these standards had been met in the case of Iraq.

A second justification for the invasion of Iraq that has received some attention is that of 'humanitarian intervention.'[5] Again, it is important to separate rhetoric designed to sway public opinion from legal argument. With the onset of hostilities, there was certainly a noticeable shift in the 'packaging' of the Iraq war for public consumption. The US and, to a lesser extent, Britain emphasized the liberation of the Iraqi people from dictatorship.[6] As a legal matter, however, no attempt was made to cast the war as a humanitarian intervention. Once again, the absence of legal argument speaks volumes. It speaks to the fact that there is no firm legal basis for asserting a right of individual states to intervene forcibly in other countries on humanitarian grounds. To be sure, there is a current of opinion suggesting that, in exceptional circumstances, armed force may be used when it is the only means to forestall an immediate, overwhelming humanitarian disaster.[7] It was this idea that animated the NATO intervention in Kosovo in 1999. But even in that case of extreme crisis, the balance of opinion remains that the notion of humanitarian intervention did not provide a legal justification for the use of armed force.[8] It is therefore hardly surprising that there was no attempt by the US or Britain legally to justify the Iraq war as a humanitarian intervention. In any case, even if one were to accept in principle that humanitarian interventions are legal in a narrow range of extreme circumstances, Iraq did not fall into that range. There is little doubt that the Iraqi government repressed and brutalized its citizens. The recent discoveries of mass graves bear witness to the regime's brutality.[9] However, there was no urgent humanitarian crisis that necessitated immediate use of force, and none was alleged by the US or British governments. In short, while the liberation of the Iraqi people may have been a positive side-effect of 'Operation Iraqi Freedom,' under existing international law it cannot convert otherwise illegal use of force into lawful action.

This takes us to the last possible legal basis for the Iraq intervention, and to the arguments that were actually deployed by the US and Britain to justify it. In essence, the argument is that the Security Council had authorized the use of force through a set of resolutions, encompassing resolution 678 (29 November 1990), resolution 687 (3 April 1991), and resolution 1441 (8 November 2002).[10] To appreciate the purchase of this argument, it is necessary to consider the relevant resolutions in some detail.

Iraq invaded Kuwait on 1 August 1990. In resolution 660 of 2 August, the Security Council called upon Iraq to withdraw from Kuwait 'immediately and unconditionally.' In light of Iraq's refusal to heed this and other calls by the Council for withdrawal, the preamble to resolution 678 'recalled and reaffirmed' a series of resolutions pertaining to Iraq, beginning with resolution 660 and ending with resolution 677 (1990). It then noted Iraq's refusal 'to comply, with its obligation to implement resolution 660 (1990) and the abovementioned subsequent resolutions.' In paragraph 2 of resolution 678, the Council therefore authorized 'Member States cooperating with the Government of Kuwait . . . to use all necessary means to uphold and implement resolution 660 (1990) and all subsequent relevant resolutions and to restore international peace and security in the area.' Several weeks later, in January 1991, 'Operation Desert Storm' was undertaken to expel Iraq from Kuwait.

Upon completion of 'Desert Storm,' resolution 686 of 2 March 1991 outlined an initial, provisional ceasefire. Resolution 687 followed to provide for a permanent ceasefire, which was contingent upon Iraq's unconditional acceptance of various conditions, including extensive disarmament obligations. In paragraph 33 of the resolution the Security Council declared that 'upon official notification by Iraq . . . of its acceptance of the provisions above, a formal ceasefire is effective between Iraq and

Kuwait and the Member States cooperating with Kuwait in accordance with resolution 678 (1990). In paragraph 34 of the resolution, the Council decided 'to remain seized of the matter and to take such further steps as may be required for the implementation of the present resolution and to secure peace and security in the area.'

As is well known, Iraq's compliance with its obligations under resolution 687 and a series of subsequent resolutions was less than satisfactory. Notably its compliance with disarmament obligations and its co-operation with UN weapons inspectors left much to be desired. In September 2002, the Bush administration vowed to put an end to a 'decade of deception and defiance.'[11] The administration called on the Security Council to enforce Iraqi compliance, if necessary through military means. However, other members of the Security Council were reluctant to set the tracks toward a military solution. After intense negotiations, a compromise was finally enshrined in resolution 1441.

The Council found that 'Iraq has been and remains in material breach of its obligations under relevant resolutions, including resolution 687' (paragraph 1) and gave Iraq a 'final opportunity to comply with its disarmament obligations' (paragraph 2). Any further non-compliance would 'constitute a further material breach,' which would be 'reported to the Council for assessment' (paragraph 4). Based on the reports of Iraq's performance, the Council would convene immediately 'in order to consider the situation and the need for full compliance ... in order to secure international peace and security' (paragraph 12). The resolution recalled 'that the Council has repeatedly warned Iraq that it will face serious consequences as a result of its continued violations of its obligations' (paragraph 13). Finally, the Council decided 'to remain seized of the matter' (paragraph 14).

In the weeks following the adoption of resolution 1441, the Security Council was not able to agree on whether Iraq's conduct warranted an armed intervention, and no resolution explicitly authorizing such intervention was adopted. The US and Britain have maintained that an additional resolution providing specific authorization of force was not required. If they had entertained discussions on a 'second resolution,' they argued, it was for political not legal reasons. According to the US government, taking action against Iraq was a question merely of will, not of authority.[12] The three resolutions outlined above—678, 687, and 1441— were said to provide all the authority needed to enforce Iraqi compliance. The argument goes roughly like this: resolution 678 authorized force against Iraq, for purposes that included restoring peace and security in the area. Resolution 687 suspended the authority provided in resolution 678, but did not terminate it. Rather, the ceasefire was contingent upon Iraq's compliance with the various conditions in resolution 687. If Iraq were in material breach of this arrangement, the authority to use force under resolution 678 would be revived. Resolution 1441 confirmed that Iraq was and continued to be in material breach. Resolution 1441 required reporting to and discussion by the Security Council of Iraq's breaches, but not an express further decision to authorize force.[13]

This line of argument has been rejected by an overwhelming majority of international lawyers, who have spoken out on the matter in unusual numbers.[14] Indeed, a senior legal adviser to the British foreign secretary resigned over the issue.[15] Why?

Security Council resolutions are carefully crafted compromises, often the product of delicate diplomatic tangos behind closed doors. But, like all treaty-based arrangements, they ultimately must be measured against the standard of the ordinary meaning of the language employed and interpreted in good faith. Add to that the fact that the Security Council has explicitly authorized the use of force only twice in its history – once during the Korean War in 1950 and once in response to Iraq's invasion of Kuwait in 1990. Given the reluctance of the Council to authorize forcible measures, it is difficult to see how resolutions 678, 687, and 1441 could in good faith be interpreted as an open-ended authorization of the use of force against Iraq. A closer look at the excerpts from these resolutions highlighted above further supports this conclusion. A number of points can be made in that regard.

First, the authority to use force provided by resolution 678 was quite clearly focused on Iraq's invasion of Kuwait. For better or for worse, it took this dramatic a transgression by Iraq to prompt the Security Council to authorize 'all necessary means.' But this authority related to compliance with resolution 660 and a specified set of subsequent resolutions relating to Iraq's invasion of Kuwait – not an indeterminate set of future resolutions on Iraq. Similarly, the phrase 'restore peace and security' was carefully chosen to confine the authority provided.

Second, the ceasefire effected pursuant to resolution 687 was contingent only upon Iraq's formal acceptance of the conditions set out in the resolution. Nowhere does the resolution indicate that the ceasefire merely suspended paragraph 2 of resolution 678 (the authorization of force), or that it could be terminated in case of Iraqi non-compliance. This silence stands in marked contrast to resolution 686, the earlier provisional ceasefire arrangement, which explicitly recognized that paragraph 2 of resolution 678 remained valid during the period required for Iraq to comply with the terms of the provisional ceasefire. In any event, a termination of the ceasefire would be a matter for the Security Council, not for individual states. Paragraph 34 of the resolution makes this plain through the decision of the Council that it will 'remain seized of the matter' and 'take such further steps as may be required.' Further, resolution 687 speaks of a ceasefire between Iraq, Kuwait, and 'Member States cooperating with the Government of Kuwait.' The latter terminology refers to the coalition of states that had pledged to assist Kuwait in collective self-defence against Iraq's invasion and that had been authorized to use force in resolution 678. This coalition of states no longer exists, and it is difficult to see how authority to use force or to end the ceasefire with Iraq could now rest with the United States or with Britain.

Third, authority for the use of force against Iraq cannot be found in resolution 1441. Yes, paragraph 13 reminds Iraq that it would face serious consequences as a result of its continued non-compliance. But, given the deep disagreements that led to the adoption of this compromise resolution, it is impossible to read this paragraph as an express or even an implied authorization of force. It is also true that resolution 1441 did not expressly require an additional resolution authorizing force, but no conclusions can be drawn from that fact. If the Council had indeed previously authorized the use of force, as the US and Britain maintain, no such additional decision, and therefore no reference to it, was needed. Conversely, if previous resolutions did not provide authority, as other Security Council members asserted, there was no need for resolution 1441 to state the obvious — that an authorizing resolution was required for lawful use of force. With respect to the question of force, then, resolution 1441 was simply a place holder. It allowed the UN process to proceed in the hope that it would resolve the Iraq situation through renewed weapons inspections. In the meantime, it preserved the legal status quo.

In short, resolution 1441 did not authorize the US and Britain to take military action against Iraq. The legality of their intervention in Iraq therefore turns on whether resolutions 678 and 687, adopted more than a decade earlier in the aftermath of Iraq's invasion of Kuwait, provided open-ended authority to enforce Iraqi disarmament with 'all necessary means.' They did not.

The UN charter has not accomplished the ambitious goal of eliminating war. Nonetheless, the rules on the use of force have done important work. They have served to constrain the resort to force by states, notably by providing a normative framework against which actions must be justified and can be assessed. In the case of the war against Iraq, neither justifications based on UN Security Council authorization, nor arguments based on self-defence or humanitarian intervention can carry the day. One may hold any number of opinions on whether or not the war against Iraq was necessary and appropriate, and even on whether or not international law should accommodate this type of intervention. But we should all be clear that, under existing international law, the use of force against Iraq was illegal.

NOTES

1. *The National Security Strategy of the United States of America*, September 2002, 13–16; available at www.whitehouse.gov.nsc/nss.pdf

2. 'Letter dated 7 October 2001 from the Permanent Representative of the United States of America to the United Nations addressed to the President of the Security Council'; available at www.un.int/usa/s2001-946.htm

3. See Abram Chayes, *The Cuban Missile Crisis: International Crisis and the Role of Law* (London and NY: Oxford University Press 1974), 63–6.

4. William Taft, IV, 'Memorandum: The Legal Basis for Preemption,' 18 November 2002; available at www.cfr.org/publication.php?id = 5250

5. Ed Morgan, 'Use of force against Iraq is legal,' *National Post*, 19 March 2003.

6. 'Village by village, city by city, liberation is coming. The people of Iraq have my pledge: Our fighting forces will press on until their oppressors are gone and their whole country is free.' President Bush, Radio Address, 5 April 2003; available at www.whitehouse.gov/news/releases/2003/04/20030405.html. See also the 'Liberation Update'; available at www.whitehouse.gov/news/releases/2003/05/iraq/ 20030506–19.html

7. For a thoughtful treatment, see International Commission on Intervention and State Sovereignty, *The Responsibility to Protect* (December 2001); available at www.dfait-maeci.gc.ca/iciss-ciise/report-en.asp

8. See Nico Krisch, 'Legality, morality and the dilemma of humanitarian intervention after Kosovo,' *European Journal of International Law* 13(no 1, 2002); available at www3.oup.co.uk/ejilaw/hdb/ Volume_13/Issue_01/

9. See Patrick E. Tyler, 'An open secret is laid bare at mass grave in Iraqi marsh,' *New York Times*, 14 May 2003; available at www.nytimes.com/2003/05/14/international/world-special/14GRAV.html

10. Security Council resolutions can be accessed at www.un.org/Docs/sc/unsc_ resolutions.html

11. See *A Decade of Deception and Defiance*, 12 September 2002; available at www.whitehouse.gov/news/releases/2002/09/iraq/20020912.html

12. President Bush, *Address to the Nation*, 17 March 2003; available at www. whitehouse.gov/news/releases/2003/03/20030317-7.html

13. On the US position, see 'Letter dated 30 March 2003 from the Permanent Representative of the United States of America to the United Nations addressed to the President of the Security Council'; available at www.un.int/usa/s2003_351.pdf. On the British position, see Attorney General, Lord Goldsmith, 'Legal basis for use of force against Iraq,' 17 March 2003; available at www.pmo.gov.uk/output/Page3287.asp

14. See, for example, 'Howard must not involve US in an illegal war,' 26 February 2003; available at www.theage.com.au/articles/2003/02/25/1046064031296.html (Australia); 'War would be illegal,' *Guardian*, 7 March 2003; at education.guardian.co.uk/Print/ 0,3858,4620124,00.html (Britain); Peter Slevin, 'Legality of war is a matter of debate – many scholars doubt assertion by Bush,' *Washington Post*, 18 March 2003; at www.commondreams.org/headlines03/0318-05.htm (US); Jeff Sallot, 'Legal experts say attack on Iraq is illegal,' *Globe and Mail*, 20 March 2003, A10 (Canada).

15. Ewen MacAskill, 'Adviser quits Foreign Office over legality of war,' *Guardian*, 22 March 2003, available at http://politics.guardian. co.uk/iraq/story/0,12956,919647,00.html

✗ NO
Why the Invasion of Iraq Was Lawful
DAVID WINGFIELD

When the United States, Britain, Australia, and their allies invaded Iraq, they claimed that they were acting in accordance with international law because resolutions passed by the United Nations Security Council had authorized the war. Many countries and international lawyers disagree. They claim that no resolution of the Security Council authorized the war and that as a consequence the invasion was illegal. Who is right?

The debate is reminiscent of Humpty Dumpty's debate with Alice. Humpty Dumpty said that when he uses a word 'it means just what I choose it to mean – neither more nor less.' In response to Alice's question of whether he could make words mean different things, Humpty Dumpty replied 'the question is, which is to be master – that's all.' Stripped to its core, the debate over the Iraq war was, and continues to be, a debate over who is to be master of the interpretation of Security Council resolutions – those countries that used force or those countries that opposed the use of force.

Democracies resolve debates within their borders about the meaning of words in statutes or other legal documents by referring the matter to a court. The international community cannot do so, however. It has no court that operates like a domestic court in a Western democracy. (The International Court of Justice can only decide disputes that the concerned states agree be submitted to it.)

For this reason, the legality of the invasion of Iraq cannot be tested in a court of law. It can be tested only by reference to reason: is there a rational basis for concluding that the invasion of Iraq was lawful under international law? If so, then the right of the United States, Britain, Australia, and their allies to invade Iraq must be conceded and the debate moved to the political question of whether the invasion was a smart thing to do. After all, international law exists for the benefit of the United States, too. The US should not be prevented from acting in accordance with its security needs by appeals to international law if it can make a rational case of legality.

The charter of the United Nations authorizes the use of force under chapter VII, which permits war under two circumstances. One circumstance is individual or collective self-defence pursuant to article 51. Countries that are attacked have the inherent right to defend themselves by war. The other is when the Security Council, on behalf of the international community, authorizes the use of force against another country.

The use of force under the charter begins with a 'determination' under article 39, the first article of chapter VII. Under article 39, the Security Council may 'determine the existence of any threat to the peace, breach of the peace, or act of aggression.' The wording of article 39 is very broad. The article gives the Security Council the power to determine that a threat short of an actual breach of peace and security exists, that a breach of peace and security short of an act of aggression exists, that an act of aggression short of an attack on another country exists, or that an actual attack has taken place. Obviously in the last case the country that is the object of the attack has the right to defend itself by force, independent of any Security Council determination under article 39.

It is interesting that article 39 does not stipulate that the threat to or breach of the peace has to be committed by a sovereign nation. Although it is doubtful that the framers of the charter of the United Nations had in mind state-sponsored terrorists when they drafted the language of the charter, article 39 is written in language that is broad enough to encompass threats or breaches to the peace by states that sponsor terrorists but which otherwise do not overtly threaten any other country.

After the Security Council makes a determination under article 39 it has two choices. One choice, pursuant to article 41, is to decide on 'measures' that do not involve the use of armed force in order to give effect to its decisions. Economic sanctions, for example, are a permitted 'measure' under this article. The second choice, pursuant to article 42, is to take 'action by air, sea, or land forces as may be necessary to maintain or restore international peace and security.'

Sharp-eyed lawyers will notice the disjunctive 'or' in article 42 between the nouns air, sea, and land and between the verbs maintain and restore. Consequently, by combining articles 39 and 42, it is clear that force can lawfully be used in antici-pation of a breach of international peace and security or as a reaction to such a breach. The threat or breach can come from the direct or indirect action of a country and the response can take any form of military action that is necessary either to maintain existing peace and security or to restore the peace and security that has been threatened or disrupted. In other words, pre-emptive attacks are perfectly lawful under international law providing that the Security Council has first 'deter-mined' that another country threatens international peace and security and has authorized 'action' against that country to restore international peace and security

The only limit on the degree of force to be used under article 42 is that the force must be 'necessary' to maintain or restore international peace and security. The whole point of using force under the charter of the United Nations is to change the behaviour of a state. Sometimes the force necessary to change a state's behaviour will consist of limited bombing of some military or political targets. Often, though, it will be necessary to destroy completely a hostile state's ability to use military power or to control territory. It is to this latter activity that one customarily applies the concept 'war.'

Lawyers look to precedent to guide their interpretation of the law. The Security Council has twice authorized war: in 1950 when North Korea invaded the Republic of Korea and forty years later when Iraq invaded Kuwait. Therefore, to understand what the Security Council must say in order to authorize war and what it does to wage that war, the best places to look are its resolutions autho-rizing the Korean and Gulf wars.

Of course, the United Nations does not possess its own military forces, and therefore it cannot itself wage war. Long before President George W. Bush coined the phrase 'coalition of the willing,' the Security Council had adopted the concept. When the Security Council declares war it requests and authorizes a 'coalition of the willing' to fight and allows that coalition to determine the tactics and strategy of the war, as well as its aims, as it did in both the Korean war and the Gulf war.

The Korean war was conducted essentially under three resolutions, resolutions 82, 83, and 84, which were enacted in June and July 1950. In those resolutions, the Security Council 'determined' that North Korea's attack on the Republic of Korea constituted a breach of the peace. The Council then 'called' upon the member states to provide assistance in enforcing these resolutions and 'recommended' that the member states assist the Republic of Korea in restoring international peace and security to the area. It is important to note that the Security Council recommended that those countries that were willing to provide military assistance should do so under United States command. Although the resolutions did not expressly refer to chapter VII or to any article of that chapter, it is clear from their language that they were enacted under that chapter. The 'determination' was obviously made pursuant to article 39, and 'calling' on all other countries to restore international peace and security was obviously an 'action' under article 42.

After China entered the Korean war, the Security Council enacted a resolution removing the complaint of aggression that had given legal sanction to the war from the list of matters of which the Council was then seized. In effect, the Council said that North Korea's breach of the peace was now off its plate. Nevertheless, the Korean war continued for almost another two-and-a-half years without any further Security Council resolutions authorizing its continuation. The Korean experience demonstrates that, once the Security Council authorizes 'action' to restore international peace and security, the actions taken under that authorization remain lawful until the countries taking those actions are satisfied that they should stop fighting or until the Security Council enacts a resolution determining that international peace and security have been restored in the area. Any such resolution would make the continuation of hostilities illegal for those countries engaged in them.

Following Iraq's invasion of Kuwait in 1990, the Security Council did not initially authorize war, although Kuwait, of course, had the right to defend itself by war. Rather, the Security Council passed resolution 660 under articles 39 and 40 of chapter VII in which the Council 'determined' that the Iraqi invasion of Kuwait was indeed a breach of international peace and security. This determination, which has been recalled in all subsequent resolutions, allowed the Security Council to decide what should be done about Iraq so that international peace and security could be restored.

What the Security Council decided to do was to pass resolution 678, which demanded that Iraq fully comply with resolution 660 and all subsequent resolutions of which it was in breach. The Security Council gave Iraq until 15 January 1991 to comply with those resolutions. If it did not do so, resolution 678 authorized the member states 'to use all necessary means' to 'restore' international peace and security and to ensure compliance with the resolutions Iraq had breached. Using 'all necessary means' is obviously an 'action' under article 42. The Security Council also requested in resolution 678 that the member states provide appropriate support for the 'actions' to restore international peace and security in the area. Unlike the Korean war resolutions, resolution 678 was expressly enacted under chapter VII of the charter in its entirety. Resolution 678 was unambiguously a declaration of war, albeit a conditional one.

As with the Korean war, the first Gulf war did not technically end. The hostilities ceased with an armistice, or a ceasefire in modern parlance, not with a treaty of peace or its Security Council equivalent. The United States, North Korea, and China, not the United Nations, agreed to the Korean war armistice. However, in the Gulf war the Security Council, not the belligerent states, enacted its terms.

The terms of the Gulf war ceasefire can be found in resolutions 686 and 687, which were enacted (as were all the other resolutions relating to Iraq's invasion of Kuwait) under chapter VII of the charter in its entirety, including the articles authorizing the use of force. Resolution 686 notes that combat operations by the coalition forces had been 'suspended,' not that the authority for those operations had been set aside. Resolution 687, which enacted the formal terms of the ceasefire, ordered Iraq unconditionally to destroy all its chemical, biological, and nuclear weapons and not to acquire new ones or the means of making new ones, amongst other things. It is clear from the terms of resolutions 686 and 687 that if Iraq was to breach the ceasefire the war could lawfully resume as if hostilities had never ceased in 1991. Indeed, the contrary cannot logically be argued.

As we all know, Iraq did breach the terms of the ceasefire and subsequent resolutions. In response to some of its more flagrant breaches, such as ejecting the weapons' inspectors in 1998, the United States and Britain bombed Iraq's military and security infrastructure. Nevertheless, over time, the Security Council ignored Iraq's non-compliance with the terms of the ceasefire. But the Council never enacted a resolution declaring that international peace and security had been restored to the area, or even a resolution similar to that which the Council enacted in January 1951 to remove the issue of Korea from its plate. Rather, in each of the resolutions it enacted, it recalled that Iraq was and remained a threat to world peace and security; the Council remained seized of the problem that Iraq presented.

In November 2002, the Security Council enacted resolution 1441, the resolution that contains the phrase 'serious consequences.' Resolution 1441 was enacted to remedy the Security Council's lack of action over Iraq's non-compliance with Security Council resolutions going all the way back to the ceasefire in 1991. In effect, the Security Council wanted to ensure that no one could argue that the legal effect of its previous resolutions had lapsed through lack of deliberate action to enforce them. Legally, this resolution was probably unnecessary. Over a dozen other resolutions enacted under chapter VII, stretching back to the ceasefire resolutions, re-affirmed the right to wage war by 'recalling' the earlier resolutions that had authorized the first Gulf war.

Thus, in resolution 1441 the Security Council was simply reaffirming that the legal basis for its declaration of war remained in effect. It did so by expressly recognizing under chapter VII that Iraq's non-compliance with the previous resolutions posed a 'threat to international peace and security.' It specifically recalled that the ceasefire declared in resolution 687 depended on Iraq's compliance with the terms of the cease-fire resolution and 'decided' that Iraq remained in breach of those terms. The Security Council then gave Iraq a 'final' opportunity to comply. Just to be sure that no one misses the point, at the end of all of this the Security Council 'recalled' that Iraq would face 'serious consequences' if it continued to violate its obligations under the many earlier resolutions. Serious consequences are, of course, 'actions.' In other words, in resolution 1441 the Security Council expressly re-affirmed the language that is its code for war and re-affirmed the right to resume the war should Iraq not immediately comply with its obligations. Short of saying 'any country that wishes to do so may attack Iraq again if it does not immediately comply with the earlier resolutions,' the meaning of resolution 1441 could not be clearer.

After resolution 1441 was passed, the Security Council authorized inspectors to enter Iraq to certify whether or not Iraq had fully complied with its disarmament obligations. The weapons' inspectors were unable to certify that Iraq had done so, thus confirming that Iraq remained in breach of its obligations. Therefore, the position of the United States, Britain, Australia, and their allies, that is, that Iraq remained in breach of the terms of ceasefire and other resolutions up to the moment of invasion, is unassailable. Iraq's breaches of the resolutions gave the coalition a rational basis in international law for resuming hostilities against Iraq for the purpose of destroying its military capability and changing its political leadership so that it would cease to threaten international peace and security. The legal basis for this war, for example, is much sounder than the legal basis for the military action against Serbia over Kosovo, which of course was not supported by any Security Council resolution before battle was joined.

The debate over the invasion of Iraq raised, and continues to raise, many funda-mental questions relating to the use of power, the best way to create a secure and stable international order, the control of weapons of mass destruction, the legitimacy of the use of force to protect or promote human and political rights, the effective-ness of Security Council resolutions, and the right of the United States to use its mil-itary forces against another country unilaterally. In the context of the invasion of Iraq, these are all political not legal questions. Dressing them in legal garb does not make them any less political. The legal issue is quite narrow and straightforward: can a rational case be made that the invasion of Iraq was supportable under international law? Such a case can be made, and therefore the debate over this war should stay where it belongs: in the arena of politics, not that of law.

POSTSCRIPT

One problem that emerges from this debate is the growing gap between international law and the actual behaviour of states. This gap is particularly evident in relation to expectation stated in the Charter of the United Nations that all members renounce war except in the "common interest" and under Security Council authorization. Critics are quick to point out that more than 126 members of the United Nations have been involved in interstate conflicts costing well over 22 million lives. How does one respond to this widening gulf between the expectations of international law and state behaviour?

One approach is to argue that we should discard international law along with the pretence that it constrains behaviour of states. In an increasingly dangerous and hostile world, those that pose the greatest danger (terrorist groups or "rogue" states) already totally disregard international laws. Thus, states must be willing to take whatever actions, unilaterally and without further authorization if necessary, in order to protect themselves. This appears to be partly the premise of the *National Security Strategy* and the Bush Doctrine. While the Bush administration was willing to seek endorsement of the Security Council for its actions, it was quite willing to act without such authorization. This reasoning is also reflected in the Bush administration's decision to withdraw from the International Criminal Court, an issue addressed later in this book.

A second approach seeks to make international law more relevant by broadening the definitions inherent in it. According to this view, we must legitimize those actions of states that must be taken as a matter of necessity in order to ensure their survival. Thus, international law must be changed to more "realistically" reflect the actual world. This perspective is adopted by those supporters of the Bush Doctrine of preemptive war who argue that the traditional definitions of self-defence need to be revised and updated to take into account present realities. Only by broadening its categories and recognizing the right to a preemptive strike in self-defence will international law be seen as legitimate and relevant in the future.

A third approach is to find new and better ways to hold states accountable to current international laws. The failure is not in the laws themselves, but in the inadequacies of current mechanisms for implementing and enforcing them. The international community must work toward building stronger international institutions, such as an International Criminal Court, while pressuring all states to continue to work within international law. Critics such as Noam Chomsky argue that the real "rogue" state is not Iraq, Iran, or North Korea, but the United States, because it insists on acting outside international law. Some of these issues will be raised again when we examine the case for an International Criminal Court in Issue Fifteen.

Suggested Additional Readings

Byers, Michael. "The Shifting Foundations of International Law: A Decade of Forceful Measures against Iraq." *European Journal of International Law* 13, no. 1 (February 2002): 21–41.

Cassese, Antonio. "Terrorism Is Also Disrupting Some Crucial Legal Categories of International Law." *European Journal of International Law* 12, no. 5 (December 2001): 993–1001.

Chace, James. "Present at the Destruction: The Death of American Internationalism." *World Policy Journal* 20, no. 1 (Spring 2003): 1–4.

Falk, Richard. "What Future for the UN Charter System of War Prevention? Reflections on the Iraq War." In Irwin Abrams and Wang Gungwu, eds., *The Iraq War and Its Consequences: Thoughts of Nobel Peace Laureates and Eminent Scholars.* New Jersey: World Scientific, 2003: 195–214.

Farer, Tom. "The Prospect for International Law and Order in the Wake of Iraq." *American Journal of International Law* 97, no. 3 (July 2003): 621–27.

Foster, Charles. "International Law: Another Casualty of the Iraq War?" *Contemporary Review* 283, no. 1651 (August 2003): 76–78.

Gray, Christine. "From Unity to Polarization: International Law and the Use of Force against Iraq." *European Journal of International Law* 13, no. 1 (2002): 1–19.

Kampfner, John. "War and the Law." *New Statesman* 133, no. 4678 (March 8, 2004): 21–22.

Lobel, Jules, and Michael Ratner. "Bypassing the Security Council: Ambiguous Authorizations to Use Force, Cease-Fires and the Iraqi Inspection Regime." *American Journal of International Law* 93, no. 1 (January 1999): 124–54.

Valasek, Tomas. "New Threats, New Rules: Revising the Law of War." *World Policy Journal* 20, no. 1 (Spring 2003): 17–24.

Williams, Jody. "Iraq and Preemptive Self-Defense." In Irwin Abrams and Wang Gungwu, eds., *The Iraq War and Its Consequences: Thoughts of Nobel Peace Laureates and Eminent Scholars.* New Jersey: World Scientific, 2003: 17–48.

Yoo, John. "International Law after the War in Iraq." *American Journal of International Law* 97, no. 3 (July 2003): 563–75.

InfoTrac® College Edition

Search for the following articles in the InfoTrac® database:

Beard, Jack M. "America's New War on Terror: The Case for Self-Defense under International Law." *Harvard Journal of Law & Public Policy* 25, no. 2 (Spring 2002): 559–90.

Bellamy, Alex J. "International Law and the War with Iraq." *Melbourne Journal of International Law* 4, no. 2 (October 2003): 497–520.

Glennon, Michael J. "The Fog of Law: Self-Defense, Inherence, and Incoherence in Article 51 of the United Nations Charter." *Harvard Journal of Law & Public Policy* 25, no. 2 (Spring 2002): 539-58.

For more articles, enter:
"Iraq war," "international law," "security council," or "laws of war" in the keyword search.

Web Resources

For current URLs for the following websites, visit www.crosscurrents.nelson.com.

THE WAR ON IRAQ: LEGAL ISSUES

www.hrcr.org/hottopics/Iraq.html

This site is maintained by the Arthur W. Diamond Law Library at Columbia Law School. It contains an extensive collection of documents, articles, and links relating to the legal aspects of the Iraq war.

ELECTRONIC IRAQ

electroniciraq.net/news/internationallaw.shtml

Electronic Iraq is a news portal on the U.S.–Iraq crisis published by Middle East alternative news publishers. The site contains publications dealing with the legality of the war.

RICHARD FALK AND DAVID KRIEGER, EDS., "THE IRAQ CRISIS AND INTERNATIONAL LAW," NUCLEAR AGE PEACE FOUNDATION BRIEFING BOOKLET (JANUARY 2003)

www.wagingpeace.org/menu/resources/publications/2003_01_iraq-reader.pdf

This booklet contains a good collection of full-text articles and documents on the topic.

WORLD PRESS REVIEW: THE UNITED NATIONS, INTERNATIONAL LAW, AND THE WAR IN IRAQ

www.worldpress.org/specials/iraq/

This page contains a selection of articles on the legality of the war in Iraq from news sources around the world.

Will a Ballistic Defence System Undermine Global Security?

✔ **YES**
ERNIE REGEHR, "Missile Proliferation, Globalized Insecurity, and Demand-Side Strategies," Waterloo: Project Ploughshares, *Ploughshares Monitor* (March 2001)

✘ **NO**
FRANK P. HARVEY, "The International Politics of National Missile Defence: A Response to the Critics," *International Journal* 55, no. 4 (Autumn 2000): 545–66

In July 2001, the Bush administration signalled its clear intent to push forward with its plans to develop and deploy a ballistic missile defence (BMD) system by requesting an increase in funding for its program to $8.3 billion for the fiscal year 2002. This represented an increase of 57 percent from the previous year's spending. The administration also made it clear that it would go ahead with expanded testing of BMD systems, even if it meant abrogating the thirty-year-old Anti-Ballistic Missile (ABM) Treaty. In addition, the defense department announced that it would begin construction on a site in Alaska that could be functional as a first BMD site by 2004. Even as American attention shifted toward the "war on terrorism" in late 2001, the Bush administration reiterated its pressing need for an effective BMD system.

The desire to develop a system for providing defence against missile attacks has been uppermost in the minds of defence planners ever since the Germans launched V-2 rockets against civilian populations in London in 1944. The advent of nuclear weapons and the subsequent development of long-range missiles only gave more urgency to the idea. In the 1960s, both the Americans and the Soviets were working on plans to develop missile defence systems.

But technologies were still at an early stage then; they relied on the development of small missiles carrying nuclear-tipped warheads that could intercept an incoming missile. The Americans began deploying such a system in Grand Forks, North Dakota; it was aimed primarily at defending their Inter-Continental Ballistic Missile (ICBM) sites. However, there were still many doubts about the effectiveness of such a system. Thus, in 1972, the Americans supported the signing of the ABM Treaty that limited both the Americans and the Soviets to the development of only two ABM sites. (This limit was later reduced by agreement to one.) The Americans eventually abandoned their BMD site in Grand Forks. Instead, the United States concentrated on deterring a nuclear attack by supporting treaties aimed at limiting the proliferation of nuclear weapons and ballistic missile technology. At the same time, the Americans continued to rely on a strategy of deterrence by pursuing a doctrine of "mutually assured destruction" (MAD), which guaranteed an attack of devastating proportions on anyone who attacked the United States with nuclear weapons.

Nevertheless, the concept of a BMD system was reborn under Ronald Reagan. As tensions rose between the Soviets and the Americans in the early years of his presidency, defence analysts warned that the U.S.S.R. appeared to be capable of launching both a first strike and a second retaliatory strike against American soil.

As part of his response, in 1983, President Reagan called for the building of a comprehensive defensive shield around the United States that would make nuclear weapons obsolete. Called the Strategic Defense Initiative (SDI), but popularly known as Star Wars, the plan called for the development of emerging technologies, such as laser weapons, to build a more effective BMD system. Although many were skeptical of the feasibility of such a system, the Reagan administration spent some $85 million on SDI research.

By the end of the 1980s, however, the strategic environment was changing. The U.S.S.R. was in a state of collapse, democratization was spreading throughout Eastern Europe, and the Cold War had effectively come to an end. The threat of a massive nuclear attack from the Soviet Union was no longer a possibility. But studies carried out for the new administration of George Bush Senior cautioned against complacency. In a review of the SDI program, analysts warned that the new threat would more likely come from an unauthorized use of nuclear weapons, including use by terrorist groups of stolen nuclear devices. In addition, a growing number of states hostile to the United States were acquiring ballistic missile technology. The use of SCUD missiles against Israel and Saudi Arabia seemed to give credence to these new concerns. As a result, the Bush administration announced that SDI would be refocused on the development of a GPAL (Global Protection against Limited Strikes) system, which would have three components: ground-based national missile defence (NMD), ground-based theatre missile defence (TMD), and space-based missile defence.

Although the Clinton administration continued work on the BMD, the program's budget was cut from $39 billion to $18 billion over five years. Intelligence reports in the mid-1990s downplayed the danger of a nuclear attack on the United States in the next fifteen years. Enthusiasm for BMD seemed to be waning.

In 1998, Donald Rumsfeld was asked to lead an independent commission examining U.S. security needs. The Rumsfeld Commission warned that a number of nations overtly hostile to the United States were pushing ahead with weapons programs and could develop the capability to use longer-range ballistic missiles, armed with biological or nuclear warheads, in the very near future. In the same year, both India and Pakistan carried out nuclear tests, while Iran and North Korea tested new, longer-range ballistic missiles. These events seemed to confirm the warnings of the Rumsfeld Commission and stimulated renewed interested in ballistic missile defence. Nevertheless, President Clinton decided to defer the deployment of a BMD system in 2000.

When President George W. Bush took office in 2001, he immediately expressed enthusiasm for the concept of BMD. In fact, his administration announced dramatic increases in spending on BMD research and said that it would press forward with deployment of such a system even if it meant violating the ABM Treaty. *The National Security Strategy of the United States* issued in 2002 noted that the "deployment of an effective missile defense system" is increasingly necessary in the face of threat posed by "rogue states."

These debates are of special relevance to Canadians. As a nation, Canada must consider the global-security implications of missile defence. But it must also respond to the possibility of participating in operating any BMD system that the United States deploys. U.S. officials have made it clear that the United States would like Canada to participate once such a system is operational.

If Canada did agree to participate, the missile defence system would be operated by the joint U.S.–Canadian North American Aerospace Defence Command (NORAD) as a Ballistic Missile Defence of North America (BMD-NA). Although Canada's contributions, monetary or otherwise, may be minimal, its participation would be valuable in helping legitimize the program in the eyes of U.S. allies and other countries around the world that remain skeptical about the wisdom of BMD.

In the following readings, we find two contrasting Canadian interpretations of BMD. Ernie Regehr, of Project Ploughshares, examines the problems with BMD and counsels against Canadian participation in the program. Frank Harvey examines the arguments made against BMD and sets out to refute them.

✔ YES
Missile Proliferation, Globalized Insecurity, and Demand-Side Strategies
ERNIE REGEHR

For the moment, demand for weapons of mass destruction remains significant, though not overwhelming. There are at least four prominent elements to reducing demand for weapons of mass destruction (WMD) and long-range ballistic missiles: promoting accountable governance, ameliorating regional insecurities, blocking ballistic missile defence, and challenging the double standard of non-proliferation.

Recent comments out of Ottawa, by the Prime Minister[1] as well as the Defence[2] and Foreign[3] ministers, have allowed that the proposed American national missile defence (NMD) "system has to be developed in a way that will not be offensive to the Russians and the Chinese," and should not be pursued without consultation with allies, with the implication that if direct Russian, Chinese, and NATO opposition can be forestalled, NMD will be acceptable. The most generous (and perhaps even correct) interpretation of that approach is that it amounts to a de facto Canadian "no" to NMD inasmuch as it makes Canada's approval conditional on that of two of the international community's most vociferous opponents of NMD (Russia and China).

But what if the main nuclear weapon states were to arrive at mutual acceptance of, or acquiescence to, ballistic missile defence, accompanied by European acceptance?[4] In other words, if a key focus of popular opposition to ballistic missile defence were to be removed, namely the fear that it would upset the fragile stability of the US/Russian/Chinese nuclear relationships and re-start the arms race, should that make NMD acceptable to Canadians?

An obvious reason why it should not is that NMD represents a commitment to the long-term retention of nuclear arsenals. American NMD proponents insist and assume that Russia and China will and must indefinitely maintain enough nuclear weapons and long-range delivery systems to overwhelm any defence system that the Americans might mount. That this posture calls into question the NPT-related "unequivocal undertaking to accomplish the total elimination of their nuclear arsenals" hardly needs further comment.

Less obvious, but no less real, is the contribution of NMD's nuclear retentionist assumptions to pressures toward the horizontal proliferation of weapons of mass destruction and long-range missiles to deliver, or threaten, them. The effective mitigation of that threat will be undermined by the pursuit of unilateral or monopolist high-cost, hi-tech protection efforts. NMD will add to the proliferation pressures, and it is only through collective international attention to the political and security issues that generate proliferation pressures – that is, through attention to the demand side of proliferation – that the threat that is said to be animating NMD interests will be successfully addressed.

HORIZONTAL PROLIFERATION PRESSURES

Even though NMD assumes continued nuclear threats from Russia and China, NMD advocates say that the focus of defence is not protection against those immediate and major threats. Rather, the focus of NMD is said to be on the few intercontinental-range ballistic missiles, tipped with nuclear, chemical, or biological warheads, that might one day be aimed at America from states nurturing a persistent hostility towards the US.

Whether such states are defined as "rogues," or "states of concern," or simply as states with a will and a capacity to acquire ballistic missiles (threshold states), they exist and represent a hard reality of current and potential missile proliferation that the international community will have to confront sooner or later – namely, the reality that neither ballistic missile technology nor the capacity to build weapons of mass destruction will indefinitely be confined to only a few major military powers under what they regard as the discipline of mutual deterrence.

And if Washington's public worrying about the likes of North Korea is indeed just a cover, as for some key American leaders it no doubt is, for its more ambitious pursuit of a robust NMD system coupled to offensive deployments in support of America's pursuit of terrestrial and space military domination, the WMD and missile proliferation pressures, horizontal and vertical, will only intensify accordingly.

GLOBALIZED VULNERABILITY

Even though the overwhelming majority of states that could become proliferators decide not to, the very fact that they could makes intercontinental or long-range ballistic missiles (ICBMs) one of the more tangible demonstrations of the globalization of insecurity. Like instantaneous currency transfers, ICBMs can erase national boundaries and cause the weak and the powerful to shudder with equal trepidation. Surface-to-surface intercontinental ballistic missiles are designed for only one payload, weapons of mass destruction, and no corner of the world from the corridors of Washington to the savannahs of Africa can elude their reach.

It is this shared vulnerability that ultimately renders "national" defence an oxymoron. ICBMs are inimical to the military protection of national territory – a stark reality that renders the American unilateral pursuit of "national" missile defence (NMD) a costly case of collective denial. The world is irrevocably interdependent, and unilateral national military responses to globalized insecurity are unlikely to be any more effective in protecting national territory than, say, strictly Canadian pollution-control regulations in protecting the Arctic environment.

NMD enthusiasts regard the struggle against proliferation as already lost. The missile threat cannot be eliminated, they say, so it's time to build our own impenetrable fortress. But the fact that there is no such thing as an impenetrable fortress, a fact confirmed by psychology as well as physics, rests on the first principle of globalized insecurity, which is that security is not amenable to national or unilateral arrangement. It is a principle that the United States, given its continuing ambitions for unilateral "space control and space superiority,"[5] does not find compelling. The rejection of unilateralism and the acceptance of mutual vulnerability are not the habits of superpowers, but it remains the case that only when the major powers join in re-inventing interdependence as a source of shared strength are they likely to set about building mutual global security regimes instead of trying to protect monopolies.

DEMAND AND NON-PROLIFERATION

A growing list of states does or could have access to those technologies of instant intercontinental destruction, and whether or not they act on that capacity depends finally on their own perceptions of self-interest and of the common interest. Israel, India, and Pakistan have thus decided to acquire both nuclear weapons and missiles of expanding range. South Africa, on the same grounds of self-interest and the common interest, has only recently decided the opposite, that is, to forgo the pursuit of such a capacity.

The proliferation or non-proliferation of weapons of mass destruction and the ballistic missiles to deliver them to distant targets depends finally on the voluntary decisions of states. States with expanding technical capabilities – and there are many of them – will in the end not be prevented, against their will, from acquiring WMD and long-range missile technologies in a world in which there continues to be a powerful demand for them.

For the moment, demand remains significant, though not overwhelming. States with grievances against, or that regard themselves as vulnerable to interventions by, distant powers, are likely to look with considerable interest at long-range missiles with which to pose a convincing counter-threat. That interest is powerfully present in all current nuclear weapon states (NWS). And, for example, it is clear that repeated military attacks on Iraq do not serve to reduce that regime's interest in acquiring WMD and extending the range of its missiles. And what guarantee is there that other countries, with the capability but no current interest in acquiring WMD and long-range ballistic missiles, will not change in ways that could produce conditions of intense demand for such weapons?

In arms control, demand tends to trump control. Efforts to control access to weapons that are not accompanied by measures to mitigate strong demand for them are in the long run not likely to be successful. The central insight of peace-building is that peace and disarmament (from small arms to WMD) do not endure through enforcement but through the building of political, social, and economic conditions conducive to restraint and stability. Regulatory and control regimes are important elements of stable security conditions, but as long as conditions produce a strong demand for weapons, it will be impossible to prevent the proliferation of WMD and ballistic missiles. And their spread to any new states promises a serious escalation of global insecurity.

There are at least four prominent elements to reducing demand for WMD and long-range ballistic missiles: promoting accountable governance, ameliorating regional insecurities, blocking ballistic missile defence, and challenging the double standard of non-proliferation.

1. Governance

It is too often overlooked, but one indispensable element of the effort to reduce the demand for ballistic missiles by states now in pursuit of them is support for the emergence of democratically accountable governments. The greatest current demand for ballistic missiles outside the acknowledged nuclear weapon states is in unaccountable repressive regimes that ignore the security of their citizens in favour of provocative policies aimed at regime aggrandizement or survival.

Strategies to isolate and demonize threshold states tend to reinforce the very vulnerabilities that produce the demand for weapons of mass destruction and the intercontinental ballistic missiles to deliver them. Regimes out of step with both the international community and their own citizens are usually inclined to try to intimidate both with increasingly threatening postures and practices, internationally and domestically. While direct engagement[6] of "outlaw" states holds the danger of rewarding threat with cooperation, the aim of diplomacy must obviously be to draw them into compliance with international norms and to encourage internal democratization. And a particular focus of engagement must be the strengthening of civil society and the impetus toward public participation and democracy.

In the end, the only credible long-term hedge against demand for weapons of mass destruction and the means of delivering them is an emboldened civil society that claims the right and acquires the capacity to give direct expression to alternative national interests and aspirations. States eschew extremism, not in response to external military threats, but in response to the emergence of an internal civil society that supports moderation and seeks a place of respect within the international community. In any state in which the people define public need, the demand is less likely to be for the acquisition of strategic missiles than for schools and hospitals.

That does beg the question of just who is defining national and collective needs in the United States and NATO. Some obviously think you can have it both ways – not only missiles and schools, but missiles for us and not for them, which gets us to the double standard problem (see The Double Standard).

2. Regional Insecurity

To date, nuclear weapons and advanced, if not yet intercontinental, missile capacity have spread beyond the traditional nuclear weapon states only in regions of intractable regional conflict. The Israel/Palestine and India/Pakistan conflicts both date back to the end of World War II and both have remained hot conflicts and involved hot wars. A call for new approaches to regional security and conflict resolution in instances such as these is both relevant and urgent, but unfortunately making the call for change is a lot easier than actually delivering alternatives. Nevertheless, the extent to which the international community and its security and peacemaking institutions can credibly address enduring regional conflicts is the extent to which we can expect real reductions in the demand for WMD and the means of their delivery.

3. NMD and Demand

Any American ballistic missile defence effort promises to increase both vertical and horizontal proliferation pressures (demand). Vertical proliferation pressures will grow in Russia and China as a result of NMD, even if they were to agree to it. As the public debate on NMD regularly points out, NMD will threaten current arms control agreements and lead both Russia and China to take escalatory steps they consider necessary to maintain a credible deterrent (e.g., maintain or shift to high alert status, and increase missile numbers to overwhelm any NMD capacity to intercept them). From there the vertical proliferation pressures will cascade to India and then Pakistan.

Horizontal proliferation pressures are also destined to increase in response to NMD deployment inasmuch as NMD signals the intention of current NWS to retain their nuclear arsenals indefinitely, while insisting that everyone else disavow them. NMD, in other words, exacerbates the problem of the double standard.

4. The Double Standard

Even if some measure of strategic stability among the NWS were to be re-established in a strategic environment that included an NMD system, the pressures toward horizontal proliferation would still have increased. The double standard, enshrined in the Nuclear Non-Proliferation Treaty, not in principle but in practice, and solemnly repeated in NATO strategic doctrine that says that in our hands nuclear weapons are agents of security, while in all others they are instruments of terror, is not sustainable.

Any state's policies towards acquiring or forgoing WMD and ballistic missiles are likely to be varied, complex, and focussed on their own perceptions of self-interest. In other words, it's not likely that any state will seek ballistic missiles just because the major powers have them, but the international community's effort to preserve a double standard in these matters is not an aid to restraint or compliance. Any state that believes it is in its interests to pursue provocative, attention-getting strategies is more likely to pursue nuclear weapons and missile capability if these enjoy some level of respectability and legitimacy in the international community by virtue of the retentionist policies of major powers. The international community cannot credibly say it is illegitimate for Iraq to acquire a ballistic missile capability if others claim that right and if Iraq is not party to any international agreement that prohibits it from acquiring them. Of course, the only point of having ballistic missiles is to deliver a weapon of mass destruction. Iraq, as a signatory to the NPT and to the biological weapons convention, and by Security Council action, is bound by international laws against any WMD acquisition. However, states like Iraq, and like the US on the matter of the first use of nuclear weapons, may find it useful to pursue a policy of provocative ambiguity.

The challenge to the international community is thus clear: to hold all states to the same standard of behaviour, and thus to reinforce principles of interdependence and mutual security with unambiguous commitments to reduce and eventually eliminate the ballistic missiles (as well as the nuclear weapons) of the major powers.[7] In the meantime, the disquietingly long meantime, during which current NWS are tasked to reduce and eventually eliminate their arsenals of long-distance mass destruction, means have to be found to make it attractive for other states to reject all WMD and long-distance delivery systems.

MULTILATERAL MISSILE MONITORING

Just as missile control measures are destined to failure unless they are complemented by vigorous demand reduction efforts, demand reduction efforts can only be sustained and harvested through control mechanisms designed to consolidate and institutionalize an international consensus of restraint leading finally to the prohibition of WMD and their means of delivery. Current and welcome discussions within the Missile Technology Control Regime (MTCR) are trying to encourage both supply and demand restraint by exploring a "set of principles, commitments, confidence-building measures and incentives that could constitute a code of conduct against missile proliferation."[8] These are not currently public discussions, but the fact that they are taking place should be understood as some movement towards an international consensus to reduce the number and limit the spread of ballistic missiles.

Russia's proposal for a global missile monitoring system (GMS) is a further effort to take advantage of, and to build on, that emerging consensus. The GMS would, among other things, incorporate the MTCR's focus on restricting technology transfers, provide security guarantees for states eschewing the pursuit of long-range ballistic missiles, and monitor missile launches.

Any mechanism to control long-range ballistic missiles faces the daunting political challenge of recognizing the current de facto, but ultimately unsustainable, monopoly on missiles, and then solidifying a commitment from all non-nuclear weapon states to themselves reject the acquisition of ballistic missiles in exchange for a commitment from the states that do have them to take discernable steps toward eliminating their long-range military ballistic missile arsenals. Sustained confidence in any arrangement by which most states agree not to acquire ballistic missiles while those with ballistic missiles for military purposes agree to reductions and movement toward their elimination[9] (and, significantly, agree not to link their offensive capabilities to missile defences) will depend on the emergence of a reliable global ballistic missile monitoring mechanism with four basic roles:

- to monitor, assess, and share information on the ballistic missile development programs of all states;

- to provide surveillance and monitoring of the pre-launch status of missiles in nuclear weapon states to facilitate and verify de-alerting measures;

- to receive and share pre-launch notification of missile launches for accepted purposes, such as satellite launches; and

- to detect and track ballistic missile launches and flights and share the information in real time.

The latter two functions are central to the proposed US/Russian Joint Data Exchange Center[10] (JDEC), which too should gradually be globalized.

Protection from weapons of mass destruction delivered across oceans and continents by ballistic missiles is not a national prerogative. It is a global imperative that will not be met through military defence. Protection is a common global responsibility that in this instance depends on eliminating the threat, and that in turn requires as much attention to removing the demand for such weapons as it does to restricting access to them.

NOTES

1. On Feb. 7, 2001, Prime Minister Chrétien told the House of Commons that he had indicated to President Bush that the NMD "system has to be developed in a way that will not be offensive to the Russians and the Chinese."

2. Paul Koring (Washington) and Jeff Sallot (Ottawa) (2001) report that Minister of Defence Art Eggleton says Canada is "open-minded" on the NMD question.

3. On Feb. 14, 2001, Foreign Affairs Minister John Manley, in response to a question from MP Svend Robinson, told the House of Commons that "it is appropriate to give the United States... time to define what the project is that is being described as national missile defence – it has indicated that it has not done that yet – and the time it has asked for to take up what its plans are, not only with its allies but with the Russians and the Chinese."

4. According to Michael Gordon (2001), "European officials now seem to accept, grudgingly, the fact that the new American team is determined to move ahead. . . . The debate is entering a new phase in which the issue is more how the United States should go about developing missile defenses, than whether it should try."

5. On the occasion of the January 2001 Space Commission report to the US Congress, the Commander in Chief of NORAD and US Space Command and the Air Force Space Command, Gen. Ralph E. Eberhart, added to the inventory of US military leaders calling for the US to control space when he counselled increased "attention to the sensitive issues of space control and superiority."

6. See, for example, Haass and O'Sullivan 2000.

7. The Nuclear Non-Proliferation Treaty states pledged their commitment to "the elimination from national arsenals of nuclear weapons *and the means of their delivery*" (emphasis added; see preamble to the Treaty).

8. The MTCR is an export control arrangement (voluntary guidelines among a suppliers' group) designed to limit the spread of ballistic and cruise missile technologies. The MTCR group has begun discussions with other states on the viability of developing a broader, formal multilateral instrument to prevent missile proliferation.

9. One proposed deal would include a worldwide missile warning system accessible to all states, the provision by missile states of satellite launch facilities and other space probes for peaceful purposes for other states, permission for other countries to build missiles for space exploration and satellite launches, and a multilateral verification agency (Dean 1998).

10. The Joint Data Exchange Center is to be established under a June 2000 agreement between Presidents Clinton and Putin and will facilitate "the exchange of information derived from each side's missile launch warning systems on the launches of ballistic missiles and space launch vehicles."

REFERENCES

Dean, Jonathan (1998), "Step-by-Step Control Over Ballistic and Cruise Missiles," *Disarmament and Diplomacy*, Issue 31, October, pp. 2–11.

Gordon, Michael R. (2001), "News Analysis: Allies' Mood on 'Star Wars' Shifts," *New York Times*, February 5.

Haass, Richard N. and Meghan L. O'Sullivan (2000), "Terms of Engagement: Alternatives to Punitive Policies," *Survival* 42, No. 2, pp. 113–35.

Koring, Paul and Jeff Sallot (2001), Feb. 2, *The Globe and Mail*.

✗ NO
The International Politics of National Missile Defence: A Response to the Critics
FRANK P. HARVEY

INTRODUCTION

To encourage more informed discussion of national missile defence (NMD) and to widen a dangerously narrow public debate on the subject, this article challenges critics of NMD to confront the logical and factual errors in their arguments against deployment. Because the American programme has important implications for Canadian foreign and security policies (and Canadian-American relations more generally), critics should be prepared to defend their positions beyond simply reiterating the same superficial criticisms. The Canadian public should expect nothing less from the academic community (not to mention our elected officials) than a sophisticated exchange of ideas on such an important issue. [. . .]

THE DEMISE OF THE NPT AND ABM

The most common criticisms of NMD are associated with warnings about the demise of the Non-Proliferation treaty (NPT) and Anti-Ballistic Missile (ABM) treaty. Signed in 1968 and 1972, respectively, these treaties are two pillars of nuclear disarmament and arms control that, according to proponents, were responsible for slowing the pace of proliferation during the cold war and stabilizing the longest nuclear rivalry in history. Because they continue to be essential for controlling proliferation and maintaining a stable nuclear environment, it is imperative that their underlying principles and fundamental logic should not be undermined.

What critics fail to point out is that the worst abuses of horizontal and vertical proliferation of nuclear weapons and technology occurred after the treaties were signed. Regardless of the indicator used to track nuclear proliferation — overall nuclear stockpiles, numbers of strategic warheads in submarine launched ballistic missiles, inter-continental ballistic missiles, strategic bombers,[1] production and stockpiles of weapons' grade plutonium, thefts of fissile material, trade in dual use technology tied to the atomic energy industry, trade in ballistic missile technology, and so on — the evidence of an increase in the pace of proliferation is clear. Recent nuclear tests by India and Pakistan are but the latest illustration of the same pattern. To claim that the NPT and the ABM treaty are essential parts of the international arms control structure doesn't say much for the treaties or for the prospects for serious arms control and disarmament in the future.[2]

Some critics — those who claim that the more relevant measure of the treaty's effectiveness is the number of nuclear weapons states in the world today — will reject my criteria for judging the NPT's success. These critics argue that there were five nuclear weapons states when the NPT was signed in 1968, and there were still five at the beginning of 1998. There are now seven with India and Pakistan. If the undeclared states (Israel) and the "wannabes" (Iraq, Iran, and North Korea) are included, the number rises to eleven. The expectation when the NPT was negotiated was that there would be far more nuclear weapons states, but that prediction was obviously wrong. The NPT would, therefore, seem to be an overwhelming success.

Applying the same logic, perhaps the success of the New York Police Department (NYPD) should be judged on the basis of how many millions of New Yorkers do not commit murder or rob liquor stores, regardless of whether they ever intended to commit those (or other) crimes.[3] Similarly, an overwhelming majority of non-nuclear states are not interested in acquiring nuclear weapons, not because their leaders find the weapons repulsive and morally reprehensible (although some probably do) but primarily because nuclear weapons provide no added security (at this time), or because security guarantees from allies are more than sufficient (as is the case in Canada). Most states, in other words, have the luxury of being able to say "no" to nuclear weapons. The success of the NPT must be measured instead by (a) how many aspiring nuclear states (signatory and non-signatory) are prevented from acquiring or developing the technology to deploy nuclear weapons and/or their delivery vehicles, and (b) how many states (signatory and non-signatory) continue to provide the requisite technology to aspiring nuclear powers. It takes only one nuclear weapon to produce the catastrophe the NPT was designed to prevent, and the capability to deliver and inflict that kind of damage is spreading.

The fate of the NPT (and perhaps its ultimate demise) will not depend upon NMD deployment. It will continue to depend upon political, military, and security environments in places such as India, Iran, Iraq, Israel, Libya, North Korea, Pakistan, and Syria. Officials in these states are convinced that ballistic missiles and nuclear weapons technology serve their security and national interests and are more than willing to accept related technology transfers from China, Russia, France, the United States, and Canada to accommodate their concerns. Critics in the arms control community refuse to acknowledge that these states will continue to be perceived as threatening whether or not the United States has a defensive shield. [. . .]

Leaders of "new" and "aspiring" nuclear weapons states are perceived by many critics as passive observers who learn from established nuclear powers and, in true Pavlovian fashion, respond accordingly. The best way to control proliferation and maintain a stable nuclear environment, critics assume, is for established nuclear powers to "teach" officials in other states to adhere to the principles, logic, and moral (read "civilized") standards entrenched in the treaties. That assumption is not only naïve but also dangerously superficial when it comes to understanding the proliferation puzzle and the myriad factors that explain most (if not all) proliferation decisions. It is particularly insulting to officials in, for example, India and Pakistan to be told that their capacity to make informed decisions about their own global and regional security interests is limited. The notion that established nuclear powers or the international arms control community command the intellectual high ground on these issues and, by extension, have a moral obligation to "guide" other cultures and peoples toward the enlightened path of nuclear sanity is reminiscent of the worst extremes of Manifest Destiny and its associated policies. While this obviously is not the intention of the arms control community, it is precisely how their pronouncements are perceived in some states.

Finally, it is particularly ironic for critics in the arms control and disarmament community to embrace the ABM treaty as the cornerstone of non-proliferation and nuclear sanity when the same critics vehemently criticized the treaty throughout the 1970s and 1980s for entrenching the logic of mutually assured destruction (MAD) in United States–Soviet rivalry. That logic was used by both sides to justify huge defence expenditures, ever-increasing nuclear stockpiles, and an exponential increase in the number of nuclear targets – all with reference to the benefits of maintaining a robust, stable, and credible second-strike capability. The rationale underlying the ABM treaty remains the same: as long as the United States and Russia have enough weapons to survive and retaliate after a pre-emptive first-strike, neither side will be tempted to launch first. Given their new-found concern for protecting the sanctity of the ABM treaty, it seems NMD critics in the arms control community have now fully embraced a thesis that was so obvious to many in the defence community during the cold war – large stockpiles of nuclear weapons on high alert can serve the global desire for nuclear stability and peace.[4] If that is not the point these critics are trying to make, perhaps they should acknowledge the logical implications (and unintended consequences) of supporting the ABM treaty and/or rejecting NMD.

NMD WILL LEAD TO NUCLEAR PROLIFERATION BY RUSSIA AND CHINA

Building on claims about the impending demise of decades of disarmament negotiations, critics predict that China and Russia will respond to NMD with a major build-up and deployment of more sophisticated weapons as they attempt to regain their security by re-establishing (or, in the case of China, strengthening) their second-strike capability. This automatic action-reaction sequence will, in turn, create security threats for officials in India and Pakistan, who will retaliate with greater numbers of nuclear weapons for their own security. A huge spiral in defence spending and arms protection will result and propel the international community back to square one of the arms control and disarmament agenda – all because of a relatively minor investment of about two per cent of the United States defence budget (or 0.3 per cent of its federal budget). Three interrelated assumptions underlie these predictions: proliferation by Russia and China is directly related to (and will be a primary consequence of) American NMD deployment; Russian and Chinese warnings convey a "real" fear that the United States is attempting to gain a first-strike advantage; and the fear of an impending American first-strike advantage justifies Russian and Chinese proliferation. Each assumption reveals logical inconsistencies and factual errors.

First, the casual chain cited by critics to predict almost automatic proliferation by Russia and China ignores evidence compiled over years of research on why states proliferate. Without exception, the research points to a complex set of political, economic, and military-strategic prerequisites.[5] If the findings and patterns identified in this body of work are correct, China can be expected to acquire and deploy more advanced systems if and when the technology becomes available and affordable, and as long as Chinese officials perceive as unfair the imbalance between their nuclear capabilities and those of the United States, Russia, Europe, and the North Atlantic Treaty Organization (NATO). Although the United States and Russia have the luxury as major nuclear powers to disarm to START II, III, or IV levels, China will continue to build up the levels befitting an ascending major power. In other words, the real incentive for China to upgrade its nuclear capabilities is Beijing's perception that its nuclear deterrent is unstable, for the same reason American and Soviet officials worried in the 1960s and 1970s – China's retaliatory capability is not sufficiently potent (or credible) in "second-strike" terms. Whether or not the United States deploys NMD is irrelevant; Chinese officials will continue to see a capability/credibility gap, at least until their stockpiles approach parity with those in Europe. Even if the United States were to decide to scrap NMD tomorrow, China would continue to upgrade its systems on the basis of worst-case scenarios and assumptions about surreptitious NMD development. I suspect that as defence technologies become available and affordable, Russia and China will do precisely the same thing, regardless of what the Americans do today.[6]

Because Russia has already deployed advanced weapons designed to circumvent missile defence systems, critics' fears of this kind of proliferation following NMD deployment are moot. The new SS-X-27 ballistic missile, for example, has an accelerated boost phase of 100 seconds (down from 180 seconds, making it harder to detect on launch), can carry three warheads, and is highly manoeuvrable. It is particularly interesting that this combination of technologies serves as an effective countermeasure not only to NMD but to the alternative missile defence system that Vladimir Putin, the Russian president, offered the Europeans in June 2000.[7] Critics predict that Russia will accelerate the pace of proliferation in retaliation for NMD, but they should at least explain what Russia would gain and why its leaders are likely to ignore the political, military, and, especially, economic costs of returning to a cold war footing. [. . .]

Second, Russian and Chinese fears of losing second-strike capabilities are based, in part, on a basic and fundamental cold war concern that effective defences will give the United States first-strike advantage. NMD deployment, therefore, will force Russia and China to acquire additional missiles to augment their retaliatory capability and, by extension, the credibility of their nuclear deterrent threat. Those critics who use such warnings to establish a case against NMD should be prepared to explain why their fears are legitimate. The only way to do so would be to explain how NMD provides the United States with a first-strike capability, and, more importantly, why the United States would sometime in the future threaten or launch a massive first-strike attack against Russia and/or China. [...]

Third, critics should explain why they are willing to accept current threats by China and Russia to proliferate in retaliation for NMD when they rejected as logically absurd the identical strategy when it was used by the United States and the Soviet Union to increase nuclear stockpiles throughout the cold war. Their arguments included the fact that most of the 30,000 missiles on each side were redundant and entirely useless; a few missiles were more often more than sufficient to inflict unacceptable damage, and this "minimum" deterrence was more than sufficient to provide effective security from a pre-emptive strike. After all, who would be foolish enough to risk provoking even one retaliatory missile? But critics in the arms control community today refuse to apply the same logic and criticism to Russia and China because it undermines the rationale tied to warnings about automatic proliferation. As an unintended consequence, nuclear proliferation becomes a reasonable and logical response to NMD.

TECHNOLOGICAL LIMITATIONS OF NMD

Two main assertions underpin the "technological limitations" critique: current defence technologies don't work; and simple decoys and countermeasures can overcome any shield. But if NMD is indeed plagued by these incredible technological hurdles, and if simple countermeasures can easily offset any investment in defence, then, aside from wasting money (see section four) what exactly is the problem for China and Russia? After all, only an effective NMD shield would justify an arms race to re-establish a stable second-strike capability. Conversely, if NMD does not (or will not) work, then any security concerns expressed by Russia or China about maintaining the credibility of their nuclear deterrent are misplaced and mistaken, as are related decisions by these states [to] proliferate in retaliation for a useless defensive system. Juxtaposed against the previous criticisms, the technological critique is, in many ways, mutually exclusive – the stronger the arguments and evidence about the deficiencies of NMD, the weaker the claims about automatic and justifiable proliferation by Russia and China because they have no reason to feel compelled to compensate for losses in security. Notwithstanding this obvious logical inconsistency, which critics rarely acknowledge and almost never attempt to address, the limits of interceptor technology are offered as sufficient reason to scrap the entire programme.

With respect to NMD architecture, the scope of the proposed project will evolve through four stages, beginning with 20 interceptors in 2005 and growing to a larger system by 2011. As William Broad points out, "the shield would require at least 2 launching sites, 3 command centers, 5 communication relay stations, 15 radar, 29 satellites, 250 underground silos and a total of 250 missile interceptors (by 2011). It would be based in Hawaii, Alaska, California, Colorado, North Dakota, Massachusetts, Greenland, Britain and possibly Maine. Two radar would be set up in Asia, possibly in Japan and South Korea. Building it would cost at least $60 billion and running it would take at least 1,455 people, and probably hundreds more."[8] According to the critics, an investment of US$60 billion simply cannot be justified on the basis of recent tests or the prospects for success in the future. The technology is not capable of satisfying even the most basic requirements for success and, according to critics among scientists and engineers, it is unlikely ever to be robust enough to deal with decoys and simple countermeasures.

Consider the argument put forward by Burton Richter (winner of the 1976 Nobel Prize for physics): "Assume for the sake of argument that an attack is composed of five missiles (the massive attack we used to worry about from the Soviet Union would have involved hundreds or thousands) and suppose that the chance of one interceptor finding and destroying the real warhead from one of the attacking missiles is four out of five, or 80 per cent. Then, the chance of killing all five incoming warheads with five interceptors would be calculated this way: 0.8 for the first interceptors on the first warhead, multiplied by 0.8 for the second on the second, and so on for all five. Work it out, and the probability of getting all five is about 33 per cent, or a two-out-of-three chance that at least one of the incoming warheads will get through. Since one warhead can kill hundreds of thousands of people, that is not good enough."[9]

There are several problems with this argument. First, even if we acknowledge the incredible technological hurdles that remain, and even if we accept the fact that the current system is far from perfect, the more relevant questions for policymakers are: how close to perfect does the technology have to be to be useful; and how prudent is deployment today if interceptor technology, speed, and precision will continue to evolve and improve? Critics have never clarified how close to perfect a defence system has to be to be useful and worthy of funding. Even the staunchest critics of NMD assign at least some probability of success. The question is whether that probability is worth an investment of two per cent of the United States defence budget.

Second, most critics in the scientific community intentionally side step the link between the number of interceptors launched at a single target and the probability of a successful hit. Current plans are to use three or four interceptors per target, applying a "hit-move-hit" strategy. According to congressional testimony by General Robert T. Kadish, director of the Pentagon's Ballistic Missile Defence Organization, if interceptors approach 80 per cent accuracy, two or three attempts would increase the probability of a successful hit to 96 per cent and 99 per cent, respectively.[10] For the sake of argument, accept the most pessimistic assessment of the technology in 2005–2008—say, about a 30 per cent probability of any given interceptor hitting its target. Critics will no doubt cite this as the fairest evaluation of contemporary interceptor technology – one out of three interceptor tests in 1999–2000 was successful. With 30 per cent accuracy, and assuming precision will not improve through trial and error, the second, third, and fourth attempts increase the probability of a successful hit to 51 per cent, 66 per cent, and 76 per cent, respectively.

Third, even if overall success rates remain as low as 30 per cent, the question American policy-makers are facing is whether to deploy a system that protects the population from three out of ten missiles (that is, eight out of ten missiles using four interceptors), or scrap the entire programme and, in so doing, face a 100 percent probability that the population will suffer the effects of all ten missiles if attacked?[11] The technological case in favour of deployment is even stronger when one considers that 30 per cent is far lower than the estimates offered by critics and proponents in the scientific community and significantly lower than estimates cited by scientists involved in all aspects of the NMD testing programme. Moreover, the 250 interceptors planned for deployment by 2011 will certainly compensate for limitations of current technology, even if they remain constant. Since that is highly unlikely, the investment of two per cent of the defence budget is a bargain.

Many critics suffer from static impressions of progress and overlook constant improvements in interceptor and decoy identification technology. That NMD has not yet reached 100 per cent accuracy is irrelevant. What is relevant is whether the pace of innovation is such that NMD will, at some future point, produce a "high enough" probability of success to warrant deployment (even 30 per cent is arguably high enough), whether the current programme provides sufficient security to offset the costs and potential risks, and whether alternatives (such as constructive engagement, transparency, economic sanctions, and so on) are cheaper and more likely to accomplish the same security objectives. Current and future decisions regarding research, development, and deployment should depend on these calculations; they should not (and mostly probably will never) depend on the status and limitations of present-day technology, especially if the technology is evolving at a rapid pace. [. . .]

The greatest technological challenge for NMD is the system's capacity to disregard countermeasures and decoys. According to some critics, decoys are extremely hard to detect and cheaper to produce than interceptors. Thus, NMD will always be a waste of time and money. There are at least two problems with this argument.

First, critics tend to downplay the problems developing countries face when incorporating countermeasures into a well-functioning ballistic missile programme. They are also quick to acknowledge the enormous costs and limitations the world's richest and most scientifically advanced country faces when developing interceptor technology. The only states with the capability to develop and deploy decoys "easily" are the very states that don't need them; they already have a stable and credible retaliatory threat. Not true, claim the critics. Developing countries also have the technology to build and deploy decoys to circumvent NMD interception. If that is true, then they most certainly have the capacity to produce ballistic missiles as well. If ballistic missile threats are real, then it makes perfect sense for the United States to increase the costs incurred by "states of concern" by forcing them to deploy decoys and countermeasures when developing their ballistic missile programmes. Just because countermeasures can be deployed does not mean the United States should accept defeat, scrap NMD, and give potential adversaries the option of disregarding those added costs. Scrapping NMD simply means that the ballistic missile threat will continue to proliferate in ways that are more affordable. The harder it is for potential opponents to threaten (implicitly or explicitly) the use of these weapons, the better. On the other hand, if ballistic missile threats are indeed fabrications to justify military expenditure on NMD, and if there is no reason to be worried about the pace of ballistic missile proliferation, then critics should be prepared to provide a more comprehensive and detailed defence of that position.[12]

A second and related set of criticisms focuses on controversies surrounding the NMD testing programme and the standards used by the Pentagon to evaluate success and failure. Some critics have accused the Pentagon of fixing the tests in order to facilitate a successful hit and, therefore, congressional funding. I'm not a ballistic scientist and do not presume to understand the physics involved in the programme, but it seems perfectly reasonable to develop and improve technology through stages by first identifying NMD's limitations; the system's maximum potential is irrelevant at this time. If the initial tests were designed to assess an interceptor's capacity to hit hundreds of targets and 20–30 different decoys, and it fails, the results provide virtually no useful information about what went wrong, why certain decoys may have been missed, or what has to be improved to move the technology forward. On the other hand, if a single interceptor misses/hits a single target, or misses/hits a simple decoy, the information obtained from that test is far more useful and relevant. [. . .]

The same critique also tends to underplay the incredible scientific achievements associated with even a very simple test. Obviously, the system cannot achieve its maximum potential today, but we should not evaluate the performance of current technology based on the requirements for a system envisioned in five, eight, or ten years – interceptor technology, like any technology, will continue to improve. Again, the question for policy-makers is whether deployment today makes sense considering the probability of success, the probability of improving future systems through trial and error, and the costs and benefits to overall security when compared to alternative strategies.[13]

NMD: A COLOSSAL WASTE OF MONEY OR A MINOR AND PRUDENT INVESTMENT?

The most straightforward way to evaluate the quality of any significant defence expenditure is to estimate the money involved in the programme (financial costs); the contribution the programme makes to state security (benefits); the probability those benefits will be realized (technology); the potential dangers associated with deployment (risks); and the probability those costs will be incurred (security costs). The results should then be compared to other security programmes that promise to accomplish the same objectives, for the same (or lower) costs, with the same (or higher) probability of success. Finally, the estimates should be compared to those for alternative programmes designed to address a different set of equally or more important security objectives. All things considered, programmes with higher utility for a state's security should be funded.

With respect to the financial costs, the proposed United States investment in NMD is approximately US$60 billion over ten years, or about $6 billion per year between 2001 and 2011. That is about two per cent per annum of a defence budget of approximately US$300 billion (or approximately 0.3 per cent of the total federal budget of $2 trillion). The numbers are likely to be lower as the defence budget increases to $317 billion in 2005 and $349 billion in 2010, but the average yearly expenditure of two per cent serves as a useful benchmark to make a few important points.

For critics, two per cent of the defence budget is a waste of money (high financial costs) for a system aimed at non-existent threats (no benefits) that will not work (technological limitations) and will probably create a host of other problems (security costs) as Russia and China automatically retaliate by proliferating nuclear weapons (high risks). I have already responded to many of these assertions by outlining important flaws and inconsistencies in the critics' case. I would like to now turn to three items I have not yet addressed: financial investment, alternative programmes that are perhaps more suited to the task, and other programmes designed to address a different set of security objectives.

How cost effective is the American investment in NMD? With the preceding analysis in mind, and for the sake of argument, accept an optimistic estimate of evolving threats tied to the proliferation of ballistic missile technology – say, only a ten-per-cent probability that by 2005–2008 one or more "states of concern" will have developed and deployed one or more medium- to long-range ballistic missiles capable of reaching the United States (even critics would find this number very low). The current annual investment is quite a bargain, especially when one looks at where the remaining 98 per cent of the defence budget ends up and the correspondingly limited contribution much of that investment makes to United States security.

Moreover, a ten-per-cent probability of a ballistic missile threat is a far more significant and relevant concern when viewed in terms of the overall defence profile; that is, all American security, defence, and threat scenarios the government considers relevant and the consequences in damage and lives should those threats become real. If only those threats the United States can tackle with at least some likelihood of success are included, then the ten-per-cent probability of a ballistic missile threat becomes even more relevant. Put differently, a 99-per-cent probability of a terrorist attack in the next three years resulting in 100 deaths is not as relevant as a ten-per-cent threat with the potential to produce tens if not hundreds of thousands of casualties. The question policy-makers are confronting is whether the strategy designed to address the ten-per-cent threat has a higher probability of success than corresponding funds and programmes to stop, for example, terrorism. Would another $60 billion invested in anti-terrorism provide an equal (or better) return in security than stopping even a single missile with NMD?

Most critics agree that the rogue-state threat is exaggerated, but few are prepared to argue that there is nothing to worry about. The real debate, then, is about time and the pace and evolution of the threat. Critics must estimate the appropriate amount of funding for their preferred solution to the problem, even if their estimate of the probability of a ballistic missile threat in 2005–2008 is, say, one percent. How much of the United States defence budget would critics be willing to allocate to address a one-per-cent threat, using whatever programme they prefer? If they conclude that one per cent (or $3 billion) of the defence budget would be enough to implement their preferred solution, then they have an obligation to explain what the money buys, how the proposed investment enhances United States security, how likely it is that the programme will succeed, and so on. Ultimately, critics should be prepared to evaluate their alternatives using the same standards they apply to NMD, with reference to the same criteria for assessing costs, risks, and probabilities for success or failure.

The "alternatives" proposed by critics usually include some combination of improved transparency, weapons verification, monitoring, import/export controls and a host of other diplomatic (for example, constructive engagement) and coercive diplomatic (for example, economic sanctions, bombing Iraq) strategies. Presumably these methods are more constructive because they address the proliferation problem from the demand and supply side and, in the process, produce none of the costs associated with NMD. But these popular policy pronouncements rarely include the details policy-makers need to compare them to NMD.

If one were to look at the money already invested, not only by the United States but also globally, on programmes tied to transparency, monitoring, verification, and economic sanctions, I suspect the total far exceeds the proposed investment in NMD. What exactly do we have to show for all these efforts, strategies, and investments? Even the most optimistic take on the proliferation record is not particularly encouraging – witness the recent failure of inspection, monitoring, verification, and sanctions regimes in Iraq, North Korea, India, and Pakistan. Where exactly is the proof that another $60 billion invested in these strategies is more cost-effective, or more likely to address (prevent) ballistic missile threats circa 2005–2008? How exactly will diplomatic efforts to "engage" Iraq, Iran, or North Korea prevent them from developing their nuclear programmes, and what is the probability of success – 76 per cent? 30 per cent? Wouldn't improved economic relations provide the same capital required for these states to augment their receptive nuclear and ballistic weapons facilities? How probable is that outcome? Ah, ask the critics, but isn't it time we took the risk? Based on the evidence so far, no it is not!

Critics in the "human security" community are fond of claiming that there are so many other, more relevant threats – drug trafficking, environmental degradation, world hunger and disease, AIDS, intrastate ethnic conflict, refugees, terrorism, chemical and biological weapons proliferation – that should receive the bulk of security-related expenditures. But the existence of a threat says nothing about how the problems can be addressed, whether transferring NMD's $60 billion from the defence budget is a better and more cost-effective investment in security, or whether the transfer will do anything to address evolving ballistic missile threats (however remote they may be). Like NMD, decisions about which programme to fund, or which security threats to solve, must be based on a balanced evaluation of the costs, risks, and the probability of accomplishing objectives.

Consider the combined investments in "human security" by some of the largest United States or European aid agencies over the last ten years (the same time frame for NMD's $60 billion procurement). Now, track the trends in drug trafficking, environmental degradation, AIDS, ethnic conflict, etc., during the same period. Notwithstanding the billions of dollars invested globally by several countries, international agencies, and non-governmental organizations, the problems have arguably become worse. How would another $60 billion help resolve these or similar "human security" problems, and are the benefits (and attendant probabilities of realizing them) likely to make an equal (or greater) contribution to United States security than $60 billion on NMD?

Obviously, I am not suggesting that we should stop funding programmes to combat other serious problems. But critics should acknowledge the fact that many of these "other" problems and related solutions are incredibly complex, perhaps even more complex than interceptor technology, because their success depends on the support, sacrifice, and sponsorship of political and military officials within developing countries. In many cases solutions are made even more difficult by ruling elite who have other priorities – environmental security and controlling child labour, for example, are not likely to be priorities in a country whose leaders are trying to encourage foreign investment through cheap labour and low production costs. In addition, many human security threats are highly interconnected and interdependent, which further complicates the search for cost-effective solutions. Critics will continue to make reference to these "other" security concerns when criticizing expenditures on NMD, but they should be honest about the costs and success rates associated with resolving their preferred security threats.

In sum, if the relative importance of these "other" threats is debatable to begin with, and if they are complex, interdependent, and very difficult to resolve because of existing international and domestic impediments, and if investing in them instead of in NMD does absolutely nothing to resolve ballistic missile threats, then how exactly does transferring $60 billion in defence funds to "human security" problems make any practical sense? The specifics remain elusive, for obvious reasons.

NMD AND CANADIAN POLICY OPTIONS

Critics have warned Canadians that NMD will be costly. What they fail to point out is that little if any of the costs will be placed on the shoulders of Canadian taxpayers. Ottawa has not been asked to contribute a red cent to the project, and, unfortunately, Canadian companies are unlikely to compete for the larger defence contracts. Some critics will continue to mention "costs" at every opportunity, but they should admit that the United States is more than willing to pay for (and develop) the technology in-house – for all of the reasons outlined above.

The failure in July 2000 of the last three crucial interceptor tests will have no significant effect on the project – scientists (and United States senators) acquired no new information about components central to the functioning of NMD.[14] The kill vehicle failed to separate from the booster rocket, but the technology has been functioning successfully for decades in particularly every major space mission, satellite launch, and shuttle project in the history of the National Aeronautical Space Administration (NASA).[15] Ironically, the only clear failure, aside from booster separation, was the balloon designed as a basic countermeasure. This is likely to be far more upsetting to those critics who offer the simplicity of countermeasure technology as a reason to scrap the programme – if the United States is having a hard time deploying a decoy, what does that suggest about the capacity of developing countries to accomplish the same task?

In the end, Canada's position on NMD will have very little to do with the costs of the programme, the success or failure of interceptor technology, the relative merits of NMD versus boost-phase strategies, the implications for arms control and disarmament, or the warnings from China or Russia. These are issues at the heart of debates in the United States – Canada's position will depend on how they are resolved south of the border. Whether or not Canadian officials accept as valid the logic and utility of NMD, Ottawa will drop the subject if the United States decides to scrap the programme (regardless of its merits). The real choice during and after the 2000 presidential campaign is not "whether" NMD will be developed but "how" it will move forward – as a Democratically sponsored NMD or as a Republican version of the Strategic Defense Initiative (SDI)? The technology has matured to the point where United States policies will continue to shift to accommodate it, especially given the prospects for improvements. More specific predictions about the system's architecture, therefore, will depend primarily on domestic politics in the United States.

Many critics in Canada claim that a decision by Ottawa to reject NMD would have little, if any, effect on Canada–United States relations. But those who make that argument never explain in detail why the United States would accept such a decision without responding, or why Canada's relations with the United States in North American Aerospace Defence (NORAD) would be unaffected. There are few, if any, historical precedents to defend that position. The critics' response is that we do not need cold war relics like NORAD. But just what is the argument here: that there will be no consequences if Canada rejects NMD, or that the consequences will be irrelevant? Few, if any, details are offered to defend either position. Ironically, a break with NORAD would have a direct effect on Canada's access to the very satellite technology required for information on transparency, verification, and monitoring – all of which are more cost-effective alternatives to the proliferation problem, according to critics.

The dilemma for Canadian policy-makers is NMD's departures from principles and precedents embedded in the ABM treaty. For a variety of domestic political reasons, it makes perfect sense for Canadian officials to hold off on major policy statements until the United States makes a definitive move. But because the United States is unlikely to scrap NMD, Canada will have to consider its support for the programme sometime. Perhaps the most effective (and politically acceptable) approach would be for Canadian officials to emphasize the benefits of NMD in comparison to a full-blown SDI programme – ironically, by using many of the arguments put forward by critics of NMD. While the arguments are not particularly relevant (or persuasive) when applied to NMD, they are useful as criticisms of SDI – a more robust system that will depend on significantly more expensive space-based lasers, none of which is essential for addressing current or short-term threats from "states of concern." NMD, in other words, is the most balanced, stable, and affordable alternative today. Canada's decision to support the programme is the right one, not because the United States favours it, but because, all things considered, NMD makes sense for Canadian security and defence.

NOTES

I am very grateful to Brian Buckley and David Mutimer for their helpful comments on an earlier draft of the paper.

1. Relevant charts can be obtained from the Natural Resources Defense Council web page: http://www.nrdc.org/nuclear/nudb/datainx.asp.

2. Note 12 lists resources that highlight the threats tied to ballistic missile proliferation and fissile material theft.

3. The analogy is less than ideal, of course, because the NYPD has the capacity and authority to arrest criminals – police can credibly threaten a myriad of punishments to prevent criminal activity. There are no parallel international institutions that can effectively monitor, prevent, or reverse proliferation by states that decide to acquire the technology or successfully sanction those who break laws or other treaty obligations.

4. This logic is used today by American nuclear strategists to justify increasing the number of targets from 2,500 (in 1995) to 3,000 today, mostly to address threats from China, Iran, Iraq, and North Korea. See Hugo Young, "Secrets of Washington's nuclear madness revealed," *Guardian Weekly*, 22 June 2000.

5. For an excellent collection of articles summarizing these patterns, see Zachary S. Davis and Benjamin Frankel, eds., *The Proliferation Puzzle: Why Nuclear Weapons Spread and What Results* (London: Frank Cass 1993). See also William C. Potter and Harlan W. Jencks, eds., *The International Missile Bazaar: The New Suppliers' Network* (Boulder, CO and London: Westview, 1994).

6. For a detailed analysis of China's evolving nuclear policy see Brad Roberts, Robert A. Manning, and Ronald N. Montaperto, "China: the forgotten nuclear power," *Foreign Affairs 79* (July/August 2000). For an interesting discussion of China's position on bombing or invading Taiwan see http://www.washingtonpost.com/wp-dyn/articles/A7467–2000Jul8.html.

7. For additional details about Russia's SS-X-27 missile programme, see http://www.softwar.net/SS27.html, which claims that: "The first deployment was reported to be in a SS-19 silo complex located at Tatishchevo in January of 1998 . . . The mobile Russian SS-27 also raises serious proliferation questions since the Moscow Institute of Thermal Technology is providing the SS-27 design to China. China intends to produce the TOPOL-M missile under the designation 'Dong Feng' (East Wind) DF-41. The DF-41 is expected to be deployed with Chinese manufactured nuclear warheads also designed with the aid of U.S. super computers."

8. The overview is from William Broad, "A missile defence with limits: the ABC's of the Clinton plan," http://www10.nytimes.com/library/world/americas/063000missileplan.html (30 June 2000). Additional details of NMD architecture can be found at: http://www.acq.osd.mil/bmdo/bmdolink/html.

9. Burton Richter, "It doesn't take rocket science," *Washington Post*, 23 July 2000, B02. http://www.washingtonpost.com/wp-dyn/articles/A25940–2000Jul22.html.

10. Ibid.

11. Why would any leader be foolish enough to launch an attack on the United States in the first place, critics will ask. But that popular question overlooks the other objective of NMD: to prevent opponents from believing that they can deter the United States (or NATO) from launching a conventional attack. Protecting United States (and Canadian/European) bargaining leverage in Bosnia, Kosovo, Iraq, Taiwan, and North Korea is as relevant to NMD as protecting North America from a missile attack. Critics may be right in claiming the North Korean leaders are not likely to launch an attack (or even issue a nuclear threat) unless some crisis (for example, one that involves the United States over South Korea) escalates out of control. But the key question for United States policy-makers is whether, in the midst of this hypothetical conventional war, the probability of confronting an explicit nuclear threat from

North Korea increases or decreases with/without NMD. In earlier stages of this crisis, does the probability of confronting a conventional war initiated by North Korea increase or decrease with/without NMD? And, to step even further back, does the probability of confronting crisis escalation by North Korea increase or decrease with/without NMD? And in terms of the initial stage of the crisis, are the incentives for crisis management and resolution higher or lower for the North Korean leadership with/without NMD? At each stage of the crisis United States NMD is likely to be more stabilizing, unless North Korean leaders are irrational. The critics respond that that is precisely the problem — North Korean leaders may be irrational and completely upset the logic associated with the simplistic, "rational choice" interpretation of the scenario offered by proponents of NMD. Fair enough, but in addition to defending the culturally insensitive assertion that North Korean leaders are less rational than Western leaders, critics are now faced with having to explain why North Korea would contemplate launching a ballistic missile, an action they previously concluded was highly unlikely and a fabrication of the military industrial complex. See Harvey, "Proliferation, rogue-states and national missile defence" (*Canadian Military Journal*, forthcoming, 2000).

12. A simple web search for keywords "nuclear proliferation" or "ballistic missile proliferation" should provide the optimists with sufficient information to reconsider their position. Here is a small sample:

   http://www.fas.org/irp/threat/bm-threat.htm;

   http://www.fas.org/nuke/guide/iran/missile/;

   http://www.stimson.org/policy/nucleardangers.htm;

   http://www.cia.gov/cia/publications/nie/nie99msl.html;

   http://www.editors.sipri.se/pubs/pressre/akbk.html;

   http://www.cato.org/pubs/fpbriefs/fpb-051es.html;

   http://www.ceip.org/programs/npp/bmtestimony.htm;

   http://www.defenselink.mil/news/Jan1999/to1201999_to120md.html;

   http://www.cns.miis.edu/pubs/npr/moltz975.htm (Center for NonProliferation Studies);

   http://www.nuclearfiles.org/prolif/;

   http://www.aph.gov.au/library/pubs/cib/1999–2000/2000cib01.htm.

13. The "technological limitations" arguments has now shifted from debates about whether a defence system should be deployed at all to debates about which system is better: NMD or the alternative offered by Putin during the Clinton-Putin summit in June 2000. Now that Russia has acknowledged United States concerns about ballistic missile proliferation, the key question is whether a theatre missile defense system (based on boost phase interceptor technology) is more likely than NMD to succeed. Russia has so far been unclear on specifics.

14. One week after the second of three failed interceptor tests, the United States Senate approved a $1.9 billion expenditure for the next stage of the NMD programme. Audrey Hudson, "Senate approves $1.9 billion for missile defense," *Washington Times*, 14 July 2000.

15. A failure with booster separation was not even considered among the thousands of potential problems, for obvious reasons. For commentary by Kadish immediately following the failed test, see http://www.cnn.com/2000/US/07/08/missile.defense.04/index.html.

POSTSCRIPT

In the introduction, mention was made of the Rumsfeld Commission's 1998 report, which highlighted the need to respond to the ballistic missile threat. Since then, Donald Rumsfeld has been appointed secretary of defense in the Bush administration and is a key figure in the "war on terrorism." In the immediate aftermath of September 11, 2001, there was some uncertainty about the future of BMD. American attention appeared to be shifting to the threat posed by potential use of biological and chemical weapons against the United States. However, the 2002 *National Security Strategy*, enunciating the Bush Doctrine, gave a prominent place to the role of missile defence in its strategy against "rogue states." Subsequent budgets of the Bush administration devoted significantly increased funds to research and development of a space-based missile defence system.

A growing number of countries have expressed support for the American BMD plans. John Howard, prime minister of Australia, announced that his government would be "recklessly negligent" if it did not have some involvement in the program. Japan also announced its support. The prime minister of India, Atal Behari Vajpayee, revealed that his government was expanding discussions with the United States on its BMD program.

In Canada, the Liberal government, despite its opposition to the war against Iraq, has shown increased interest in the American BMD program. In January 2004, David Pratt, the Canadian defence minister, wrote to Donald Rumsfeld to express interest in entering into negotiations on the role that Canada might play in the development of such a missile shield. In his letter, he made it clear that the discussion should take place in the context of NORAD, the North American Aerospace Defence Command. But he appeared to place no real conditions on the talks, thus seeming to signal a growing willingness to participate directly in the missile defence program.

How do such discussions fit into Canada's traditional support for multilateral anti-proliferation efforts? Would participation in the plan represent a reversal of Canada's previous opposition to the militarization of space? If, as the critics suggest, Canada chose not to support the American plans, what would be the repercussions on Canadian–American relations? Given the growing American preoccupation with "homeland security," does Canada have much political leeway in choosing not to participate in the program?

Suggested Additional Readings

Axworthy, Lloyd. "Canada and Ballistic Missile Defence." Vancouver: Liu Institute for Global Issues, February 15–16, 2001. Available at www.ligi.ubc.ca.

Boese, Wade. "Missile Defense Post–ABM Treaty: No System, No Arms Race." *Arms Control Today* 33, no. 5 (June 2003): 20–24.

Cirincione, Joseph. "Why the Right Lost the Missile Defense Debate." *Foreign Policy* 106 (Spring 1997): 38–55.

_____, and Frank von Hippel. *The Last Fifteen Minutes: Ballistic Missile Defense in Perspective*. Washington, D.C.: Coalition to Reduce Nuclear Dangers, 1996.

Dean, Jonathon. "Step-by-Step Control over Ballistic and Cruise Missiles." *Disarmament and Diplomacy* 31 (October 1998): 2–11.

Fergusson, James. "Round Table: Missile Defence in a Post-September 11th Context." *Canadian Foreign Policy* 9, no. 2 (Winter 2002): 111–30.

Fitzgerald, Francis. *Way Out There in the Blue*. New York: Simon & Schuster, 2000.

Gimblett, Richard. "A Strategic Overview of the Canadian Security Environment." *Canadian Foreign Policy* 9, no. 3 (Spring 2002): 7–20.

Gronland, Lisbeth, and David Wright. "Missile Defense: The Sequel." *Technology Review* (May–June 1997): 29–36.

Handberg, Roger. *Ballistic Missile Defense and the Future of American Security: Agendas, Perceptions, Technology, and Policy*. Westport, Conn.: Praeger Publishers, 2001.

Hentz, James J. "The Paradox of Instability: United States 'Primacy,' China, and the National Missile Defense (NMD) Debate." *Defense & Security Analysis* 19, no. 3 (September 2003): 293–99.

Karp, Aaron. *Ballistic Missile Proliferation: The Politics and Technics*. Stockholm: Stockholm International Peace Research Institute, 1995.

Lewis, George, et al. "Why National Missile Defense Won't Work." *Scientific American* (August 1999): 36–41.

Mason, Dwight. "Canada and Missile Defense." *Canada Alert*. Washington: Hemisphere Focus, Center for Strategic and International Studies, June 6, 2003.

Mendelsohn, Jack. "Missile Defense: And It Still Won't Work." *Bulletin of the Atomic Scientists* (May–June 1999): 29–31.

Regehr, Ernie. *Full Report: Canada and Ballistic Missile Defence*. Vancouver: Liu Institute for Global Issues/Simon Centre for Peace and Disarmament Studies, December 20, 2003. Available at www.ligi.ubc.ca/simons.htm.

InfoTrac® College Edition

Search for the following articles in the InfoTrac® database:

Kennedy, Brian. "Protecting Our Nation: The Urgent Need for Ballistic Missile Defense." *Vital Speeches of the Day* 68, no. 6 (January 1, 2002): 165–69.

Denoon, David. "Review of Fatal Choice: Nuclear Weapons and the Illusion of Missile Defense." *Ethics & International Affairs* 16, no. 2 (October 2002): 175–77.

Garwin, Richard L. "Review of Defending America: The Case for Limited National Missile Defense." *Political Science Quarterly* 117, no. 2 (Summer 2002): 311–12.

For more articles, enter:
"BMD" in the keyword search.
"ballistic missile defense" in the subject guide.

Web Resources

For current URLs for the following websites, visit www.crosscurrents.nelson.com.

CARNEGIE ENDOWMENT FOR INTERNATIONAL PEACE

www.ceip.org

This site offers extensive list of resources on missile defence issues.

CENTER FOR DEFENSE INFORMATION

www.cdi.org

This website provides extensive information on ballistic missile defence, including a regular CDI Defense Monitor.

CENTER FOR SECURITY POLICY

www.centerforsecuritypolicy.org

The website of this conservative think tank offers an extensive collection of publications on BMD.

COUNCIL FOR A LIVABLE WORLD

www.clw.org/nmd.html

This lobby opposed to BMD provides a range of resource materials. Check out its detailed *Briefing Book on Ballistic Missile Defense*.

PROJECT PLOUGHSHARES

www.ploughshares.ca

Canada's leading peace-research institute has a large archive of resources on BMD addressing the issue from various perspectives.

Has NATO Become Irrelevant in an Age of Terrorism?

✔ **YES**
STEVEN MEYER, "Carcass of Dead Policies: The Irrelevance of NATO,"
Parameters 33, no. 4 (Winter 2003–04): 83–97

✗ **NO**
REBECCA JOHNSON AND MICAH ZENKO, "All Dressed Up and No Place
to Go: Why NATO Should Be on the Front Lines in the War on Terror,"
Parameters 32, no. 4 (Winter 2002–03): 48–63

On March 29, 2004, the leaders of seven states — Bulgaria, Estonia, Latvia, Lithuania, Romania, Slovakia, and Slovenia — met in Washington, D.C., to present their "instruments of accession" to the North Atlantic Treaty Organization. With the addition of these states, the membership in NATO is now twenty-six, an increase of ten members since the end of the Cold War. Representatives from three other countries hoping to join the alliance organization in the future — Albania, Croatia, and Macedonia — also attended the ceremonies.

In a speech marking the event, U.S. secretary of state, Colin Powell, recalled that NATO was originally founded to provide "defense of a common territory." Now, he proclaimed, "our enemies seek not only the death of multitudes but the death of liberty itself . . . we stand united in the global war against terrorism, a war that compels the resistance of all free peoples and must be won by free peoples together in alliance." Secretary Powell noted that rather than simply preventing aggression, the future role of NATO would be "to promote freedom, to extend the reach of liberty, and to deepen the peace." He concluded, "I am confident that with the new energy that these seven nations bring to our alliance, our alliance will be as successful in the future as it has been in the past." Secretary Powell's prediction of a positive and expansive future for NATO stands in contrast to the view held by many others who have increasingly questioned the relevance of NATO, especially in an age of terrorism, when the principal threat to security comes from non-state actors. It also appears to stand in contrast to the policies of an American administration that has emphasized its willingness to act unilaterally to protect its national interests. In order to understand this debate, it is useful to briefly recall the history of NATO.

Founded in 1949, NATO originally consisted of ten European nations, Canada, and the United States. The original European members (Belgium, Britain, Denmark, France, Iceland, Italy, Luxembourg, the Netherlands, Norway, and

Portugal) were later joined by Greece, Turkey, West Germany, and Spain. NATO forces are composed of members' armed forces, while the United States, as the dominant partner in the alliance, provides the Allied Commander, Europe. Political accountability is assured through the North Atlantic Council, composed of ministers from each member state and a permanent ambassador in residence in Brussels, Belgium, the location of NATO headquarters.

From its inception, the major purpose of NATO was to deter, and repel if necessary, an armed attack on Western Europe by the Soviet Union and its allies in the Warsaw Pact. In this sense, NATO was a classical defensive alliance. It existed principally because of the perceived threat from the Soviets. In addition, NATO was intended to foster political cooperation and reduce conflict within Europe so that the Soviets could not take advantage of any perceived weaknesses in Western solidarity.

When the Soviet Union collapsed and the Cold War came to an end, the future of NATO came increasingly into question. If the U.S.S.R. is no longer a security threat, from whom is NATO protecting Europe? Without a clear security threat to consolidate support from its members, can NATO hope to survive at all? One response to these questions has been to identify a broader field of concern for NATO security interests. In 1993, the NATO alliance agreed to the general principle of participating in peacekeeping operations outside its traditional sphere of influence. It was argued that unless NATO played some role in helping to mitigate regional hostilities, the ethnic conflicts in the Balkans, Southern and Eastern Europe, and Russia itself could drag the neighbouring NATO members into a wider European war. As a result, when the former Yugoslavia disintegrated into ethnic fighting, NATO became involved in both Bosnia and Kosovo, launching military strikes and later providing ground forces in an attempt to quell the fighting. These interventions were seen by many as a test to demonstrate the future relevance of NATO. To some this intervention showed that NATO was willing to respond to security threats on its perimeter, while others perceived it as demonstrating the limitations of the NATO alliance for responding to the "new" threats. For example, some American military officials complained that the lengthy time that it took to obtain approval from all of the participants for every list of bombing targets had severely damaged the effectiveness of NATO actions.

The terrorist attacks on the United States on September 11, 2001, raised new questions about the future relevance of NATO. Article 5 of the North Atlantic Treaty, which states that an attack against any member is an attack against all members, was invoked by NATO for the first time in response to these attacks. However, all of the subsequent military actions in relation to Afghanistan, Iraq, and more generally as part of the "war on terrorism" have been organized by the United States through an ad hoc "coalition of the willing" and not under the aegis of NATO. In fact, the opposition of key NATO members such as France and Germany to the war in Iraq has revealed deep divisions with the alliance itself.

The new Bush Doctrine, while mentioning the continuing importance of alliances, placed significant weight on the necessity of taking unilateral actions in order to secure the national interest.

Despite these concerns about the future role of NATO, expansion of membership in the alliance itself has remained a high priority. In January 1994 at the NATO summit, allied leaders committed themselves to accepting new members into the alliance, as provided for under article 10 of the North Atlantic Treaty. The 1994 Brussels Declaration of NATO Heads of State and Government affirmed that membership in the alliance was open to other European states, as long as they were willing to contribute to the security of the North Atlantic area and to further the principles of the Washington Treaty. In other words, they must be committed to democratization. After a series of negotiations, in 1999, three former Warsaw Pact members — Hungary, Poland, and the Czech Republic — joined the alliance. The ceremonies in Washington in March 2004 marked the second round of membership expansion since the end of the Cold War.

Does this continued expansion of membership mark the beginning of a new and hopeful future for the NATO alliance? Or does it just mask the ongoing irrelevance and decline of an outdated artifact of the Cold War? In the following essay, Steven Meyer argues that NATO has become largely irrelevant in the current security context. He contends that it is time for members of NATO to admit to the myth of the alliance's continuing relevance and to dissolve the organization. In response, Rebecca Johnson and Micah Zenko argue that NATO is far from being irrelevant and that more attention should be invested in giving it a larger role in facing the new security threats. They call on the members of NATO to take their potential role in the war on terrorism more seriously and on the United States to invest more attention in supporting such a role for the alliance.

✔ **YES**

Carcass of Dead Policies: The Irrelevance of NATO*

STEVEN MEYER

In 1877, Lord Salisbury, commenting on Great Britain's policy on the Eastern Question, noted that "the commonest error in politics is sticking to the carcass of dead policies."[1] Salisbury was bemoaning the fact that many influential members of the British ruling class could not recognize that history had moved on; they continued to cling to policies and institutions that were relics of another era. Salisbury went on to note that the cost was enormous because this preoccupation with anachronism damaged Britain's real interests. Despite Salisbury's clever words, his observation is nothing new. Throughout Western history policymakers often have tended to rely on past realities, policies, and institutions to assess and deal with contemporary and future situations.

Post-Cold War American policymakers have not been immune from falling into this trap. Indeed, this inertial approach, characterized by Washington's unbending support for NATO and its expansion, has defined American foreign and security policy since the collapse of the Soviet Union and the bipolar world. During the Cold War, NATO provided the proper linchpin of American – and West European – security policy, and served as a useful, even fundamental deterrent to Soviet military might and expansionism. However, NATO's time has come and gone, and today there is no legitimate reason for it to exist. Although the strong differences exhibited in the Alliance over the war against Iraq have accelerated NATO's irrelevancy, the root causes of its problems go much deeper. Consequently, for both the United States and Europe, NATO is at best an irrelevant distraction and at worst toxic to their respective contemporary security needs.

THE INERTIAL IMPERATIVE

The end of the Cold War presented a problem similar to the one faced by post-World War II American leaders. A tectonic shift had occurred that required innovation, creativity, and a real understanding of the evolving world. For some experts – both in government and academia, as well as on both sides of the Atlantic – the collapse of the Soviet Union and the Warsaw Pact called into question the need for NATO. They recognized that an era had ended and the time was ripe for a basic debate about the future of NATO and Western security policies and structures.

*The views expressed in this article are personal ones and do not reflect the official policy or position of the National Defense University, the Department of Defense, or the U.S. Government.

Unfortunately, the policymakers in Washington who established the priorities for the post-Cold War era reacted quite differently from their predecessors. A small, influential coterie of policymakers in the elder Bush and then the Clinton administrations reacted reflexively and inertially, cutting off what should have been useful debate on the future. Moreover, virtually all of the officials who helped define the foreign and security policy in the Bush "41" Administration have resurfaced in the current Bush Administration. According to them, the existence and viability of NATO was not to be questioned. It was to remain basically the same successful alliance of American and European foreign and security policy that it had been since 1949. But a fundamental change was taking place in the post-Cold War security environment. In 1949, a genuine, measurable security threat justified NATO for all its members. Now, with the end of the Cold War, the inertial attachment to NATO meant that the alliance had to seek or invent reasons to justify its existence and relevance.

American officials recognized the threats to the alliance. NATO needed props. Expansion into the former Warsaw Pact was one. Not only did expansion provide a whole new raison d'etre for the alliance, but – perhaps more important – it spawned a large new bureaucracy and the accompanying "busyness" that provide the lifeblood of institutions trying to justify their existence. At the same time, the theological mantra changed. Since there was no longer an enemy, NATO could not be described as a defensive alliance, it now was to be a combination of a wide-ranging political and collective security alliance. There were only two avenues the countries of Central and Eastern Europe could take if they wanted to join the West: NATO for security interests, and the European Union for economic interests. No other avenues were acceptable.

Consequently, in 1999 Poland, Hungary, and the Czech Republic joined NATO, and in November 2002 the Baltic countries, Slovakia, Slovenia, Bulgaria, and Romania accepted invitations to join the alliance.

In addition to expansion, the crisis in the Balkans also came to NATO's rescue. For the Clinton Administration, the former Yugoslavia was never really the most important point. NATO credibility was. This distinction is fundamental because policies that were designed to justify NATO were not necessarily the same as those that would deal successfully with issues in the former Yugoslavia. Clinton Administration spokesmen often pointed out that our vital interest was in preserving the alliance and vindicating our leadership of it. [. . .]

Although the current Bush Administration's focus has been riveted on the post-9/11 war on terrorism and Iraq, it has remained staunchly committed to NATO and its expansion. In its approach to the NATO Summit in Prague in November 2002, the alliance's serious problems were ignored, downplayed, or glossed over. For example, in congressional testimony in February 2002, a high-level Administration official said that NATO expansion was an exercise in "how much we can do to advance the cause of freedom," and that we must strengthen

NATO's military capability and political solidarity.[2] In October 2002, in an address to the NATO Parliamentary Assembly, another Administration official noted that NATO "remains the essential link between Europe and North America—the place for free nations to secure peace, security, and liberty."[3]

But no one explains what all of this means — whose freedom, peace, security, and liberty are endangered? Who, after all, is the enemy? How is it possible to argue that there is any sense of political solidarity in the wake of the alliance's deep split over Iraq? NATO enthusiasts repeat their mantra by rote, but none of it justifies supporting a failing alliance.

INEVITABLE DECLINE

There are five interrelated reasons why post-Cold War rhetoric and inertial symbolism no longer conform to reality.

- *First, the legitimate threat that justified NATO really is gone.* All three
  US administrations since the collapse of the Soviet Union have paid lip service to this aphorism. For more than a decade, US security has advocated cooperation with Russia, but the structural and functional reality is quite different. Essentially, we are following a modified version of the post-World War I model, which excluded the defeated Germany from European and Western councils, rather than the more positive post-1815 and post-1945 models of including former enemies as quickly and completely as possible into the new security system. Consequently, the NATO-Russia Founding Act, the old Permanent Joint Council, and the new NATO-Russia Council speak more to separation and isolation than they do to cooperation and inclusion. They reinforce the fault line in Europe, unnecessarily dividing the continent into "ins" and "outs," with Russia clearly still "out."[4]

  The fundamental problem has been the inability of the post-Cold War American—and European—leadership to move beyond old organizations, policies, and philosophies to build organizations, policies, and philosophies that are more appropriate to the current age. Ever since the end of the Cold War and the ascendancy of the United States as the world's only superpower, American foreign policy has been formulated and controlled by a very small coterie of elites from both the Democratic and Republican parties who share a remarkable synonymy of interests, values, and outlooks, differing only at the margins.

- *Second, the whole nature of contemporary European politics has changed so fundamentally that it has outgrown NATO-type alliances.* For the first time in about 1,800 years, there is no world-class threat to or from any European state or combination of European states that requires a wide-ranging, comprehensive alliance such as NATO.[5] For the most part, borders are set, uncontested, and peaceful. Aggressive nationalism (although not nationalism itself) and the race for arms and empire that so dominated the politics of every major power from the 16th through the early 20th centuries are gone.

In Western Europe, the political struggle has replaced many of the characteristics of Westphalian sovereignty with a more intricate system of regions, states, and supranational organizations. The "constitutional conference" launched in March 2002 ultimately may determine what happens to the residue of traditional sovereignty in Western Europe. The situation is different in Central Europe, where states are trying to reestablish democracy and civil society after years of Nazi and communist tyranny, while at the same time struggling to meet the requirements to join the European Union. And the collapse of the Stalinist system has resolved the "Soviet Question" that dominated much of the second half of the 20th century. Although we can't predict Russia's future exactly, it is highly unlikely that the Stalinist system will be reestablished, and by including Russia as an equal we greatly enhance her prospects for a stable political order and a more traditional, non-antagonistic relationship with the United States and the rest of the West.

The modern sense of security in Europe not only is broader than what even the new form of NATO is built for, it is different in *kind*, and it is best summarized in the (Maastricht) Treaty on European Union (1990–92) and the follow-up Treaty of Amsterdam (1997). These treaties speak to an understanding of security that includes issues of justice, environment, ethnicity, economic development, crime, and terrorism, in addition to references to more narrowly military definitions of security. In those sections of the Maastricht and Amsterdam treaties that deal with a "common foreign and security policy," NATO is not mentioned, but several references are made to the Western European Union. Neither treaty envisions NATO as an integral part of Europe's security future, and a major reason it has been so difficult to implement the "common foreign and security policy" parts of these treaties is because NATO stands as both an impediment and an intimidation to Europe's future.

Of course, the United States does have interests in common with the Europe that is emerging, but without the kind of overall mutual threat we faced in the past, they are much more issue-specific. For example, economic ties now provide America's single most important relationship with Europe— both as partner and competitor. However, we are doing much less than we should do to prepare for the future of this relationship, in part because we are distracted by an anachronistic security relationship. We also have other common interests in such areas as the environment, terrorism, and others, none of which are particularly well suited to resolution by NATO or any other like alliance. Occasionally, the United States and specific European countries or groups of countries may need to engage in joint military activities – the Gulf War in the early 1990s and the more recent war in Afghanistan provide two excellent examples. In both cases coalitions were put together to deal with specific issues and, during both, NATO was little more than a "truck stop." But these conflicts were unique. It was impossible to recreate the Gulf War alliance to confront Iraq in 2003, and within a year or two we probably will be saying the same thing about multilateral cooperation in Afghanistan. At the same time, there also are strong differences between the United States and much of Western Europe on a growing number of issues – such as how to deal with Iraq, the Israeli-Palestinian horror, abrogation of the ABM Treaty, disagreement over the Kyoto Treaty, and accusations in the European press and among European officials about "American hegemony" or "American hyperpower."

As Robert Kagan argues, the differences between the United States and Europe go to much deeper philosophical and anthropological levels.[6] As the US view of engaging the world has become increasingly ideological, that of the Europeans has become increasingly pragmatic. Both sides retain a sense of superiority and arrogance when dealing with the third world. For the Europeans, however, this tends to be more cultural, while for the United States it is a divine mission. Consequently, the United States takes more seriously what Anthony Padgen describes as the "vision of a single 'orbis terrarum'" – the notion "of a presumed right of lordship over the entire world," which, ironically, had been a hallmark of the European empire in America.[7]

In an environment of shifting interests and philosophies between Europe and the United States, Americans and Europeans still share – at least in theory – a respect for democratic values. But that is not enough to hold NATO together. There also is a growing transatlantic split over a range of primary issues: the size, sophistication, and use of military power; environmental issues; budget priorities, including welfare expenditures; the role of state sovereignty, involving especially the evolution of the European Union; and more.[8]

- *Third, as NATO's relevance has declined as a security organization in the West, it also has become less important for Russian security interests.* For a while after the Cold War, NATO enlargement was a top Russian foreign policy concern, and Russia's leaders almost uniformly opposed enlargement as a direct threat to their country's vital interests.

But while opposition to NATO remains strong in the Russian military, for President Putin and his primary leadership circle, the salience of NATO for Russia's security interests has declined dramatically since the 9/11 terrorist attacks. For example, the opposition of Putin and other Russian officials to the inclusion of the Baltic states in NATO – a crisis in Russian-Western relations just a few years ago–has become virtually a non-issue. The Putin government supported the establishment of US military bases in Central Asia after 9/11, an area still considered part of the Russian "near abroad," which was unthinkable before the terrorist attacks. In addition, there has been only mild opposition to the Bush Administration's decision to abrogate the 1972 ABM Treaty. Finally, the serious bickering between the United States and NATO partners in "Old Europe" over Iraq apparently has convinced Putin that Russian interests are best served by holding the alliance at arm's length. [. . .]

For most Russian leaders – more so than for their American counterparts – the events of 11 September 2001 finally brought the Cold War to an end. Concern about terrorism has prompted Putin to seek a new strategic relationship with the West that preferably would replace NATO and end the artificial divide between east and west. Shortly after 9/11, Putin observed that "all nations are to blame for the terrorist attacks on the United States because they trust outdated security systems. . . . [W]e have failed to recognize the changes of the last 10 years."[9] [. . .]

- *Fourth, expansion to the east actually damages the legitimate interests of the new NATO members.* NATO membership does not protect the countries of Central and Eastern Europe from any recognizable security threat. The usual argument advanced by NATO enthusiasts is that the new members will become "consumers" of security rather than "providers" of security. But, again, security against or from what? What, for example, is the security threat to Hungary, or Slovenia, or the Czech Republic, or even Poland that requires NATO membership? There is no traditional security threat to these countries that could not be handled by the Europeans themselves – if they have the political will to do so. [. . .]

Enlargement puts the Central and East European members in an unnecessary and rapidly debilitating political and financial position. In particular, the countries of Central and Eastern Europe are becoming increasingly enmeshed in a conflict of loyalty between NATO and the European Union. Despite the propaganda that NATO and the EU are two legitimate, complementary avenues of development, in fact they are becoming increasingly competitive – for attention, loyalty, and resources. Although this problem is gaining momentum in Western Europe, it is becoming especially acute in Central and Eastern Europe, where the resource base is considerably smaller and political affiliations more fragile.

As a result, "since their accession on March 12, 1999, Poland, Hungary, and the Czech Republic have all experienced integration difficulties,"[10] because the real demands of economic and social issues lead to "economic constraints" and "a failure of political will."[11] And still, NATO and EU authorities continue to press these strapped economies to live up to difficult and at times mutually exclusive commitments that undermine pressing economic and social programs. [. . .]

In addition, NATO membership — including vulnerability to Western arms merchants — damages the ability of these countries to deal with genuine emerging security issues. Issues of social and economic justice, crime and corruption, environmental degradation, and ethnic reconciliation bear more directly on the security futures of these countries than does their struggle to satisfy NATO's arcane demands for membership. Consequently, instead of pressing these countries to spend scarce resources on NATO, Washington should encourage them to focus exclusively on European and regional organizations that are better geared to help address the real, pressing interests of the countries of Central and Eastern Europe.[12]

- *Fifth, since the end of the Cold War, NATO's programs and instruments have expanded seemingly exponentially, and its organizing rationale has changed.* Virtually every summit — especially since the fall of communism — has been concerned with attempts to "redefine" or "reinvent" NATO in an effort to ignore history and make NATO relevant to the new reality. [. . .]

As the Cold War faded into history, NATO enthusiasts began to argue that the very nature of the alliance had to change if it was to continue to exist. Consequently, as Henry Kissinger noted, NATO "has become more akin to a collective security organization, like the United Nations, than to a traditional alliance."[13] If the alliance was to survive, it had to find a rationale that did not depend on a clearly defined enemy, or even a potential enemy. A loosely formed "collective security organization" was the answer.

In reality, these two types of alliances represent a distinction without a difference. Even in a collective "security alliance," there must be at least some overriding common security bond that holds the participants together. As noted before, quite the opposite is happening — not only on security issues, but in the political realm as well. The NATO that has emerged since the end of the Cold War does not satisfy even the most rudimentary tests of what an alliance is supposed to do. For example, it fails both Stephen Walt's "five . . . explanations for international alliances" and Glenn Snyder's theory of alliance formation and management.[14] And, the further we get from the Cold War, the more serious those frictions will become as the nexus of values and interests between the United States and Europe continues to widen. Two recent examples illustrate the point.

First, after 9/11, NATO's European members declared "Article 5" support for the United States in its war against terrorism generally and the military action in Afghanistan. This was the first time in NATO's history that Article 5 had been formally invoked – and it is likely to be the last, despite the argument that "modern-day terrorism and WMD proliferation are 'Article 5 threats.'"[15] The United States spurned the European action, and in doing so Washington signaled that it did not need NATO and that the European allies counted for little in the greatest threat to US vital interests since perhaps the attack on Pearl Harbor.

Second, differences over Iraq illustrate the widening gap in interests and values between the United States and several important European countries, especially France and Germany. These differences are not superficial; they are rooted in a basic philosophical divergence that will not be explained away by the normal admonition that "there have always been differences among NATO countries." This time, the political survival of the German – and perhaps the French – government depends on it. In both cases, political success depends increasingly on disagreeing with Washington on many of the most important international issues. At the same time, US policy – either by design or by accident – is dividing Europe and thereby damaging the Europeans' efforts to find common ground on the future of Europe and underscoring Europe's irrelevancy for US security interests.

GETTING PAST THE PAST

The Europeans will have to take the initiative to move beyond security anachronisms such as NATO, because it will not happen as a result of US leadership. Washington will cling to NATO even more desperately and continue to manufacture complicated, ineffective, even deleterious mechanisms to "prove" NATO's importance and viability. For Washington, NATO is the security institution that best exemplifies the static world it prefers – it makes no difference that the alliance no longer serves any useful security function. The American political class will not be voluntarily shaken from that perspective, no matter how much the world changes.

The Europeans, on the other hand, have been more ready to recognize and embrace the changes that are taking place in the structure of the international system. They are struggling with the transition and are more fully engaged in the transformation than is the United States. The Europeans have reached a critical juncture in the construction of the "European space." Certainly, questions of "widening versus deepening," problems of a multiple-speed Europe, the lasting soundness of the Euro, the equity of the Common Agricultural Policy, and even issues of consensus versus majority rule are very important, and they will be handled one way or another in time. But the critical issue that will ultimately define the nature and character of European cooperation is the whole arena of foreign and security policy – an issue that the Europeans currently are not handling very well.

If the United States is blinded by its own self-righteousness, the Europeans are crippled emotionally by their timidity. For different reasons, then, both sides are unable to shed NATO's Cold War grip, despite the Europeans' greater potential to break this inertia. To do so, they will have to recognize that the conduct of foreign and security policy is perhaps the most fundamental arena that defines any polity. The Europeans are now "a de facto military protectorate of the United States,"[16] unable to fully provide for their own relations with other states and other political organizations on the international stage. To have one's security and foreign policy agenda set by another is the height of servitude.

The Europeans have made a halting start by trying to construct the Common Foreign and Security Policy (CFSP) and the European Security and Defense Policy (ESDP). Efforts in both areas have a long history, beginning in the 1960s and 1970s when the "member states of the European community cooperated and endeavored to consult with one another on major international problems."[17] These efforts progressed through the Single European Act in 1986, received a major boost in the Maastricht Treaty of 1993 and the Amsterdam Treaty of 1999, the Nice Treaty in 2001, and, in security specifically, at the 1999 Cologne Council meeting (including the Petersburg tasks), and the Helsinki Headline Goals (HHG), which are supposed to be achieved by 2003.[18]

But the effort has stalled, and it is likely to remain stalled as long as the Europeans are tied to the myth that NATO and its lore is the appropriate linchpin for the future. Although discussion under the current European Constitutional Convention does not presently provide a major role for foreign and security policy, there is no reason it cannot be extended to do so.[19] The platform and the precedent are available; only the political will is lacking. The Europeans should begin to chart their own course now by exercising their option under Article 13 of the NATO Treaty and announcing their intention to withdraw from the alliance. Ironically, the bitter transatlantic dispute over Iraq may already have started the process.

NOTES

1. David Steele, *Lord Salisbury — A Political Biography* (New York: Routledge, 1999), p. 121.

2. Comments by Undersecretary of Defense for Policy, Douglas Feith; see the Armed Forces Press Service, 28 February 2002.

3. Statement by Undersecretary of State for Political Affairs, Marc Grossman; see *Department of State Bulletin*, 9 October 2001.

4. *The Financial Times*, 15 May 2002.

5. Terrorism does not fit the bill because it is diffuse, sporadic, and of much less salience in Europe than in the United States. All of this requires a different kind of response than NATO can provide. In short, NATO does not have the tools to fight terrorism.

6. Robert Kagan, "Power and Weakness," *Policy Review*, No. 113 (June & July, 2002).

7. Anthony Padgen, *Lords of All the World—Ideologies of Empire in Spain, Britain, and France (1500–1800)* (New Haven, Conn.: Yale Univ. Press, 1995), pp. 5, 8.

8. Clearly, as disagreements within Europe over Washington's Iraq policy demonstrate, European countries are not always of one mind on all transatlantic issues. But intra-European divisions do not undermine the basic point, and once the immediate crisis over Iraq fades, the centrifugal issues separating the United States from the Europeans will accelerate.

9. BBC World News Report, 25 September 2001.

10. Jeffrey Simon, "NATO's Membership Action Plan and Defense Planning," *Problems of Post-Communism*, 48 (May–June 2001), 28.

11. Ibid., p. 30.

12. Although the EU is the most important organization for the future of Central and Eastern Europe, other organizations, such as the Southeast Europe Brigade (SEEBRIG) and the Southeastern Europe Defense Ministerial (SEEDM) process are potentially more important to the specific security issues of these countries than is NATO.

13. "A Dangerous Divergence," *The Washington Post*, 10 December 2002, op-ed.

14. Stephen M. Walt, *The Origins of Alliances* (Ithaca, N.Y.: Cornell Univ. Press, 1987), ch. 2; Glenn H. Snyder, *Alliance Politics* (Ithaca, N.Y.: Cornell Univ. Press, 1997), chs. 2, 6.

15. Richard L. Kugler, "Preparing NATO to Meet New Threats: Challenge and Opportunity," US Department of State, International Information Programs, 27 March 2002, http://usinfo.state.gov/topical/pol/nato/02032800.htm.

16. Zbigniew Brzezinski et al., "Living With the New Europe," *The National Interest*, No. 60 (Summer 2000).

17. Council of the European Union, "Common Foreign and Security Policy/European Security and Defense Policy," http://ue.eu.int/pesc/pres.asp?lang=en.

18. Some scholars argue that European efforts to find common ground in foreign and security policy can be traced back to the European Defense Community idea (Pleven Plan) of 1966–67.

19. Title III, Article 13, of the preliminary draft Constitutional Treaty provides ample justification for bold moves in the area of foreign and security policy.

✗ NO

All Dressed Up and No Place to Go: Why NATO Should Be on the Front Lines in the War on Terror
REBECCA JOHNSON AND MICAH ZENKO

Following the 2000 American presidential election, some analysts worried that transatlantic relations would be strained by the policies proposed by the incoming Bush Administration. From disagreements over the Kyoto Treaty to the decision to proceed quickly with the deployment of ballistic missile defenses, a functional split between America and its European allies threatened to emerge.[1] While the attacks of 11 September 2001 changed US interests and priorities overseas, these disagreements will not dissolve completely. They have receded, however, in immediate importance to the American goal of fighting terrorists with a global reach. As European officials were quoted to have told an American official after 9/11, "Kyoto is an issue you argue about when all else is well."[2]

Retaining the commitment of a broad-based coalition is critical to the success of America's evolving war against terrorism. Although the North Atlantic Treaty Organization (NATO) is an obvious hub from which to organize this coalition, and alliance members have shown their eagerness to respond to common threats such as terrorism, Washington has held true allied support at arm's length. While officials in Washington have endorsed NATO's invocation of Article 5 for the first time in the alliance's history and accepted limited contributions of troops and equipment for the military campaign and later support for the restricted peacekeeping mission in Afghanistan, they have refused to allow NATO to engage in the sort of operations the alliance embraced when it affirmed its Article 24 commitments in April 1999. This refusal, while puzzling given the consistent willingness of the European allies to contribute troops and resources, is even more surprising when one remembers that it was the United States, not Europe, that initially pushed for the inclusion of Article 24 during the Washington Summit in April 1999.[3]

This article argues that the United States should work with its NATO allies in fulfilling their Article 24 commitments. It is organized in three sections. First, we examine the decisionmaking procedures immediately following 9/11 to determine the reasons behind the Bush Administration's opposition to a muscular NATO presence in the war against terrorism. In this section we answer Washington's objections that an active NATO role would undermine US operational autonomy and reveal stark inequalities in alliance readiness.

In the second section we argue the advantages of coordinating the war through NATO under the auspices of Article 24. First, given the undeniable links between al Qaeda and terrorist networks operating in Europe and elsewhere around the globe, it is important that the US campaign is not isolated to a few obvious spots in Afghanistan and Iraq. To do the job right, American military, diplomatic, and intelligence services will need serious, coordinated support from their allies, and working through – rather than past – NATO would help to ensure that important information does not slip through the cracks. Second, in its capacity as the preeminent institution for collective defense, NATO provides the support the United States needs to conduct such a comprehensive campaign. NATO has the mandate through its Article 24 provisions; it has the experience of running a coordinated campaign through its missions in Bosnia, Kosovo, and Macedonia (where alliance troops face many of the same issues of porous borders, trafficking, and militancy that must now be addressed in Afghanistan); and it has the will of its European members. Finally, in the conclusion we offer suggestions for what a NATO-centered effort would look like in practice, drawing from the alliance's ongoing operations in the Balkans.

NATO'S NEWEST CHALLENGE

Since the collapse of the Soviet Union in 1991, NATO has undertaken a series of missions unprecedented in the alliance's history. The alliance conducted military strikes and later provided ground forces for peace support operations in Bosnia and Kosovo, created institutional arrangements to engage with former Warsaw Pact countries, and expanded its membership to include three historically pivotal states of Central Europe – the Czech Republic, Hungary, and Poland.

Some have debated whether this expansion of NATO's responsibilities, combined with the disappearance of the unifying threat portrayed by the Soviet Union, could harm the centrality of NATO's mission – providing for the collective defense of all its members.[4] NATO's response to 9/11 has shown how quickly the alliance can refocus its sprawling interests when one member faces a direct attack.

Within 30 hours of the attacks on New York and Washington, the alliance invoked Article 5 of the North Atlantic Treaty. Article 5 states quite simply that "an armed attack against one or more of" the NATO members "shall be considered as an attack against them all." Though its original intent changed dramatically with the end of the Cold War, it has remained a core element of NATO's raison d'etre. The new rationale for Article 5 was found in the Strategic Concept statement released during NATO's 50th Anniversary Washington Summit in April 1999. An update of the first Strategic Concept publicly released in 1991, the 1999 version went further than the alliance's previous doctrinal declarations in embracing out-of-area operations of a sort that differed from the traditional understanding of defending against a Soviet invasion. Article 24 of the Strategic Concept declared:

> Any armed attack on the territory of the allies, from whatever direction, would be covered by Articles 5 and 6 of the Washington Treaty. However, alliance security must also take account of the global context. Alliance

security interests can be affected by other risks of a wider nature, including acts of terrorism, sabotage, and organized crime, and by the disruption of the flow of vital resources.[5]

While far-reaching, the declaration was actually a scaled-back compromise from language that the United States initially hoped to introduce regarding the declaration of new purposes.[6] European governments sought to limit the Strategic Concept to deal with threats directly related to Europe – including those originating in the Balkans and the Mediterranean. The United States pushed for an expansive declaration to consider threats from organized crime, terrorism, and especially weapons of mass destruction.[7]

When NATO officials met in Brussels on 12 September 2001 to discuss the alliance's response to the attack on America, 18 of the 19 NATO nations were prepared to fulfill the commitments laid out in Article 24. While the attacks were carried out on the territory of the United States, alliance members recognized that they were all vulnerable to future acts of terrorism. America absorbed the attacks, but the loss to the world included citizens of 80 countries. Within the alliance itself, all but three of its 19 member nations lost citizens either in Washington or New York. Direct threats to the European continent and its periphery included the US Embassy in Paris, synagogues in Strasbourg and Tunisia, Jewish and American properties in Germany, the water supply system in Morocco, and several other sites not revealed by European police for fear of making them more attractive.[8] Furthermore, there is evidence that NATO itself was threatened. Quoting sources within the German police agency (BKA), the newsmagazine *Stern* reported that NATO headquarters was itself the target of an attack similar to the ones committed on 11 September in the United States.[9]

THE WAR AGAINST TERRORISM: NATO ON THE SIDELINES

The only state that hesitated to embrace NATO's decision was the United States – the same state that had lobbied so forcefully for the creation of the new NATO mandate two years earlier. Two concerns featured prominently in the minds of decisionmakers in Washington: Washington's reluctance to cede operational autonomy, and its concern that the European allies lack the capabilities to conduct a military campaign outside the North Atlantic theater.

Washington's hesitancy to jeopardize operational control was evidenced in its response to the alliance's decision to invoke Article 5 in September. According to one NATO official, the allies requested "a commitment to be consulted by Washington before anything happens" in return for invoking Article 5.[10] European governments had sought enhanced consultations from the United States over a number of international issues long before the arrival of the Bush Administration, and they did not waste this opportunity to increase their leverage.

The reaction in Washington was quick and decisive — NATO could not be allowed to reign in any US response. According to a senior State Department official speaking to reporters after the first emergency meeting on 12 September, the United States was pushing for a resolution that would mention that the article could be invoked, without actually voting on the measure itself. A senior Administration official said that it was the Europeans who were "desperately trying to give us political cover and the Pentagon was resisting it." Eventually, Secretary of Defense Rumsfeld relented and agreed to accept the clause.[11]

Even in agreeing to the invocation of Article 5, Secretary Rumsfeld tried to distance himself from the NATO alliance, however, stating publicly to its members, "The mission determines the coalition. The coalition doesn't determine the mission."[12] The reason for America's tentative approach to accepting the invocation of Article 5 is most certainly related to the US desire to retain maximum flexibility in its military planning and operations. This concern would turn out to be overblown in that even after Rumsfeld relented, the alliance left it up to Washington to determine the nature of the response and whether the United States would need NATO assistance.[13]

Since it began planning a global response to the terror attacks of September 2001, the Bush Administration has worked from the assumption that at some point in the future America might have to operate alone.[14] During the Afghanistan operations, the United States relied primarily on its own capabilities for conducting the military strikes and allowed European peacekeepers to oversee the International Security Assistance Force (ISAF), the stability force sanctioned by the UN Security Council.

While placing NATO on the sideline may have been necessary for military efficiency and to avoid politically difficult decisions, Europe's ancillary role has meant that since the initial outpouring of support immediately following the attacks there has been less sympathy and support from mainstream society on the continent. As the war against terrorism verges further from one of specific military goals in Afghanistan to one of crucial global financial, intelligence, and legal cooperation, European governments may feel less attachment to what has been largely a unilateral American mission. Consequently, the United States may not be able to quickly enlist the support of its allies whenever its needs to, as some have suggested.[15] This has been most clearly visible in the allies' stark opposition to America's stated intention to pursue Saddam Hussein as part of its broader campaign.

Overriding and related to the American decision to operate outside of NATO's command structure is the fact that few NATO allies have the military capability to conduct combat operations outside the North Atlantic theater. None of the European allies possesses long-range strike attack aircraft that do not require forward basing, such as the American B-52H, B-1, and B-2 bombers. Meanwhile, the United States maintains over 150 such bombers in service.[16]

Europe also has severe limitations in its power-projection capabilities, with few assets in the fields of strategic air and sealift, air-to-air refueling, and reconnaissance and strategic intelligence. [. . .]

This is not to say that the European NATO members have had no military role in the first stages of the campaign against global terrorism. The most significant contribution has come from the NATO ally with the greatest capacity to provide the United States support for its operations in Afghanistan – the United Kingdom. Reflecting their long-standing special relationship with the United States, the British have been the most vocal American ally in the aftermath of the attacks, with Prime Minister Tony Blair at times appearing out in front of Washington in his condemnation and demands of the Taliban and the al Qaeda terror network. Militarily, the British provided three nuclear-powered submarines armed with precision-guided munitions, tactical fighter aircraft, 600 Royal Marine Commandos, and permission to use its strategically important air base on Diego Garcia. All told the British have contributed more than 6,000 military personnel to the South Asian theater of operations during the military campaign, with 1,700 infantry troops committed to Operation Jacana in the mountainous regions along the Afghan-Pakistani border.[17] The British also led the initial International Security Assistance Force that provided stability during the transition period for the interim government in Kabul.

The importance of this contribution should not be overlooked. According to Anthony Cordesman, senior scholar at the Center for Strategic and International Studies in Washington, "The US and British experience in Afghanistan may indicate that the US and NATO have overstressed the high technology and high investment aspects of coalition warfare and interoperability, and paid too little attention to the value of being able to draw on a pool of highly trained lighter forces, like the SAS, or their Australian, Canadian, German, and other equivalents."[18] Not only have British troops played a critical role in strategic operations on the ground in Afghanistan, they also have taken the lead in reconstruction efforts and are responsible for rebuilding airfields, de-mining large segments of land in and around Kabul, and rebuilding roads from the capital to the countryside.[19]

The rest of the NATO alliance also has participated in the war against terrorism in smaller though still important ways.[20] Although they were not included directly in combat operations in Afghanistan, as Colin Powell noted, "Not every ally is fighting, but every ally is in the fight."[21] [. . .]

The European military contribution has been useful to backfill those US forces that are needed to operate in the theater surrounding Afghanistan. Seven German-based AWACS planes, with Germans composing one-third of those on board, were deployed to America to relieve similar US assets, providing air interdiction support on the East Coast and other areas of interest.[22] Before the mission's termination in late April, the alliance's crew, including ground support for the AWACS operation, reached 830 personnel from 13 countries.[23] NATO also has dispatched seven frigates, a destroyer, and an auxiliary oiler to the Mediterranean to take the place of American naval assets there that moved into the Indian Ocean closer to Afghanistan.[24] And NATO forces will likely replace low-intensity, high-demand American forces in the Balkans in order to free them up for operations elsewhere.[25]

WASTED POTENTIAL

But NATO's contribution to the evolving effort should be greater than providing special forces for reconnaissance and limited combat in Afghanistan, and for keeping the peace in Afghanistan's capital. The alliance publicly codified its need to adapt its capabilities in the new fight against terrorism in its 18 December 2001 statement, but its troops and assets have largely been made to cool their heels.[26]

One need look only to alliance efforts in the Balkans to understand NATO's capacity to undertake operations like those needed to eradicate terrorist networks. Currently, NATO has troops involved in peacekeeping missions in Bosnia, Kosovo, and Macedonia, with European members providing roughly 80 percent of the forces for these missions.[27] The United States contributes around 5,000 of the 42,000 troops in KFOR,[28] and 3,100 of the 18,000 troops in Bosnia.[29] NATO's deployment in Macedonia is far smaller; a 3,000 troop, British-led operation finished in September 2001; that was followed by a 1,000 troop, German-led follow-on mission; in late June 2002, the mission was extended through October, with the number of German troops being reduced and the Netherlands taking over the lead nation role. Each of these missions must coordinate with the other international agencies at work in the area in order to control the region's porous borders and corrupt institutions that facilitate the development of transnational organized crime and extremist groups.

These missions are no longer combat missions; they more closely resemble the sort of low-intensity, on-the-ground, long-term engagement the United States has committed itself to in the current phase of Operation Enduring Freedom and must undertake in other areas if it realistically hopes to eradicate terrorism. It is important to be clear on this point. There are two components to the current war against terrorism, just as there were two components to NATO's interventions in the Balkans: a large-scale military engagement, and a long-term policing and reconstruction mission. [. . .]

The links between terrorist organizations like al Qaeda and regional crime syndicates in southeastern Europe have been trumpeted by specialists in Washington at luncheon talks and in the news since 9/11.[30] But the NATO troops on the ground in the Balkans realized long ago that these networks are the main obstacles to peaceful and sustainable reconstruction. Indeed, these networks are even more corrosive to the region than any lingering ethnic radicalism. According to

British defense sources, "All NATO troops in the Balkans will be contributing to the campaign [against terrorism] because a lot of terrorist activity is funneled through the region in terms of arms-trafficking, money-laundering, and drugs."[31]

In addition, these troops themselves are targets in the region. According to a report from the International Crisis Group, "Given the presence of ex-mujahidin in Bosnia, the tens of thousands of former military and paramilitary fighters in Bosnia, Kosovo, and Macedonia who are Muslims by tradition, if not for the most part by observance, and the large deployments of US and other troops in the region, some (though by no means all) senior Western sources describe the potential terrorist threat as significant."[32]

So long as these criminal networks are allowed to operate in the Balkans, Western Europe remains vulnerable to attack. One common practice, "identity laundering," allows potential extremists to slip into Western Europe virtually unseen. In one striking example, British peacekeepers in Bosnia helped track down Bensayah Belkacem, one of Osama bin Laden's key associates who may have been responsible for obtaining the Western passports used by the terrorists in the attacks in the United States.[33]

Al Qaeda singled out Europe as the launching point for its terrorist attacks against the West. Islamic militants targeted ghetto Arab immigrant communities to propagate the radical message of bin Laden, recruited foot soldiers in slums and mosques, and used this foothold in Europe to plan their attacks.[34] Once mid-level al Qaeda officials had fomented sufficient human and financial support inside a city, compartmentalized sleeper cells were left in place awaiting opportunities to strike.[35] Despite vigorous efforts by local law enforcement officials in Germany, Spain, Italy, Britain, and the Netherlands, many of these cells may still exist unnoticed and be awaiting their signal to act.[36]

Europe has pursued its investigations on terrorism with an eye to integrating Muslim communities and protecting civil and human rights. National and continental-wide police forces have made renewed efforts to target potential suspects and break up radical Islamic networks. Despite these increased investigations into Islamic fundamentalism on the continent and arrests of suspected terrorists, however, after three months of the policing effort, an estimated 60 percent of radical Islamic networks were yet to be discovered, according to Western European intelligence officials.[37] Furthermore, law enforcement officials believe that European-based militants who trained and fought in Afghanistan have returned to the continent with the intent of conducting additional terrorist operations.[38]

Lord Robertson has called Afghanistan a "black hole" that lacks any sustainable state structure, and has argued, "That is why NATO is engaged in South-East Europe — to prevent such black holes from emerging on our doorstep."[39] He is right, and in order to avoid having the Balkans serve as the same sort of fertile breeding ground for extremism that is present in Afghanistan, a coordinated approach must be developed to respond effectively to these concerns.

This approach exists in the Balkans. NATO troops operate alongside representatives of the UN, the Organization for Security and Cooperation in Europe (OSCE), and the European Union (EU), as well as aide workers from numerous international relief agencies. In Bosnia and Kosovo, NATO takes responsibility for security, policing, and border monitoring.[40] The UN runs civil administration; the OSCE is in charge of democratization and institution-building; and the EU takes the lead in reconstruction and economic development. One can see how these missions overlap — civil administration and effective institution-building rely on security, and economic development relies on effective policing. For all the criticism levied against civil reconstruction campaigns in Bosnia and Kosovo, the parties are closer to a peaceful, stable existence than at any time in the past decade. NATO security forces are conducting an effective campaign to combat criminal and extremist networks in the region.

But localized success in some areas in the Balkans is not sufficient. If either mission — the war on terrorism or peacekeeping in the Balkans — is to be successful, the two need to be better integrated, not dissociated. The United States needs to remain active in both, not just in the assault on Afghanistan, and the European allies need to coordinate planning and intelligence on a scale larger than the Balkans. They should employ the lessons they have learned from their operations in the Balkans to coordinate efforts with other international institutions. This means capitalizing on strong communications networks, launching an aggressive outreach campaign with Muslim countries through the Euro-Atlantic Partnership Council (EAPC), and retaining operating autonomy to ensure that individual missions can be carried out with minimal bureaucratic delay. In brief, they should take their experience from the Balkans — both the successes and the failures — and adopt operational procedures that closely resemble the procedures and structures witnessed in the terrorist networks they are trying to combat.

PUTTING NATO ON THE FRONT LINES

The first of these procedures that should be adopted is operational autonomy. Effective coordination will be the linchpin of the international war against terrorism, and this coordination will fail unless each of the components is allowed to carry out its tasks unimpeded. By making NATO the hub that synchronizes the array of international institutions that will contribute to this effort, operational autonomy will be enhanced.

Skeptics will argue that the need for unimpeded action is precisely why the United States should lead the international effort. They will contend that placing NATO front and center in the international response will only stymie action. But while the United States may be able to carry out a military campaign in Afghanistan largely on its own, it is not able to fight the kind of war that is needed to cripple international terrorism. This "war" has many fronts, arguably the least important of which is being conducted south of Tajikistan today. An effective campaign against terrorism requires accurate and timely intelligence to locate cells and their planned activities. It requires alert, trained law enforcement, immigration services, and border patrols, as well as flexible teams ready to respond when important information is revealed. Finally, it requires time, dedication, and resources. With its membership, partners, and shared experience, NATO can commit each. The alliance might not be the most efficiently run organization, but it has both the breadth and depth to make it the best suited for the job of ringleader.

What does this mean in practice? John Arquilla and David Ronfelt have released a new edited volume on networks and "netwars."[41] A network is a distinct organizing concept that has developed along with technological advances. It requires not just that individuals' interactions link them in a network, but that they recognize and foster their form of organization (in contrast to a traditional, hierarchical form of organization). A network is generally characterized by diffuse clusters of individuals who relate to one another through hubs. The authors of the RAND study argue, "The West must start to build its own networks and must learn to swarm the enemy, in order to keep it on the run or pinned down until it can be destroyed."[42] "Swarming" refers to attacking the enemy in different ways simultaneously. Small, nimble networks are key to this endeavor, which means that NATO will be called on to operationalize smaller, more adaptable units operating with a large degree of autonomy to respond to their environments. This is not to advocate the abolition of traditional military force structures (corps, divisions, brigades, regiments, etc.), but to suggest NATO can best fulfill its Article 24 provisions by positioning itself at the center of the war against terrorism within its existing commitments. NATO forces tracking small arms in Bosnia should be given the discretion to make changes to their mission to respond to developments on the ground. Likewise, NATO troops working with Uzbekistan and Turkmenistan on border security through the Partnership for Peace program should be given leeway in how they carry out their missions.[43] So long as the contingents that are deployed to any one mission are all of the same nationality, there should be few problems concerning how changes in orders travel up the chain of command.

While the OSCE and the EU will likely fight having some of their core responsibilities usurped, NATO should take the lead in military, anti-crime, and border activity. The OSCE's track record on combating trafficking is poor, and a concerted policing effort is needed to counter the trails of drugs, arms, and people that snake across Central Asia, Russia, and the Balkans into Western Europe. NATO, with contributions from its member countries and support from its partners, has the heft that is needed to undertake this important job. Without question the alliance should consult closely with the OSCE and the EU to ensure that their security, political, and economic programs reinforce, not undermine, each other, but the programs all should be engineered with attention to shutting down transnational crime and building stable governments and economies. The OSCE lacks the institutional capacity to carry out this critical task, and NATO should take it over. While some may worry that EU and OSCE countries would resist NATO's enhanced role, these countries recognize that they are out of the loop in the war against terrorism. By positioning NATO at the hub of European anti-terror efforts, it would provide them with a voice in the planning and implementation of these efforts, as well as bring them in contact with the alliance's substantial assets and capabilities.

Working through NATO also gives the alliance the opportunity to continue to build strong working bonds with Russia. It is true that many in Russia still hold lingering suspicions about the alliance's true intentions, but NATO and Russia have been able to work very well together on joint missions in Bosnia and Kosovo. SFOR and KFOR are enduring examples of the good that can come from NATO-Russian cooperation, and the West should not shrink from using NATO as the center for the international response merely because they fear opposition from Moscow.

Luckily this is precisely what the alliance has undertaken with the new relationship that will be embodied in the NATO-Russian Council, or "NATO at 20."[44] The West can learn much more from Russia than the lessons of its military experiences in Afghanistan. Russian police also face traffickers transiting their territory; they contribute soldiers to secure Tajikistan's border with Afghanistan; and they still retain intelligence sources across the globe. NATO should work with Moscow to help neutralize the networks operating in Russia at the same time that they employ Russian assets to the larger military, police, and intelligence effort.[45]

Seen in this way, NATO would serve as the hub of an international network against terrorism. It would coordinate its own military and policing missions within Europe and offer training, intelligence, and potentially troops or logistical support to out-of-area efforts. [. . .]

The effectiveness of this coordination will rest on intelligence sharing. Before 9/11, NATO members were already providing relatively good intelligence estimates about terrorist threats to the United States. [. . .]

The future burden will be on the allies to more quickly process the analyses provided by US and European intelligence sources. Institutionally, the alliance needs to create mechanisms that assure such sharing will not be done in an ad hoc manner, in response to specific threats and crises, but as a part of the normal operating procedure of a network that faces transnational threats. [. . .]

NATO's ability to work with the other dominant European institutions has been battle-tested and improved throughout the 1990s with the alliance crisis management efforts in the Balkans. This high level of coordination will need to be even further enhanced by expanding ties outside Europe.

One of the most important institutions that NATO will need to coordinate with is the OSCE. Mircea Geoana, the Romanian Foreign Minister and former holder of the OSCE's rotating chairmanship, announced that the 55 OSCE member states had adopted an action plan against terrorism at their meeting in Bucharest on 3-4 December 2001.[46] While this plan was little more than a gesture, it can have important symbolic meaning in enhancing solidarity in the American-led campaign. Speaking at the meeting, US Secretary of State Colin Powell called the document "a resolute expression of our collective will."[47]

Reports are growing more insistent that in the war against terror, "Washington employs the rhetoric of political multilateralism, on the one hand, and the reality of military unilateralism, on the other."[48] If the operation in Afghanistan becomes associated with mere retaliation, or even worse, aggression, US goals become compromised and US interests become even more endangered. The Muslim countries in the Balkans, Central Asia, and the Caucasus are all members of the OSCE. Incorporating their support of this effort through their commitment to the action plan at the December 2001 meeting was an important step to gaining greater legitimacy. [. . .]

CONCLUSION

Although the 9/11 attacks on the United States were horrific and unprecedented, a worst-case scenario could arise in which America's European allies remember 11 September as an once-in-a-lifetime event. Even only a few months after the attacks there was evidence that Europe was viewing them as "an aberration that is now behind us."[49] Should the world be so fortunate that another large-scale unconventional attack does not occur, Washington will have to reinvigorate allied enthusiasm to make sure Brussels does not lose focus in the fight against terror. If no more attacks happen, and Europe loses its concentration, the American-led campaign could look increasingly like a global version of the decade-long enforcement of the no-fly-zones over Iraq, where all the allies dropped out except for Great Britain. For America's European allies to express outrage against terrorism but then forget the horror would send the wrong message to the world, and could be the source of the perpetually feared rift within the alliance.

A better course of action would be for the NATO allies to endorse a mission that retains transatlantic cohesion and that builds on the strengths of the alliance – its ability to work in conjunction with other organizations, its strong communications network, its reach into the Muslim world through the EAPC, and its ability to provide wide operating autonomy to coalition partners. To combat transnational terrorist networks effectively, NATO should more closely resemble a network itself. It has taken the initial steps in this direction following the end of the Cold War, and it should make further progress now and after the coming Prague summit if it is to retain a central role in the new security environment.

It has always been a central maxim of Brussels that the solidarity of the alliance is more important that the concerns of any single country. The threat of terrorism is a threat to the entire world, let alone NATO, and the victory over global terrorism is not inevitable, nor probable in the short-term. Thus, the alliance needs to maintain its solidarity in the face of this threat. It should find a way to do so, however, that does not undermine NATO's current missions or long-term health. This will require that the United States dedicate significant attention and resources to the alliance at precisely the time that its attention is being pulled elsewhere. For the continuing stability of Europe and lasting strength of the alliance, one hopes that the United States will make this necessary investment.

NOTES

1. Lord George Robertson, "The Future of the Transatlantic Link," Lisbon, Portugal, 24 October 2001.

2. Dana Milbank and T. R. Reid, "New Global Threat Revives Old Alliance," *The Washington Post*, 16 October 2001, p. A10.

3. Suzanne Daley, "Europeans Pledge Troops, if Necessary," *The New York Times*, 9 October 2001, p. B8; Alan Sipress and Vernon Loeb, "U.S. Welcoming Allies' Troops," *The Washington Post*, 11 November 2001, p. A38.

4. David S. Yost, *NATO Transformed: The Alliance's New Roles in International Security* (Washington: United States Institute of Peace Press, 1998).

5. NATO, "The Alliance's Strategic Concept," Press Release NAC-S(99)65, 24 April 1999.

6. Richard Sokolsky, Stuart Johnson, and F. Stephen Larrabee eds., *Persian Gulf Security: Improving Allied Military Contributions* (Santa Monica, Calif.: RAND, 2000), p. 40.

7. Shahram Chubin, Jerrold Green, and F. Stephen Larrabee, *NATO's New Strategic Concept and Peripheral Contingencies: The Middle East*, workshop proceedings, 15–16 July 1999 (Santa Monica, Calif.: RAND, 1999); and William Drozdiak and Thomas W. Lippman, "NATO Widens Security 'Map,'" *The Washington Post*, 25 April 1999, p. A1.

8. Phillip Jaklin and Hugh Williamson, "Terror Suspects Detained in Germany," *Financial Times*, 24 April 2002, p. 6; Richard Bourdeaux, "4 Terror Suspects Arrested in Italy," *Los Angeles Times*, 21 February 2002, p. A1; and Barry James, "17 Suspected of Qaeda Links Arrested Across Europe," *International Herald Tribune*, 25 April 2002, p. 4.

9. Florian Gless and Regina Weitz, "Explodiert die Welt?" *Stern*, 20 September 2001.

10. Bruce Wallace, "We'll Stand Behind the U.S.," *The Gazette* (Montreal), 13 September 2001, p. B5.

11. Suzanne Daley, "After the Attacks: The Alliance," *The New York Times*, 13 September 2001, p. A17; and Elaine Sciolino and Steven Lee Myers, "Bush Says 'Time is Running Out'; U.S. Plans to Act Largely Alone," *The New York Times*, 7 October 2001, p. B5.

12. Martin Fletcher, Michael Evans, and Damian Whitworth, "U.S. Warns of Possible London Attack," *The Times* (London), 19 December 2001, p. 1.

13. Daley, "After the Attacks: The Alliance," p. A17.

14. Bob Woodward and Dan Balz, "At Camp David, Advise and Dissent," *The Washington Post*, 31 January 2002, p. A1.

15. Jim Hoagland, "Enlist America's Allies," *The Washington Post*, 13 January 2002, p. B7; and Martin Walker, "New Europe: Uneasy, Necessary Ally," *San Diego Union-Tribune*, 30 December 2001, p. G5.

16. International Institute for Strategic Studies, *The Military Balance: 2000–2001* (Oxford, Eng.: Oxford Univ. Press, 2000), p. 30.

17. Michael R. Gordon, "Britain Allots Troops for Afghan Ground Combat, and Australia is Contributing, Too," *The New York Times*, 27 October 2001, p. B2; and Richard Norton-Taylor, "1,700 UK Troops to Fight in Afghan War," *The Guardian*, 19 March 2002, p. 1.

18. Anthony Cordesman, "The Lessons of Afghanistan: Warfighting, Intelligence, Force Transformation, Counterproliferation, and Arms Control," Center for Strategic and International Studies, Washington, D.C., 28 June 2002.

19. Interview with Julian Lindley-French, Senior Research Fellow, Institute for Security Studies, Paris, 16 July 2002.

20. For an accounting of these contributions through June 2002, see Anthony Cordesman's "The Lessons of Afghanistan," pp. 26–35.

21. Robin Wright, "NATO Promises Cohesive Stand Against Terrorism," *Los Angeles Times*, 7 December 2001.

22. Haig Simonian, "Berlin Flexes its Muscles," *Financial Times*, 13 October 2001, p. 13; and "NATO Adds Planes For U.S. Sky Patrols," *USA Today*, 17 January 2002, p. 8.

23. NATO, "Statement by the Secretary General on the Conclusion of Operation Eagle Assist," press release (2002) 057, 30 April 2002.

24. Norman Kempster, "NATO Sends Military Planes to U.S.," *Los Angeles Times*, 11 October 2001, p. A4; Paul Mann, "Europe Wary Of Prolonged Bombing," *Aviation Week and Space Technology*, 22 October 2001, p. 32.

25. Keith B. Richburg and DeNeen L. Brown, "NATO to Send Radar Planes to Patrol U.S. Coast," *The Washington Post*, 9 October 2001, p. B9.

26. NATO, "Statement on Combating Terrorism: Adapting the Alliance's Defence Capabilities," press release (2001) 173, 18 December 2001.

27. Charles Grant, "Does this War Show that NATO No Longer has a Serious Military Role?" *The Independent*, 16 October 2001, p. 4.

28. "French General Takes over Command of NATO-Led Force in Kosovo," *Agence France Presse*, 3 October 2001.

29. James Dao, "Americans Plead to Remain in Bosnia," *The New York Times*, 22 October 2001, p. B3.

30. Misha Glenny, "Balkan Instability Could Create a Terrorist Haven," *The New York Times*, 16 October 2001, p. A31; Judy Dempsey, "EU in Wrangle on Balkan Stability Pact," *Financial Times*, 30 October 2001, p. 12; and NATO/SFOR Press Conference, 25 September 2001.

31. Michael Evans, "British Soldiers Leaving Balkans," *The Times* (London), 27 September 2001, p. 13.

32. "Bin Laden and the Balkans: The Politics of Anti-Terrorism," ICG Balkans Report No. 119, 9 November 2001.

33. Daniel McGrory, "Bin Laden Aide Arrested in Bosnia," *The Times* (London), 11 October 2001, p. 9.

34. Sam Dillon with Emma Daly, "Spain Pursues Terrorists Among Its Muslim Immigrants," *Los Angeles Times*, 4 December 2001; Sebastian Rotella, "Europe Holds Fertile Soil for Jihads," *Los Angeles Times*, 5 December 2001; Susan Sachs, "North Africans in Europe Said to Preach War," *The New York Times*, 11 December 2001, p. B2; and Steven Erlanger and Chris Hedges, "Terror Cells Slip Through Europe's Grasp," *The New York Times*, 28 December 2001, p. A1.

35. Sebastian Rotella and David Zucchino, "Hunt Is On for Middle Managers of Terrorism," *Los Angeles Times*, 23 December 2001, p. A1.

36. Edmund Andrews, "German Officials Find More Terrorist Groups, and Some Disturbing Parallels," *The New York Times*, 26 April 2002, p. A12.

37. Bob Drogin and Paul Watson, "Battlefield Clues Key to Bush's Next Step," *Los Angeles Times*, 9 December 2001.

38. Erlanger and Hedges, "Terror Cells Slip Through Europe's Grasp"; and Vivienne Walt, "Terrorists 'Spread all Over Europe,'" *USA Today*, 22 July 2001, p. A4.

39. Theodor Troev and Stefan Wagstyl, "NATO Plans Eastward Shift," *Financial Times*, 6 October 2001, p. 3.

40. Lord George Robertson, "Kosovo One Year on: Achievement and Challenge," NATO, 21 March 2000, internet, http://www.nato.int/kosovo/repo2000/index.htm, accessed 12 September 2002.

41. John Arquilla and David Ronfelt, eds., *Networks and Netwars: The Future of Terror, Crime, and Militancy* (Washington: RAND, 2001).

42. Ibid., p. 369.

43. Because of its recent civil war, Tajikistan is currently not a member of the Partnership for Peace (PfP) program. Given their crucial position in Central Asia and the porous nature of their shared border with Afghanistan, Tajikistan should be allowed to become a PfP member.

44. Michael Wines, "Accord is Near on Giving Russia a Limited Role in NATO," *The New York Times*, 23 April 2002, p. A3.

45. Of course a large component of the war against terrorism is financial. We omit it here only because NATO has no particular role to play in that area. Efforts to block terror financing will be complex and long-lasting.

46. "OSCE Ministerial Ends with Anti-Terror Declaration, Action Plan," US State Department website, 4 December 2001, http://usinfo.state.gov/topical/pol/terror/01120404.htm, accessed 11 September 2002.

47. Quoted in BBC News, "OSCE Moves Against Terror," 4 December 2001, internet, http://news.bbc.co.uk/1/hi/world/europe/1689179.stm, accessed 11 September 2002.

48. Julian Lindley-French, *Terms of Engagement: The Paradox of American Power and the Transatlantic Dilemma post-11 September*, Chaillot Paper No. 52 (Paris: Institute for Security Studies, May 2002), p. 14. See also Donald McNeil, "More and More, Other Countries See the War as Solely America's," *The New York Times*, 4 November 2001, p. B1.

49. Suzanne Daley, "Many in Europe Voice Worry U.S. Will Not Consult Them," *The New York Times*, 31 January 2002, p. A12.

POSTSCRIPT

This debate has focused primarily on the future of permanent multilateral military alliances, particularly NATO. An alliance generally involves making a formal commitment, usually through a treaty, to come to the aid of fellow members if they are attacked. As in the case of NATO, an alliance can take on a degree of permanence through the development of formal bureaucratic institutions and structures. To the extent that alliance members share a common set of cultural values and interests, the cohesion of the alliance will be strengthened. Thus, even when the threat that led to the formation of the alliance recedes, the alliance structure itself may continue, often searching for new tasks or missions.

An alternative to an alliance is the formation of more informal coalition. By definition, coalitions are temporary combinations of states that come together to address an immediate threat. Because a coalition, unlike NATO, lacks an institutional base, it may be harder to sustain for very long, especially as the security situation evolves. Therefore coalitions are highly dependent on some combination of diplomatic pressures and financial rewards and punishments to maintain them. In the case of the "war on terrorism," for example, where the enemy is virtually unseen, clear victories are few, and the conflict may be long-term, the challenge of maintaining the cohesiveness of a coalition is enormous.

Nevertheless, some analysts suggest that international coalitions are more likely to be the wave of the future than permanent alliances such as NATO. They note that the two wars in Iraq, the war in Afghanistan, and the war against terrorism have all been fought by broad-based coalitions. The Bush Doctrine, while making reference to multilateral alliances, seems to rely more on a combination of temporary international "coalitions of the willing," bilateral alliances, and a willingness to act unilaterally. However, given their fluidity and the high investment required to maintain their cohesiveness, are such international coalitions likely to replace permanent multilateral alliances altogether in the future?

Suggested Additional Readings

Asmus, Ronald D. "Rebuilding the Atlantic Alliance." *Foreign Affairs* 82, no. 5 (September–October 2003): 20.

Davis, Jacquelyn K. *Reluctant Allies and Competitive Partners: U.S.–French Relations at the Breaking Point?* Herndon, Va.: Brassey's, 2003.

Dibb, Paul. "The Future of International Coalitions: How Useful? How Manageable?" *The Washington Quarterly* 25, no. 2 (Spring 2002): 131–32.

Gvosdev, Nikolas K. "Diplomatic Gobblygook: Alliances and the National Interest." *The National Interest* 2, no. 27 (July 9, 2003). Available at www.inthenationalinterest.com/Articles/Vol2Issue27/Vol2Issue27Realist.html.

Hanson, Victor Davis. "So Long to All That: Why the Old World of Bases, Alliances, and NATO Is Now Coming to an End." *National Review Online* (January 31, 2003). Available at www.nationalreview.com/hanson/hanson013103.asp.

Jentleson, Bruce W. "Tough Love Multilateralism." *The Washington Quarterly* 27, no. 1 (Winter 2003–04): 7–24.

Kolko, Gabriel. "Iraq, the United States, and the End of the European Coalition." *Journal of Contemporary Asia* 33, no. 3 (2003): 291–98.

Legault, Albert. "The Aftermath of the War: New Tasks for the Institutions." *European Foreign Affairs Review* 8, no. 4 (December 2003): 505–08.

Pasicolan, Paolo, and Balbina Y. Hwang. "The Vital Role of Alliances in the Global War on Terrorism." Washington, D.C.: The Hertiage Foundation, Backgrounder no. 1607 (October 24, 2002). Available at www.heritage.org/Research/NationalSecurity/bg1607.cfm.

Tertrais, Bruno. "The Changing Nature of Military Alliances." *The Washington Quarterly* 27, no. 2 (Spring 2004): 135–50.

Walt, Stephen M. "Why Alliances Endure or Collapse." *Survival* 39, no. 1 (Spring 1997): 156–79.

Yost, David S. *NATO Transformed: The Alliance's New Roles in International Security.* Washington, D.C.: Institute of Peace Press, 1998.

InfoTrac® College Edition

Search for the following articles in the InfoTrac® database:

Gordon, Philip H. "NATO and the War on Terrorism: A Changing Alliance (The Shock Wave Abroad)." *Brookings Review* 20, no. 3 (Summer 2002): 36–38.

Rupp, Richard E. "NATO Enlargement: All Aboard? Destination Unknown." *East European Quarterly* 26, no. 3 (Fall 2002): 341–63.

Valasek, Tomas. "The Fight against Terrorism: Where's NATO?" *World Policy Journal* 18, no. 4 (Winter 2001): 19–25.

For more articles, enter:

"NATO" or "military alliances" in the keyword search or subject guide.

Web Resources

For current URLs for the following websites, visit www.crosscurrents.nelson.com.

NORTH ATLANTIC TREATY ORGANIZATION

www.nato.int

The official website of the NATO contains many official documents of the organization, texts of speeches, and news updates.

CENTRE FOR EUROPEAN SECURITY AND DISARMAMENT

www.cesd.org

This site contains many resources on NATO from a European perspective. In the past, the organization published a regular newsletter called *NATO Notes*, which contains articles discussing developments in NATO.

GLOBAL BEAT RESOURCES ON NATO

www.nyu.edu/globalbeat/nato.html

Maintained by the Center for War, Peace and the News Media at New York University, this website contains resources relating to NATO, especially on the topic of expansion.

ARMS CONTROL ASSOCIATION

www.armscontrol.org

The Arms Control Association is a nonpartisan organization promoting an understanding of arms control issues. The site contains articles on NATO and related issues.

FAS MILITARY ANALYSIS NETWORK

www.fas.org/man/nato/index.html

The Federation of American Scientists sponsors this website, which offers an extensive collection on materials on NATO from a variety of differing national perspectives.

Do Biological Differences Predispose Men to War?

✔ **YES**

FRANCIS FUKUYAMA, "Women and the Evolution of World Politics," *Foreign Affairs* 77, no. 5 (September–October 1998): 24–40

✘ **NO**

J. ANN TICKNER, "Why Women Can't Run the World: International Politics According to Francis Fukuyama," *International Studies Review* 1, no. 3 (Fall 1999): 3–11

In a recent article in a leading international relations journal, Martin van Creveld writes: "From North America through Europe to Australia, the military of developed countries are in retreat." He notes that during the last decade, "scarcely a day goes by in any developed country without some military program being cancelled, a procurement decision postponed, or personnel being made redundant" ("The Great Illusion: Women in the Military," *Millennium: Journal of International Studies* 29, no. 2 [2000]: 429).

In examining this trend, van Creveld notes several critical factors. The proliferation of nuclear weapons after World War II made serious conflict between major states virtually unthinkable. With the end of the Cold War, there was less justification for maintaining military budgets. During the past decade, a preoccupation with deficits and a desire to reduce financial costs has made development of new weapons systems unattractive politically.

But van Creveld notes that something else appears to be happening. The decline of Western militaries is taking place at the same time that there has been an unprecedented influx of women into the military. Before 1914, very few women took active part in wars and no military force included them as a regular part of its establishment. The two world wars, and the unprecedented demands for personnel, led to a rethinking of the role for women. For the first time, nations established women's auxiliary corps. In World War I, some 150 000 women served. In World War II, this number increased to 1.5 million women, 800 000 from the Soviet Union alone. Despite this increase, women in uniform still played primarily a support role. Most served in clerical positions or as doctors and nurses. Even in the Soviet Union, where the communist ideology placed more emphasis on the equality of women, few women filled combat positions. Less than one percent of Soviet pilots were women.

This situation began to change in the late 1960s. As the Vietnam War lost popular support in the United States, it became more difficult to recruit men into the military. As a result, military planners became more willing to open the doors to female recruits. By the late 1970s, women made up about seven percent of the American armed forces. Soon other European countries joined in, recruiting larger numbers of women into their armed forces. Once in the military, women insisted that they have the same opportunities for advancement as their male counterparts. Since advancement in the military is limited to those with combat experience, women demanded that all positions, not just non-combat ones, be open to them. Thus, the 1980s and 1990s saw not only an expansion in the number of women serving in the military, but their growing presence in combat positions. During recent war efforts in the Persian Gulf, Kosovo, and Afghanistan, it was not unusual to see press pictures of young mothers in combat fatigues kissing a baby goodbye as they are shipped out to the front.

How should this changing role of women in the military be interpreted? Does it represent a victory for the feminist movement and an indicator of the progress that women are making in competing with men more successfully in all endeavours? Van Creveld claims that the growing role of the women in the military is not a gain for the equality of women. The reason women are enlisting in larger numbers is not to enter into combat as equals with men, but because "they hope that they will not be obliged to fight." Thus, for van Creveld, the "feminization" of the military is not so much a sign of the advancement of women as it is a symptom of the continuing decline of militaries in the West. In fact, van Creveld argues that in countries where wars continue to be fought, women rarely play key leadership and combat roles and instead are involved "overwhelmingly as eggers-on, camp followers, and victims" (441).

Van Creveld's article raises intriguing questions about the relationship between gender and war. Traditionally, war and military service have been the most gendered forms of human activity. Yet they have rarely received sustained attention from international relations scholars. Long dominated by males who work largely within a realist framework, the gendered nature of war has largely been taken for granted. In the past fifteen years, a growing feminist literature on war has tried to address these issues; mainstream international relations scholarship, however, has largely ignored these findings. Joshua Goldstein, in analyzing this situation, notes that a recent major survey of the literature on war and peace showed that only one-tenth of one percent of the writings were devoted to the issue of gender and war.

The gender blinders in mainstream international relations studies carry over to the foreign policy establishment. The influential monthly *Foreign Affairs* did not carry a single article about gender issues between 1990 and 1996. In 1998, however, it published an article on gender and war that attracted considerable debate. Written by Francis Fukuyama, the article addresses the issues raised by van Creveld — what should one make of the "feminization" of the military? Fukuyama argues that biological differences make women more peaceful. As a result, he says, the "feminization of world politics" over the last century (since the suffrage movement) has been a significant contributor to today's "democratic zone of peace."

Although the article was entitled "Women and the Evolution of World Politics," the editors of *Foreign Affairs* chose the more sensational title "What If Women Ran the World?" to run on the front cover. Fukuyama's response appears at first to be largely in sympathy with feminist perspectives. If women ran the world, he says, it would likely be more peaceful and less violent. But Fukuyama bases his argument on an appeal to sociobiology and the inherited biological characteristics of men and women. Thus, he critiques those feminists who argue that war is largely a socially constructed cultural institution that reflects the values of a patriarchal society. In drawing out the implications of his argument, he comes to conclusions that could be used as a basis for arguing against the continued feminization of world politics.

In the second reading, J. Ann Tickner, a leading feminist scholar, critiques Fukuyama's argument. She warns of the dangers of debating the merits of Fukuyama's appeal to sociobiology, arguing that this approach deflects attention away from the real issues about gender and war that need to be addressed.

✔ YES
Women and the Evolution of World Politics
FRANCIS FUKUYAMA

World politics has become increasingly feminized in the 20th century as women have gained political power and exercised it. This evolution in the sexual basis of politics should be reflected in changes in international relations as the correlation between gender and antimilitarism decreases the use of force to solve international problems.

CHIMPANZEE POLITICS

In the world's largest captive chimp colony at the Burger's Zoo in Arnhem, Netherlands, a struggle worthy of Machiavelli unfolded during the late 1970s. As described by primatologist Frans de Waal, the aging alpha male of the colony, Yeroen, was gradually unseated from his position of power by a younger male, Luit. Luit could not have done this on the basis of his own physical strength, but had to enter into an alliance with Nikkie, a still younger male. No sooner was Luit on top, however, than Nikkie turned on him and formed a coalition with the deposed leader to achieve dominance himself. Luit remained in the background as a threat to his rule, so one day he was murdered by Nikkie and Yeroen, his toes and testicles littering the floor of the cage.

Jane Goodall became famous studying a group of about 30 chimps at the Gombe National Park in Tanzania in the 1960s, a group she found on the whole to be peaceful. In the 1970s, this group broke up into what could only be described as two rival gangs in the northern and southern parts of the range. The biological anthropologist Richard Wrangham with Dale Peterson in their 1996 book *Demonic Males* describes what happened next. Parties of four or five males from the northern group would go out, not simply defending their range, but often penetrating into the rival group's territory to pick off individuals caught alone or unprepared. The murders were often grisly, and they were celebrated by the attackers with hooting and feverish excitement. All the males and several of the females in the southern group were eventually killed, and the remaining females forced to join the northern group. The northern Gombe chimps had done, in effect, what Rome did to Carthage in 146 B.C.: extinguished its rival without a trace.

There are several notable aspects to these stories of chimp behavior. First, the violence. Violence within the same species is rare in the animal kingdom, usually restricted to infanticide by males who want to get rid of a rival's offspring and mate with the mother. Only chimps and humans seem to have a proclivity for routinely murdering peers. Second is the importance of coalitions and the politics that goes with coalition-building. Chimps, like humans, are intensely social creatures whose lives are preoccupied with achieving and maintaining dominance in status hierarchies. They threaten, plead, cajole, and bribe their fellow chimps to join with them in alliances, and their dominance lasts only as long as they can maintain these social connections.

Finally and most significantly, the violence and the coalition-building is primarily the work of males. Female chimpanzees can be as violent and cruel as the males at times; females compete with one another in hierarchies and form coalitions to do so. But the most murderous violence is the province of males, and the nature of female alliances is different. According to de Waal, female chimps bond with females to whom they feel some emotional attachment; the males are much more likely to make alliances for purely instrumental, calculating reasons. In other words, female chimps have relationships; male chimps practice realpolitik.

Chimpanzees are man's closest evolutionary relative, having descended from a common chimp-like ancestor less than five million years ago. Not only are they very close on a genetic level, they show many behavioral similarities as well. As Wrangham and Peterson note, of the 4,000 mammal and 10 million or more other species, only chimps and humans live in male-bonded, patrilineal communities in which groups of males routinely engage in aggressive, often murderous raiding of their own species. Nearly 30 years ago, the anthropologist Lionel Tiger suggested that men had special psychological resources for bonding with one another, derived from their need to hunt cooperatively, that explained their dominance in group-oriented activities from politics to warfare. Tiger was roundly denounced by feminists at the time for suggesting that there were biologically based psychological differences between the sexes, but more recent research, including evidence from primatology, has confirmed that male bonding is in fact genetic and predates the human species.

THE NOT-SO-NOBLE SAVAGE

It is all too easy to make facile comparisons between animal and human behavior to prove a polemical point, as did the socialists who pointed to bees and ants to prove that nature endorsed collectivism. Skeptics point out that human beings have language, reason, law, culture, and moral values that make them fundamentally different from even their closest animal relative. In fact, for many years anthropologists endorsed what was in effect a modern version of Rousseau's story of the noble savage: people living in hunter-gatherer societies were pacific in nature. If chimps and modern man had a common proclivity for violence, the cause in the latter case had to be found in civilization and not in human nature.

A number of authors have extended the noble savage idea to argue that violence and patriarchy were late inventions, rooted in either the Western Judeo-Christian tradition or the capitalism to which the former gave birth. Friedrich Engels anticipated the work of later feminists by positing the existence of a primordial matriarchy, which was replaced by a violent and repressive patriarchy only with the transition to agricultural societies. The problem with this theory is, as Lawrence

Keeley points out in his book *War Before Civilization,* that the most comprehensive recent studies of violence in hunter-gatherer societies suggest that for them war was actually more frequent, and rates of murder higher, than for modern ones.

Surveys of ethnographic data show that only 10–13 percent of primitive societies never or rarely engaged in war or raiding; the others engaged in conflict either continuously or at less than yearly intervals. Closer examination of the peaceful cases shows that they were frequently refugee populations driven into remote locations by prior warfare or groups protected by a more advanced society. Of the Yanomamo tribesmen studied by Napoleon Chagnon in Venezuela, some 30 percent of the men died by violence; the !Kung San of the Kalahari desert, once characterized as the "harmless people," have a higher murder rate than New York or Detroit. The sad archaeological evidence from sites like Jebel Sahaba in Egypt, Talheim in Germany, or Roaix in France indicates that systematic mass killings of men, women, and children occurred in Neolithic times. The Holocaust, Cambodia, and Bosnia have each been described as a unique, and often as a uniquely modern, form of horror. Exceptional and tragic they are indeed, but with precedents stretching back tens if not hundreds of thousands of years.

It is clear that this violence was largely perpetrated by men. While a small minority of human societies have been matrilineal, evidence of a primordial matriarchy in which women dominated men, or were even relatively equal to men, has been hard to find. There was no age of innocence. The line from chimp to modern man is continuous.

It would seem, then, that there is something to the contention of many feminists that phenomena like aggression, violence, war, and intense competition for dominance in a status hierarchy are more closely associated with men than women. Theories of international relations like realism that see international politics as a remorseless struggle for power are in fact what feminists call a gendered perspective, describing the behavior of states controlled by men rather than states per se. A world run by women would follow different rules, it would appear, and it is toward that sort of world that all postindustrial or Western societies are moving. As women gain power in these countries, the latter should become less aggressive, adventurous, competitive, and violent.

The problem with the feminist view is that it sees these attitudes toward violence, power, and status as wholly the products of a patriarchal culture, whereas in fact it appears they are rooted in biology. This makes these attitudes harder to change in men and consequently in societies. Despite the rise of women, men will continue to play a major, if not dominant, part in the governance of postindustrial countries, not to mention less-developed ones. The realms of war and international politics in particular will remain controlled by men for longer than many feminists would like. Most important, the task of resocializing men to be more like women — that is, less violent — will run into limits. What is bred in the bone cannot be altered easily by changes in culture and ideology.

THE RETURN OF BIOLOGY

We are living through a revolutionary period in the life sciences. Hardly a week goes by without the discovery of a gene linked to a disease, condition, or behavior, from cancer to obesity to depression, with the promise of genetic therapies and even the outright manipulation of the human genome just around the corner. But while developments in molecular biology have been receiving the lion's share of the headlines, much progress has been made at the behavioral level as well. The past generation has seen a revival in Darwinian thinking about human psychology, with profound implications for the social sciences.

For much of this century, the social sciences have been premised on Emile Durkheim's dictum that social facts can be explained only by prior social facts and not by biological causes. Revolutions and wars are caused by social facts such as economic change, class inequalities, and shifting alliances. The standard social science model assumes that the human mind is the terrain of ideas, customs, and norms that are the products of man-made culture. Social reality is, in other words, socially constructed: if young boys like to pretend to shoot each other more than young girls, it is only because they have been socialized at an early age to do so.

The social-constructionist view, long dominant in the social sciences, originated as a reaction to the early misuse of Darwinism. Social Darwinists like Herbert Spencer or outright racists like Madsen Grant in the late nineteenth and early twentieth centuries used biology, specifically the analogy of natural selection, to explain and justify everything from class stratification to the domination of much of the world by white Europeans. Then Franz Boas, a Columbia anthropologist, debunked many of these theories of European racial superiority by, among other things, carefully measuring the head sizes of immigrant children and noting that they tended to converge with those of native Americans when fed an American diet. Boas, as well as his well-known students Margaret Mead and Ruth Benedict, argued that apparent differences between human groups could be laid at the doorstep of culture rather than nature. There were, moreover, no cultural universals by which Europeans or Americans could judge other cultures. So-called primitive peoples were not inferior, just different. Hence was born both the social constructivism and the cultural relativism with which the social sciences have been imbued ever since.

But there has been a revolution in modern evolutionary thinking. It has multiple roots; one was ethology, the comparative study of animal behavior. Ethologists like Konrad Lorenz began to notice similarities in behavior across a wide variety of animal species, suggesting common evolutionary origins. Contrary to the cultural relativists, they found that not only was it possible to make important generalizations across virtually all human cultures (for example, females are more selective than males in their choice of sexual partners) but even across broad ranges of animal species. Major breakthroughs were made by William Hamilton and

Robert Trivers in the 1960s and 1970s in explaining instances of altruism in the animal world not by some sort of instinct towards species survival but rather in terms of "selfish genes" (to use Richard Dawkins' phrase) that made social behavior in an individual animal's interest. Finally, advances in neurophysiology have shown that the brain is not a Lockean tabula rasa waiting to be filled with cultural content, but rather a highly modular organ whose components have been adapted prior to birth to suit the needs of socially oriented primates. Humans are hard-wired to act in certain predictable ways.

The sociobiology that sprang from these theoretical sources tried to provide a deterministic Darwinian explanation for just about everything, so it was perhaps inevitable that a reaction would set in against it as well. But while the term socio-biology has gone into decline, the neo-Darwinian thinking that spawned it has blossomed under the rubric of evolutionary psychology or anthropology and is today an enormous arena of new research and discovery.

Unlike the pseudo-Darwininsts at the turn of the century, most contemporary biol-ogists do not regard race or ethnicity as biologically significant categories. This stands to reason: the different human races have been around only for the past hundred thousand years or so, barely a blink of the eye in evolutionary time. As countless authors have pointed out, race is largely a socially constructed category: since all races can (and do) interbreed, the boundary lines between them are often quite fuzzy.

The same is not true, however, about sex. While some gender roles are indeed socially constructed, virtually all reputable evolutionary biologists today think there are profound differences between the sexes that are genetically rather than culturally rooted, and that these differences extend beyond the body into the realm of the mind. Again, this stands to reason from a Darwinian point of view: sexual reproduction has been going on not for thousands but hundreds of millions of years. Males and females compete not just against their environment but against one another in a process that Darwin labeled "sexual selection," whereby each sex seeks to maximize its own fitness by choosing certain kinds of mates. The psychological strategies that result from this never-ending arms race between men and women are different for each sex.

In no area is sex-related difference clearer than with respect to violence and aggression. A generation ago, two psychologists, Eleanor Maccoby and Carol Jacklin, produced an authoritative volume on what was then empirically known about differences between the sexes. They showed that certain stereotypes about gender, such as the assertion that girls were more suggestible or had lower self-esteem, were just that, while others, like the idea that girls were less competitive, could not be proven one way or another. On one issue, however, there was virtu-ally no disagreement in the hundreds of studies on the subject: namely, that boys were more aggressive, both verbally and physically, in their dreams, words, and actions than girls. One comes to a similar conclusion by looking at crime statis-tics. In every known culture, and from what we know of virtually all historical time periods, the vast majority of crimes, particularly violent crimes, are committed by men. Here there is also apparently a genetically determined age specificity to violent aggression: crimes are overwhelmingly committed by young men between the ages of 15 and 30. Perhaps young men are everywhere socialized to behave violently, but this evidence, from different cultures and times, suggests that there is some deeper level of causation at work.

At this point in the discussion, many people become uncomfortable and charges of "biological determinism" arise. Don't we know countless women who are stronger, larger, more decisive, more violent, or more competitive than their male counterparts? Isn't the proportion of female criminals rising relative to males? Isn't work becoming less physical, making sexual differences unimportant? The answer to all of these questions is yes: again, no reputable evolutionary biologist would deny that culture also shapes behavior in countless critical ways and can often overwhelm genetic predispositions. To say that there is a genetic basis for sex differences is simply to make a statistical assertion that the bell curve describing the distribution or a certain characteristic is shifted over a little for men as compared with women. The two curves will overlap for the most part, and there will be countless individuals in each population who will have more of any given characteristic than those of the other sex. Biology is not destiny, as tough-minded female leaders like Margaret Thatcher, Indira Gandhi, and Golda Meir have proven. (It is worth pointing out, however, that in male-dominated societies, it is these kinds of unusual women who will rise to the top.) But the statistical assertion also suggests that broad populations of men and women, as opposed to exceptional individuals, will act in certain predictable ways. It also suggests that these populations are not infinitely plastic in the way that their behavior can be shaped by society.

FEMINISTS AND POWER POLITICS

There is by now an extensive literature on gender and international politics and a vigorous feminist subdiscipline within the field of international relations theory based on the work of scholars like J. Ann Tickner, Sara Ruddick, Jean Bethke Elshtain, Judith Shapiro, and others. This literature is too diverse to describe succinctly, but it is safe to say that much of it was initially concerned with understanding how international politics is "gendered," that is, run by men to serve male interests and interpreted by other men, consciously and unconsciously, according to male perspectives. Thus, when a realist theorist like Hans Morganthau or Kenneth Waltz argues that states seek to maximize power, they think that they are describing a universal human characteristic when, as Tickner points out, they are portraying the behavior of states run by men.

Virtually all feminists who study international politics seek the laudable goal of greater female participation in all aspects of foreign relations, from executive mansions and foreign ministries to militaries and universities. They disagree as to whether women should get ahead in politics by demonstrating traditional masculine virtues of toughness, aggression, competitiveness, and the willingness to use force when necessary, or whether they should move the very agenda of politics away from male preoccupations with hierarchy and domination. This ambivalence was demonstrated in the feminist reaction to Margaret Thatcher, who by any account was far tougher and more determined than any of the male politicians she came up against. Needless to say, Thatcher's conservative politics did not endear her to most feminists, who much prefer a Mary Robinson or Gro Harlem Brundtland as their model of a female leader, despite – or because of – the fact that Thatcher had beaten men at their own game.

Both men and women participate in perpetuating the stereotypical gender identities that associate men with war and competition and women with peace and cooperation. As sophisticated feminists like Jean Bethke Elshtain have pointed out, the traditional dichotomy between the male "just warrior" marching to war and the female "beautiful soul" marching for peace is frequently transcended in practice by women intoxicated by war and by men repulsed by its cruelties. But like many stereotypes, it rests on a truth, amply confirmed by much of the new research in evolutionary biology. Wives and mothers can enthusiastically send their husbands and sons off to war; like Sioux women, they can question their manliness for failing to go into battle or themselves torture prisoners. But statistically speaking it is primarily men who enjoy the experience of aggression and the camaraderie it brings and who revel in the ritualization of war that is, as the anthropologist Robin Fox puts it, another way of understanding diplomacy.

A truly matriarchal world, then, would be less prone to conflict and more conciliatory and cooperative than the one we inhabit now. Where the new biology parts company with feminism is in the causal explanation it gives for this difference in sex roles. The ongoing revolution in the life sciences has almost totally escaped the notice of much of the social sciences and humanities, particularly the parts of the academy concerned with feminism, postmodernism, cultural studies, and the like. While there are some feminists who believe that sex differences have a natural basis, by far the majority are committed to the idea that men and women are psychologically identical, and that any differences in behavior, with regard to violence or any other characteristic, are the result of some prior social construction passed on by the prevailing culture.

THE DEMOCRATIC AND FEMININE PEACE

Once one views international relations through the lens of sex and biology, it never again looks the same. It is very difficult to watch Muslims and Serbs in Bosnia, Hums and Tutsis in Rwanda, or militias from Liberia and Sierra Leone to Georgia and Afghanistan divide themselves up into what seem like indistinguishable male-bonded groups in order to systematically slaughter one another, and not think of the chimps at Gombe.

The basic social problem that any society faces is to control the aggressive tendencies of its young men. In hunter-gatherer societies, the vast preponderance of violence is over sex, a situation that continues to characterize domestic violent crime in contemporary postindustrial societies. Older men in the community have generally been responsible for socializing younger ones by ritualizing their aggression, often by directing it toward enemies outside the community. Much of that external violence can also be over women. Modern historians assume that the Greeks and Trojans could not possibly have fought a war for ten years over Helen, but many primitive societies like the Yanomamo do exactly that. With the spread of agriculture 10,000 years ago, however, and the accumulation of wealth and land, war turned toward the acquisition of material goods. Channeling aggression outside the community may not lower societies' overall rate of violence, but it at least offers them the possibility of domestic peace between wars.

The core of the feminist agenda for international politics seems fundamentally correct: the violent and aggressive tendencies of men have to be controlled, not simply by redirecting them to external aggression but by constraining those impulses through a web of norms, laws, agreements, contracts, and the like. In addition, more women need to be brought into the domain of international politics as leaders, officials, soldiers, and voters. Only by participating fully in global politics can women both defend their own interests and shift the underlying male agenda.

The feminization of world politics has, of course, been taking place gradually over the past hundred years, with very positive effects. Women have won the right to vote and participate in politics in all developed countries, as well as in many developing countries, and have exercised that right with increasing energy. In the United States and other rich countries, a pronounced gender gap with regard to foreign policy and national security issues endures. American women have always been less supportive than American men of U.S. involvement in war, including World War II, Korea, Vietnam, and the Persian Gulf War, by an average margin of seven to nine percent. They are also consistently less supportive of defense spending and the use of force abroad. In a 1995 Roper survey conducted for the Chicago Council on Foreign Relations, men favored U.S. intervention in Korea in the event of a North Korean attack by a margin of 49 to 40 percent, while women were opposed by a margin of 30 to 54 percent. Similarly, U.S. military action against Iraq in the event it invaded Saudi Arabia was supported by men by a margin of 62 to 31 percent and opposed by women by 43 to 45 percent. While 54 percent of men felt it important to maintain superior world wide military power, only 45 percent of women agreed. Women, moreover, are less likely than men to see force as a legitimate tool for resolving conflicts.

It is difficult to know how to account for this gender gap; certainly, one cannot move from biology to voting behavior in a single step. Observers have suggested various reasons why women are less willing to use military force than men, including their role as mothers, the fact that many women are feminists (that is, committed to a left-of-center agenda that is generally hostile to U.S. intervention), and of partisan affiliation (more women vote Democratic than men). It is unnecessary to know the reason for the correlation between gender and antimilitarism, however, to predict that increasing female political participation will probably make the United States and other democracies less inclined to use power around the world as freely as they have in the past.

Will this shift toward a less status- and military-power-oriented world be a good thing? For relations between states in the so-called democratic zone of peace, the answer is yes. Consideration of gender adds a great deal to the vigorous and interesting debate over the correlation between democracy and peace that has taken place in the past decade. The "democratic peace" argument, which underlies the foreign policy of the Clinton administration as well as its predecessors, is that democracies tend not to fight one another. While the empirical claim has been contested, the correlation between the degree of consolidation of liberal democratic institutions and interdemocratic peace would seem to be one of the few nontrivial generalizations one can make about world politics. Democratic peace theorists have been less persuasive about the reasons democracies are pacific toward one another. The reasons usually cited — the rule of law, respect for individual rights, the commercial nature of most democracies, and the like — are undoubtedly correct. But there is another factor that has generally not been taken into account: developed democracies also tend to be more feminized than authoritarian states, in terms of expansion of female franchise and participation in political decision-making. It should therefore surprise no one that the historically unprecedented shift in the sexual basis of politics should lead to a change in international relations.

THE REALITY OF AGGRESSIVE FANTASIES

On the other hand, if gender roles are not simply socially constructed but rooted in genetics, there will be limits to how much international politics can change. In anything but a totally feminized world, feminized policies could be a liability.

Some feminists talk as if gender identities can be discarded like an old sweater, perhaps by putting young men through mandatory gender studies courses when they are college freshmen. Male attitudes on a host of issues, from child-rearing and housework to "getting in touch with your feelings," have changed dramatically in the past couple of generations due to social pressure. But socialization can accomplish only so much, and efforts to fully feminize young men will probably be no more successful than the Soviet Union's efforts to persuade its people to work on Saturdays on behalf of the heroic Cuban and Vietnamese people. Male tendencies to band together for competitive purposes, to dominate status hierarchies, and to act out aggressive fantasies toward one another can be rechanneled but never eliminated.

Even if we can assume peaceful relations between democracies, the broader world scene will still be populated by states led by the occasional Mobutu, Milosevic, or Saddam. Machiavelli's critique of Aristotle was that the latter did not take foreign policy into account in building his model of a just city: in a system of competitive states, the best regimes adopt the practices of the worst in order to survive. So even if the democratic, feminized, postindustrial world has evolved into a zone of peace where struggles are more economic than military, it will still have to deal with those parts of the world run by young, ambitious, unconstrained men. If a future Saddam Hussein is not only sitting on the world's oil supplies but is armed to the hilt with chemical, biological, and nuclear weapons, we might be better off being led by women like Margaret Thatcher than, say, Gro Harlem Brundtland. Masculine policies will still be required, though not necessarily masculine leaders.

The implications of evolutionary biology for the hot-button issue of women in the military is not as straightforward as one might think. The vast majority of jobs in a modern military organization are in the enormous support tail that trails behind the actual combat units, and there is no reason that women cannot perform them as well if not better than men. While men have clearly evolved as cooperative hunters and fighters, it is not clear that any individual group of women will perform less well than any individual group of men in combat. What is much more problematic is integrating men and women into the same combat units, where they will be in close physical proximity over long periods of time. Unit cohesion, which is the bedrock on which the performance of armies rests, has been traditionally built around male bonding, which can only be jeopardized when men start competing for the attention of women. Commanders who encourage male bonding are building on a powerful natural instinct; those who try to keep sexual activity between healthy 20-year-old men and women in check through "zero tolerance" policies and draconian punishments are, by contrast, seeking to do something very unnatural. Unlike racial segregation, gender segregation in certain parts of the military seems not just appropriate but necessary.

THE MARGARET THATCHERS OF THE FUTURE

The feminization of democratic politics will interact with other demographic trends in the next 50 years to produce important changes. Due to the precipitous fall in fertility rates across the developed world since the 1960s, the age distribution of countries belonging to the Organization of Economic Cooperation and Development will shift dramatically. While the median age for America's population was in the mid-20s during the first few decades of the twentieth century, it will climb toward 40 by 2050. The change will be even more dramatic in Europe and Japan, where rates of immigration and fertility are lower. Under the UN Population Division's low-growth projections, the median age in Germany will be 55, in Japan 53, and in Italy 58.

The graying of the population has heretofore been discussed primarily in terms of the social security liability it will engender. But it carries a host of other social consequences as well, among them the emergence of elderly women as one of the most important voting blocs courted by mid-21st century politicians. In Italy and Germany, for example, women over 50, who now constitute 20 percent of the population, will account for 31 percent in 2050. There is no way, of course, of predicting how they will vote, but it seems likely that they will help elect more women leaders and will be less inclined toward military intervention than middle-aged males have traditionally been. Edward Luttwak of the Center for Strategic and International Studies has speculated that the fall in family sizes makes people in advanced countries much more leery of military casualties than people in agricultural societies, with their surpluses of young, hotheaded men. According to demographer Nicholas Eberstadt, three-fifths of Italy's offspring in 2050 will be only children with no cousins, siblings, aunts, or uncles. It is not unreasonable to suppose that in such a world tolerance of casualties will be even lower.

By the middle of the next century, then, Europe will likely consist of rich, powerful, and democratic nations with rapidly shrinking populations of mostly elderly people where women will play important leadership roles. The United States, with its higher rates of immigration and fertility, will also have more women leaders but a substantially younger population. A much larger and poorer part of the world will consist of states in Africa, the Middle East, and South Asia with young, growing populations, led mostly by younger men. As Eberstadt points out, Asia outside of Japan will buck the trend toward feminization because the high rate of abortion of female fetuses has shifted their sex ratios sharply in favor of men. This will be, to say the least, an unfamiliar world.

LIVING LIKE ANIMALS?

In Wrangham and Peterson's *Demonic Males* (said to be a favorite book of Hillary Rodham Clinton, who has had her own to contend with), the authors come to the pessimistic conclusion that nothing much has changed since early hominids branched off from the primordial chimp ancestor five million years ago. Group solidarity is still based on aggression against other communities; social cooperation is undertaken to achieve higher levels of organized violence. Robin Fox has argued that military technology has developed much faster than man's ability to ritualize violence and direct it into safer channels. The Gombe chimps could kill only a handful of others; modern man can vaporize tens of millions.

While the history of the first half of the twentieth century does not give us great grounds for faith in the possibility of human progress, the situation is not nearly as bleak as these authors would have us believe. Biology, to repeat, is not destiny.

Rates of violent homicide appear to be lower today than during mankind's long hunter-gatherer period, despite gas ovens and nuclear weapons. Contrary to the thrust of postmodernist thought, people cannot free themselves entirely from biological nature. But by accepting the fact that people have natures that are often evil, political, economic, and social systems can be designed to mitigate the effects of man's baser instincts.

Take the human and particularly male desire to dominate a status hierarchy, which people share with other primates. The advent of liberal democracy and modern capitalism does not eliminate that desire, but it opens up many more peaceful channels for satisfying it. Among the American Plains Indians or the Yanomamo, virtually the only way for a man to achieve social recognition was to be a warrior, which meant, of course, excelling at killing. Other traditional societies might add a few occupations like the priesthood or the bureaucracy in which one could achieve recognition. A modern, technological society, by contrast, offers thousands of arenas in which one can achieve social status, and in most of them the quest for status leads not to violence but to socially productive activity. A professor receiving tenure at a leading university, a politician winning an election, or a CEO increasing market share may satisfy the same underlying drive for status as being the alpha male in a chimp community. But in the process, these individuals have written books, designed public policies, or brought new technologies to market that have improved human welfare.

Of course, not everyone can achieve high rank or dominance in any given status hierarchy, since these are by definition zero-sum games in which every winner produces a loser. But the advantage of a modern, complex, fluid society is, as economist Robert Frank has pointed out, that small frogs in large ponds can move to smaller ponds in which they will loom larger. Seeking status by choosing the right pond will not satisfy the ambitions of the greatest and noblest individuals, but it will bleed off much of the competitive energy that in hunter-gatherer or agricultural societies often has no outlet save war. Liberal democracy and market economies work well because, unlike socialism, radical feminism, and other utopian schemes, they do not try to change human nature. Rather, they accept biologically grounded nature as a given and seek to constrain it through institutions, laws, and norms. It does not always work, but it is better than living like animals.

✗ NO
Why Women Can't Run the World: International Politics According to Francis Fukuyama
J. ANN TICKNER

Feminist perspectives on international relations have proliferated in the last ten years, yet they remain marginal to the discipline as a whole, and there has been little engagement between feminists and international relations (IR) scholars. As I have suggested elsewhere, I believe this is largely due to misunderstandings about feminist IR scholarship that are reflected in questions that feminists frequently are asked when presenting their work to IR audiences.[1] Many of these misunderstandings reflect considerable ontological and epistemological differences, which are particularly acute with respect to mainstream IR approaches. In other words, feminists and IR scholars frequently talk about different worlds and use different methodologies to understand them.[2]

A different kind of misunderstanding, also prevalent, arises from the fact that talking about gender involves issues of personal identity that can be very threatening, even in academic discourse. Feminists are frequently challenged by their critics for seeming to imply (even if it is not their intention) that women are somehow "better" than men. In IR, this often comes down to accusations that feminists are implying that women are more peaceful than men or that a world run by women would be less violent and morally superior. Critics will support their challenges by reference to female policymakers, such as Margaret Thatcher, Golda Meir, or Indira Gandhi, who, they claim, behaved exactly like men.[3]

Most IR feminists would deny the assertion that women are morally superior to men. Indeed, many of them have claimed that the association of women with peace and moral superiority has a long history of keeping women out of power, going back to the debates about the merits of female suffrage in the early part of the century. The association of women with peace can play into unfortunate gender stereotypes that characterize men as active, women as passive; men as agents, women as victims; men as rational, women as emotional. Not only are these stereotypes damaging to women, particularly to their credibility as actors in matters of international politics and national security, but they are also damaging to peace.

As a concept, peace will remain a "soft" issue, utopian and unrealistic, as long as it is associated with femininity and passivity.[4] This entire debate about aggressive men and peaceful women frequently comes up when issues about women and world politics are on the table. Moreover, it detracts from what feminists consider to be more pressing agendas such as striving to uncover and understand the disadvantaged socioeconomic position of many of the world's women and why women are so poorly represented among the world's policymakers.

A current version using the claim that women are more peaceful than men to women's disadvantage, and the types of agenda-deflecting debates it may engender, can be found in Francis Fukuyama's recent article, "Women and the Evolution of World Politics," in *Foreign Affairs*, as well as in the commentaries on it in the subsequent issue.[5] Unlike the type of criticism mentioned above that, often mistakenly, accuses feminists of claiming the morally superior high ground for women, Fukuyama boldly asserts that indeed women *are* more peaceful than men. But, as has so often been the case, Fukuyama deploys his argument to mount a strong defense for keeping men in charge. Not only does this type of reasoning feed into more strident forms of backlash against women in international politics, but it also moves our attention further away from more important issues. Hypothesizing about the merits or disadvantages of women in charge, or debating the relative aggressiveness of men and women, does little to address the realities of a variety of oppressions faced by women worldwide. Fukuyama's views not only deflect from important feminist agendas, but they also support some disturbing trends in IR more generally, which are reinforcing polarized views of the world in terms of civilization clashes and zones of peace versus zones of turmoil.[6]

Foreign Affairs chose to publish Fukuyama's article under the cover title (in red) "What If Women Ran the World?" This title was surely designed to provoke (and perhaps frighten) its readers, most of whom are probably unfamiliar with IR feminist scholarship. More problematically, it is likely that this will be the only article that mentions feminist IR scholarship to which readers of *Foreign Affairs* will be exposed.[7] Responses in the subsequent issue of *Foreign Affairs* were, for the most part, quite hostile to Fukuyama's position, and asked what was wrong with his argument. Katha Pollitt asserts, "just about everything."[8] Nevertheless, by focusing on the need to rebut Fukuyama's sociobiological and over-generalized portrayal of warlike men and peaceful women, these responses, like the article itself, refocus conversations in unproductive ways that do little to clarify many of the issues with which IR feminists are concerned.

Fukuyama's article is not overtly antifeminist. Indeed, he cites what he calls "a vigorous feminist subdiscipline within the field of international relations" (p. 32) quite favorably, albeit chastising postmodernism for its commitment to social constructionism and radical feminism for its misguided utopianism (p. 40).[9] Curiously, in light of his misgivings about utopianism, Fukuyama offers a seemingly optimistic, even radical vision of a different, relatively peaceful, "feminized" world (in the West at least), where men's aggressive animal instincts have been tamed and channeled into productive activities associated with liberal democracy and capitalism. Fukuyama supports his central claim — that men have "naturally" aggressive instincts — by comparing their behavior to the aggressive and even Machiavellian behavior of male chimpanzees in Gombe National Park in Tanzania. This type of aggression, which, Fukuyama argues, is atypical of most intraspecies behavior, is as true of male humans as it is of their nearest evolutionary relatives, male chimpanzees.

Fukuyama notes that, as with chimps, violence in all types of human societies has been perpetrated largely by men. He develops this claim by documenting recent discoveries in the life sciences and evolutionary psychology that find profound differences between the sexes, especially in areas of violence and aggression. Whereas he is careful to say that culture also shapes human behavior, Fukuyama believes that this line of thinking will replace social constructionist views of gender differences that came about as a reaction to the misuse of Darwinism to reinforce racial superiority and class stratification. In other words, these findings have profound implications for all the social sciences.

Fukuyama also notes that feminists prefer to see such behavior as a product of patriarchal culture rather than rooted in human biology because biologically rooted behavior is harder to change: therefore, they will not be happy with his claims. Fukuyama goes on to hypothesize about a feminized world that would follow different rules. He sees the realization of such a world as a distinct possibility, at least in the West, as women gain more political power. What he calls the "feminization" of world politics has been taking place gradually as women have won the right to vote. The right to vote, along with a relative increase in numbers of elderly women, has resulted in a gender gap with respect to voting on issues of foreign policy and national security, with women being less supportive of national defense spending and involvement in war than men. In spite of these trends, Fukuyama predicts that men will continue to play an important role, particularly in international politics where toughness and aggression are still required.

Given the difficulties of changing genetically programmed behavior and presuming that this new world would have to include socially constructed feminized men, this hypothetical picture seems like a considerable leap from reality. Even though Fukuyama's portrait of this feminized world is seemingly sympathetic, I believe that his message is, in fact, deeply conservative – offering one more iteration of the well-established argument that a "realistic" view of international politics demands that "real" men remain in charge. Accepting its premises actually silences, rather than promotes, feminist agendas and women's equality. Although many of his claims can be successfully challenged on empirical grounds, as his critics demonstrated by their rebuttals in *Foreign Affairs*, his views feed into a conservative agenda that serves not to put women in control, but to keep them out of positions of power.

Why is this the case? Because Fukuyama tells us that no matter how attractive it may seem, we should not move further toward this feminized world; instead, we must keep things the way they are – with strong men at the helm. He argues that women are not able to deal with today's threats that come from violent leaders, such as Slobodan Milosevic, Saddam Hussein, and Mobutu Sese Seko. On the horizon are threats from states in the Middle East, Africa, and South Asia, led by aggressive younger men unsocialized in the ways of mature democracies. Fukuyama claims that people in agricultural societies, presumably outside the zone of peace, with their surpluses of young, hotheaded men, are less concerned with military casualties and therefore more prone to pick fights (p. 38), an assertion that appears to have disturbingly racist overtones.

Closer to home, citing the necessity for combat readiness in the face of these dangers, Fukuyama, by advocating separation of men and women in single-sex military units, effectively advises against women in combat positions. Although he does not deny that women could do as well in combat as men (which was indeed demonstrated in the Gulf War), he claims that their presence destroys combat units' cohesion, which he believes is built on male bonding (p. 37). This "false necessity," together with the need to channel what he calls biologically rooted male desire to dominate into successful competition in universities, corporations, and political arenas, seems to imply fewer rather than more opportunities for women in both military and civilian life.[10]

And what of men's biological or naturally aggressive tendencies?[11] As feminists have pointed out, one of the main reasons why today's military is recruiting women is because not enough "aggressive" men are joining up. Much of basic training involves overcoming men's reluctance to kill. Advances in military technology have depersonalized warfare so that the problems associated with the long-standing reluctance of men in combat to fire their weapons have been lessened.[12] Violence inside states, which is more prevalent in the United States than in many states outside the western democratic "zone of peace," about which Fukuyama speaks so favorably, stems at least as much from lack of economic opportunities as it does from innate male aggression.[13] Tenure in universities and corporate success are not just about satisfying the need for social recognition of alpha males; they are much-needed guarantees of income and job security, important to both men *and* women.

If we were to accept that men do have aggressive tendencies, the leap from aggressive men to aggressive states is problematic, as many international relations scholars have pointed out.[14] Do men's aggressive tendencies really get channeled into international war, thus leading to the possibility of domestic peace between wars? The high homicide rate in the United States makes one skeptical of this possibility, whereas Switzerland, a country with one of the lowest homicide rates in the world, is rarely an international aggressor. If most men, particularly young men, have violent tendencies, as Fukuyama claims, why is it that some states are so much more peaceful than others? Statesmen do not choose war lightly. Nor is war generally decided at the ballot box where, according to Fukuyama, significant numbers of women are voting for peace. It has often been older men who send young men off to war to fight for what they see as legitimate national interests. Would American policymakers in the 1960s or today's Vietnam veterans be satisfied with the explanation that America fought in Vietnam as an outlet for the aggressive tendencies of its young men?

Now to turn to some of the real feminist agendas for international politics — agendas that are completely silenced by Fukuyama's article. I know of no international relations feminists who hypothesize about or advocate women running the world, as the cover title of Fukuyama's article and the turn-of-the century illustration depicting a woman in boxing gloves "flooring her beau" (p. 29) suggest. Although Fukuyama includes socially feminized men (who must have overcome their aggressive genes) in the ruling coalitions of his feminized world, such a world is unappealing and sure to threaten, or perhaps amuse, those presently in charge, as well as reinforce culturally defined gender stereotypes about international politics and women.

What IR feminists *have* argued for is getting rid of idealistic associations of women with peace. Associations of women with peace, idealism, and impracticality have long served to disempower women and keep them in their place, which is out of the "real world" of international politics.

When Fukuyama claims that sociobiology was misused at the turn of the century, with respect to race and ethnicity, he too, is misusing it. He does this under the guise of evidence about profound genetically rooted differences between the sexes by inferring that these differences predetermine men's and women's different (and unequal) roles with respect to contemporary international politics.[15] Of course, feminists want women to participate more fully in global politics and contribute to making the world a less dangerous place. But, rather than killing each other, haven't many men been working toward this goal also?

Wherever men's genes may have pointed, they founded the discipline of international relations by trying to understand why states go to war and trying to devise institutions to diminish its likelihood in the future. Preferred futures are not feminized, but ones in which women *and* men participate in reducing damaging and unequal hierarchical social structures, such as gender and race.

Many feminists would agree that biology may indeed be a contributing factor to certain aggressive behaviors. Yet understanding and working to lessen various insecurities that women face can only be achieved if we acknowledge a need for diminishing socially constructed gender hierarchies that result in the devaluation of women's lives and their economic and social contributions to society. In spite of Fukuyama's assertion that social constructionism is being effectively challenged by new findings in evolutionary biology, the fact that the majority of subsistence farmers in Africa are women, while men are more frequently found in the more prosperous cash crop sector, can hardly be explained by biology alone. Culturally assigned roles, which have little to do with biology, diminish women's socioeconomic position in most societies. Speculating about women in charge, whether their boxing gloves are on or off, seems far removed from the lived reality of the vast majority of the world's women. Katha Pollitt states that even in the United States, where Fukuyama claims that women are fast gaining political power, women constitute only 12 percent of Congress and, after 80 years of female suffrage, have not even won the right to paid maternity leave or affordable day care.[16] Running foreign policy, she concludes, seems like a fantasy.[17] Nevertheless, by focusing on these unlikely futures, Fukuyama effectively silences more pressing agendas and deflects investigations away from trying to understand why the world's women are so often disempowered and even oppressed.

Of course, IR feminists are concerned with issues of war and peace. But rather than debating whether men are aggressive and women peaceful, they are asking new questions about conflict, as well as trying to expand conventional agendas. Feminist agendas include human rights issues such as rape in war, military prostitution, refugees (the majority of whom are women and children), and more generally issues about civilian casualties.[18] Even though civilians now account for well over 80 percent of wartime casualties, understanding the reasons for and consequences of these disturbing trends has not been at the center of international relations investigations. Feminists have also joined the debate about whether security should be defined more broadly to include issues of structural and ecological violence. With this question in mind, feminists are investigating the often negative effects of structural adjustment and economic globalization on women, as well as problems associated with the degradation of the environment.[19] All of these issues seem closer to women's lived realities than debates about their likelihood of running the world.

By asserting that developed democracies tend to be more feminized than authoritarian states, and by linking this to the popular claim about the relative peacefulness of democracies, Fukuyama obscures deeper truths and hides more progressive practical possibilities.

Kal Holsti has suggested that a better explanation for "zones of peace," which actually extend well beyond Western democracies, is the diminished likelihood of war between strong states with governments seen as legitimate by their populations.[20] There are very few states where some have reached a critical mass in political decisionmaking, which makes any link between the democratic peace and the political participation of women tenuous at best. A more fruitful line of investigation is one that is illustrated by a study outlining the results of survey data collected in several Middle Eastern countries, democratic and otherwise. The data show that in the case of the Arab-Israeli dispute, women are not less militaristic than men, but both women and men who are more supportive of gender equality are also more favorably disposed to compromise.[21] A cluster of such attitudes could be the building blocks not for a more feminized world, whatever that may mean, but for a more just and peaceful world in which gender and other social hierarchies of domination, which have resulted in the subordination of women, are diminished.

The debate surrounding Fukuyama's article appears to have stimulated a race to demonstrate who can be more aggressive than whom. Marshaling evidence of women's participation in wars, with pictures of female soldiers on parade and documenting women's violence in matters of abuse of children and servants, Ehrenreich and Pollitt assure us that women can be every bit as aggressive as men.[22]

Are these the debates we should be having? Surely they deflect from the real issues with which international relations scholars are struggling – namely to try to understand the roots of war and what can be done to prevent it. Investigating the enormous variations in levels of conflict across history and societies is surely a more promising place to begin than in deterministic, biologically rooted theories about the aggressive nature of men. International relations feminists have added a new and important dimension to these investigations.

Rather than joining debates about aggressive men and peaceful women, IR feminists are striving to better understand unequal social hierarchies, including gender hierarchies, which contribute to conflict, inequality, and oppression. Evidence suggests that war is more likely in societies with greater gender inequality. Intentionally or not, Fukuyama's musings about women running the world deflect attention away from this more pressing agenda of working toward a world with increased gender equality. Such a world could, I believe, be a less conflictual one for both women and men. Let us turn our attention to more productive conversations between feminist and international relations scholars about the evolution of world politics, conversations that strive to better understand how such a world could be realized.

NOTES

1. J. Ann Tickner, "You Just Don't Understand: Troubled Engagements Between Feminists and IR Theorists," *International Studies Quarterly* 41, No. 4 (1997), pp. 611–632.

2. The symposium in *International Studies Quarterly* 42, No. 1 (1998), pp. 193–209 is an exception to the lack of engagement. It also demonstrates some of the conversational difficulties to which I refer.

3. Tickner, "You Just Don't Understand," p. 613.

4. For elaboration on this claim, see Jean B. Elshtain, "The Problem with Peace," in Jean Elshtain and Sheila Tobias, eds., *Women, Militarism and War* (Savage, Md.: Rowman and Littlefield, 1990), pp. 255–266; and Christine Sylvester, "Some Dangers In Merging Feminist and Peace Projects," *Alternatives* 12, No. 4 (1987), pp. 493–509.

5. Francis Fukuyama, "Women and the Evolution of World Politics," *Foreign Affairs* 77, No. 5 (1998), pp. 24–40; and Barbara Ehrenreich, Katha Pollitt, et al., "Fukuyama's Follies: So What If Women Ran the World?" *Foreign Affairs* 78, No. 1 (1999), pp. 118–129.

6. See, for example, Samuel Huntington, *The Clash of Civilizations and the Remaking of World Order* (New York: Simon and Schuster, 1996); and Max Singer and Aaron Wildavsky, *The Real World Order: Zones of Peace, Zones of Turmoil* (Chatham, N.J.: Chatham House Publishers, 1993). Fukuyama also draws on the democratic peace argument to support his global polarization view. For further discussion of this point, see Miriam Fendius Elman, "The Never-Ending Story: Democracy and Peace," in this issue of *International Studies Review*.

7. Indeed, Fukuyama's article has received much worldwide attention in the press, as well as in the foreign policy community. See, for example, Katie Grant, "Why We Need Men in Our New Feminine World," *Glasgow Herald*, January 11, 1999, p. 13.

8. Katha Pollitt, "Father Knows Best," *Foreign Affairs* 78, No. 1 (1999), p. 123.

9. Since *Foreign Affairs* does not allow footnotes, it is often difficult to know to which specific literature Fukuyama refers when making such criticism.

10. This type of argument has shown up in more virulent forms. See, for example, Harvey Mansfield, "Why a Woman Can't Be More Like a Man," *Wall Street Journal*, November 3, 1997, p. A22. Mansfield accuses feminists of "feminizing America." He argues that

women are not cut out for war and that men must be allowed to fulfill their traditional role as protectors, a role that is being undermined as women gain equal access to jobs outside the home. Fukuyama also addresses some of these issues in his new book *The Great Disruption: Human Nature and the Reconstitution of Social Order* (New York: Free Press, 1999).

11. R. Brian Ferguson, "Perilous Positions," *Foreign Affairs* 78, No. 1 (1999), p. 125 claims that chimpanzees' naturally aggressive tendencies are also questionable. He contends that the Gombe chimps became aggressive only after human-induced changes in their feeding patterns.

12. While there has been evidence documenting soldiers' reluctance to kill, I realize this is a controversial argument. For further discussion of this issue, including positions that refute this hypothesis, see Joanna Bourke, *An Intimate History of Killing: Face to Face Killing in Twentieth Century Warfare* (London: Granta Books, 1999).

13. The recent dramatic drop in the crime rate in the United States seems to support this position.

14. For examples, see Kenneth Walz, *Theory of International Politics* (Reading, Mass.: Addison Wesley, 1979), Chap. 2; and Jane Jaquette, "States Make War," *Foreign Affairs* 78, No. 1 (1999), pp. 128–129.

15. The popularity of sociobiological arguments about sex differences is evidenced by a cover story in *Time*, March 8, 1999, p. 57, by Barbara Ehrenreich entitled "The Real Truth about the Female." Ehrenreich's position is much more sympathetic to women — she cites feminist scholars who are doing serious work in this area — but it is indicative of a trend toward emphasizing the sociobiological roots of human behavior and its appeal to wider audiences. Many feminists would probably argue that biology and culture are mutually constitutive of each other.

16. Pollitt, "Father Knows Best," p. 125.

17. Katie Grant points out that if, as Fukuyama claims, men can become feminized, we do not necessarily need women to run things, even in this new gentler world. Grant, "Why We Need Men."

18. Ruth Seifert, "The Second Front: The Logic of Sexual Violence in Wars," *Women's Studies International Forum* 19, No. 1–2 (1996), pp. 35–43; Cynthia Enloe, *Bananas, Beaches and Bases: Making Feminist Sense of International Politics* (Berkeley: University of California Press, 1990); Katharine Moon, *Sex Among Allies: Military Prostitution in US-Korean Relations* (New York: Columbia University Press, 1997); and Susan Forbes Martin, *Refugee Women* (London: Zed Books, 1992).

19. Eleonore Kofman and Gillian Youngs, eds., *Globalization: Theory and Practice* (London: Pinter, 1996); Maria Mies and Vandana Shiva, *Ecofeminism* (London: Zed Books, 1993); and Rosi Braidotti et al., *Women, the Environment and Sustainable Development: Towards a Theoretical Synthesis* (London: Zed Books, 1994).

20. Kalevj Holsti, *The State, War, and the State of War* (Cambridge, U.K.: Cambridge University Press, 1996).

21. Mark Tessler and Ina Warriner, "Gender, Feminism, and Attitudes Toward International Conflict: Exploring Relationships with Survey Data from the Middle East," *World Politics* 49, No. 2 (1997), pp. 250–281.

22. Barbara Ehrenreich, "Men Hate War Too," *Foreign Affairs* 18, No. 1 (1999), pp. 120–121; and Katha Pollitt, "Father Knows Best," p. 123.

POSTSCRIPT

In discussing this topic, it is useful to note that feminists do not take a single approach to the issue of war and peace. Some feminists believe that women's experiences are fundamentally different from men's. According to this view, the problem is not that men and women are different but that sexist cultures devalue "feminine" qualities instead of celebrating and promoting them. Women, because of their greater experience with nurturing and human relations, are generally more effective than men in conflict resolution and group decisionmaking. But they are less effective than men in combat. Such feminists see these gender differences as partly biologically based, as Fukuyama claims. But others see them as entirely culturally constructed. Many of these feminists see the role of women as primarily to oppose the male-constructed war system and all the symptoms of male dominance that go with it.

Other feminists argue that women are in fact equal to men in ability and that biological differences are not important. The gendering of war reflects male discrimination against women, like other forms of sexism. Women have the right to participate in all social and political institutions (including military ones) without facing discrimination. The exclusion of women from positions of power in international relations is unfair and prevents women from making important contributions to society. However, such feminists do not believe that the inclusion of women in the military will fundamentally change the international system, a given country's foreign policy, or war itself. Unlike Fukuyama, they see no hidden dangers in the "feminization" of world politics.

Suggested Additional Readings

Damousi, Joy, and Marilyn Lake, eds. *Gender and War.* Cambridge: Cambridge University Press, 2001.

Elshtain, Jean Bethke. *Women and War.* New York: Basic Books, 1987.

Enloe, Cynthia. *Bananas, Beaches and Bases: Making Feminist Sense of International Politics.* Berkeley: University of California Press, 1989.

Pierson, Ruth Roach, ed. *Women and Peace: Theoretical, Historical and Practical Perspectives.* New York: Croom Helm, 1987.

Tickner, J. Ann. *Gender in International Relations: Feminist Perspectives on Achieving Global Security.* New York: Columbia University Press, 1992.

Van Der Dennen, J., and V. Falger. *Sociobiology and Conflict: Evolutionary Perspectives on Competition, Cooperation, Violence and Warfare.* New York: Chapman & Hall, 1990.

Weinstein, Laurie, and Christie White. *Wives and Warriors: Women and the Military in the United States and Canada.* Westport, Conn.: Bergin & Garvey, 1997.

Whitworth, Sandra. *Feminism and International Relations: Towards a Political Economy of Gender in Interstate and Non-Governmental Institutions.* New York: St. Martin's, 1994.

Wicks, Stephen. *Warriors and Wildmen: Men, Masculinity, and Gender.* Westport, Conn.: Bergin & Garvey, 1996.

Wrangham, Richard, and Dale Peterson. *Demonic Males: Apes and the Origins of Human Violence.* New York: Houghton Mifflin, 1996.

York, Jodi. "The Truth(s) about Women and Peace." *Peace Review* 8, no. 3 (1996): 323–29.

InfoTrac® College Edition

Search for the following articles in the InfoTrac® database:

Cooke, Miriam. "Gender Camouflage: Women and the U.S. Military." *NWSA Journal* 13, no. 3 (Fall 2001): 181–88.

Jernigan, Pat. "Women at War: Gender Issues of Americans in Combat." *Minerva: Quarterly Report on Women and the Military* 19, no. 1 (Spring 2001): 51.

Rabrenovic, Gordana, and Laura Roskos. "Civil Society, Feminism, and the Gendered Politics of War and Peace." *NWSA Journal* 13, no. 2 (Summer 2001): 40.

For more articles, enter:
"gender and war," "women and war," "women and military," or "war and feminism" in the keyword search.

Web Resources

For current URLs for the following websites, visit www.crosscurrents.nelson.com.

Feminist Theory Website

www.cddc.vt.edu/feminism/enin.html

This page, from Virginia Tech University, provides research materials and information on a range of gender issues.

Feminist Theory and Gender Studies

csf.colorado.edu/isa/sections/ftgs/

A section of the International Studies Association website, this page offers a variety of resources and links on feminist theory and international relations.

H-Minerva: Women and War

www.h-net.org/~minerva/

H-Minerva is a discussion network devoted to the study of women in war and the military, worldwide and in all historical areas. The site also has links to related journals, announcements, and other websites.

War and Gender

www.warandgender.com

This site, maintained by Joshua Goldstein, includes materials and discussions relating to his book, *War and Gender: How Gender Shapes the War System and Vice Versa.* It includes full text of the first chapter of this book.

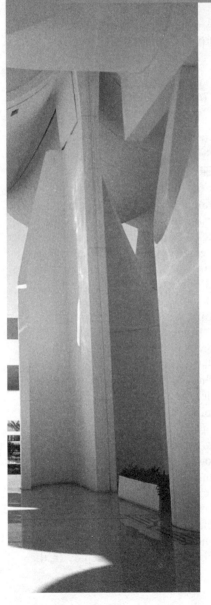

PART THREE

GLOBAL POLITICAL ECONOMY

Does globalization cheat the
world's poor?

Was the "Battle in Seattle" a significant
turning point in the struggle against
globalization?

Would a North American currency
union benefit Canada?

Will the Kyoto Protocol undermine
economic growth and competitiveness
in Canada?

Will debt relief address the needs of
highly indebted countries?

Does Globalization Cheat the World's Poor?

✔ **YES**
MICHEL CHOSSUDOVSKY, "Global Poverty in the Late 20th Century,"
Journal of International Affairs 52, no. 1 (Fall 1998): 293–312

✗ **NO**
GAUTAM SEN, "Is Globalisation Cheating the World's Poor?" *Cambridge
Review of International Affairs* 14, no. 1 (Autumn–Winter 2000): 86–106
(revised)

There is little doubt that the globalization of the world's economy is taking place at an extraordinarily rapid pace. World merchandise exports have expanded at an average annual rate of approximately 6 percent since 1950, compared with a 4.5 percent rate in world output. In 1913, the entire flow of goods in world trade totalled only U.S. $20 billion. In contrast, in 1994, international trade in goods and services stood at U.S. $4.3 trillion a year. Foreign direct investment (FDI) has been growing at an even faster pace than trade. During recent decades, FDI has been reported to have expanded by 27 percent per year, representing an average growth of U.S. $205 billion a year. Today, there are more than 2000 large multinational corporations (operating in six or more countries) and well over 8000 smaller ones. Together, these 10 000 multinationals are estimated to control over 90 000 subsidiaries.

At the same time, technology has been undergoing a similar process of globalization. Miniaturization and computerization have speeded up communications and transportation times while reducing costs. Rapid developments in communications, when combined with the globalization of financial markets, have led to a sharp increase in the movement of capital. Together, these developments have helped propel an expansion of the global economy, which is not limited by traditional geographical constraints. Factors such as geography and climate no longer give a particular region a comparative advantage.

For some observers, the rapid pace of globalization is a welcome trend. The lowering of economic barriers, greater openness to competitive market forces, and the reduction of artificial market restraints are seen as promoting higher economic growth and prosperity. Consumers have access to cheaper, more diverse, and more advanced products. Expansion of trade and investment generates jobs. At the same time, globalization is said to generate positive political dividends. States that adjust to the changing market are able to generate higher rates of economic growth and technological innovation. They have more resources to deploy in the international arena to both promote and defend their interests. Countries that are linked by economic ties and have a mutual interest in promoting economic growth are more likely to seek stable, peaceful, and cooperative ties with other states. Similarly, firms and workers with a stake in trade advancement and economic growth are more likely to be supportive of active and constructive foreign policies that are aimed at maintaining these benefits. Edward Mansfield, in *Power, Trade, and War* (Princeton, N.J.: Princeton University Press, 1994), suggests that the data clearly support the contention that trade and peace are closely related — higher levels of trade are usually associated with lower levels of international hostility and antagonism.

Despite this optimistic picture, economic globalization clearly has its downside. An increasingly liberalized economic world imposes severe adjustment burdens on certain segments of workers and firms. The distribution of wealth, both within and between states, has become more unequal. Exposure to the uncertainties and insecurities of foreign competition has led to demands for protectionist measures and the abandonment of multilateral cooperation. Critics are concerned that unfettered global competition creates overwhelming pressures to abandon domestic social policies, environmental regulations, and human-rights protections.

Such concerns have in turn given rise to a growing backlash against globalization itself. Globalization for many people, it is argued, has become a "race to the bottom." At the heart of globalization is growing poverty and inequality, which can be reversed only if the forces of globalization themselves are curtailed. As the massive demonstrations at several international summits have shown, anti-globalization movements have grown significantly in recent years.

The following essays examine the implications of globalization, particularly for global poverty. Michel Chossudovsky examines the various forces that have contributed to the globalization of poverty and famine in recent decades. Gautam Sen argues that globalization itself need not cheat the world's poor. In fact, economic growth and globalization are important to the economic and social progress of the poor. While rejecting the arguments of anti-globalization theorists and activists, Sen argues for more attention to the ways in which the benefits of globalization can be more effectively redistributed to marginalized segments of society.

✔ YES

Global Poverty in the Late 20th Century
MICHEL CHOSSUDOVSKY

THE GLOBALIZATION OF POVERTY

The late 20th century will go down in world history as a period of global impoverishment marked by the collapse of productive systems in the developing world, the demise of national institutions and the disintegration of health and education programs. This "globalization of poverty" – which has largely reversed the achievements of post-war decolonization – was initiated in the Third World, coinciding with the onslaught of the debt crisis. Since the 1990s, it has extended its grip to all major regions of the world including North America, Western Europe, the countries of the former Soviet block and the Newly Industrialized Countries (NICs) of South East Asia and the Far East.

In the 1990s, famines at the local level have erupted in sub-Saharan Africa, South Asia and parts of Latin America; health clinics and schools have been closed down; and hundreds of millions of children have been denied the right to primary education. In the Third World, Eastern Europe and the Balkans, there has been a resurgence of infectious diseases including tuberculosis, malaria and cholera.

IMPOVERISHMENT — AN OVERVIEW

Famine Formation in the Third World

From the dry savannah of the Sahelian belt, famine has extended its grip into the wet tropical heartland. A large part of the population of the African continent has been affected: 18 million people in Southern Africa (including 2 million refugees) are in "famine zones" and another 130 million in 10 countries are seriously at risk.[1] In the Horn of Africa, 23 million people (many of whom have already died) are "in danger of famine" according to a United Nations estimate.[2]

In the post-independence period extending through the 1980s, starvation deaths in South Asia had largely been limited to peripheral tribal areas. But in India today, there are indications of widespread impoverishment among both the rural and urban populations following the adoption of the 1991 New Economic Policy under the stewardship of the Bretton Woods institutions. More than 70 percent of rural households in India are small marginal farmers or landless farm workers, representing a population of over 400 million people. In irrigated areas, agricultural workers are employed for 200 days a year and in rain-fed farming for approximately 100 days. The phasing out of fertilizer subsidies – an explicit condition of the International Monetary Fund (IMF) agreement – and the increase in the prices of farm inputs and fuel is pushing a large number of small- and medium-sized farmers into bankruptcy.

A micro-level study conducted in 1991 on starvation deaths among handloom weavers in a relatively prosperous rural community in Andhra Pradesh sheds light on how local communities have been impoverished as a result of macroeconomic reform. The starvation deaths occurred in the months following the implementation of the New Economic Policy: with the devaluation and the lifting of controls on cotton yarn exports, the jump in the domestic price of cotton yarn led to a collapse in the pacham (24 meters) rate paid to the weaver by the middle-man (through the putting-out system). "Radhakrishnamurthy and his wife were able to weave between three and four pachams a month, bringing home the meagre income of 300 to 400 rupees (U.S. $12 to 16) for a family of six; then came the Union Budget of 24 July 1991, the price of cotton yarn jumped and the burden was passed on to the weaver. Radhakrishnamurthy's family income declined to 240 to 320 rupees a month (U.S. $9.60 to 13.00)."[3] Radhakrishnamurthy of Gollapalli village in Guntur district died of starvation on 4 September 1991. Between 30 August and 10 November 1991, at least 73 starvation deaths were reported in only two districts of Andhra Pradesh.[4] There are 3.5 million handlooms throughout India supporting a population of some 17 million people.

Economic "Shock Therapy" in the Former Soviet Union

When assessing the impact on earnings, employment and social services, the post-Cold War economic collapse in parts of eastern Europe appears to be far deeper and more destructive than that of the Great Depression. In the former Soviet Union (starting in early 1992), hyperinflation triggered by the downfall of the ruble contributed to rapidly eroding real earnings. Economic "shock therapy" combined with the privatization program precipitated entire industries into immediate liquidation, leading to lay-offs of millions of workers.

In the Russian Federation, prices increased one hundred times following the initial round of macroeconomic reforms adopted by the Yeltsin government in January 1992. Wages, on the other hand, increased tenfold. The evidence suggests that real purchasing power plummeted by more than 80 percent in the course of 1992.[5]

The reforms have dismantled both the military-industrial complex and the civilian economy. Economic decline has surpassed the plunge in production experienced in the Soviet Union at the height of the Second World War, following the German occupation of Byelorussia and parts of the Ukraine in 1941 and the extensive bombing of Soviet industrial infrastructure. The Soviet gross domestic product (GDP) had by 1942 declined by 22 percent in relation to pre-war levels.[6] In contrast, industrial output in the former Soviet Union plummeted by 48.8 percent and GDP by 44.0 percent between 1989 and 1995, according to official data, and output continues to fall.[7] Independent estimates, however, indicate a substantially greater drop and there is firm evidence that official figures have been manipulated.[8]

While the cost of living in eastern Europe and the Balkans was shooting up to western levels as a result of the deregulation of commodity markets, monthly minimum earnings were as low as ten dollars a month. "In Bulgaria, the World Bank and the Ministry of Labor and Social Assistance separately estimated that 90 percent of Bulgarians are living below the poverty threshold of U.S.$4 a day."[9] Old age pensions in 1997 were worth two dollars a month.[10] Unable to pay for electricity, water and transportation, population groups throughout the region have been brutally marginalized from the modern era.

Poverty and Unemployment in the West

Already during the Reagan-Thatcher era, but more significantly since the beginning of the 1990s, harsh austerity measures are gradually contributing to the disintegration of the welfare state. The achievements of the early post-war period are being reversed through the derogation of unemployment insurance schemes, the privatization of pension funds and social services and the decline of social security.

With the breakdown of the welfare state, high levels of youth unemployment are increasingly the source of social strife and civil dissent. In the United States, political figures decry the rise of youth violence, promising tougher sanctions without addressing the roots of the problem. Economic restructuring has transformed urban life, contributing to the "thirdworldization" of western cities. The environment of major metropolitan areas is marked by social apartheid: urban landscapes have become increasingly compartmentalized along social and ethnic lines. Poverty indicators such as infant mortality, unemployment and homelessness in the ghettos of American (and increasingly European) cities are in many respects comparable to those prevailing in the Third World.

Demise of the "Asian Tigers"

More recently, speculative movements against national currencies have contributed to the destabilization of some of the world's more successful "newly industrialized" economies (Indonesia, Thailand, Korea), leading virtually overnight to abrupt declines in the standard of living.

In China, successful poverty alleviation efforts are threatened by the impending privatization or forced bankruptcy of thousands of state enterprises and the resulting lay-offs of millions of workers. The number of workers to be laid off in state industrial enterprises is estimated to be on the order of 35 million.[11] In rural areas, there are approximately 130 million surplus workers.[12] This process has occurred alongside massive budget cuts in social programs, even as unemployment and inequality increase.

In the 1997 Asian currency crisis, billions of dollars of official central bank reserves were appropriated by institutional speculators. In other words, these countries are no longer able to "finance economic development" through the use of monetary policy. This depletion of official reserves is part and parcel of the process of economic restructuring leading to bankruptcy and mass unemployment. In other words, privately held capital in the hands of "institutional speculators" far exceeds the limited reserves of Asian central banks. The latter acting individually or collectively are no longer able to fight the tide of speculative activity.

GLOBAL FALSEHOODS

Distorting Social Realities

The increasing levels of global poverty resulting from economic restructuring are casually denied by G7 governments and international institutions (including the World Bank and the IMF); social realities are concealed, official statistics are manipulated, economic concepts are turned upside down. In turn, public opinion is bombarded in the media with glowing images of global growth and prosperity. As expressed in one *Financial Times* article, "Happy days are here again . . . a wonderful opportunity for sustained and increasingly global economic growth is waiting to be seized."[13]

The world economy is said to be booming under the impetus of "free market" reforms. Without debate or discussion, so-called "sound macroeconomic policies" (meaning the gamut of budgetary austerity, deregulation, downsizing and privatization) are heralded as the key to economic success. In turn, both the World Bank and the United Nations Development Programme (UNDP) assert that economic growth in the late 20th century has contributed to a remarkable reduction in the levels of world poverty.

Defining Poverty at "A Dollar a Day"

The World Bank framework departs sharply from established concepts and procedures for measuring poverty.[14] It arbitrarily sets a "poverty threshold" at one dollar a day, labeling population groups with a per capita income above one dollar a day as "nonpoor."

This subjective and biased assessment is carried out irrespective of actual conditions at the country level.[15] With the liberalization of commodity markets, the domestic prices of basic food staples in developing countries have risen to world market levels. The one-dollar-a-day standard has no rational basis: population groups in developing countries with per capita incomes of two, three or even five dollars remain poverty stricken (i.e., unable to meet basic expenditures on food, clothing, shelter, health and education).

Arithmetic Manipulation

Once the one-dollar-a-day poverty threshold has been set, the estimation of national and global poverty levels becomes an arithmetic exercise. Poverty indicators are computed in a mechanical fashion from the initial one-dollar-a-day assumption. The data is then tabulated in glossy tables with forecasts of declining levels of global poverty into the 21st century.

These forecasts of poverty are based on an assumed rate of growth of per capita income; growth of the latter implies pari passu a corresponding lowering of the levels of poverty. For instance, according to the World Bank's calculations, the incidence of poverty in China should decline from 20 percent in 1985 to 2.9 percent by the year 2000.[16] Similarly, in the case of India (where according to official data more than 80 percent of the population [1996] have per capita incomes below one dollar a day), a World Bank "simulation" (which contradicts its own "one-dollar-a-day" methodology) indicates a lowering of poverty levels from 55 percent in 1985 to 25 percent in the year 2000.[17]

The entire framework built on the one-dollar-a-day assumption is tautological; it is totally removed from an examination of real life situations. No need to analyze household expenditures on food, shelter and social services; no need to observe concrete conditions in impoverished villages or urban slums. In the World Bank framework, the "estimation" of poverty indicators has become a numerical exercise.

The UNDP Framework

While the UNDP Human Development Group has in previous years provided the international community with a critical assessment of key issues of global development, the 1997 *Human Development Report* devoted to the eradication of poverty conveys a viewpoint similar to that advanced by the Bretton Woods institutions. According to the UNDP, "the progress in reducing poverty over the 20th century is remarkable and unprecedented. . . . The key indicators of human development have advanced strongly."[18] The UNDP's "human poverty index" (HPI) is based on "the most basic dimensions of deprivation: a short life span, lack of basic education and lack of access to public and private resources."[19]

Based on the above criteria, the UNDP Human Development Group comes up with estimates of human poverty which are totally inconsistent with country-level realities. The HPI for Colombia, Mexico and Thailand, for instance, is around 10 to 11 percent (see Table 1). The UNDP measurements point to achievements in poverty reduction in sub-Saharan Africa, the Middle East and India which are totally at odds with national estimates of poverty.

The human poverty estimates put forth by the UNDP portray an even more distorted and misleading pattern than those of the World Bank. For instance, only 10.9 percent of Mexico's population is categorized by the UNDP as "poor." Yet this

TABLE 1

THE UNDP HUMAN POVERTY INDEX, SELECTED DEVELOPING COUNTRIES

Country	
Trinidad and Tobago	4.1
Mexico	10.9
Thailand	11.7
Colombia	10.7
Philippines	17.7
Jordan	10.9
Nicaragua	27.2
Jamaica	12.1
Iraq	30.7
Rwanda	37.9
Papua New Guinea	32.0
Nigeria	41.6
Zimbabwe	17.3

Source: *Human Development Report* 1997, Table 1.1, p. 21.

estimate contradicts the situation observed in Mexico since the early 1980s: a collapse in social services, the impoverishment of small farmers and a massive decline in real earnings triggered by successive currency devaluations. According to one report:

[R]eal income [in Mexico] fell between 1982 and 1992 [following the adoption of IMF prescriptions]. Infant deaths due to malnutrition tripled. The real minimum wage lost over half its value; and the percentage of the population living in poverty increased from just under one-half to about two-thirds of Mexico's 87 million people.[20]

A recent OECD study confirms unequivocally the mounting tide of poverty in Mexico since the signing of the North American Free Trade Agreement (NAFTA).[21]

Double Standards in the "Scientific" Measurement of Poverty

Double standards prevail in the measurement of poverty. The World Bank's one-dollar-a-day criterion applies only to "developing countries." Both the Bank and the UNDP fail to acknowledge the existence of poverty in Western Europe and

North America. Moreover, the one-dollar-a-day standard contradicts established methodologies used by western governments and intergovernmental organizations to define and measure poverty in "developed countries."

In the West, methods for measuring poverty have been based on minimum levels of household spending required to meet essential expenditures on food, clothing, shelter, health and education. In the United States, for instance, the Social Security Administration (SSA) in the 1960s set a "poverty threshold" which consisted of "the cost of a minimum adequate diet multiplied by three to allow for other expenses." This measurement was based on a broad consensus within the U.S. Government.[22] The U.S. "poverty threshold" for a family of four (two adults and two children) in 1996 was U.S.$16,036. This figure translates into a per capita income of U.S.$11 a day (compared to the one-dollar-a-day criterion of the World Bank used for developing countries). In 1996, 13.1 percent of the U.S. population and 19.6 percent of the population in central cities of metropolitan areas were below the poverty threshold.[23]

Neither the UNDP nor the World Bank undertakes comparisons in poverty levels between "developed" and "developing" countries. Comparisons of this nature would no doubt be the source of "scientific embarrassment," as the poverty indicators presented by both organizations for Third World countries are in some cases of the same order of magnitude as (or even below) the official poverty levels in the United States, Canada and the European Union. In Canada, which occupies the first rank among all nations according to the same 1997 *Human Development Report* published by the UN, 17.4 percent of the population is below the national poverty threshold, compared to 10.9 percent for Mexico and 4.1 percent for Trinidad and Tobago, according to UNDP's HPI.[24]

Conversely, if the U.S. Bureau of Census methodology (based on the cost of meeting a minimum diet) were applied to the developing countries, the overwhelming majority of the population would be categorized as "poor." While this exercise of using "Western standards" and definitions has not been applied in a systematic fashion, it should be noted that with the deregulation of commodity markets, retail prices of essential consumer goods are not appreciably lower than in the United States or Western Europe. The cost of living in many Third World cities is higher than in the United States. Moreover, household budget surveys for several Latin American countries suggest that at least 60 percent of the population in the region does not meet minimum calorie and protein requirements. In Peru, for instance, according to household census data, 83 percent of the Peruvian population was unable to meet minimum daily calorie and protein requirements following the 1990 IMF sponsored "Fujishock."[25] The prevailing situation in sub-Saharan Africa and South Asia is more serious, where a majority of the population suffers from chronic undernourishment.

Poverty assessments by both organizations take official statistics at face value. They are largely office-based exercises conducted in Washington and New York with insufficient awareness of local realities. For example, the 1997 UNDP Report points to a decline of one-third to one-half in child mortality in selected countries of sub-Saharan Africa, despite declines in state expenditures and income levels. What it fails to mention, however, is that the closing down of health clinics and massive lay-offs of health professionals (often replaced by semi-illiterate health volunteers) responsible for compiling mortality data has resulted in a de facto decline in recorded mortality.

Vindicating the "Free" Market System

These are the realities which are concealed by the World Bank and UNDP poverty studies. The poverty indicators blatantly misrepresent country-level situations as well as the seriousness of global poverty. They serve the purpose of portraying the poor as a minority group representing some 20 percent of world population (1.3 billion people).

Declining levels of poverty including forecasts of future trends are derived with a view to vindicating free market policies and upholding the "Washington Consensus" on macroeconomic reform. The "free market" system is presented as the most effective means of achieving poverty alleviation, while the negative impact of macroeconomic reform is denied. Both institutions point to the benefits of the technological revolution and the contributions of foreign investment and trade liberalization, without identifying how these global trends might exacerbate rather than abate poverty.

THE CAUSES OF GLOBAL POVERTY

Global Unemployment: "Creating Surplus Populations"[26] in the Global Cheap-Labor Economy

The global decline in living standards is not the result of a scarcity of productive resources as in preceding historical periods. The globalization of poverty has indeed occurred during a period of rapid technological and scientific advance. While the latter has contributed to a vast increase in the potential capacity of the economic system to produce necessary goods and services, expanded levels of productivity have not translated into a corresponding reduction in levels of global poverty.

On the contrary, downsizing, corporate restructuring and relocation of production to cheap labor havens in the Third World have been conducive to increased levels of unemployment and significantly lower earnings to urban workers and farmers. This new international economic order feeds on human poverty and cheap labor: high levels of national unemployment in both developed and developing countries have contributed to the depression of real wages. Unemployment has been internationalized, with capital migrating from one country to another in a perpetual search for cheaper supplies of labor. According to the International Labor Organization (ILO), worldwide unemployment affects one billion people, or nearly one third of the global workforce.[27]

National labor markets are no longer segregated: workers in different countries are brought into overt competition with one another. Workers' rights are derogated as labor markets are deregulated. World unemployment operates as a lever which "regulates" labor costs at a world level. Abundant supplies of cheap labor in the Third World (e.g., China with an estimated 200 million surplus workers) and the former Eastern bloc contribute to depressing wages in developed countries. Virtually all categories of the labor force (including the highly qualified, professional and scientific workers) are affected, even as competition for jobs encourages social divisions based on class, ethnicity, gender and age.

PARADOXES OF GLOBALIZATION

Micro-Efficiency, Macro-Insufficiency

The global corporation minimizes labor costs on a world level. Real wages in the Third World and Eastern Europe are as much as seventy times lower than in the United States, Western Europe or Japan: the possibilities of production are immense given the mass of cheap impoverished workers throughout the world.[28]

While mainstream economics stresses efficient allocation of society's scarce resources, harsh social realities call into question the consequences of this means of allocation. Industrial plants are closed down, small and medium-sized enterprises are driven into bankruptcy, professional workers and civil servants are laid off and human and physical capital stand idle in the name of "efficiency." The drive toward an "efficient" use of society's resources at the microeconomic level leads to exactly the opposite situation at the macroeconomic level. Resources are not used "efficiently" when there remain large amounts of unused industrial capacity and millions of unemployed workers. Modern capitalism appears totally incapable of mobilizing these untapped human and material resources.

Accumulation of Wealth, Distortion of Production

This global economic restructuring promotes stagnation in the supply of necessary goods and services while redirecting resources toward lucrative investments in the luxury goods economy. Moreover, with the drying up of capital formation in productive activities, profit is sought in increasingly speculative and fraudulent transactions, which in turn tend to promote disruptions on the world's major financial markets.

In the South, the East and the North, a privileged social minority has accumulated vast amounts of wealth at the expense of the large majority of the population. The number of billionaires in the United States alone increased from 13 in 1982 to 149 in 1996. The "Global Billionaires Club" (with some 450 members) has a total worldwide wealth well in excess of the combined GDP of the group of low-income countries with 56 percent of the world's population.[29]

Moreover, the process of wealth accumulation is increasingly taking place outside the real economy, divorced from bona fide productive and commercial activities. As noted in *Forbes Magazine*, "Successes on the Wall Street stock market [meaning speculative trade] produced most of last year's [1996] surge in billionaires."[30] In turn, billions of dollars accumulated from speculative transactions are funneled toward confidential numbered accounts in the more than 50 offshore banking havens around the world. The U.S. investment bank Merrill Lynch conservatively estimates the wealth of private individuals managed through private banking accounts in offshore tax havens at U.S. $3.3 trillion.[31] The IMF puts the offshore assets of corporations and individuals at U.S. $5.5 trillion, a sum equivalent to 25 percent of total world income.[32] The largely ill-gotten loot of Third World elites in numbered accounts is placed at U.S. $600 billion, with one-third of that held in Switzerland.[33]

Increased Supply, Reduced Demand

The expansion of output in this system takes place by "minimizing employment" and compressing workers' wages. This process in turn backlashes on the levels of consumer demand for necessary goods and services: unlimited capacity to produce, limited capacity to consume. In a global cheap labor economy, the very process of expanding output (through downsizing, layoffs and low wages) contributes to compressing society's capacity to consume. The tendency is therefore toward overproduction on an unprecedented scale. In other words, expansion in this system can only take place through the concurrent disengagement of idle productive capacity, namely through the bankruptcy and liquidation of "surplus enterprises." The latter are closed down in favor of the most advanced mechanized production. Entire branches of industry stand idle, the economy of entire regions is affected and only a part of the world's agricultural potential is utilized.

This global oversupply of commodities is a direct consequence of the decline in purchasing power and rising levels of poverty. Oversupply contributes in turn to the further depression of the earnings of the direct producers through the closure of excess productive capacity. Contrary to Say's Law of Markets, heralded by mainstream economics, supply does not create its own demand. Since the early 1980s, overproduction of commodities leading to plummeting (real) commodity prices has wreaked havoc, particularly among Third World primary producers, but also (more recently) in the area of manufacturing.

Global Integration, Local Disintegration

In developing countries, entire branches of industry producing for the internal market are eliminated while the informal urban sector — which historically has played an important role as a source of employment creation — has been undermined as a result of currency devaluations and the liberalization of imports. In sub-Saharan Africa, the informal sector garment industry has been wiped out and replaced by the market for used garments, imported from the West at U.S. $80 a ton.[34]

Against a background of economic stagnation (including negative growth rates recorded in Eastern Europe, the former Soviet Union and sub-Saharan Africa), the world's largest corporations have experienced unprecedented growth and expansion of their share of the global market. This process, however, has largely taken place through the displacement of pre-existing productive systems, i.e., at the expense of local-level, regional and national producers. Expansion and profitability for the world's largest corporations is predicated on a global contraction of purchasing power and the impoverishment of large sectors of the world population.

Survival of the fittest: the enterprises with the most advanced technologies or those with command over the lowest wages survive in a world economy marked by overproduction. While the spirit of Anglo-Saxon liberalism is committed to "fostering competition," G-7 macroeconomic policy (through tight fiscal and monetary controls) has in practice supported a wave of corporate mergers and acquisitions as well as the bankruptcy of small- and medium-sized enterprises.

In turn, large multinational companies (particularly in the U.S. and Canada) have taken control of local-level markets (particularly in the service economy) through the system of corporate franchising. This process enables large corporate capital ("the franchiser") to gain control over human capital, cheap labor and entrepreneurship. A large share of the earnings of small firms and/or retailers is thereby appropriated, while the bulk of investment outlays is assumed by the independent producer (the "franchisee").

A parallel process can be observed in Western Europe. With the Maastricht Treaty, the process of political restructuring in the European Union increasingly heeds dominant financial interests at the expense of the unity of European societies. In this system, state power has deliberately sanctioned the progress of private monopolies: large capital destroys small capital in all its forms. With the drive toward the formation of economic blocks both in Europe and North America, the regional- and local-level entrepreneur is uprooted, city life is transformed, individual small scale ownership is wiped out. "Free trade" and economic integration provide greater mobility to the global enterprise while at the same time suppressing (through non-tariff and institutional barriers) the movement of small, local-level capital.[35] "Economic integration" (under the dominion of the global enterprise), while displaying a semblance of political unity, often promotes factionalism and social strife between and within national societies.

THE ONGOING INTERNATIONALIZATION
OF MACROECONOMIC REFORM

The Debt Crisis

The restructuring of the global economic system has evolved through several distinct periods since the collapse of the Bretton Woods system of fixed exchange rates in 1971. Patterns of oversupply started to unfold in primary commodity markets in the second part of the 1970s, following the end of the Vietnam War. The debt crisis of the early 1980s was marked by the simultaneous collapse of commodity prices and the rise of real interest rates. The balance of payments of developing countries was in crisis, and the accumulation of large external debts provided international creditors and "donors" with "political leverage" to influence the direction of country-level macroeconomic policy.

The Structural Adjustment Program

Contrary to the spirit of the Bretton Woods agreement of 1944, which was predicated on "economic reconstruction" and stability of major exchange rates, the structural adjustment program (SAP) has, since the early 1980s, largely contributed to destabilizing national currencies and ruining the economies of developing countries.

The restructuring of the world economy under the guidance of the Washington-based international financial institutions and the World Trade Organization (WTO) increasingly denies individual developing countries the possibility of building a national economy. The internationalization of macroeconomic policy transforms countries into open economic territories and national economies into "reserves" of cheap labor and natural resources. The state apparatus is undermined, industry for the internal market is destroyed, national enterprises are pushed into bankruptcy. These reforms have also been conducive to the elimination of minimum wage legislation, the repeal of social programs and a general diminution of the state's role in fighting poverty.

"Global Surveillance"

The inauguration of the WTO in 1995 marks a new phase in the evolution of the post-war economic system. A new "triangular division of authority" among the IMF, the World Bank and the WTO has unfolded. The IMF has called for more effective "surveillance" of developing countries' economic policies and increased coordination among the three international bodies, signifying a further infringement on the sovereignty of national governments.

Under the new trade order (which emerged from the completion of the Uruguay Round at Marrakesh in 1994), the relationship of the Washington-based institutions to national governments is to be redefined. Enforcement of IMF-World Bank policy prescriptions will no longer hinge upon ad hoc country-level loan agreements (which are not "legally binding" documents). Henceforth, many of the mainstays of the structural adjustment program (e.g., trade liberalization and the foreign investment regime) have been permanently entrenched in the articles of agreement of the WTO. These articles set the foundations for "policing" countries (and enforcing "conditionalities") according to international law.

The deregulation of trade under WTO rules combined with new clauses pertaining to intellectual property rights will enable multinational corporations to penetrate local markets and extend their control over virtually all areas of national manufacturing, agriculture and the service economy.

Entrenched Rights for Banks and MNCs

In this new economic environment, international agreements negotiated by bureaucrats under intergovernmental auspices have come to play a crucial role in the remolding of national economies. Both the 1997 Financial Services Agreement under the stewardship of the WTO and the proposed Multilateral Agreement on Investment under the auspices of the OECD provide what some observers have entitled a "charter of rights for multinational corporations."

These agreements derogate the ability of national societies to regulate their national economies. The Multilateral Agreement on Investment also threatens national-level social programs, job creation policies, affirmative action and community-based initiatives. In other words, it threatens to lead to the disempowerment of national societies as it hands over extensive powers to global corporations.

CONCLUSION

Ironically, the ideology of the "free" market upholds a new form of state interventionism predicated on the deliberate manipulation of market forces. Moreover, the development of global institutions has led to the development of "entrenched rights" for global corporations and financial institutions. The process of enforcing these international agreements at national and international levels invariably bypasses the democratic process. Beneath the rhetoric of so-called "governance" and the "free market," neoliberalism provides a shaky legitimacy to those in the seat of political power.

The manipulation of the figures on global poverty prevents national societies from understanding the consequences of a historical process initiated in the early 1980s with the onslaught of the debt crisis. This false consciousness has invaded all spheres of critical debate and discussion on the "free" market reforms. In turn, the intellectual myopia of mainstream economics prevents an understanding of the actual workings of global capitalism and its destructive impact on the livelihood of millions of people. International institutions including the United Nations follow

TABLE 2

POVERTY IN SELECTED DEVELOPED COUNTRIES, BY NATIONAL STANDARDS

Country	Poverty Level
United States (1996)(*)	13.7
Canada (1995)(**)	17.8
United Kingdom (1993)(***)	20.0
Italy (1993)(***)	17.0
Germany (1993)(***)	13.0
France (1993)(***)	17.0

Sources: (*) U.S. Census Bureau

(**) Center for International Statistics, Canadian Council on Social Development

(***) European Information Service

suit, upholding the dominant economic discourse with little assessment of how economic restructuring backlashes on national societies, leading to the collapse of institutions and the escalation of social conflict.

NOTES

1. See Food and Agricultural Organization of the United Nations, *Food Supply Situation and Crop Prospects in Sub-Saharan Africa, Special Report*, no. 1 (April 1993). While there are no data at a regional level, one can infer from country-level figures that at least a quarter of Sub-Saharan Africa's population is at risk of famine. Ten million peasants in the Sertao region of Northeast Brazil suffer from famine and lack of water according to official figures. See "Dix millions de paysans ont faim et soif," *Devoir*, 16 April 1993, p. B5.

2. For further details see Claire Brisset, "Risque de famine sans precedent en Afrique," *Monde Diplomatique* (July 1992), pp. 24–25, and Claire Brisset, "Famines et guerres en Afrique subsaharienne," *Monde Diplomatique* (June 1991), pp. 8–9.

3. K. Nagaraj, et al., "Starvation Deaths in Andhra Pradesh," *Frontline*, 6 December 1991, p. 48.

4. Ibid.

5. See Michel Chossudovsky, *The Globalization of Poverty* (London: Zed Books, 1997), chapter 11.

6. World Bank, *World Development Report 1997* (Washington, DC: World Bank, 1997), Fig. 2.1, p. 26.

7. United Nations *Economic Commission for Europe, Economic Survey of Europe, 1995–96* (Geneva: UNECE, 1996).

8. Interviews conducted by the author with academic economists and international organizations based in Moscow, November 1992.

9. Jonathan C. Randal, "Reform Coalition Wins Bulgarian Parliament," *Washington Post*, 20 April 1997, p. A21.

10. "The Wind in the Balkans," *Economist*, 8 February 1997, p. 12.

11. Eric Ekholm, "On the Road to Capitalism, China Hits a Nasty Curve: Joblessness," *New York Times*, 20 January 1998.

12. Ibid.

13. "Let Good Times Roll," *Financial Times*, 1 January 1995 (editorial commenting on OECD economic forecasts), p. 6.

14. For a methodological review on the measurement of poverty see Jan Drewnowski, *The Level of Living Index* (Geneva: United Nations Institute for Social Research and Development (UNRISD), 1965). See also the extensive research on poverty thresholds conducted by the U.S. Bureau of the Census.

15. See World Bank, *World Development Report, 1990* (Washington, DC: World Bank, 1990).

16. See World Bank (1997), table 9.2, chapter 9.

17. Ibid.

18. United Nations Development Programme, *Human Development Report, 1997* (New York: United Nations, 1997), p. 2.

19. Ibid., p. 5. Introduced in the 1997 *Human Development Report*, the human poverty index (HPI) attempts "to bring together in a composite index the different features of deprivation in the quality of life to arrive at an aggregate judgement on the extent of poverty in a community." A high HPI indicates a high level of deprivation. See www.undp.org/undp/hdro/anatools.htm#3.

20. Soren Ambrose, "The IMF Has Gotten Too Big for Its Riches," *Washington Post*, 26 April 1998, p. C2.

21. See Clement Trudel, "Le Mexique subit le choc de l'internationalization," *Devoir*, 28 March 1998, p. A4.

22. See U.S. Bureau of the Census, *Current Population Reports, Series P60-198, Poverty in the United States: 1996* (Washington, DC: U.S. Bureau of the Census, 1997).

23. Ibid., p. 7.

24. According to the official definition of Statistics Canada (1995). For country ranks based on the UNDP's Human Development Index, see United Nations Development Programme (1997), table 6, p. 161.

25. See Chossudovsky, *El Ajuste Economico: El Peru bajo el Dominio del FMI* (Lima: Mosca Azul Editores, 1992), p. 83.

26. See Leonora Foerstel, *Creating Surplus Populations* (Washington, DC: Maisonneuve Press, 1996).

27. International Labour Organization, *Second World Employment Report* (Geneva: International Labour Organization, 1996).

28. See Saulma Chaudhuri and Pratima Paul Majumder, *The Conditions of Garment Workers in Bangladesh, An Appraisal* (Dhaka: Bangladesh Institute of Development Studies, 1991). According to this study, monthly wages in the garment industry were on the order of U.S.$20 a month (including overtime) in 1992 − less than ten cents an hour.

29. "International Billionaires, the World's Richest People," *Forbes Magazine*, 28 July 1997.

30. Charles Laurence, "Wall Street Warriors Force their Way into the Billionaires Club," *Daily Telegraph*, 30 September 1997.

31. "Increased Demand Transforms Markets," *Financial Times*, 21 June 1995, p. II.

32. "Global Investment Soars," *Financial Times*, 7 June 1996, p. III.

33. See Peter Bosshard, "Cracking the Swiss Banks," *Multinational Monitor*, November 1992.

34. Based on the author's research and interviews in Tunisia and Kenya, December 1992.

35. For instance, while the large multinational enterprises move freely within the North American free trade area, non-tariff restrictions prevent small-scale local capital in one Canadian province from extending into another Canadian province.

✗ **NO**

Is Globalisation Cheating the World's Poor?

GAUTAM SEN

INTRODUCTION

Globalisation pertains to integration between economies of all types, at different levels of development and encompasses developed and developing countries. The discussion below is principally concerned with the absorption of developing economies into the wider world economy, dominated by developed countries. Some radical critics of globalisation consider it the contemporary manifestation of Western expansionism and cultural hegemony. As a corollary, globalisation is held to conceal the mundane imperatives of exploitation and dominance in the language of economic determinism and progress.[1] The key concepts underpinning globalisation are, first and foremost, economic progress itself as well as its unspoken, but universally acknowledged, correlate, the international division of labour. The second set of references pertains to the vehicles for their attainment, which are export orientation, the import of technology and transnational corporations, the crucial institutional conduit for wider economic interaction with the outside world. Finally, two contextual elements, good governance and structural adjustment, or transition in the former planned economies have come to be associated with globalisation. They are invariably presented as the preconditions that enable the instruments for achieving the putative goals to operate. These goals, means and preconditions are embodied in the so-called "Washington consensus," shared by the IMF, the World Bank and US official agencies.

The radical riposte to this depiction is that, in reality, the global economy is characterised by a growing concentration of wealth and inequality owing to exploitation, equalling plunder, as well as revolutionary new methods for generating wealth denied to developing countries.[2] Thus, globalisation is condemned as a neo-imperial ideology, a self-serving obfuscation that cajoles and ensures the consent of subordinate peoples. The dichotomy is between the promise of escape from dire material necessity and improved living standards through global economic integration and the failure to achieve it. And the discourse on globalisation supposedly diverts attention from the failure to promote its ostensible aim of welfare and, perhaps, the autonomy of its intended beneficiaries, to a self-absorbed intellectual teleology of economic integration.

This "Washington consensus" could be regarded as an ideology in the Marxist sense because it conceals social contradictions, but nevertheless aspires to the progressive historical outcome of economic advancement.[3] However, while a Marxist perspective could agree that the goals are progressive, the role and dynamics of the means for achieving it are questioned, as are the conception of governance and adjustment, suggested as necessary. Nevertheless, it is pertinent to note that these disagreements about globalisation now occur within the categories and assumptions of conventional economic analysis rather than some materialist conception of social contradictions that require different issues to be addressed. In relation to the Gramscian notion of ideology, to the extent that the victims of globalisation do not accept the ideological discourse on globalisation, but acquiesce in the prescriptions of its protagonists, the issue becomes one of power, or more exactly their lack of it.[4] A contrasting liberal view would question the idea that globalisation and economic integration are primarily conflictual or a failure. In this view, if globalisation is an ideology it is a useful symbolic representation for simplifying complex reality, by compressing its multi-dimensional character in a form of shorthand. The pro-market ideology of globalisation could then be regarded as both a convenient generalisation and a source of "satisficing" action in the face of uncertainty and the absence of a complete knowledge of options and consequences or their comprehension within a meaningful time frame. For example, the standard explanation of gains from trade can be allowed to settle policy questions when the general equilibrium outcome of a situation is difficult to predict.

The contention of the present discussion is that, firstly, globalisation is positive for the economic welfare of the majority, including the poor. Indeed, it is judged to be a precondition for it, even if the benefits are not immediate. Secondly, the only vehicle for easing poverty and deprivation in the short run is redistribution, which requires political decisions and specific programmes. However, there is little evidence of political support for effective and meaningful redistributive measures, either in the advanced or developing countries. Thirdly, on the contrary, not only are the poor ignored, they are the victims of various forms of discrimination in the market place because they only possess a weak political voice. Such discrimination occurs because the politicisation of markets primarily benefits the powerful and acts against the interests of the vulnerable, especially those in developing countries. Thus, it is argued that it is the political character of globalisation that distorts economic development and hurts the poor rather than any features inherent in the economic dynamics of globalisation, per se, which is the world-wide spread of capitalism.

Globalisation has multiple empirical dimensions, but both those who question its novelty or assert that it is an uniquely important contemporary phenomenon, if not altogether new, agree that globalisation is primarily an economic phenomenon.[5] Critics of globalisation condemn its economic consequences as well as many of its socio-political manifestations. But the issue of its economic configuration remains a critical nodal point that needs to be outlined in order to comprehend the differing views of globalisation. In order to appreciate globalisation as a historical phenomenon it needs to be situated in relation to an older intellectual tradition and the ideas of classical political economists, like Adam Smith and David Ricardo on the one hand and Karl Marx and his followers on the other. It is also necessary to identify the protagonists in the globalised economy and their interests in order to understand how the political economy of globalisation impacts on developing countries. The main actors are governments, domestic interests within them, transnationals (who likely have a political role in more than one national society) and inter-governmental organisations, who reflect government preferences but, perhaps, not with symmetric correspondence.

THE EMPIRICAL ECONOMIC DIMENSIONS OF GLOBALISATION

Economic interaction in the contemporary global economy contains both familiar and novel forms of interaction. It particularly highlights the enhanced importance of new institutional forms and the role of non-state actors, principally, the transnational corporation. The most important economic relationships are trade and investment, which overlap and encompass different types of capital as well as technology flows. There is also a rapid growth of international trade in services that is integrating global production and consumption distinctively as well as on a bigger scale.[6]

The most spectacular manifestations of globalization are capital mobility and the Internet. There has been a huge increase in the turnover of global capital, especially in foreign exchange markets. In 1998 $1.5 trillion of foreign exchange was swapped daily, an amount equal to one-sixth of annual US output and more than 50 times the value of trade in goods and services. The number of Internet hosts world wide increased from around 2 to 45 million between 1993 and 1999. There has also been steady growth of international trade, as measured by trade/GDP ratios. The ratio of trade to output has doubled since 1950, with a significant increase in the past decade. In fact, its impact has been greater because non-tradable services have contributed a large share of the growth in output during this period. Price changes in fuel also understate the magnitude of increased interdependence during the period. Tariff barriers on imports of manufactured goods were expected to fall to 3% after the Uruguay Round, as compared to 47% in 1947.[7]

Between 1995 and 1998 alone foreign direct investment flows rose from $315 to $644 billion, more than a rise by a factor of twelve since 1981-5. Although the share of developing countries fell in the aftermath of the Asian financial crisis in 1997, it had been growing steadily to reach 37% of total inward flows by then.[8] Transnational corporations (TNCs) are also responsible for a quarter of total international trade and a fifth of world output. Intra-firm trade is estimated to account for a third of all merchandise trade and a further third of it occurs between different TNCs. A high degree of monopoly and oligopoly therefore prevails in two thirds of all international trade transactions. It suggests that the architecture of the world economy has become institutionalized and acquired deeper roots than would be the case if international trade were dominated by arms-length, third-party transactions, which lack a similar "internalized" character. To the extent that the world economy exhibits elements of structural institutionalisation and continuity, similar to that which exists at the national level, globalisation can be said to have occurred. [. . .]

ECONOMIC ANALYSIS AND GLOBALISATION

Ultimately, there is no coherent alternative economic analysis for the international division of labour that might be counterposed to the classical political economy tradition that reaches back to Adam Smith and culminates with modern neo-classical economists like, Eli Hecksher, Bertil Ohlin and Paul Samuelson.[9] The infant industry argument and more recent departures, deriving from the issue of market imperfections, arising from technology gaps and highlighting increasing returns, do not either completely controvert or reject the older tradition, but seek to account for anomalies in the patterns of international specialisation.[10] The functioning of the globalising economy can therefore be judged theoretically in relation to a spectrum that ranges from an idealised free market model rooted in classical political economy, of which Milton Friedman is one of its purest modern adherents, and an interventionist one associated with both List and Keynes.[11] The characterisation is itself idealised because prescriptions for economic policy can contain disparate elements that belong to alternative ideological traditions. Thus, the phenomenon of globalisation, which represents the expansion of capitalism, albeit a distinctive variant dependent on contingent circumstances, needs to be judged in relation to a set of goals that are both economic and philosophical, concerning notions about what is the "good life."[12]

The idealised market of general equilibrium belongs to the realm of logical possibilities, but the alternative of routine economic intervention also largely occurs within a context of markets and private property. The analysis of socio-economic transformation therefore pertains to the functioning of markets. [. . .] A crucial related issue for judging the impact of globalisation is the extent to which political intervention alters economic outcomes, i.e., income redistribution (not necessarily in a progressive direction) and/or institutional features that create privileges like rent.

The economic consequences of globalisation for the disadvantaged, the key ethical question, can be evaluated according to three criteria. The first is its association with reductions in absolute poverty, the second, its relationship with inequality, the issue of relative deprivation, and third, its impact on political systems, which either gain greater autonomy or remain excessively vulnerable to events beyond their own boundaries that affect the poor. Subsumed under these specific questions are issues like economic growth and the socio-political transformation of individual and community life, including their cultural identity and autonomy. But clearly, being left out of the globalised economy is worse than the failure to get a larger share of the fruits of world economic growth, as Africans have been discovering for more than two decades.[13] As a first approximation, the relevant unit of analysis remains the international system and therefore the fate of its component units, states, although some judgements require the isolation of subjects at lower levels of socio-political aggregation.

A further set of socio-political issues arises in relation to the economics of globalisation. These are questions that economists have tended to ignore because much of modern economic theory is based on abstractions that require heroic assumptions about individual behaviour and the institutional framework within which it takes place, e.g., the need for labour markets to clear speedily in response to market signals. The issue might be approached at a high level of generality in order to highlight the problem. One of the consequences of the globalisation of markets is to alter the nature of the changes that society and governments have to deal with. To the extent that markets are global, citizens of the individual countries that comprise it are subject to a variety of forces of change that originate outside their own borders and impact more frequently. Governments also need to respond to external forces that potentially limit their ability to cater to the needs and demand of their own citizens. Thus, poorer citizens with limited political salience are likely losers when governments respond to capital market volatility in order to placate very much wealthier foreigners.

POLITICAL POWER IN THE GLOBAL ECONOMY: INTERNATIONAL TRADE AND STRUCTURAL ADJUSTMENT

Economists spend a great deal of time demonstrating the existence of efficient outcomes and the conditions necessary for their achievement. The issue of market failures leads to policy prescriptions designed to minimise welfare losses. Yet the governance of the world economy has never occurred on the basis of efficiency criteria alone and certainly not according to its implied teleology of global welfare.[14] The reasons for government policies that fail to optimise global welfare have been subjected to analytical scrutiny, as have the possibility of trade-offs between global and national welfare.[15] The rules and regulations that govern the operations of the globalised market do not issue immaculately out of economic models designed to maximise global welfare. They are intimately connected to the politics of national interest and the parochial aspirations of constituents within them. As far as the analysis of globalisation and its consequences are concerned, the main interest is in actual outcomes and their causes rather than the demonstration of the technical possibility of maximising long-run global welfare by adopting appropriate policies. It is this nexus that explains the pay-off for developing societies as well as the disadvantaged of affluent countries in the context of globalisation.

INTERNATIONAL TRADE

The impact of the global economy on developing countries is substantially a product of politicised markets, excluding the significance of the initial distribution of national and private assets. Domestic labour in advanced countries resists and curtails market access for their exports. Contemporary environmental and human rights lobbies, despite tenuous economic justification for their demands, are reinforcing this resistance. In fact, both sources of resistance to exports from developing countries ultimately stem from the desire to protect employment. The history of protectionist policies need not be recounted in detail here, except to note that developing countries only have circumscribed access to the markets of advanced economies in sectors especially crucial for their economic development. The export of labour-intensive goods like clothing, shoes and light consumer goods, critical for the livelihood of surplus labour, released by rising agricultural productivity or demographic change, has been subject to detailed regulation and persistent barriers in the form of quotas and tariff peaks.[16] Protectionist practices, as noted below, are institutionalised in the agricultural sector of the principal advanced economies and cause great harm to the prospects of a large number of Asian, African and Latin American developing countries, especially large economies like Indonesia and Argentina that enjoy a singular comparative advantage in agriculture. Genuine markets, the perceived expression of globalisation, would require the end of political intervention and free trade in these products, which are sold at marginal cost by developing countries since they do not wield market power in them.

The oligopolistic structure of retail markets in advanced countries also militates against a fair distribution of the final prices of mass-produced, non-branded products, originating in poor countries. Intermediaries resident in advanced countries capture the largest share of the final selling price. Competition policies that place poor countries at less of a disadvantage in dealings with oligopolistic agents in advanced countries would therefore be justifiable on welfare grounds. However, the blatant interference by the governments of advanced countries in favour of their own citizens highlights clear conflicts of interest with producers in poor countries that asymmetrical political power and regulatory practices are intended to perpetuate.

The history of international trade negotiations during the post-WWII period under the aegis of the GATT reflects these political imperatives. Politically weak countries usually fail to achieve their objectives and often depend on the calculated goodwill of powerful countries, which recognise that unbridled ruthlessness in translating their power capabilities into the norms and operating procedures of the regime would be counterproductive because the disenfranchised might revolt, despite costs to them. A further unhappy perversity arises because liberalisation can impose prolonged adjustment costs on the most vulnerable countries, since increased competition often eliminates their existing opportunities, for example, the loss of export quotas under the multi-fibre arrangement.[17]

The two sectors of particular interest to developing countries, clothing and agriculture, remained outside the purview of the GATT trade order until the recent Uruguay Round, although their future is not yet unambiguously clear. Paradoxically, their inclusion within the multilateral framework of international trade may be attributed to the success of globalisation, since the growing prominence of developing countries made some concessions to them unavoidable. In order to secure their agreement on other issues like the General Agreement on Trade in Services (GATS), trade-related intellectual property services (TRIPS) and trade-related investment measures (TRIMs), a negotiated quid pro quo was thought necessary. By contrast, during earlier rounds of GATT advanced countries were indifferent to tariff reductions in sectors that would have benefited developing countries, since the latter were exempted from offering reciprocity and the principal supplier rule disqualified them from taking the initiative, because of their modest shares in the relevant sectors. Once again, asymmetric political influence rather than economic criteria explains the result.

The scope and time horizon for intellectual property protection embodied in the TRIPS regime are also the product of the political power wielded by advanced economies rather than a balance between the interests of producers of intellectual property and the generality of users. The rationale for the rigidity of the regime is justified by the analytical insight that it is in the national interest of producing countries to limit the diffusion of technology beyond their own borders.[18] Once again, the economics of globalisation don a national mask. The major defeat for developing countries at the Uruguay round was to be deprived, on weak intellectual grounds, of the critical policy tool of infant industry protection, which remains a thorny issue that has not been disavowed by either compelling economic logic or policy experience. A considerable body of economic analysis continues to highlight the disadvantages of being a latecomer country, owing to the relevance of learning by doing, market size, etc.[19] These arguments are evident in the advocacy of strategic trade policies and the arbitrary nature of specialisation due to temporary technological leads rather than relative national factor endowment. But this debate was largely conceded during the Uruguay round by developing countries, on the anvil of insistent assertion by powerful national interests, rather than reasoned persuasion.

The importance of the dynamics of relative power, including the preferences of influential national constituents, as opposed to the calculus of global welfare, has thus been in sustained evidence in the outcomes of the Uruguay round negotiations. The precise contours of various agreements on most issues reflect the scope for discretion in moulding market outcomes and the historic salience of transnational corporations in guiding much of the agenda; for example, on the GATS, TRIPS and TRIMs. The most blatant was the reaffirmation of national autonomy in determining anti-dumping and countervailing actions, which most observers acknowledge to be capricious.[20] Their misuse against the exports of developing countries has less to do with maximising welfare than national and parochial interests. Significantly, protestors against globalisation from the advanced countries, frequently associated with trade unions, wish to strengthen such malpractice in the name of international brotherhood and justice. Many of them were present at the demonstrations against the WTO Ministerial meeting at Seattle. The importance of power politics, as opposed to the cogency of welfare arguments and notions of sovereign equality, was underlined by the exclusion of developing countries from the Green Room discussions at Seattle in December 1999. It was this miscalculation rather than the protesters outside in the streets that precipitated the Seattle debacle, because the debarred countries consequently decided to oppose any private understanding, as a matter of principle.[21]

STRUCTURAL ADJUSTMENT

Structural adjustment programmes (SAPs) have been another important issue for the critics of globalisation and do indeed constitute a specific and important historic crossover point for developing countries. They embody policies that are dictated by external agencies and enforce a form of globalisation on them. Quite clearly, many, if not most, developing countries would have been unlikely to adopt the retrenchment and liberalisation required by SAPs voluntarily, if only because the resulting domestic political fall-out is costly. At the same time, the harsh medicine of SAPs is administered in less potent doses to politically well-connected regimes and fuels resentment even further, since mitigated application is obviously not available to all. Recently, the most important adviser on development policy in Washington, the distinguished chief economist of the World Bank, Joseph Stiglitz, denounced SAPs as frequently ill-conceived and their architect, the IMF, as mediocre.[22] It may well be, however, that the IMF is a prisoner of circumstances, seeking to square the circle and constrained by powerful private economic interests from rich countries who are in a position to press their preferences through the US Treasury. Their concern is to retrieve local currency assets before exchange rate depreciation makes them worthless, which prompts advocacy of orthodox macroeconomic measures under the aegis of the IMF.

SAPs highlight two distinctive issues that go to the heart of the difficulties posed by globalisation for developing countries, irrespective of its economic merits and historical inevitability. The first is the problem of financial volatility in global markets that arises from the intrinsic difficulty of exchange rate management, for which policy prescription remains uncertain. For example, the circumstances in which fixed or floating exchange rates are appropriate, given the degree of exposure to international trade, etc., are far from self-evident. These novel conditions were the permissive background for the widespread corruption and mismanagement highlighted by the crisis in financial liquidity in Southeast Asia during 1997.[23]

A more intractable issue is the reality that the increase in objective global economic interdependence has not been accompanied by greater subjective societal integration that could underwrite the cost of volatility. Thus, the emerging global world economy lacks the corresponding social structures that cushion economic vicissitudes within domestic society.[24] The absence for indebted countries of the equivalent of Chapter 11 of US law, which protects agents facing bankruptcy, illustrates this dilemma. The failure of IMF SAPs to substantially mitigate their especially harsh impact on the poor adequately also reflects the inability, of wealthy governments, to protect citizens of other societies from the painful consequences of adjustment, required for participation in the world market. In fact, in recent decades the largesse of the richest countries has been diminishing, and, indeed, the US has withheld and, then, arranged for forgiveness of some of its UN dues.

The issue of good governance highlights complex problems that cannot be comprehended by slogans about the exploitative character of globalisation. It cannot be automatically assumed that the reason for the failure of socio-economic transformation in much of the developing world, and its painfully slow progress in yet other parts, is primarily economic as well as external in origin, i.e., globalisation. A passing acquaintance with the functioning of governments and bureaucracies in many Asian, African and Latin American countries cannot fail to underline the deep indigenous roots of corruption and mismanagement, independent of any external fortification.[25] The phenomenon of state capture and the theft of investment funds – which therefore ends up in consumption – as well as transfer payments intended for the poor are routine and involve many at the highest levels of government. However, blaming globalisation for the consequences diverts attention from such criminal misdeeds and also misdirects analysis of their underlying causes. The absence of good governance in a significant number of countries can undoubtedly be blamed on external factors, but these reasons were essentially political in character rather than economic.

The prolonged survival of kleptocracies in countries like Zaire, the Philippines, Indonesia and much of Latin America can be blamed on the Cold War rather than the imperatives of the global market place. The fact that Western economic interests often benefited through association with such regimes is more a consequence rather than a cause of their being in power, a by-product of narrow Cold War imperatives to maintain friendly regimes in power regardless of the wider consequences for the countries concerned. It is no coincidence that most of these kleptocratic regimes are now out of power in the aftermath of the Cold War. However, globalisation is altering the context of state action by imposing powerful constraints of external origin that can crowd out responses to local needs. The capacity for exit of external agents and its severe and immediate disruptive impact on the functioning of economies results in neglect of local constituents, especially those without a voice.[26] This is the reason for the failure to cater adequately to the needs of the poor during economic crises that impose budgetary cuts.

GLOBALISATION AND POVERTY

The causes of poverty are complex and require both careful conceptual analysis and empirical examination.[27] However, the obvious questions that can be posed are: does globalisation cause, intensify or relieve poverty? There is little evidence that globalisation, per se, causes poverty or intensifies it, unless population growth, capital market volatility and SAPs, which are usually the immediate causes of increased poverty, are primarily attributed to globalisation rather than policy failure. On the contrary, globalisation does indeed relieve poverty, albeit only slowly and, according to conventional wisdom, it worsens inequality, though these are dissimilar phenomena, because growth is likely to be associated with greater income differentials. However, recent studies challenge the inference that adjustment and globalisation either worsen poverty or increase inequality.[28] A major reason for the prevalence of poverty in the first place, as opposed to periodic variations owing to the impact of globalisation, is the absence of political will to redistribute income and assets and no amount of theorising about epistemology can obscure this stark reality.[29]

Three general issues need to be borne in mind before rushing to judgement. The first is how economic benefits can accrue to the poor. Second, the fact that although globalisation has historical antecedents, it is a phenomenon that is still at an early stage of evolution. An assessment of its eventual consequences therefore justifies some caution, for the present. Third, economic growth is a precondition for the alleviation of poverty, although whether or not globalisation inhibits development, as compared to inward development strategies, remains a separate question.

The situation of the poor improves through employment, redistributive measures or increases in the value of any assets they possess. The latter cannot be regarded as significant because subsistence at the margin for the very poor (under $1 per day) implies that such assets are liquidated quickly to ensure physical survival. Redistributive measures in regions like South Asia and especially Latin America, where a numerical majority of the world's poor live, are not significant, except during crises, though there are notable exceptions within them. Meaningful redistributive measures would first need to address the problem of unequal land ownership, which persists because the dominant elites are the landed minority. The paucity of land availability should also be borne in mind (e.g., Bangladesh), although the salience of the issue of political power is the principal explanation for skewed ownership and landlessness. The only realistic long-term solution to poverty is therefore improved employment opportunities, generated by economic growth. Such growth needs to be labour-intensive and may possess other redistributive spin-offs, but cannot be sustained in isolation from the global economy.

Recent changes in poverty indices, in the context of the increased globalisation of national economies, are ambiguous. They suggest that the largest single geographical concentration of the poor, located in the South Asian region, has experienced little or no improvement in their living standards.[30] The debate as to whether or not their numbers have grown slightly, as one recent survey seems to suggest, does not refute the main inference that the poor have benefited little from liberalisation, the precursor of globalisation, in the recent past. However, it needs to be borne in mind that the period under purview is relatively short and an enduring resolution to the long-standing historical problem of poverty is unlikely to be speedy. The relief of dire poverty, which is the outcome of the vulnerability of the very poor to economic volatility, requires periodic public intervention that depends on political will and humanitarian endeavour. Experience also shows that economic growth and the greatest recent historical successes in combating poverty have taken place in economies, like the Republic of Korea, Taiwan and now evident in the rapid socio-economic transformation of China, that have internationalised.[31] In the case of the Republic of Korea and Taiwan, substantial economic development had occurred in the first half of the twentieth century during colonial rule and the subsequent redistribution of land under US occupation ensured a critical condition for the alleviation of poverty.[32]

Thus, although globalisation, the contemporary manifestation of engagement with the international economy, may not be the ultimate catalyst of economic advance, it accompanies economic growth, as the association of rises in per-capita incomes with successive increments to international trade and foreign investment demonstrates. However, the first necessary step for economic advance is political stability, the protection of property rights and the rule of law. They may be inimical for the sharpening of contradictions, as a prelude to the revolutionary seizure of power by a vanguard on behalf of the masses, labouring under false consciousness, but it is essential for capitalist development. These conditions are absent in large swathes of Africa and only weakly enforced in much of South Asia and Latin America and are a powerful reason for faltering economic performance, as potential investors, both domestic and foreign, shy away and urgent infrastructure remains undeveloped or is misapplied.

CONCLUSION

The rejectionist critics of globalisation have sought to locate it historically by engaging in metaphysical socio-political speculation at high levels of abstraction. Their preoccupation with the apocalyptic, meta-historical implications of globalisation, as well as proneness for opportunistic critiques of it on behalf of displaced labour in advanced countries, has deflected a more pragmatic assessment. It might account for their failure to give adequate attention to some of its serious negative consequences for the most vulnerable. For example, one of the meta-historical characteristics of globalisation has been the communications revolution, transporting ideas, goods and people in large volumes across space and instituting unprecedented integration of the global economy and society. Even its critics regard this phenomenon as largely positive because it has empowered them by allowing the NGOs, through which they operate, to organise opposition over the Internet. The latter is the quintessential expression of globalisation and increasingly defining its economic scope in the phenomenon of e-commerce.[33] However, it has also ensured rapid transmission of diseases like AIDS that many politically incoherent and weak administrative systems cannot cope with, as its dramatic incidence in Africa and

Asia shows. This is surely a more urgent issue for those affected, requiring international intervention, than the bemoaned indignity of economic dependence or cultural homogeneity? Climate change, whose causes are still imperfectly understood, also requires global endeavour to mitigate its negative impact on poor societies that do not possess the resources to overcome recurrent floods or droughts, for example. In fact, the world is now undergoing a historic transformation that is simultaneously a centripetal economic force and a centrifugal political one. It is the source of negative feedback that needs considered attention.

The rejection of globalisation, for being supposedly inimical to the emancipation of the poor, implies a paradoxical consequent espousal of a nationalist and territorial basis for addressing their situation, the unavoidable historical alternative to it. The affirmation of such a normative outlook might be regarded as incongruous from an ideological perspective that implicitly rejects capitalism as well. Instead, it might have been expected that the privileged place of the state might also be counterposed to a potentially more radical, however weakly articulated, and cosmopolitan alternative. A further irony of the politics of rejection is the simultaneous affirmation of interests that are clearly in conflict. The protest against so-called "social dumping" (i.e., cheap imports) to protect jobs in the advanced countries cannot serve the interests of those in the third world whose livelihoods depend on it, both purported victims of a globalised market, integrated by footloose multinationals. However, one of the key complaints against globalisation that turn out to possess serious normative implications, perhaps inadvertently, is the criticism of the social cost of economic adjustment in general and its structural variety in particular. In effect, such a critique asserts the cosmopolitan character of the political right to be protected against adjustment, for all affected. The policy implication, from which its protagonists may well recoil when its true costs are known, would, in fact, entail international redistribution, depriving their own fellow citizens, who are creditors, to benefit debtors who are not.

Markets are inherently political because agents deploy their differential access to political and military resources to influence economic outcomes. In slave societies and during the feudal-mercantilist period such politicisation was unambiguous because forced labour and physical control were self-evident in determining economic outcomes. In capitalist markets, prices play a critical role in integrating the economic system as well as the distribution of income and political interference to influence economic outcomes is pervasive, but not universal. It almost certainly serves the less well-off better than previous historical alternatives as well as socialist central economic planning. "Exploiting classes," in Marxist terms, extract relative rather than absolute surplus because competition between capitalists makes it unavoidable. But there is more direct political intervention in the globalised economy than within the domestic economic sphere. The advocates of greater international economic integration systematically underrate its durability, while the critics of globalisation seek more of it without reflecting on the likelihood that it will be captured by the powerful. The political nature of such neo-mercantilist interference would merely add to the disadvantage of participation in markets without adequate human or physical assets. However, globalisation cannot provide the conditions for its own efficient operation by providing public goods like good governance and installing infrastructure.

Thus, the greatest enemies of the poor are those who wish to politicise the world economy further, because the resulting policies will be captured by dominant groups, however lofty the motives for their promulgation. The immediate alleviation of poverty requires significant redistribution of income and assets, particularly land. In the long run international economic integration constitutes the unavoidable basis for the alleviation of poverty, although globalisation can instigate negative political feedback, by privileging the voices of the newer global factors in the calculations of governments in developing countries. Such an outcome is likely to weaken the relative political salience of existing policies that benefit the poor. However, if it can be agreed that the worst drawbacks of globalisation stem from its politicisation the appropriate response to it cannot be the halting of capitalist development, but the curbing of politicisation, because it favours the powerful. The economics of the marketplace may not reduce poverty quickly, but, unlike the marketplace for political activity, it is not inherently biased against the poor.

NOTES

1. Walter D. Mignolo, "Globalization, Civilization Process and the Relocation of Languages and Cultures," in Fredric Jameson and Masao Miyoshi, eds., *The Cultures of Globalization*, Durham and London, Duke University Press, 1998, pp. 32–53.

2. See for example, Serif Hetata, "Dollarization, Fragmentation and God" in Frederic Jameson and Masao Miyoshi, pp. 273–90.

3. Jorge Larrain, *Marxism and Ideology*, London and Basingstoke, The Macmillan Press Ltd., 1983, pp. 1–45, esp.

4. For a brief summary see Antonio Gramsci, "Culture and Ideological Hegemony," in Jeffrey C. Alexander and Steven Seidman, eds., *Culture and Society Contemporary Debates*, Cambridge, UK, Cambridge University Press, 1990, pp. 47–54.

5. Paul Hirst and Grahame Thompson, *Globalisation in Question: The International Economy and the Possibilities of Governance,* Oxford, Polity Press, 1995. Robert Boyer and Daniel Drache, eds., *States Against Markets: The Limits of Globalisation*, London, Routledge, 1996.

6. World export of services grew by 25% between 1994 and 1997. "Entering the 21st Century," The World Bank, *World Development Report*, Oxford, Oxford University Press, 2000, p. 64.

7. *World Development Report; UNDP Human Development Report*, UNDP, Oxford, Oxford University Press, 1997, p. 83.

8. UNCTAD, *Overview World Investment Report 1999*, New York, UN 1999, pp. XXI–XXXIV. *Human Development Report 1997* and *UNDP Human Development Report.*

9. Douglas A. Irwin, 1996, op. cit.

10. Paul R. Krugman, ed., *Strategic Trade Policy and the New International Economics,* Cambridge, Mass., The MIT Press, 1988.

11. Milton Friedman, *Capitalism and Freedom,* Chicago, University of Chicago Press, 1962; and J.M. Keynes, "The Postulates of the Classical Economics and the Principle of Effective Demand," (General Theory, chapters 1–3) in Alvin H. Hansen, *A Guide to Keynes,* New York, McGraw Hill Book Company Inc., 1953, pp. 3–35.

12. Alan Ryan, "John Rawls," in Quentin Skinner, *The Return of Grand Theory in the Human Sciences,* Cambridge, UK, Cambridge University Press, 1985, pp. 101–20; and Partha Dasgupta, *An Inquiry into Well-Being and Destitution,* Oxford, Oxford University Press, 1993; also Roger Tooze and Craig N. Murphy, "The Epistemology of Poverty and the Poverty of Epistemology in IPE: Mystery, Blindness, and Invisibility," *Millennium Journal of International Studies,* Special Issue Poverty in World Politics: Whose Global Era? Winter 1996, Volume 25, Number 3, pp. 681–708.

13. The paltry share of foreign investment is more of a complaint than the prospect of being exploited as a result of gaining a larger proportion of it. Cf. UNCTAD, New York, UN 1999. op. cit. pp. XXIII–XXIV.

14. On the political constraints faced by governments in allowing unhindered market outcomes see James Mayall, *Nationalism and International Society,* Cambridge, UK: Cambridge University Press, 1990, pp. 108–10. Also see Strange, Susan, *States and Markets,* London, Pinter Publishers, 2nd edition, 1994.

15. Ronald Rogowski, *Commerce and Coalitions: How Trade Affects Domestic Political Alignments,* Princeton, New Jersey Princeton University Press, 1989 and an extension to it by Paul Midford, "International Trade and Domestic Politics: Improving on Rogowski's Model of Political Alignments," *International Organization,* 47, 4 Autumn 1993, pp. 535–64.

16. Sam Laird, "Multilateral Approaches to Market Access Negotiations," Staff Working Paper, Trade Policy Review Division, 98–102, Geneva, Switzerland, May 1998, WTO, pp. 1–21. On the scale of income losses for developing countries owing to textile quotas see UNDP, 1997, p. 86.

17. UNDP, 1997, ibid. calculated that overall the least developed countries would lose $600m and Sub-Saharan Africa $1.2 billion as a result of the Uruguay Round, p. 82.

18. On the logic for curbing the diffusion of technology, which the stringent trade-related intellectual property services regime that the Uruguay Round Agreement embodies cf., "A 'Technology Gap' Model of International Trade," in Paul R. Krugman, 1996. op. cit. pp. 152–64. For a critique of the current WTO intellectual property rights regime see Jagdish Bhagwati, *A Stream of Windows,* Cambridge, Mass., The MIT Press, 1998, pp. 77–82. On the importance of technology, as opposed to factor accumulation, for economic growth, cf. William Easterly and Ross Levine, "It's Not Factor Accumulation: Stylized Facts and Growth Models," Policy Research Group, *The World Bank,* January 2000, pp. 1–50, www.worldbank.org/research/growth/wpauthor.htm.

19. The idea that an efficient capital market, mainly evidenced by its absence in a majority of developing countries, can finance industries with a comparative advantage suggests a degree of wilful disingenuosness on the part of professionals.

20. Anne O. Krueger, editor, "Introduction" in *The WTO as an International Organization,* Chicago, Chicago University Press, 1998, pp.1–30.

21. See the comments of the Indian official at Seattle, Mr. N.K. Singh, in "The Seattle Ministerial Conference: Road Ahead for Developing Countries," *ICRIER*, December 1999, pp. 3–4. www.icrier.res.in/public.panel13.dec.html.

22. Joseph Stiglitz's scathing account is titled, "What I Learned at the World Economic Crisis: The Insider," *The New Republic*, 17–24, April, 2000.

23. Paul R. Krugman, "What Happened to Asia," January 1998, web.mit.edu/krugman/www/. Also Steven Radelet and Jeffrey Sachs, "The East Asian Financial Crisis: Diagnosis, Remedies, Prospects," Harvard Institute for International Development, Paper presented to the Brookings Panel, Washington, D.C. March, 1998.

24. For a clutching at straws that merely underlines the grievous weakness of a functioning global civil society that might mitigate the consequences of interdependence, see Jan Aart Scholte, "Global Civil Society," in Ngaire Woods editor, *The Political Economy of Globalization*, Basingstoke, Hants., The Macmillan Press, 200, pp. 173–201.

25. For a graphic account of the situation in Africa see "Africa," *The Economist*, Volume 355, Number 8170, March 13–19, 2000, pp. 23–25.

26. Albert O. Hirschman, *Essays in Trespassing, Economics and Politics and Beyond*, Cambridge, UK, Cambridge University Press, 1981, pp. 209–45.

27. For an exhaustive discussion see Michael Lipton and Martin Ravallion, "Poverty and Policy," in J. Behrman and T. N. Srinivasan, *Handbook of Development Economics, Volume III*, Elsevier Science, 1995, pp. 2553–657.

28. For a thorough review denying that globalisation causes poverty see David Dollar and Aart Kraay, "Growth *Is* Good For You," Development Research Group, *The World Bank*, March 2000, www.worldbank.org/research/growth/wpauthor.htm. Also IMF Staff, "Globalization: Threat or Opportunity?" *IMF*, April, 2000, www.imf.org/external/gifs/space.gif.

29. Mary Durfee and James N. Rosenau, "Playing Catch-UP: International Relations Theory and Poverty," Julian Saurin, "Globalisation, Poverty and the Promises of Modernity," *Millennium*, 1996, op. cit. pp. 521–46; 657–80.

30. "Indian Poverty and the Numbers Game," *The Economist*, Volume 355, Number 8168, April 29–5 May 2000, pp. 69–70.

31. Gautam Sen, "Post-Reform China and the International Economy Economic Change and Liberalisation Under Sovereign Control," *EPW*, Volume XXXV, Number 11, March 11 2000.

32. On the development of Taiwan during the first half of the nineteenth century see Christopher Howe, *The Origins of Japanese Trade Supremacy*, London, Hurst & Company, 1996, pp. 335–65. An account of the US-sponsored redistribution of land in Japan, Korea and Taiwan in the aftermath of WWII is provided by Gary L. Olson, *US Foreign Policy and the Third World Peasant*, New York, US, Praeger, 1974.

33. See Danny Quah, "The Weightless Economy in Economic Development," London: *Centre for Economic Policy Research*, Discussion Paper Number 417, 1998.

POSTSCRIPT

The authors take the term "globalization" for granted, assuming that it is in fact taking place. Not everyone has accepted this fundamental assumption. Michael Veseth, for example, has questioned whether globalization is as far developed as analysts generally assume. In examining a number of "global" firms, Veseth found that their actual behaviour often was not genuinely global in nature. This finding led him to conclude that "actual global firms are relatively rare and the process of globalization is far less developed than most people imagine." Instead, globalization has become popular as a focus of discussion because it is vague and hence a variety of policies and projects can be attached to the concept. (See Michael Veseth, *Selling Globalization: The Myth of the Global Economy* [Boulder: Lynne Rienner Publishers, 1998.]) To better understand the debate, it is worthwhile to examine further the meaning of the term "globalization" and the various forms that it takes. Jan Aart Scholte's *Globalization: A Critical Introduction* (New York: St. Martin's Press, 2000) is a good starting point.

Suggested Additional Readings

Bakan, Joel. *The Corporation: The Pathological Pursuit of Profit and Power.* Toronto: Penguin Canada, 2004.

Bello, Walden. *The Future in the Balance: Essays on Globalization and Resistance.* San Francisco: Food First and Focus on the Global South, 2001.

Birdsall, Nancy. "Life Is Unfair: Inequality in the World." *Foreign Policy* 111 (Summer 1998): 76–93.

Brecher, Jeremy, and Tim Costello. *Global Village or Global Pillage: Economic Reconstruction from the Bottom Up.* New York: South End Press, 1994.

Chossudovsky, Michel. *The Globalisation of Poverty—Impacts of IMF and World Bank Reforms.* London: Zed Books, 1997.

_____. Gerry Mander, and Edward Goldsmith, eds. *The Case Against the Global Economy – And a Return to the Local.* San Francisco: Sierra Club Books, 1998.

Deaton, Angus. "Is World Poverty Falling?" *Finance & Development* 39, no. 2 (June 2002): 4–7.

Friedman, Thomas L. *The Lexus and the Olive Tree.* New York: Farrar, Straus and Giroux, 1999.

Grieder, William. *One World, Ready or Not—The Manic Logical of Global Capitalism.* New York: Simon and Schuster, 1997.

Martin, Hans-Peter, and H. Schumann. *The Global Trap: Globalization and the Assault on Prosperity and Democracy*. London: Zed Books, 1997.

Scott, Bruce R. "The Great Divide in the Global Village." *Foreign Affairs* 80, no. 1 (January–February 2001): 160–77.

InfoTrac® College Edition

Search for the following articles in the InfoTrac® database:

Amann, Edmund, and Werner Baer. "Neoliberalism and Its Consequences in Brazil." *Journal of Latin American Studies* 34, no. 4 (November 2002): 945–59.

"Globalization and Inequality: A Norwegian Report." *Population and Development Review* 26, no. 4 (December 2000): 843.

Korzeniewicz, Roberto Patricio, and Smith, William C. "Poverty, Inequality, and Growth in Latin America: Searching for the High Road to Globalization." *Latin American Research Review* 35, no. 3 (Summer 2000): 7.

For more articles, enter:
"globalization and poverty" or "globalization and inequality" in the keyword search.
"globalization" in the subject guide.

Web Resources

For current URLs for the following websites, visit www.crosscurrents.nelson.com.

Centre for the Study of Globalisation and Regionalisation

www.warwick.ac.uk/fuc/soc/CSGR

The website of this leading academic research centre on globalization at the University of Warwick contains a collection of working papers on various dimensions of globalization.

ELDIS

www.eldis.org

This "gateway to development information" hosted by the Institute of Development Studies (at the University of Sussex) provides access to an extensive range of materials relating to trade, development, and globalization. Look for its useful research subject guides, including one on globalization.

PovertyNet

www.worldbank.org/poverty

This subsection of the official website of the World Bank includes papers and studies dealing with poverty and development. Especially useful is the annual *World Development Report*, with statistics on economic growth and world poverty.

International Monetary Fund

www.imf.org

The official website of the IMF contains papers examining the relationship between trade and poverty. Both the World Bank and IMF sites give helpful insight into the "Washington consensus."

Róbinson Rojas Archive

www.rrojasdatabank.org/dev3000.htm

The Róbinson Rojas website archives a large collection of material on various aspects of globalization and international political economy.

Globalisation Guide

www.globalisationguide.org

The site poses a number of questions that relate to the relationship between global poverty and globalization. It also contains numerous links and other resources.

Poverty, Inequality, and Globalization

are.berkeley.edu/~harrison/globalpoverty

This website, maintained by Professor Ann E. Harrison at the University of Berkeley, offers an extensive collection of papers and lectures on the relationship of globalization and poverty. It is a good starting point for research on globalization and poverty.

Was the "Battle in Seattle" a Significant Turning Point in the Struggle against Globalization?

✔ **YES**
STEPHEN GILL, "Toward a Postmodern Prince? The Battle in Seattle as a Moment in the New Politics of Globalisation," *Millennium: Journal of International Studies* 29, no. 1 (2000): 131–40

✗ **NO**
JAN AART SCHOLTE, "Cautionary Reflections on Seattle," *Millennium: Journal of International Studies* 29, no. 1 (2000): 115–21

Significant turning points in history have come to be symbolized by a particular event or set of events. The Boston Tea Party became identified as the beginning of the American Revolution, and the storming of the Bastille is still celebrated as the spark of the French Revolution. In more recent times, specific events have also been interpreted as significant signposts in a changing world order. The dismantling of the Berlin Wall symbolically marked the end of the Cold War. The launch of the Persian Gulf War was seen by some as a harbinger of a "New World Order."

For many, the "Battle in Seattle" has come to symbolize one such critical turning point. The immediate context was the Third Ministerial Conference of the World Trade Organization (WTO), which was scheduled to meet in Seattle from November 30 to December 3, 1999. Two previous ministerial conferences had taken place in Singapore in 1996 and in Geneva in 1998, with little public fanfare. But as delegates from 130 nations descended on Seattle for deliberations, the conference took on a totally different character.

Thousands of demonstrators took to the streets of Seattle, virtually shutting down the city and seriously disrupting WTO deliberations. As demonstrators and police clashed in increasingly violent confrontations, the "Battle in Seattle" captured headlines around the world. When the conference ended without agreement on a new Millennium Round of talks to further liberalize world trade, activists declared that they had achieved a significant victory.

The "Battle in Seattle" was in many ways reminiscent of the anti-Vietnam and anti-nuclear demonstrations of the 1960s and 1970s. However, unlike these movements, which focused on issues relating to war and peace, the Seattle demonstrations focused on issues of economic justice, corporate power, and inequality. Unlike the anti-Vietnam demonstrations of the 1960s, which were driven more by disillusioned youth, the anti-globalization demonstrations in Seattle have been described as multi-generational, multi-class, and multi-issue — environmentalists, animal-rights supporters, union members, human-rights activists, and anarchists representing a broad spectrum of causes and goals.

Since Seattle, it has become virtually impossible to hold a significant meeting of world leaders to discuss global economic issues without triggering massive demonstrations. Subsequent international meetings in Quebec City, Genoa, and Cancún featured similarly dramatic confrontations between demonstrators and policymakers.

Why has the arcane world of international economics and trade become the focus of popular mass protest? Some see these events as signifying an important setback for globalization. As resistance to globalization deepens, we are entering a new phase of de-globalization. But others suggest that we are seeing a significant shift in the politics of globalization as new voices and forces, which have been excluded from global economic governance, demand access to decision-making structures. What we are witnessing is the emergence of a "global civil society." This term refers to growth in independent NGOs, social movements, and other nonprofit sector actors that increasingly operate across national borders. It is argued that these actors are increasingly seeking access to international policy discussions, including those involving trade and finance. As a result, a process that was once the exclusive domain of power elites is being democratized.

In the following readings, we encounter two different interpretations of the meaning of Seattle. Stephen Gill of York University sees the events in Seattle as a harbinger of new political alignments and forces that are seeking to "develop a global and universal politics of radical (re)construction around values such as democratic human development, human rights, and intergenerational security." Jan Aart Scholte of Warwick University is more cautious in his interpretation of these same events. Although Scholte is hopeful that a more humane global economic order will emerge, he emphasizes that the concept of global civil society has serious limits and that developments in Seattle could be ephemeral.

✔ **YES**

Toward a Postmodern Prince?
The Battle in Seattle as a Moment in the New Politics of Globalisation
STEPHEN GILL

The modern prince, the myth-prince, cannot be a real person, a concrete individual. It can only be an organism, a complex element of society in which a collective will, which has already been recognised and has to some extent asserted itself in action, begins to take concrete form.[1]

This essay analyses recent protests against aspects of neoliberal globalisation, as for example at the World Trade Organisation (WTO) Ministerial Meeting in Seattle in late 1999 and in Washington, DC, in spring 2000 to coincide with the IMF and World Bank Annual Meetings. I first examine the reason for the failure of the Seattle talks, and secondly, evaluate the protests and their political significance. Finally, I analyse some emerging forms of political agency associated with struggle over the nature and direction of globalisation that I call the "the postmodern Prince." This concept is elaborated in the final section of this essay. It is important to stress at the outset, however, that in this essay the term "postmodern" does not refer, as it often does, to a discursive or aesthetic moment. In my usage, "postmodern" refers to a set of conditions, particularly political, material, and ecological, that are giving rise to new forms of political agency whose defining myths are associated with the quest to ensure human and intergenerational security on and for the planet as well as democratic human development and human rights. As such, the multitude and diverse political forces that form the postmodern Prince combine both defensive and forward-looking strategies. Rather than engaging in deconstruction, they seek to develop a global and universal politics of radical (re)construction.

The battle in Seattle took place both inside and outside the conference centre in which the meetings took place; the collapse of the discussions was partly caused by the greater visibility of trade issues in the everyday lives of citizens and the increasing concern over how international trade and investment agreements are undermining important aspects of national sovereignty and policy autonomy, especially in ways that strengthen corporate power. These concerns – expressed through various forms of political mobilisation – have put pressure upon political leaders throughout the world to re-examine some of the premises and contradictions of neoliberal globalisation.

WHY THESE TALKS FAILED

Why specifically did the Seattle talks fail? The first and most obvious reason was US intransigence, principally in defence of the status quo against demands for reform by other nations concerned at the repercussions of the liberalisation framework (the built-in agenda) put in place by the GATT Uruguay Round.[2] The GATT Uruguay Round was a "Single Undertaking," a generic all-or-nothing type of agreement that meant signatories had to agree to all its commitments and disciplines, as well as to the institutionalisation of the WTO. The wider juridical-political framework for locking in such commitments can be called the new constitutionalism of disciplinary neoliberalism. This encompasses not only trade and investment, but also private property rights more generally (and not just intellectual property rights). It also involves macroeconomic policies and institutions (for example independent central banks and balanced budget amendments) in ways that minimise, or even "lock out" democratic controls over key economic institutions and policy frameworks in the long term.[3]

In this context, the US mainly wanted to sustain commitments to existing protections for intellectual property rights and investment and stop any attempts to weaken the capacity of existing agreements to open new markets for American corporations. The US position was based on intelligence work by government agencies, academics, and corporate strategists co-ordinated by the CIA.[4]

So it would be easy to say that protests outside the Seattle Convention Centre and confronted by the Seattle riot police, the FBI, and the CIA had little or no effect on the failure of the talks, other than the fact that many delegates could not get into the building because of the disruptions outside. However, this would be to misunderstand the link between public concern and the negotiating positions of states in the WTO. Indeed, it is becoming clear that the central reasons for the failure of the Seattle Ministerial were linked to the fact that the establishment of the WTO has gone well beyond the traditional role of the GATT in ways that have begun not only increasingly to encroach on crucial domestic policy areas and national sovereignty, but which also have repercussions for international law. In addition, key areas of concern to the public such as food safety, biotechnology, the environment, labour standards, and broader questions of economic development add to the popular disquiet and mobilisation over cultural, social, and ethical questions linked to the globalisation project.

In this regard – and this is very relevant to the concerns of the protesters as well as many governments – the new services negotiations that will occur in Geneva as a result of the Single Undertaking have a wide mandate and the new trade disciplines will have potentially vast impact across major social institutions and programs, such as health, education, social services, and cultural issues. This will allow for wider privatisation and commercialisation of the public sector and indirectly, of the public sphere itself, for example in social programs and education.[5] The logic of the negotiations will likely inhibit many government programs that could be justified as being in the public interest, unless governments are able to convince WTO panels that these programs are not substantially in restraint of trade and investment on the part of private enterprise. Indeed, because the built-in agenda will proceed in Geneva, many divisions among governments, especially between North and South, are emerging. The North-South divisions also revolved around dissatisfaction on the South's part at concessions made in the earlier GATT Uruguay Round, coupled with their frustration in failing to open Northern markets for their manufactured and agriculture exports.

With this agenda in mind, the protesters — although drawn from a very diverse range of organisations and political tendencies — believe there is centralisation and concentration of power under corporate control in neoliberal globalisation, with much of the policy agenda for this project orchestrated by international organisations such as the WTO, the IMF, and the World Bank. Thus, it was not surprising that the battle in Seattle moved to Washington, DC, in mid-April where the same set of progressive and environmental activists and organisations, including trade unions, protested the role of the IMF, the World Bank, and the G-7.

What is significant here is that the new counter-movements seek to preserve ecological and cultural diversity against what they see as the encroachment of political, social, and ecological mono-cultures associated with the supremacy of corporate rule. At the time of writing, the protests were set to move on to lay siege to the headquarters of Citicorp, the world's biggest financial conglomerate.

THE CONTRADICTIONS OF NEOLIBERAL GLOBALISATION AND THE SEATTLE PROTESTS

Implicitly or explicably, the failure of the talks and indeed much of the backlash against neoliberal globalisation is linked to the way that people in diverse contexts are experiencing the problems and contradictions linked to the power of capital and more specifically the projects of disciplinary neoliberalism and new constitutionalism. So what are these contradictions and how do they relate to the Seattle protests?

The first is the contradiction between big capital and democracy. Central here is the extension of binding legal mechanisms of trade and investment agreements, such as the GATT Uruguay Round and regional agreements, such as NAFTA. A counter-example, which pointed the way towards Seattle in terms of much of its counter-hegemonic political form, was the failed OECD effort to create a Multilateral Agreement on Investment. The MAI was also partly undermined by grass-roots mobilisation against corporate globalisation, as well as by more conventional political concerns about sovereignty. The protesters viewed agreements such as NAFTA and organisations such as the WTO as seeking to institutionalise ever-more extensive charters of rights and freedoms for corporations, allowing for greater freedom of enterprise and world-wide protection for private property rights. The protesters perceived that deregulation, privatisation, and liberalisation are a means to strengthen a particular set of class interests, principally the power of private investors and large shareholders. They are opposed to greater legal and market constraints on democracy.

Put differently, the issue was therefore how far and in what ways trade and investment agreements "lock in" commitments to liberalisation, whilst "locking out" popular-democratic and parliamentary forces from control over crucial economic, social, and ecological policies.

The second set of contradictions are both economic and social. Disciplinary neoliberalism proceeds with an intensification of discipline on labour and a rising rate of exploitation, partly reflected in booming stock markets during the past decade, whilst at the same time persistent economic and financial crises have impoverished many millions of people and caused significant economic disloca-tions. This explains the growing role of organised labour – for example American-based trade unions such as the Teamsters – in the protests, as well as organisations representing feminists, other workers, peasants, and smaller producers world-wide. In this regard, the numbers do not lie: despite what has been the longest boom in the history of Western capitalism, the real incomes of average people have been falling. So if this happens in a boom, what happens in a bust? This question has been answered already in the East Asia crisis when millions were impoverished.

Third, for a number of years now, discipline has become linked to the intensi-fication of a crisis of social reproduction. Feminist political economy has shown how a disproportionate burden of (structural) adjustment to the harsher, more competitive circumstances over the past twenty years has fallen on the shoulders of the less well-paid, on women and children, and on the weaker members of society, the old and the disabled. In an era of fiscal stringency, in many states social welfare, health, and educational provisions have been reduced and the socialisation of risk has been reduced for a growing proportion of the world's population. This has generated a crisis of social reproduction as burdens of adjust-ment are displaced into families and communities that are already under pressure to simply survive in economic terms and risk becomes privatised, redistributed, and generalised in new forms.[6]

The final set of contradictions are linked to how socio-cultural and biological diversity are being replaced by a social and biological mono-culture under corporate domination, and how this is linked to a loss of food security and new forms of generalised health risk. Thus, the protesters argued that if parts of the Seattle draft agenda were ratified, it would allow for a liberalisation of trade in genetically modified crops, provisions to allow world water supplies to be privatised, and the patenting of virtually all forms of life including genetic material that had been widely used across cultures for thousands of years. The protesters also felt particu-larly strongly about the patenting of seeds and bio-engineering by companies like Novartis and Enron, and other firms seen to be trying to monopolise control over food and undermine local livelihood and food security.[7]

Hence protesters opposed the control of the global food order by corporate inter-ests linked to the new constitutionalism. These interests have begun to institutionalise their right "to source food and food inputs, to prospect for genetic patents, and to gain access to local and national food markets" established through the GATT Uruguay Round and WTO.[8] Transnational corporations have managed to redefine food security in terms of the reduction of national barriers to agriculture trade, ensuring market rule in the global food order. The effect is the intensification of the centralisation of control by "agri-food capital via global sourcing and global trading," in ways that intensify world food production and consumption relations through

> unsustainable monocultures, terminator genes, and class-based diets [in ways] premised on the elimination of the diversity of natural resources, farm cultures, and food cultures, and the decline of local food self-sufficiency and food security mechanisms.[9]

Together, these contradictions contribute to what might be called a global or "organic crisis" that links together diverse forces across and within nations, specifically to oppose ideas, institutions, and material power of disciplinary neoliberalism. Much of the opposition to corporate globalisation was summed up by AFL-CIO President John Sweeny, who alongside President Clinton, was addressing the heads of the 1,000 biggest transnational corporations at the annual meeting of the self-appointed and unelected World Economic Forum in Davos in February 2000. Sweeny stated that the protests from North and South represented "a call for new global rules, democratically developed" to constrain "growing inequality, environmental destruction, and a race to the bottom for working people," warning that if such rules were not forthcoming "it will generate an increasingly volatile reaction that will make Seattle look tame."[10] Indeed, Clinton's remarks made at Davos

> seemed designed as a reminder that these fears – even expressed in unwelcome and sometimes violent ways, as they were in Seattle – have a legitimacy that deserves attention in the world's executive suites and government ministries.[11]

We know by now, of course, that the violence in Seattle was almost completely carried out by the heavily armed police militias who took the battle to the protesters. In Washington, in April 2000, police pre-emptively arrested hundreds of demonstrators, in actions justified by the local police chief as a matter of prudence. Another example of this was the repression of peaceful protests at the Asia-Pacific Economic Co-operation meeting in Vancouver in 1998. The protests focused on the contradiction of separating free trade from political democracy, dramatised by the presence of the Indonesian dictator, President Suharto. In sum, state authorities will quickly act to restrict basic political rights and freedoms of opposition by alternative members of civil society – rights supposedly underpinned by the rule of law in a liberal constitutional framework – when business interests are threatened. At Seattle, the anonymous, unaccountable, and intimidating police actions seemed almost absurd in the light of the fact that the protests involved children dressed as turtles, peaceful activists for social justice, union members, faith groups, accompanied by teachers, scientists, and assorted "tree huggers," all of whom were non-violent. Indeed, with the possible exception of a small number of anarchists, virtually none of the pro-testers was in any way violent. In Washington, the police protected the meetings wearing heavy armour from behind metal barricades, in the face of protesters carrying puppets and signs that read "spank the Bank." Moments such as these, how-ever, illustrate not only comedy of the absurd but also the broader dialectic between a supremacist set of forces and an ethio-political alternative involved in a new inclu-sive politics of diversity.

Indeed, since the Seattle debacle the protesters have been able to extend their critique of what they see as the political mono-culture by showing how one of its key components, the "quality press" and TV media, reported what occurred. In the US, for example, the mainstream media found it impossible to represent the violence as being caused by the authorities in order to provoke and discredit the opposition as being Luddite, anti-science, and unlawful. Seen from the vantage point of the protesters, "the *Washington Post* and the *New York Times* are the keepers of 'official reality,' and in official reality it is always the protesters who are violent."[12]

TOWARD A POSTMODERN PRINCE?

In conclusion, I advance the following hypothesis: the protests form part of a world-wide movement that can perhaps be understood in terms of new poten-tials and forms of global political agency. And following Machiavelli and Gramsci, I call this set of potentials "the postmodern Prince," which I understand as something plural and differentiated, although linked to universalism and the construction of a new form of globalism, and of course, something that needs to be understood as a set of social and political forces in movement.

Let us place this hypothesis in some theoretical context. Machiavelli's *The Prince* addressed the problem of the ethics of rule from the viewpoint of both the prince (the *palazzo*, the palace) and the people (the *piazza*, the town square). Machiavelli sought to theorise how to construct a form of rule that combined both *virtù* (ethics, responsibility, and consent) and fear (coercion) under conditions of *fortuna* (circumstances). *The Prince* was written in Florence, in the context of the political upheavals of Renaissance Italy. Both Machiavelli and later Gramsci linked their analyses and propositions to the reality of concrete historical circumstances as well as to the potential for transformation. These included pressing contemporary issues associated with the problems of Italian unification, and the subordinate place of Italy in the structures of international relations. And it was in a similar national and international context that Gramsci's *The Modern Prince* was written in a Fascist prison, a text that dealt with a central problem of politics: the constitution of power, authority, rule, rights, and responsibilities in the creation of an ethical political community. Nevertheless, what Gramsci saw in *The Prince* was that it was "not a systematic treatment, but a 'live' work, in which political ideology and political science are fused in the dramatic form of a 'myth.'"[13] The myth for Machiavelli was that of *condottiere*, who represented the collective will. By contrast, for Gramsci *The Modern Prince* proposed the myth of the democratic modern mass political party — the communist party — charged with the construction of a new form of state and society, and a new world order.

In the new strategic context (*fortuna*) of disciplinary neoliberalism and globalisation, then, a central problem of political theory is how to imagine and to theorise the new forms of collective political identity and agency that might lead to the creation of new, ethical, and democratic political institutions and forms of practice (*virtù*). So in this context, let me again be clear that by "postmodern Prince" I do *not* mean a form of political agency that is based on postmodern philosophy and the radical relativism it often entails. What I am intending to communicate is a shift in the forms of political agency that are going beyond earlier modernist political projects. So the "postmodern Prince" involves tendencies that have begun to challenge some of the myths and the disciplines of modernist practices, and specifically resisting those that seek to consolidate the project of globalisation under the rule of capital.

Thus, the battles in Seattle may link to new patterns of political agency and a movement that goes well beyond the politics of identity and difference: it has gender, race, and class aspects. It is connected to issues of ecological and social reproduction, and of course, to the question of democracy. This is why more than 700 organisations and between 40,000 and 60,000 people — principally human-rights activists, labour activists, indigenous people, representatives of churches, industrial workers, small farmers, forest activists, environmentalists, social justice workers, students, and teachers — all took part collectively in the protests against the WTO's Third Ministrial on 30 November 1999. The protesters seem aware of the nature and dynamics of their movement and have theorised a series of political links between different events so that they will become more than what James Rosenau called "distant proximities" or simply isolated moments of resistance against globalisation."[14]

In sum, these movements are beginning to form what Gramsci called "an organism, a complex element of society" that is beginning to point towards the realisation of a "collective will." This will is coming to be "recognised and has to some extent asserted itself in action." It is beginning to "take concrete form."[15] Indeed the diverse organisations that are connected to the protests seek to go further to organise something akin to a postmodern transitional political party, that is one with no clear leadership structure as such. It is a party of movement that cannot be easily decapitated. This element puzzled mainstream press reporters at Seattle since they were unable to find, and thus to photograph or interview, the "leaders" of the protests. However, this emerging political form is not a signal of an end to the protests. It is also not a signal of an end to universalism in politics as such, since many of the forces it entails are linked to democratisation and a search for collective solutions to common problems. It seeks to combine diversity with new forms of collective identity and solidarity in and across civil societies. Thus, the organisers of the April 2000 Washington demonstrations stated that "Sweeny's prediction" made at Davos was in fact a description of events that were going on right now, but that are largely ignored by the media:

> The Zapatista uprising in Mexico, the recent coup in Ecuador, the civil war in the Congo, the turmoil in Indonesia, and the threat of the U'Wa people to commit mass suicide, are all expressions of the social explosion that has arisen from the desperation caused by the politics of the World Bank, IMF, and their corporate directors. . . . Fundamental change does not mean renaming their programs of other public relations scams. Fundamental reform means rules that empower the people of the world to make the decisions about how they live their lives — not the transitional CEO's or their purchased political leaders.[16]

In this regard, the effectiveness of the protest movements may well lie in a new confidence gained as particular struggles come to be understood in terms of a more general set of inter-connections between problems and movements world-wide. For instance, the Cartagena Protocol on Biosafety on genetically modified life forms was signed in late January 2000 in Montreal by representatives from 133 governments pursuant to the late 1992 UN Convention on Biological Diversity for the trade and regulation of living modified organisms (LMOs). The draft Protocol ensures that sovereign governments have rights to decide on imports of LMOs provided this is based on environmental and health risk assessment data. The Protocol is founded on the "precautionary principle," in effect meaning that where scientific uncertainty exists, governments can refuse or delay authorisation of trade in LMOs. Apart from pressure from NGOs, the negotiations were strongly influenced by scientists concerned about genetic and biological risks posed by the path of innovation. The process finally produced a protocol with significant controls over the freedoms of biotechnology and life sciences companies. Indeed, linkages and contradictions between environmental and trade and investment regulations and laws are becoming better understood by activists world-wide, for instance, how the Biosafety Protocol and the rules and procedures of the WTO may be in conflict.

Nevertheless, it must be emphasised that, although they may represent a larger proportion of the population of the world in terms of their concerns, in organised political terms the protest groups are only a relatively small part of an emerging global civil society that includes not only NGOs but also the activities of political parties, churches, media communication corporations, and scientific and political associations, some progressive, others reactionary. Transnational civil society also involves activities of both transnational corporations, and also governments that are active in shaping a political terrain that is directly and indirectly outside the formal juridical purview of states. Indeed, as the UN Rio conference on the environment and its aftermath illustrated, corporate environmentalism is a crucial aspect of the emerging global civil society and it is linked to what Gramsci called *transformismo* or co-optation of opposition. For example, "sustainable development" is primarily defined in public policy as compatible with market forces and freedom of enterprise. When the global environment movement was perceived as a real threat to corporate interests, companies changed tack from suggesting the environmentalists were either crackpots or misguided to accepting a real problem existed and a compromise was necessary. Of course a compromise acceptable to capital was not one that would fundamentally challenge the dominant patterns of accumulation.

I have not used the term postmodern in its usual sense. Rather, I apply it to indicate a set of conditions and contradictions that give rise to novel forms of political agency that go beyond and are more complex than those imagined by Machiavelli's *The Prince* or Gramsci's *The Modern Prince*. Global democratic collective action today cannot, in my view, be understood as a singular form of collective agency, for example, a single party with a single form of identity. It is more plural and differentiated, as well as being democratic and inclusive. The new forms of collective action contain innovative conceptions of social justice and solidarity, of social possibility, of knowledge, emancipation, and freedom. The content of their mobilising myths includes diversity, oneness of the planet and nature, democracy, and equity. What are we discussing is, therefore, a political party as well as an educational form and a cultural movement. However, it does not act in the old sense of an institutionalised and centralised structure of representation. Indeed this "party" is not institutionalised as such, since it has a multiple and capillary form. Moreover, whilst many of the moments and movements of resistance noted above are at first glance "local" in nature, there is broad recognition that local problems may require global solutions. Global networks and other mobilizing capabilities are facilitated with new technologies of communication.

A new "postmodern Prince" may prove to be the most effective political form for giving coherence to an open-ended, plural, inclusive, and flexible form of politics and thus create alternatives to neoliberal globalisation. So, whilst one can be pessimistic about globalisation in its current form, this is perhaps where some of the optimism for the future may lie: a new set of democratic identities that are global, but based on diversity and rooted in local conditions, problems, and opportunities.

NOTES

I would like to thank Cemal Acikgoz, Isabella Bakker, Adam Harmes, and Ahmed Hashi for their comments and help in preparing this essay.

1. Antonio Gramsci, *Selections from the Prison Notebooks of Antonio Gramsci*, trans. Quintin Hoare and Geoffrey Nowell Smith (New York: International Publishers, 1971), 129.

2. Scott Sinclair, "The WTO: What happened in Seattle? What's Next in Geneva?" *Briefing Paper Series: Trade and Investment* 1, no. 2 (Ottawa: Canadian Centre for Policy Alternatives, 2000), 6.

3. Stephen Gill, "Globalisation, Market Civilisation, and Disciplinary Neoliberalism," *Millennium: Journal of International Studies* 23, no. 3 (1994): 399–423.

4. See "CIA Spies Swap Cold War for Trade Wars," *Financial Times*, 14 August 1999, 1.

5. Editorial, "New Trade Rules Education," *Canadian Association of University Teachers Bulletin*, 7 September 1999, 1. The *Bulletin* added that Educational International representing 294 educational unions and associations world wide expressed great concern about how WTO initiatives would undermine public education.

6. See the essays in Isabella Bakker, ed., *The Strategic Silence: Gender And Economic Policy* (London: Zed Books, 1994).

7. Paul Hawken, "The WTO: Inside, Outside, All Around The World" [http://www.co-intelligence.org/WTOHawken.html] (26 April 2000).

8. Phillip McMichael, "The Crisis of Market Rule in the Global Food Order" (paper presented at the British International Studies Annual Meeting, Manchester, 20–22 December 1999).

9. Ibid., 2.

10. John Sweeny, "Remember Seattle," *Washington Post*, 30 January 2000, B7.

11. Ann Swardson, "Clinton Appeals for Compassion in Global Trade; World Forum Told Don't Leave 'Little Guys' Out," *Washington Post*, 30 January 2000, A18.

12. Posted on http://www.peoples@psot4.tele.dlk (26 April 2000) on behalf of the NGO network "Mobilization for Global Justice" that organised the Washington protests. Their website [http://www.a16.org] passed 250,000 visitors at the time of the protests.

13. Gramsci, *Selections from the Prison Notebooks*, 125.

14. James Rosenau, "Imposing Global Order: A Synthesised Ontology for a Turbulent Era," in *Innovation and Transformation on International Studies*, Stephen Gill and James H. Mittleman, eds. (Cambridge: Cambridge University Press, 1997), 220–35.

15. Gramsci, *Selections from the Prison Notebooks*, 129.

16. Posted by the NGO network "Mobilization for Global Justice" on http://www.peoples@post4.tele.dk (26 April 2000).

✗ **NO**

Cautionary Reflections on Seattle
JAN AART SCHOLTE

"The Battle of Seattle": stage one on a global popular revolution? Nail in the coffin of neoliberalism? Harbinger of a more secure, equitable, and democratic world order? While I count myself a proponent of far-reaching reform of globalisation, my reactions to recent events in the city of my youth are somewhat cautious.[1]

The demonstrations of late 1999 in Seattle against the World Trade Organisation (WTO) are the latest in a string of street protests against prevailing global economic regimes. The windows of McDonald's in Geneva suffered a similar fate to the panes of Pike Street when the WTO Ministerial Conference met on the shores of Lac Leman in 1998. Most of the Annual and Spring Meetings of the International Monetary Fund (IMF) and the World Bank have witnessed opposition rallies since several thousand people crowded the squares of Berlin in 1988. Throughout the 1990s, protesters also raised their voices outside the yearly summits of the Group of Seven (G7), most notably when tens of thousands of campaigners for the cancellation of Third World debt encircled the Birmingham G7 Summit in 1998. In early 2000, the annual Davos gathering of the World Economic Forum (WEF) became the latest occasion for "civil society" to raise the banners against "globalisation."

This popular mobilisation has made an impact. The launch of the Millennium Round in Seattle was abandoned in part due to public unease as expressed in the streets. Similarly, co-ordinated opposition from many non-governmental organizations (NGOs) played an important role in halting moves toward a Multilateral Agreement on Investment (MAI) in late 1998. Grassroots pressure for debt relief has helped prompt some reductions of bilateral and multilateral claims on poor countries. Lobbying by NGOs, trade unions, and reform-oriented think tanks has also encouraged greater attention by global and regional institutions to alleviating the social costs of economic restructuring in the face of globalisation. In 1999 the IMF even went so far as to recast its "Enhanced Structural Adjustment Facility" as the "Poverty Reduction and Growth Facility." Following pressure from civil society, the IMF, the Organisation for Economic Cooperation and Development (OECD), the WTO, and the World Bank have all intensified public relations efforts, including marked increases in disclosure about their decisions and policy processes.

These developments are welcome. Civic action has pushed issues of social justice and democracy high up the agenda of global economic governance. We may hope that these new priorities retain and indeed increase their current prominence and generate concrete benefits.

Yet "victory" in the "Battle of Seattle" is no occasion for exuberance or complacency about the future of globalisation or the role of civil society in shaping its course. Halting a new round of trade liberalisation is not the same thing as building a better world order. Nor have civic initiatives in the Seattle scenario provided full confidence in the contributions of civil society to progressive global politics.

The following comment elaborates three cautionary notes. First, we should not overestimate the significance of Seattle in terms of policy change. Second, when assessing Seattle we should not romanticise civil society as an inherently powerful and progressive force. Third, we should look beyond the dismantlement of neoliberal globalisation to the construction of something better.

SMALL HARVESTS

My first cautionary note relates to the scale of change represented by the disruption of the proceedings in Seattle. The Millennium Round has only been deferred, not dropped altogether. Social movements have sought major reform of the WTO since its inception in 1995. Development activists pursued change in the General Agreement on Tariffs and Trade (GATT) for several decades before that. These long efforts have booked only modest gains to date. Thanks in good part to pressure from certain civic groups, the WTO has since 1996 added competition issues, development concerns, environmental problems, and labour standards to its agenda. However, little has happened on these matters beyond occasional meetings of committees and working groups.[2] The core mission of the WTO has remained that of the widest and fastest possible liberalisation of cross-border flows of goods and services.

Thanks in part to pressure from churches, NGOs, and trade unions, the Bretton Woods institutions have in recent years made some greater policy revisions than the WTO; nonetheless, so far, they too have retained a mainly neoliberal orientation.[3] The IMF's recent stress on poverty has brought a striking change of rhetoric, as the World Bank's adoption in 1999 of the so-called Comprehensive Development Framework. However, we have yet to see what concrete improvements in social and environmental conditions these changes will bring. To date, "structural adjustment" in a globalising world economy has for the Bretton Woods agencies continued in the first place to mean liberalisation, privatisation, and deregulation.

Meanwhile, civic campaigns for change have had little to say — let alone achieved much — in respect of global finance. The previously mentioned campaigns for debt reduction in the South constitute an exception in this regard, though the actual sums of relief have thus far remained fairly small. Following crises in Asia, Latin America, and Russia, much discussion spread in the late 1990s regarding a new global financial architecture, but present prospects point toward emergency rewiring rather than major reconstruction.

In short, social movements of the kind represented on the streets of Seattle have achieved only marginal reforms of global economic governance to date. Instead of the unadulterated neoliberalism that prevailed in the 1980s and early 1990s, we now have neoliberalism with some fringes of social and environmental policy. Advocates of change have succeeded in placing neoliberal approaches to globalisation under more critical public scrutiny, but the supertanker is slow to turn.

LIMITS OF CIVIL SOCIETY

My second cautionary note relates to limitations in the practices of civil society regarding global economic governance.[4] Many civic activists have assumed rather uncritically that civil society efforts inherently contribute to human betterment. Some academic accounts of global civil society have reinforced these presumptions. Such romanticism does little to advance actual reform of globalisation and indeed can encourage detrimental complacency. Measured − and at times even sceptical − assessments of global civil society are needed to maximise its contributions and sustain its integrity.

By no means does this sober stance deny the significant positive potentials of civil society for progressive global politics. For one thing, community-based organizations, labour unions, and NGOs can play substantial roles in citizen education about globalisation. Civic groups can also give voice to stakeholders who tend not to be heard through official channels. Actors in global civil society can furthermore fuel policy debates by advancing alternative perspectives, methodologies, and proposals. Pressure from civic circles can thus increase transparency and accountability in the governance of globalisation. Moreover, at a time when official channels do not provide adequate mechanisms for democracy in globalisation, civic activism can help legitimise (or delegitimise) prevailing rules and governance institutions. In all of these ways, civil society can strengthen social cohesion, countering various other aspects of contemporary globalisation that have tended to weaken it. In principle, then, a lot of good can come out of global civic mobilisation.

Events in Seattle bore out these potential benefits in a number of ways. With regard to civic education, for example, the commotion (and more particularly the media attention that it attracted) made a larger public aware of the WTO and some of the downsides of the current neoliberal global trade regime. In terms of giving voice, the streets of Seattle (briefly) handed the microphone to grassroots associations that are not often heard in policy processes surrounding global trade. With respect to fuelling debate, the demonstrations in Seattle made it plain that alternatives to currently prevailing regimes are conceivable and perhaps desirable. This pressure has also compelled proponents of the neoliberal trading order to formulate their own case more clearly, precisely, and − we may hope − self-critically. The activists of Seattle have also impressed on regulators of world trade the need to open up and be accountable to citizens. Finally, the "Battle of Seattle" illustrated the importance of civil society in legitimating − or in this case delegitimating − multilateral laws and institutions. Global economic governance cannot rest on technocratic expertise alone: it requires popular consent as well.

Yet, events in Seattle also illustrated various limitations on civil society involvement in global economic governance. For one thing, we must not exaggerate the scale of the benefits just mentioned. Much more civic education is needed about the WTO and globalisation in general. We have yet to see whether Seattle will have launched a lasting, searching, inclusive public debate about the nature of the global economy and its governance. While the managers of global economic institutions have clearly been shaken by the Seattle episode, this experience does not so far appear to have substantially raised their attention to direct public accountability.

The coalition of resistance forces in Seattle may have also proved to be ephemeral. Does this movement have the necessary levels of resources and commitment for a long-haul campaign of global economic reform and/or transformation? A core of activists has devoted itself to the cause full-time, but wider public backing has to date generally been episodic and shallow. For example, a flurry of civic actions has surrounded the IMF/World Bank Annual and Spring Meetings for the last dozen years, but between these gatherings the day-to-day pressure for change (occasional upsurges in one or the other programme country aside) has been largely restricted to a handful of professional NGO campaigners.

In Seattle, as elsewhere, campaigners for change in the global economy have faced major resource disadvantages in their struggle with forces for neoliberal continuity. Oxfam and Fifty Years Is Enough have not begun to match the World Economic Forum and the Institute of International Finance in terms of staff, funds, equipment, office premises, and access to information. Thus far, proponents of change in the global economic order have also rarely developed effective symbolic capital, that is, ideas, images, and slogans that can mobilise a large constituency in a sustained way.

Nor should we forget that most of the nonofficial actors in Seattle did not subscribe to the street protesters' rejection of neoliberal global trade. As at earlier WTO meetings in Geneva and Singapore, far and away the largest sector of civil society present in Seattle was the business lobby. Likewise, bankers have far outnumbered other non-governmental groups at meetings of the multilateral financial institutions. Business associations and individual firms have influenced the shape of contemporary global economic governance much more than reformers and radicals in other quarters. If we take the scope of civil society to include commercial lobbies and policy think tanks as well as trade unions, NGOs, and community groups, then organised non-governmental forces have on balance actually *favoured* the neoliberal status-quo, not opposed it.

This situation points to a more general problem of equitable and democratic representation in global civil society as it has developed to date. In terms of class, for instance, the non-state actors that influence global economic governance have drawn disproportionately from propertied, professional, computer-literate, and English-speaking circles. In terms of countries, the people who have congregated in Seattle, Geneva, and Washington have come disproportionately from the North. In terms of civilisational inputs, most organized civic engagement with global economic institutions has come from Western circles, with Buddhist, Hindu, Islamic, and other cultures largely left out of the loop. In terms of gender and race, women and people of colour have been severely underrepresented in the academic, business, and trade union sectors of global civil society. In addition, urban residents have tended to obtain far easier access to civic campaigns on global economic governance than people from the countryside.

In short, there is a significant danger that global civic activism can reproduce the exclusions of neoliberal globalisation, even in campaigns that mean to oppose those inequities. How can we ensure that civil society indeed gives voice to all, and not just to those who speak the right language and can afford an airfare to Seattle?

Other deficits in democratic practice can also undermine the credentials of civic campaigners for global economic change. For example, global associations — no less than a government department or a business corporation — can be run with top-down managerial authoritarianism. In addition, policy making in global civic organizations can be quite opaque to outsiders: who takes the decisions, by what procedures, and for what reasons? Civic groups may be further deficient in respect to transparency when they do not publish financial statements or even a declaration of objectives, let alone full-scale reports of their activities. Moreover, the leadership of many NGOs is self-selected, raising troubling questions of accountability and potential conflicts of interest. In short, there is nothing inherently democratic in global civil society, whether we are talking about the WEF or the demonstrators of Seattle.

LOOKING AHEAD

My final cautionary note regarding recent events in Seattle concerns the way forward. Regrettably, campaigners for change in the global economy have on the whole held underdeveloped visions of the alternative worlds that they desire. Thus far, the energies of anarchists, consumer advocates, development campaigners, environmentalists, trade unions, and women's movements have, on balance, concentrated far more on undermining the neoliberal agenda than on mapping a different course. To be sure, certain critics have articulated some fairly specific ways forward, but many opponents have not moved beyond protest to proposal, offering reconstruction as well as destruction, specifying what they are for as well as what they are against. The demonstrators of Seattle spoke forcefully about what they rejected, but they offered comparatively few details about what they wanted in place of the Millennium Round, the WTO regime, and the current global economy more generally.

In particular, calls for "deglobalisation" have not been satisfactory in this regard. Many critics of neoliberalism have sought to unravel globalisation and to regain a purportedly better pre-global past. These circles have included economic nationalists (among them some old-style socialists) and a number of environmentalists. Many religious revivalists and xenophobic groups have also wanted to turn back the clock on globalisation.

These negative stances are understandable in light of the pains of neoliberal economic restructuring for many social circles. However, calls to reverse gear are misguided. For one thing, proponents of deglobalisation have greatly romanticised the local community and national sovereignty, neither of which have produced utopia in the past. Reactive opponents of neoliberalism have also tended to discount some of the benefits of globalisation, including indeed the possibility of developing transborder solidarities of the oppressed in global civil society. Moreover, deglobalisation is impracticable. The ideational, productive, regulatory, and technological forces behind globalisation have reached such magnitude that any return to a pre-global status quo ante is currently out of the question.[5]

The challenge, then, is to reorient globalisation, to steer the process in a different direction. Like many critics, the demonstrators in Seattle, Davos, and elsewhere have often conflated globalisation with neoliberalism. They have denounced "globalisation" when their actual target is the neoliberal approach to globalisation. Other policy frameworks could handle global economic governance in more effective, equitable, and democratic ways. The problem is not globalisation, but the way we handle it.

Progressive elements in global civil society therefore face a far greater challenge than disrupting summits on global economic governance. If neoliberal globalisation has unacceptable adverse consequences, and deglobalisation is not a viable option, then new forms of globalisation need to be developed. Fortunately some academic and civil society practices are beginning to explore these potentials.[6] If the energy of protest could be coupled with the inspiration of innovation, than more humane global futures could result.

NOTES

1. See Jan Aart Scholte, *Globalization: A Critical Introduction* (Basingstoke: Macmillan, 2000), especially chap. 12.

2. Jan Aart Scholte, Robert O'Brien, and Marc Williams, "The WTO and Civil Society," *Journal of World Trade* 33, no 1 (1999): 107–24.

3. See Paul J. Nelson, *The World Bank and Non-Governmental Organizations: The Limits of Apolitical Development* (Basingstoke: Macmillan, 1995); Jonathan A. Fox and L. David Browns, eds., *The Struggle for Accountability: The World Bank, NGOs and Grassroots Movements* (Cambridge, MA: MIT Press, 1998); and Robert O'Brien et al., *Contesting Global Governance: Multilateral Economic Institutions and Global Social Movements* (Cambridge: Cambridge University Press, 2000).

4. The following points draw on Jan Aart Scholte, "Global Civil Society," in *The Political Economy of Globalization*, Ngaire Woods, ed. (Basingstoke: Macmillan, 2000), 173–201.

5. This assessment is elaborated in *Globalization: A Critical Introduction*, chap. 4.

6. See, for instance, Samir Amin, *Capitalism in the Age of Globalization: The Management of Contemporary Society* (London: Zed Books, 1997); James H. Mattelman, *The Globalization Syndrome: Transformation and Resistance* (Princeton, NJ: Princeton University Press, 2000); Jan Nederveen Pieterse, ed., *Global Futures: Shaping Globalization* (London: Sage, 2000); and Michael Edwards and John Gaventa, eds., *Global Citizen Action: Perspectives and Challenges* (Boulder, CO: Lynne Rienner, forthcoming).

POSTSCRIPT

One problem in understanding the significance of events such as the "Battle in Seattle" is sorting out the different groups participating in the demonstrations and their wide range of tactics and strategies. The more radical anti-globalization groups seemed focused primarily on disruptive techniques aimed at bringing the work of the WTO to a halt. Others were concerned with finding ways to hold the WTO accountable by demanding a greater popular voice in decisionmaking processes surrounding trade policies.

Events such as those in Seattle have led some to draw attention to the "dark side" of global civil society. In an article cited below, David Robertson argues that if NGOs want to hold institutions such as the WTO accountable to the public and make their work more transparent, then NGOs themselves must be prepared to do the same. He notes that many NGOs do not hold elections for officers and do not reveal their sources of funding or their expenditures. What makes them, he asks, any more representative of the population than the governments participating in WTO negotiations? Robertson suggests that NGOs should sign a code of conduct before they are given greater accessibility and participation. What would such a code of conduct contain? Would it even be feasible or desirable?

Suggested Additional Readings

Bhagwati, Jagdish. "Responding to Seattle." *Challenge* 44, no. 1 (January–February 2001): 6–19.

Clarke, Tony. "Taking on the WTO: Lessons from the Battle of Seattle." *Studies in Political Economy* 62 (Summer 2000): 7–16.

Hoad, Darren. "The World Trade Organisation: The Events and Impact of Seattle 1999." *Environmental Politics* 9, no. 4 (Winter 2000): 123–29.

Kaldor, Mary. "'Civilising' Globalisation? The Implications of the 'Battle in Seattle.'" *Millennium: Journal of International Studies* 29, no. 1 (2000): 105–14.

Kiely, Ray. "Globalization: From Domination to Resistance." *Third World Quarterly* 21, no. 6 (December 2000): 1059–71.

Levi, Margaret, and David Olson. "The Battles in Seattle." *Politics & Society* 28, no. 3 (September 2000): 309–30.

McMichael, Philip. "Sleepless since Seattle: What Is the WTO About?" *Review of International Political Economy* 7, no. 3 (September 2000): 466–75.

Robertson, David. "Civil Society and the WTO." *World Economy* 23, no. 9 (September 2000): 1119–35.

InfoTrac® College Edition

Search for the following articles in the InfoTrac® database:

Buttel, Frederick H. "Some Observations on the Anti-Globalisation Movement." *Australian Journal of Social Issues* 38, no. 1 (February 2003): 95–116.

Bendle, Mervyn. "Trajectories of Anti-Globalism." *Journal of Sociology* 38, no. 3 (September 2002): 213–23.

Scholte, Jan Aart. "Civil Society and Democracy in Global Governance." *Global Governance* 8, no. 3 (July–September 2002): 281–304.

For more articles, enter:
"anti-globalization" or "Battle in Seattle" in the keyword search.

Web Resources

For current URLs for the following websites, visit www.crosscurrents.nelson.com.

BBC News: The Battle for Free Trade

news.bbc.co.uk/1/hi/special_report/1999/11/99/battle_for_free_trade/534014.stm

This page offers a collection of written and audio-visual reports on the events in Seattle as covered by the BBC.

Global Action

flag.blackened.net/~global/

This site is devoted to reports and analyses of Seattle from the viewpoint of anti-globalization activists.

Free Trade and Globalization: WTO Protests in Seattle

www.globalissues.org/TradeRelated/Seattle.asp

This page contains a collection of resources on the Seattle protests, with special emphasis on the media coverage of the events.

Trade Observatory

www.tradeobservatory.org

The site of this resource centre sponsored by the Institute for Agriculture and Trade Policy contains many documents and updates on the World Trade Organization and issues related to trade and globalization.

Would a North American Currency Union Benefit Canada?

✔ **YES**
THOMAS J. COURCHENE, "The Case for a North American Currency Union," *Policy Options* 24, no. 4 (April 2003): 20–25

✘ **NO**
ANDREW JACKSON, "Why the 'Big Idea' Is a Bad Idea," *Policy Options* 24, no. 4 (April 2003): 26–28

In order to trade with one another, nations must have some basis for exchanging currencies. In 1944, when the leaders of the Western capitalist countries gathered at the New England resort Bretton Woods, they were concerned about developing a reliable mechanism for determining the value of one country's currency in relation to another's. Fluctuating currency exchange rates and the resulting temptation to competitively devalue one's currency had been an important contributor to the economic and political turmoil that preceded the outbreak of World War II. The leaders meeting at Bretton Woods based their hope for postwar economic recovery and prosperity on the establishment of a regime of fixed exchange rates. Participating governments were given primary responsibility for enforcing the rules of the new regime, while the newly created International Monetary Fund (IMF) was to encourage the stability of exchange rates by assisting states facing balance-of-payments crises that could tempt them to devalue their currencies.

Key to this system was the American dollar and the role of the United States as the leading, hegemonic power in this new monetary regime. The value of currencies would be determined in relation to the dollar, the value of which in turn was based on a fixed rate of $35 per ounce of gold. To maintain a stable value for their currencies, the central banks of other countries would buy or sell their own currencies using the U.S. dollar to raise or lower their value. Thus, while the Bretton Woods system sought to maintain a fixed exchange rate of currencies, it demanded a measure of coordinated intervention by governments.

While the system worked relatively well initially, it broke down in 1971, when President Nixon, without prior consultation with allies, announced that the United States would no longer exchange dollars for gold. Cutting the dollar loose from the gold standard meant that its value, like the value of other currencies, would reflect changes in the marketplace. This led to a period of floating exchange rates during which market forces, not government interventions, determined currency values. What resulted was a period of volatility, with currencies fluctuating more wildly, financial crises occurring more frequently, and various countries defaulting on loans. Efforts of the Group of Seven (and later the G-8) countries to coordinate global monetary policies had not been successful. Many observers came to believe that a world of more than a hundred fluctuating currencies was not compatible with the continued globalization of the economy.

Two options appear open to states in response to this issue. One is for a nation to "dollarize" its economy, that is, replace its national currency with the U.S. dollar. A country can do this either with a formal agreement with the United States or informally, by allowing the U.S. dollar to increasingly become the accepted currency for transacting business in its economy. Some countries, such as Ecuador and El Salvador, have officially dollarized their economies, while many others have at least partially dollarized on an informal basis. For some countries, the thought of abolishing their national currencies is politically unacceptable because of the role that these currencies play as a symbol of national independence. In addition, those countries that dollarize in effect surrender control of their monetary policies, since they have no say in American institutions that regulate the U.S. monetary policy.

A second option is to abolish national currencies in favour of the creation of a new regional currency. The model for this solution has been the creation of the common currency union by the European Union for its population of 305 million people. In 2002, twelve members of the European Union abolished their national currencies, many of them dating back centuries, and adopted the euro. It was hoped that the creation of single currency would facilitate the process of making the European community into a single continent-wide market for business. Although the introduction of the euro has been seen largely as a success, it is not without its detractors. Three EU states – Britain, Denmark, and Sweden – decided not to adopt the euro. To many critics in these countries, the euro is simply a symbolic representation of a larger political agenda of integration, intended to erase national distinctiveness and weaken national sovereignty.

The issues of dollarization and currency unions have gained increased attention in Canada in recent years. Two factors in particular have contributed to this interest. First, the performance of the Canadian dollar in relation to the U.S. dollar has caused concern in many quarters. Until September 2002, the Canadian dollar had been performing poorly, reaching an all-time low of 62 cents to the American dollar. Many feared that the declining dollar was contributing to a decline in living standards and making Canadian assets vulnerable to foreign acquisition as they declined in international value. When the Canadian dollar began to rise in relation to the U.S. dollar again in 2003, some sectors feared that the rising dollar would negatively affect Canada's trade balance and employment levels. Such fluctuations in value of the Canadian dollar gave rise to new calls for somehow stabilizing currency exchange rates.

Second, the success of the euro has sparked renewed discussion of the potential value of regional currency unions. As the euro increased in strength globally and became a potential competitor with the U.S. dollar, some analysts have suggested that the time has come to consider the merits of a North American currency union. Some have even suggested that a new currency for North and South America, the amero, would compete with the euro.

A prominent figure in the debate about currency rates and monetary policy is Thomas Courchene, an economist at Queen's University. Courchene has been a proponent of a currency union with the United States. In the following article, he sets out some of the arguments for this approach and examines the issues involved in the implementation of such a union. Andrew Jackson, a senior economist with the Canadian Labour Congress, provides a response to Courchene's article. Jackson sees many of the same dangers in a monetary union as in the free trade debate. While it is argued that a monetary union would ease Canada's economic problems in its relations with the United States, Jackson warns that these gains would come at the loss of many important distinctive Canadian values.

✔ YES

The Case for a North American Currency Union

THOMAS J. COURCHENE*

In making the case for a Canada–US or perhaps a NAFTA currency union, I shall elaborate upon and hopefully substantiate the following propositions:

- that our system of flexible exchange rates has not served Canada well;

- that a fixed-exchange-rate system is preferable to our current floating rate system, given the degree of North American integration, the nature of this integration (north-south economic regions) and the shift away from a resource-based economy and society to a human-capital-based economy and society;

- that North American Monetary Union (NAMU) along euro lines is the logical longer term goal toward which a fixed-exchange-rate regime should evolve; and

- that the last time that Canada had a common currency with the US (the Pearson era) represented one of the most creative periods in terms of enacting policies that have made us socio-economically unique in the upper half of North America.

Appropriately, however, the analysis begins with reference to one of the most significant events in the annals of monetary and economic history – the advent of the euro.

Whenever the subject of the euro arises, we are immediately informed by our policy officials that the political objectives that motivated monetary union in Europe do not have a parallel in North America. I agree with this. But now that the euro is alive and running it has major implications for currency arrangements in other trading blocs. Among other things, the euro signals:

- the "denationalization" of national monetary regimes;

- the emergence of common currencies as supra-national public goods; and

- a dramatic shift toward currency consolidation, with well over two-dozen countries already using or committed to using the euro.

One does not have to believe that the future will involve only a handful of currencies in order to recognize the wisdom of investigating the options for the future of Canada's exchange rate regime.

Admittedly, the Spring of 2003 would not appear to be the most propitious time to levy a broadside against Canada's flexible rate regime. After all, Canada has avoided the US recession, has the highest GDP growth of the G7 and is the

---

*This article is based on joint research undertaken with Richard Harris.

only G7 country running a fiscal surplus. Moreover, the Canadian macro environment is, arguably for the first time ever, characterized by workable and transparent fiscal and monetary targets. While I am happy to assign excellent grades for implementation to our macro managers over this recent period, my quarrel lies with the longer-term appropriateness of the underlying framework itself. Why, in a progressively integrating North American economic space, and where Canada is more integrated trade-wise to the US than is any European country to its Euro partners, would we want to pursue a monetary policy independent of that of the US?

Among the concerns that have been raised about the falling and volatile Canadian dollar over the last decade are that it has

- led to a quite dramatic fall in living standards for Canadians (relative to those of Americans);

- led to fire-sale prices for those of our assets that generate a Canadian-dollar income stream;

- led to cost and competitive uncertainty as a result of the inherent exchange rate volatility, which uncertainty becomes more problematical as we shift to a knowledge-based economy and may be playing an important role in our falling share of inward North American foreign direct investment.

- led to a serious currency "misalignment" for long periods of time, where substantial overvaluation leads to downsizing, off-shoring, and exit, while undervaluation provides incentives for migration of human capital and underinvestment in productivity-enhancing technology, the net result of which will be a more resource-based and less human-capital-intensive economy than would otherwise be the case.

At one level, there are some easy counters to these claims — the falling dollar provides an important stimulus to exports and, a related point, that having the dollar fall in line with falling resource prices (see the figure "Canadian Dollar and Real Commodity Prices") provides a "buffer" to price shocks to the commodity sectors. I agree with both of these "facts." However, this stimulus and/or buffering is a very mixed blessing over the medium term. Specifically, commodity-price buffering may well be one of the causes of our productivity shortfall vis-à-vis the Americans. The story would go as follows. Cushioning Canadian dollar commodity prices, that is to say, depreciating the Canadian dollar in line with the fall in relative commodity prices provides incentives for labour and capital to remain in the commodity sector rather than shift to the "new economy." Moreover, assuming that the capital equipment and technology that drives the new economy is priced in US dollars, a falling Canadian dollar means that the price of this equipment will have risen apace.

Figure 11.1 Canadian Dollar and Real Commodity Prices

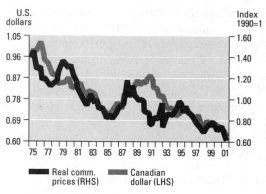

Source: Bank of Canada, Statistics Canada

These incentives point in the direction of a smaller new economy, and less technology investment in both the old and new economies. In turn, this implies lower productivity growth than would be the case if there were no buffering, namely lower productivity growth than if there were a fixed exchange rate. As an important corollary, this also suggests that Canada's relative productivity slowdown will gradually offset the impact of the depreciation, so that any export stimulus from a falling dollar may well be temporary, that is, eroded by lower productivity growth. While this theoretical approach fits well into the managerial theories of the firm, and while there is plenty of anecdotal evidence suggesting that this actually may be the case in many sectors, flexible-rate advocates let alone our macro officials steadfastly maintain that there is *no* causation going from exchange rates to productivity. In the interests of our collective economic futures, they had better be correct. I do not believe that they are.

Apart from the commodity-price buffering argument, much of the rest of the case for flexible rates rests on the related assumption that only floating exchange rates can accommodate asymmetric Canada-US shocks. This too, I believe to be incorrect, especially once one recognizes that Canada's trade has dramatically veered north-south by region (see Table 1 on page 288 for Canada and the chart for Ontario's interprovincial and US trade). In effect, these trends suggest that Canada is moving in the direction of becoming a series of north-south, cross-border economies. In this context, assume that both the Canadian and American components of each of these cross-border economies (e.g. Ontario and Michigan, B.C. and Washington) are in some sort of cost/competitive equilibrium. Now assume that there is a commodity price increase. Initially, this affects both sides of the cross-border regions similarly (Michigan and Ontario; B.C. and Washington; Alberta and the Texas Gulf; Prairies and Montana, Quebec and New York).

But if we attempt to *buffer* this price hike by appreciating the exchange rate, then *all of the Canadian regions are offside vis-à-vis their US counterparts.* Why would we do this? The key continental asymmetries are typically east-west, that is between B.C. and Ontario (Washington vs. Michigan), or Alberta vs. Ontario (Texas vs. Mid-West) and not between the two sides of the cross-border regions. National flexible rates *cannot* address these internal east-west asymmetries. Much better to keep exchange rates fixed and to address east-west asymmetries via national redistributive

Figure 11.2 Ontario's Interprovincial and International Exports

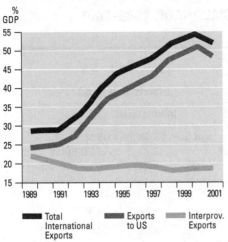

Total International Exports   Exports to US   Interprov. Exports

Source: Trade Update 2002: Third Annual Report on Canada's State of Trade, Department of Foreign Affairs and International Trade Canada

instruments such as taxation, equalization, employment insurance and, where appropriate, sub-national stabilization policies. Phrased differently, let Ontario and B.C. adjust in the same way that Michigan and Washington adjust with the caveat that Canada, unlike the US, has regionally redistributive instruments to provide a helping hand, as noted in the previous sentence.

Given, therefore, that it is clearly possible to mount a case for fixed exchange rates, what range of options is available?

Contrary to the majority view, fixed exchange rate regimes *are* sustainable a) when countries are highly integrated and b) where policy is geared to making the fixed exchange rate the keystone of national economic policy. The best examples are the very successful Austrian and Dutch fixes to the DM, which even held through the union of East and West Germany. And since Canada is more highly integrated, trade-wise, with the US than are Austria/Holland with Germany, this should be eminently feasible were we to clearly commit ourselves to a fixed rate.

If, nonetheless, even greater certainty is desired, one can go the currency board route. Currency boards are arrangements where circulating local currencies are fully backed by the anchor currency, usually the US dollar, e.g. Argentina and Hong Kong. Argentina's unhappy experience with a currency board is usually raised in this context. However, in terms of the issue at hand, namely the sustainability of the currency board's parity value, Argentina's problem, among others, was that the currency board held too well. Hence, Argentina had no way to respond to Brazil's 40 percent devaluation against the peso, short of abandoning the currency board which it ultimately did. The real lesson here is along somewhat different lines. Do not adopt a currency board that is anchored to the US dollar if the US is not your major trading partner. With 87 percent of our trade destined for US markets, this would not be our concern if we established a currency board relationship with the US dollar.

Over the longer term, however, the appropriate evolution would be toward a euro-type North American Monetary Union (NAMU).

When up and running, NAMU might be organized along the following lines. There would be a supra-national central bank — say the Reserve Bank of North America (RBNA). The Bank of Canada would be on the board of the RBNA, just as the Bank of France is on the board of the ECB (European Central Bank).

TABLE 1

INTERNATIONAL AND INTERPROVINCIAL TRADE, 1989–2001

	1989 Exports as % of GDP				2001 Exports as % of GDP			
	International				International			
	% of GDP (1)	US Share (2)	US as % of GDP (3)	Inter- provincial (4)	% of GDP (5)	US Share (6)	US as % of GDP (7)	Inter- provincial (8)
Canada	25.4	73.2	18.6	22.5	43.1	87.3	37.6	19.7
Nfld	31.0	68.4	21.2	11.9	37.1	65.6	24.3	20.3
PEI	14.7	60.2	8.8	30.6	31.8	89.9	28.5	27.7
NS	15.8	66.0	10.4	21.0	29.0	82.7	23.7	21.1
NB	26.2	66.5	17.4	30.0	45.7	89.1	42.3	31.2
Que	21.2	75.7	16.0	22.9	39.6	84.8	33.6	19.4
Ont	28.6	85.9	24.6	22.6	51.5	93.3	48.0	18.7
Man	18.5	62.6	11.6	28.0	30.7	80.0	24.6	29.7
Sask	22.7	45.0	10.2	25.6	44.2	59.0	26.1	25.4
Alta	24.5	75.7	18.5	28.5	41.3	88.8	36.7	22.1
BC	28.7	83.4	12.5	13.5	31.3	70.9	22.2	14.1

Source: Canada Department of Foreign Affairs and International Trade (2002), Tables 1A and 9E.
Notes: Nfld (Newfoundland), PEI (Prince Edward Island), NS (Nova Scotia), NB (New Brunswick),
    Que (Quebec), Ont (Ontario), Man (Manitoba), Sask (Saskatchewan), Alta (Alberta), BC (British
    Columbia).

The US would retain majority control of the RBNA — indeed, they would likely retain 12 seats, corresponding to their current Federal Reserve Districts, while probably granting Canada only one. The US dollar would continue to exist (why would anyone, least of all the Americans, want to replace the world's most important currency?) and would be the circulating currency in the USA. Canada would create a new currency that would exchange one-for-one with the US dollar. Suppose the "entry" exchange rate was 150 current Canadian cents for one US dollar. Then 100 new Canadian dollars would be equivalent to 150 current Canadian dollars — items that cost 150 old dollars would now cost 100 new dollars, and similarly for wages. Hence, we would maintain the existing relative price differences between Canada and the US. For example, if it now takes one day's work to pay the weekly rent, this would also be the case under the new currency. This is exactly the currency-conversion process that every euro country has just come through. Note that our new currency could still have Canadian symbolism on one side, with one side adorned with a picture of the rockies and the other indicating that this new $5 bill, for example, is the liability of the RBNA and identical to and freely exchangeable for a US $5 bill. At the eleventh hour, the Europeans abandoned the notion of allowing one side of their new currency to vary across countries. But they have allowed this for the 1 and 2 euro coins. Seigniorage would stay with Canada, but the exchange rate would disappear.

As befits a unified monetary area, the RBNA would control the amount of currency outstanding at any given time, presumably in line with RBNA goals such as price stability, economic growth, etc. Canada's share of this total currency would be "demand determined" — for example, faster Canadian growth under NAMU would result in a larger Canadian share of the overall North American currency.

It took the Europeans more than a decade to converge to a series of "entry rates" for the various currencies. We would likely have to repeat this gradual entry process for NAMU as well, hopefully replete with some version of the Maastricht guidelines. One frequently expressed concern is that if we lock ourselves in at, say, 66 US cents for one Canadian dollar (or 150 Canadian cents for 1 US dollar) then we are underpricing our assets, vis-à-vis the Americans, *for all time*. This is *not* the case. Suppose we enter NAMU, or a fixed-exchange-rate regime, at 66 cents. If we perform better than the US, our wages and non-traded-goods prices will rise relative to those in the US. *This is how we will close the current income gap with the Americans.* And this is precisely what happened to the Irish — they entered the EMS/euro at an undervalued rate and have performed so well that they now have per capita incomes above the EU average.

Alternatively, we could simply adopt the US dollar as our currency. Many or most of the above benefits on the economic front would also apply to dollarization. However, there would be some significant policy and societal costs. We would lose seigniorage and lose currency symbolism. The clearings system would likely follow the north-south trading patterns and become north-south by region, (e.g., Toronto clearing with the US eastern seaboard and Vancouver with San Francisco), thereby beginning a process of undermining our east-west comity. In contrast, under NAMU, clearings would occur nationally before we cleared internationally, as is the case in Euroland. Under dollarization, our financial structure and financial policy would likely fall under the US ambit and orbit. Not only would there be no rationale for maintaining the Bank of Canada, but with no fall-back institutions in place, this option would be difficult to reverse, at least over the short term. Indeed, one of the reasons why I got involved in this issue in the first place was to provide a range of currency options that would dominate and/or preclude dollarization.

Would the US ever agree to NAMU?

The almost unanimous answer from both sides of the border appears to be *No*. But many on both sides of the border would have also claimed that the US would never sign a free trade agreement with Canada, let alone with Mexico. At the very least this answer surely needs to be nuanced. First, the euro is making a big splash — one can foresee a day when close to 50 countries could be in the Euro zone, which will make the euro highly competitive with the dollar as a means of payment, as a unit of account, and as a store of value. At some point, the United States and the Fed will surely get concerned: Can one maintain and sustain economic hegemony without also having the dominant currency? Second, while we fully recognize that Canada's regions and the northern tier of Mexican states are progressively integrating into North American economic space, it has gone largely unnoticed that 38 US states now have Canada as their largest (international) trading partner, and I would guess that many of the remaining states would have Mexico as their largest export market. While it is true for many of these states that exports to the rest of the US dominate exports to Canada, the fact remains that the US itself is becoming more fully integrated into North American economic space, and it is not difficult to foresee a day when Canada and Mexico will account for 50 percent of US exports. Beyond this, the spate of currency crises across Central and South America and their cost to the US in terms of loan guarantees, bailouts, lost markets and the like suggest that, at some point, US self-interest will force it to play a larger and more interventionist role in enhancing hemispheric currency stability.

Yet none of this is intended to suggest that the US will, out of the blue as it were, offer to internationalize its central bank, even if it were to maintain the overwhelming decision-making authority. Rather, if a move to a NAMU or a hemispheric monetary union emerges it will probably come about in a roundabout way. For example, several key countries would dollarize, perhaps responding to US incentives so that they choose the dollar rather than the euro. After a while, these countries will quite naturally want some input into US monetary policy. Among other things, they will request periodic meetings with the US or the Federal Reserve System as to the likely evolution of US monetary policy, during which meetings they will also state their own priorities. Gradually, these meetings will become more frequent and perhaps more formalized and, almost unwittingly, this process begins to move in the direction of a US-dominated RBNA and NAMU. Alternatively, as part of deepening NAFTA, Canada, Mexico and the US might acquire "observer status" on the boards of some of each others' institutions, including the central banks. Again, these informal linkages could then become more formalized and eventually prepare the way for some version of a RBNA.

Our last experience with fixed rates was over the period 1962–70, when the Canadian dollar was set at 92.5 US cents. As already noted, this covered the Pearson years when we initiated, or finalized, our comprehensive range of social programs that distinguish us from the Americans. This provides tangible counter-evidence to the claim that we lose "sovereignty" over a wide range of policy areas if we tie our currency to the US dollar. Naturally, under fixed exchange rates, we do lose "monetary sovereignty": this is the very reason for fixing the exchange rate. But the NAMU variant of fixing would restore some say in overall monetary policy.

As an aside, when we finally floated the dollar in 1970, it *appreciated* from 92.5 cents to the 105 cent range in the mid-1970s. This is evidence that we *were* converging to the US (à la Ireland in Euroland) under this 1962–1970 "common currency."

What might drive the system toward fixed rates and, perhaps, NAMU? One factor will be the position that Britain takes on the euro. The British do not want political union with Europe, so that in this they are like Canada in the North American context. Their options are – keep the floating pound, fix the pound to the euro, allow eurorization, or embrace the euro and the ECB. Note that they will have one vote out of thirteen now, and one vote out of 25 or so in a year or two. My guess is that they will opt to join the euro, which should send a key message to Canada that currency integration is not inherently about sovereignty.

A move by Mexico to dollarize, which would give them monetary stability at favourable wages, may trigger moves on our part to deepen NAFTA economically and, eventually, monetarily. In this context, it is important to recognize that any progress in the area of deepening NAFTA to incorporate framework policies relating to countervail, subsidy and anti-dumping will surely require that our exchange rates are fixed, or at least jointly managed. By way of illustration, it has not escaped the Americans that our exchange rate has depreciated significantly over the last dozen years. Phrased differently, the amount of the levy on softwood lumber is not unrelated to the amount of the depreciation.

There is a related storm cloud on the horizon. Over the 1990–2001 period, our real exchange rate depreciated from an index of 100 in 1990 to 70 in 2001. Over this same period our current account balance with the US went from a deficit of 1 percent of GDP in 1990 to a current account *surplus* of over 6 percent in 2001. If and when the Americans finally got around to focus on their trade deficit, we may well become the target for much of the adjustment in either or both of the exchange rate and the trade balance. I simply leave it to the reader to mull over the possible scenarios here, replete with how much sovereignty flexible rates will have provided us with.

On the purely domestic front, as was the case for the FTA, not much is likely to happen until business comes on side. Were the recent statement by Alcan favouring a North American currency to be endorsed by several other prominent companies, the game would be afoot. It is important to note, however, that much of the Canadian economy is already outside of the Canadian dollar area. The fortunes of the largest Canadian companies can rise and fall with hardly an impact on the Canadian dollar since most of the stock trading takes place in US dollars. Let me speculate that this is beginning to worry the Bank of Canada, in the following sense. In the current time frame, we are outperforming the Americans. If this is part of the long-awaited convergence (à la Ireland), one would expect wages to rise and the prices of non-traded goods and services to be subject to upward pressure as well. If this is really convergence, then productivity will increase and this will not show up as inflation. But measurement problems with respect to productivity are manifold, so that convergence may reveal itself in the data, initially at least, as inflation. And if this is so, it will be difficult for the Bank of Canada not to hike interest rates to choke off this inflation and, with it, *choke off the convergence.* One of the ways to interpret the Governor's recent statement that he would hope that the exchange rate will increase (appreciate) as Canadian economic activity increases is that this would help stem the potential rise in measured inflation and, therefore, facilitate convergence. This issue would not arise under a common currency, since there would be no assumption that Canada could affect NA inflation anymore than Ireland could affect EU inflation.

Those in favour of the flexible-rate status quo tend to take refuge in the following argument:

Fixed exchange rates are unsustainable and a common currency is unattainable. Therefore, the real choice is between flexible rates and dollarization. Since dollarization is unacceptable, flexible rates shall rule!

Except for "dollarization is unacceptable," this argument is, I respectfully submit, completely wrong. Given the pace of currency consolidation, it is unlikely that a floating or flexible exchange rate will even be in the longer-term choice set. Rather, the choice will likely be between North American monetary union (or some version of exchange-rate fixity) on the one hand, and dollarization on the other. Faced with this decision set, most Canadians would surely vote for NAMU!

As a final comment, it is fair to say that it was because Canada had done its homework that we were able to say "yes" to the Canada-US Free Trade Agreement when the opportunity arose. The situation with respect to NAMU or a common currency is analogous. We need to assess the pros and cons of alternative approaches to currency consolidation in North America, so that if and when a window of opportunity arises our homework/research will likewise be done. One cannot preclude that, as a result of this in-depth analysis, flexible rates will emerge as the "winner," so to speak. But let's do the requisite analysis first, before pre-judging the results.

✗ **NO**
Why the "Big Idea" Is a Bad Idea
ANDREW JACKSON

In recent months, the same people who championed the FTA and NAFTA have been promoting the "big idea" of still closer economic integration with the United States. What Tom D'Aquino of the Canadian Council of Chief Executives, former prime minister Brian Mulroney and Wendy Dobson of the C.D. Howe Institute have in mind is a grand "strategic bargain" in which Canada would give the US a strong North American security perimeter (including close co-ordination of immigration and defence policies), and even greater access to Canadian energy resources. In return, we would (yet again!) supposedly obtain secure access to the US market.

The "big idea" seeks to strike down US trade and border measures through negotiation of a customs union. As noted by the recent House of Commons Committee Report on North American Relations, a customs union features common external tariffs and border measures which involves a loss of national autonomy in international trade and investment policy. The European Union, for example, speaks with just one voice at the WTO. While the precise shape of any future North American deal is hard to predict, not least given the distinct lack of interest in Washington, it is clear that Canadian business is prepared to surrender a lot of policy levers in return for the holy grail of Canadian trade policy, "protection from US protectionism."

The "big idea" is a bad idea for many reasons, not least the explicit threat it poses to the expression of distinctive Canadian values on defence, international affairs, and immigration and refugee issues. It is also a very bad idea in terms of its implications for economic and social policy. Specifically, the "big idea" challenges our necessary ability to shape industrial development, to control our energy sector and move toward a more environmentally sustainable economy; to levy taxes at the level needed to maintain a distinctive Canadian social model, and to limit the impacts of international trade and investment agreements on our social and cultural policies.

Canadians are commonly told that "free trade" has been a huge success in terms of boosting exports to the US. In truth, almost all of our export growth has been due to the growth of the American market in the 1990s, the low level of the Canadian dollar, soaring energy exports, and the historical strength of the auto sector. The trade deals have dramatically failed to do what they were supposed to do: close the long-standing Canada-US gap in manufacturing sector productivity. Between 1992 and 2000, manufacturing output per hour worked rose by just 16 percent in Canada compared to 43 percent in the US, and the gap grew wider as the decade wore on. This carries a significant price in terms of foregone wage growth and prospects for our future prosperity.

Ironically, the large and growing productivity gap is constantly lamented by the same people who said that free trade would give a major boost to industrial efficiency. But, NAFTA has done little to solve the underlying structural problem: an industrial sector which is still too heavily tilted to the production of crude resource-based and basic industrial goods (45 percent of exports), and far too weak when it comes to the production of sophisticated finished products. To be sure, we have some strong non-resource sectors like auto, steel, and telecom equipment. But, less than one-sixth of Canadian manufacturing production is of machinery and equipment, well under half the US level, and it is this key gap which explains our weak productivity growth. Canadians do as well or better than the US in the resource sector, steel and auto industries, but the greatest productivity gains have taken place in the advanced capital goods sectors, where we are still very weak.

One problem with the "big idea" is that it distracts attention from our real problem, a collective failure by corporate Canada to innovate and to invest adequately in research and development, "workers" skills, and new plant and equipment. Worse, a new deal would almost certainly limit our ability to pursue national industrial polices to help build "knowledge-intensive" industries. Would we retain our (regrettably largely unused) right to screen foreign takeovers of Canadian industrial leaders? (Would we really want Nortel or Bombardier to be taken over, given that Canadian taxpayers have sunk huge amounts of research and development subsidies into these companies to build our innovation base?) Could Canada and the US really speak with one voice at the WTO when it comes to the negotiation of future industrial subsidies rules? Our interest lies in building up capacity in sectors where we lack a historical advantage, while the US wants to challenge threats to its dominance in advanced industries.

When it comes to industrial policy, a much more sensible approach would be to retain and expand our room for manouevre under the current WTO rules, while exploring possibilities for closer North American co-operation in the few very closely integrated sectors where we have joint interests. It is possible, for example, to think about common trade policies to expand North American content and jobs in auto, steel, aerospace, and lumber.

Proponents of the "big idea" favour closer continental energy integration, even though we surrendered most tools of control, such as differential export pricing and quantitative export controls under NAFTA. Canadians should be deeply concerned about our fast-rising natural gas exports and high oil level of exports given rapid depletion of the cheapest, most accessible conventional resources, and the prospect of rising real prices as the US rapidly exhausts its own resource base. While it is far from clear that we would want to return to a Trudeau-era regulatory regime, it is surely reasonable to make use of our right under WTO rules to make sure that exports of non-renewable resources do not hinder our ability to meet future Canadian needs.

Rather than even closer integration in the oil and gas sector and joint development of environmentally-fragile Arctic resources, we need to restore export regulation by the National Energy Board for conservation purposes. And, tight integration of electricity grids is a very bad idea indeed. Today, cheap hydroelectric power gives most Canadians much lower prices than American consumers and industries. In the wake of the Enron and California power deregulation fiascos, the case for publicly owned and regulated power utilities is much more compelling than that for deregulated continental markets.

Moreover, deeper energy integration would undermine our ability to build a more sustainable economy and deal with the very serious challenge of global warming. Ratification of the Kyoto protocol and its first stage targets prompted a storm of criticism from Alberta and most of the oil and gas industry, on the grounds that charges for carbon emissions would undercut the development of the tar sands and frontier resources. The primary oil and gas sector is a major producer of greenhouse gas emissions, and the carbon intensity of nonconventional resource development which will dominate the future of the industry is very high. Initially, Kyoto will have a very limited impact. But, the fact remains that there is a fundamental longer-term contradiction between completely integrated continental energy markets and rapid primary energy sector development on the one hand, and energy conservation measures, slower resource development, and the fostering of "green industries" and soft energy paths, on the other. We should retain control of our own energy future.

When it comes to preserving the Canadian social model, proponents of the "big idea" like to talk of a purely economic arrangement. That is hardly surprising since the great majority of Canadians remain deeply committed to a more egalitarian and secure society than that to be found south of the border. But, there is no such thing as a purely economic deal. As soon as the ink was dry on the FTA, business began to complain vociferously that the Canadian model was a barrier to competitiveness. Canada is a significantly more equal society than the US because of a higher level of tax-funded social programs and public services, and a higher floor of labour rights and standards. The 15 percent US per capita income advantage over Canadians is enjoyed only by the top one-third or so of the income distribution. Canadian poverty rates, by a common definition of less than half of median income, are much lower than in the US (10 percent vs. 17 percent), and the minimum gap between the top and bottom deciles of the family after-tax income distribution is 4 to 1 in Canada compared to 6.5 to 1 in the US. The private sector unionization rate is more than double that of the US.

Canada's more social democratic model is positive in economic terms in many respects. It gives us a more highly skilled work force, and more cost-effective and accessible social protections (with health care being the key example). But, the same organizations promoting the "big idea" have consistently lobbied for cutting income taxes on corporations and high earners to US levels, not to mention more privatized delivery of social services. The "tax cuts for competitiveness" argument has clearly had an impact on public policy. After the elimination of the federal deficit through deep cuts to social programs in the early to mid-1990s, the lion's share of the growing federal surplus went to the Martin tax cuts. As a share of GDP, federal taxes have fallen by about two percentage points since 1997, notwithstanding the consistently strong support of most Canadians for re-investment in social programs and public services. Public opinion research shows that only the very affluent have strongly supported the tax cut agenda, not least because the US model of low taxes and low social provision would leave them better off. At a cultural level, it is only the corporate elite who routinely compare their level of after-tax income to that of Americans.

The "tax cuts for competitiveness" economic argument was hugely exaggerated. But, it had credibility because of the threatened shift of investment and jobs to the US. Extending deep economic integration from the goods sector to the many parts of the services sector still not greatly impacted by NAFTA would lead to much higher levels of cross border movement of professionals and managers, and would surely strengthen downward competitive pressures on the tax base. The Canadian social model has been strained rather than undercut by NAFTA. It would not automatically disappear because of closer economic integration. But, the equalizing impact of progressive taxes would be further diminished, and there would be strong pressures not to increase general tax levels to finance better social programs and public services.

The Canadian social model would also be directly threatened by a customs union with its implication of a common (read US) voice in international trade and investment negotiations. The current formal position of the Canadian government is that social and public services should not be "on the table" for WTO services negotiations, and that our ability to maintain not-for-profit delivery of public services should be maintained. There are already clear threats under NAFTA, as argued in the Romanow report. If a province privatized hospital or home care services, for example, it would be difficult for a future government to return to not-for-profit delivery without paying compensation to the US corporate health care interests which are a growing presence in the system. It is in Canada's interests to defend measures to "carve out" social services and culture from WTO negotiations to preserve the space for choice and to shut out a US commercial presence. But, the US is promoting further liberal-ization in both areas at the WTO. The direct implications of a common trade policy for sovereignty in "non-economic areas" is a hidden time-bomb in the "big idea" of a customs union.

To conclude, on a wide range of policy fronts, the "big idea" is a bad idea that would undercut the necessary space for defending distinctive Canadian values and interests. That does not mean that the *status quo* of NAFTA is ideal. On some fronts, we should seek to reverse NAFTA constraints, such as the Chapter 11 investment provisions which threaten legitimate government regulation, and the one-sided commitment to unimpeded energy exports. On other fronts, we might want to deepen the relationship through new arrangements. Simplifying a lot of border procedures clearly makes sense. And, sectoral trade deals could work in closely integrated sectors. Also on the agenda should be replacement of the largely toothless side-deals of NAFTA with more effective means to create a high floor of labour rights and environmental standards. Pressures to tax harmonization in a world of mobile capital and transnationals could be countered by explicit agreements to create a North American tax floor.

The future of North America is open, but it does not lie in further reinforcing the neo-liberal economic and social model which lies at the heart of the "big idea." Canadians have no desire to abandon our distinctive social model, and every reason to doubt that "free markets" are the path to prosperity. They want sensible working arrangements to manage economic linkages, measures to stop destructive competition which serves only transnational corporate interests, and preservation of sovereignty in those areas where it is most important.

POSTSCRIPT

As mentioned in the introduction, there are two policy options for maintaining a fixed exchange rate of currencies: dollarization and monetary union. In some ways, dollarization is the easy solution, since it is a policy that can be adopted unilaterally. Canada could simply chose to adopt the U.S. dollar as its official currency. Because the U.S. would not relinquish any control of its own monetary policy, it would not even have to be part of the decisionmaking process.

Interestingly, there has been some support for dollarization in Quebec among pro-independence forces. Bernard Landry, former Parti Québécois premier of Quebec, argued in favour of the use of the U.S. dollar as a common currency. Currently, if Quebec declared its independence, it would have to engage in potentially lengthy and costly negotiations in order to continue using the Canadian dollar. However, if Canada were to adopt the U.S. dollar now, the costs of any adjustments would be shared across the country. If Quebec separated in the future, it would be able to continue using the U.S. dollar without seeking permission or incurring further adjustment costs.

If Canada were to opt for a currency union with the United States, there would have to be substantial negotiations between the two countries. Each would have to relinquish some control over its monetary policy and work with its partner to establish a common set of institutions to manage the new currency. Such negotiations would require two things. First, each side would need to have sufficiently strong commitment to make the necessary concessions to achieve a mutually satisfactory agreement. Second, each partner would need to be convinced that such an arrangement would provide sufficient benefits to justify the surrender of a degree of sovereignty over monetary and fiscal policies. Since September 11, 2001, the United States has been increasingly preoccupied with tightening border controls for homeland security and with strengthening its sovereignty. Is there sufficient political will on both sides to enter into such negotiations? If the two countries did, what types of concessions might Canada have to make to form a new currency union? Would these concessions be politically sellable at home?

Suggested Additional Readings

Buiter, Willem H. "The EMU and NAMU: What Is the Case for North American Monetary Union?" *Canadian Public Policy* 25, no. 3 (September 1999): 285–305.

Carr, Jack. "Defending the Current Monetary System." *ISUMA: Canadian Journal of Policy Research* 1, no. 1 (Spring 2000): 97–100.

Courchene, Thomas, and Richard Harris. "From Fixing to Monetary Union: Options for North American Currency Integration." *C.D. Howe Institute Commentary*, no. 127 (June 1999).

Grubel, Herbert. "The Case for the Amero: The Economics and Politics of a North American Monetary Union." *Critical Issues Bulletin* (Vancouver: The Fraser Institute, September 1999).

_____. "The High Dollar, the Bank of Canada, & Monetary Union." *Fraser Forum* (December 2003): 17, 27.

_____, et al. "Round Table on a North American Currency." *Canadian Parliamentary Review* 22, no. 2 (Summer 1999): 5–13.

Harris, Richard G. "The Case for North American Monetary Union." *ISUMA: Canadian Journal of Policy Research* 1, no. 1 (Spring 2002): 93–96.

Laidler, David. "Canada's Exhange Rate Options." *Canadian Public Policy* 25, no. 3 (September 1999): 324–32.

Marceau, Richard. "A Quebec Perspective on a North American Currency." *Canadian Parliamentary Review* 22, no. 2 (Summer 1999): 2–5.

InfoTrac® College Edition
Search for the following articles in the InfoTrac® database:

"Beyond NAFTA: A Forum — Toward a North American Economic Community." *The Nation* 272, no. 21 (May 28, 2001): 9.

Blanchard, Mark. "'Loonie' Bin: The U.S. Dollar May Force the Struggling Canadian 'Loonie' into Extinction." *Insight on the News* 18, no. 8 (March 4, 2002): 27.

Chriszt, Michael. "Perspectives on a Potential North American Monetary Union." *Economic Review* (Atlanta, Ga.) 85, no. 4 (October 2000): 29.

For more articles, enter:
"currency union," "monetary union," or "dollarization" in the keyword search or subject guide.

Web Resources
For current URLs for the following websites, visit www.crosscurrents.nelson.com.

CENTER FOR STRATEGIC AND INTERNATIONAL STUDIES (CSIS)
csis.org/about/index.htm

Go to Programs, then choose Canada Project (under Americas Program) for resources on Canadian–American relations, including a regular column titled *North American Integration Monitor*.

C.D. Howe Institute

www.cdhowe.org

C.D. Howe Institute is one of Canada's leading public policy institutes. This site contains papers relating to monetary union with the United States and the state of Canadian economy generally.

Canada Association for Business Economics (CABE)

www.cabe.ca/cbe/

Go to Articles and select volume 7, number 4 (December 1999) issue of *Canadian Business Economics* for articles devoted to the subject of a North American monetary union.

Institute for Research on Public Policy

www.irpp.org

The website of this Canadian public policy research institute contains papers dealing with Canadian relations with the United States, including monetary relations.

Will the Kyoto Protocol Undermine Economic Growth and Competitiveness in Canada?

✔ **YES**
KENNETH GREEN, "Kyoto Krazy," *Fraser Forum* (January 2003): 6–7;
and "Martin Joins the Kyoto Follies," Editorial, Fraser Institute,
February 4, 2004

✗ **NO**
DÉSIRÉE MCGRAW, "The Case for Kyoto: A Question of Competitiveness,
Consultations, Credibility, Commitment and Consistency," *Policy
Options* 24, no. 1 (December 2002–January 2003): 35–39

Few issues better demonstrate the complex relationships and tradeoffs between economic growth, trade, and the environment than the debate over global climate change. An important focal point of this debate has been the 1997 Kyoto Protocol. This agreement was intended to set targets for the nations of the world to reduce the emission of man-made greenhouse gases (GHGs), which are seen as a major contributor to global warning. The attempt to set specific targets for reducing GHGs has sparked a debate that has pitted environmental forces against economic and industrial interests. This discussion took on greater significance when the United States, the single greatest contributor of greenhouse gas emissions in the world, announced that it was pulling out of the Kyoto Protocol in order to protect both its economy and the American "way of life." This decision has intensified debates in Canada over the likely environmental benefits that will be achieved by the Kyoto Protocol in relation to the economic costs that it might impose on participating governments.

In order to understand the debate on the economic impact of the Kyoto Protocol, it is necessary to be familiar with the origins of the agreement itself. In the 1980s, scientists expressed growing concern about a gradual increase in temperature on a global scale and the impact that this increase could have on the environment and the economies of the world. In 1988, Canada, in cooperation with the United Nations and the World Meteorological Programme, hosted a conference entitled The Changing Atmosphere: Implications for Global Security. In examining the various studies prepared by scientists, the conference delegates concluded that the global climate changes observed in the 1980s resulted in large part from man-made causes. They called for a global reduction in carbon dioxide emissions of 20 percent below 1988 levels by 2005.

The following year, as a follow-up to the conference, the United Nations created the Intergovernmental Panel on Climate Change (IPCC). The IPCC is composed of leading scientists appointed by governments and is charged with reviewing the latest scientific findings on climate change and providing policymakers with advice. Their work helped form the basis for the largest meeting of heads of government to discuss climate change and the environment ever held. Known as the Rio Earth Summit, this 1992 UN-sponsored conference focused global attention as never before on environmental issues. However, the results of the conference received mixed reviews. Although a Framework Convention on Climate Change was successfully negotiated and signed by most nations, the final document was significantly watered down. The framework agreement acknowledged that climate change posed a serious threat to the world. It called on all nations to take actions that would reduce the continuing build-up of greenhouse gases, which were seen as contributing to global warming. However, the government of George Bush Senior threatened to boycott the summit unless specific targets or deadlines for implementation were removed from the document. As a result, the final treaty contained no set deadlines or targets for the reduction of GHG emissions.

In addressing global warming, it was hoped that the world would follow the same model that was adopted in addressing the problem of ozone depletion. In 1987, nations of the world signed the landmark Montreal Protocol on Substances That Deplete the Ozone Layer. This agreement set specific targets for elimination of emissions that cause depletion of the ozone layer. Initially, industrialized countries, which were seen as the principal culprit of ozone depletion, agreed to begin reducing their emissions while developing countries were temporarily allowed to increase theirs. Over time, successive ozone protocols were negotiated in which industrial countries sped up their reduction of ozone depleting emissions while developing countries began to reduce theirs. The initial success of the Montreal Protocol was seen as a good model for dealing with other issues, such as global warning.

Although the Framework Convention on Climate Change contained no specific targets or deadlines, it did establish a process by which signatories would undertake negotiations leading to the establishment of such targets in the future. Three rounds of negotiations were held, culminating in the Kyoto Protocol in 1997. In the negotiations leading up to the protocol, the most contentious issue was the levels of cuts to GHG emissions that each nation was to make. The European nations wanted the protocol to mandate emission reductions of 15 percent. The United States, Japan, and Canada lobbied hard for lower levels. Before going into the negotiations, the federal government had agreed with the provincial governments that it would negotiate for a target of 3 percent. U.S. President Bill Clinton, a supporter of the Kyoto Protocol, pressed Canada to accept a higher target. The United States ended up agreeing to a target of 7 percent reduction in

GHG emissions for itself, while Canada agreed to a 6 percent reduction. At the same time, Canada was successful in negotiating some loopholes, such as "credits" for its large forests, arguing that forests create a benefit by holding carbon dioxide out of the atmosphere.

The finalization of the Kyoto Protocol triggered considerable debate both worldwide and in Canada. Canadian provincial governments complained that the federal government had committed them to GHG emissions cuts far exceeding what the provinces had agreed to. The federal government countered that the loophole provisions effectively reduced provincial emissions to a 3 percent level of reduction. Environmental groups decried Canada's persistence in seeking new and ever larger loopholes as a dangerous watering down of the agreement that would effectively undermine the environmental impact of the protocol. Many economic interests and provincial governments argued that even with these loopholes implementation of Kyoto would have a serious negative impact on Canadian economic growth and job creation.

The debate over the Kyoto Protocol gained greater importance when the newly elected government of George W. Bush announced that it was withdrawing from the Kyoto Protocol. The American withdrawal presented a significant threat to the success of the protocol. In order to come into force, the protocol required that 55 nations accounting for 55 percent of the world's GHG emissions sign on. The withdrawal of the United States, which accounts for 25 percent of the world's total GIIG emissions, posed an important threat to implementation of the protocol. The participation of Canada, with its 2 percent of the world's total GHG permissions, took on increased significance. The Chrétien government restated its commitment to forge ahead with implementation despite domestic opposition, particularly from the provinces.

To mollify domestic criticisms about the potential negative impact on the Canadian economy, the federal government has taken a two-pronged approach. Internationally, it has continued to press for expansion of the loopholes that would allow Canada more "credits," thereby reducing the amount of reductions that Canada would have to make. Domestically, it set up a federal-provincial consultation process for implementing the Kyoto Protocol, with Alberta Premier Ralph Klein, one of the most vocal critics of Kyoto, as co-chair. This process was dealt a serious blow when Ralph Klein withdrew from his role and the Albertan government issued its own highly critical report on Kyoto.

In the following readings, two opposing approaches to the Kyoto Protocol are presented. Two articles published under the auspices of the Fraser Institute make the case that implementation of the Kyoto Protocol will cause significant damage to Canada's economic growth, trade, and job prospects. In contrast, Désirée McGraw argues that implementation of the protocol will be good not only for the environment but also for Canada, as it will allow it to remain competitive and prosperous at the same time.

✔ **YES**

Kyoto Krazy

KENNETH GREEN

Canada's ratification of the Kyoto Protocol on Climate Change is now a done deal. Prime Minister Jean Chretien has forced ratification of the Protocol, committing Canada to return emission levels for carbon dioxide and other gases suspected of warming the earth to 6 percent below the levels emitted in 1990. Because emission rates have grown since 1990 and are predicted to continue doing so, Canada's target of 6 percent below 1990 levels equates to a 30 percent reduction from predicted emission levels by about 2012.

As always seems to be the case in these situations, environmental pressure groups such as the David Suzuki Foundation have joined the government in claiming that their support of the Protocol rests on the most robust scientific evidence. They believe that the law is on their side, that they've been terribly conscientious about consultation and cooperation, that there really is a free lunch, and Canada can achieve draconian reductions in energy use at low cost – or even at a profit (Torrie *et al.*, 2002).

But as more pragmatic researchers in the private sector and academia have shown, Kyoto Protocol ratification will provide little benefit, and will likely lead to real and wrenching economic impacts that will negatively affect the well being of Canadians (McKitrick and Essex, 2002). Indeed, when examined from a public policy perspective, signing and implementing the Kyoto Protocol is a profoundly poor idea that will generate a great deal of pain, but little or no gain, in terms of making a safer world for ourselves and our grandchildren.

First, consider the science behind the proclaimed benefits of Canada's ratification of the Kyoto Protocol. Canada's federal government has justified ratification of the Kyoto Protocol by citing groups such as the United Nations Intergovernmental Panel on Climate Change, which has published reports suggesting that a warmer climate would cause major ecological disruption necessitating urgent action (IPCC, 2001). But other scientists, in both Canada and the United States, have shown that the threat of global warming is overstated by the United Nations (McKitrick and Essex, 2002). Indeed, scientists such as Harvard University's Sallie Baliunas explain that most observed global warming has been a natural, and largely beneficent phenomenon, primarily related to the increase of energy output from the sun (Soon, Baliunas *et al.*, 2001).

But even if one believes that global warming poses significant risks for future generations, the science of greenhouse gas reductions suggests that implementing the Kyoto Protocol is largely a waste of effort. On a global basis, Canada only emits about two percent of the gases accused of causing global warming. If Canada managed to achieve the Kyoto Protocol targets, Canadian emissions would decline to about 1.4 percent of global emissions by 2012, while emissions of countries like India

304

and China continue to grow rapidly. That is not a significant difference when one considers that the world's biggest emitters have not endorsed the protocol, and are unlikely to do so in the foreseeable future. Even NASA scientist James Hansen, who some consider the modern "father of climate change" agrees that it would take 30 Kyoto-like reductions – with full global compliance – to negate what the United Nations climate panel sees as the threat of manmade global warming (Hansen, 2000).

Second, consider the cost. Cost and job-loss estimates vary tremendously, but Canadian university research economists Mark Jaccard, John Nyboer, and Bryn Sadownik estimate that Kyoto implementation could cost 3 percent of Canada's gross domestic product, could cost the average Canadian family four percent of its annual disposable income, and could cause energy prices to rise substantially (Jaccard, Nyboer and Sadownik, 2002). Presuming that energy producers pass on increased costs to consumers (a good assumption even for Canada's heavily-regulated energy sector), Jaccard *et al.* predict that electricity costs would likely rise up to 85 percent in some Canadian provinces; natural gas prices would likely rise by 40 to 90 percent; and the after-tax price of gasoline would likely rise by 50 percent.

Applying the Jaccard *et al.* estimates to the household economy of a Canadian family of four earning $40,000 per year, and living in a modest 1,200 square-foot single-story home in Toronto, the total annual cost of Kyoto would include $1400 in lost income, $400 per year in additional electricity costs, $700 per year in additional natural gas costs, and about $800 per year in added gasoline costs. That puts the total Kyoto bill for a moderate-income family of four at over $3,300, or nearly 10 percent of total pre-tax income.

Finally, there is the question of international trade. About 87 percent of Canada's exports go to the United States, accounting for over 40 percent of Canada's gross domestic product. US President George W. Bush has refused to ratify the Kyoto Protocol on Climate Change, and the United States is moving ahead with an alternative greenhouse gas control plan that avoids the kind of economic losses that Canada will soon inflict upon itself. Meanwhile, other countries, such as Mexico, are not bound by Kyoto, and will offer more attractive options for importing goods and exporting services.

The overarching question in a public policy sense regarding the Kyoto Protocol is straightforward: "Has signing the Kyoto Protocol made Canadians better off?" Given that the threat of climate change is far more modest than governments claim; given that the costs of reducing greenhouse gas emissions are likely to be far higher than government claims; and given that compliance with the Kyoto Protocol will make Canada a less competitive country, the answer is clearly *no*. In fact, rather than make Canadians safer, as its proponents claim it will, the weight of the evidence suggests that Kyoto compliance will make Canadians less safe. Though it will provide virtually no environmental, health, or safety benefit, Kyoto compliance will deprive future Canadians of the resources and economic resilience they will need to face the unpredictable challenges they will invariably confront.

REFERENCES

Hansen, James (2000). "Global Warming in the 21st Century: An Alternative Scenario." *Proceedings of the National Academy of Sciences USA.* Vol. 97, Issue 18 (September 12): 9875–880. Available digitally at *http://www.pnas.org/cgi/content/full/97/18/9875.*

Jaccard, Mark, John Nyboer, and Bryn Sadownik (2002). *The Cost of Climate Policy.* Vancouver: UBC Press.

McKitrick, Ross and Christopher Essex (2002). *Taken by Storm, the Troubled Science Policy and Politics of Global Warming.* Toronto: Key Porter Books.

Michaels, Patrick J. and Robert C. Balling Jr. (2000). *The Satanic Gases: Clearing the Air About Global Warming.* Washington DC: Cato Institute.

Soon, Willie, Sallie L. Baliunas, Arthur B. Robinson, and Zachary W. Robinson (2001). *Global Warming, a Guide to the Science.* Vancouver: The Fraser Institute.

Torrie *et al.* (2002). *Kyoto and Beyond, the Low Emission Path to Innovation and Efficiency.* Vancouver: David Suzuki Foundation.

United Nations Intergovernmental Panel on Climate Change (2001). *Climate Change 2001: Impacts, Adaptation, and Vulnerability.* Cambridge, UK: Cambridge University Press.

Martin Joins the Kyoto Follies
KENNETH GREEN

Paul Martin's throne-speech pledge that Canada will meet – and even exceed – its greenhouse gas reduction targets under the Kyoto Protocol bodes ill for the competitive ability of Canadian industry and the economic well-being of individual Canadians.

First, as has been written in several open letters to Paul Martin by Canadian and International scientists, the science of Kyoto is anything but settled. Uncertainty is far too high, and computer models much too simple, to allow confidence in the predictions of politically influenced science bodies such as the United Nations Intergovernmental Panel on Climate Change. Don't just take my word for it, go and read the petition of 19,000 scientists at the Oregon Petition (www.oism.org), which states, in part, that "There is no convincing scientific evidence that human release of carbon dioxide, methane, or other greenhouse gasses is causing or will, in the foreseeable future, cause catastrophic heating of the Earth's atmosphere and disruption of the Earth's climate. Moreover, there is substantial scientific evidence that increases in atmospheric carbon dioxide produce many beneficial effects upon the natural plant and animal environments of the Earth."

Second, Martin's Kyoto position shows gross ignorance of the key role that affordable energy plays in producing the quality of life that Martin says he wants for Canadians. Greenhouse gases are emitted when fossil fuels are burned, whether it's coal, oil, or natural gas. Reducing greenhouse gas emissions, therefore, can only be done in three ways: using less fuel, switching from higher-carbon fuels (such as coal and oil) to lower-carbon fuels such as natural gas, or switching to non-carbon energy sources such as wind and solar power to displace energy now generated from fossil fuels. But nobody is interested in building more dams, and wind and solar power can provide only the tiniest fraction of the energy needed for a competitive technological society. A study at Cornell University showed, for example, that for the U.S. to replace half of its fossil fuel use with alternative energy it would have to cover 17 percent of the continental United States — about 1/6th of the entire landmass — with power generation facilities.

Without a significant share of energy available from alternatives, Canada's ability to meet the Kyoto Protocol comes down to forcing rapid switches to more efficient equipment burning lower-carbon fuels. Many Canadians might think that's a great idea, but wait until they get the bill. The fact of the matter is, more efficient equipment is more expensive equipment, and installing it before older equipment is ready for retirement represents an economic loss that businesses will have to recoup those costs one way or another. Meanwhile, lower-carbon fuels are more expensive fuels. Natural gas has recently shown massive price fluctuations, and Canada's consumption of natural gas has been outpacing its production for years. Alternative energy sources are more expensive still. Since firms can't simply raise prices in competitive markets, such costs are likely to be borne by Canadians in lowered wages, or lower return to investors. Again, this is not idle speculation. Before Kyoto was ratified, Simon Fraser university professor Mark Jaccard estimated that Kyoto compliance could raise the cost of electricity by 80 percent, raise the cost of natural gas from 40 percent to 90 percent, and raise the cost of gasoline by 50 percent. While paying those higher energy bills, Jaccard estimates that the average household would take a pay cut of about 4 percent.

Energy is the master resource behind virtually everything that gives Canadians the quality of life we enjoy. We use a lot of energy not because we're profligate, but because we're a highly dispersed, cold climate, technologically advanced country. Fortunately, we have still been blessed with enough domestic energy sources to be able to compete well against the United States, even exporting power and natural gas to our largest trading partner. But under Kyoto, those exports are likely to vanish as Canada leaves its oil and coal in the ground, and burns the natural gas it currently exports.

The United States has refused to ratify the Kyoto treaty for precisely these reasons. If Canadian firms are to remain competitive against U.S. firms, abundant, affordable energy is a must. Martin's plan to "go beyond" Kyoto virtually assures less abundant, more expensive energy, more expensive technology, and less money in Canadian pockets to pay for it all.

Paul Martin has said that he intends to improve Canadian quality of life, and reduce western alienation, but his embrace of Kyoto bodes poorly for either goal. One can only hope that in his Kyoto pledge, Martin was paying lip-service to an idea that has attained the status of religion, while in reality, he intends to do little to actually implement measures that would cripple Canada's competitiveness.

✗ NO

The Case for Kyoto: A Question of Competitiveness, Consultations, Credibility, Commitment and Consistency
DÉSIRÉE MCGRAW

Ratifying the Kyoto Protocol does not preclude Canadians from developing a Made-in-Canada action plan on climate change; it compels us to do so. Kyoto provides an internationally-agreed framework for meeting targets on greenhouse gas (GHG) reductions; it does not dictate how countries are to meet these objectives. In fact, through a series of market-based and other broad mechanisms, the accord augments, not diminishes, the flexibility with which individual countries can meet their climate change commitments. In short, Kyoto sets the conditions for action on climate change; it does not dictate how a nation must meet its international commitments.

After a decade of international negotiations and national consultations on climate change, the first draft of a federal action plan was presented to a meeting of energy and environment ministers on October 28. Further formal discussions on the accord took place in late November – a matter of weeks, if not days, before Parliament is expected to vote on whether Canada should be legally bound to Kyoto by ratifying it.

There is no doubt that Canada's "ratification readiness" would be greatly enhanced by a comprehensive national implementation plan to ensure we can meet our Kyoto commitments. However, the foot-dragging of the past decade has made it clear that no such plan will materialize until ratification is assured. For better or worse, implementation is now contingent upon ratification – not, as some prominent political and business leaders would have it, the other way around. By protracting the debate on ratification, we are running out the clock on implementation. The longer Canada postpones ratification, the more difficult it will become to implement Kyoto, if not impossible. Failure to meet our global climate change commitments may well become a self-fulfilling prophecy.

Ottawa's continued mixed messages on Kyoto have confounded our international counterparts: while the EU was assured that we were on board, the US was convinced we would follow their lead and reject the accord. Domestically, the policy vacuum left by Ottawa has encouraged special interest groups and provinces such as Alberta and Quebec to present their own alternatives to Kyoto.

In 1992, under the Conservative government of Brian Mulroney, Canada was one of the first industrialized countries to both sign and ratify the United Nations Framework Convention on Climate Change, one of two treaties to emerge from the Rio Earth Summit. As such, Canada was one of the original champions of the principles underlying the Kyoto Protocol (named after the Japanese city in which it was adopted in 1997), which is a subagreement to the 1992 climate convention. The accord calls for industrialized countries to reduce their GHG emissions by 6 percent below 1990 levels by the period 2008–2012. But Kyoto represents only the first, but nonetheless critical, step to meeting our climate change commitments. These entail a total reduction of 50–75 percent in greenhouse gases globally in this century alone. The most recent round of climate negotiations in New Delhi sought to bring emerging economies and major greenhouse-gas-emitting countries in the developing world, such as Brazil, China and India, on board the regime.

In the decade since the Rio Earth Summit, Canada is widely seen to have gone from environmental leader to laggard, both at home and abroad. So, at last month's World Summit on Sustainable Development in Johannesburg, the prime minister's pledge that Parliament would ratify the Kyoto Protocol by year's end came as a surprise to the UN community, to Canadians and, apparently, to his own Cabinet. Nonetheless, Mr. Chrétien's was a critical announcement at a critical time. Kyoto now stands poised to become legally binding on all countries which have ratified it. To be operational, the accord requires ratification by a minimum of 55 countries responsible for at least 55 percent of the globe's GHG emissions. Although Kyoto has long surpassed the first criterion for entry into force, the second has remained elusive, especially in light of the Bush administration's refusal to ratify the agreement. While the US contributes roughly 25 percent to total GHG emissions, Canada produces a mere 2 percent. But person-for-person, it is Canadians – not Americans – who are the biggest energy consumers in the world. Our country should compensate for its vast size and extreme climate not with more GHG emissions, but with greater innovation and investment in efficient sources of energy.

Current opponents of Kyoto claim that Canada can't afford to ratify, and thus implement, the accord because it would damage Canada's economic competitiveness. However, it is the policy uncertainty created by the government's continued hesitation regarding ratification that is most costly for corporate decisionmaking. Canadian corporations have a legitimate concern about the negative effects of uncertainty to their competitiveness and ability to attract investment. Ratification of the accord and effective negotiation of details of the implementation plan with key industrial sectors as well as the provinces and territories is the best way to deal with such uncertainty.

Moreover, according to the Alberta-based Pembina Institute for Appropriate Technology, Canada's competitiveness is likely to benefit, not suffer, from a decision by Parliament to ratify the Kyoto Protocol. Their report finds that by taking a lead on environmental policy, governments position firms to be more efficient and competitive. In a survey of corporations in several key sectors (such as oil and gas, electricity, chemicals, transportation and manufacturing) with major operations in Canada, those firms which took early action to improve efficiency and effect emission-reduction strategies in anticipation of Kyoto ratification, also increased their competitiveness. For example, from 1990 to 2000, Dupont reduced its GHG emissions by 60 percent while production increased by 10 percent and shareholder return quadrupled. Between 1995 and 2001, Interface (a flooring products firm) reduced GHG emissions (per unit of production) by 64 percent in its Canadian operations while the company's waste reduction program produced savings of over $185 million worldwide. Canadian policy now needs to recognize and credit this progress, and set clear and realistic targets for further improvements.

Also prominent in the rhetoric of Kyoto critics is the notion that Canada cannot afford to implement the agreement because our largest trading partner has rejected it, and therefore so must we. This argument confuses lack of leadership by the Bush administration on climate change with lack of action by American states, cities, companies and citizens. Indeed, state and municipal governments in the US have taken far more significant action to reduce GHG emissions than their Canadian counterparts. If these trends continue, the US may well reduce its GHG emissions in line with Kyoto targets despite not having formally ratified the accord. And although it is unlikely to do so under the Bush administration's watch, the US may well ratify under a future administration. With American ratification would come a stronger push for enforcement mechanisms, and thus trade measures. So, Canada has a choice: we can pay now or pay more later.

Although the US appears to be making progress on climate change outside the Kyoto framework, Canada's track record remains very weak. In the absence of legally binding targets, Canada has invoked the voluntary Rio pledge to stabilize its GHG emissions at the 1990 level by 2000. Instead, despite a slew of federal and provincial plans purporting to address climate change, Canada's emissions levels have grown by 20 percent in the last decade. Given our evergrowing emissions levels, the federal government estimates that Canada will need to reduce its current levels by 25 percent in order to meet its Kyoto target by 2010.

Ratifying Kyoto will not only allow Canada to contribute to the global effort to curb climate change, it will have the practical effect of narrowing – not widening – the gap with the US. Moreover, ratification would not preclude us from strengthening this global commitment with national or indeed regional (NAFTA-based) ones, so long as these enhance rather than erase our Kyoto targets.

Contrary to popular belief, Canada's commitment to ratify the Kyoto Protocol did not come with the prime minister's pledge at the Johannesburg Summit. The Liberal government initially signalled its intent to ratify Kyoto when it signed the accord in 1997. Why then, in the five years since first signing the accord, has Ottawa failed to produce a viable national action plan to implement the agreement? This failure is not, as some would have it, due to lack of consultations or technical know-how: Canada has some of world's best people in both the private and public sectors working on climate change issues. The failure to craft a clear, comprehensive and timely implementation program is due purely to a lack of political will.

against

w]

Current complaints regarding the federal government's failure to fully consult with the provinces, key sectors and stakeholders are disingenuous in light of the real record: Kyoto has arguably been more extensively consulted upon than any other treaty signed by Canada. Imagine, if you will, the federal government consulting Canadians this much on whether it should adhere to international institutions – such as NAFTA or the WTO – which meet the approval of powerful sectors of the Canadian economy. The objection here is not to consultations per se, but to their selective use for purely opportunistic or PR purposes. As decisions once enacted by elected representatives in national legislatures are increasingly made by non-elected officials at international summits, it is critical that citizens and parliamentarians become more informed and involved at all levels and stages of the policymaking process. But tackling the "democratic deficit" in international decision-making should not be a discriminatory undertaking, nor should it be used as a delaying tactic regarding matters on which the government would rather avoid taking decisive action. Which brings us back to Kyoto.

Ottawa's mistake lies not in its failure to consult but, rather, in its failure to consult the right people on the right question: until now, selective discussions with elites and experts have been framed by "whether to ratify" Kyoto; instead, the Chrétien government should have been consulting Canadians directly on "how to implement" the accord from the start. This is what Ottawa is now doing in late 2002 – but only after years of procrastination and vacillation.

Despite the initial praise it inspired in international and environmental circles, the commitment made by Mr. Chrétien in Johannesburg is still not clear-cut. Canada's position now appears to be contingent upon two additional and improbable conditions:

- Nationally, ratification seems to depend upon the environmental and economic equivalent of a "Clarity Act on Kyoto" – a level of detail rarely required by other international agreements Canada has signed.

- On the international scene, the condition for ratifying Kyoto appears to be credits for clean energy exports – a scheme which has so far failed to secure any substantive support during previous rounds of international negotiations.

  This equivocation seriously undermines the Government of Canada's credibility on this critical issue, both at home and abroad. Far from reestablishing the country's credentials as an environmental champion, the confusion following the prime minister's remarks in Johannesburg may ultimately serve to alienate important stakeholders on all sides of this issue.

- The international community, especially the EU, would likely block any additional amendments to Kyoto, particularly those proposed by a country widely seen to have already watered down the accord. In this light, the position – held by several prominent political and business leaders – that Canada should not ratify Kyoto because it is too feeble proves perverse: If Kyoto does not do enough to curb climate change, it is in part because countries such as Canada have consistently negotiated additional concessions which have served to weaken its effect. Having successfully softened the accord, Canada's walking away from it now would be viewed by the international community as an act of bad faith, if not betrayal. This is the American approach to international treaties, not the Canadian one. Concretely, rejection of Kyoto would also mean that Canada would have little if any influence in the future rounds of global climate negotiations, which are expected to bring key developing countries into the fold. Thus, from an international perspective, non-ratification is a non-starter: it would damage Canada's reputation and its leverage in future international negotiations on critical issues beyond climate change.

- Environmentalists who strongly support Kyoto view the Johannesburg announcement as a last-ditch, legacy-driven effort to reverse the country's decade-long slide from environmental leader to laggard. Some perceive the *Jean-come-lately* support for the accord as an act of "ecological oppor-tunism" stemming from the prime minister's preoccupation with his legacy rather than from a real concern for the environment.

- Business will resent the added burden of having to now scramble to meet Kyoto targets within a much tighter timeframe. Had Canada not only signed but also ratified the protocol following its 1997 adoption, energy producers and consumers would have had more time to transition to a cleaner, less carbon-dependent economy. The policy confusion created by the govern-ment's protracted hesitation regarding Kyoto has also proven problematic for corporate decisionmaking, which thrives in conditions of certainty. It is time to bring clarity to this issue and get on with business of implementation. This is what the corporate world does so well — it sets clear rules and works to meet them.

- Some provinces have decried the federal government's "breach of public trust" in changing the focus of this fall's cross-Canada discussions on Kyoto from ratification to implementation. There is no doubt that the fed-eral government has circumvented a public consultation process that it had itself laid out. But this process was ill-conceived and over-extended from the start. Consent of the provinces is not required for ratification of international agreements; this authority rests strictly with the federal government. However, given the provinces' shared jurisdiction over natural resources, the federal government does have a responsibility to consult its provincial counterparts on how it arrives at implementing these treaties and must work to involve the provinces in areas of implementa-tion under their jurisdiction. Indeed, without securing the full cooperation of the provinces, a number of key instruments may be unavailable for implementation.

Therefore, if one views ratification as a matter of foreign policy (to be exercised by the federal government for the common good) and implementation as a matter of domestic environmental and economic policy (to be jointly agreed by the federal and provincial governments), the revised focus of the current deliberations – from consultations on whether to ratify to real negotiations on how to implement – is not only more acceptable, it is preferable (again, notwithstanding the delay).

Once Parliament ratifies Kyoto, the treaty becomes domestic law and Canada has six to ten more years to reach its targets. The country does not – as Prime Minister Chrétien has stated – have another ten years to work out the plan. 2008–2012 is the deadline for achieving the plan, not developing it. This reality check leads some to want to abandon Kyoto altogether. It leads others to the opposite conclusion: Canada must expedite ratification as a matter of utmost priority and then consult the stakeholders on how – not whether – to achieve them. It's a matter of commitment.

Perhaps Canada should follow the example of Norway and other parties to Kyoto. After assembling a team of high-profile, popular individuals to both champion Kyoto with domestic audiences and coordinate its implementation, Norway produced a solid national action plan in a matter of six weeks.

This Liberal government has already proven it can muster the massive political will and resources to successfully tackle seemingly intractable problems. The fiscal deficit provides a compelling case in point: the rationale presented was short-term pain for long-term gain; it would be irresponsible to leave such a burden on future generations. The same logic applies, if not more so, to the ecological debt.

Among a broad range of worthy ecological issues and initiatives, Kyoto has become the litmus test on the environment. Any government, sector or individual seen to be stalling on Kyoto will be seen to be stalling on the environment. Kyoto will help determine whether Canada's citizens and leaders are up to the challenge of bringing our country into the carbon-constrained reality of the 21st century. It will also provide very substantial opportunities to make a transition to a more efficient and competitive economy.

For all its imperfections (the inevitable result of the trade-offs inherent in international negotiations), Kyoto represents the only global game in town for addressing climate change. The result of ten years of tough negotiations, the accord reflects careful compromises made by some 170 states with divergent interests at vastly different stages of their economic development. Domestic disagreements within Canada about how to address climate change only serve to reinforce Kyoto's value as an international agreement. Indeed, the Protocol embodies innovative principles – such as "intergenerational equity" and "common but differentiated responsibility" – which may prove instructive for Canada as it seeks to establish a fair and equitable regime without unduly burdening particular provinces, sectors or stakeholders.

The near-universal support enjoyed by the protocol has led countries that remain outside the regime to be dubbed "environmental rogue states." Just as there is little doubt the US — even going it alone — would prevail militarily against Iraq, a Made-in-the-USA alternative to Kyoto would undoubtedly help curb climate change. But international relations and the rule of law are about means — not just ends. These unilateral actions represent inadequate responses to what are collective-action problems. At least the US is fairly consistent — if not misguided — in its go-it alone approach to foreign affairs. Will Canada be consistent in its foreign policy and apply its general preference for multilateralism to the problem of climate change?

The question Canada faces is not whether to adopt Kyoto or develop a made-in-Canada solution; this is a false choice since adopting the former implies the latter. At issue is whether Canada will adopt a unilateral or international approach to the global problem of climate change.

Let it be stated emphatically that there is no moral equivalence between the potential deployment of weapons of mass destruction by Saddam Hussein and the dangers posed by climate change. While the former would represent a deliberate evil act of a single madman, the latter reflects the seemingly benign actions of countless producers and consumers largely in the industrialized world. However, there is a clear double standard in international affairs: the burden of proof for taking collective action against an environmental threat appears to far exceed that required for responding to a military one.

Within the hierarchy of international relations, "hard" security and trade matters have traditionally trumped "soft" social and environmental ones. The reality, however, is that ecological degradation is a growing source of conflict in the world and thus represents a real threat to collective security. Pervasive climate change has been described as second only to nuclear war in terms of its catastrophic effects globally. In this sense, climate change is far more than a matter of environmental policy; it is increasingly a matter of national security.

The evidence underlying global climate change is objective, far-reaching and compelling. Indeed, few issues on the global agenda have galvanized such widespread consensus within political and scientific communities. The Intergovernmental Panel on Climate Change — representing 1,500 of the world's leading atmospheric scientists, economists and technologists — have repeatedly concluded that: (1) the current scope, scale and pace of climate change are unprecedented, and (2) human activity — mainly through the production of greenhouse gases such as carbon dioxide — is increasingly influential in this regard. Canadian scientists from across the country have been active in their areas of expertise in the work of this international panel. Even sceptical nations find the science convincing. Thirteen national academies of science — including the American counterpart whose members were hand-picked by President George W. Bush himself — concur with these findings.

Still, international affairs are not susceptible to courtroom proofs beyond reasonable doubt. It is precisely for this reason that a "Precautionary Principle" underlies many environmental agreements such as the Kyoto Protocol. While the US and, to some extent, Canada have sought to expel direct reference to this principle in international treaties, its intent is straightforward: where there is a threat of serious or irreversible harm, lack of scientific certainty should not preclude action. Otherwise, positive proof would come too late. The principle essentially asserts that it is better to err on the side of action that turns out to be unnecessary than to expose ourselves to preventable devastation through inaction.

POSTSCRIPT

An interesting issue related to this debate concerns the role of "epistemic communities" in the formation of international agreements such as the Kyoto Protocol. An epistemic community is a group of experts who, based on their knowledge derived from application of recognized scientific methods, develop a consensus about the nature of an international problem and formulate the preferred solution to that problem. International relations scholars have noted that epistemic communities can play a significant role in advising governments and assist them in identifying a course of action in responding to global problems.

In the case of the Kyoto Protocol, the proposed solution was highly influenced by the 1996 scientific assessment report issued by the Intergovernmental Panel on Climate Change (IPCC), a UN advisory board composed of noted scientists. The IPCC's report concluded that "the balance of evidence suggests a discernible human influence on global climate." This conclusion was taken by many to mean that climatic disasters are likely to occur if significant action is not taken to reduce GHG remissions immediately.

The subsequent debate focused to a large extent on whether the proposed cuts were adequate, in terms of reducing the dangers of global warming, while not causing undue costs in terms of job loss and economic disruption. The readings included here show that analysts differ widely in their assessments, which makes it difficult to come to a consensus on the economic impact of the Kyoto Protocol. More recently, opponents of environmental agreements such as the Kyoto Protocol have started to question the science on which the IPCC work has been based. Is global warming in fact occurring, as scientists claim? Temperature rises in recent years, some argue, are just a part of the natural cycles that the world goes through. How will the political dynamics of implementation change if the scientific consensus is undermined?

Suggested Additional Readings

Alberta. *Albertans & Climate Change: Taking Action.* Edmonton, October 2002. Available at www3.gov.ab.ca/env/climate/actionplan/docs/takingaction.pdf.

Blomqvist, Åke. "Comment on 'Kyoto Protocol: Implications of a Flawed but Important Environmental Policy.'" *Canadian Public Policy* 27, no. 2 (June 2001): 235–37.

Broadhead, Lee-Anne. "Canada as a Rogue State: Its Shameful Performance on Climate Change." *International Journal* 56, no. 3 (Summer 2001): 461–80.

Canada. *Climate Change Plan for Canada.* Ottawa, November 2002. Available at www.climatechange.gc.ca/plan_for_canada/plan/.

Canadian Manufacturers and Exporters. *Pain Without Gain: Canada and the Kyoto Protocol*. Ottawa, 2002. Available at www.cme-mec.ca/kyoto/documents/kyoto_release.pdf.

May, Elizabeth. "From Montreal to Kyoto: How We Got From Here to There – or Not," *Policy Options* 24, no. 1 (December 2002–January 2003): 14–18.

Paehlke, Robert. "Environmentalism in One Country: Canadian Environmental Policy in an Era of Globalization." *Policy Studies Journal* 28, no. 1 (2000): 160–75.

Rollings-Magnusson, Sandra, and Robert C. Magnusson. "The Kyoto Protocol: Implications of a Flawed but Important Environmental Policy." *Canadian Public Policy* 26, no. 3 (September 2000): 347–59.

Smith, Heather. "Chicken Defence Lines Needed: Canadian Foreign Policy and Global Environmental Issues." In Fen Hampson, Norman Hillmer, and Maureen Appel Molot, eds., *Canada among Nations 2001: The Axworthy Legacy*. Toronto: Oxford University Press, 2001: 213–33.

Sonneborn, Carrie. "Generating Jobs: Sustainable Energy Initiatives Deliver More Jobs and Lower Greenhouse Emissions." *Alternatives Journal* 26, no. 2 (Spring 2000).

Van Kooten, G. Cornelis. "Smoke and Mirrors: The Kyoto Protocol and Beyond." *Canadian Public Policy* 29, no. 4 (December 2003): 397–415.

Weibust, Inger. "Implementing the Kyoto Protocol: Will Canada Make It?" In David Carment, Fen Hampson, and Norman Hillmer, eds., *Canada among Nations 2003: Coping with the American Colossus*. Toronto: Oxford University Press, 2003: 287–311.

InfoTrac® College Edition

Search for the following articles in the InfoTrac® database:

Barrett, Scott. "Political Economy of the Kyoto Protocol." *Oxford Review of Economic Policy* 14, no. 4 (Winter 1998): 20.

Bayon, Richardo, "More Than Hot Air: Market Solutions to Global Warming." *World Policy Journal* 19, no. 3 (Fall 2002): 60–68.

Gardiner, Stephen M. "The Global Warming Tragedy and the Dangerous Illusion of the Kyoto Protocol." *Ethics & International Affairs* 18, no. 1 (April 2004): 23–40.

For more articles, enter:
"Kyoto Protocol" in the keyword search or subject guide.

Web Resources

For current URLs for the following websites, visit www.crosscurrents.nelson.com.

UNITED NATIONS FRAMEWORK CONVENTION ON CLIMATE CHANGE

unfccc.int

The official website of the UN Framework Convention on Climate Change includes the text of the Kyoto Protocol and the list of signatory countries, as well as regular updates on ratification of the protocol.

GLOBAL WARMING

www.globalwarming.org

This site, designed for students, contains documents on the politics and economics of the global warming debate, including updates on the Kyoto negotiations.

THE PEMBINA INSTITUTE

www.pembina.org

An independent environmental policy research organization, the Pembina Institute offers extensive materials on climate change from a pro-environmental point of view. It especially focuses on the impact of environmental measures on the energy industry in Canada.

DAVID SUZUKI FOUNDATION

www.davidsuzuki.org

The website of this think tank, which was founded by the noted Canadian scientist David Suzuki, contains studies relating both to the Kyoto Protocol and the economic impacts of environmental measures.

THE FRASER INSTITUTE

www.fraserinstitute.ca

The Fraser Institute is an independent policy institute with an emphasis on free market approaches. Its website contains articles and editorials highly critical of the potential economic impacts of the Kyoto Protocol.

ISUMA: CANADIAN JOURNAL OF POLICY RESEARCH

www.isuma.net

The entire Winter 2001 issue of this online policy journal is devoted to climate change and contains several articles specifically dealing with the Kyoto Protocol.

RATIFICATION OF THE KYOTO PROTOCOL: CITIZEN'S GUIDE TO THE CANADIAN CLIMATE CHANGE POLICY PROCESS

www.sustainabletoronto.ca/publications/kyotocitizensguide.pdf

This 176-page document was prepared by the faculty and students at Innis College, University of Toronto. It includes a comprehensive overview of the various governmental, economic, and environmental interests at stake in the climate change debate.

Will Debt Relief Address the Needs of Highly Indebted Countries?

✔ **YES**

ROMILLY GREENHILL, "The Unbreakable Link — Debt Relief and the Millennium Development Goals," Jubilee Research/New Economics Foundation (February 2002)

✘ **NO**

DENISE FRONING, "Will Debt Relief Really Help?" *The Washington Quarterly* 24, no. 3 (Summer 2001): 199–211

For many in the developing world, particularly in Africa and Latin America, the 1980s have come to be referred to as the "lost decade." By the beginning of the decade, it was evident that the call for a new international order, launched with much fanfare in the late 1960s, had become bogged down in fruitless debate. Instead of moving toward a more prosperous and hopeful future, many in the developing world found themselves facing deepening economic crises, deteriorating environmental conditions, and, in Africa, recurring famines. But the main story of the decade became the mounting debt crisis faced by a growing number of less developed countries (LDCs). By the end of the 1980s, this debt was estimated to be about U.S. $1.4 trillion. (All amounts henceforth are given in U.S. dollars.) Efforts to repay it have led to a net transfer of resources from the South to the North. In 1988 alone, $32.5 billion more was transferred to the North, mostly in the form of debt service payments, than was received in the South in aid and loans. Instead of moving toward a new and more equitable international economic order, North–South relations in the 1980s became preoccupied with crisis management and the politics of debt.

The international response to the debt crisis can best be described in terms of two phases, labelled after two successive American secretaries of the treasury who took leadership of the North's reaction to the debt crisis. The first phase, the Baker Plan, unveiled by then-U.S. Treasury Secretary James Baker, called for an additional $40 billion to be lent to the fifteen largest, mostly middle-income, debtors. Half of the funds would come from the World Bank and regional development banks, while the other half would come from "voluntary" loans from commercial banks. Access to these loans would be conditional on acceptance of International Monetary Fund–approved (IMF) programs. New sources of funding were also promised for the smaller, lower-income African states whose debts, owed mainly to donor governments and international financial institutions (IFIs), were in many cases more onerous.

However, the Baker Plan soon lost momentum, and support from many donors fell short of promised levels. Private financial flows dropped as commercial banks withdrew from all but the most risk-free loans. Resentment in the South mounted as governments struggled with the political consequences of implementing many of the austerity measures demanded by the IMF. LDC governments complained that the IMF-imposed structural adjustment programs, which typically included sharp cuts in government services and subsidies, undermined their political legitimacy without really resolving their economic crisis. Throughout the 1980s, "IMF riots" became commonplace in many LDCs. More countries were falling into arrears, not only to banks, governments, and their export credit agencies, but also to the IFIs, such as the IMF and the World Bank, whose debt payments cannot be rescheduled.

In 1989, James Baker's successor, Nicholas Brady, launched a new initiative to deal with the debt crisis. The centrepiece of the Brady Plan was to make up to $35 billion available to finance debt-reduction deals negotiated between selected debtor countries and their creditor banks. The plan was adopted by the IFIs and the G-7 industrialized countries as their primary approach to the debt crisis. But from the beginning, critics charged that the plan was fundamentally flawed and woefully inadequate. The South Commission, chaired by the former president of Tanzania, Julius Nyerere, pointed out that the plan dealt only with debt owed to commercial banks and that reduction of even this debt was still up to those banks. Further, the commission argued that the pool of funds available was clearly inadequate to achieve any real measure of debt reduction. In reviewing Northern efforts to deal with the debt crisis, the commission's report, *The Challenge to the South* (Oxford: Oxford University Press, 1990), concluded: "The upshot is that debt has become a form of bondage, and the indebted economies have become indentured economies – a clear manifestation of neo-colonialism. This state of affairs cannot go on. The debt and its service must be reduced to a level that allows growth to proceed at an acceptable pace" (p. 227).

At the end of the 1990s, it was increasingly evident that the fears of the South Commission had come true, especially in the case of African countries. In its 1986 *World Development Report*, the World Bank predicted with confidence that by the mid-1990s developing-country debt would, in the worst-case scenario, amount to about $864 billion, and that the amount owed by African low-income countries would be only about $29 billion. However, by 1994, according to the World Bank's own figures, the external debt of all developing countries stood at nearly $2 trillion, while the debt of sub-Saharan African countries was $210 billion (Susan George, "Rethinking Debt," *Development* 2 [1996]: 54).

The continuing debt crisis has led some people to question whether more radical debt-relief measures are needed to address the problems facing developing countries. One voice in this movement has been the Jubilee 2000 campaign, a grassroots movement started in the United Kingdom to mobilize support for debt remission. The co-founders of Jubilee 2000, William Peters and Martin Dent, liken their campaign to the struggle against slavery in an earlier century. They developed their case for debt relief by drawing on the Hebraic concept of the jubilee as a model for debt forgiveness today.

In part as a result of the work of the Jubilee campaign, debt forgiveness has become a major international issue in recent years; the Pope and celebrities such as Bono of the pop band U2 have become spokespeople for the cause. There has also been a number of promising developments recently. One of these is the World Bank's Highly Indebted Poor Countries (HIPC) Initiative. Announced in 1996 and implemented in September 1997, HIPC aims debt-relief funding at the poorest and most heavily indebted countries. After initial projects in Uganda and Bolivia, the World Bank expanded the initiative; it is now known as the Enhanced Highly Indebted Poor Countries Initiative. The overall goal is to combine HIPC debt relief with more traditional forms of debt forgiveness and forgive up to $55 billion, a little more than half the total outstanding debt of these countries. Mozambique qualified for an additional $600 million of debt relief in April 2000, bringing its total to $4.3 billion of debt forgiven. Burkina Faso was approved for an additional $700 million in June 2000 after meeting previous guidelines. The World Bank has also established a Trust Fund for the HIPC to assist multilateral development banks with the costs they incur when forgiving debt. Since then, some individual countries have announced measures to forgive a substantial portion of developing-country debt.

Despite this progress, many feel that not enough has been done to address the debt issue. With the passing of the Jubilee year of 2000, less attention has been focused on debt forgiveness. The Jubilee 2000 campaign has been renamed the Jubilee Debt Campaign. Increasingly, the international community has turned its focus to the United Nations Millennium Development Goals announced in 2000. In the Millennium Declaration passed by the United Nations General Assembly, the leaders of the world committed themselves to reducing the number of those who live in poverty and hunger by half by the year 2015. They also set other goals, such as the achievement of universal primary education, the reversal of the spread of HIV/AIDS and malaria, and the reduction of child and material mortality rates by half in the same time period.

In the first reading, Romilly Greenhill looks at the issue of debt relief in the context of these new goals. In this report prepared for the Jubilee campaign, she examines the achievements of the HIPC debt-relief initiative and finds that the results have fallen far short of the hopes of debt campaigners. She then focuses on what it will take to achieve the goals set by the United Nations in the Millennium Declaration. Greenhill concludes that it is only through 100 percent debt cancellation and a significant increase in aid-giving that there is any hope of achieving these goals. Denise Froning provides another perspective by looking at some of the problems with reliance on debt forgiveness. She examines the internal problems of developing countries that need to be addressed and also looks at the changes needed in the policies of industrialized countries.

✔ **YES**

The Unbreakable Link — Debt Relief and the Millennium Development Goals

ROMILLY GREENHILL

At the start of the new millennium, the world's leaders met in the United Nations General Assembly to set out a new global vision for humanity. In their Millennium Declaration, the statesmen and women recognised their 'collective responsibility to uphold the principles of human dignity, equality and equity at the global level.'[1] They pledged to 'spare no effort to free our fellow men, women and children from the abject and dehumanising conditions of extreme poverty.'[2]

From these fine words, a set of goals was born: to eliminate world poverty by the year 2015; to achieve universal primary education; to promote gender equality and empower women; to reduce child mortality; improve maternal health; to combat HIV/AIDS and other diseases; and to ensure environmental sustainability. According to Clare Short, the UK's Secretary of State for International Development, these goals have the potential to 'transform the lives of hundreds of millions of poor people, and make the planet a better and safer place for our children and grandchildren.'[3]

Since then, the Millennium Development Goals — as they were subsequently named — have been adopted by all major donor agencies as guiding principles for their strategies for poverty eradication. The OECD 'confirmed their commitment to reducing poverty in all its dimensions and to achieving the seven International Development Goals.'[4] The IMF and World Bank have co-ordinated their efforts behind this set of goals, and the UK Government has made them the centrepiece of its overall aid strategy. More importantly, the adoption of the targets has motivated a fundamental shift within development thinking — away from a narrow focus on inputs, towards a fundamental concern with outcomes for the poor of the world.[5]

Moreover, since the adoption of the MDGs in the year 2000, events have conspired to reinforce the urgent need for poverty reduction in the world. According to Gordon Brown, the aftermath of September 11th has shown that 'the international community must take strong action to tackle injustice and poverty ... [and to] achieve our 2015 Millennium Development Goals.'[6]

But meeting the 2015 targets requires resources. Ernest Zedillo, in his report of the High Level Panel for Financing for Development, has assessed that total additional resources of $50bn per year will be needed to meet these targets worldwide, over and above the current level of spending in key areas. This estimate is based on detailed costings in some of the key goal areas by UN bodies such as UNICEF, the World Health Organisation, and others such as the World Bank.[7]

The UN Millennium Declaration was not the only remarkable event of the year 2000. Equally notable – though perhaps more poignant – was the winding down of the Jubilee 2000 campaign, described by Kofi Annan as 'the voice of the world's

BOX 1
PROGRESS IN THE HIPC INITIATIVE AS OF END 2001

1. Completion Point Countries (4)

Bolivia

Mozambique

Tanzania

Uganda

2. Decision Point Countries (20)

Benin

Burkina Faso

Cameroon

Chad

Ethiopia

The Gambia

Guinea

Guinea-Bissau

Guyana

Honduras

Madagascar

Malawi

Mali

Mauritania

Nicaragua

Niger

Rwanda

Sao Tome and Principe

Senegal

Zambia

3. Other Countries (18)

Angola

Burundi

Cape Verde

Central African Republic Comoros

Comoros

Congo DR

Congo Rep

Cote D'Ivoire

Ghana

Lao PDR

Liberia

Myanmar

Sierra Leone

Somalia

Sudan

Togo

Vietnam

Yemen

conscience and indefatigable fighters for justice.'[8] The Jubilee 2000 coalition had campaigned for the cancellation of the un-payable debts of the poorest countries by the end of 2000, under a fair and transparent process. Their petition – the largest ever – had been signed by 24 million people worldwide.

The central message of the Jubilee 2000 campaign was that human rights should not be subordinated to money rights. Poor countries prepared to commit resources to meeting the basic needs and economic rights of their populations should not be prevented from doing so because of the need to pay back debts to rich creditor countries and institutions.

The Jubilee 2000 campaign had won a commitment to a $110bn write off of un-payable debts. This was to be achieved partly through an extension of the World Bank's Heavily Indebted Poor Countries (HIPC) initiative, and partly through additional bilateral commitments from creditors such as the UK.

But it is now clear that the HIPC initiative is not delivering enough either to produce the promised 'robust exit' from unsustainable debts or to meet internationally agreed poverty reduction goals. As shown in Box [1], by the end of 2001 – a full year after the millennium deadline called by the Jubilee 2000 coalition – only four countries had passed through all the hoops of the HIPC initiative. Out of the 42 countries included in the process, almost half of these had not even reached 'decision point', after which they receive some interim relief on their debt service payments. Moreover, even when relief is provided, research by Jubilee Plus[9] has shown that debt burdens remain unsustainable. **HIPC is a failure.**

For this reason, debt campaigners have argued that debt relief can no longer be based on arbitrary debt-to-export ratios, designed by rich country creditors and multilateral institutions so as to minimise their own losses. Instead, poor countries should be able to call for debt relief when it is clear that debt repayments are crowding out payments for services fundamental to human rights.

Debt campaigners were encouraged, therefore, by indications that the up-coming UN Financing for Development Conference would be prepared to consider linking debt relief to each country's capacity to raise the finance needed to achieve the millennium development goals.[10] But hopes were dashed when this proposal was rejected by the G7 countries, including the EU, Japan, and Canada. In the usual round of horse-play which precedes these conferences, the G77 countries have been forced to make concessions in this area, merely in order to keep the rich countries on board.[11]

We believe that this is wrong.

We show in this report that if poor country governments are to have sufficient resources to meet the MDGs, as well as to meet other essential expenditure needs and pro-poor investments, **the 42 HIPC countries as a whole cannot afford to make any debt service payments.** In fact, we find that **even if all the debts of these 42 countries are cancelled, the HIPCs will need an additional $30bn in aid each year if there is any hope of meeting goal 1 while for the other goals, a total of $16.5bn will be needed.** [...]

DEBT SERVICE PAYMENTS TAKE RESOURCES FROM THE MDGS

Calculating the resources needed to meet the MDGs in each country is no easy task. Data on the number of poor people in each country, the current level of indicators such as HIV and malarial prevalence, or even the number of children in school, is often not available, or not reliable. Moreover, working out the exact amount that will need to be spent across different countries to meet common objectives requires making heroic assumptions about costs in each country. Some of the goals – such as 'reversing the loss of environmental resources' are inherently very difficult to evaluate.

In this report, we make use of country specific estimates prepared by key international bodies such as the World Bank, UNICEF, World Health Organisation, and Water Vision 21. These estimates form the basis of the $50bn estimated by Ernest Zedillo and are widely used by the international community in their assessments of the resource requirements of the MDGs.[12] For goals and targets for which no estimates have been prepared, we use the total figures provided in the Zedillo Report. [. . .]

It should be emphasised that our approach is not new. Others, including CAFOD,[13] Christian Aid, Joe Hanlon,[14] and Eurodad[15] have undertaken similar exercises. Here, our aim is mainly to update these analyses with the most recent global estimates of the costs of meeting the 2015 targets, and the most recently available figures of current spending on both debt services and key social expenditures.

Goal 1: Eradicate extreme poverty and hunger

- Halve, between 1990 and 2015, the proportion of people whose income is less than one dollar a day
- Halve, between 1990 and 2015, the proportion of people who suffer from hunger.

Eradicating mass poverty is often seen as the most fundamental of the MDGs. In the simplistic world of the donor community, extreme poverty is defined as living on less than one dollar a day. This is a very problematic assumption, not least because people's well-being, or ill-being, depends on much broader factors than absolute income. Moreover, using an absolute international poverty line does not reflect differences in relative poverty across countries. While it represents gross numbers, or incidence, of those who are counted as poor, it says nothing about the depth of poverty or the inequalities amongst the poor, or between the poor and rich. But, as DFID argues, the $1 target 'represents an internationally agreed operational method of identifying the number of people who by any standards have unacceptably low incomes.'[16]

Of all the MDGs, this goal is also the most difficult to relate to debt service payments. It is clear that debt repayments are taking resources that could be spent to reduce poverty, but quantifying the exact linkages is much more difficult. [. . .]

Goal 2: Achieving universal primary education

- Ensure that, by 2015, children everywhere, boys and girls alike, will be able to complete a full course of primary schooling

Access to primary education is a basic human right. Education benefits individuals, their families, and also society as a whole, by enabling greater participation in democratic processes. Education serves to empower individuals, helps them to take advantage of economic opportunities, and improves their health and that of their family.

Yet, in 2000, **one in three** children across the developing world did not complete the 5 years of basic education which UNICEF belives in the minimum required to achieve basic literacy.[17] We are clearly a long way from achieving the Millennium Development Goal of achieving Universal Primary Education by 2015.

UNICEF has calculated the amount that countries will need to spend in order to meet the MDGs.[18] They found that almost all of the HIPCs will need to increase spending on education – with larger countries such as Ethiopia needing to spend an extra $203m, and the poorer HIPCs such as Burkina Faso and Niger needing an extra $60m.

We added these estimates to current level of spending on education, taken from the World Development Indicators 2001.[19] From this, we were able to calculate the total spending that would be required in each of the HIPCs each year if the MDGs are to be met. [. . .]

The HIPC countries will only need to spend $6.5bn each year in order to ensure that every child gets an education sufficient to ensure basic literacy. While large relative to the incomes of HIPCs, on a global scale this figure is miniscule – representing, for example, less than half of one percent of the projected US defence budget of $1,600bn over the next five years. And only $1.2bn of this is additional to what governments are currently spending – although [. . .] countries like Burkina Faso will need much larger increases in spending than some of the other HIPCs.

Goal 4: Reducing child mortality

- Reduce, by two-thirds, between 1990 and 2015, the under-five mortality rate

Goal 5: Improving maternal health

- Reduce by three quarters, between 1990 and 2015, the maternal mortality ratio

Goal 6: Combating HIV/AIDS, malaria and other diseases

- Have halted by 2015, and begun to reverse, the spread of HIV/AIDS
- Have halted by 2015, and begun to reverse, the incidence of malaria and other related diseases.

A tragedy is unfolding in Africa. Within the last 24 hours, 5,500 Africans were killed by HIV/AIDS. One in five of all adults in Africa are infected by the virus, while 17 million Africans have died from AIDS since the start of the epidemic. AIDS has so far left 13 million children orphaned, a figure which will grow to 40 million by 2010 if no action is taken.[20]

Moreover, AIDS is not the only killer. Other diseases such as malaria, TB, childhood infectious diseases, maternal and prenatal conditions and micronutrient deficiencies abound. Average life expectancy in Africa has *fallen* since 1980, from 48 to 47 – and in individual countries, the fall is much more extreme. Life expectancy in Zambia is now only 38 years, down from 50 years in 1980, while Sierra Leone has a life expectancy of only 37 years. And even these figures mask the catastrophic impact on children. In Africa, 161 children out of every 1,000 children will die before their fifth birthday; in Niger, this figure is as high as one in four.[21]

Yet, the Global Commission on Macroeconomics and Health has estimated that **eight million** lives could be spared each year if a simple set of health interventions needed to meet the MDGs were put in place.

The Commission, which is chaired by Professor Jeffrey Sachs of Harvard University, was launched by Gro Harlem Bruntland, Director General of the World Health Organisation, in 2000. In a recent report into Macroeconomics and Health, it stated that 'the vast majority of the excess disease burden [in poor countries] is the result of a relatively small number of identifiable conditions, each with a set of existing health interventions that can dramatically improve health and reduce the deaths associated with these conditions. **The problem is that these interventions don't reach the world's poor.** Some of the reasons for this are corruption, mis-management and a weak public sector, but in the vast majority of countries, there is a more basic and remediable problem. **The poor lack the financial resources to obtain coverage of these essential interventions, as do their governments.**'[22] [. . .]

The Commission recommends that some of the increase in spending needed should come from domestic revenues. But as they note, 'for the low-income countries, we still find a gap between financial means and financial needs, which can be filled only by the donor world if there is to be any hope of success in meeting the MDGs.[23] But 'there is another method to raise more revenues for health in low income countries: deeper debt relief, with the savings allocated to the health sector.'[24]

The need for more debt relief is evident. The Commission Report has shown that vast improvements in the lives of millions of people in poor countries are achievable, with an increase in expenditure totalling only 0.1% of GDP of the rich donor and creditor countries. Yet, despite this overwhelming imperative, the poorest countries are still paying debt service of $8bn per year.

Target 10: Halve, by 2015, the proportion of people without sustainable access to safe drinking water

Like education and health care, access to safe water is a basic right. Safe water is vital for proper health and hygiene, including the prevention of water borne diseases. Distances travelled to fetch water result in a huge loss of time for poor people, particularly women and children. Yet, **one billion** people currently lack safe drinking water and almost **three billion** – half the world's population – lack adequate sanitation. **Two million** children die each year from water-related diseases. As the Vision 21 Framework for Action states, this situation is 'humiliating, morally wrong and oppressive.'[25]

This is the more so, given that the resources required to ensure universal access to basic water and sanitation are comparatively small. Water Vision 21, a report produced by partners in the Water Supply and Sanitation Collaborative Council, has estimated that providing access to safe water and sanitation will only cost $25 per rural dweller – $15 to provide access to safe water, $10 for rural sanitation and hygiene promotion – and $75 per urban dweller, of which $50 is for urban water and $25 for peri-urban sanitation. These are additional to the costs currently borne by households and communities. These are one-off costs of providing access to basic water, and do not include the continuing costs, for example of operations and maintenance of current water supplies.

In order to meet the MDG of halving the proportion of people without sustainable access to safe drinking water, our calculations [...] find that in total, the HIPCs would have to spend only $2.4bn per year on water and sanitation – less than Europe spends on alcohol over ten days.

Target 11: By 2020, to have achieved a significant improvement in the lives of at least 100 million slum dwellers

Slums are defined by the World Bank as 'neglected parts of cities where housing and living conditions are appallingly poor.'[26] Hundreds of millions of the urban poor in developing countries currently live in unsafe and unhygienic environments where they face multiple threats to their health and security. The tenth millennium development target commits the international community to over-turning this unacceptable situation, and improving the lives of at least 100 million slum dwellers by 2020.

The World Bank has calculated that programmes of upgrading that would provide services to all slum areas in all developing countries could be implemented at a cost of approximately 0.2% to 0.5% of GDP.[27] When the costs of investment in infrastructure, land acquisition and necessary institutional support are added, the total comes up to around 1% to 2% of GDP. Because the MDG only refers to improving the lives of 100 million slum dwellers worldwide, we take the lower of these estimates, and assume that the HIPCs will need to spend 1% of GDP annually on improving slum conditions. In total, this comes to **$1.7bn** for all the 39 HIPCs considered.

OTHER GOALS AND TARGETS

Goal 3: Promoting gender equality and empowering women

- Eliminate gender disparity in primary and secondary education preferably by 2005 and to all levels of education no later than 2015

Target 9: Integrate the principles of sustainable development into country policies and programmes and reverse the loss of environmental resources

Providing basic health, education and water to the populations of poor countries is clearly vital and should be given preference over debt service payments. But at the same time, other dimensions of development — such as promoting gender equality and protecting environmental resources, are also needed if development is to be sustainable in the long run.

Unfortunately, however, these goals are inherently difficult to cost, and are therefore difficult to compare with debt service payments. Promoting gender equality and empowering women will, according to the Zedillo report, require a total yearly sum of $3bn, but we cannot tell how this will be allocated across the HIPCs and non HIPCs. Ensuring environmental sustainability will require a much greater change in resource use and energy use, particularly the need for contraction and convergence in energy use between rich and poor countries.

TOTAL REQUIRED TO MEET MDGS

Our analysis shows that the total funds required each year to meet MDGs 2 to 7 are not exorbitant. In order to meet the UN Millennium Declaration's intention to 'free our fellow men, women and children from the abject and dehumanising conditions of extreme poverty, to which more than a billion of them are currently subjected',[28] a mere $30.6bn per year is required.

This figure may be small in global terms. But [. . .] it represents 18% of GDP for the 42 HIPCs as a whole, and a staggering 355% of their debt service. [. . .]

LINKING DEBT SERVICING TO THE MILLENNIUM DEVELOPMENT GOALS

Even without servicing their external debts, it is clear that the 39 HIPCs face a formidable challenge if they are to raise the level of resources required to meet the MDGs.

While it is true that governments can raise their own revenues by taxing their domestic populations, in most of the HIPC countries the extreme poverty experienced means that governments find it very difficult to raise the kind of resources needed.

Debt servicing worsens this position by diverting preciously needed resources, which could be used for saving lives, and educating children, towards rich country creditors.

Moreover, governments cannot be spending all their revenues on social expenditures. Crucial expenditures such as maintaining law and order, public administration, essential infrastructures such as roads, policing and defence are also needed. Following Joe Hanlon, who bases his analysis on work done by Jeffrey Sachs, we argue that the HIPCs should be spending 10% of GDP on other essential expenditures.[29]

Given the current ability of the HIPC governments to raise revenues, and given the essential expenditures needed to meet the MDGs and for other essential expenditures, we now ask: how much can the HIPCs afford to pay to their rich country creditors in debt service payments? [. . .]

Our analysis shows that, as whole, **the HIPCs have no spare resources available that could be used for debt servicing**. In fact, even with 100% debt cancellation, **the HIPCs will require an additional $16.5bn if goals 2 to 7 are to be met**, and this is without the additional $30bn needed for goal 1. [. . .]

Our conclusion, therefore, is simple. All of the 39 HIPCs here — and the three not included in our data set — will need 100% debt cancellation if the MDGs are to be met.

COUNTER ARGUMENTS

This conclusion has far reaching implications, and in particular shows that the current process for debt service reduction, the HIPC initiative — which will bring down debt service payments by only around 27% in nominal terms — is woefully inadequate.

We know that our conclusion will not be welcomed by everyone, in particular the rich country creditors and multilateral institutions who collect the meagre interest payments paid by poor countries. Accordingly, we now deal with two popular counter arguments: firstly, that it is impossible to ensure that the money saved in debt service payments is not siphoned off elsewhere; and secondly, that we should be increasing grants, rather than providing debt relief.

Objection 1: How can we ensure that the savings made in debt service payments will in fact be channelled towards meeting the MDGs?

This is a common objection to any form of debt relief mechanism, and generally reflects a patronising view of poor country leaders as being corrupt and incompetent. Certainly corruption is an issue, and as such has been the target of much action by Jubilee 2000 campaigners in heavily indebted nations. However, it is somewhat ironic that multilateral and bilateral creditors are concerned about corruption when discussing debt relief – yet pay little attention to issues of corruption when making new loans.

Moreover, experience in the use of HIPC resources to date has shown that, if civil society is involved, mechanisms can be developed to ensure that all debt relief funds are dedicated to key expenditure areas as required to meet the MDGs. Encouragingly, Uganda's experiences with costing her Poverty Eradication Action Plan – the Ugandan Poverty Reduction Strategy Paper – have shown that debt relief can be channelled towards those expenditures most likely to have an impact on poverty targets.

Objection 2: We should provide more aid, not reduce debts.

The colossal financing needs of the poorest countries if the MDGs are to be met have not gone unnoticed by world leaders. Gordon Brown's new proposed trust fund, into which major donors would contribute funds towards the overall target of $50bn per year, is a commendable example of the concern of some of the leaders of rich countries to meet these goals. So, why not forget about debt relief, and just provide for more aid?

As we have already argued, there is little point in providing more aid to poor countries if it is just to be swallowed up in debt service payments. But more importantly, there are many arguments to suggest that debt relief will be much more effectively used than increased aid.

Firstly, global aid flows are, despite the 0.7% of GDP commitment, in long term decline. The US recently termed ODA as an 'obsolete form of development assistance.' Even the UK currently gives less than half the 0.7% aid target.

Secondly, debt relief acts as de facto budget support – meaning that it is money that can be used by the government according to its own strategic priorities, just like its own revenues. Traditional project aid – through which donors provide funds for a particular purpose, such as building a road or an individual food security project – faces multiple difficulties. These include donor co-ordination; priorities being determined by donors' strategic interests rather than by recipient governments; tying of aid to procurement from the host country; and transactions costs. More importantly, however, debt relief is highly predictable – it is the securest form of revenue, stretching over a 20 year period.

In many countries, debt relief also has greater ownership within debtor countries, particularly amongst civil society groups. People see the savings from debt relief as 'their' money to be spent wisely, rather than donors' money which is seen as having little to do with domestic needs.

CONCLUSION: THE NEED FOR A SABBATH ECONOMICS

Our conclusion is clear. If the Millennium Development Goals are to be met, all of the HIPCs will need full cancellation of all of their debts. This is not an act of charity, but a moral imperative. While eight million die each year for want of the funds spent by the rich countries on their pets; when millions of children stay out of school for want of half a percent of the US defence budget; and when the amount spent on alcohol in a week and a half in Europe would be adequate to provide sanitation to half the world's population, something is very wrong.

Maybe it is time, once again, to call on biblical principles. The 'Jubilee' principle – which provides ways of reversing the relentless flow of resources from the poor to the rich, and narrowing the gap between – formed the foundation of one of the most successful global campaigns ever. But there are others. The central tenets of 'Sabbath Economics' are that the world is abundant and provides enough for everyone – but that human communities must restrain their appetites and live within limits. For Sabbath Economics, disparities in wealth and power are not natural, but come about through sin, and must be mitigated within the community through redistribution.[30]

We do not have to believe in God – or indeed any religion – to accept these principles. It is enough for us to recognise that more than a billion people do not need to live in poverty while their debts continue to be repaid. The current HIPC initiative does not and cannot do enough to bring down the unsustainable debt burden of the world's poorest countries. If the Millennium Development Goals are to be met, there is no alternative but to provide a new framework for debt relief – one which respects the human rights of the poor.

NOTES

1. United Nations Millennium Declaration, Resolution 55/2.

2. ibid.

3. Foreword to 'Halving world poverty by 2015: economic growth, equity and security' DFID 2001.

4. OECD/DAC Guidelines on Poverty Reduction: In the Face of Poverty.

5. Sir John Vereker, Permanent Secretary of the UK's Department for International Development, at a speech at the All Party Group on Overseas Development (APGOOD), January 23rd 2002.

6. Statement from the Rt Hon Gordon Brown MP to the IMFC on Saturday November 17th 2001.

7. Report of the High Level Panel on Financing for Development, United Nations.

8. Cited in 'The world will never be the same again' Jubilee 2000 Coalition, December 2000.

9. See 'Flogging a Dead Process', a Report by Jubilee Plus, September 2001.

10. UN General Assembly, Preparatory Committee for the International Conference on Financing for Development, 4th Session: Revised draft outcome prepared by the Facilitator, 7 December 2001.

11. Source: Financial Times, Monday January 28th, 'US blocks move for big rise in aid to poor countries', by Carola Hoyos and Allan Beattie.

12. It should be noted that in most cases, we have used the most conservative estimates of the required spending, for example by excluding the capital costs of education spending.

13. For example, 'Further and deeper debt cancellation is vital for development' Presentation at the UN's Financing for Development Preparation Committee, by Henry Northover, October 2001; and 'The Human Development Approach to Debt Sustainability Analysis for the World's Poorest' CAFOD Policy Paper.

14. Cancelling debt to promote development: Paper by Joseph Hanlon, Policy Advisor to Jubilee 2000 Coalition.

15. Putting Poverty Reduction First: Why a poverty approach to debt sustainability must be adopted. Eurodad, October 2001.

16. DFID: Halving world poverty by 2015: economic growth, equity and security.

17. Is EFA affordable? Estimating the Global Minimum cost of 'Education for All', UNICEF Innocenti working paper no. 87.

18. UNICEF did this by: estimating the number of children enrolled in school in 2000; estimating the number of children who will be in school in each year between 2000 and 2015 assuming that enrolment rates don't change, based on projected levels of population growth; estimating the number of children who will need to be in school each year if enrolment ratios move from current levels to 100% by 2015, in a linear fashion; calculating the number of new school places that will be needed each year, by subtracting the total number of children who will need to be in school to reach 100% by 2015, from the baseline scenario; multiplying the number of additional children to be added into school by country specific educational costs relative to expenditure levels in the year 2000; and then dividing the additional costs by 15 to get average annual costs. It should be noted that we take the lower range of UNICEF's estimates, excluding, for example, the capital costs of building classrooms and the recurrent costs of improving educational quality.

19. It should be noted that these include all forms of educational spending, i.e. including secondary and tertiary spending. However, in most countries secondary and tertiary spending are small in comparison with primary spending.

20. Source: 'Reality Check: The Need for Deeper Debt Cancellation and the Fight Against HIV/AIDS' Drop the Debt Report, April 2001.

21. Source: World Development Indicators 200128 Report of the Commission on Macroeconomics and Health, Page 4.

22. Report of the Commission on Macroeconomics and Health, Page 4.

23. Source: Decision Point paper for Ethiopia, World Bank.

24. ibid., page 62.

25. Vision 21: A Shared Vision for Hygiene, Sanitation and Water Supply p.1.

26. World Bank: Cities Alliance for Cities Without Slums: Action Plan, page 1.

27. Ibid.

28. United Nations Millennium Declaration, op. cit.

29. This is broken down into 2% on public administration; 3% on police and defence; and 5% on essential infrastructures such as roads.

30. Myers, C. (2001) 'The Biblical Vision of Sabbath Economics'.

✗ NO
Will Debt Relief Really Help?
DENISE FRONING

In 2000, debt relief for what the International Monetary Fund (IMF) and World Bank term Heavily Indebted Poor Countries (HIPCs) was the cause of the moment in development theory, attracting international attention and broad agreement that it was the single most important piece of the poor-country development puzzle. Widespread consensus emerged that international lenders must forgive the HIPCs' debt burden. In the ebb and flow of development trends, debt relief thus had its moment in the sun, and rich countries rightly agreed to forgive some of the debt — although the World Bank and the IMF did not.

This relief, although limited to bilateral debt, will help. But when the G-7 and other advocates of development move on to the latest fad in the quest for solutions to the problems of the world's poorest countries — whether disease, education, or some yet unmentioned ill — all the attendant causes of debt relief will still need to be addressed.

All of these problems are long-term concerns. None of these countries will be wealthy tomorrow, nor will they solve all their troubles immediately. For G-7 nations, perhaps especially the United States, accustomed to focusing on the next quarter's profits rather than long-term returns, the temptation will likely be to give up too soon. That decision would be a mistake.

The fact is that these poor countries face far too many problems in addition to overwhelming debt, many of which are precisely what caused the debt accumulation in the first place. Many factors — disease, poverty, lack of education, lack of institutions, lack of transportation infrastructure, lack of food, lack of business, lack of security, lack of foreign investment, and lack of prospects — continue to stifle the economic growth of these countries, and they will continue to do so after debt relief. Without a change in these circumstances, debt relief will be only a short-term palliative, and these countries will find themselves back in the same predicament that they now face.

WHAT IS THE PROBLEM?

Bad policies and their attendant outcomes, both within and outside these countries, contribute to the "problem of poverty." Poor countries must improve domestically in a number of areas; their poverty cannot be attributed entirely to external factors. Although these countries face some valid domestic woes, many of the excuses for poverty are invalid. A lack of natural resources, for instance, does not fully account for the poverty the HIPCs face. Africa, where most of the world's 41 HIPCs are located, is awash in natural wealth, from diamonds, gold, and oil to arable agricultural land.[1] As George Ayittey observes, the continent has abundant natural potential. This potential, however, remains largely unrealized. Citing examples such as Russia, some have argued that such resources are more a curse than a blessing, but that argument does not explain the lack of development. Country after country has become rich based on these very resources.

Some maintain that lack of progress among HIPCs is due in part to geographical location and the affliction of disease that accompanies that location. The impact of disease, from malaria to cholera to AIDS, is indeed debilitating; but even if disease were entirely eliminated, the lack of institutions (or the persistence of corrupt ones) would keep the people of these countries poor.

I do not belittle the effects of disease or suggest that people should abandon attempts to mitigate the health crisis in the HIPC countries. Rather than quibble about which cause of poverty should be considered paramount, however, we must first acknowledge that the troubles of these countries are legion and that each must be addressed for lasting development to take place. For example, a couple of years ago, before the debt-relief craze, corruption was the cause du jour. The World Bank and other august institutions held conferences, everyone nodded their heads sagely, and learned people everywhere agreed that corruption was corrosive and that something must be done. Although work to address this particular problem undoubtedly continues, the international focus on corruption has shifted to other contributing factors of poverty; yet corruption's effects remain as debilitating as ever.

The construction of sound institutions, as one example, ought not to be abandoned because other problems exist. In fact, admitting that the impediments are many and related reduces the risk of "fad" development, in which whatever currently fashionable panacea that captures popular attention reigns while other crucial issues are forgotten.

Bad Leaders

Ayittey makes the important distinction between the African people and the leaders of African nations. It is not the African people who squander development opportunities. Too often, it is African leaders, as Ayittey has observed, who seize both native wealth and foreign aid while plunging their countries into war and plundering their money, both through the exploitation of resources like diamonds and by stealing massive amounts of foreign aid.[2] As the Freedom House annual survey of political freedom points out, "Only 21 African countries (40 percent) are electoral democracies."[3] The African people do not choose these leaders, but they must suffer the consequences of these leaders' poor decisions.

Corruption

Despite its trendiness as an issue, corruption is a truly debilitating factor in the poorest countries. Indeed, much of Africa reflects the results of corruption undermining efforts to foster emerging market economies. Corruption is a cancer on the most legitimate efforts at development in many African countries, affecting regulation as well as property rights and discouraging economic progress. Although hardly unique to Africa or to developing nations, corruption is all the more damaging to them; it creates obstacles to development that an already established, large-scale economy might survive but that can prove fatal to fledgling efforts at market development in small economies.

Part of Africa's development problem, as economist John Mukum Mbaku writes, is bureaucrats who are often

> members of the politically dominant group and have significant influence over the allocation of resources. Under these conditions, civil servants behave like interest groups whose primary objective is to put pressure on the political system in an effort to redistribute wealth to themselves. "In countries with poorly constructed, inefficient, and non-self-enforcing constitutional rules, opportunistic behavior (including rent seeking) [is] usually quite pervasive.... Excessive regulation of economic activities creates many opportunities for rent seeking, including bureaucratic corruption.[4]

Mukum Mbaku's solution: reform the laws to remove the state from direct control over the economy – a system which leads to profit skimming, if not outright profit seizure.

Corruption compounds itself. Sometimes because of profit seizure, lower level bureaucrats themselves are underpaid and regard taking bribes as necessary for their survival. The whole system becomes rotten in layers, with the entire structure threatening to tumble down if one attempts to reform one part of it.

Bad Institutions

Ayittey delineates four institutional pillars[5] that are essential for lasting development in Africa: an independent judiciary, an independent central bank, free media, and neutral armed forces. In HIPCs and other poor countries, these pillars are often missing, which is why foreign assistance – even by those agencies whose sole purpose is giving aid – has proved ineffective overall. World Bank analysis of past loans and credits concludes that assistance "has a positive impact on growth [only] in countries with good fiscal, monetary, and trade policies."[6] In countries with poor policies, aid has had a negative impact. Robert Barro's analysis reveals that countries with "good fiscal, monetary, and trade policies" are more likely to experience positive economic growth whether they receive assistance or not.[7] Meanwhile, regardless of how much assistance they have received, countries with poor economic policies have not experienced sustained economic growth.[8] Clearly, sound economic policies, not foreign assistance, are the key to development.

HOW RICH NATIONS EXACERBATE THE PROBLEM

For poor countries to succeed in the international economy, they must have access to the markets of developed countries. Yet the United States levies the most onerous of its tariffs – as high as 45 percent – against some of these impoverished nations.

The U.S. weighted-average tariff rate of only 2 percent on worldwide imports is low by global standards,[9] but rather than apply this rate evenly among nations, the United States applies tariffs according to the type of product imported. The goods that face the highest U.S. tariffs are precisely those that the poorest countries produce: agricultural goods, textiles, and apparel. Combined with the impact of quotas, the U.S. tariff structure presents a significant obstacle to any country struggling to create even an initial presence in the world economy.

U.S. weighted-average tariff rates vary widely when plotted along lines of the exporting countries' economic wealth. Countries whose inhabitants earn an annual per capita gross domestic product (GDP) of more than $25,000 face an average U.S. tariff rate of 2 percent. Twenty-five countries with annual per capita GDPs of less than $1,000 – approximately the amount that a minimum-wage worker in the United States earns in one month – face tariff rates greater than the U.S. average.

This disparity in U.S. tariff rates exists because poor countries tend to export many of the commodities that are subject to high tariffs in the United States and other wealthy markets. Low-income nations develop industries in which they have a comparative advantage and which provide goods and services that meet the basic needs of their people. The agricultural, textile, and apparel industries are labor-intensive and do not require sophisticated machinery or large amounts of capital to make a profit. The resource they do require, and the resource – sometimes the only resource – that developing countries have, is people.

The United States imposes absurdly high duties on the very goods for which poor countries most need a market, effectively pricing HIPCs out of the market. For example, Gambia, which has a GDP per capita of about $325 per year, faces duty rates on exports to the United States ranging from 8.8 percent on woven cotton fabrics to 11.8 percent on textile outerwear to 15.4 percent on women's clothing; the tariff on women's clothing is almost eight times the U.S. average tariff rate of 2 percent. The notion that women's skirts from Gambia are going to flood the U.S. market, overwhelm American textile factories, and send Ann Taylor out of business is clearly preposterous. In fact, if Gambia exported its entire economy to the United States, it would amount to less than 0.005 of 1 percent of total U.S. GDP.

Other examples of U.S. protectionism against HIPCs are just as absurd and needlessly damaging. Burkina Faso, a landlocked nation subject to droughts and desertification (both of which make agriculture a difficult endeavor, to say the least), has an annual GDP per capita of about $215. Its main exports are cotton and gold, and the United States is not one of its principal markets. Nonetheless, Burkina Faso faces a 33.3 percent tariff on whatever outerwear it might attempt to send to the

United States. If Burkina Faso — which faces high costs in exporting everything because of its poverty and landlocked nature — somehow manages to get a coat to the United States, that coat is instantly taxed at a third against its cost.

Likewise, Malawi produces a total GDP of only $1.8 billion — just 0.02 percent the size of the U.S. economy — but faces a U.S. tariff rate of 32.8 percent on exports of suits and coats (raincoats excluded). Presumably, raincoats fall under "outerwear," which faces a 15.3 percent tariff when entering the U.S. market.

Ironically, the United States has said it wants to help these very countries! The entire economies of these HIPCs, much less their total exports, are a raindrop in the ocean of the U.S. economy. The same situation is true for other wealthy nations like those of the European Union (EU). It would cost nothing for developed nations such as the G-7 countries to eliminate all duties and quotas on HIPCs, but that act could mean a lot to the Malawian who can expect to earn $160 this year — the proverbial "less than a dollar a day."

An opportunity to use the resources they do possess — people — to build the sort of labor-intensive industries that are the only comparative advantage of poor countries could lead to long-term development. These high tariffs and continuing quotas, however, discourage development of such industries. Who in these poorest countries can afford to risk precious money to build a factory producing goods for which no market exists?

On the other hand, by gaining access to the world market, where the demand and remuneration are much higher than in domestic markets, poor countries can acquire more capital. This capital in turn fuels further production, increases savings, and fosters the development of new industries that can create further economic growth.

WHAT IS THE SOLUTION?

Breaking the cycle of indebtedness will require several actions.

Forgive Debt

Among those actors who must act on debt forgiveness are the World Bank and IMF, which refuse to forgive the debt HIPCs owe to them even though multilateral debt accounts for as much as 80 percent of overall debt in some of these countries. The policies of these lenders perpetuate the debt cycle, forcing indebted countries to continue to depend on new aid in order to pay off old debts. This situation will never lead to sustainability.

The debt crisis in poor countries is real. A long-term solution requires total forgiveness of existing bilateral and multilateral debt, which is unlikely to be repaid in any event, and ending the debt cycle by eliminating bilateral and multilateral assistance. Countries must foster their own economic policies that attract private-sector credit and investment and that have proven to be the best means of achieving long-term, sustainable economic growth.

Remove Barriers to Globalization

Dani Rodrik cites "a long list of admission requirements" imposed on countries that try to join the world economy today.[10] He's right: a thicket of protectionist policies has sprung up around the global market, impeding developing countries' progress toward wealth. Of course, regardless of the protectionist behavior of other nations, rich or poor, it is crucial to HIPC development that the HIPCs themselves unilaterally lower their own barriers to trade and foster sound institutions internally. These measures will benefit the HIPCs regardless of what other countries do.

Nonetheless, the impediments to which Rodrik refers do exist. Therefore, rich countries should give the HIPCs time to implement the Uruguay Round obligations to which they have committed themselves in the World Trade Organization (WTO), recognizing that poor countries face very high costs in their efforts to liberalize. Among the WTO's 140 members are 109 developing or transition economies. The cost of implementing just three WTO agreements—the sanitary and phytosanitary measures, the customs valuation, and the TRIPS (Trade-Related Aspects of Intellectual Property Rights) agreements – is $150 million for each developing country.[11]

For such countries where, as Rodrik remarks, $150 million may amount to a full year's development budget, implementation is a huge task. Clearly, for these countries to comply with the TRIPS or other agreements in any reasonable amount of time (reasonable from any perspective, rich or poor), they need some assistance. Thus, wealthy countries should increase their commitment to providing educational advice on how to implement such agreements and should be receptive to creative alternatives with respect to implementation by those countries that may lack the infrastructure developed countries take for granted. Also, rich countries must be patient and recognize that obstacles will have to be resolved along the way.

Encourage Trade through Regional Customs Arrangements

Encouragement can include strengthening the free-trade role of such existing customs unions as the Southern African Development Community (SADC). For many of the HIPCs, multilateral agreements on the WTO scale may simply be too big an aspect of modern globalization to undertake at present. Without giving up on the multilateral endeavors to which they have already committed, they may need to focus on more manageable liberalization, through bilateral or regional negotiations.[12] Multilateral advancement of free trade is ideal, but in an imperfect world, the perfect often must give way to the achievable.

Establishing a common trading system such as a regional trade union will allow these poor countries to pool their limited resources to establish a customs framework. At the same time, each country can gain expertise in building the institutional elements of a modern economy without bearing the cost of modernizing on its own. Regional customs arrangements also alleviate the trade burden for landlocked countries, including some HIPCs, which face dramatically higher trading costs because they must transport goods through a neighboring country to reach a port.

Notably, however, these regional customs unions often have not met their own trade liberalization commitments for various reasons. Sometimes, members delay pledged liberalization due to war or the fear that trade constitutes a threat to their own industries – as Tanzania did when withdrawing from COMESA (the Common Market for Eastern and Southern Africa). In such circumstances, the HIPCs and other poor countries must take responsibility for their own actions and honor the free-trade commitments they have already made, which will foster economic growth in the long run even if trade flows do not rise significantly in the short term.

Eliminate All Tariffs and Quotas on HIPCs

Rich countries should lower the entry fees HIPCs pay to join the global economy by removing trade barriers imposed on these countries. Both the United States and the EU have passed legislation intended to increase market access for developing countries. The EU recently proposed duty-free access to its market for 48 poor countries in its "Everything But Arms" plan; the United States enacted the Trade and Development Act of 2000 to increase access to the U.S. market for poor African and Caribbean countries.

Both of these initiatives, however, offer only limited market access improvements in sectors that would most benefit these developing countries: textiles and some agricultural goods in the U.S. market; sugar, rice, and bananas in the EU. Moreover, both efforts serve domestic protectionist interests far more than they promote economic development in poor countries. For example, under the EU's proposal, tariff reductions on rice and sugar would not even begin until 2006. Because 2006 is also the year in which the EU's agricultural subsidy program, or Common Agricultural Policy (CAP), is due for its next review, the likelihood that those tariffs will be eliminated or even reduced is questionable.

Aside from denying market access to developing countries, the CAP is very costly to the world economy, around \$75 billion annually.[13] Two-thirds of the cost (\$49 billion) is borne by Europeans in the form of higher prices, inefficient production, and economic distortions. The remaining \$25 billion – roughly equal to the total output of Burkina Faso, Gambia, Malawi, Cameroon, Guinea-Bissau, Madagascar, Mali, and Mozambique – falls on countries outside the EU in the form of lost agricultural export opportunities in Europe.

The United States also maintains barriers in the textile and apparel sector that impose enormous costs on U.S. citizens as well as on developing countries. The annual cost imposed on foreign countries by U.S. textile and apparel barriers ranges from \$4 billion to \$15.5 billion.[14]

The European CAP and U.S. textile and apparel barriers impose a significant burden on the world economy and are clearly an impediment to trade liberalization. As illustrated above, the cost to rich nations of eliminating these barriers for HIPCs is minimal; but for many low-income countries, agricultural and textile exports are a vital source of income and an important path to development.

Institute Economic Freedom

Ultimately, establishing sound institutions is crucial to development. For development to take place, a country must first establish a rule of law on which its people can rely. Laws must ensure protection of personal property rights, as Barro established in his studies.

Other actions to maximize economic freedom are also essential, including minimizing the level of corruption and reducing the regulation that stifles economic development and hinders individual liberty. Hernando de Soto details the very real way in which red tape can prevent the legal purchase of property in some developing countries, requiring a number of steps that can reach into the hundreds through a number of agencies and last for years.[15] Free-trade flows are also a key component of development.

The benefits of economic freedom are not just ivory-tower musings. They appear as tangible evidence in the real world. Regardless of geography or culture or the unique conditions of different nations and regions, economic freedom, and through it the seeds of prosperity, can develop globally. Examples include Chile in Latin America, Hong Kong and Singapore in the Asian tropics, and Estonia among the former Communist republics of Eastern Europe, not just the already vibrant Western economies.

Critics often dismiss such examples of success as isolated incidents that are exceptions to the rule. They say, for example, that Hong Kong and Singapore are too small to be representative, or that Taiwan and South Korea succeeded economically in a different era, and so on. These criticisms are excuses, not reasoned arguments. The fact that so few countries in the tropics have developed is indeed a sign of more things wrong than right in the region, but to dismiss Hong Kong and Singapore is counterproductive when examples of success are needed instead. In addition, the notion of an "exception proving a rule" is scientifically backward: theories are proven wrong when an exception is found, not vice versa. The development of Hong Kong and Singapore, two tropical countries, disproves the theory that development of the Western kind cannot occur in the tropics.

The next argument that inevitably arises about Hong Kong and Singapore — that they are not viable tropical success stories because of their territorial size — is equally invalid. As Jagdish Bhagwati observes,

The exceptionalism cited to explain away the East Asian performance has taken some strange forms. For instance, it used to be asserted that Hong Kong and Singapore were small "city states" and therefore somehow not subject to the economic laws applying to other "normal" nations. Of course, many nations around the world are even smaller on dimensions such as population.[16]

Such exceptionalism was likewise applied to "exceptionally large" countries like India to justify development failures without regard to the success of the United States, a large country in every sense of the word.[17] Is the economic growth of the United States then to be regarded as an exception? Where does one draw the line? Is Switzerland too small to be anything other than an exception to development success? Is Chile? Or Estonia?

In truth, countries will succeed or fail regardless of their size. Their performance depends far more on implementing successful institutions and addressing their unique problems, as well as taking advantage of the unique attributes that each finds in its own situation. In a variation on the Anna Karenina principle,[18] each troubled country is troubled in its own way.

The standard excuses for lack of HIPC development, then, fall short. Tropics are not the reason: there are examples of tropical success stories. Lack of resources is not the reason: the tropics possess abundant natural resources, far more in fact than many other regions. Countries in the tropics do have the problem of disease. Along with the admitted problems of their tropical location, however, their natural wealth offers a potential solution. A country like Nigeria that has an abundance of oil could spend all its petroleum proceeds on vaccines if its government so chose. But it does not. Instead, the money vanishes into private bank accounts. Why? Corruption and lack of sound institutions, as well as the lack of a viable rule of law that could, if present, minimize the siphoning of profits into private hands.

REASON TO HOPE

Success stories exist, often in places few would predict. Upon its establishment in 1949, the Republic of China on Taiwan had a poor, agricultural economy that was inefficient and overregulated, and its people were not politically free. In the 1960s, however, the government began to institute economic reforms. It guaranteed private property and set up a legal system to protect it, reformed the banking and financial sectors, stabilized taxes, gave public lands to private citizens, and allowed the free market to expand. Taiwan has become one of the world's fastest growing economies in recent years; in the 1990s, its growth rate was 11 percent.

Taiwan also has developed a functional democracy and has conducted successful multiparty elections in both the legislative and executive branches of government after years of rule by a repressive, one-party system. It is proof that a nation that was under an authoritarian regime little more than a quarter-century ago can evolve into an economically thriving democracy.

For those who are convinced by the argument that Taiwan's development took place at a time in which the costs of globalization were lower, Chile, whose GDP per capita has grown steadily since the government imposed economic reforms (except during a recession in the mid-1980s), offers a more recent example. Although the costs of this economic liberalization were often high, Chile demonstrates that institutions of economic freedom can impel political liberalization as well, for it was Augusto Pinochet's military regime that first began to institute the reforms that continued and intensified under subsequent democratic governments. Today, Chile has a market-oriented economy characterized by a high level of foreign trade.

An even more recent example of poor-country growth took place in the 1990s, when the costs of joining the world economy were about as high as they are now: Estonia, which emerged from half a century of Soviet domination in 1991 only to find that its standard of living, which in 1939 had been on par with Scandinavian cousin Finland, now lagged far behind. (Even today, Estonia's GDP per capita is one-seventh the level of Finland's.) Lacking an education in Western-style economic or political theory and having been taught in the Soviet system, Estonians began building sound economic institutions, privatizing state-owned industries, establishing a sound legal framework to attract foreign investment, liberalizing trade barriers, balancing the budget, and stabilizing the currency (by tying it to the German mark). In 10 short years, Estonia has become a model of economic development.

Of course, some could argue that Estonia's location — near its Scandinavian neighbors, which were already developed countries — has eased its progress; certainly, having a high volume of trade with Finland has proven beneficial. Yet some could also argue that Estonia's location — next to an unpredictable giant that just 50 years earlier overran it and destroyed its economic prosperity along with its sovereignty — is a distinct liability. Fundamentally, Estonia, like Chile, Singapore, Taiwan, and the rest of the world's economic success stories, has maximized its assets and sought to minimize its liabilities. All countries must do the same, no matter how insurmountable the liabilities may seem, in order to develop.

Three countries in three distinct regions, with three different cultural backgrounds, and in three different time frames: all examples of the possibilities of growth through sound institutional reform. Addressing the plight of the HIPCs may seem an overwhelming endeavor, but that does not mean it cannot be done. Far from it; anyone who sees a solution to a particular HIPC problem should be encouraged to tackle it, for these countries need assistance in many areas.

I myself advocate the fundamental necessity of institution building. Economic freedom is vital and, in the end, the only truly humane solution, for history demonstrates that only under such a system do people have the chance to use free will to achieve maximum prosperity. But creating economic freedom also means building sound, corruption-resistant, independent institutions that minimize the ability of anyone, native or foreign, rich or poor, to meddle in individual lives. Only then will debt relief really help.

NOTES

1. George Ayittey, *Africa in Chaos* (New York: St. Martin's Press, 1998).

2. Ayittey, "How the West Compounds Africa's Crisis," *Intellectual Capital*, June 29, 2000, located at <http://207.87.15.232/issues/Issue387/item9858.asp>.

3. Adrian Karatnycky, *Freedom in the World: 2000–2001*, located at <http://www.freedomhouse.org/research/freeworld/2001/essay1.htm>.

4. John Mukum Mbaku, "Bureaucratic Corruption in Africa: The Futility of Cleanups," *Cato Journal* 16, no. 1, located at <http://www.cato.org/pubs/journal/cj16n1–6.html>.

5. Ayittey, "How the West Compounds Africa's Crisis."

6. Craig Burnside and David Dollar, "Aid, Policies, and Growth," World Bank, Policy Research Department, Macroeconomic and Growth Division, June 1977.

7. See Robert J. Barro, "Rule of Law, Democracy, and Economic Performance," in Gerald P. O'Driscoll, Kim R. Holmes, and Melanie Kirkpatrick, eds., *2000 Index of Economic Freedom* (Washington, D.C.: Heritage Foundation and Dow Jones & Co., 2000), 31–51.

8. David Dollar and Lant Pritchett, "Assessing Aid: What Works, What Doesn't and Why," *World Bank Policy Research Report*, 1998, 2.

9. U.S. International Trade Commission, information available at <http://www.usitc.gov>.

10. Dani Rodrik, "Trading in Illusions," *Foreign Policy* (March/April 2001), located at <http://www.foreignpolicy.com/issue_marapr_2001/rodrick.html>.

11. J. Michael Finger, remarks at workshop on "Developing Countries and the New Round of Multilateral Trade Negotiations," Harvard University, November 5-6, 1999.

12. Traci Phillips, "Copyrights and Wrongs," *Marquette Intellectual Property Law Review* 4 (2000), in *Foreign Policy* (January–February 2001), located at <http://www.foreignpolicy.com/issue_janfeb_2001/gnsjanfeb2001.html>.

13. Brent Borell and Lionel Hubbard, "Global Economic Effects of the EU Common Agricultural Policy" in *Reforming the CAP* (Institute of Economic Affairs, 2000), 21.

14. Robert Feenstra, "How Costly Is Protectionism?" *Journal of Economic Perspectives* 6, no. 3 (Summer 1992): 163. See also Laura Baughman et al., "Of Tyre Cords, Ties and Tents: Window-Dressing in the ATC?" *World Economy* 20, no. 4, 409.

15. Hernando de Soto, *The Mystery of Capital* (New York: Basic Books, 2000).

16. Jagdish Bhagwati, *The Wind of the Hundred Days* (MIT Press, 2000), 31.

17. See generally Bhagwati, *The Wind of the Hundred Days*.

18. The opening line of Leo Tolstoy's *Anna Karenina*: "Happy families are all alike; every unhappy family is unhappy in its own way."

POSTSCRIPT

An interesting dimension of the issue of debt relief has been the success of the Jubilee 2000 movement in winning some concessions. In the past, advocacy campaigns on complex technical issues such as international trade and finance have met with limited results. Campaigns such as the International Campaign to Ban Landmines have been successful because they focus on an issue of physical harm that is readily identifiable; as well, the link between cause and effect can be easily drawn. In many cases, the answer to the question of whom to "blame" can be fairly easily identified.

The situation is quite different in the case of debt relief. Given the complexity of the issue, it is sometimes difficult to identify who was responsible for the accumulation of the debts. The Jubilee campaigners have often focused on the notion of international debt as a form of "bondage" or "slavery" in an effort to prod the conscience of the North to respond to the issue. But not everyone agrees that the industrialized countries need to share this responsibility by offering debt forgiveness. Peter Bauer, in his article "Ethics and the Etiquette of Third World Debt" (*Ethics and International Affairs* 1 [1987]: 73–84), provides a neoclassical economic case against debt relief. Bauer believes that the debt problems are largely the creation of LDC governments themselves, who must take the responsibility for dealing with them. In fact, he argues, it is unethical to offer debt relief to those who were responsible for creating the debt in the first place, since this may only cause them to continue their irresponsible behaviour. Does the question of who is to blame for the debt crisis have a direct bearing on how the burden should be shared? From the discussion above, is it clear who is "responsible" for these debts? How should the response to this question shape our decision on whether to support debt forgiveness?

Suggested Additional Readings

Addison, Tony, and Mansoob Murshed. "Debt Relief and Civil War." *Journal of Peace Research* 40, no. 2 (March 2003): 159–76.

Ayittey, Geroge B.N., and Michelle Denise Carter. "Should Western Donors Impose Strict Conditions for African Debt Relief." *CQ Researcher* 13, no. 29 (August 29, 2003): 713–15.

Bulow, Jeremy, and Kenneth Rogoff. "Cleaning Up Third World Debt Without Getting Taken to the Cleaners." *Journal of Economic Perspectives* 4, no. 1 (Winter 1990): 31–42.

Collins, Carole, et al. "Jubilee 2000: Citizen Action across the North–South Divide." In Michael Edwards and John Gaventa, eds., *Global Citizen Action*. Boulder: Lynne Rienner, 2001; 135–48.

Dent, Martin, and Bill Peters. *The Crisis of Poverty and Debt in the Third World*. Aldershot: Ashgate, 1999.

Easterly, William. "How Did Heavily Indebted Poor Countries Become Heavily Indebted? Review Two Decades of Debt Relief." *World Development* 30, no. 10 (October 2002): 1677–96.

Garg, Ramesh C. "The Case for Debt-Forgiveness for Latin America and the Caribbean Countries." *Intereconomics* 28, no. 1 (January–February 1993): 30–4.

Jaggar, Alison M. "A Feminist Critique of the Alleged Southern Debt." *Hypatia* 17, no. 4 (Fall 2002): 119–44.

Keet, Dot. "The International Anti-Debt Campaign: A Southern Activist View for Activists in 'the North' . . . and 'the South.'" *Development in Practice* 10, no. 3/4 (August 2000): 461–78.

Stiglitz, Joseph. "Odious Rulers, Odious Debts." *Atlantic Monthly* 292, no. 4 (November 2003): 39–41.

Thomas, M.A. "Getting Debt Relief Right." *Foreign Affairs* 80, no. 5 (September–October): 36–45.

InfoTrac® College Edition

Search for the following articles in the InfoTrac® database:

Rowden, Rick. "A World of Debt." *The American Prospect* 12, no. 12 (July 2, 2001): S29.

Sachs, Jeffrey D. "Resolving the Debt Crisis of Low-Income Countries." *Brookings Papers on Economic Activity* 1 (Spring 2002): 257–86.

Sharma, Sohan, and Surinder Kumar. "Debt Relief–Indentured Servitude for the Third World." *Race and Class* 43, no. 4 (April–June 2002): 45–56.

For more articles, enter:
"debt relief," "debt forgiveness," "Jubilee Debt Campaign," or "Third World debt" in the keyword search or subject guide.

Web Resources

For current URLs for the following websites, visit www.crosscurrents.nelson.com.

DEBT RELIEF INTERNATIONAL

www.dri.org.uk

Debt Relief International runs a program to build the capacity of the governments of the HIPCs to manage their own debt strategy and analysis, without having to rely on international technical assistance.

GLOBAL POLICY FORUM

www.globalpolicy.org/socecon/develop/debt/index.htm

This site contains a large number of documents and articles relating to debt relief.

JUBILEE RESEARCH

www.jubilee2000UK.org

The website of the British-based Jubilee campaign has extensive documentation and links to other national Jubilee campaigns around the world.

ONEWORLD: DEBT GUIDE

www.oneworld.org/guides/debt/index.html

This guide, prepared by UK-based OneWorld, is a good starting point for learning about debt issues.

THE WORLD BANK GROUP: HIPC

www.worldbank.org/hipc

The HIPC site, maintained by the World Bank, offers official documents and reports relating to debt relief.

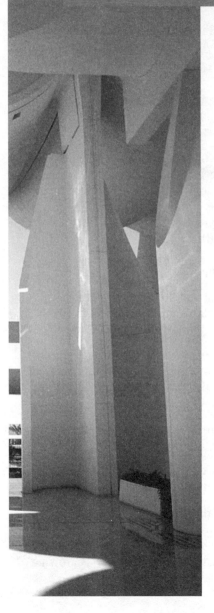

PART FOUR

GLOBAL COOPERATION AND HUMAN SECURITY

Should human security be the core value of Canadian foreign policy?

Do we need an international criminal court?

Are truth commissions useful in promoting human rights and justice in transitional societies?

Should states pursue an open-border policy toward migrants?

Do we need a world environmental organization?

Should Human Security Be the Core Value of Canadian Foreign Policy?

✔ **YES**

LLOYD AXWORTHY, "Human Security: Safety for People in a Changing World," Ottawa: Department of Foreign Affairs and International Trade, 1999

✘ **NO**

WILLIAM W. BAIN, "Against Crusading: The Ethics of Human Security and Canadian Foreign Policy," *Canadian Foreign Policy* 6, no. 3 (Spring 1999): 85–98

During much of the twentieth century, most policymakers and academics had a common understanding of the concept of security as the basis for foreign policy. It was generally assumed that the study of security had to do with the ways in which force or threats to use force were employed to ensure the physical safety of a country's citizens and the protection of that country's core values. Thus, security was closely associated with the state's role in providing "national security."

This approach is based on several realist assumptions:

1. The international system is characterized by a state of anarchy — that is, a lack of overarching authority. As a result, states must pursue their own self-interest, even if at times it conflicts with the larger collective interest.

2. The danger of a foreign attack is a constant and overriding threat to the physical well-being of the state and its inhabitants. States must therefore be vigilant to recognize threats as they emerge and take appropriate action to counter them.

3. Ensuring national security is rooted in the effective management of military force and the balance of power.

4. Since the state is the ultimate guarantor of security, the security of individuals is subsumed in the broader quest for "national security."

In this traditional formulation, the notion of threat was primarily associated with military threats posed by other states, or in some cases threats posed by non-state actors such as terrorist groups. As policymakers and analysts assessed the changes taking place in the post–Cold War international order, there was growing dissatisfaction with the traditional concept of national security. Many began to question the definition of security itself. They have argued that we should move beyond some abstract notion of the state and "national interests" and instead focus on "security" as it affects the well-being of individual human beings and groups where they actually live.

Typical of this approach was the *Human Development Report, 1994*, issued by the United Nations Development Programme. In this report, a case is made for developing a concept of "human security" that is universal, human-centred, and multidimensional. The report maintains that security, rather than being a military concept, has many components: economic, nutritional, environmental, personal, community, and political. In reconceptualizing security, the report proposes that states move away from the unilateralism that typifies traditional national security policies toward a more collective and cooperative approach. This change would give rise to a new form of diplomacy in which states would increasingly cooperate not only with other states and international governmental organizations but also with non-governmental organizations (NGOs) and other civil society actors.

The "human security" agenda reflects what Nicholas Wheeler calls a "solidarist" approach to international society. Solidarists argue that a state's claim to sovereignty and non-intervention is limited by the duty of all states to maintain a minimal standard of humane treatment of all citizens within their borders. Where such basic humane standards are not maintained, others have a responsibility, if not a duty, to come to the aid of those suffering.

Lloyd Axworthy took up the human security concept when he became the minister of foreign affairs and made it the focal point of the Liberal government's foreign policy. As a result, a whole set of issues gained prominence on the Canadian foreign policy agenda: human rights and democratization, landmines, peacebuilding, and the ways in which the plight of war affects children, to name only a few. To Axworthy, the human security agenda builds naturally on the liberal internationalist principles that have long shaped Canadian foreign policy.

Although Axworthy has since left his government post, the human security agenda officially remains a key element in the Canadian foreign policy agenda. But how useful is the focus on human security? Should this continue to be the lens through which we view the world and shape our foreign-policy interests?

Two perspectives on these questions are presented here. In the first reading, Lloyd Axworthy lays out his vision of human security and the role it should play in Canadian foreign policy. In the second reading, William W. Bain offers a more skeptical perspective. He argues for a more pluralist understanding of international society that gives greater priority to the notions of sovereignty and non-interference and respects the right of states to pursue their own vision of the good life. Bain doubts that the kind of moral principles that underlie the concept of human security have in fact become universally accepted.

He fears that a foreign policy driven by a human security agenda would mean an overly moralized policy. Such a crusading spirit could lead to charges of cultural imperialism abroad and cynicism at home if Canada cannot live up to its promises to deliver. A more prudent approach to foreign policy, Bain argues, is more in keeping with the traditions of Canadian foreign policy than with this crusading spirit.

✔ YES
Human Security: Safety for People in a Changing World
LLOYD AXWORTHY

I. THE NEED FOR A NEW APPROACH TO SECURITY

Since the end of the Cold War, security for the majority of states has increased, while security for many of the world's people has declined.

The end of the superpower confrontation has meant greater security for states touched by that rivalry. Yet during this decade we have seen new civil conflicts, large-scale atrocities, and even genocide. Globalization has brought many benefits, but it has also meant a rise in violent crime, drug trade, terrorism, disease, and environmental deterioration. It clearly does not follow that when states are secure, people are secure.

Security between states remains a necessary condition for the security of people. The principal objective of national security is the protection of territorial integrity and political sovereignty from external aggression. While declining in frequency, the threat of inter-state war has not vanished, and the potential consequences of such a war should not be underestimated. Technological advances and proliferation of weaponry mean that future wars between states will exact a horrific toll on civilians. At the same time national security is insufficient to guarantee people's security.

A growing number of armed conflicts are being fought within, rather than between, states. The warring factions in these civil wars are often irregular forces with loose chains of command, frequently divided along ethnic or religious lines. Small arms are the weapon of choice and non-combatants account for eight out of ten casualties. Once considered merely "collateral damage," civilians are being thrust into the epicentre of contemporary war.

Greater exposure to violence is not limited to situations of armed conflict. It is also directly related to the erosion of state control. This decline is most evident in failed states, where governments are simply incapable of providing even basic security for people threatened by warlords and bandits. Challenges to state control can also be seen in the expansion of organized crime, drug trafficking, and the growth of private security forces.

Security for people is also affected by a broadening range of transnational threats. In an increasingly interdependent world we routinely experience mutual, if unequal vulnerability. Opening markets, increased World trade, and a revolution in communications are highly beneficial, but they have also made borders more porous to a wide range of threats. A growing number of hazards to people's health — from long-range transmission of pollutants to infectious diseases — are global phenomena in both their origins and their effects. Economic shocks in one part of the world can lead rapidly to crises in another, with devastating implications for the security of the most vulnerable.

These broad trends are clearly not new to the 1990s; each has been intensifying over recent decades. During 40 years of superpower rivalry, however, nuclear confrontation and ideological competition dominated the security agenda. As a result, these other challenges have only been widely acknowledged in more recent years. Outside the confines of the Cold War, the opportunity exists to develop a comprehensive and systematic approach to enhancing the security of people.

II. BACKGROUND TO THE CONCEPT OF HUMAN SECURITY

While the term "human security" may be of recent origin, the ideas that underpin the concept are far from new. For more than a century — at least since the founding of the International Committee of the Red Cross in the 1860s — a doctrine based on the security of people has been gathering momentum. Core elements of this doctrine were formalized in the 1940s in the UN Charter, the Universal Declaration of Human Rights, and the Geneva Conventions.

The specific phrase "human security" is most commonly associated with the 1994 UNDP *Human Development Report,* an attempt to capture the post-Cold War peace dividend and redirect those resources towards the development agenda. The definition advanced in the report was extremely ambitious. Human security was defined as the summation of seven distinct dimensions of security: economic, food, health, environmental, personal, community, and political. By focusing on people and highlighting non-traditional threats, the UNDP made an important contribution to post-Cold War thinking about security.

The very breadth of the UNDP approach, however, made it unwieldy as a policy instrument. Equally important, in emphasizing the threats associated with underdevelopment, the Report largely ignored the continuing human insecurity resulting from violent conflict. Yet by the UNDP's own criteria, human insecurity is greatest during war. Of the 25 countries at the bottom of the 1998 Human Development Index, more than half are suffering the direct or indirect effects of violent conflict. The UNDP definition of human security was proposed as a key concept during the preparatory stages of the 1995 Copenhagen Summit on Social Development. But it was rejected during the Summit and has not been widely used thereafter.

Over the past two years the concept of human security has increasingly centred on the human costs of violent conflict. Here, practice has led theory. Two initiatives in particular, the campaign to ban landmines and the effort to create an International Criminal Court, have demonstrated the potential of a people-centred approach to security. Anti-personnel landmines are a clear example of a threat to the security of people. While contributing only marginally to the security of states, mines have a devastating impact on ordinary people attempting to rebuild their lives in war-torn societies. The International Criminal Court establishes a mechanism to hold individuals accountable for war crimes and crimes against humanity, and holds the promise of preventing the future abuse of people by governments and other parties to conflicts. Both measures are practical, powerful applications of the concept of human security.

III. DEFINING HUMAN SECURITY — A SHIFT IN THE ANGLE OF VISION

In essence, human security means safety for people from both violent and nonviolent threats. It is a condition or state of being characterized by freedom from pervasive threats to people's rights, their safety, or even their lives. From a foreign policy perspective, human security is perhaps best understood as a shift in perspective or orientation. It is an alternative way of seeing the world, taking people as its point of reference, rather than focusing exclusively on the security of territory or governments. Like other security concepts — national security, economic security, food security — it is about protection. Human security entails taking preventive measures to reduce vulnerability and minimize risk, and taking remedial action where prevention fails.

The range of potential threats to human security should not be narrowly conceived. While the safety of people is obviously at grave risk in situations of armed conflict, a human security approach is not simply synonymous with humanitarian action. It highlights the need to address the root causes of insecurity and to help ensure people's future safety. There are also human security dimensions to a broad range of challenges, such as gross violations of human rights, environmental degradation, terrorism, transnational organized crime, gender based violence, infectious diseases, and natural disasters. The widespread social unrest and violence that often accompanies economic crises demonstrates that there are clear economic underpinnings to human security. The litmus test for determining if it is useful to frame an issue in human security terms is the degree to which the safety of people is at risk.

IV. A NECESSARY COMPLEMENT TO NATIONAL SECURITY

Human security does not supplant national security. A human security perspective asserts that the security of the state is not an end in itself. Rather, it is a means of ensuring security for its people. In this context, state security and human security are mutually supportive. Building an effective, democratic state that values its own people and protects minorities is a central strategy for promoting human security. At the same time, improving the human security of its people strengthens the legitimacy, stability, and security of a state. When states are externally aggressive, internally repressive, or too weak to govern effectively, they threaten the security of people. Where human security exists as a fact rather than an aspiration, these conditions can be attributed in large measure to the effective governance of states.

From a human security perspective, concern for the safety of people extends beyond borders. Although broadening the focus of security policy beyond citizens may at first appear to be a radical shift, it is a logical extension of current approaches to international peace and security. The Charter of the United Nations embodies the view that security cannot be achieved by a single state in isolation. The phrase "international peace and security" implies that the security of one state depends on the security of other states. A human security perspective builds on this logic by noting that the security of people in one part of the world depends on the security of people elsewhere. A secure and stable world order is built both from the top down, and from the bottom up. The security of states, and the maintenance of international peace and security, are ultimately constructed on the foundation of people who are secure.

V. AN ENABLING ENVIRONMENT FOR HUMAN DEVELOPMENT

The two concepts of human security and human development are mutually reinforcing, though distinct. The UNDP report itself, while proposing a very broad definition of human security, was clear that the two concepts were not synonymous. Together, human security and human development address the twin objectives of freedom from fear and freedom from want.

People's freedom to act can be constrained by both fears; and for the poorest and most vulnerable members of society, poverty and insecurity are linked in a vicious circle. Breaking that cycle requires measures to promote human development, through access to reliable employment, education, and social services. But it also requires measures to promote human security by offering protection from crime and political violence, respect for human rights including political rights, and equitable access to justice. The absence of such guarantees of human security constitutes a powerful barrier to human development. Regardless of levels of income, if people lack confidence in society's ability to protect them, they will have little incentive to invest in the future. A development optic highlights this positive dimension of the concept – namely the opportunity that human security provides to liberate the potential for growth.

Human security provides an enabling environment for human development. Where violence or the threat of violence makes meaningful progress on the developmental agenda impractical, enhancing safety for people is a prerequisite. Promoting human development can also be an important strategy for furthering human security. By addressing inequalities which are often root causes of violent conflict, by strengthening governance structures, and by providing humanitarian assistance, development assistance complements political, legal, and military initiatives in enhancing human security.

VI. FOREIGN POLICY IMPLICATIONS

Human security provides a template to assess policy and practice for their effects on the safety of people. From a foreign policy perspective, there are a number of key consequences.

First, when conditions warrant, vigorous action in defence of human security objectives will be necessary. Ensuring human security can involve the use of coercive measures, including sanctions and military force, as in Bosnia and Kosovo.

At the same time, the human costs of strategies for promoting state and international security must be explicitly assessed. This line of argument dates back to the 19th-century movement to ban the use of inhumane weapons, but, as we have seen in the recent campaign to ban anti-personnel landmines, it continues to have contemporary relevance. Other security policies, such as comprehensive economic sanctions, should take into account the impact on innocent people.

Third, security policies must be integrated much more closely with strategies for promoting human rights, democracy, and development. Human rights, humanitarian, and refugee law provide the normative framework on which a human security approach is based. Development strategies offer broadly based means of addressing many long-term human security challenges. One of the dividends of adopting a human security approach is that it further elaborates a people-centred foreign policy.

Fourth, due to the complexity of contemporary challenges to the security of people, effective interventions involve a diverse range of actors including states, multilateral organizations, and civil society groups. As the challenges to the safety of people are transnational, effective responses can only be achieved through multilateral cooperation. This is evident in the array of new international instruments developed in the last decade to address transnational organized crime, drug trafficking, terrorism, and environmental degradation. These threats link the interest of citizens in countries which enjoy a high level of human security with the interests of people in much poorer nations, who face a wider range of threats to their safety.

Fifth, effective responses will depend on greater operational coordination. For example, successful peace-support operations are multi-dimensional, and depend on the close coordination of political negotiators, peacekeepers, human rights monitors, and humanitarian aid personnel among others. Furthermore, development agencies are now engaged in promoting security sector reform, while security organizations have helped channel development assistance in post-conflict countries. Managing these overlapping mandates and objectives is one of the principal challenges for a human security agenda.

Sixth, civil society organizations are seeking greater opportunity and greater responsibility in promoting human security. In many cases, non-governmental organizations have proven to be extremely effective partners in advocating the security of people. They are also important providers of assistance and protection to those in need of greater security. At the same time, the business sector, potentially a key actor in enhancing human security, could be more effectively engaged.

VII. TOWARDS AN AGENDA FOR HUMAN SECURITY

Human security offers a new angle of vision and a broad template for evaluating policies. It also yields a concrete set of foreign policy initiatives. Focusing systematically on the safety of people highlights the need for more targeted attention to key issues that are not yet adequately addressed by the international community. Current examples of such gaps include the unchecked proliferation of small arms and the inadequate protection of children in circumstances of armed conflict.

Human security is enhanced by reducing people's vulnerability and by preventing the conditions which make them vulnerable in the first place. Assisting people in highly insecure situations, particularly in the midst of violent conflict, is a central objective of the human security agenda. Refugees have long been the focus of international attention. The same focus on vulnerability highlights the immediate needs of the internally displaced, and demobilized combatants. At the same time, a human security agenda must go beyond humanitarian action, by addressing the sources of people's insecurity. Building human security, therefore, requires both short-term humanitarian action and longer-term strategies for building peace and promoting sustainable development.

Two fundamental strategies for enhancing human security are strengthening legal norms and building the capacity to enforce them. New standards are needed in areas such as restricting the illegal trafficking in small arms, banning the use and recruitment of children as soldiers, prohibiting exploitative child labour, providing greater protection for the internally displaced, and ensuring the applicability of legal standards to non-state actors and to violence below the threshold of armed conflict.

There is little point in defining new norms and rights, however, if societies have no capacity to enforce existing norms or to protect already recognized rights. For this reason, improving democratic governance within states is a central strategy for advancing human security. So is strengthening the capacity of international organizations, in particular the United Nations, to deliver on their agreed mandates. Yet the range of protection tasks assigned to UN-mandated operations is increasing, at the same time as the UN's capacity to organize and fund such operations is dwindling.

Building institutional capacity without strengthening respect for norms would undermine a human-centred standard of security. Strengthening norms without building the capacity to protect them only invites disillusionment with the possibility of constraining power by the rule of law. Both are essential strategies if we are to move towards a more humane world.

✗ **NO**

Against Crusading: The Ethics of Human Security and Canadian Foreign Policy
WILLIAM W. BAIN

Recent efforts to include the ethic of human security as one of the core objectives of Canada's foreign policy lack the necessary coherence required to be a useful guide for the conduct of statecraft. Canada's foreign policy seeks to achieve three key objectives: (1) to promote prosperity and employment; (2) to protect security within a stable international framework; and (3) to protect abroad Canadian values and culture (Canada 1995: 10). In the practice of statecraft these objectives are not always reconcilable and, consequently, they sometimes – though not always – demand conflicting action. Ottawa has traditionally emphasized its economic and security interests above other goals, even though Canada has been at the forefront of the effort to promote the global observance of human rights, the rule of law, and good governance. More recently, the discourse of Canada's foreign policy, especially as it is articulated by Foreign Minister Lloyd Axworthy, may indicate a significant change in this order of priorities and in the moral substance of Canada's interests abroad. But the practical implementation of Ottawa's emerging doctrine of human security may impede efforts to secure other equally fundamental, but conflicting, values and it may commit Canada to principles that it is not entirely prepared to fulfill.[1]

The ethic of human security challenges and possibly undermines the moral foundation of international society as it has existed for nearly four hundred years. Exponents of human security reject the sovereign state as the paramount moral community of international society; they do not believe that these communities ought to be the principal referents of security. Rather, the ethic of human security accords moral priority to the security of individual human beings. Therefore, the difference between human security and our traditional understanding of national security presupposes an important change in the moral character of world politics; indeed, it may foreshadow a change which is nothing short of revolutionary. By investigating the ethical foundation of Ottawa's nascent doctrine of human security we can gain important insight into Canada's basic values and how these values impact its foreign policy and sense of purpose in world politics. It will become evident as a result of this investigation that Canada's doctrine of human security emphasizes certain norms which are often at odds with the prevailing norms of present-day international society, norms which also constitute an important part of Canada's traditional foreign policy objectives. Moreover, this doctrine may engender excessive moralism; that is, a tendency to encounter the world as if Canada were engaged in a moral crusade. Indeed, a foreign policy which is guided, at least in part, by a universal doctrine such as human security is difficult to reconcile with the practical realities and fundamentally pluralist nature of inter-national society. In its effort to include human security as one of its core foreign policy objectives, Ottawa must recognize the circumstantial character of world pol-itics and how this contingent condition affects the achievement of certain values. Recognizing this state of affairs entails relying upon prudent judgment, rather than indiscriminate universal principles, to guide Canada's foreign relations. An approach which carefully weighs competing and conflicting moral claims permits the greatest opportunity to criticize others for unjust practices, to stand in soli-darity with those resisting oppression, to refrain from recklessly imposing our values on others, and to achieve the key objectives of Canada's foreign policy.

ALTERNATIVE ETHICS OF SECURITY IN THE POST-COLD WAR WORLD

The tremendous change brought about by the end of the cold war compelled scholars and practitioners of world politics to question and to reconceptualize the meaning of security. It is often said that focusing upon nuclear deterrence, mili-tary balances, zero-sum games, competing power blocs, and interstate relations is overly narrow or even out of date in the post-cold war world.[2] Replacing this cold war security discourse are several discourses which centre upon issues such as the environment, equity, human potential, multilateralism, religion, ethnicity, gender, identity, and cooperative and common security. Following from this ongoing process of critical reflection and redefinition is an approach which not only rejects the traditional cold war understanding of security, but proposes instead an ambi-tious set of principles that, if implemented fully, would signal a revolutionary change in the practice of diplomacy.

Given the lofty goals proposed by the advocates of human security, we might be inclined to view the concept as mere rhetoric or we might be tempted to dismiss it as unrealizable, albeit well-intentioned, ideals in much the same way as the aspira-tions of the inter-war idealists were disparaged by those who subscribed to a more "realistic" approach to world politics.[3] But human security is an idea which is much larger than Minister Axworthy and his aspirations for Canada's foreign policy. It is an idea which enjoys considerable support throughout the world. And the discourse of world politics indicates clearly that the idea of human security amounts to a great deal more expedient, idealistic, naïve, and foolish rhetoric. For example, the principles and imperatives of human security command a prominent place in the activities of the UN, they are at the centre of the Report of the Commission on Global Governance, and they are a pervasive theme in the discourse of global civil society.[4] Similarly, the purpose and value of global initiatives such as the Ottawa Treaty, which prohibits anti-personnel mines, the proposed International Criminal Court, efforts to define the rights of the child, and attempts to confront the global problem posed by the spread of AIDS are all intelligible and are frequently justified in the discourse of human security. These developments indicate that, far from being more rhetoric, at least some people associate human security with a set of ends which are good in themselves; that is, their enjoyment needs no further justification. And while advocates of human security often differ in areas of emphasis and in matters of prescription, they share a common belief that human security is a better way to engage the complexities of an emerging world that is challenged less by interstate threats than by threats which are contained within states or which transcend the jurisdiction of particular states.

The ethical foundation of human security differs in several important ways from the ethic of national security which has heretofore dominated both theoretical and practical understanding of security. The ethic of human security incorporates into the security discourse a cluster of values which broadens significantly the scope and substance of the word "security." In articulating the idea of human security, Minister Axworthy proposes an understanding which recognizes the elementary importance of "human rights and fundamental freedoms, the right to live in dignity, with adequate food, shelter, health and education services, and under the rule of law and good governance" (Axworthy 1996c: 3–7). In addition to these values, he suggests that human security also embraces a commitment to democratic development and ensuring quality of life and equity for all human beings. Collectively, these values are to form an integral part of a Canadian foreign policy, which is designed to confront the post-cold war world.

Human security has gained currency in large part because of the dilemmas presented by the practice of national security.[5] National security is concerned with the safety of particular political communities: sovereign states. Individual security is assumed to follow from national security by virtue of our membership in a particular political community. Thus, national security presupposes the assumption that states are worth preserving; that is, sovereign states are thought of as moral communities in their own right. In fact, preserving the fortunes of the political community is such a deeply held norm that national security is one of the few norms that, in certain circumstances, may justifiably pre-empt other fundamental norms of international society. But the practice of world politics reveals a more troubling side of national security: some states do not provide adequate security for their citizens and they fail to deliver the most basic social goods. Failed or unjust states, such as Somalia, Liberia, Rwanda, and the former Yugoslavia, are typically bastions of tyranny, sources of great misery, and are often themselves the most immediate threat to their citizens' security. In states such as these, the term "national security" is nothing more than a misnomer; it refers to a juridical entity rather than a sociological nation. Ironically, the constitutive norms of international society sustain this condition in a rather perverse way: the rights of sovereign equality, nonintervention, and political independence help to ensure the survival of what are otherwise unviable states.[6]

That some states do not provide adequate security for their citizens, yet manage to ensure their own survival, casts doubt upon their worth as moral communities and upon the doctrine of national security.

Recognizing the principal difficulty of national security — individual security does not necessarily follow from the security of the political community — underscores the key normative difference between national security and human security. Whereas national security postulates states as the principal recipients of security, human security confers moral priority on the security of individual human beings. Human security, or what Minister Axworthy calls "real" security, is concerned foremost with the protection of the individual (1996b: 2). An ethic of human security does not permit us to remain detached from, or indifferent to, human suffering on account of deeply ingrained injunctions against interfering in the domestic affairs of sovereign states. For Canada, this means that a commitment to human security requires a "broadening of the focus of security policy from its narrow orientation of managing state-to-state relationships, to one that recognizes the importance of the individual and society for our shared security" (Canada 1995: 25). Thus, in a departure from the classical ethic of national security, human security discloses a cosmopolitan ethic which posits the community of humankind as resting above the society of states.

IS HUMAN SECURITY A SOUND FOUNDATION FOR CANADA'S FOREIGN POLICY?

A tension exists between the practical implications of a foreign policy which seeks to secure the values of human security and the prevailing moral disposition of the society of states. The moral substance of international society is disclosed in a constellation of constitutive norms which reflect the common values and interests of its constituent members. These norms are not given by any philosophical treatise; they are not discovered by power of human reason; and they are not theorized by the spectators of world politics in relation to how they think the world ought to be. The norms of international society are products of human activity: they are the distillation of centuries of diplomatic, military, economic, and other international practice. And because these norms are artifacts of human experience they are historically situated: over time they have varied in their incarnation, strength, importance, and interpretation.

Although international society is embedded in, and is a product of, history, it should not be confused with any purposive enterprise or any evolutionary view of human progress: international society is not justified by the achievement of specific ends, such as welfare or human dignity. The definite mark of international society "[lies] not in the shared purposes of its members states ... but in their acknowledgement of formal rules of mutual accommodation"(Nardin 1983: 309). The constitutive norms of international society represent moral injunctions which circumscribe the exercise of power. And by imposing limits on the exercise of power these norms stand opposed to certain policies, even when they represent the most expedient way of fulfilling the requirements of the national interest. The constitutive norms of international society restrict the means that states may employ to obtain national advantage and the ends for which states may aspire (Morgenthau 1948: 80). Thus, in a key and basic way, the norms of international society provide the basis for mutual coexistence; collectively they admit that there are different conceptions of the "good life." In recognizing different conceptions of the good life, international society affords individual states the opportunity to pursue their own notion of the good life without being subject to interference on the part of others. Located at the heart of this notion of society is an ethic of pluralism: "the conception that there are many different ends that men may seek and still be fully rational, fully men, capable of understanding each other" (Berlin 1991: 11).

To argue that international society is fundamentally pluralist in its organization is not to say that the theory of pluralism is the only basis of human organization and association. For example, medieval Europeans ordered themselves on the principle that all European states constituted the *respublica Christiana* — the Christian Commonwealth of Europe. In this mode of association, human relations are intelligible in one universal pattern, a pattern which determines the place of all persons, their rights and duties, their function and purpose. It is a pattern which presupposes the acceptance of a singular common good, or common good life, to be shared by all. And while there is no logical or empirical reason not to believe that a universal association or commonwealth could again exist in contemporary world politics, the history and discourse of world politics suggest that large groups of human beings do not believe that they live in such a world today. In terms of foreign policy, we continuously debate the most profitable course of action; we complain that we give too much or not enough; we blame others for failing to fulfill their obligations and they, in turn, respond that they have done so; and in our relations with others, we are concerned to answer the question: to whom do we owe our primary obligations — to members of our own political community or to those persons who are not members?

These moral conversations may indicate that many of us do not properly understand the common good and purpose of our world or that perhaps we know too little or that we are too feeble-minded to comprehend its significance. These conversations may indicate also that the ends and purposes of human beings are many; that they speak to ends that are of the category "good" but which do not necessarily entail one another and are not reconcilable in one systematic, uniform, and all-encompassing pattern.[7] We find that these different ends of human life may "come into conflict, and lead to clashes between societies, parties, individuals, and not least within individuals themselves; and furthermore that the ends of one age and county differ widely from those of other times and other outlooks" (Berlin 1969: 102). And because the ends of human beings are many, the world in which they live is not intelligible in the context of a single moral theory. Rather we live in a world in which moral voices and perspectives coexist and sometimes conflict; over the course of history they advance and retreat; and we discern and evaluate their importance in the context of varying degrees of strength or weakness. Thus, it might be the case our present world discloses some degree of universalism and that our world may once again be ordered on principles of a universalist ethic. However, it seems as if the ethic of pluralism, at least for the moment, best describes the dominant ethic of international society.

It is precisely this ethic of pluralism which potentially conflicts with human security. Human security does not allow full expression of different conceptions of the good life: it does not recognize that there are ways of organizing our lives which are both different and moral. The doctrine of human security imposes upon all a universal good life that is determined by values whose meaning is derived mainly from Canadian and western experience and which rest above the diversity and particularisms of individual political communities. Thus, a Canadian foreign policy based upon the doctrine of human security would not stop at securing the moral and material interests of Canadians; rather it would transcend this proper purpose in an attempt to secure the interests of humanity in its entirety. This universal mission is revealed inasmuch as "Canadians hold deeply that we must pursue our values internationally. They want to promote them for their own sake, but they also understand that our values and rights will not be safeguarded if they are not enshrined throughout the international environment" (Canada 1995: 34). And in asserting that Canadians speak with one moral voice, Minister Axworthy suggests that "[i]t is critical that this voice be heard internationally as it both validates our worth as a country and promotes the value of human dignity around the globe" (1996a: 1). But in a society of states which values pluralism, this view wrongly identifies the aspirations of Canada with the aspirations of the world.

This excessive moralism which may infect Canada's sense of purpose in world politics is an unsuitable foundation for a nation's foreign policy. For a foreign policy of this type does not acknowledge the circumstantial nature of human relations; and it is indicative of an attitude or mood which does not differ significantly from the indiscriminate cold war injunction, "stop communism," which led the US to oppose all communist regimes everywhere without assessing their origin or their specific character. And it was the pursuit of this (indiscriminate) universalist mission that entangled the US in the catastrophe of Vietnam. Like all realms of human relations, world politics is marked by contingency, chance, change, and unpredictability. But Minister Axworthy's notion of human security takes scant notice of this conditional state of affairs. Rather it is imbued with inchoate references and ill-considered commitments to a multitude of abstract ideals and universal principles of which the implications have not been sufficiently thought through. A foreign policy which endorses abstract principles before appraising the circumstances which impose upon the statesperson, is bound to fail. The actions of the stateperson are bound by practical limits: "human activity, with whatever it may be concerned, enjoys a circumscribed range of movement. The limits which define this range are historic, that is to say, they are themselves the product of human activity" (Oakeshott 1996: 116). And that is why words such as "possibility," "necessity," "requirement," "likely," "compromise," "restraint," and "contingent," constitute the substance of the vocabulary of statecraft. But abstract principles are divorced from the practical world of statecraft. They are ahistorical, they take no notice of human experience, they are not susceptible to limitation, they are ignorant of circumstance, and they are not amenable to compromise. Indeed, human conduct which is guided wholly by abstract principle has difficulty recognizing that the achievement of one end may, in some circumstances, conflict with another desirable end (Mill 1988: 138).

The danger of permitting abstract principle to guide foreign policy is evident, for example, in Canada's human rights policy. Human rights are a central part of Canada's foreign policy agenda: they are accorded the status of a "threshold" issue which colours significantly Canada's international relations. Indeed, Minister Axworthy submits that "[r]espect for human rights is a critical component of the Canadian identity and therefore must play an important role in our foreign policy agenda" (1997: 1). But in these pronouncements it is difficult to find any moral reason to qualify how Canada's human rights policy is to be implemented. There is acknowledgement that Canada's "ability to effect change can be limited," and that its efforts are sometimes construed as unjustified interference in the internal affairs of others (Axworthy 1997: 1–7). There is also recognition that Canada's ability to force change is limited by a paucity of economic leverage and international clout. However, these conditions speak to instrumental problems: they refer only to limitations of the means with which to achieve the end and not to the achievement of the end itself. Canada's foreign policy establishment, in its commitment to secure human rights, is noticeably silent on questions concerning moral conflict: it does not acknowledge that fundamental values sometimes clash. And it seems as if Canada's doctrine of human security does not recognize that the pursuit of human rights may sometimes impede securing other fundamental values; that obtaining the good of human rights may entail a loss of order, or of security, or some other value; and that an occasion may arise when human rights ought to be subordinated to the achievement of other fundamental values.

In the absence of these qualifications, Canada's stated human rights objectives are not the result of careful deliberation which weighs interest, power, obligations, rights, competing claims, and the circumstances in which they are embedded. A human rights policy which is guided wholly by abstract principle quickly transforms itself into a doctrine of universal human salvation. And it is in this spirit of universal salvation that Canada charts a course which asserts that: "it is important that we pursue the issue of human rights internationally. It is important as an extension of our own beliefs" (Axworthy 1997: 1). A foreign policy of this type is less about securing Canadian interests than it is about validation and affirmation of national righteousness. This is when the conduct of foreign policy ceases to be a useful instrument of statecraft: it becomes the servant of justice for the sake of doing justice.

A foreign policy which seeks justice, but is unaware of circumstance, rival claims, and conflicting obligations, can see no diversity or difference in human experience. Universalism and uniformity are all that is intelligible in a mission to extend our beliefs and to validate our worth as a country. It is at this point that we seek to repress difference, not because difference contributes to disorder or insecurity, but because it is identified with error. Thus, the chief duty of government and the purpose of foreign policy becomes one of suppressing as error all opposition to the enterprise of securing the greater justice of human rights for all.[8] And in its missions to secure a particular notion of justice for all of humanity, Canada runs the risk of inflicting injustice of a greater magnitude than that which it seeks to remedy. Instead of recognizing the circumstantial nature of world politics and the diversity of human existence, Canada seems intent on pursuing a universalist mission in an attempt to perfect the inherently imperfect nature of the human condition.

But we must be quick to note that recognizing and celebrating diversity does not require us to remain silent in the face of injustice. We are not required to accept an extreme relativist position which precludes all communication with members of other cultures and civilizations. We are not muted prisoners of our own cultural practices, unable to understand the practices of others. Because human beings are moral creatures, we are able to comprehend injustice, even when it occurs in circumstances quite different from our own. And because we are able to communicate with members of other cultures, we are able to criticize unjust practices and stand in solidarity with other human beings against injustice. Canada ought to criticize oppressive governments and it ought to stand in solidarity with those who are resisting oppression.

But in criticizing others for human rights abuses, for example, Canada must remain acutely aware of how this criticism affects the realization of other fundamental values, both for Canadians and for others. Occasion may arise when the achievement of order, security, or peace may be threatened by an overly progressive human rights policy. A foreign policy which is conscious of circumstances is aware of something which foreign policy guided by abstract principle is not: the norms of international society sometimes demand conflicting action. There is no predetermined way to disentangle these conflicting obligations. Good and right in international society are not derived from any particular norm such as order or justice. We can comprehend no universal and common chief good for which all the world's statespersons strive to secure. And we cannot resolve conflicting moral demands by appealing to a single authoritative norm; we cannot discern a definite and permanent hierarchy in which the norms of international society are arranged; nor is it evident that these norms are equal to each other at all times and in all circumstances. The norms of international society are an eclectic group which merely reflect the contradictions, tensions, and imperfections of the creatures that created them.

RECONCILING HUMAN SECURITY AND CANADA'S FOREIGN POLICY OBJECTIVES

The moral dilemmas and conflicts of world politics are not resolved in the abstract, but in the practice of statecraft. In the practice of world politics, the circumstances of our world, at times, oblige some norms to yield to others. The practice of statecraft suggests that, in extreme cases, the rights of sovereign states may be abrogated or suspended when it is in the interest of international society as a whole. Likewise, when human rights injunctions clash with the imperatives of national security, human rights usually lose. And in the absence of an authoritative norm to guide the practice of statecraft, the statesperson must rely upon a particular type of judgment, a type of judgment we call prudence, to resolve conflicting obligations.

Prudence, which is often described as the supreme virtue of politics, is a species of practical wisdom: it discloses a mode of common sense which is the antithesis of abstract intellectualism. Prudence is the name we give to that type of wisdom which is associated with careful consideration, deliberation, restraint, and foresight. It is a type of sound judgment which guides the statesperson through the difficult choices and which makes some sense of conflicting demands and obligations. And through all the complexity, mystery, and uncertainty of our world, it is the prudent statesperson who is able to choose the best course of action under these trying conditions. Thus, the prudent statesperson demonstrates the ability to make the right decision at the right time – the ability to solve real problems, to get things done, to select the most profitable course among the many possible paths on which to travel. However, prudence ought not to be mistaken for ordinary common sense; rather it is a kind of wisdom with which few are endowed. For prudence is not a technical subject: we do not become prudent simply by reading philosophy or by observing world politics from the sidelines. And prudence is not learned mechanically or by rote. The practice of statecraft, like human conduct in general, is indeterminate, uncertain, and susceptible to chance, and it is quite unlike exact sciences which require no deliberation (Aristotle 1963: 49). Therefore, it is not possible to stipulate in advance a prudential principle, apply it to our subject, and expect successful political action to follow. Rather, prudence is imparted and learned by way of practice and experience.

The prudent statesperson must consider a multitude of parties and circumstances in the conduct of statecraft. Prudential statecraft refuses to judge and solve problems in the abstract. In contrast, abstract principles know only absolute truth: they cannot discriminate between the circumstances which distinguish a problem's moral significance. The prudent statesperson is obligated to attend first to the interests of his/her own citizens – those to whom he/she is directly accountable. Performing this task is the chief duty of the statesperson. And in a democratic society, fulfilling this duty may sometimes require that the statesperson ignore popular opinion. But the statesperson's work is not finished after the requirements of the national interest have been satisfied. He/she must also consider the legitimate interests of other claimants and he/she must contemplate the interests of innocent third parties before deciding upon a particular course of action. Indeed, considering the legitimate interests of others is a basic and necessary ingredient of successful foreign policy; for a "nation that is too preoccupied with its own interests is bound to define those interests too narrowly. It will do this because it will fail to consider those of its interests which are *bound up in a web of mutual interests* with other nations. In short, the national interest when conceived only from the standpoint of the self-interest of the nation is bound to be defined too narrowly and therefore to be self-defeating [italics in original]"(Niebuhr, 1958: 40). The virtuous statesperson must assess all legitimate claims and decide which one, under the circumstances, appears to be closest to the truth. The prudent statesperson, in carefully weighing different claims and circumstances, adjusts to the contours of the problem (Vico 1965: 34). In contrast, the moral crusader applies to the problem a universal principle in the effort to obtain a solution.

It is not yet clear how Ottawa intends to reconcile its doctrine of human security with the circumstantial nature of human relations; for there appears to be little allowance for contingency, unpredictability, accident, and chance. Human security is a universalist doctrine which takes little notice of the pluralist nature of international society; instead it posits a community of humankind above the society of states. And this cosmopolitan commitment supposes that Canadian values are those of the entire world without ascertaining if this sense of right is a truth held by others. As such, human security is an unsuitable objective of Canada's foreign policy. However, this does not mean that Canada must abandon its commitment to issues concerning human rights, democracy, the rule of law, and good governance. Canada may legitimately, and ought to, criticize Indonesia's human rights record in East Timor, China's suppression of pro-democracy activists, child labour practices in India, military rule in Burma, war crimes in Yugoslavia, and genocide in Rwanda.

But caution must be exercised while expressing opposition to the practices of others. Canada must avoid undermining other constitutive norms of international society while pursuing these ends. This means that Canada may recognize injustice and may express solidarity with those who are resisting oppression; that is to say, that we can share with them an opposition to injustice and therefore "march in their parade" (Walzer 1994). This also means that purposive efforts to remedy injustice may be, in some cases, better left to those directly engaged. When we move from a position of moral solidarity to one of direct engagement, we inevitably retreat into our own particular morality (Walzer 1994). It is at this point that universalist schemes of human salvation manifest themselves and begin to erode the pluralist nature of international society. A prudent foreign policy allows us to "march in the parade" without indiscriminately imposing our values on others. A policy which abstains from moral crusading is important both for the moral development of others and for Canada. Canada has demonstrated that it is not always prepared to undertake the responsibilities that the ethic of human security entails. For example, when faced with choosing between human rights and economic interests, Canada has often demonstrated a willingness to secure the latter at the expense of the former. We see in the past that Canada has softened its human rights agenda in order to advance its economic interests abroad.[9] But in the absence of a willingness to consistently fulfill the requirements of a policy of human security, and in the absence of a forthright acknowledgment that the fundamental objectives of Canadian foreign policy may sometimes conflict, any ongoing commitment to a policy sustained by self-righteousness invites charges of hypocrisy and threatens to fray the moral fabric that is distinctly Canadian.

Surely this advice will meet profound dissatisfaction, and even indignation, from the prophets of human security and other similar universalist doctrines. They will criticize the prudent course as being conservative and slow to work. They are right. But Canada ought to be most reticent and cautious before it begins to subvert international society as it presently exists. International society has provided the basis for some countries – Canada among them – to strive for and achieve some notion of the good life. And enshrined in international society is an ethic that permits Canada to pursue an understanding of the good life which is distinctly its own. Thus, Canada ought to pursue its foreign policy objectives in such a way that it preserves and, indeed, sustains the pluralism of international society. However, a Canadian foreign policy based upon the principles of human security would not be favourably disposed toward securing this good. Rather it would likely suffer from an unacknowledged contradiction which may hinder the practical conduct of statecraft by infusing Canada's international relations with excessive moralism. And insofar as Ottawa fails to acknowledge that Canada's foreign policy objectives may sometimes demand conflicting action, it invites allegations of hypocrisy which threaten to undermine Canada's credibility, both at home and abroad.

The potential danger of a foreign policy which does not acknowledge that conflicting demands may confound the best attempts to secure basic values is evident in recent events concerning Canada and the Asia-Pacific region. Canada's efforts to increase its economic presence in the region are often met with strident criticism because of Indonesia's human rights record in East Timor, China's treatment of pro-democracy activists, and child labor practices in India and Pakistan. Likewise, attempts to pursue Canada's human rights agenda regularly provoke attitudes of apathy and skepticism at home, and accusations of cultural imperialism from abroad. Canada's leaders are likely to evoke feelings of uncertainty and disbelief when, on the one hand, Minister Axworthy openly questions the value and relevancy of APEC because it does not address human rights issues and, on the other hand, Prime Minister Jean Chrétien emphasizes that APEC "means business" by indicating that it is primarily a free-trade group in which human rights concerns are to be raised "on the margin in private bilateral talks" (Sallot 1997). And we are apt to encounter confusion when foreign policy statements are less about Canada's interests abroad than with concerns at home. Canada may do harm to its international reputation and credibility, and it may unnecessarily complicate its foreign relations, to the extent that human security "must play a important role in our foreign policy agenda" because it "validates our worth as a country" and affirms Canada's national identity. The inevitable contradictions and hypocrisies of a foreign policy which is not grounded in the substance of international affairs, but is directed toward fostering national unity or some other domestic concern, is likely to breed mistrust, doubt, and suspicion. Thus, we should not be surprised that demonstrators protesting the recent APEC summit in Vancouver accused Ottawa of putting "profits before people," "indulging murderers," and being "indifferent to human suffering." The anti-APEC protesters, in their anger, passion, and skepticism, are pointing to the principal difficulty of committing Canada to a policy of human security: Canada is not always prepared to achieve the ambitious set of ideals that human security entails.

In abandoning its moralist pretensions and in tempering its aspirations with regard to human security, Ottawa need not abandon its commitment to human rights, democracy, the rule of law, and good governance. Canada ought to pursue these objectives in such a way that the statesperson, after carefully deliberating over competing and conflicting moral claims, determines a course of action which is most appropriate given the particular circumstances that distinguish the problem. This means that we ought to pursue human rights, democracy, the rule of law, and good governance when the circumstances permit us to do so. It is this middle ground, that area between relativism which accords validity to all truth claims and a universalism which imposes one pattern of life on all, for which Canada's foreign policy ought to aim. This area is, admittedly, difficult to find; it is something which is constantly shifting: its boundaries are blurred and uncertain and its content is always open to change, challenge and revision. However, the substance of this middle ground is sufficiently stable so that we are able to speak of it in a meaningful way. The middle ground of which we speak is that area in which we secure the greatest possible amount of the many obtainable goods, but which does not permit injustice of a magnitude that would be rightly called intolerable. We ought to aim at achieving those goods which are associated with human security insofar as the circumstances permit us to do so; but in doing so, we ought to aim also at maintaining values such as political independence and noninterference — goods which are essential to the maintenance of the society of states. Thus, we see that the middle ground between relativism and universalism is an area whose procedural basis rests upon the virtue of compromise.

But in aiming for this middle ground, we ought to be forthright in acknowledging that occasions may arise when we ought not pursue certain policies for the sake of other fundamental values. Recognizing that fundamental values clash; that it may not be possible to secure all things considered to be good at all times and in all places; and that sometimes it is best to accept a state of affairs which does not satisfy all the requirements of justice, is only to realize that finding the middle ground is often difficult. And it is difficult to maintain ourselves in this area precisely because our values may clash and because our moral injunctions may demand conflicting action. That is why a foreign policy which is based upon prudential ethics does the greatest justice to Canada and to its neighbors. Thus, in the effort to secure these goods while, at the same time, preserving the good of pluralism, Canada's foreign policy toward Asia Pacific, and elsewhere, ought to be guided by the wisdom of Vico's learned sage, "who through all the uncertainties of human action keeps his eye steadily focused on eternal truth, manages to follow in a roundabout way whenever he cannot travel in a straight line so as to be as profitable as the nature of things permit" (Vico 1965: 35).

REFERENCES

Annan, Kofi (1998). *Annual Report of the Secretary-General on the Work of the Organization* The Fifty-Third Session of the General Assembly (New York: United Nations).

Aristotle (1963). *Ethics* John Warrington ed. & trans. (London: J.M. Dent and Sons).

Axworthy, Lloyd (1997). *Notes for an Address by the Honourable Lloyd Axworthy, Minister of Foreign Affairs, at the Consultations with Non-Governmental Organizations in Preparation for the 53rd Session of the United Nations Commission on Human Rights* (Ottawa: February 5).

_____ (1996a). *Notes for an Address by the Honourable Lloyd Axworthy, Minister of Foreign Affairs, at the Consultations with Non-Governmental Organizations in Preparation for the 52nd Session of the United Nations Commission on Human Rights* (Ottawa: February 13).

_____ (1996b). *Notes for an Address by the Honourable Lloyd Axworthy, Minister of Foreign Affairs, to the 52nd Session of the United Nations Commission on Human Rights* (Geneva, Switzerland: April 3).

_____ (1996c). *Notes for an Address by the Honourable Lloyd Axworthy, Minister of Foreign Affairs, to the 51st General Assembly of the United Nations* (New York, NY: September 24).

Baldwin, David (1997). "The Concept of Security" *Review of International Studies* 23: 1–26.

Berlin, Isaiah (1969). "Historical Inevitability" *Four Essays on Liberty* (Oxford: Oxford University Press).

_____ (1991). "The Pursuit of the Ideal" *The Crooked Timber of Humanity* Henry Hardy ed. (London: Fontana Press).

Canada (1995). *Canada in the World* (Ottawa: DFAIT).

Carr, E. H. (1946). *The Twenty Year Crisis: 1919–1939* (London: Macmillan).

Commission on Global Governance (1995). *Our Global Neighbourhood* (Oxford: Oxford University Press).

Gilles, David (1996). *Between Principle and Practice: Human Rights in North-South Relations* (Montreal: McGill-Queen's University Press).

Jackson, Robert H. (1990). *Quasi-States: Sovereignty, International Relations and the Third World* (Cambridge: Cambridge University Press).

_____ (1995). *Human Security in a World of States* Paper Presented at the Annual Conference of the International Studies Association (Toronto: March 18–22).

Krause, Keith and Michael Williams (1996). "Broadening the Agenda of Security Studies: Politics and Methods" *Mershon International Studies Review* 40: 229–54.

Lipschutz, Ronnie D. ed. (1995). *On Security* (New York: Columbia University Press).

Mill, John Stuart (1988). *The Logic of the Moral Sciences* (La Salle, IL: Open Court).

Morgenthau, Hans J. (1948). "The Twilight of International Morality" *Ethics* 58:2.

Nardin, Terry (1983). *Law, Morality, and the Relations of States* (Princeton: Princeton University Press).

Niebuhr, Reinhold (1958). "America's Moral and Spiritual Resource" in Earnest W. Lefever ed. *World Crisis and American Responsibility* (New York: Association Press).

Oakeshott, Michael (1996). *The Politics of Faith and the Politics of Scepticism* Timothy Fuller ed. (New Haven: Yale University Press).

Roberts, Adam and Benedict Kingsbury eds. (1993). *United Nations, Divided World: The UN's Role in International Relations* (Oxford: Clarendon Press).

Sallot, Jeff (1997). "Axworthy Warns APEC of Irrelevancy" *The Globe and Mail* (24 November): A1, A6.

Vico, Giambattista (1965). *On the Study Methods of Our Time* Elio Gianturco trans. (Indianapolis: Bobbs-Merrill Company, Inc.).

Waltzer, Michael (1994). *Thick and Thin: Moral Argument at Home and Abroad* (Notre Dame: University of Notre Dame Press).

NOTES

This essay was first presented at the Annual Meeting of the International Studies Association, Washington DC, February 16–20, 1999. The author would like to thank Barbara Arneil, Megan Gilgan, K.J. Holsti, Robert Jackson, Brian Job, Samuel LaSelva, Heather Owens, Hamish Telford, Mark Zacher, and the two anonymous reviewers for their helpful comments and suggestions.

1. The category "human rights," unless indicated otherwise, refers to the restrictive civil and political conception rather than the more permissive conception which includes economic, social, and cultural rights. The more inclusive category "fundamental values" refers to a cluster of issues such as peace, order, security, and justice.

2. For example see Lipschutz (1995); Krause and Williams (1996); and Baldwin (1997).

3. For example see Carr (1946).

4. For example see Roberts and Kingsbury (1993); Annan (1998); Commission on Global Governance (1995). It should be noted that global civil society, or transnational society, performs a very important role in promoting human security and shaping the content of national and international security discourse. But the importance and significance of this role does not indicate a parallel foreign policy which exists apart from state activity. Rather global civil society and states are part of the same process of foreign relations, although they serve different purposes and functions. For the purpose of this article it is most appropriate to focus upon states and the issues that

affect them because the ultimate authority to conduct foreign relations is endowed in states and it is states, in spite of role and influence of global civil society, who bear ultimate responsibility for the success or failure of foreign policy.

5. The following discussion on security is derived from and heavily influenced by Jackson (1990) and Jackson (1995).

6. For a detailed explication of this argument see Jackson (1990).

7. This discussion is derived from Berlin (1969).

8. This thought is derived from Oakeshott (1996: 60–64).

9. For example, see Gillies (1996).

POSTSCRIPT

It is worth noting that Canada has taken a lead role in promoting the human security agenda among other states. Following a bilateral meeting between Lloyd Axworthy and the foreign minister of Norway in 1998 to launch the idea, a larger forum was held that included foreign ministers from Austria, Chile, Ireland, Jordan, the Netherlands, Slovenia, South Africa, Switzerland, and Thailand.

Although Bain questions whether the concept of human security is in keeping with Canadian foreign policy traditions, one can certainly argue that Canada's promotion of the idea follows the country's traditional role as a middle power. Axworthy, a former political scientist and university professor, has long been an advocate of the notion of "soft power." According to this view, Canada's power in the international community lies not in its military might, but in its ability to promote powerful ideas. Canadian efforts to build an international coalition of "like-minded" states around humanitarian issues in the 1990s can be seen a perpetuation of Canada's traditional role as middle power.

In his critique of human security, Bain is fearful that Canada may pursue a moralistic and interventionist foreign policy. In examining cases where Canada has pursued human security as the goal, is there evidence that Canada has tried to impose its claims on other states?

It is worth noting that Bain also suggests that "abandoning its moralist pretensions and . . . tempering its aspirations" does not mean that Ottawa should "abandon its commitment to human rights, democracy, the rule of law, and good governance." But it should pursue these objectives only "when the circumstances permit us to do so." If Bain's advice had been taken during the past decade, how different would Canadian foreign policy be? What issues might Canadian foreign policymakers have chosen not to promote?

Suggested Additional Readings

Axworthy, Lloyd. "Human Security and Global Governance: Putting People First." *Global Governance* 7, no. 1 (January 2001): 19–23.

Hampson, Fen Osler, and Dean F. Oliver. "Pulpit Diplomacy: A Critical Assessment of the Axworthy Doctrine." *International Journal* 54, no. 3 (1998): 379–406.

Hampson, Fen Osler, et al. *Madness in the Multitude: Human Security and World Disorder.* Don Mills: Oxford University Press, 2002.

Jockel, Joe, and Joel Sokolsky. "Lloyd Axworthy's Legacy: Human Security and the Rescue of Canadian Defence Policy." *International Journal* 56, no. 1 (Winter 2000 – 2001): 1–18.

McRae, Robert, and Don Hubert. *Human Security and the New Diplomacy: Promoting People, Promoting Peace.* Montreal: McGill-Queen's University Press, 2001.

Nef, Jorge. *Human Security and Mutual Vulnerability: An Exploration into the Global Political Economy of Development and Underdevelopment.* Ottawa: International Development Research Centre, 1995.

Suhrke, Astri. "Human Security and the Interests of States." *Security Dialogue* 30, no. 3 (1999): 265–76.

InfoTrac® College Edition

Search for the following articles in the InfoTrac® database:

Khong, Yuen Foong. "Human Security: A Shotgun Approach to Alleviating Human Misery?" *Global Governance* 7, no. 3 (July–September 2001): 231.

King, Gary, and Christopher J.L. Murray. "Rethinking Human Security." *Political Science Quarterly* 116, no. 4 (Winter 2001): 585–611.

Ogata, Sadako, and Johan Cels. "Human Security: Protecting and Empowering the People." *Global Governance* 9, no. 3 (July–September 2003): 273–82.

For more articles, enter:
"human security" in the keyword search or subject guide.

Web Resources

For current URLs for the following websites, visit www.crosscurrents.nelson.com.

Freedom from Fear: Canada's Human Security

www.humansecurity.gc.ca

This site, from the Department of Foreign Affairs and International Trade, offers a definition of the term *human security* and discusses Canada's approach to human security.

Center for Basic Research in Social Sciences: Program on Human Security

www.cbrss.harvard.edu/programs/hsecurity.htm

This site from a centre at Harvard University offers papers relating to human security.

Human Security Network

www.humansecuritynetwork.org

The Human Security Network supports and encourages initiatives that protect human security.

GEORGE MACLEAN, "THE CHANGING PERCEPTION OF HUMAN SECURITY: COORDINATING NATIONAL AND MULTILATERAL RESPONSES"

www.unac.org/en/link_learn/Canada/security/perception.asp

This paper defines and illustrates how human security can create a more peaceful global climate. It also looks at modern threats to human security.

UNESCO SECURIPAX FORUM

www.unesco.org/securipax/

The online UNESCO Forum on Human Security contains a large collection of UN publications and materials by other agencies on human security.

Do We Need an International Criminal Court?

✔ YES
DOUGLAS CASSEL, "Why We Need the International Criminal Court,"
Christian Century 116, no. 15 (May 12, 1999): 532–36

✗ NO
ALFRED P. RUBIN, "Some Objections to the International Criminal Court,"
Peace Review 12, no. 1 (March 2000): 45–50

How are notions of justice and human security to be implemented in a world composed of nation-states? One answer to that question is the argument that the state should remain the primary arena where issues such as justice, human rights, and civil liberties are defined and protected. The best hope for pursuing justice then is in the maintenance of orderly and stable relations between states. In a society of states, this order can best be achieved by observance of two fundamental legal and moral principles: respect for national sovereignty of all states and non-intervention in the domestic affairs of another sovereign state. These principles were largely built on the belief, rooted in the turmoil of the sixteenth and seventeenth centuries, that the greatest threat to peace and the pursuit of justice stemmed from the widespread intervention in the affairs of other states. They assumed that the priority should be placed on promoting peace and justice between states rather than addressing the issues of peace and justice within states; issues of domestic justice are placed beyond the concerns of the international community.

This way of thinking has had an important impact on the way that human justice has been viewed in the international system. As Hedley Bull notes, "the basic concept of coexistence between states, expressed in the exchange of recognition of sovereign jurisdiction, implies a conspiracy of silence entered into by governments about the rights and duties of their respective citizens" (*The Anarchical Society: A Study of Order in World Politics* [London: Macmillan, 1977]: 83). It is this conspiracy of silence that has increasingly come to bother many people. While some have seen in the notion of sovereignty the promise of security and protection from the wanton harm of outsiders, others have experienced sovereignty as a cloak of protection for oppression and injustice. The worst crimes against humanity and the most oppressive human-rights abuses, they argue, have taken place under the legal protection of national sovereignty. In fact, studies of contemporary conflicts show that in the twentieth century, more people have been killed in intrastate fighting than in interstate wars. For many people, the greatest threat to personal security is not a foreign military force but their own government.

How do we address this situation? Some have suggested that the world needs a permanent international criminal court. Such an idea is not new. As long ago as 1474, Peter van Hagenbach was tried by the Court of the Holy Roman Empire for the torture of civilians. At the Congress of Vienna in 1815, states debated whether there should be trials for those engaged in the slave trade. And, in 1872, Gustave Moynier, a founder of the International Committee of the Red Cross, drew up a proposal for an international criminal court to try violators of the Geneva Conventions of 1864.

Although discussions of the concept of an international criminal court continued in the twentieth century, actual efforts at implementing such a plan proceeded largely on an ad hoc basis. Following the atrocities of World War II, the International Military Tribunal at Nuremberg and the International Military Tribunal for the Far East were established to prosecute war criminals. But these efforts have long been subject to criticism for being driven by political imperatives rather than representing a triumph of the rule of law. Some critics argued that they were nothing more than "victor's tribunals."

During the Cold War, the ideological struggle between the East and the West created little political will to move forward with the idea of an international criminal court. However, the end of the Cold War and the experience of conflicts in Yugoslavia and Rwanda with devastating civilian casualties and human-rights abuses created new momentum for such a project. In 1994, an Ad Hoc Committee on the Establishment of the International Criminal Court, composed of state representatives, was set up to begin working on a draft statute. This work eventually led to the convening in Rome of a UN Diplomatic Conference of Plenipotentiaries on the Establishment of an International Criminal Court in June 1998. These negotiations in turn led to the adoption, in July 1998, of a treaty calling for the creation of an International Criminal Court (ICC). A total of 120 countries voted in favour, 21 abstained, and 7 were opposed. The United States and Israel joined China, Iran, Iraq, Libya, and Sudan in opposing the treaty.

The Rome Statute declares that the signatories recognize that international crimes "threaten peace and security" and affirms that these crimes "must not go unpunished." At the same time, signatory states promise to ensure "an end to impunity" for individual perpetrators. Proponents of the treaty see its provisions as a significant advancement of the norms of human justice in the international system. The ICC would provide a means of non-military intervention to protect the welfare of individuals. Advocates argue that it is a significant advancement in the development of cosmopolitan values. However, the Rome Statute has strong critics who are skeptical about whether anything like a commonly understood notion of international criminal law exists between nations. Further, the growing intrusion into national sovereignty is seen as having potentially dangerous side effects in the future.

In the first essay, Douglas Cassel, a professor of international law, makes the case for the International Criminal Court. Then Alfred P. Rubin, also a professor of international law, argues against implementing the ICC.

✔ **YES**
Why We Need the International Criminal Court
DOUGLAS CASSEL

This has been a good century for tyrants. Stalin killed millions but was never even charged with a crime. Pol Pot slaughtered well over 1 million but never saw the inside of a prison cell. Idi Amin and Raoul Cedras are comfortably retired. Despite recent legal complications, Chile's General Augusto Pinochet, too, will probably escape trial. Ditto for Slobodan Milosevic, who has chosen to close out the century by brutalizing Kosovo.

There have been few exceptions to this pattern of impunity. The most notable exceptions are the Nazis who faced judgment at Nuremberg. Joining the short list of adjudged are the Greek colonels, the Argentine junta, the genocidal regime in Rwanda and some leaders in the former Yugoslavia. But the odds have overwhelmingly favored those who commit atrocities. Will the 21st century be any better?

The answer may well depend in large part on the success − or failure − of the world's first permanent court with global jurisdiction over the most serious international crimes. Last summer in Rome, by a vote of 120 nations in favor, seven opposed and 21 abstentions, a United Nations diplomatic conference adopted a treaty to establish an International Criminal Court (ICC) in The Hague in the Netherlands. It will hear cases of genocide, war crimes and crimes against humanity that national governments are unable or unwilling to prosecute.

The ICC will differ from the existing World Court, officially called the International Court of Justice, also located in The Hague. The World Court hears only lawsuits between governments and cannot prosecute individuals. As a permanent global court, the ICC will likewise differ from the special International Criminal Tribunals created by the UN Security Council to address atrocities in the former Yugoslavia and Rwanda.

Nearly all the world's democracies − Europe plus such countries as Argentina, Australia, Canada, Costa Rica, South Africa and South Korea − supported the Rome treaty. Seventy-eight nations have now signed the treaty, indicating their intention to join it. Once 60 countries complete the ratification process (to date only Senegal has done so), the treaty will go into effect and the ICC will be created.

Late blooming 20th-century tyrants have little to fear; the ICC will have power to try only crimes committed after it is established. The current carnage in Colombia, Congo and Sierra Leone, for example, will either go unpunished or be addressed in some other way.

Only two democracies – Israel and the United States – opposed the ICC, thereby joining a rogue's gallery of regimes like China, Iran, Iraq, Libya and Sudan. Israel's opposition is regrettable but understandable: the Jewish state has lost so many lopsided UN votes that it fears giving power to an international prosecutor.

The U.S., too, professes to fear frivolous or politically motivated prosecutions of American soldiers and officials. However, the ICC has so many built-in safeguards against unwarranted prosecutions that the odds of abuse are minimal. Otherwise, the ICC would hardly have garnered support from Britain, France and other countries with extensive military and peacekeeping forces overseas.

Washington's real grievance is that it cannot control the court. In 1995, on the 50th anniversary of the Nuremberg trials, President Clinton became the first U.S. president to announce support for an ICC. But the U.S. insisted on an ICC that would be an arm of the UN Security Council, which would make prosecutions subject to a U.S. veto and insulate Washington from unwanted trials.

The rest of the world found this vision uninspiring. Still, in a fruitless effort to induce U.S. participation, backers of the ICC at Rome offered numerous concessions, including a significant role for the Security Council. The council will be empowered to refer cases to the ICC. Indeed, at least in the early years, council referral is likely to be the primary route by which cases reach the court. While cases can also be referred by states that are party to the treaty or by the prosecutor, the obstacles to doing so will initially be so high that the ICC will depend heavily on the council. The council can also block investigations by voting to defer them for one year, renewable indefinitely.

But these and other concessions were not enough to dispel Washington's fears that if American troops commit war crimes in another country, that country could have those troops tried in The Hague (unless the U.S. would agree to investigate the case itself). Also, other nations with veto power on the Security Council could block a resolution to defer a case. In short, U.S. control is less than fully assured under the ICC, which pleased neither the Pentagon nor Senate Foreign Relations Committee Chair Jesse Helms, who declared that any treaty to create a court that could conceivably prosecute Americans would be "dead on arrival" on Capitol Hill.

U.S. opposition to the ICC is of a piece with its vote a year earlier against the treaty to ban antipersonnel landmines, its refusal to pay UN dues, its economic sanctions on allies that do business in Cuba and its implicit foreign policy of demanding a "superpower exemption" from international rules. It lends further support to the views held by "elites of countries comprising at least two-thirds of the world's people," according to Harvard scholar Samuel Huntington, writing in *Foreign Affairs*, that Uncle Sam is "intrusive, interventionist, exploitative, unilateralist, hegemonic, hypocritical, and applying double standards." Small wonder that following the 120-7 humiliation of the U.S. in Rome, delegates applauded for 15 minutes.

U.S. opposition to the ICC not only undermines American credibility and diplomacy but also strains the human rights banner Washington purports to carry. The rest of the world cannot fail to notice that the U.S. supports the prosecution of Yugoslavs and Rwandans for human rights crimes but not the prosecution of Americans. If human rights is no more than a flag of convenience, its rallying power diminishes.

But American participation, while important, is not indispensable. The world's democracies are likely to go ahead without us. Americans who care more for the dignity of humanity than for the color of their passports should support the ICC, despite its shortcomings, as a first step toward international justice for crimes against humanity.

But does "justice" for atrocities require a court, let alone a criminal court, much less an international criminal court? Volumes have been devoted to defining justice. For ICC purposes, however, we can focus on an operational definition. Justice calls for identification, exposure, condemnation and proportionate punishment of individuals who violate fundamental norms recognized internationally as crimes, and it calls for reparations to victims, by means of fair investigations and fair trials by an authorized judicial body. Thus defined, justice requires criminal courts, including − as experience has shown − at least the possibility of prosecution before international courts.

Like other efforts to capture "justice" in words, this account covers both too little and too much. As Martha Minow has observed, some crimes are so horrific or massive that no amount of punishment can be proportional. And no form of court-ordered reparation can truly repair the loss of even a single loved one, much less of an entire people. At best, successful prosecutions can deliver only a measure of justice.

On the other hand, criminal punishment may not always contribute to a just society. As argued eloquently by Donald Shriver in these pages (August 26, 1998), "living with others sometimes means that we must value the renewal of community more highly than punishing, or seeking communal vengeance for, crimes." And while "some forms of justice sow the seeds of justice, some do not. Without peaceful public acceptance of their decisions, courts risk irrelevance at best and social chaos at worst."

The case for an ICC must acknowledge the wisdom of such insights. Yet these comments do not so much counsel against the existence of the ICC as remind us of its inherent limitations. Criminal justice is not, by itself, sufficient to heal either victims or societies.

Still, without at least the credible prospect of criminal punishment, victims and societies are unlikely to wield the leverage necessary to pry out the truth, which is an essential prerequisite to genuine repentance, forgiveness and reconciliation. Pervasive impunity is therefore the enemy of justice in all its dimensions.

How might the ICC contribute to justice?

First, in particular cases, it may identify, expose, condemn and punish perpetrators and provide reparations to victims. It may do so either by its own prosecutions or by stimulating prosecutions in national courts, brought by governments reluctant to see their officials and soldiers hauled off to The Hague for trial. Either way, an effective ICC could lift the blanket of impunity that now covers atrocities almost everywhere. By so doing, it could provide a measure of justice to some victims. That by itself would justify creation of the ICC.

But such a court would have even broader impact. It would serve to reinforce moral norms. There is no more powerful social condemnation of evil than to label it as a serious crime, for which serious punishment may be imposed. The preamble adopted in Rome elevates ICC crimes to the status of the "most serious crimes of concern to the international community as a whole." The ICC's every indictment, arrest, conviction and sentence may serve to remind governments, the media and the public that there is "zero tolerance" for crimes against humanity.

The pedagogical and practical import of such moral messages is illustrated by the current case of General Pinochet. In strictly legal terms, he has suffered no more than deprivation of liberty and freedom of movement for some months. He may never actually be prosecuted. But his hopes of becoming a respected senior statesman and to go down in history as his country's savior have been dashed. He will now be remembered, above all, as a torturer who got nabbed. Not only has he suffered loss of honor and reputation, but Chile will now understand its history differently. In Chile and elsewhere, a generation of youth has been taught that his alleged crimes, most of which took place before they were born, are so unconscionable that he is pursued for them even today.

Such messages sensitize global consciousness. This, in turn, has practical consequences. Governments may find it more difficult to grant visas, confer political asylum or otherwise treat alleged torturers as if their crimes could be forgotten. Voices of conscience may be empowered; their demands to treat future Pinochets as pariahs will be legitimized. Of course, to the extent the ICC proves to be ineffective, its moral message will be undermined. An impotent ICC may serve merely to stoke the fires of cynicism. This is one reason why the extensive compromises made at Rome are troubling.

To succeed, however, the court need not be perfect. Consider the case of former Bosnian Serb leader Radovan Karadzik. In 1995 he was indicted for genocide by the International Criminal Tribunal for the former Yugoslavia. Yet he remains at large, because NATO troops in Bosnia to date have not dared to arrest him. Does his case show that genocide is tolerated in practice?

Prior to the Dayton peace agreements, that may indeed have been the message. Until then, few of the suspects indicted by the International Tribunal had been arrested. Karadzik still strutted the world stage as head of the Bosnian Serb "government." But he was barred from Dayton, because he had been indicted and would have to be arrested if he left Yugoslavia. The agreements reached at Dayton also excluded him from any future position in government because, again, he had been indicted. Since then he has lost his official position, and remains hunkered down in Serb territory, unable to travel. Dozens of other suspects have now been arrested or have surrendered.

A similar point may be made on the question of the court's deterrent value. The prospect of prosecution will not deter a Pol Pot or a Slobodan Milosevic. But not all dictators are fanatics like Pol Pot. And at times, calculating manipulators like Milosevic may be restrained by the threat of indictment. How often this happens may depend on how credible the threat is. That, in turn, depends on how the compromises made at Rome play out in practice.

Two of the Rome compromises are especially troublesome. The first imposes a "state consent" requirement on the ICC's jurisdiction (except in cases referred by the Security Council). In cases referred by states or by the prosecutor on his or her own motion, the ICC will not be free to prosecute crimes regardless of where they are committed. It will have jurisdiction only by consent of either the state where the crime was committed or the state in which the accused is a citizen. States that ratify the Rome treaty are parties to the court and automatically consent to its jurisdiction. Other states may consent on a case-by-case basis.

The treaty negotiations suggest the significance of this limitation. Germany proposed that the ICC have "universal" jurisdiction, that is, be able to prosecute crimes wherever they are committed. This made legal sense. For centuries individual states have had the right to prosecute piracy, regardless of where it takes place. Treaties now allow states to prosecute genocide, torture and serious war crimes — all within ICC jurisdiction wherever they are committed. If individual states have universal jurisdiction over such heinous international crimes, why can they not agree to delegate it to an international court?

This legally sensible proposal did not, however, attract much diplomatic support. Most states were unwilling to give the court a worldwide license to prosecute.

South Korea proposed a compromise: Let the ICC hear any case that has the consent of any one of four states — the state where the crime took place, the state of nationality of the defendant, the state of nationality of the victim, or the state having custody of the suspect. While far short of universality, this proposal would have given the ICC jurisdiction in most cases. But the U.S. strenuously objected. Allowing so many states to invoke ICC jurisdiction would allow the court to bypass the Security Council.

In a last-ditch effort to bring the U.S. on board without gutting the court's jurisdiction, the Canadian chair of the Rome conference whittled the four states in South Korea's proposal down to two: the territorial state and the state of nationality of the accused. Over U.S. objections, this proposal became part of the final text of the treaty.

To understand the effect of this provision, consider a hypothetical case involving Saddam Hussein. If he commits atrocities in Kuwait, either of two states could consent to ICC jurisdiction: Kuwait, where the crimes were committed, or Iraq, the state of Saddam's nationality. Since Kuwait would be likely to consent, in such cases – international wars – state consent is not a major obstacle.

But suppose Saddam commits atrocities against Kurds or political dissidents inside Iraq. Then the territorial state and the state of his nationality are one and the same: Iraq, which he controls. In such cases – regimes that repress ethnic minorities or others within their own borders – the ICC may be unable to act.

This kind of situation poses a serious threat to the effectiveness of the court. Except on referral by the Security Council, the ICC could not, for example, prosecute Milosevic for atrocities committed in Kosovo, nor Pol Pot for killing Cambodians, nor Pinochet for "disappearing" Chileans.

Another potentially crippling compromise allows the ICC to hear cases (again, except for those referred by the Security Council) only when the states involved are unable or unwilling to do so. The U.S. likes this provision; it can avoid ICC jurisdiction simply by conducting its own good-faith investigation – even if the result is a decision not to prosecute, or an acquittal.

But what if, say, a Milosevic promises to investigate alleged war crimes by his troops in Kosovo? Unlike the International Criminal Tribunal for Yugoslavia, which has primary jurisdiction, the ICC would have to defer to a Yugoslav national investigation unless the ICC prosecutor can prove that it is a sham. But how can the prosecutor impeach a national investigation before it starts? In most cases, the ICC will have to wait until the individual nation has a chance to show its true colors. In the meantime, what may happen to fingerprints, blood samples, autopsies and witnesses? ICC prosecutor and judges will have to keep careful watch lest national prosecutors merely go through the motions, stall and possibly ruin the ICC's case.

Despite such weaknesses and uncertainties, the agreement on the ICC reached in Rome is the best we are likely to get for the foreseeable future. It deserves support as an essential first step. Once created, it will have a chance to prove itself. If it fails, the need to strengthen it will be demonstrated.

Neither the Clinton administration nor the U.S. Senate is likely to accept the ICC. This is no reason, however, for American supporters to sit on their hands.

It should be stressed that the ICC has significant safeguards against abuse. For example, its judges must have expertise in criminal or international law, and can be elected only by a two-thirds majority of states which are parties to the treaty, most of which will be democracies. Its prosecutor cannot begin an investigation of an American without first notifying the U.S. and allowing it to take over the investigation and any prosecution. Even if the U.S. consents, the ICC prosecutor still cannot begin an investigation without reasonable grounds and the prior approval of a three-judge panel, which may be appealed to a five-judge panel. Once the investigation is complete, no trial can be held without another prior approval by the three-judge panel. Even then there are extensive fair-trial safeguards. No judicial system is airtight, but this one comes close.

Supporters can also dispel Pentagon claims that because American troops undertake so many overseas missions they are uniquely exposed to ICC prosecution. In Bosnia as of mid-1998, for example, our troops represented less than 20 percent of NATO forces and only 10 percent of the International Police Task Force.

Bringing international criminals to justice is no easy task. But the ICC gives humanity in the coming century a chance to administer justice that wasn't available in the 20th century. Let us not miss the opportunity.

THE PINOCHET PRECEDENT

Chile's General Augusto Pinochet would be a prime candidate for trial before the International Criminal Court — if the court existed. Since it does not, a makeshift substitute — extraditing him from Britain for trial in Spain — has been attempted.

In 1973, assisted by the U.S., Pinochet overthrew the democratically elected government of socialist Salvador Allende. His military regime then set out to eliminate and terrorize its political opponents. According to reports based on official Chilean investigations, Pinochet's regime was responsible for over 2,000 assassinations, more than 1,000 disappearances and countless cases of torture.

Numbers cannot tell the full story. As noted by Lord Steyn in the British extradition proceedings, "The case is not one of interrogators acting in excess of zeal." Rather, as Lord Steyn described the alleged torture, "The most usual method was the 'grill,' consisting of a metal table on which the victim was laid naked and his extremities tied and electrical shocks were applied to the lips, genitals, wounds or metal prosthesis."

Nor is Pinochet accused merely of failing to prevent crimes by underlings. Chile's intelligence agency responsible for torture, the notorious DINA, "was directly answerable to General Pinochet rather than to the military junta." According to the Spanish charges, DINA killed, disappeared and tortured victims "on the orders of General Pinochet."

To date Pinochet has enjoyed both de facto and de jure impunity in Chile. In 1978, after the worst was over, he awarded himself and his men an amnesty for any crimes that might have been committed by their regime. When he finally restored civilian rule in 1990, he warned against "touching a hair on the head of one of my men." The new constitution also made him senator for life, immune from prosecution. For added insurance, military courts retain jurisdiction over any alleged crimes by the military.

Pinochet was so safe from prosecution in Chile that he presumed he was safe anywhere. He was wrong. Assisted by human rights activists, Spanish Judge Baltasar Garzon has in recent years accumulated enough evidence to charge the general not only for murdering Spanish citizens but also for committing crimes against a far larger number of Chileans.

As Pinochet recuperated from back surgery in London last October, Judge Garzon asked British authorities to arrest him for extradition to Spain. Britain obliged. As of this writing, the general has been under house arrest in England for six months. Three British courts have now ruled on the case. Most recently a committee of Law Lords, Britain's highest court, voted six to one against the general's claim that as a former head of state he is immune from prosecution. The United Nations Convention Against Torture, they ruled, requires member states either to extradite or prosecute alleged torturers. Sitting heads of state are immune, but former heads are not.

Since Britain did not join the convention until 1988, however, the lords authorized the government to extradite Pinochet only for torture committed after 1988. British Home Secretary Jack Straw decided in April that the post-1988 cases submitted by the Spanish judge justify extradition. However, lengthy legal proceedings, followed by a final opportunity for Straw to reconsider, could take months or even years.

Whatever the ultimate outcome, the rulings in this case by the highest courts of Britain and Spain make clear that international law now permits third countries to prosecute torturers whose home country is unwilling or unable to bring them to court. But the case also shows the unreliability of this approach. What if Britain had not joined the torture convention? Or if Downing Street were still occupied by Tories and not Tony Blair? Would Britain have arrested Pinochet? Whatever the outcome, the Pinochet case thus underlines the need for an ICC.

✗ NO
Some Objections to the International Criminal Court
ALFRED P. RUBIN

Perhaps it is unwise to comment on the structure of the proposed International Criminal Court (ICC) while the negotiations to define it still continue. Nevertheless, there are underlying inconsistencies between the dominant conceptions of the ICC's operations and the realities of the international legal (and political and economic) order. These inconsistencies cannot be remedied by tinkering with the details. As currently conceived by its supporters, the ICC cannot work as envisaged without massive changes in the international legal order. But those changes cannot be accomplished without losses that nobody realistically expects and few really want.

The ICC assumes there is such a thing as international criminal law. But what is its substance? Who exercises law-making authority for the international legal community? Who has the legal authority to interpret the law once supposedly found?

While ample precedents for the international equivalent of common law can be found in the claims and property areas, the criminal law is different. Some acts by individuals have been historically deemed to violate it, whatever it is − piracy, war crimes, international traffic in slaves, and now genocide and perhaps aggression and other atrocities. But until now those "crimes" have not been defined by international law as such. They have been defined instead by the municipal laws of many states and in a few cases by international tribunals set up by victor states in an exercise of positive law making. Thereby, the tribunal's new rules were "accepted," under one rationale or another, by the states in which the accused were nationals.

Some Nazis were convicted at Nuremberg of planning aggressive war, but the Nazi attack on Poland in 1939 was preceded by the Molotov-Ribbentrop Pact. The notion that the Soviets did not help plan the "aggressive war" was regarded by many as hopelessly unconvincing, so it was agreed among the Nuremberg prosecutors not to allow any mention of that treaty at the trial. As to "war crimes," Grand Admiral Doenitz, Hitler's successor in Germany, was convicted at Nuremberg among other things of authorizing unrestricted submarine warfare in violation of a 1936 treaty. Admiral Nimitz, the American hero, sent a letter to the tribunal pointing out that he had issued almost identical orders in the Pacific on December 7, 1941. Of course, Nimitz was not tried for anything by anybody.

As for "crimes against humanity," it was agreed to define those as acts connected with Word War II itself. Thus, the Soviet Union's deliberate starvation of the Ukraine and the establishment of the Gulag Archipelago were not within the Nuremberg charge. Nor were American acts of wartime hysteria, such as the mass displacement of Americans of Japanese heritage from the three West Coast states but not from Hawaii. The nuclear bombing of Nagasaki was not mentioned either, although it could be said to have raised serious questions about American observance of the laws of war even assuming the Hiroshima bomb was a legitimate wartime act. In sum, the victors did not apply to themselves the rules they purported to find in the international legal order. The deeper question is whether rules asserted by victors and applied only to losers represent "law" at all.

Another theory has been that if all or nearly all "civilized" states define particular acts as violating their municipal criminal laws, then those acts violate "international law." Far from being new to the international arena, that conception attempts to revive jus gentium theory, which failed when Lord Mansfield, Sir William Scott, and Joseph Story, among many others, developed conflict-of-law and choice-of-law theory in a civil claims context so as to make it unnecessary to determine which states are "civilized" and which rules are universal.

Occasionally, the same theory has been urged under the argument that some acts violate "general principles of law recognized by civilized states," and thus violate general international law. But to define states that agree with us as "civilized" and those that disagree as not worth considering would eliminate most of the human race from the rubric "civilized." That might be correct as far as we are concerned, but it will not likely represent any universal "law." And it does not make even acknowledged wicked acts "criminal" in any known sense.

Suppose it was possible to define as universal crimes acts defined and punished as criminal by various municipal legal orders. If that were done it still would not confer "standing" in the international community to expand any single state's municipal jurisdiction, to create a "universal" jurisdiction over the acts of foreigners abroad, no matter how horrendous.

Early attempts to resolve these problems abound. For example, in the United States, the first statute criminalizing "piracy" was enacted in April 1790. It made criminal by U.S. law any "offense which if committed within the body of a county, would by the laws of the United States be punishable by death" and various lesser acts such as running away with goods "to the value of $50" (not saying whether lesser valuations or greater valuations would be included in the definition), yielding up a "vessel voluntarily to any pirate" (not defining "pirate"), or mutiny (without using the word). The statute was found defective in early cases and was supplemented with another in 1819 which made criminal by U.S. law "the crime of piracy as defined by the law of nations" and apparently asserted universal jurisdiction over those committing "piracy" as so defined by subjecting them to the American criminal process if they were "afterwards . . . brought into or found in the United States," even if they were foreigners acting solely against foreign interests or persons.

That statute was upheld by the Supreme Court in 1820, but reduced in its effect, as to both definition and jurisdiction, and eventually abandoned, although it still appears in the U.S. Code. The principal problem was that Joseph Story and some other judges felt they knew how the "law of nations" defined "piracy" but very few others did. Despite Story's objections, in all but "piracy cases," "common law crimes" were abandoned in the United States federal courts because prosecutors refused to bring such cases.

A similar fate met attempts to establish an international criminal court to hear cases involving the international traffic in slaves. When such a court was proposed by the British in the 1830s and 1840s, it was rejected by the U.S. A close examination of the British proposal showed how it would authorize British warships to arrest vessels of any nationality in only some parts of the world, but did not authorize American or other warships to arrest British vessels near the British Isles. Indeed, when Haiti established its own anti-slave-trade legislation based on identical assertions of universal jurisdiction in 1839, the British objected, claiming that the universal law of the sea allowed no universal jurisdiction in any case outside of the exercise of belligerent fights in wartime.

Turning to attempts to incorporate universal jurisdiction in an ICC by treaty construction, consider that the Genocide Convention and the four 1949 Geneva Conventions on the protection of the victims of armed conflict leave the traditional jurisdictional arrangements of general international law untouched. All four Geneva Conventions refer to some "grave breaches," generally acts that individuals might commit or order that seem to harm persons or property that need not be harmed in order for the conflict to proceed in the usual miserable ways. The obligation is on the High Contracting Parties severally to enact municipal legislation. The Conventions provide in identical language in each Convention that "The High Contracting Parties undertake to enact any legislation necessary to provide effective penal sanctions for persons committing, or ordering to be committed, any of the grave breaches of the present Convention defined [sic] in the following Article."

In fact, the various wicked acts are not "defined" in the Geneva Conventions. For example, each of the Conventions lists "willful killing" as such a "grave breach." But soldiers routinely "willfully kill" the enemy. All known legal orders excuse or authorize "willful killing" in self-defense or to defend a protected class of others, such as family members. The 1949 Conventions do not attempt to draw the necessary distinctions between a "willful killing" that is legally a "grave breach" to be made the subject of criminal sanctions in all contracting states, and one that remains legally within a soldier's privilege.

Nor do they define who is a "soldier" for those purposes. The attempt to define who is entitled to prisoner-of-war treatment if captured by an enemy might be interpreted as such a definition, but not necessarily, and itself leads to serious complications. Indeed, in the Prisoners of War Convention itself (Convention III of 1949), questions about status are to be resolved by "a competent tribunal" (Article 5) with no clue as to who should convene the tribunal or determine its criteria. And there is much more that is doubtful about the interpretation of the key provisions of this part of the Prisoners of War Convention, indeed of all four Conventions.

Similarly, the Genocide Convention of 1948, although calling "genocide" a "crime under international law," restricts the definition and enforcement of this "crime" to the municipal tribunals of the various parties who alone are "to provide effective penalties for persons guilty of genocide." And persons charged with genocide "shall be tried by a competent tribunal of the State in the territory of which the act was committed, or by such international penal tribunal as may have jurisdiction with respect to those Contracting Parties which shall have accepted its jurisdiction." Clearly those who sought to establish in 1948 a universal jurisdiction by means of the positive law failed.

It has been argued that at least the 1949 Geneva Conventions resolve the universal jurisdiction issue by providing that "[e]ach High Contracting Party shall be under the obligation to search for persons alleged to have committed, or to have ordered to be committed, such grave breaches, and shall bring such persons, regardless of their nationality, before its own courts." But there are many problems with this interpretation. First, so severe have been the practical difficulties that there have been no cases in the 50 bloody years since 1949 in which any High Contracting Party has fulfilled that "obligation." Second, even if the "obligation" were taken seriously, it would be impossible in many cases for the accused to defend themselves. How could General Schwarztkopf, for example, produce the evidence to show that before he ordered the bombing during the Gulf War of what later appeared to be a civilian bomb shelter, his best intelligence – derived from intercepts and possibly infiltrators or other eye-witnesses – was that the supposed bomb shelter was actually an illegal overlay of civilians above a military communications site?

It can be argued that the law has progressed from the days of Nuremberg and the 1948 and 1949 Conventions: that universal jurisdiction is now an accepted custom. But is it? What states, under what circumstances, have accepted the custom? Even where it has been enacted, has it been accepted outside of a positive commitment? Accepted as law? We should have serious doubts about the assertions of customary law that are occasionally used in this context.

What about the ICC Convention itself as a positive law document under which states agree to submit to the Court and to have it exercise jurisdiction over specified offenses? That would seem to fit the caveat in the Genocide Convention and make the "world community" the "victor," setting up a victor's tribunal for which Nuremberg and Tokyo would be the precedents. Indeed, similar tribunals with non-combatant "victors" were set up regarding events in the former Yugoslavia and Rwanda. But that has not and would still not solve the deeper problems as they appear on the surface.

To illustrate the difficulties, let us agree that to be "law" the rule to be applied must be applied universally. Some villains will escape, of course, as they do in municipal legal orders' criminal subsets. But are the jurisdictional rules and the substantive rules themselves applicable? Would they apply, for example, to

Russian soldiers in Chechnya? To Chechens who infiltrate Russia and blow up civilian housing? If conceptually the rules did apply regardless of Russian or Chechen legislation defining their soldiers' status and privileges, which might otherwise exempt their own personnel from liability, the next question is whether Russian or Chechen officials would agree that American or other police have the authority to investigate or make arrests in Russian or Chechen controlled territory. Is their agreement necessary?

In East Timor it was thought to be necessary, and the formal government of Indonesia did agree to the introduction of foreign forces in its territory, apparently to apply some notion of law (although precisely what law, how it is to be applied and by whom are open questions) while East Timor remained part of the Indonesian state. If so, then this returns us to the world of positive law and national discretion. If not, before what forum is the point to be argued? By whom? What if the Russians or Chechens still disagree? Would Americans agree to Russian or Chechen investigators or police, unauthorized by American law, making arrests of American military personnel in U.S. territory and placing them before their own or some "international" tribunals to be tried under their concept of "criminal law"?

But, it may be argued, we are not speaking of Russian or Chechen officials. We are speaking of representatives of the international community. Surely we cannot object to an evolution of the international legal order to allow international inspectors and police to make arrests for offenses defined by positive law. But Iraq has made exactly that objection to the United Nations. And Iraq turns out not to be friendless, regardless of the American notion of the Iraqi legal argument and however villainous Saddam Hussein may be. We are left with the notion that positive submission is probably required both to define the evil acts and to enforce their proscription against individuals. But that positive submission has not yet been given by anybody outside various victors' or similar situations (such as with the former Yugoslavia). As a matter of positive law, once the agreement has been given it is subject to interpretation and it cannot be reasonably supposed that the state whose leaders are accused of violating the undefined law will agree with those officials of any institution on all their interpretations of the "law."

These theoretical difficulties obviously arise in practice, and no amount of new theory can resolve the problems as I see them. The issue is not the politicization of tribunals. It is the value systems in the minds of honorable judges. For example, in 1970 Mohammed Bedjaoui, later President of the International Commission of Jurists, argued that newly independent states retain a discretion to renounce their debts and nationalize foreign-owned property based on the primacy of national self-determination over property rights in the international legal order. Who can say definitively that he was wrong? Despite the ringing assertions of "reasonableness" we have heard on all sides since the days of Cicero, arguments over value systems, about which reasonable people do in fact disagree, are not the same as having political biases.

In practice, the issues arise in yet another form. Not only are the value systems in the minds of the ICC's officials very much in question, but the questions extend to the entire process. For example, when is an indictment to be handed down or carried out? If it is to be immediately upon discovering convincing evidence of an indictable atrocity, then is a general to be arrested in the midst of a battle? By whom? And what of the battle? Assuming, as I suppose we must, that Article 2.4 of the United Nations Charter makes international armed conflict itself unthinkable, what about internal battles? Or have we reached a stage in world development in which all existing constitutions are to be protected by the international community from revolutionary change? Who is to determine that rebels, using the best tools available to them, are to fail because there are legal questions surrounding the use of some of those tools that seem to outside parties to be disproportionate in the death and destruction they bring to innocents?

Is war and revolution to be reduced to the status of a game with an impartial umpire blowing a whistle when his or her conception of the rules is violated? Then is the world supposed to stop while the case is brought to a tribunal that might in fact find that the umpire blew the whistle prematurely? And if the umpire blows the whistle after the battle ends, is the victorious military leader to be tried? Was Admiral Nimitz or President Truman or "Bomber" Harris or Josef Stalin responsible for the transgressions of which they have been accused?

The notion that any society should be ruled by the "best," regardless of the will of ordinary folks, has been with us since at least the days when Plato wrote his *Republic*. But who is to discover the "best"? Who is to convince the traditional holders of authority to yield that authority to others whom yet others regard as the "best"? I forbear to cite examples when this approach has been tried, including the attempt by Dionysus II to apply it in his Kingdom of Sicily with Plato himself present. It has always failed.

The reasons why it has failed were eloquently illustrated in a naively arrogant book by Sherard Osborn, a British Navy Captain publishing in 1857 about events during the 1830s when he served British interests in the Malay Peninsula:

> Such are the cruelties perpetrated by these wretched native monarchies . . . and yet philanthropists and politicians at home maunder about the unjust invasion of native rights, and preach against the extension of our rule. As if our Government, in its most corrupt form, would not be a blessing in such a region, and as much if not more, our duty to extend, as a Christian people, than to allow them to remain under native rulers, and then to shoot them for following native habits.

Those who agree with the moral rationales for 19th-century European imperialism and ignore the other things that went with it, such as the exercise of force to implement that fancied moral and political superiority, might support the ICC. I cannot.

POSTSCRIPT

When analyzing the debate over the ICC, it is instructive to examine the very different approaches taken to this issue by Canada and the United States. Under the umbrella of its commitment to promoting human security, Canada has been a strong supporter of the concept underlying the ICC from the beginning. The Canadian government chaired the "Like-Minded Group," a coalition of nearly 60 countries advocating the ICC. Canada was active in the negotiations leading up to the establishment of the ICC and contributed to the UN trust fund that helped many developing countries participate in the deliberations. On June 29, 2000, Canada became the first country to adopt legislation to implement the provisions of the Rome Statute in its national law. The Crimes Against Humanity and War Crimes Act was adopted by the Canadian Parliament in order to bring Canadian law into conformity with the ICC. In February 2003, a Canadian lawyer was elected as the first presiding chief justice of the ICC.

In contrast, the American government has persistently expressed doubts about the ICC. Despite a variety of concerns, President Clinton finally signed the treaty in the dying days of his administration in December 2000. But he recommended that the incoming administration not ratify the treaty in the Senate. Almost immediately upon taking office, the Bush administration expressed its concerns about the ICC. President Bush focused particularly on the fear that American government officials and military personnel might be unfairly tried for war crimes for political reasons. He thus sought an exemption for American personnel participating in overseas missions. Finally, in May 2002, the U.S. government informed UN Secretary-General Kofi Annan that the United States would not seek to ratify the treaty and that is was renouncing any legal obligations flowing from its signing of the treaty. Subsequently, the United States requested that the Security Council grant exemptions from prosecution to U.S. military personnel before the U.S. government approves participation in any UN peacekeeping missions. In addition, President Bush signed into law the American Servicemembers Protection Act. This law gives the president the authority to use military force to free any Americans held by the ICC in the Hague, to suspend military assistance to any country ratifying the ICC treaty, and to restrict U.S. participation in UN peacekeeping operations unless prior immunity to prosecution is granted to U.S. military personnel.

Suggested Additional Readings

Anderson, John B. "An International Criminal Court—An Emerging Idea." *Nova Law Review* 15 (1991): 433–47.

Arsanjani, Mahnoush. "The Rome Statute of the International Criminal Court." *American Journal of International Law* 93, no. 1 (1999): 22–43.

Bass, Gary J. *Stay the Hand: The Politics of War Crimes Tribunal.* Princeton: Princeton University Press, 2000.

Bassiouni, Cherif. "From Versailles to Rwanda in Seventy-Five Years: The Need to Establish a Permanent International Criminal Court." *Harvard Human Rights Law Journal* 10 (1997): 11–62.

Cogan, Jacob. "International Criminal Courts and Fair Trials: Difficulties and Prospects." *Yale Journal of International Law* 27 (Winter 2002): 111–41.

Gallarotti, Giulio M., and Arik Y. Preis. "Toward Universal Human Rights and the Rule of Law: The Permanent International Criminal Court." *Australian Journal of International Affairs* 53, no. 1 (April 1999): 95–112.

Rieff, David. "Court of Dreams." *New Republic* 219, no. 10 (1998): 16–18.

Rubin, Alfred P. "Challenging the Conventional Wisdom: Another View of the International Criminal Court." *Journal of International Affairs* 52 (Spring 1999): 783–95.

Sewall, Sarah B., and Carl Kaysen, eds. *The United States and the International Criminal Court: National Security and International Law.* Lanham, Md.: Rowman & Littlefield Publishers, 2000.

Stromseth, Jane E., ed., *Accountability for Atrocities: National and International Responses.* Ardsley, N.Y.: Transnational Publishers, 2003.

InfoTrac® College Edition

Search for the following articles in the InfoTrac® database:

Tochilovsky, Vladimir. "Globalizing Criminal Justice: Challenges for the International Criminal Court." *Global Governance* 9, no. 3 (July–September 2003): 291–99.

Tucker, Robert W. "The International Criminal Court Controversy." *World Policy Journal* 18, no. 2 (Summer 2001): 71–81.

Scharf, Michael P. "The ICC's Jurisdiction over the Nationals of Non-Party States: A Critique of the U.S. Position." *Law and Contemporary Problems* 64, no. 1 (Winter 2001): 67.

For more articles, enter:

"international criminal court," "war crimes," or "war crimes tribunal," in the keyword search or subject guide.

Web Resources

For current URLs for the following websites, visit www.crosscurrents.nelson.com.

COALITION FOR AN INTERNATIONAL CRIMINAL COURT

www.iccnow.org

This website, established by a coalition of NGOs supporting the ICC, contains not only textual material but also audio documentaries and links.

HUMAN RIGHTS WATCH: INTERNATIONAL CRIMINAL COURT

www.hrw.org/campaigns/icc/

This is the website of the NGO Human Rights Watch's campaign, which supports the ICC.

HUMAN RIGHTS FIRST

www.humanrightsfirst.org

This lawyers' site dealing with human rights offers a good collection of materials on the ICC and other international tribunals.

ROME STATUTE OF THE INTERNATIONAL CRIMINAL COURT

www.un.org/law/icc

The official UN website for the ICC contains the text of the statute, information regarding current status of ratification, and related documentation.

INTERNATIONAL CRIMINAL COURT: RESOURCES IN PRINT AND ELECTRONIC FORMAT

www.lib.uchicago.edu/~llou/icc.html

This page from the University of Chicago Library offers an annotated list of materials on the topic of the ICC.

Are Truth Commissions Useful in Promoting Human Rights and Justice in Transitional Societies?

✔ **YES**

JOANNA R. QUINN, "Truth Commissions and Restorative Justice"

✘ **NO**

RICHARD ASHBY WILSON, "Challenging Human Rights as Restorative Justice"

In October 2000, when the first freely elected president of Yugoslavia (now Serbia and Montenegro) took office, the first thing he did was announce the creation of a truth commission. The purpose of this commission was to investigate the crimes and human-rights abuses that had taken place during the wars of Yugolsav succession. In the nine months following this announcement, at least eleven other truth commissions were established in various parts of the world, from East Timor to Sierra Leone and from Panama to Bosnia.

The recent interest in truth commissions has stemmed partly out of the experiences of Latin America and South Africa in searching for ways to assist their societies in making a transition from a period of protracted civil conflict and human-rights abuses to a stable, functioning democracy based on rule of law and observance of human rights. These efforts have been supported by the international community, and other countries have been encouraged to see them as models.

Supporters of truth commissions argue that they are necessary in helping transitional nations overcome the limitations of a more traditional criminal justice approach embodied in the concept of war-crimes tribunals and international criminal courts discussed in Issue Fifteen. The International Criminal Court or an ad hoc war-crimes tribunal cannot deal with situations where massive or systemic human-rights abuses have occurred over a period of time. Because of the high demand for proof in criminal trials, the number of those who are actually prosecuted and found guilty still represents only a very small fraction of those culpable. International tribunals can be expensive, move slowly, and produce only limited results. In war-torn societies that are trying to rebuild fragile institutions, it is too much to expect that the domestic judicial system will pick up the slack. In Rwanda, for example, there were over 100 000 prisoners waiting for years in jail to be tried for their involvement in tribal genocide. Ten years after the genocide occurred, only a small percentage of those implicated in the events had been successfully prosecuted. In the end, the emphasis on criminal prosecution may have a limited role in preventing new outbreaks of strife and violence.

These difficulties have led some to advocate the use of additional human-rights initiatives, especially the establishment of truth commissions. Such commissions can play an important role in fostering reconciliation, forging mutual understanding, and aiding victims. By providing the victims of a conflict with a platform to tell their stories, they reveal the terrible human cost of human-rights abuses, war, and dictatorship. Often, people from one side come to see the suffering and pain experienced by those on the other side of the conflict. Such meetings can provide the basis to move beyond the formal "peace process" at the highest levels to a deeper process of reconciliation within the society. By moving beyond narrow, legalistic definitions of guilt, truth commissions may foster a broader national process of introspection that encourages all sectors of a society to examine their role in past conflicts. By focusing on recovering the "truth" about its past, a society can reform its institutions in order to prevent recurrences of abuses. Because truth commissions downplay the notion of punishment and retribution, governments can then pursue more proactive strategies aimed at promoting reconciliation along ethnic, racial, linguistic, or religious lines.

In many transitional societies, truth commissions are attractive for some very pragmatic reasons. In some cases, oppressive leaders have sought immunity from prosecution in return for surrendering power or making peace. Often, large numbers of civil servants or military officials implicated in abuses remain in office. It is simply not possible to purge a government of everyone implicated in a previous regime without causing a collapse of the government and its bureaucracy. In other cases, the extent of the human-rights abuses has been so extensive that prosecution of all those implicated is not possible without overwhelming the already fragile national judicial system. The placing of such a high burden on the judicial system may further weaken its credibility and legitimacy.

Because of these factors, there is a growing interest in how the international community can facilitate the establishment and functioning of truth commissions. According to a database established by the United States Institute of Peace, at least twenty-four truth commissions have been established since 1982, the majority of them since 1990. Nearly a dozen countries have also established commissions of inquiry or similar bodies that function somewhat like truth commissions.

Despite this growing interest, truth commissions are not without their share of controversy. Within the international human-rights community itself, there is growing debate over the value of truth commissions in helping transitional societies in the long term. On one side are those who argue that truth commissions embody an approach to national reconciliation based on the principle of "restorative justice." By downplaying the importance of prosecution and punishment and placing an emphasis on forgiveness, truth commissions provide a basis for national reconciliation that will lead to more stable, just societies in the future. On the other side, a growing number of analysts have challenged the concept of restorative justice as a basis for truth commissions. These analysts argue that it is important not to overlook the role that retribution plays in establishing justice. Unless the perpetrators of past war crimes and human-rights abuses are seen to suffer some punishment for their actions, it is difficult to build a society that respects human rights in the future.

This debate is taken up in the following two articles. Joanna Quinn is a Canadian scholar who has studied truth commissions in Haiti and Uganda. She argues that the principles of restorative justice are important to an understanding of the positive role that truth commissions play in aiding transitional societies in re-establishing social order. In response, Richard Wilson, who has studied and written extensively on the Truth and Reconciliation Commission in South Africa, argues that the emphasis on forgiveness and reconciliation that underlies truth commissions may in fact undermine the legitimacy of the human-rights and domestic judicial systems that are necessary to the task of nation-building.

✔ YES
Truth Commissions and Restorative Justice
JOANNA R. QUINN

In recent years, a debate has emerged about what should be done in societies where egregious human rights violations have taken place. Societies like these are often at a stand-still, needing to do something to move forward, but worried in case the choice they make might somehow not be enough. Throughout most of the world, it is common practice to subject the perpetrators of crimes, both large and small, to trials in which they are held accountable for what they have done. Yet these kinds of proceedings are simply unable to address many of the other aspects of the crimes which have been committed, including the impact on victims and their families, as well as implications for the larger society.

RETRIBUTIVE VS. RESTORATIVE JUSTICE

The distinction that must be made here is between retributive and restorative justice. The first of these, trials, are a form of *retributive justice*. The term *retribution* is defined by the *Canadian Oxford Dictionary* as "punishment for a crime, injury, etc.; vengeance." Centred around principles such as accountability and punishment, retributive mechanisms bring the person charged with a particular crime before a judge or panel of judges who hear evidence as to the crime committed, whereupon a decision as to the person's guilt or innocence is taken, and a proportional response or sentence is meted out. Such legal prosecutions follow from the rule of law, the parameters of which have long been established. "In the Western liberal legal tradition, the rule of law . . . entails the presumption of innocence, litigation under the adversary system, and the ideal of a government by laws, rather than by persons."[1]

Retributive justice can take many forms. In the Western world, trials are commonly held to deal with criminal charges. In such cases, decisions are often made by a combination of judge and/or jury to determine not only a person's guilt or innocence, but also decide what penalty he or she should incur. These trials are held under the jurisdiction of national laws.

Another more recent development in retributive justice is the advent of retributive tribunals. Starting with the Nuremberg trials, which were held post–World War II to deal with Nazi war crimes, and again with the appointment of the International Criminal Tribunal for the Former Yugoslavia (ICTY) and the International Criminal Tribunal for Rwanda (ICTR), as well as the recent initiation of the International Criminal Court (ICC), the international community has begun to take a significant interest in the prosecution of perpetrators of crimes of mass atrocity, genocide, and war crimes. Often, such bodies derive their authority from international agreements and international treaties; the ICC, for example, came into being through the signing by state parties of the Treaty of Rome. In these cases, too, panels of judges hear evidence before deciding a person's guilt or innocence and determining an appropriate sentence.

Such bodies, however, are both labour- and knowledge-intensive. Often, a dichotomy of responses is carried out. In the first and very common scenario, hundreds of people are needed to run these complex organizations: courtrooms staffed by clerical and security staff, judges assisted by legal staff, and prisons. In other cases, the legal system is simply unable to deal with the onslaught of cases that would inevitably be brought before it. The Cambodian case provides a useful illustration. In 2000, its weak court system comprised judges 80 percent of whom did not hold law degrees and many of whom had never received formal education at all, let alone training in legal matters.[2] Another difficulty is that the sheer magnitude of the period of mass atrocity would make it nearly impossible to deal effectively with the cases at hand. In Rwanda, for example, approximately 120,000 Rwandans remained in prison in 2000, six years after the genocide of approximately 800,000 Rwandans in 1994. It is estimated that if the regular court system tried to deal with these cases, it would take upwards of 180 years. Those constructing the model of restorative justice must recognize and deal with these constraints and the perceptions of the system and its limitations.

Other societies have taken a different approach; they have opted instead to use a form of *restorative justice*. As I define it, restorative justice is a process of active participation in which the wider community deliberates over past crimes, giving centre stage to both victim and perpetrator in a process that seeks to bestow dignity and empowerment upon victims, with special emphasis placed upon contextual factors.[3] Quite unlike in the retributive system described above, however, the applicability of punishment is absent from this type of justice. And unlike in the process of retribution, wherein the perpetrator is the sole focus of the proceedings, in restorative processes the victim receives special attention.

Any number of instruments may be employed to bring about restorative justice. In most cases, the instrument itself is developed with regard to the specificities of the situation in which it is to be employed; as opposed to retributive trials and tribunals, instruments of restorative justice are not merely cookie-cutter solutions. Among the methods available to states grappling with past atrocity are reparation, which might include apology or restitution, like that granted to Canadians and Americans of Japanese descent who were interned during World War II. In 1988, the American government gave those Japanese who had been interned US$20,000 per survivor as a form of compensation under the Civil Liberties Act, while in the same year, the Canadian government awarded $21,000 per survivor under the Japanese Canadian Redress Agreement.

Another response to mass human rights abuses by the state has been the truth commission. In the spirit of restorative justice, the truth commission often avoids retribution and sentencing. Rather, it pushes for the provision of an apology or reparation to the citizens of a country who have been wronged by human rights abuses. This tendency is due in part to the relative cost associated with other forms of reparation, resources that are often thought to be better allocated to other social programs in a transitional society. Certainly, truth commissions may not be appropriate in every context. They do, however, have the potential to generate many benefits for societies in transition.

TRUTH COMMISSIONS

A relatively new instrument of justice following a period of atrocity, the truth commission provides a forum in which a society can learn about the abuses of the past. Generally, a truth commission's main task is to collect information about such abuses and to compile this information to produce a coherent account of the history of that society. This can be particularly important in societies where abuses have been government-sponsored and have therefore gone unrecorded in any official way. It is often the case that these abuses are unsubstantiated or even denied by the governments in question. For this reason, a truth commission can play a vital role in uncovering and chronicling the events of a society's collective past.

By my definition, a truth commission is made up of four components: it is (a) a non-judicial investigatory body established, sanctioned, or empowered by the state (or by a dominant faction within the state) to (b) determine the truth about widespread human rights violations that occurred in the past in order to (c) discover which parties may be blamed for their participation in perpetrating such violations over (d) a specified period of time. These four characteristics adequately address the various needs of the truth commission.

The first-ever truth commission was convoked in Uganda in 1974, although it completely failed to promote either truth or acknowledgement. Since that time, more than twenty truth commissions have been appointed by national governments, among them highly successful commissions in Argentina, Chile, and South Africa. Truth commissions may be variously concerned with other aspects of reparation, including property and/or loss of income. Truth commissions are, however, effectively prohibited from dealing with aspects *other* than past human rights abuses because of the relative cost associated with other forms of retributive justice, monies that might better be allocated to other facets of the transitional society.

Among the most highly celebrated (and successful) truth commissions is the Truth and Reconciliation Commission (TRC) that was held in South Africa to consider the human rights abuses that had taken place during apartheid. It was established under the 1995 Promotion of National Unity and Reconciliation Act by the South African parliament. The Act gave the TRC the power to grant individualized amnesty, as well as search and seizure powers, subpoena powers, and witness-protection powers. The TRC had three separate yet inter-related capacities: the Human Rights Violations Committee, the Amnesty Committee, and the Reparations and Rehabilitation Committee. The TRC took testimony from 23,000 victims and witnesses, 2000 of whom appeared in public hearings. The TRC process seems to have been able to bring about a societal recognition and responsibility for the abuses perpetrated under apartheid-era governments. It was also pivotal in publicizing truth commissions around the world.

Another commission of note is the National Commission on Truth and Reconciliation (NCTR) that took place in Chile between May 9, 1990, and February 9, 1991. During that nine months, the Commission received evidence from more than 3400 victims and their families, considered such evidence, and finally prepared a report. The NCTR compiled lists of victims and the details of their cases. Testimony was heard, evidence gathered, and decisions made; in the end, all of the evidence was referred to the courts, except for the testimony of those who had been granted a blanket amnesty. The acknowledgement of the suffering of the people of Chile brought about in Chilean society appears to have played a vital role in helping Chile to regain democracy.

The success of truth commissions appears to depend upon the creation of a common and official "truth narrative" that can lead to the outward and public acknowledgement of past events. This hearing of the experiences of oneself and others might well validate the experience of those involved in past crimes. The discussion of group and individual experiences and the recognition of others' experiences as valid are required. This acknowledgement of past events is a critical step in the process of reconciliation between victims and perpetrators. And it is influential in bringing a sense of healing to the community.

HOW TRUTH COMMISSIONS CAN PROMOTE RESTORATIVE JUSTICE

The very definition of the relative "success" of truth commissions, however, is based on a different set of evaluative criteria than that of its retributive justice counterpart, acknowledgement trials. In a restorative context, the process is not at all perpetrator-centric. As such, truth commissions are focused less on prosecuting and sentencing those who have committed past atrocity. Rather, the aim of restorative mechanisms of all stripes, but particularly of truth commissions, is to determine the truth about such events, by means of a collaborative and often very public process.

Critics often argue that people who have lived through abuse are hungry for justice and revenge. They contend that only by holding people accountable can any kind of societal reconciliation take place. Certainly, if conducted properly, national accountability trials can showcase the ability of a country's judicial system to function, which can in turn have a deterrent effect on the future commission of human rights abuses. Sadly, however, the underpinnings necessary for traditional judicial function are often simply not in place, as in the case of Cambodia, mentioned above.

Truth commissions have many advantages over more traditional forms of retributive justice. I have identified six reasons that the restorative process is preferable, each of which is discussed in greater detail below.

First, restorative justice does not merely deal with a particular case among the many thousands that may exist; it is a process with a significantly broader focus, which allows it to begin to work at a broader societal level. This is so because of the broad mandate of most truth commissions. The Ugandan truth commission, for example, was mandated to "inquire into all aspects of violations of human rights, breaches of the rule of law and excessive abuses of power committed against any persons" between 1962 and 1986.[4] Whereas trials traditionally focus on only one case and collect information pertaining to that one case, truth commissions are able to consider a broad spectrum of cases and to collect information pertaining to them all. In a ground-breaking use of applied technology, the Haitian truth commission collected information regarding more than 8,000 individual cases of abuse. The commission was then able to compile this information into a database that could be used to cross-reference the details of each crime committed and to provide an overall picture of the many thousands of abuses that had taken place. The scope of most trials is such that an investigation of this magnitude is not possible.

Second, truth commissions can also have a popular educative effect. Because their activities concern such a broad spectrum of the wider society, its activities are often widely publicized. In turn, this gives the commission the opportunity to effect a great degree of change within that society. One outcome of truth commission activity after a period of atrocity that is often felt is that people begin to learn about the sanctity of their rights and the state's responsibility to uphold them. Especially where the state itself has sponsored and carried out human rights abuses, people often have no idea of the rights to which they are entitled. One additional benefit that can be brought about by truth commission activity is that the society can begin to build a shared understanding and public record of the events that took place. This is particularly important because often people are aware only of their own circumstances; through the building of a common understanding of shared past events, people in a society can more readily come to terms with their shared history and begin to move forward.

Third, a truth commission can help strengthen and build a new judicial infrastructure. Although it is not concerned with the retributive aspects of the justice system and cannot replace a trial, a truth commission can begin to carry out some of the functions that a functioning judicial system should be able to encompass.

It is particularly important, for example, that a society should feel able to trust in the judicial process. By appointing as commissioners people of integrity who are beyond reproach, and by carrying out proceedings in a way that honours everyone involved, this trust in the judicial system can be augmented. Moreover, in some cases, the truth commission may actually be afforded quasi-judicial powers that allow it to turn the evidence collected over to authorities involved in other retributive mechanisms. In this way, the truth commission and national trials, for example, may actually work in tandem.

Fourth, as mentioned above, truth commissions are often tailored to a society's particular circumstances. This specificity allows the appointed truth commission the opportunity to address directly the crimes committed within a given society. Obviously, the situation in each society will be different. The Guatemalan Commission for Historical Clarification was agreed to in 1994 by the Guatemalan government and leftist rebels after nearly thirty years and more than 200,000 deaths and disappearances. The Guatemalan commission, when it began work in 1997, was mandated to work with the armed forces and guerrilla organizations and even appointed a liaison team to carry out a special investigation of both organizations. Conversely, the Argentine National Commission on the Disappeared was established in 1983 to uncover the details of disappearances carried out under several successive military juntas. To date, no truth commission has borne more than a slight resemblance to the next. Yet each has gone some distance to specifically attend to the abuses that were carried out within the society in question.

Fifth, and more importantly, truth commissions are often able to operate in a much less costly fashion than their retributive counterparts. After a period of mass atrocity, societies are left devastated. The impact is often felt both physically and socially. The destruction of the physical infrastructure becomes apparent in crumbling hospitals, bullet-riddled buildings, and collapsed roads and bridges. The social infrastructure, too, is ruined. People no longer feel able to trust in their friends, neighbours, or government institutions. Yet in most cases, the finite financial resources of the society enable it to tackle either the physical *or* the social problems. Truth commissions require less staff to be able to operate at full capacity and are able to address significantly more cases in a shorter period of time. As a result, the truth commission presents itself as an attractive option to many societies in the early stages of transition.

Lastly, and above all, the truth commission acts to foster aspects of reconciliation. Although truth commissions have been variously concerned with finding details of disappearances, government complicity, or guerrilla activity, among others, the main desired outcome implicit in the mandate and goals of each commission is reconciliation. That is to say, one of the underlying purposes of any truth commission is to bring the factions of society that have been at odds to a point where they are once again able to live and work together. Such individual and societal reconciliation can lead to strengthened civil society and even the re-establishment of democracy among the population.[5] By its very nature, then, the truth commission, as a mechanism of restorative (rather than retributive) justice, is significantly better able to provide the foundation for these desired effects.

CONCLUSION

One must be careful not to confuse the very different processes of retributive and restorative justice. It is clear that retributive processes such as the accountability trial are able to perform a particular function. It is also clear that, given the proper support and resources, they can do it well. Restorative mechanisms such as the truth commission, however, perform a substantially different set of tasks. Indeed, trials and truth commissions fulfill a disparate set of functions and must be recognized as being distinctly different. For a variety of reasons, detailed above, truth commissions are better suited to bring about the processes of restorative justice, including societal healing and reconciliation.

NOTES

1. Martha Minow, *Between Vengeance and Forgiveness: Facing History after Genocide and Mass Violence* (Boston: Beacon Press, 1998), 25.

2. Kay Johnson, "Will Justice Ever Be Served?" *Time*, 10 April 2000, 17.

3. Adapted from Sinclair Dinnen, "Restorative Justice in Papua New Guinea," *International Journal of the Sociology of Law* 25 (1997): 245–62.

4. The Republic of Uganda, *The Report of the Commission of Inquiry into Violations of Human Rights* (Kampala: UPPC, 1994), 3.

5. Consideration of the outcomes of societal reconciliation and acknowledgement are only now beginning to emerge. See, for example, Joanna R. Quinn, "Acknowledgement: The Road to Forgiveness," Institute on Globalization and the Human Condition Working Paper Series, McMaster University, January 2003, available at www.humanities.mcmaster.ca/~global/wps/Quinn.pdf.

✗ **NO**
Challenging Human Rights as Restorative Justice
RICHARD ASHBY WILSON

In the 1990s in democratizing countries of Latin America, Eastern Europe, and South Africa, human rights emerged as a universal panacea to authoritarianism. Human rights were demanded by ordinary citizens massed in the squares of Leipzig or on the streets of Bisho in South Africa, and they became the bedrock of the new constitutional order. Human rights legislation became a central component in the transformation of repressive state institutions and the establishing of the rule of law after authoritarian rule. In each society, new political leaders had to face the question of how to deal with the gross human rights violations of the past, and they set up new institutions and commissions to reaffirm human dignity and prevent the reoccurrence of mass atrocities.

One result of their increasing popularity was that human rights became detached from their legal foundations and transformed into a generalized moral and political discourse, which is then used to address all manner of power relations among individuals, groups, and states. The broad extension of human rights talk intensified as democratizing regimes, with crumbling economies and fractured social orders, grasped for unifying metaphors. Human rights seemed to provide an ideological adhesive through their emphasis on truth and reconciliation. Indeed, the ideological promiscuity of human rights – their ability to appeal to diverse and often opposed political constituencies – is one explanation for their wide-ranging globalization in the 1990s.

Now over a decade after the wave of democratic transitions, it is time to take stock and to evaluate critically the role of human rights ideas and institutions. It has became possible to move on from simply extolling human rights as a universally "good thing" to examining what happened when human rights institutions were established in the context of political compromise, where neither opposing side in a civil war had won an outright military victory and where key perpetrators of the era of repression (from Vice-President F.W. de Klerk in South Africa to Senator Augusto Pinochet in Chile) still occupied positions of political power.

This evaluation requires a political analysis of the concrete conditions faced by new political elites and, in particular, of the fractured nation identity and lack of legitimacy of state institutions. It focuses on how new political leaders often used human rights to re-imagine the nation and to manufacture legitimacy for key state institutions. By focusing on how new elites have used human rights to legitimate their own regimes, we can understand one reason why, ten years or so after the transitions, human rights have come to lack authority in the eyes of many citizens in Latin America and South Africa. In South Africa, human rights became less and less legitimate as an emergent political elite used human rights to shore up bargains made with the outgoing authoritarian political establishment.

Even though the new vision of nation-building appeared to be characterized by liberal values of tolerance and decency, it had its own morally coercive implications, as new amnesty provisions deprived victims of their right to prosecute perpetrators. In South Africa, retributive justice[1] based upon punishment of perpetrators was defined as "un-African" by former Archbishop Desmond Tutu, chair of the country's Truth and Reconciliation Commission (or TRC), which functioned in its entirety from 1996 to 1998. Desmond Tutu's religious vision of reconciliation stressed public confession by victims, created meaning for suffering through a narrative of sacrifice and liberation, and encouraged the forsaking of revenge. Reconciliation portrayed retributive justice as blood-lust and as an affront to democratization and the new political order. In place of retribution, Tutu promoted a restorative justice view of human rights, which has as its aim the restoration of social bonds and the repairing of the torn fabric of society.

The TRC's version of reconciliation was conveyed to the population primarily through the Human Rights Violations (HRV) hearings. For two years during the historical moment in which the fledgling "new South Africa" was born, the TRC's hearings became national rituals of "reconciliation," forgiveness, and truth-telling. Reconciliation is a quasi-religious concept that became a guiding principle for new rituals of civic nationalism. HRV hearings were emotionally intense public ceremonies that generated collective moral values and sought to inculcate them in all who participated, including those watching hearings on television each night. Like all rituals, they were met with a complex mixture of compliance, acceptance, indignation, and resistance.

There were a number of positive benefits to South Africa's experiment in truth and reconciliation. Transitions from authoritarianism require the breaking of hegemonic silences and the construction of a new public space where ordinary citizens can speak openly about the consequences of state terror. Public recognition of formerly repressed stories allowed greater mutual understanding between the sections of South African society that had been separated by the racialized boundaries of apartheid. This made possible a greater "fusion of horizons," to use the phrase of philosopher Hans-Georg Gadamer, a base line of understanding, and it defined the parameters of discussion on the past. As Michael Ignatieff (2001) has contended, the recognition and acceptance of these formerly repressed truths, as well as their integration into a public narrative about the past, circumscribes the range of impermissible lies. After the South African Truth and Reconciliation Commission, one can no longer maintain, as the National Party once attempted to argue, that apartheid was a benevolent, "good neighbor" policy somehow gone awry. Nor can one deny that tens of thousands were killed by the operatives of an abhorrent political system.

However, the identification of human rights with restorative justice was not without serious drawbacks. In the South African transition, reconciliation became a symbol of the pact between the old, outgoing apartheid elite and the incoming elite, a pact that perpetuated an aspect of authoritarian legality – namely impunity – in the present. Here, reconciliation became the language not of principle and inalienable individual rights, but of compromise, political hedging, and trade-offs that included amnesty — an official pardon — for human rights offenders. This strategy of reconciling with past enemies became more widespread beyond South Africa and was reinforced in countries such as El Salvador and Sierra Leone by United Nations missions and international nongovernmental organizations seeking diplomatic solutions to conflicts. In these situations, reconciliation helps to forge a new nation-building ideology that values political expediency over legality and consolidating the rule of law. But this is done at the cost of sacrificing the individual rights and dignity of victims, and especially their right to justice as enshrined in new bills of rights in national constitutions. As Borneman (1997) contends, the most successful postauthoritarian regimes are those that place accountability and retributive justice at the center of their moral and political project.

Advocates of restorative justice often maintain that truth commissions can fulfill a need for public education on human rights and democratic values of tolerance. In the case of South Africa, the TRC's objectives of creating reconciliation and building a new inclusive and benevolent image of the nation were only partially fulfilled, as maintained in my book *The Politics of Truth and Reconciliation in South Africa* (2001). For all their media coverage, TRC hearings were often little more than a symbolic and ritualized performance with a weak impact on vengeance in urban townships. The transfer of reconciling values from an elite to the masses was uneven and ambiguous. In the case of South Africa and its impressive array of new human rights institutions, the involvement of victims did not necessarily mean a deep loyalty to nation-building or a new language of rights.

Even some members of the South African Truth and Reconciliation Commission came to recognize that reconciliation demanded too much of victims, and that the concept was excessively infused with Christian connotations of "turning the other cheek" and "love thine enemy." Commissioners consequently abandoned the practice of asking victims at the Human Rights Violation hearings whether they forgave their persecutor. Reconciliation implies a shared set of moral values that may not actually exist on the ground, especially in societies ravaged by long-standing conflicts. Thus, it has the potential to coerce individuals into compliant positions they would not adopt of their own accord. In the post-conflict order, everyone is required to co-exist peacefully and to forsake individual acts of revenge, but, beyond that, it could be argued that individuals have the right to think and feel what they like, including hatred for their former enemy. This is a central tenet of liberalism — that governments legislate actions, not beliefs.

My own ethnographic research in the townships of Johannesburg had led me to the conclusion that, contra the established view within the Truth and Reconciliation Commission, retributive understandings of justice are more salient in South African society than ideas of reconciliation and forgiveness. The main reason why the TRC could not convert many South Africans to its view of restorative justice was that, as a result of many years of state violence and counter-violence, most citizens held a punitive, "eye-for-an-eye" vision of justice. This is not a result of "African culture" but of the specific historical conditions created by apartheid and the anti-apartheid struggle. In the African townships surrounding metropolitan centers such as Johannesburg and Durban, the anti-apartheid movement had militarized the youth in response to the counter-insurgency strategy of the apartheid state. In 1990, a war erupted between the anti-apartheid African National Congress (ANC) and the Inkatha Freedom Party, the party of Zulu nationalism, which was armed and trained by apartheid state operatives. There were also battles within the ANC that followed generational lines, where youths were organized into Special Defense Units and older men were members of a separate ANC military structure – MK.

In the absence of gainful employment after the first multi-racial elections in 1994, many hardened cadres of the political struggle turned to criminality. Post-apartheid African townships became characterized by a patchwork of warring gangs who terrorized the local population. In the ten years after apartheid, South Africa had some of the world's worst crime figures for homicide, rape, and car hijackings, and it also has one of the highest incarceration rates in the world. These harsh realities ensure that revenge remains a feature of the political landscape and they hamper lofty sentiments of reconciliation.

Advocates of restorative justice such as Joanna Quinn argue persuasively that truth commissions can strengthen the new judicial infrastructure by acting inclusively and building trust. Yet I would argue that in practice, the South African TRC was not particularly effective in creating a new culture of human rights or greater respect for the rule of law. Because of its emphasis on reconciliation, the South African Truth and Reconciliation Commission did not sufficiently engage with popular understandings of justice based in widespread practices of revenge. Instead, the TRC demonized understandable feelings of retribution as dangerous to the well-being of the new "rainbow nation." This approach simply did not take into account the widespread views on justice of many South Africans. As long as human rights institutions worked to undermine criminal prosecutions and financial reparations from perpetrators, they would be resisted by some victims and denounced as a "sell-out" by informal justice institutions such as community courts.

Because Africans were neglected for so many years by the formal legal system,[2] they set up local courts to mediate and adjudicate many of their own problems. In the 1990s, this took place with little reference to the criminal justice system or bodies such as the TRC, which was seen by many people I interviewed as weak and ineffectual. The low level of reparations and the amnesty process within the TRC combined to strengthen the view that human rights were really about the violation of principles of "natural justice." Instead of appealing to human rights commissions to solve problems of social order, many Africans turn to over

400 local courts in rural and urban areas across the country. Local legal structures deal mostly with petty crimes and domestic disputes, but they have also taken on the legacy of past political violence. In particular, they have protected returning black councilors and their families who were chased out of the townships in 1984, when their houses were burned and some family members were "necklaced." Unlike human rights commissions, many community members take the view that local courts will always find out the guilty and achieve justice through vengeful punishment, rather than "reconciliation" and amnesties. Thus, a discontinuity between legal systems has emerged in the South African transition through the opposition between local, retributive justice versus national, restorative justice.

The unintended consequences of popular justice are worth remarking upon here. Despite the opposition of local African courts to the TRC, there is a strong convergence in the aims and objectives of local and human rights institutions around co-existence. I hesitate to use the word *reconciliation*, since no one I interviewed thought that it accurately described the process of reincorporation of former "apartheid collaborators." Reconciliation is clearly the moral discourse of national-level institutions. Yet it is ironic that neighborhood courts that portray themselves as a "tribal" authority and that reject the TRC's humanitarian view of human rights for a more punitive and retributive view of justice are in the end promoting similar solutions to the TRC. They do so not through notions of reconciliation derived from Christian ethics and human rights talk, but through expressions of legitimate traditionalist authority and the possibility of punitive sanction against any who transgress its decisions.

The empirical evidence from other democratizing countries shows that retributive justice can itself lead to reconciliation (in the sense of peaceful co-existence and the legal, non-violent adjudication of conflict) in the long run. The most damaging outcome of truth commissions results from their equating of human rights with reconciliation and amnesty. This delegitimizes them enormously in relation to popular understandings of justice and can lead to greater criminalization in society. There is growing evidence from Eastern Europe and elsewhere (Borneman 1997) that it is necessary for democratizing regimes to challenge directly the impunity created during the authoritarian order if they are going to avoid an upsurge in criminality and a lack of respect for state institutions.

Ironically, human rights became the language of restorative justice and forgiveness of human rights offenders in South Africa, whereas at the same time in international contexts human rights were developing in just the opposite direction with the establishing of the International Criminal Court and a number of successful prosecutions brought by the UN war crimes tribunals for the former Yugoslavia and Rwanda. Pursuing more criminal trials of perpetrators within South Africa not only would have had the advantage of fortifying the rule of law and indirectly addressing wider criminalization in society, but also would have linked human rights to popular understandings of justice and accorded human rights-oriented institutions much greater legitimacy in the process. This, in turn, could have helped resolve the wider legitimacy crisis of post-apartheid state institutions in a more effective manner. A policy of allowing more civil prosecutions of offenders would have made the transformation of the judiciary clearer and more evident.

This view is backed up by a salient interpretation of international human rights treaties, which holds that those responsible for gross human rights violations must be brought before a court of law and held accountable. In the pages of the *Yale Law Journal*, Diane Orentlicher (1991: 2540) reiterated the international legal imperative to punish that transcends national political contexts:

> [T]he central importance of the rule of law in civilized societies requires, within defined but principles limits, prosecution of especially atrocious crimes ... [I]nternational law itself helps assure the survival of fragile democracies when its clear pronouncement removes certain atrocious crimes from the provincial realm of a country's internal politics and thereby places those crimes squarely within the scope of universal concern ... A state's complete failure to punish repeated or notorious instances of these offenses violates its obligations under customary international law.

I am persuaded that Orentlicher has articulated correctly the ideal relationship between international human rights and national processes of democratization and the establishment of the rule of law. The international character of human rights laws and institutions exists to reinforce national processes of delivering retributive justice for victims of human rights violations. The rule of law cannot meaningfully be said to exist if it is predicated upon impunity for gross human rights violations committed in the authoritarian past, since, as Orentlicher (1991: 2542) states:

> If law is unavailable to punish widespread brutality of the recent past, what lesson can be offered for the future? ... Societies recently scourged by lawlessness need look no further than their own past to discover the costs of impunity. Their history provides sobering cause to believe, with William Pitt, that tyranny begins where law ends.

The justice advanced by international criminal law and ad hoc human rights tribunals is retributive justice: punishment for offenders and just compensation for victims. In transitional contexts such as South Africa, human rights institutions should ideally reinforce this understanding of justice. However, in countries emerging from authoritarian rule, human rights commissions often come to undermine accountability in favor of nation-building, thus thwarting the intention of national and international human rights courts. Truth commissions often signify individual or blanket amnesty for perpetrators and a limited "truth finding" operation as a parallel compromise solution.

In sum, we can say that in the 1980s and 1990s, human rights at the national level often became the language of pragmatic political compromise rather than the language of principle and accountability being pursued through international legal institutions. This is the main obstacle to popular acceptance of human rights in newly democratized countries. The redefinition, and some would say deformation, of human rights during democratic transitions to mean amnesty and reconciliation conflicted not only with widespread notions of justice in society, but also, it could be argued, with a state's duty to punish human rights offenders as established in international criminal law.

The appropriation of human rights by nation-building politicians and their identification with forgiveness, reconciliation, and restorative justice elevates social stability as the greatest social good. This image of human rights undermines accountability and the rule of law, and with it the breadth and depth of the democratization process. If human rights are associated instead with a principled position of accountability of key human rights offenders, then this would bring human rights into line with the views of the majority, who see justice as proportional punishment for wrongdoing. This would also connect national change to international human rights law, which increasingly takes the view that there are no conditions under which a torturer or a mass murderer should go free.

With the establishment of the International Criminal Court in 2002 and extradition proceedings against General Augusto Pinochet in Britain in 1999, which established that heads of state do not enjoy immunity from prosecution for human rights violations such as torture, the stage seems increasingly set for international human rights law to transcend national legal systems and to prosecute those involved in gross human rights violations with greater vigor. The arrest and extradition to the UN war crimes tribunal of Slobodan Milosevic in June 2001 sets an international precedent, as Milosevic is the first head of state to stand trial for human rights abuses at an international tribunal. The tide of global justice is now turning in favor of legality, prosecution, and punishment rather than diplomacy, reconciliation, and forgiveness.

Despite the protestations of some political leaders who replace the dictators, international prosecutions are seen as wholly just by many of those who lived through periods of violence, terror, and authoritarianism. In an international context where the jurisdiction of human rights institutions is intensifying and broadening, it is misguided to delegitimize human rights at the national level by detaching them from a retributive understanding of justice and attaching them to a religious notion of reconciliation-forgiveness, regrettable amnesty laws, and an elite project of nation-building. Democratizing regimes should seek legitimacy less through nation-building efforts to forge a moral unity and communitarian ideology and more through accountability and justice, defined as proportional retribution and procedural fairness. The role of human rights commissions in all of this is to create the bedrock of accountability upon which democratic legitimacy can be built.

REFERENCES

Borneman, Jon. 1997. *Settling Accounts: Violence, Justice and Accountability in Postsocialist Europe.* Princeton: Princeton University Press.

Ignatieff, Michael. 2001. "Introduction." In Jillian Edelstein, *Truth and Lies: Stories from the Truth and Reconciliation Commission in South Africa*: 15–21. London: Granta Books.

Nozick, R. 1981. *Philosophical Explanations.* Cambridge, MA: Harvard University Press.

Orentlicher, Diane. 1991. "Settling Accounts: The Duty to Prosecute Human Rights Violations of a Prior Regime." *Yale Law Journal* 100: 2539–2615.

Wilson, Richard Ashby. 2001. *The Politics of Truth and Reconciliation in South Africa: Legitimizing the Post-Apartheid State.* Law and Society Series. Cambridge: Cambridge University Press.

NOTES

1. By retributive justice, I mean the prosecution of alleged criminal acts in a recognized court according to standard procedures and rules of legal evidence, and if guilt is established, sentencing (as punishment) proportional to the gravity of the harm and the degree of responsibility of the wrongdoer. My understanding follows Robert Nozick's (1981: 363–97) "non-teleological retributivism" that does not have as its aim the moral improvement of the offender.

2. There are other important state institutions to consider apart from the TRC – namely the criminal justice system itself, which has received only a fraction of the international interest that the TRC has enjoyed. The TRC deflected attention from the more serious project of making the legal system more representative, efficient, and fair.

POSTSCRIPT

This debate raises some interesting questions regarding the process of democratization and peacebuilding in conflict-torn societies and the ways in which the international community can best facilitate such efforts. Both human-rights advocates and conflict resolution specialists, through the work of non-governmental organizations (NGOs) and international organizations, have become involved in the efforts of transitional nations to transform themselves into more stable, just societies. It is clear, however, that these two groups have a different orientation to the task of nation-building.

Conflict resolution specialists are focused on a more pragmatic, interest-based approach that desires to build a sense of cooperation in divided communities. Thus, they appear more willing to make compromises and avoid sensitive issues that may cause further division and strife. Hence, the concept of restorative justice discussed by Joanna Quinn has considerable appeal to them. In contrast, human-rights advocates tend to focus on a more principle-driven, rights-based approach. To many peace groups, this approach appears to be overly legalistic and punitive in nature; they fear that an emphasis on retributive justice may prolong the conflict and continue to exacerbate tensions. As a result, there is a tendency to see human-rights and peacemaking as being in competition. But do these two approaches necessarily stand in contradiction to one another? Is there a way in which a human rights focus can been integrated into peace work in a way that will contribute to the promotion of human security? A useful starting point for answering these questions is the Winter 2002 issue of *Human Rights Dialogue* on integrating human rights and peace work, available at www.cceia.org.

Suggested Additional Readings

Adam, Heribert. 1998. "Trading Justice for Truth." *The World Today* 54 (January 1998): 11–13.

Dugard, John. "Reconciliation and Justice: The South African Experience." *Transnational Law & Contemporary Problems* 8, no. 2 (1998): 277–311.

Goldstone, Richard. "Exposing Human Rights Abuses: A Help or Hindrance to Reconciliation?" *Hastings Constitutional Law Quarterly* 22 (Spring 1995): 607–21.

____. "Justice As a Tool for Peace-Making: Truth Commissions and International Criminal Tribunals." *New York University Journal of International Law and Politics* 28, no. 3 (1996): 485–503.

Graybill, Lyn S. "Pursuit of Truth and Reconciliation in South Africa." *Africa Today: A Quarterly Review* 45 (1998): 103–33.

____. *Truth and Reconciliation in Africa: Miracle or Model?* Boulder, Colo.: Lynne Rienner, 2002.

Hayner, Priscilla B. *Unspeakable Truths.* New York: Routledge, 2003.

Kritz, Neil J., ed. *Transitional Justice: How Emerging Democracies Reckon with Former Regimes,* vols. 1–3. Washington, D.C.: United States Institute of Peace, 1996.

Little, David. "A Different Kind of Justice: Dealing with Human Rights Violations in Transitional Societies." *Ethics and International Affairs* 13 (1999): 65–80.

Minow, Martha. *Between Vengeance and Forgiveness: Facing History after Genocide and Mass Violence.* Boston: Beacon Press, 1998.

Pankhurst, Donna. 1999. "Issues of Justice and Reconciliation in Complex Political Emergencies: Conceptualizing Reconciliation, Justice and Peace." *Third World Quarterly* 20, no. 1 (1999): 239–56.

Quinn, Joanna R. "Dealing with a Legacy of Mass Atrocity: Truth Commissions in Uganda and Chile." *Netherlands Quarterly of Human Rights* 19, no. 4 (December 2001): 383–402.

Rotberg, Robert I., and Dennis Thompson, eds. *Truth v. Justice: The Morality of Truth Commissions.* Princeton, N.J.: Princeton University Press, 2000.

Tepperman, Jonathan. "Truth and Consequences." *Foreign Affairs* 81, no. 2 (March–April 2002): 128–45.

Zegeye, Abebe, and Ian Liebenberg. "Pathway to Democracy? The Case of the South African Truth and Reconciliation Process." *Social Identities* 4, no. 3 (1998): 319–20.

InfoTrac® College Edition

Search for the following articles in the InfoTrac® database:

Garkawe, Sam. "The South African Truth and Reconciliation Commission: A Suitable Model to Enhance the Role and Rights of the Victims of Gross Violations of Human Rights?" *Melbourne University Law Review* 27, no. 2 (August 2003): 334–80.

Hayner, Priscilla B. "Fifteen Truth Commissions —1974 to 1994: A Comparative Study." *Human Rights Quarterly* 16, no. 4 (November 1994): 597–655.

Kaye, Mike. "The Role of Truth Commissions in the Search for Justice, Reconciliation and Democratisation: The Salvadorean and Honduran Cases." *Journal of Latin American Studies* 29, no. 3 (October 1997): 693–716.

For more articles, enter:

"truth commissions" or "restorative justice" in the keyword search.

Web Resources

For current URLs for the following websites, visit www.crosscurrents.nelson.com.

TRUTH COMMISSIONS DIGITAL COLLECTION

www.usip.org/library/truth.html

This site provides a complete list of truth commissions along with links to key documents and reports related to the work of each commission.

INCORE GUIDE TO INTERNET RESOURCES ON TRUTH AND RECONCILIATION

www.incore.ulst.ac.uk/cds/themes/truth.html

INCORE is a joint project between the University of Ulster and United Nations University focusing on peace and reconciliation efforts. This site has an extensive list of resources on all aspects of truth commissions and peacemaking.

CENTRE FOR THE STUDY OF VIOLENCE AND RECONCILIATION

www.csvr.org.za

The website of this South African NGO contains some good studies on various aspects of truth commissions; click on Publications to access these materials.

INTERNATIONAL INTERNET BIBLIOGRAPHY ON TRANSITIONAL JUSTICE

userpage.zedat.fu-berlin.de/~theissen/biblio/index.htm

This page, prepared by Gunnar Theissen, offers an extensive list of resources on transitional justice, with a special focus on South Africa and Germany.

Should States Pursue an Open-Border Policy toward Migrants?

✔ **YES**
ANDREW COYNE, "The Case for Open Immigration: Why Opening Up Our Borders Would Be Good for the Country and Good for the Soul," *The Next City* (Winter 1995): 34–40, 60–66

✘ **NO**
G.E. DIRKS, "Why States Are Justified in Limiting Their Entry of Migrants"

Mass migrations provoked by disasters or political upheaval have recurred throughout history. With the institutionalization of a global system of states, the acceptance of migrants rests on the will of the receiving state. Historically, many states, such as Canada and the United States, took an open-door policy toward migrants, seeing them as a potential resource in the process of nation-building. Migrants helped settle underpopulated regions of the country, brought with them new skills, and were often a source of cheap labour, especially when they were willing to take on the menial, low-paid, and frequently dangerous jobs that local populations shunned. Receiving countries such as Canada advertised and actively recruited immigrants, providing incentives to those willing to take up the offer to leave their homes and emigrate abroad. In the early part of the twentieth century, Canada even took some 100 000 orphaned and destitute children from Great Britain for cheap farm labour.

The open-door policy of this period of history contrasts sharply with the growing hostility to immigrants in traditional destination countries today. International migration has come to be seen by many as a potential threat that recipient countries must take steps to control. This changed perception is partly rooted in the changing patterns of migration in the 1990s. Today, an estimated 125 million people live in countries not of their birth. The nature of international migration flows has become much more complex. Each year, an average of one million people are admitted to traditional receiving countries as legally admitted, permanent immigrants. An estimated twenty million people are living in other countries as legally admitted seasonal labourers or contract workers. Another twenty million are classified by the United Nations High Commissioner for Refugees (UNHCR) as "refugees and other peoples of concern." These people have been displaced outside of their country because of political conflict, natural disasters, or other factors. An estimated one million are asylum-seekers asking for refugee status in foreign countries. Finally, it is estimated that there are thirty to forty million illegal, undocumented migrants.

Several factors have contributed to this dramatic rise in international migration. During the Cold War, communist regimes, fearing a mass exodus of dissatisfied citizens, prevented their residents from emigrating or even travelling abroad. Since the collapse of the U.S.S.R., Central and Eastern European countries now see emigration as a way of reducing domestic unemployment levels while generating foreign exchange from remittances of workers abroad. Economic crises and a growing gap in income and lifestyles have led to an increased flow of migrants from developing countries in the South to industrialized countries in the North. The growing number of "complex political emergencies" in regions of Africa has produced large numbers of "forced migrants," people who have been compelled to flee their homelands because of ethnic violence, political instability, or economic collapse.

As the number of migrants has grown and the situations these migrants are leaving have become more complex, traditional distinctions between political refugees and economic migrants have become blurred. Are Haitian migrants to the United States political refugees fleeing persecution or are they economic migrants seeking a better standard of living in a wealthier neighbouring country? In addition, the traditional distinctions between sending, transit, and recipient countries are breaking down. For example, Germany, which has historically produced large numbers of migrants, is now an important transit country for migrants from Eastern Europe and the Third World. And it is under increasing pressure to permanently settle larger numbers of migrants.

As a result of this increasingly complex situation, international migration has become a sensitive political issue in many receiving states. Fears are expressed regarding the impact of migration on unemployment levels and the ability of government to maintain social and health services, which are already facing pressure from deficit-reduction measures. The growing diversity of geographical sources of migrants has raised questions about the impact of migration on national identity and the ability of societies to cope with cultural diversity. For example, in the United States, citizens of some states have been asked to vote on propositions designed to protect English as the official language of the United States and to strip illegal immigrants of any social or education benefits.

At the same time, governments have increasingly looked at ways to tighten the regulation of international migration flows by narrowing the definition of refugees, establishing stricter procedures for processing claims of asylum-seekers, and reducing the movement of illegal immigrants across the borders. Such efforts raise important questions about the role of international migration today and the rights of states to regulate their borders.

In the first article, Andrew Coyne, a noted Canadian journalist and columnist, discusses the historical role of immigration in Canada. He contends that immigration has made and continues to make a positive contribution to Canadian society. He argues that what Canada needs is not a more restrictive regulation of immigration but a policy of welcoming even larger numbers of immigrants in the future. On the other hand, Gerry Dirks of Brock University examines the reasons states are justified in seeking to regulate the flow of migrants across their borders.

✔ **YES**

The Case for Open Immigration: Why Opening Up Our Borders Would Be Good for the Country and Good for the Soul

ANDREW COYNE

Somewhere around the 15th century, cities began to lose their walls. Since their rebirth from the rubble of the Dark Ages four centuries before, the cities of Europe had sheltered within layers of protective fortifications, adding new ones as expansion demanded. Town and country were then separate in tradition, hierarchy and poverty; cities were dynamic, egalitarian and wealthy. It was only natural that they should be separate in a physical as well as spiritual sense.

The medieval city filled the role the New World would play in later centuries. It was a place of escape, an island of liberty, where the serf, if he could evade recapture by his lord for a year and a day, became a freeman, with the special rights and privileges that city residents enjoyed. Yet it also offered security, a sanctuary for the merchants and artisans against the depredations of the nobility — and of competitors. Cities had their own currencies, their own weights and measures, their own tolls and tariffs. Outsiders were restricted to a particular corner of the marketplace, their stay limited to a certain number of days. They were often required to register the name of their innkeeper with the authorities.

As the influx from the countryside progressed, however, and as the town was a centre of production as well as commerce, the original urban preference for autarchy gave way in succeeding centuries to a high level of trade between city and hinterland. This mutual interdependence, besides greatly enriching them both, blurred many of the distinctions between them. With the rise of the nation-state, the walls withered away. The nation-state now provided protection; a transcendent national identity bolstered the community of city life.

Social differences remained, of course. But the two tribes, urban and rural, no longer viewed each other as alien. They were, they realized, countrymen, subjects of the same king. Today, we would consider it absurd not only to put up walls, but to place virtually any barrier to the flow of people, trade or capital across city limits. The outside world starts at the international boundary, where we now place barriers.

These have grown ever fewer over the last two centuries. Since the publication of Adam Smith's *Wealth of Nations*, freedom of trade between nations has fought a slow, unsteady but still inexorable path to fruition. The 19th century's gold standard and today's electronic integration of financial markets gave us first the free and now the instantaneous flow of capital around the world.

But in one crucial respect, the movement of people, progress has curiously been reversed. Controls on immigration have multiplied. Until the 19th century, when nearly 60 million Europeans crossed the seas, their numbers were not even recorded. Immigration quotas are largely a 20th-century invention. Indeed, passports didn't exist before the First World War.

While restrictions on trade and capital flows remain only in the face of concerted intellectual attack, the notion that immigration can and should be controlled stands as unquestioned orthodoxy. Even economists, who generally agree that the free movement of people, like any other productive resource, would benefit the world economy — some studies suggest the gains would exceed those from removing all other trade restrictions combined — rarely support open immigration. Rival camps of restrictionists dominate the immigration debate. Both agree there must be a ceiling; they differ only on its level. Both accept that immigrants must be selected; they differ solely on the criteria. I propose to challenge these assumptions. I question not merely whether we should have more or less immigration, nor whether we should use this or that basis of selection, but whether the whole moral premise of the enterprise — that is, that the current inhabitants of a country may rightfully bar others from joining them — is sustained by anything more than the force of habit. I argue not merely that we liberalize immigration controls, but that we abolish them. [. . .]

Any proposal to add to the population through immigration inevitably raises a wide range of fears that might be grouped together under the heading of "too many people." These fears may revolve around unemployment, wages, social programs, cultural values or the environment; they may focus on the level of population, its density or its rate of growth; but they are invariably and unshakably rooted in a belief, not only that there exists a natural level of population for Canada, but that by a remarkable coincidence, we are precisely at it.

This is most plainly stated in that most antique of complaints, that immigration adds to unemployment. If there are just so many jobs to go around, it is reasoned, and if a certain number of workers are added to the labor force, unemployment will rise in like measure. But there is no natural limit to the demand for labor. As the economist Herbert Grubel puts it, every immigrant "brings along hands and a mouth." The money immigrants earn at their jobs fuels the consumption that creates jobs.

That is why the United States, with a population of 250 million, can have a lower unemployment rate than Canada, with a population of 29 million. It is also why, in the 1950s, West Germany could absorb 13 million refugees into a prewar population of 39 million, yet emerge from the decade with the lowest unemployment rate in Europe: just one percent. The Economic Council commissioned a battery of econometric studies seeking a link between the unemployment rate and either the level of population or its growth rate, using data from many different countries, and from different periods of time in Canada. It found none.

A related concern is that immigrants tend to depress wages. With more competition for jobs, workers are forced to undercut each other. For some current residents, especially unskilled workers, the distributional consequences would seem potentially painful. That's the theory.

In practice, the very increase in profits arising from all cheap labor just as quickly attracts an offsetting flood of capital from abroad. The almost perfect mobility of international capital is one of the most widely remarked phenomena of our times. Again, empirical research supports the thesis that countries with larger or faster-growing populations have no tendency to suffer low or declining wages. China is not poor because it is populous. It may, however, be populous because it is poor. It is poor because it is communist. Now that it is getting less communist, it is getting less poor.

If anything, the effects on incomes are positive. The Economic Council estimates, on the basis of scale efficiencies alone, an increase of 0.3 percent in per capita GDP for every additional million people over current population levels, or about $71 per resident citizen in 1991 dollars, every year, forever. Put another way, that's a gift to the native-born population of almost $2,000 per immigrant per year. Capitalizing the discounted value of all future gains, that works out to a lump-sum benefit to the native-born population of $76,000 per immigrant family of four. The returns from each added million diminish at higher levels of population. At current rates of investment, the Economic Council estimates the "optimal" population for Canada to be 100 million, at which point real per capita incomes would be about seven percent higher than at present – which would seem consistent with the actual gap between Canadian and U.S. incomes.

An objection might be that the same economies of scale could be captured simply through trade with other countries. But recent research, including that by Michael Porter in his best-selling *The Competitive Advantage of Nations*, stresses the special intensity of trading activity within domestic markets. The volume of trade, and with it the opportunity for specialization, is much greater among 100 million people inside one set of borders with one set of laws than it is between two countries of 50 million each, even where these are partners in a free trade area. Not least of the gains, of course, are those that stem from the mobility of labor – a freedom enjoyed within a full-blown economic union, but not within most free trade areas.

And these are just the measured gains. Some analysts, notably Julian Simon of the University of Maryland, point to other economic benefits less easily captured in the data. Large populations, Simon notes, produce "more Einsteins," bright people with bright ideas, which can benefit the rest of the population, beyond the returns accruing to the Einsteins themselves. More firms mean more competition, more products and more choices for consumers; larger and more competitive national markets offer more scope for firms to learn how to make and sell products for a world market. Immigrants, moreover, are more likely than the general population to be in their peak saving years (nearly half arrive between the ages of 20 and 39), with still more incentive to save: The older they are on arrival, the less their eligibility for contributory pensions. Higher national savings reduce the need for foreign capital to finance domestic borrowing, including government deficits, which helps the balance of payments.

Indeed, in the decades to come, the demographic role of immigration will assume increasing importance. The fertility rate has declined to 1.7, less than half the baby boom pace of the 1950s, and well below replacement level. With no immigration (and with existing emigration of about 50,000 per year), population would peak around the year 2015, dwindling to 10 million by the end of the following century. We'll need about 200,000 immigrants a year just to keep the population from falling. Of more immediate concern, as the baby boomers age, the costs of the elderly's pensions and health care will increase dramatically. With no net immigration, the "dependency ratio" − the number of children and old people as a proportion of the working age population − would rise to more than 85 percent by 2040, from 65 percent today. True, immigration, at least at the levels most people envisage, cannot stem the aging tide. But it can't hurt. Even at a net immigration rate of 0.8 percent of the population, only slightly higher than present rates, the dependency ratio could be held to about 72 percent.

Which brings us to perhaps the most direct and tangible economic benefit from immigration: its contribution to the public purse. Yes, contribution. The most common current fear about immigrants, that they impose an intolerable burden on the rest of us through their use of welfare and other public services, is the least defensible in fact.

Research by economist Ather Akbari of Saint Mary's University in Halifax, using data from Statistics Canada's Survey of Consumer Finances, shows no significant difference between immigrants and native-born Canadians in their total consumption of public services: They use more of some services, like education, but less of others, like pensions. Of particular note, immigrants are 23 percent less likely to draw unemployment insurance than native-born Canadians. They are also less likely to be on welfare. Even among recent (1981–85) immigrants, the 1986 census shows 12.5 percent on social assistance − higher than the 6.7 percent among those in the 1976–80 cohort, but lower than the 13.8 percent of native-born Canadians. Some provinces have done better than others. While immigrants make up 22 percent of British Columbia's population, they accounted for just 2.7 percent of its social assistance caseload in 1989.

But the other side of the ledger is just as important. Akbari's research confirms what other studies have shown: Immigrants as a group earn more than native-born Canadians, and hence pay more in taxes. While recent immigrants earn less than the national average − whether because of language and other adjustment difficulties, or simply because they tend to be younger and less advanced in their careers − within a decade or so they have caught up and surpassed it. Total household earnings of immigrants in 1990 averaged between $34,125 (for those who arrived in 1981–85) and $47,366 (for arrivals in the 1966–70 period), compared to $32,127 for all non-immigrant households.

Not only does the average immigrant household pay more than twice as much in taxes as it consumes in services, but the gap between the two is wider than in native-born households: That is, immigrant families pay more than their fair share in net contributions to the public treasury. Moreover, immigration spreads the cost of "pure public goods" like defence across a larger population, which reduces the bill to the average taxpayer: according to Akbari, by about $1,215 per immigrant household in 1990.

Far from a burden, in sum, immigrants transfer income to current residents. Akbari reckons that the average immigrant family paid the native-born population a premium of $1,813 in taxes net of services in 1990: a total annual transfer on the order of $2.6 billion, or about $100 per current resident. Or to put it another way, the typical young immigrant family arriving in 1990 would generate a discounted sum of $46,695 in net fiscal transfers to the native-born population over the next 45 years, in 1990 dollars. [. . .]

Those who insist on the necessity of selectivity, or fear the social costs of immigration, underestimate the high degree of self-selection involved when an immigrant, as the Confederation orator D'Arcy McGee put it, "heaves up the anchor of his heart from its old moorings." People are not normally inclined to leave their soil, their language, their culture, their family and friends, to travel 3,000 miles in the bottom of a boat to a strange and frozen land just to spend the rest of their lives on welfare. Nor is the survivor of a famine or pogrom likely to lack the basic resourcefulness required to succeed in such a land of peace and plenty as Canada. As immigration lawyer Peter Rekai has written, even the humblest immigrant brings "an intangible, immeasurable source of energy. It is a blend of hope, toil and ambition. It is the excitement generated by opportunities to break through previously impenetrable barriers of class and social standing. It is the movement generated by people on the climb: the bricklayers becoming builders, the clerks becoming supervisors, the cooks becoming restaurateurs."

That sort of human capital is not caught by such conventional measures as years of schooling – though here, too, immigrants have the edge. The median immigrant has 12.8 years of schooling, compared to 12.5 for his native-born counterpart. Indeed, a Statistics Canada review of 1991 census data, *Canada's Changing Immigrant Population*, indicates the "quality" of the immigrant population has been rising in recent years, even as the proportion passing through the points system has been falling. The obsession of so many with the supposed decline in quality of recent immigrants is out of all proportion to the available evidence. Studies purporting to show a decline generally use data from the early 1980s – a period of unusually restrictive entry – or else focus on those just off the proverbial boat, who always, in any period, underperform the average.

While immigrants form a slightly smaller proportion of the labor force than native-born Canadians, that's due to earlier arrivals, not later: Immigrants of the 1960s, 70s and 80s have higher than average participation rates. Immigrants are also, on average, more likely to be highly educated than those born in Canada: 14.4 percent have a university degree, compared with 10.5 percent among the native-born population. Of the more recent immigrants, arriving between 1981 and 1991, 17 percent had a university degree, compared with nine percent of those arriving before 1961. More than 55 percent of total immigrants are professional, skilled or semiskilled workers; that proportion has been rising steadily since the early 1980s and now stands at an all-time high.

The social characteristics of immigrants are even more striking. According to Statistics Canada, immigrants are more likely to be married than the average Canadian (66 percent to 52 percent), 22 percent less likely to be divorced. Fewer children of immigrants live with only one parent: 12 percent, in 1986, compared with more than 14 percent. Perhaps because of this stronger family structure, immigrants are, notwithstanding a few high-profile cases, less likely to land in jail than the rest of us, accounting for barely half as many penitentiary inmates in 1991 as their share of the population would warrant. (Similar results have been reported in Australia and the United States; the same trend has consistently been observed in Canada for several decades.) They are more likely to own their own home, more likely to be self-employed, save more, have higher net worths — in short, the very model of the stable, self-reliant citizen we profess to admire.

What about the cost of resettlement and language programs? The Economic Council estimated the combined cost to the federal and provincial governments to be about $20 per capita annually. The federal share this year, $271 million, includes the social assistance costs of refugee applicants, who were until recently prohibited from working while their claims were assessed. This $271 million is about a fifth as much as immigrants transfer directly to native-born taxpayers every year, not counting any gains from scale economies and the like. The difficulties of integration are wildly overstated in any case. While it is true that 40 percent to 50 percent of current immigrants speak neither English nor French on arrival, within three years that proportion has halved, and within eight years it has halved again. The 1991 census recorded only 378,000 Canadians who spoke neither official language.

Likewise, the Economic Council's research on popular attitudes towards immigrants, especially visible minorities, confirms what ought to be obvious from any reading of our own history: Familiarity breeds respect. The Council's study drew on 62 public opinion surveys between 1975 and 1990, on subjects such as the acceptability of interracial marriages and other indicators of "social distance." It found that the higher the proportion of visible minority immigrants in a community, such as one might find in Toronto or Vancouver, the more tolerant was popular opinion of racial or ethnic differences. Likewise, if found increasingly favorable attitudes over time towards both the level and composition of immigration. The exceptions were in periods of high unemployment or rapid change in the ethnic makeup of immigrants, both of which might be regarded as transitional stages.

It is often said that today's mix of immigrants differs from [that of] the past. Whatever distinctions existed among people from diverse European countries, it is argued, pale (as it were) beside the differences between Europeans and, say, Asians or Africans. But this perspective views the past through today's eyeglasses. Social differences that today seem trivial, such as between Catholic and Protestant, were once the stuff of civil wars (in some places, they still are). The charge of being unable to "fit in" has been leveled against every arriving immigrant group, in every succeeding wave: the Irish, the Germans, the Ukrainians, even the English. It was not uncommon at the turn of the century to see help-wanted ads accompanied by the admonition "No English Need Apply" since, as it was explained to a visiting English journalist, "the Englishman is too cocksure; he is too conceited, he thinks he knows everything and he won't try to learn our ways." The founder of Canadian socialism, J.S. Woodsworth, demanded that "non-assimilable elements" should be "vigorously excluded," while in Quebec, Henri Bourassa, the great French-Canadian nationalist, stormed that Canada had become "a refuge for the scum of all nations." Somehow the country survived.

Immigrants from the Third World are in fact among the most eager to participate in Canadian society, from politics to business to the arts. Asian and African immigrants apply for Canadian citizenship, for example, an average of five years after arriving, compared to the 15 years typical of American or Western European immigrants. Multiculturalism may be official policy, but in *The Illusion of Difference: Realities of Ethnicity in Canada and the United States*, University of Toronto sociologists Jeffrey Reitz and Raymond Breton show that, far from the "mosaic" of mythology, immigrants to Canada assimilate into the mainstream faster than their American counterparts. There is little tendency to ethnic segregation in Canadian cities, other studies have found, and what there is shows up less among visible minorities than other groups: "It is scarcely sensible to talk of ghettos in Canadian cities," concludes sociologist John Mercer. Rates of ethnic endogamy – marriage within the ethnic group – have been falling since 1931. Less than 10 percent of Canadians speak a language other than English or French at home. We are not Babel, and we are not about to become one. So long as we avoid minefields like multiculturism, antiracism and employment equity – which many immigrants themselves oppose – the country shows every sign of tolerating its differences tolerably well.

Nonetheless, communitarians fret that immigration will irreparably alter our national culture and identity in some indefinable fashion. Probably it will. What of it? What is the Canadian way of life? Which one should we choose? Today's? That of 50 years ago? One hundred years ago? The chauvinism this implies is not so much directed against outsiders as against anything but the here and now. It is a false conservatism, a myopic fixation on the present, the product of what G.K. Chesterton decried as "the small and arrogant oligarchy of those who merely happen to be walking about at the time." The way of life that nativists fear is in jeopardy would itself be unrecognizable to an earlier generation of nativists, who themselves struggled to preserve a way of life entirely novel to the generation before. Our culture exists not only in the present, but over time. It does not belong only to us, but to all who went before and all who will come after. It is an organic whole, a constantly evolving, living thing. When we deny that evolution, we are not preserving our culture, we are embalming it. [. . .]

Ultimately, however, this issue cannot be resolved empirically. Those who believe that Canada is "full" are no more likely to be persuaded by mere statistical evidence than the chief executives of tobacco companies. No matter how many studies may conclude that the effects of immigration are on balance positive, the true nativist will not be shaken from his fundamentalist faith. And so long as the case for immigration is put in empirical terms, it remains hostage to next year's study. What if it were found that immigration's effects were negative? Would that make the case for shutting the doors?

Only if you accept the underlying premise of the restrictionists: That the existing members of a nation-state should have the power to stop others from joining them; that the right of citizenship should depend not on a willingness to assume its obligations, but on the accident of birth. "Citizenship in Western liberal democracies is the modern equivalent of feudal privilege – an inherited status that greatly enhances one's life chances," University of Toronto political scientist Joseph Carens has written. "Like feudal birthright privileges, restrictive citizenship is hard to justify when one thinks about it closely."

The true case for open immigration depends not on its advantages or otherwise to the native-born population, but rather on the simple observation that all human beings are created equal. As such, we are obliged to consider not only our losses (if any), but their gains. Immigrants typically start out much poorer than other Canadians. So each dollar in income adds more to the average immigrant's quality of life than the average native-born Canadian loses from an equivalent decline in income. If that sounds too altruistic, try this thought experiment, made famous by the philosopher John Rawls. Suppose, in deciding what immigration policy to choose, we did not yet know which ticket we ourselves would draw in the lottery of life: Canadian-born, or foreign-born. We should then be obliged to decide in a way that would be fair to all. Indeed, it would be in our own interest to ensure both groups had an equal right to live in Canada, lest we find ourselves among those left outside.

If that is the case, then it is just as wrong to keep them out as to keep us in. On what basis, then, do we distinguish between the right to emigrate and the right to immigrate? The former is unquestionably a moral absolute, one of the first points of distinction between free and unfree states. If a Canadian wishes to leave the country, we pride ourselves on his freedom to do so. It would violate his human rights, we say, to prevent him from living where he chooses. Yet that is what we do to immigrants. If it were suggested that, in order to upgrade the labor stock of the country, we subject native-born Canadians to the "points test" and deport anyone who failed, decent people would likewise recoil in horror. Yet we cheerfully put those born elsewhere through this same degrading ritual.

Immigration undoubtedly has some unpleasant social side effects. But so does emigration. If Canada were to start hemorrhaging people by the hundreds of thousands, the effect on those remaining would be bleak. Think of East Germany after the wall. If anything, emigration is more disruptive. Which is worse for society — to have too many doctors or too few?

Whatever the effects of immigration, moreover, they are surely no greater than those induced by internal population movements. Consider first the vast annual influx of newborn children. In 1960, at the height of the baby boom, the crop of new arrivals numbered 480,000 — twice current immigration levels into a population barely half as large. Without doubt, this historic demographic bulge has had untold consequences, good and bad, for society. Yet no one suggested that, to avoid this disruption, women should be prevented from giving birth. At the same time, the work force was being invaded by millions of women, many of them unskilled; in 30 years, the participation rate has doubled, from 30 percent to 60 percent, causing an enormous social upheaval, at home and at work. Yet no one demanded that their numbers be restricted in line with some alchemistic calculation of "absorptive capacity."

Only when a national border is crossed does the movement of people suddenly become an issue. When hundreds of thousands of people migrate from province to province every year — British Columbia absorbed 85,000 people from other provinces in 1992, plus 37,000 immigrants from other lands, for a total per capita rate of immigration four times that of Canada — they are not put through endless hearings to divine whether they are moving for economic or political reasons. Just as when, earlier, millions of people migrated from the country to the city, they did not have to climb a wall to get in.

Why not? Because people have, we recognize, a right to live and work where they choose. But somehow, those who are not Canadian citizens are not considered to possess the same rights.

For some rights, restrictions are defensible. We would not extend the right to vote in Canadian elections to citizens of other countries. We pay the taxes, we get to vote. These are rights of citizenship. But we would not deprive someone of the right to, say, a fair trial, merely because he was not a Canadian citizen. That was confirmed in 1985, when the Supreme Court ruled that refugee claimants were protected by the Charter of Rights and Freedoms. Some rights, in other words, are portable. They inhere in the individual himself, whatever his nationality, solely by virtue of his humanity. These are human rights. The freedom to live where one likes, subject to the laws of the state in which one finds oneself, is surely one of those rights. It is not a right of citizenship in itself; it merely qualifies one to become a citizen.

I am not suggesting we impose no controls on immigration, but only that we apply the principle of "national treatment," familiar from the free trade debate. The same rules should determine which persons are fit to live and work among us, whether they were born here or elsewhere. That would permit excluding escaped criminals and other threats to society, and, in the rare cases where necessary, quarantining those with highly infectious diseases. Other than that, no special rules need apply.

Once we stop looking at immigrants as something other than ourselves, we see that many of the problems commonly identified with immigration are in fact problems of the whole society. Even if it were true, for example, that too many immigrants were trapped on welfare, that's not an immigration problem, it's a welfare problem. Fix the incentives in the system, and most people will choose to work, wherever they are from. If it is important to instil Canadian values in immigrants it is no less essential to instil those same values in Canadians born here. Indeed, an understanding of what it means to choose to be a Canadian might prove enlightening to the rest of us. How many Canadians have ever heard the oath of allegiance a new citizen learns by heart?

Perhaps there is a limit to Canada's "absorptive capacity." But no one knows what it is, much less how to calculate it. All we know is what we are used to, which is no guide to anything. [. . .]

An open immigration policy invariably provokes the sovereignty argument — that open immigration denies the very legal basis of nation-states, that is, self-determination.

Certainly a state has the legal power to declare limits on immigration; only its moral right to do so is in question. A state is no less sovereign with open borders than with closed; it is no less an act of sovereignty to renounce immigration controls than it is to impose them. A state obviously has a right to defend itself against armed invasion, or to protect its citizens' property from unlawful seizure. But immigrants are not coming to take our land: They are coming to bid for it, to buy or rent property the same as anyone else. The right of self-determination, so far as it has any meaning, means only that a given people living in a given territory has the right to govern itself according to its own laws. If immigrants agree to be found by the same laws, that condition is not disturbed.

The thought of open immigration also provokes some variant of "it's our country," usually accompanied by an analogy to home ownership. This is the community argument, nicely summarized by Jack Pickersgill, Louis St. Laurent's immigration minister. "Immigration is a privilege which we have a perfect right to grant or deny as we see fit," he said. "When an alien applies for admission to Canada, he is like someone applying for membership in a club."

The property rights analogy – that our right to restrict immigration is akin to membership in a club or an individual's right to forbid entry to his house – rests on a false foundation. There cannot be a collective ownership of something called Canada. Property rights have already been assigned throughout. There is private property, and there is public property. The sum of private plus public property equals all the territory of Canada. To assert, in the name of community, a sort of overarching third right to property is to negate the first two.

Certainly a society, like a club, is entitled to dictate certain terms of membership. But whatever terms apply must apply equally to all, and all who meet these terms should have equal right to admission. The social contract cannot be so defined as to exclude a class of people from even the choice of accepting it or rejecting it.

Why not? That's what clubs do, isn't it? But what clubs may do, the state may not. A private group may use any grounds it pleases in deciding who it will allow to join it. But the state, having authority over every inhabitant of a given territory, carries with it the obligation of equal treatment, without regard to national origin. (Indeed, it is even debatable whether clubs, being neither wholly public nor wholly private organizations, may decide who to admit on just any basis: Connections, comportment, or ability to pay may be acceptable grounds, but not, increasingly, race or sex.)

"To say that membership is open to all who wish to join is not to say that there is no distinction between members and non-members," writes the University of Toronto's Carens. "Those who choose to cooperate together in the state have special rights and obligations not shared by non-citizens. . . . What is not readily compatible with the ideal of equal moral worth is the exclusion of those who want to join. If people want to sign the social contract, they should be permitted to do so."

So even though states obviously have the power to restrict immigration, they cannot claim a philosophical justification for it, whether in property rights or self-determination. What's left? We were here first? But if by "we" you mean anyone but the aboriginal people, we weren't. The laws we now apply to others would have kept our own grandfathers out. Far from fearing immigration, we ought to embrace it as part of our national mission. Not only was Canada founded on it, the migration of peoples is the very motive force of human history. As my *Encyclopaedia Britannica* notes, as late as A.D. 900, "there was not one German in Berlin, not one Russian in Moscow, not one Hungarian in Budapest; Madrid was a Moorish settlement; no Turks lived in Ankara, and the few in what is now Istanbul were slaves and mercenaries."

Every Canadian schoolchild knows the proud boast of Sir Wilfrid Laurier that the 20th century would be Canada's. Very few know what it was based on: immigration. "For the next 75 years, nay the next 100 years, Canada shall be the star towards which all men who love progress and freedom shall come," Laurier said in 1904. "There are men living in this audience . . . who before they die . . . will see this country with at least 60 millions of people." This was only a commonplace of the time. "Growing, growing, growing," Stephen Leacock saw his country, "with a march that will make us 10 millions tomorrow, 20 millions in our children's time and a 100 millions ere the century runs out."

As every schoolchild also knows, neither prediction came true. As the century winds down, Canadians are edgily aware their country has failed to live up to its potential. Could the contrast between our present timorousness and the robust self-confidence of Laurier's day be linked to the shift in immigration policy? Many of our difficulties, indeed, stem directly from the scarcity of our population. The insecurity of our position relative to the United States is only the most obvious result. It shows itself, too, in our internal imbalances, in the vast spaces between us that weaken our sense of connection to one another. To be so few in number makes us more prone to domination by narrow elites, whether in business, politics or the media. It is reflected in the parochialism of our concerns, in the mediocrity of our expectations, in our relative insignificance on the world stage. And mostly, in lost momentum.

We first began to lose our way as a nation when we rejected free trade in 1911; when we shut down mass immigration, we threw away all hope of greatness. Within the cloister of our borders, Canada retreated into self-delusion and provincialism. And of all the many myths we have spun about ourselves, the worst is this: That we have done well enough, thank you, and have nothing left to do. We have become a caretaker society, when we have much work before us.

Laurier's century is not out. In a rededication to greatness, we can rediscover our sense of common purpose. Indeed, the very act of opening the borders would be a tonic in itself. Liberty and community need not be opposed, where the community is rooted in the values of liberty. Far from weakening our sense of nationhood, free immigration offers the hope of planting it in firmer soil: a nationalism with nativism. As long as immigration is still a matter of deciding how many we should "let" in, we remain stuck in the national identity cul-de-sac, forever obsessed with defining the differences between "us" and "them." Free immigration, on the other hand, recalls Laurier's sense of the nation as a gathering, like a crowd that draws nearer to hear a speaker, its cohesion growing as its numbers swell. A nation, it says, is not something you are, it's something you join.

We might then come to see the border not as a barrier, but as a contour line, defining only where a common system of laws prevails, and no more. Like borders, nations and states would still exist. They just wouldn't define themselves by their ability to exclude others. Nations would then be understood not as immutable divisions of humanity, but as self-determined associations of free people, distinguished not by the trivial differences of race or culture, but in the diverse paths to justice they pursue. In this model, the individual, the nation and humanity are but points on a continuum; the nation is the means by which the individual is led to that wider allegiance he owes humanity.

Free immigration seems radical only because of the moral blind spot that allows us to look upon immigrants as having lesser human rights than ourselves. It may be the convention now to restrict immigration, but we should not be so vain as to think it the natural order of things. It has not "always been this way," nor need it be in future. The idea that the state should concern itself with restricting the flow of people across its borders will seem in time as quaint as the notion that cities should have walls seems today. The issue thus turns not on what we can do for immigrants or on what they can do for us, but on the simple recognition, long delayed, of our common humanity — city to nation to world, the completion of the paradigm shift begun five centuries ago.

To forbid people from spending their short time on earth in whatever place offers them the best chance for a happy and fulfilling life will then seem a peculiarly backward and selfish tyranny, the more so given the false assumption — that immigration harms, rather than helps, the host community — on which it is based. The course before us, then, is clear: It is to open our hearts, open our eyes — and open the doors.

✗ NO
Why States Are Justified in Limiting Their Entry of Migrants
G.E. DIRKS

Human migration is a phenomenon that stretches back to the earliest days of our species. The factors motivating ancient and contemporary migration are numerous, many of them arising from prevailing economic conditions but others reflecting chronically undesirable political and social circumstances. Today, it is estimated that more than 100 million people globally are outside their states of origin, and the number is expected to rise significantly during the next quarter-century. Some of the people on the move have travelled comparatively short distances, seeking an improved life in neighbouring countries, often in Africa, Asia, and South and Central America, regions considered by North American standards as less developed and frequently containing politically unstable governments. Yet in relative terms, such destinations are nevertheless seen by millions of people as better locations than where they are now. Other migrants, usually with a small nest egg and a greater amount of initiative than most, have travelled greater distances to destinations in the developed, affluent, and stable parts of the world, including Canada, in search of what they hope will be economic prosperity, social security, and political tranquillity. These millions of migrants, if no effective restrictive steps are taken, soon will be joined by sizable numbers of despairing relatives, friends, and acquaintances, all examples of what is labelled "chain migration." These desperate people are fleeing from such conditions as poverty, urban squalor, famine, environmental degradation, political oppression, and civil unrest. Such would-be migrants, whether seeking nearby or distant destinations, routinely possess minimal wealth, few occupational skills, and limited education. They are all pushed by intolerable conditions at home and are pulled by the expectation of improved living conditions elsewhere.

This essay contends that massive worldwide migration and its anticipated intensification in the near future demands some strong action by the governments of both sending and destination states, aimed at its management and constraint. The argument that follows asserts that international migration cannot and should not be entirely prevented or curtailed. It can and must, however, be effectively channelled and regulated. The position adopted here is not particularly derived from moral philosophy but, rather, has its basis in the widely endorsed neorealist paradigm, primarily that aspect relating to the ongoing preeminence of the principles underlying the sovereign state. While the classical concept of sovereignty may be under some challenge today from a number of factors and forces, one cannot convincingly question that the world is still organized into sovereign states, such as Canada, that possess the legitimate capacity to coerce when necessary and owe their citizens protection and security from external and internal threats to their physical, economic, social, and cultural well-being. Thus, this paper argues that governments, Canada's being no exception, continue to have the obligation to adopt policies for the overall benefit of their existing populations. The claims of outsiders wishing to enter a state are superseded by the principles of national sovereignty. There is an obligation to do what is best for the state's own citizens. One widely accepted role for governments in an effort to protect the prevailing culture and way of life of citizens is to determine who and how many newcomers will be either temporarily or permanently welcomed into their midst.

Humans are social creatures and have organized themselves into groups or communities that as early as the 17th century in Europe came to be known as sovereign states. These political entities strive to achieve and maintain control over their own affairs and protect their societies' territories, values, and culture. State communities, particularly but not exclusively ethnically homogeneous ones, are frequently closely knit entities, possessing strong emotional attachments based on a number of factors, including a common language, religion, and history. Many communities have acquired the status of sovereign states. Such states then provide their societies with the legitimate capacity to establish rules aimed at preserving overall group identity and aspects of life that are deemed desirable. Moreover, governments, acting for the state, can determine the grounds for the admission or rejection of persons wishing to gain temporary or permanent entry into the society. Community members tend to believe that outsiders — foreigners, in common parlance — may not share the prevailing culture, preferences, and value system, and thus such aliens are to be shunned or excluded. Those outsiders, however, who may ultimately be accepted into the society will need to possess characteristics the community members find to be similar to their own or believe the would-be newcomer can quickly acquire. While states like Canada have numerous purposes, the focus in this essay is on their role as agents for protecting and preserving what their societies or members consider valuable. Screening aliens so as not to endanger the prevailing general welfare of society constitutes one of the fundamental tasks the Canadian and other governments fulfill.

The impetus for communities to gain independence so as to govern themselves is extremely powerful and pervasive and is not easily neutralized, as the inexorable move to self-determination for peoples around the world this past century has indicated. Once the status of sovereignty has been attained, liberal democratic traditions call for states to be in a position to offer their societies, through responsive and accountable governments, orderliness, stability, and protection from threats, whether they emanate from within or beyond the territorial preserve of the community. With respect to discouraging immigration, the state sets out to prevent the entry of aliens perceived to be actually or potentially capable of destabilizing the community by proving to be an economic burden or by not adhering to the prevailing values and popular expectations.

The intensification of the sense of threat to what is valued has become especially apparent among those states having limited or unpleasant experiences with foreigners and whose citizens feel they have most to lose. Frequently, these are the comparatively affluent countries of the North, where a semi–siege mentality has in some instances taken root. Western and Southern European societies illustrated this first, adopting an attitude of "drawing the wagons into a circle" during the mid- and late 1980s. More latent but nevertheless still noticeable strains of this anxiety are to be found today even in states with long traditions of admitting immigrants, such as the United States, Canada, and Australia. Today, even refugees, the recipients in the past of genuine and profound humanitarian concern in many developed countries like Canada, who were offered sanctuary, sustenance, and at times permanent residence, are no longer welcome. This reticence is understandable. Migrants of all types are perceived today by formerly generous societies as an unneeded burden and a drain on social service budgets. Given the endless number of human tragedies that have followed on the heels of other tragedies, we should not be surprised to be witnessing among developed countries growing signs of compassion fatigue.

In many cases, the population constituting the society of a state places profound importance on preserving and even strengthening its sense of identity and belonging. This sense of identity has taken generations to develop and flourish and ranks high among the desired features or values shared by members of a state's society. Communities with concern for the viability and durability of their identity may perceive would-be migrants as an unwanted threat. Governments of such states will be expected to take steps through legislation and regulation to limit or eradicate threats to societal identify. While it is not a sovereign state – at least at the time this piece is written – the Canadian province of Quebec is a good example of a society that perceives itself as culturally vulnerable and where the provincial authorities strenuously work to protect the French language and other valued cultural features of the society.

Governments, acting on behalf of their citizens, confronted by actual or potential demands from aliens for entry into their communities, are, not surprisingly, compelled to choose a variety of cost-benefit analyses when evaluating the question of admission. Certainly, the positive aspects of admitting immigrants can be significant. Would-be newcomers may, in some instances, provide needed labour. Similarly, immigrants, if legally in the country, can be expected to pay taxes, thereby contributing to the public treasury. But the perception in many countries today is that the immediate and long-term costs of admitting large numbers of migrants outweigh any benefits. Here it is important to recognize the possible distinction between perceived and actual costs. It is, after all, what governments and their citizens believe, even if it is not or only partly valid, that usually prompts legislative and other action. Thus, if societies and their leaders perceive an unacceptable cost, not only a financial cost, to be the result of large-scale migrant admission, policies to prevent this are in order.

In most cases, the anticipated negative economic implications of immigrant entry, often assumed to be probable by the home society, play a major part in determining the responses of destination countries. As crucial as these anxieties are in comparatively affluent countries, they may be still more acute for less-developed states and their societies. In these latter situations, authorities may be unable to provide basic necessities for their own citizens. Permitting outsiders from neighbouring countries to freely enter their territories can only exacerbate already desperate economic and social conditions. For the "have" countries, the economic costs might be less, but for their citizens, already complaining about high taxes and large national debts, the idea of thousands of migrants being added to welfare rolls, drawing upon medical and educational services, and seeking other types of subsidization, is highly irritating and exposes responsible, accountable governments such as Canada's to the potential wrath of the electorate. In the past decade, grassroots movements in several European states, concerned about economic and social costs and not accustomed to admitting immigrants, have fuelled extremist political parties and resulted in restrictive moves against potential newcomers by those parties already in power. In North America, anti-immigrant propositions have appeared on ballots in California and other American states accommodating large numbers of legal and illegal foreigners. Similarly, in larger Canadian cities, municipal authorities and school boards have expressed alarm over the funds needed to mount language programs for non–English-speaking people already here, let alone for those yet to come.

Destination states have been the focus of this essay to this point. This reflects the prevailing circumstances whereby governments of sending states have done comparatively little to discourage population outflow. At least three considerations account for this. First, the funds or remittances migrants send back to their families and friends in the homeland are substantial, even enormous by some standards. These funds quickly enter the economies of those countries. The treasuries of such countries as Bangladesh, the Philippines, and smaller states in Africa and the Western hemisphere obtain a vast amount, in some cases the majority of their foreign exchange, usually desperately needed hard currencies, from such remittances. Second, unrestricted emigration provides a useful safety valve to release pressure in societies where high rates of unemployment can contribute to social unrest and potential political instability for the governments of such states. Third, there have been few occasions, since migration pressures have intensified, in which the governments of destination countries have meaningfully striven to involve sending-state governments in deliberations aimed at regulating and managing global migration. Thus, for these and other reasons, authorities in sending countries see little if any justification for impeding population outflow, especially as in several United Nations conventions and declarations, the freedom to exit one's homeland is considered a right. With the establishment of liberal democratic political systems in the former communist countries of Central Europe and the disintegration of the Soviet Union, governments have adopted these freedom-of-exit principles and hundred of thousands of migrants have exercised this right. There is, of course, no equivalent right of entry to another state.

Some destination countries today are treating population pressures at their frontiers and at ports of entry as a question of genuine national security. Security can be an elusive concept. Fundamentally, it calls upon government to not only protect the territory of the state but also to prevent threats to the overall well-being of society. Included in the provision of security is the task of precluding any feeling among citizens that the community is in danger of being culturally or politically overwhelmed. Under this admittedly expanded definition of security, the perceived danger is not from conventional military aggression but rather from threats to societal stability and economic well-being potentially the result of any mass entry of unwanted immigrants. Concern for the maintenance of stability within the state is a particularly high priority for governments. Unwanted cross-border population movements can create or exacerbate conflict and social dishar-mony. In some instances, it has proven to be easier to defend the state and its citizens against the threat of military aggression than from challenges caused by uncontrolled mass migration.

To this point, this essay has asserted that the ability to freely enter a state other than the one we are born in cannot be considered as a basic human right. The claims of outsiders wishing to enter are superseded by the principles of state sovereignty. A state's first obligation is to its own society. This essay does not question that the contemporary world contains innumerable economic, political, and social inequities and injustices. Opening borders to permit the unimpeded flow of millions of people, however, will not halt or prevent these inequities and injustices, deplorable as they may be. Conceivably, opening state frontiers in those destination countries most attractive to would-be migrants would result in horrific consequences. Unprecedented strains would be placed on every aspect of the economic, social, and political infrastructure of the so-called affluent states, causing the standards of living, measured by any criteria, to plunge. In fact, the conditions in the formerly desirable destination state would reflect those in the states of origins being evacuated by the migrants.

Individually, the citizens in liberal democratic countries such as Canada have often demonstrated their generosity toward genuine refugees and in other human-itarian causes. Individuals, in fact, may be willing to accommodate an indigent migrant or refugee in their homes, but that is not an argument for a government policy to admit unlimited numbers of people from impoverished states. Personal ethics are not an appropriate basis for making public choices because they do not take into consideration the consequences such choices impose upon others in the community. An act should be judged by its probable consequences and not by its intent. Many well-intentioned policies can have and have had unsettling, unexpected results.

States under the conventions of sovereignty, with primary obligations to their own societies, are justified in selecting and limiting the types of persons permitted to temporarily or permanently gain entry. What options then are available to governments to enable them to effectively enforce the regulations they have established to manage this restricted migration? While the idea of enforcement appears particularly negative and exclusionist, in the final analysis the only approach governments can adopt consists in explicitly indicating and executing regulations and procedures based on the number and types of migrants perceived as desirable. With this in mind, and as an example, what course has Canada adopted?

Put succinctly, Canada's approach to immigration for at least a quarter-century has been to base admissions policy on three categories of potential arrivals: family, refugee, and independent. During the 1990s, the annual number of persons accepted for permanent settlement from all categories has stood at approximately 200 000, a figure deplored by many critics who argue that Canada's absorptive capacity is far less. Efforts are made by officials to ensure that the family class does not dominate the annual intake level, although it regularly exceeds one-third of yearly arrivals. Refugees, as defined by the United Nations, constitute approximately ten to fifteen percent of annual arrivals, reflecting Canada's long-standing commitment to humanitarian and compassionate principles. The independent class is composed of persons selected because of a number of criteria weighing their attributes. Points are awarded on the basis of such aspects as education, employment skills, language capabilities, and age.

By the early 1990s, the Canadian government, reflecting growing public anxiety, adopted a series of immigration policy and regulatory modifications aimed at addressing a number of problems perceived as threats to Canada's values and self-interests. Some of the issues of concern to the public and government included the following: an enormous, unmanageable backlog of applications from would-be immigrants; the rising costs to the Canadian treasury of administering the prevailing policy; the need to avoid a migrant onslaught at Canada's ports of entry as European countries close their doors to migrants; the increase in the number of aliens seeking to enter with fraudulent identity documents or no papers at all; and the unprecedented demands on government education, health, and welfare budgets from migrants requiring language training or waiting to have claims for refugee status resolved.

In an attempt to respond to these and other factors, legislation came into force in 1993 placing a cutoff point on the number of applications for entry officials would annually accept, enabling the priority for processing applicants among the three admissible classes to be altered, and tightening controls to restrict still further the admission of illegal migrants, often people with fraudulent or no identification papers.

Canada continues to be one of the few countries that maintain an active immigration program. But as this paper has argued, increased controls on international migration, even by comparatively liberal societies such as Canada's, are essential and are being strengthened to maintain a way of life believed to be worth preserving. The Canadian regulations pale compared with restrictions adopted by countries not seeing themselves as needing or wanting foreign newcomers. By embracing rigorous control methods, governments do so with the approval of their societies as well as of the conventions of sovereignty and international law. The time when open borders become the norm in our world of sovereign states is certainly nowhere in sight.

Inequities persist throughout the world. Yet, with technological advances in communications such as television, videos, and the Internet, tens of millions of people who experience poverty and oppression are now acutely aware of the comparatively better lives led by others in Europe, North America, and parts of Australia. Moreover, improvements in transportation now facilitate the movement of people over large distances. Humanity now finds itself embroiled in a profoundly serious competition between desperate, innovative people with little to lose striving to move to more attractive destinations and the governments of those destination states doing more and more to limit if not prevent the entry of these people. The state, with its monopoly on the legitimate use of coercion to enforce laws and regulations, now stands the best chance of achieving its objectives. Nevertheless, the would-be migrants will persist in their efforts to move until circumstances in their own communities are made more tolerable. And when will that be?

BIBLIOGRAPHY

Appleyard, R. *International Migration: Challenge for the Nineties.* Geneva: International Organization for Migration, 1992.

Castles, S., and M. Miller. *The Age of Migration.* New York: Guilford Press, 1993.

Collinson, S. *Europe and International Migration.* London: Pinter Publishers, 1993.

Dirks, G.E. *Controversy and Complexity: Immigration Policy-Making in the 1980s.* Montreal and Kingston: McGill-Queen's University Press, 1995.

_____. "International Migration in the Nineties: Causes and Consequences." *International Journal* 48, no. 2 (1993).

Freeman, G. "Can Liberal States Control Unwanted Migration?" *Annals of the American Academy of Political and Social Sciences* 534 (July 1994).

Jervis, R. *Perception and Misperception in International Politics.* Princeton, NJ: Princeton University Press, 1976.

Keely, C., and S. Russell. "Responses of Industrialized Countries to Asylum-Seekers." *Journal of International Affairs* 47, no. 2 (Winter 1994).

Loescher, G. *Beyond Charity: International Cooperation and the Global Refugee Crisis.* New York: Oxford University Press, 1993.

Weiner, M. "Ethics, National Sovereignty and the Control of Immigration." *International Migration Review* 30, no. 1 (Spring 1996).

_____. *The Global Migration Crisis: Challenge to States and Human Rights.* New York: HarperCollins, 1995.

Weiner, M. (ed.). *International Migration and Security.* Boulder, CO: Westview Press, 1993.

POSTSCRIPT

The issue of immigration poses a number of difficult dilemmas. Is immigration a fundamental human right? The United Nations Universal Declaration of Human Rights and the Helsinki Accords assert the universal right of emigration. If emigration is a fundamental human right, how do we reconcile this with claims of states to national sovereignty and the right to control immigration? If governments have the right to determine whom they will admit and to whom they will grant citizenship, what criteria should be used to make these decisions? Whom exactly do states have an obligation to admit? Refugees? Migrants from poor countries? Only those who have the skills and cultural background deemed necessary to contribute to society? Should those who want to reunite with family members already in the destination country be given preference?

This issue cannot be discussed without some reference to the increased concerns about terrorism and the need for stricter border controls. Since Canada has been an immigrant nation, its future vitality, as Coyne argues, depends on maintaining fairly high levels of immigration. How can this necessity be reconciled with the contention that immigration must be more tightly regulated in order to keep out suspected terrorists?

Suggested Additional Readings

Carens, Joseph H. "Aliens and Citizens: The Case for Open Borders." *The Review of Politics* 49, no. 2 (Spring 1987): 251–73.

_____. "Realistic and Idealistic Approaches to the Ethics of Migration." *International Migration Review* 30, no. 1 (Spring 1996): 156–69.

_____. "Reconsidering Open Borders." *International Migration Review* 33, no. 4 (Winter 1999): 1082–97.

_____. "Who Should Get In? The Ethics of Immigration Admissions." *Ethics and International Affairs* 17, no. 1 (2003): 95–110.

Dirks, Gerald E. *Controversy and Complexity: Canadian Immigration Policy During the 1980s.* Montreal: McGill-Queen's University Press, 1995.

Hawkins, Freda. *Canada and Immigration: Public Policy and Public Concern.* Montreal: McGill-Queen's University Press, 1998.

Knowles, V. *Strangers at Our Gates: Canadian Immigration and Immigration Policy, 1540–1997.* Toronto: Dundurn, 1997.

Pulido, Laura, "Race, Immigration, and the Border." *Antipode* 36, no. 1 (January 2004): 154–57.

Weiner, Myron. "Ethics, National Sovereignty and the Control of Immigration." *International Migration Review* 30, no. 1 (Spring 1996): 171–97.

_____. *The Global Migration Crisis.* New York: HarperCollins, 1995.

_____, and Rainer Münz. "Migrants, Refugees and Foreign Policy: Prevention and Intervention Strategies." *Third World Quarterly* 18, no. 1 (1997): 25–51.

InfoTrac® College Edition

Search for the following articles in the InfoTrac® database:

Akbari, Ather H. "Immigrant 'Quality' in Canada: More Direct Evidence of Human Capital Content, 1956–1994." *International Migration Review* 33, no. 1 (Spring 1999): 156–57.

Cam, Surhan. "Open Borders: The Case against Immigration Controls." *Capital & Class* 80 (Summer 2003): 215–18.

Roy, Arun S. "Job Displacement Effects of Canadian Immigrants by Country of Origin and Occupation." *International Migration Review* 31, no. 1 (Spring 1997): 150–61.

For more articles, enter:
"immigration policy" or "open borders" in the keyword search or subject guide.

Web Resources

For current URLs for the following websites, visit www.crosscurrents.nelson.com.

CENTER FOR IMMIGRATION STUDIES (WASHINGTON, D.C.)

www.cis.org

According to its website, the Center for Immigration Studies "is animated by a pro-immigrant, low-immigration vision which seeks fewer immigrants but a warmer welcome for those admitted." The site offers a variety of resources on immigration issues.

CENTRE FOR REFUGEE STUDIES (YORK UNIVERCITY)

www.yorku.ca/crs

The site houses a good collection of resources on refugee issues.

CENTER FOR MIGRATION STUDIES (NEW YORK)

www.cmsny.org

Although American-focused, this site offers a lot of useful information on population migration issues.

CITIZENSHIP AND IMMIGRATION CANADA

www.cic.gc.ca

Check this website for information on the Canadian government's current position on immigration.

Do We Need a World Environmental Organization?

✔ **YES**
FRANK BIERMANN, "Green Global Governance: The Case for a World Environment Organisation," *New Economy* 9, no. 2 (June 2002): 82–86

✗ **NO**
ADIL NAJAM, "The Case against a New International Environmental Organization," *Global Governance* 9, no. 3 (July–September 2003): 367–84

In the last half of the twentieth century, international organizations began focusing the world's attention on global environmental issues. In 1968, the UN Economic and Social Council adopted a resolution calling for initiatives to address the "human environment." This led to the hosting of the Stockholm Conference on the Human Environment in 1972, the first global international conference of its size on environmental issues. Twenty years later, at the Earth Summit held in Rio de Janeiro, delegates and observers expressed disappointment in the limited progress that had been made in addressing many key environmental issues. As a further follow-up, a second Earth Summit, referred as the World Summit on Sustainable Development (WSSD), was held in Johannesburg, South Africa, in 2002.

One issue that permeated the discussions at each of these meetings was how the global community should organize to address environmental issues. The Stockholm Conference and the Rio Summit have been successful in helping to raise global awareness of environmental issues. However, the response of the international community has been largely ad hoc and fragmented in nature. The Stockholm Conference led to the creation of the United Nations Environment Programme (UNEP). Based in Nairobi, Kenya, the UNEP was intended to serve as the focal point of UN discussions on the environment and help coordinate the various environmental activities of the United Nations.

Yet, most of the more than 500 environment-related treaties that have been negotiated since Stockholm are either bilateral or regional. Many of these have their own secretariat to monitor the implementation of the agreement. In addition, more than a dozen international organizations have some environmental activities in their mandates. For example, the UN Food and Agriculture Organization (FAO) is involved in protecting depleting fisheries and promoting sustainable agriculture. The UN Development Programme (UNDP) has created a Sustainable Energy and Environment Division (SEED) to consolidate its environmental initiatives, including work on energy and atmosphere issues, natural resources management, and management of desertification. The World Meteorological Organization co-sponsors the Intergovernmental Panel on Climate Change, which has had an important impact on debates about climate change. The World Health Organization promotes the development of guidelines regarding air and water pollution standards.

Despite these many developments, the United Nations Environment Programme has remained a relatively small player in the global environment picture. The UNEP's annual budget is less than U.S. $100 million. Its total spending since its inception is less than the annual budget of the UN Development Programme. The resources of the UNEP are minuscule in comparison to those of other international organizations, such as the World Bank or the International Monetary Fund. Its location in Nairobi, far from the agencies that it was intended to coordinate, has further contributed to the limited role that the UNEP can play in global environmental diplomacy.

These developments have led some to argue for a new approach to global environmental governance. This approach is based on the argument that existing institutions and agreements are inadequate for the environmental challenges facing the world today. The ad hoc, fragmented approach, which lacks any centralized, effective enforcement mechanism is a major impediment to effective environmental action. What is needed is a comprehensive restructuring at a global level that would put in place new institutional structures in order to overcome the current inertia on many environmental issues.

During the past two decades, a number of proposals for such a restructuring have been put forward. In 1989, the prime ministers of France, the Netherlands, and Norway proposed the creation of a new United Nations body that would have the power to both legislate on environmental regulations and impose punitive sanctions on any states failing to abide by them. While this proposal did not result in the adoption of a concrete plan, various governments, scholars, and activists have put forward similar schemes in the years that followed. Interest in some sort of global or world environmental organization increased following the establishment of the World Trade Organization (WTO). Some environmentalists hoped that the WTO could serve as a model for establishing a world environmental organization (WEO) with real enforcement powers. However, many states have been unwilling to support such a proposal, arguing that they were reluctant to surrender any of their national sovereignty in such a crucial area. At the same time, in looking at the experience of the WTO, many developing countries expressed fears that a WEO would provide one more mechanism for the interests of industrialized nations to intervene in the sovereignty of their countries.

Nevertheless, the topic of global environmental governance has remained on the international agenda. During its time in the presidency of the European Union, France actively campaigned in support of a world environmental organization. Global environmental governance was an important focus of the discussions and negotiations leading up the WSSD in South Africa. The UNEP played a key role in facilitating these discussions.

In the following readings, we examine the debate concerning the form that future global environmental governance should take. In the first article, Frank Biermann, a leading exponent of reform, sets out the case for a world environmental organization. After reviewing the need for such a body, Biermann explains how such a world environmental organization could be structured. In particular, he looks at the World Heath Organization, the World Trade Organization, and the Security Council as possible models. In response, Adil Najam argues that too much attention has been paid to organizational restructuring as a solution to environmental problems. Making a distinction between "institutions" and "organizations," Najam argues that the international community should not get bogged down in organizational minutiae but should focus instead on how to improve the current institutional framework for environmental action. He argues that more effort should be made to support and enhance existing institutions such as the UNEP rather than creating a new, centralized environmental organization.

✔ **YES**
Green Global Governance: The Case for a World Environment Organisation
FRANK BIERMANN

The present discourse on 'greening' the global governance system expresses the frustration felt in many quarters with the state of international environmental policy. Many observers have pointed to the paradoxical situation that powerful international bodies oriented towards economic growth – such as the World Trade Organisation (WTO), the World Bank or the International Monetary Fund – are matched only by a modest UN sub-programme for environmental issues, the United Nations Environment Programme (UNEP). The imbalance is even more apparent when UNEP is compared to the plethora of influential UN specialised agencies in the fields of labour, shipping, agriculture, communication or culture.

As a mere programme, UNEP has no mandate to adopt treaties or any regulations upon its own initiative. It cannot avail itself of regular and predictable funding, and it is subordinated to the UN Economic and Social Council. UNEP's staff hardly exceeds 300 professionals – a trifle compared to its national counterparts such as the German Federal Environment Agency with 1,043 employees and the United States Environmental Protection Agency with a staff of 18,807.

AN IDEA WHOSE TIME HAS COME

This situation has led to a multitude of proposals to grant the environment what other policy areas have long had. a strong international agency with a sizeable mandate, significant resources and sufficient autonomy – a 'World Environment Organisation' (WEO). Ideas for such an international environmental organisation were first floated before the 1972 Stockholm Conference on the Human Environment, but the reform debate has only now gained momentum after a number of governments and senior experts have expressed their support.

Amongst the idea's supporters are the former heads of the World Trade Organisation (WTO), Renato Ruggiero, and of the UN Development Programme (UNDP), Gustave Speth, as well as the designated new WTO director, Supachai Panitchpakdi. Several academics and expert commissions have also advocated

Frank Biermann, "Green Global Governance: The Case for a World Environment Organisation," reprinted with permission from *New Economy* 9, no. 2 (June 2002): 82–86.

a world environment organisation. Likewise, a number of national governments have come forward with proposals for a new agency, among them Brazil, France, Germany, New Zealand, Singapore and South Africa.

The discourse has reached the early stages of intergovernmental negotiation. In February 2001, UNEP established an open-ended intergovernmental group of Ministers or their Representatives on International Environmental Governance to systematically assess the existing institutional weaknesses and define future needs and reform options. The UN General Assembly has also created a bi-annual Global Ministerial Environment Forum to upgrade the governing council of UNEP, and an Environmental Management Group (EMG) to coordinate environmental activities within the UN system. The next major political event, which could spark new initiatives and decisions, will be the World Summit on Sustainable Development in September 2002 in Johannesburg.

The creation of several new international bodies over the past few decades – including the UN Industrial Development Organisation (UNIDO), the World Intellectual Property Organisation (WIPO), the WTO and the International Criminal Court – suggests that states are still prepared, in certain situations, to strengthen global governance by setting up organisations that can evolve into semi-autonomous actors. The launch of a WEO that would integrate existing programmes and bodies may not seem desirable or feasible for some, but given the support this idea has already mustered among some governments, it no longer seems entirely unrealistic.

THE NEED FOR A WORLD ENVIRONMENT ORGANISATION

Why do we need a new body? In short, there are three major shortcomings of the present state of global environmental governance that support the case for a WEO.

Co-ordination Deficit

First, there is a co-ordination deficit in the international governance architecture that results in substantial costs and sub-optimal policy outcomes.

When UNEP was set up in 1972, it was comparatively independent and had a clearly defined agenda. Since then, however, the increase in multilateral environmental regimes has led to a considerable fragmentation of the system. Norms and standards in each area of environmental policy are set up by distinct legislative bodies – the conferences of the parties to the environmental treaties – without much respect for repercussions and linkages with other policy fields. This situation is made worse by the organisational fragmentation of the various convention secretariats that have evolved into distinct medium-sized bureaucracies with strong centrifugal tendencies.

In addition, most specialised international organisations and bodies with some relation to environmental protection, such as the UN Food and Agriculture Organisation (FAO), have initiated environmental programmes of their own over the years. But there is not much co-ordination among these organisations and their policies.

By analogy with national politics, the current situation might come close to abolishing national environment ministries and transferring their programmes and policies to the ministries of agriculture, industry, energy, economics or trade – a policy proposal that would not find much support in most countries. An international body with a clear strategy to ensure global sustainable development would seem to be an idea whose time has come. Just as within nation states, where environmental policy has been institutionally strengthened through the introduction of independent environmental ministries, global environmental policies could be made stronger through an independent WEO that helps to contain the special interests of individual programmes and organisations and to limit duplication, overlap and inconsistencies.

Disparate Processes

Second, a WEO would be in a better position to support regime-building processes, especially by initiating and preparing new treaties.

The International Labour Organisation (ILO) could serve as a model here. While the ILO has developed a comprehensive body of conventions that come close to a global labour code, global environmental policy remains far more disparate and cumbersome in its normsetting processes. It is also riddled with various disputes among UN specialised organisations regarding their competencies, with UNEP in its current setting being unable to adequately protect environmental interests. A WEO would also improve the overall implementation of international environmental standards, for example by a common comprehensive reporting system on the state of the environment and on the state of implementation in different countries as well as by stronger efforts in raising public awareness.

Ad Hoc Support for Developing Countries

Third, a WEO could assist in the build-up of environmental capacities in developing countries.

The demand for financial and technological North-South transfers in this area is certain to increase when climate, biodiversity and other global environmental policies are more intensively implemented in the developing world. Yet the current organisational setting for financial transfers is too ad hoc and too fragmented to meet the requirements of transparency, efficiency and participation of the parties involved.

A WEO could link the normative and technical aspects of financial and technological assistance and could overcome the fragmentation of the current system. The organisation could co-ordinate various financial mechanisms and administer the funds of sectoral regimes in trust, including the future clean development mechanism and emissions trading system under the Kyoto Protocol on climate change. These responsibilities do not need to imply the set-up of large new bureaucracies. Instead, a WEO could make use of the extensive expertise of the World Bank or the United Nations Development Programme (UNDP), including their national representations in developing countries.

A WEO might meet the interests especially of developing countries, because it would provide for a more efficient and more effective transfer of technology and financial assistance to the South. A more centralised body would also create a more efficient negotiation system that would increase the opportunities of small developing nations to raise their voices in global fora. This would include the chance for developing countries to co-ordinate their positions better, which will strengthen their collective bargaining power. In addition, decision-making procedures based on North-South parity could ensure that the WEO would not evolve into a conduit of 'eco-colonialism' as many developing country actors suspect.

POSSIBLE MODELS FOR A WORLD ENVIRONMENT ORGANISATION

What might a WEO look like? What are the best organisational models for such a new body?

Model 1 — The WHO

The least-demanding option would be to maintain the current system of decentralised, issue-specific international environmental regimes along with existing specialised organisations active in the environmental field, but to upgrade UNEP at the same time from a mere UN programme to a fully-fledged international organisation with its own budget and legal personality, increased financial and staff resources and enhanced legal powers. In this model, a WEO would function — as a co-operating, not co-ordinating unit — among the other international institutions and organisations whose member states might then be inclined to shift some environment-related competencies to the new WEO.

The elevation of UNEP to a WEO of this type could be modelled either on the World Health Organisation and the ILO — that is, independent international organisations with their own membership — or on the UN Conference on Trade and Development (UNCTAD), a UN internal body established by the UN General Assembly for debate and co-operation on international trade policy.

A WEO as a specialised UN agency could approve a set of regulations to bind all members, by qualified majority voting. Its general assembly could also adopt draft treaties negotiated by subcommittees under the auspices of the organisation.

The ILO Constitution, for example, requires parties to process, within one year, all treaties adopted by the ILO General Conference to the respective national authorities (such as national parliaments) and to report back to the organisation on progress in the ratification process. This influence goes much beyond the powers of the UNEP Governing Council, which can initiate intergovernmental negotiations but cannot adopt legal instruments on its own.

Model 2 — The WTO

A second, more far-reaching model would alter the current system of decentralised, issue-specific international environmental regimes by attempting a stronger integration within a common framework of a WEO. Again, UNEP would form the core of this new organisation, which would, however, be empowered to co-ordinate other organisations and regimes. By large measure, a WEO of this type would follow the WTO model. This would require a basic Agreement on Establishing the World Environment Organisation, which would contain a number of general principles — maybe building on the 1992 Rio Declaration on Environment and Development — as well as coordinating rules that govern the organisation and its relationship with the issue-specific environmental regimes. Environmental regimes covered by the organisation could be divided into multilateral and plurilateral environmental agreements. As for multilateral agreements, ratification would be compulsory for any new member of a WEO, but plurilateral agreements would still leave members the option to remain outside. The multilateral agreements would thus form the global environmental law code under the WEO, with the existing conferences of the parties — say, to the climate convention — being transformed into subcommittees under the ministerial conference of the organisation.

This integration would enable the WEO to develop a common reporting system for all multilateral environmental agreements (eg an annual national report to the WEO); to develop a common dispute settlement system; to develop mutually agreed upon guidelines that may be followed — based on an interagency agreement — for the activities of the World Bank and the WTO dispute settlement system; and to develop a joint system of capacity-building for developing countries along with financial and technological transfers. The establishment of such an organisation would create a number of welfare gains by increasing the overall efficiency in the system. For example, the sometimes minuscule secretariats of multilateral environmental agreements would be integrated into the WEO.

Likewise, negotiations could be centralised geographically, which would especially benefit developing countries that are often not in a position to send diplomats with sufficient expertise to the various environmental treaty conferences around the world. A WEO at one specific seat — most likely in Africa — would allow especially smaller developing countries to build up specialised environmental embassies with a highly qualified staff able to follow various complicated negotiations. The same could be said for non-governmental organisations that could participate in global negotiations at lower cost.

Model 3 — UN Security Council

A third theoretical option would be to envisage a world authority for the protection of the global environment or the global commons entrusted with enforcement powers against states that fail to implement certain standards (possibly agreed upon by majority vote). The model for this option would be the UN Security Council with its far-reaching powers under Chapter VII of the UN Charter. Such an organisation seems unlikely, however, to muster sufficient support among states in the next decades. Many proposals in this vein would necessitate an amendment of the UN Charter, which would require ratification by two-thirds of UN members including China, France, Russia, the United Kingdom and the United States.

Such far-reaching restrictions of national sovereignty seem difficult to envision. Current experiences with global environmental policy indicate that for the near future, any kind of hierarchic institutionalisation of the state system will encounter insurmountable resistance in both North and South. In practice, comprehensive, even punitive enforcement and sanctioning mechanisms administered by a WEO would be feasible only against relatively small developing countries that already perceive themselves as threatened by new forms of environmental 'colonialism'. A WEO with 'sharp teeth' thus appears counterproductive at the present. Most nations would stay away from the organisation or, conversely, demand weaker standards than those devised under current environmental regimes. The aim of environmental protection would hardly be served.

CONCLUSION

Creating a World Environment Organisation would pave the way for the elevation of environmental policies on the agenda of governments, international organisations and private actors. It could assist in developing the capacities for environmental policy in African, Asian and Latin American countries, and it would improve the institutional environment for the negotiation of new conventions and action programmes as well as for the implementation and co-ordination of existing ones. Establishing a cooperative body, akin to the World Health Organisation, should be our realistic short-term goal, keeping the option open for further international integration over the course of the century.

✗ **NO**

The Case against a New International Environmental Organization
ADIL NAJAM

[World Organizations] are credited with an importance they do not possess; they are blamed for not doing what they are not given the means to do; faults that are often imaginary are ascribed to them, while their real faults go unnoticed; mythical explanations are invented to explain their ineffectiveness; and finally, there is very little recognition of the few significant results that they do achieve.[1]

–Maurice Bertrand

The premise of this article is that the current debate about global environmental governance with its still dominant focus on establishing a superorganization for the environment represents a serious misdiagnosis of the issues, is unfair to the United Nations Environment Programme (UNEP), and is likely to distract attention from other more important challenges of global environmental governance.

This is not to suggest that there is no crisis of global environmental governance. The crisis, however, is one of governance, of which organizational structure is but one element and, in this case, a relatively small element at that.[2] By coopting the larger discussions on global environmental governance, the discourse on organizational tinkering – under whatever grandiose name such proposals are advertised – are distracting from the more important and immediate challenges of global environmental governance that we face as the Rio compact on environment and development crumbles around us. The thought that any of the competing plans for a World, or Global, Environmental Organization (WEO or GEO) that are being peddled might actually be taken seriously by the world's governments – as it sometimes seems possible – is even more disturbing.[3] Not only do they show very little promise of actually doing much good to the cause of improved global environmental governance, but some could actually do harm by distracting international attention from more pressing issues.

It is not the purpose of this article to reexamine, or critique, the details of different schemes for organizational restructuring. Critiques are available elsewhere in the larger literature.[4] Moreover, to do so would be to cede to the premise on which such proposals are based, and it is that very premise that needs to be questioned. It should be noted, however, that there is a certain variety in the proposals – ranging from Daniel C. Esty's GEO, which would focus only on global issues;[5] to Frank Biermann's WEO, which would also incorporate more local concerns;[6] to John Whalley and Ben Zissimos's desire to create a global bargaining-based entity;[7] to David L. Downie and Marc A. Levy's notion of a super-UNEP.[8] However, all such schemes share a strong supposition that the problem of global environmental governance can largely be reduced to, and resolved by, playing around with the design of global environmental organizations. It is the fundamental flaws of this premise, and the dangers of taking it too seriously, that I focus on in this article.

THE DANGERS OF CONFUSING INSTITUTIONS AND ORGANIZATIONS

Although the WEO/GEO literature routinely refers to its enterprise in terms of *institutions*, it tends to use the term as if it were the plural of organization.[9] The distinction, of course, is not merely semantic; it is well established in the literature and is absolutely critical to this context.[10] Institutions, as Konrad von Moltke reminds us, are "social conventions or 'rules of the game,' in the sense that marriage is an institution, or property, markets, research, transparency or participation."[11] Therefore, institutions need not necessarily have a physical existence. Organizations, on the other hand, are much more circumscribed; according to Oran Young, they are "material entities, possessing physical locations (or seats), offices, personnel, equipment, and budgets."[12] The WEO/GEO discourse is clearly preoccupied with organizations and often ignores fundamental questions about *why* environmental degradation happens, or *why* global cooperation founders, or even *why* global environmental governance is a good idea.[13]

This confusion has the effect of trivializing global environmental governance. To place the spotlight on organizational tinkering and label it institution building is to imply that the institutional will − in terms of societal conventions and rules of the game − for global environmental cooperation already exists, and all that remains is to set up an appropriate organizational framework;[14] that global cooperation is a function of inappropriately designed organizations rather than a reflection of a fundamental absence of willingness on the part of states;[15] that the lack of implementation of international regimes stems from dispersed secretariats rather than the failure of these very same regimes "to target those actors that create the problems that regime arrangements set out to address";[16] that improved global environmental governance is a puzzle of administrative efficiency rather than a challenge of global justice.[17] None of the institutional challenges identified here are likely to be resolved by merely rearranging the organization of chairs on our planetary Titanic. Unless the core institutional questions are somehow first addressed, any new organization will fall prey to the exact same pathologies that confront existing arrangements.

The focus on organizational minutia is dangerous precisely because it distracts attention from the more real and immediate institutional challenges to global environmental governance. Two such challenges are of particular importance; both are treated only peripherally by GEO/WEO proponents, if at all.

The first relates to the near demise of the much-celebrated Rio compact on sustainable development – the supposed understanding between the developing countries of the South and their more industrialized counterparts from the North that environment and development will be dealt with as an integrated complex of concerns within the context of current and future social justice and equity. The compact, to whatever extent it did exist, was always understood to be an expression of desire rather than reality – what Tariq Banuri has called "a triumph of hope over experience."[18] The hope, obviously misplaced, was that in time the compact would become real; that both North and South would somehow learn not simply to accept it but to operationalize it. That was not to be.[19] In fact, the optimism was shed rather quickly – the North soon became wary of the fuzziness of sustainable development while the South began to fear that the supposed definitional problems with the concept were being used as an excuse for maintaining the status quo.[20]

The implication of this for the future of global environmental governance is profound. To whatever extent the concept of sustainable development embodied the semblance of an *institutional* bargain on how environmental issues should be contextualized globally, that bargain is now functionally defunct – and so is the very tentative and always nebulous accord that might once have existed on why global environmental governance may be a good thing, for whom, and on what terms. It is not a surprise, then, that the immediate reaction of many in the South is to shirk at the first mention of a GEO or a WEO; or that the addition of development-related flourishes to these proposals fail to woo the South and are either rejected or ignored.[21] Frankly, the glib and lofty goals of finding "thoughtful ways to manage our ecological interdependence"[22] or of "[elevating] environmental policies on the agenda of governments, international organizations, and private actors"[23] or even of "equitably and effectively [managing] planet Earth"[24] are no longer credible, or necessarily appealing, to those who have lived through the last ten years of broken global promises on sustainable development. In essence, the very basis of global environmental cooperation – and thereby governance that might have seemed to exist a decade ago, is under threat today. As Anil Agarwal, Sunita Narain, and Anju Sharma point out, no effective governance is possible under the prevailing conditions of deep distrust; organizational rearrangements might distract attention from deeper problems but are unlikely to solve them.[25] This sense of frustration by the developing countries was particularly apparent during the buildup to the 2002 World Summit on Sustainable Development (WSSD) in Johannesburg. Although the issue of global environmental governance was on the table during the preparatory phase, developing countries saw little value in discussions that remained focused on organizational redesign rather than on institutional restructuring.

The second critical challenge to the cause of improved global environmental governance pertains not to the exclusion of the concerns of Southern governments from the emerging "New Global Environmental Order" but to the meaningful inclusion of civil society concerns, especially those of the South.[26]

This is important because the very nature of the environmental problématique is different from many other international concerns (for example, defense and security) in that a greater proportion of key environmental decisions lie beyond the direct ability or authority of states. This underscores the need for a society-centric view of global environmental governance – one that includes state organs but goes beyond them.[27] This, of course, stands in contradiction to the predominantly state-centered view of global governance in the organizationally inclined literature. This is not to suggest that interstate organizations are unimportant. Far from it, they will have to be an integral – probably a central – component of improved global environmental governance. From an institutional perspective, however, the quality of such governance will be determined by how interstate organizations connect with emerging global public policy networks (GPPNs), of which civil society organizations are a key part.[28] In ignoring, downplaying, or at the very least distracting from the centrality of such integration, the organizational debate fails to rise to the challenge of what could have been a very timely discourse on meaningful institutional reform.

There are, however, other streams of scholarship on global governance that recognize that the key challenge is to create institutions that can integrate the multitude of voices that now feel alienated from the official chatter on global environmental issues. For example, those who talk in terms of GPPNs see better governance emanating not just from decisions taken at centralized interstate organizations or via coordinated legal frameworks, but also through networks of dispersed decision points spread out globally, across all sectors: state, market, and civil.[29] This leads one to a very different set of organizational questions – with the emphasis shifting from a search for better management as measured by administrative efficiency to better networking as gauged by broad-based legitimacy.[30]

The centrality that has been assumed by the GEO/WEO debate within the global environmental discourse translates to a distraction from these other pressing issues. It is not only that new organizational maneuvering is likely to be insufficient to revive the spirit of the Rio compact or to integrate with civil society networks; it is also that any new organizational arrangement is likely to remain as stymied as the current arrangement until these other issues of global environmental governance are tackled first.

NEW LAMPS FOR OLD

Ever since *Aladdin and the Magic Lamp*,[31] those of us who come from what used to be called the Orient have learned to be wary of anyone offering "new lamps for old!" Therefore, when someone offers to replace existing organizational arrangements with a new and improved architecture, one instinctively asks, "What is it that is so bad about the old or so different about the new?" In the case of global environmental organizations, the answer is, "Not much!"

Proponents of organizational rearrangement invariably begin with the standard scare tactics – global ecological systems are under growing threat. While this assessment is correct, the jump between acknowledging the ecological crisis and pointing to organizational inefficiency as the culprit is a rather wide one. Beyond assertion, there is no attempt to establish causality, or even correlation, between the continuing ecological crisis and the nature of the existing organizational arrangements. Two questions need to be asked. First, would things have been worse had the existing system *not* been in place? I argue later that the answer is that certainly they would have been worse. Second, could things be better under an alternative system?

Proponents of large-scale organizational rearrangement obviously believe that things would, in fact, be improved if the organizational architecture were rearranged. They accuse the existing arrangements of a coordination deficit, deficient authority, and insufficient legitimacy and they promise that setting up a new organization would streamline organizational coordination, accelerate financial and technology transfers, and improve the implementation and development of international environmental law.[32] What is not made clear, however, is why the pathologies that inflict the existing arrangements would simply not be transferred to any new arrangement? If coordination is the real roadblock to better environmental performance, then why should one believe that a new organization could achieve it better than UNEP? After all, UNEP's very raison d'être has been to coordinate and catalyze. Why should one assume that rich nations that have been so stingy in meeting their global fiscal responsibilities in the past—in environmental as well as other arenas – will suddenly turn generous for a new organization? If fragmentation is what makes the current arrangements unwieldy, could that not be addressed within the framework of Section 38.22(h) of Agenda 21, which called for the co-location of various treaty secretariats under the UNEP umbrella? What in the new system would make Northern governments – who have consistently reneged on their international commitments regarding financial and technology transfer – suddenly reverse this trend? In short, the most interesting questions are never asked, and certainly not answered.

The problems that these proposals seek to solve through reorganization are not organizational problems at all. If UNEP has been denied authority and resources, it is because the nation-states wish to deny it (and any successor superorganization) authority and resources. They have certainly never demonstrated the willingness to provide UNEP with the resources that would be required to do what they claim it ought to do. The coordination deficit is not something that crept in; it was something that was painstakingly designed into the system—because the countries that are most responsible for the global ecological crisis have never demonstrated the intention of owning that responsibility and because intense turf battles between UN agencies forced an unmanageable coordination mandate upon UNEP.[33] The coordination deficit is indeed real, but it is not organizational. It is institutional and is unlikely to go away through cosmetic architectural renovations. With due apology for sounding cynical, the point to be made is that the global environmental governance crisis at hand is not about organizational minutia; it is about the now glaring lack of willingness to embrace global environmental cooperation. This lack of will has been evident in a variety of recent environmental negotiations, most notably those related to climate change and WSSD.

The problems that the proponents of organizational rearrangement identify are, for the most part, real problems. The goals they identify for the rearranged system are laudable goals. One has no qualms about either. The issue is with how the dots are connected — or, in this case, not connected. The proposals inspire no confidence that the problems confronted by the current setup will not simply transfer to a new setup, or that new arrangements would be any more likely to succeed where the current arrangements have failed. This seems to be one more incidence of "hope triumphing over experience."[34]

VIVA LA UNEP!

Although not always intentional, the immediate casualty of the misdiagnosis on the part of WEO/GEO proponents is the reputation of the UNEP. Even though some view UNEP as the central core of the ultimate superstructure for global environmental governance — and some within UNEP may well find this notion appealing — the fact is that, implicitly or explicitly, UNEP is portrayed as being at the root of the problem. After all, when the existing organizational structure is accused of being inefficient, ineffective, and insufficiently legitimate, then UNEP — which is the centerpiece of that structure — must also stand accused, even if indirectly. Indeed, one should concede that like any other UN agency, UNEP has much that can be improved. However, the stings — implied or explicit — showered on it either ignore or underplay its very significant achievements.

The tragedy is not just that such proposals are based on the assumption that the much-trumpeted weakness of UNEP lies at the heart of the crisis of global environmental governance. Nor is it just that even the critics of such schemes nearly never question this assumption. The real tragedy is that UNEP's own leadership seems to have bought into this assumption. The rampage of exaggerated external criticism and unwarranted self-doubt cannot bode well for UNEP or for the morale of its staff. Indeed, in this article I argue that while UNEP is certainly not the perfect agency, and while there is much that can and should be improved, it is not the weakling or underachiever that it is portrayed as. Arguably, it has performed relatively well in comparison to other agencies of the UN family both in terms of performance and legitimacy, and it has every right to stand proud of its remarkable achievements, which came despite all the limitations that its critics are so fond of enumerating.

Similar to much of what is being proposed in the current round, UNEP was originally conceived as the "environmental conscience of the UN system" and was charged to act as the "focal point for environmental action within the

United Nations system."[35] In defining this mandate of coordination, it was charged with "perhaps one of the most difficult jobs in the entire UN system."[36] It has been hinted that UNEP may have been designed for failure, or at least for something less than success.[37] As John McCormick points out, "It had severe obstacles placed in its path from the outset. It had too little money, too few staff, and too much to do, it had the thankless task of coordinating the work of other UN agencies against a background of interagency jealousy and suspicion, and national governments were unwilling to grant UNEP significant powers."[38] Given the sprawling and bickering nature of the UN machinery, its own lack of executive status, and the dismal resources at its command, "UNEP could no more be expected to 'coordinate' the system-wide activities of the UN than could a medieval monarch 'coordinate' his feudal barons."[39] It should therefore be no surprise that UNEP has not been able to fulfill what Ken Conca has called "its hopeless mandate as system-wide coordinator on environmental matters."[40]

Yet, while there is agreement that UNEP has not been allowed to fulfill its coordination mandate,[41] it is also argued that it "can be credited with having achieved more than it was in reality empowered to do."[42] Those who have studied it in depth agree that it is "generally well-regarded,"[43] "relatively effective,"[44] and, given its meager resources and authority, it "has been a remarkable success."[45] While this is not the place to evaluate UNEP's achievements, I list here a sampling of reasons why it should be considered a successful international organization.

MAKING THE ENVIRONMENT A GLOBAL ISSUE

The single most important, and totally unappreciated, achievement of UNEP is its role in converting the environment into a global issue. It is easy to forget the hostility with which the developing countries had greeted the Stockholm conference of 1972 and the subsequent establishment of UNEP.[46] The placement of UNEP in Nairobi was not just a symbolic act; it was a strategic necessity without which the developing countries might never have accepted the creation of an environmental organ.[47] The fact that this became the first, and only, UN organ to be based anywhere in the developing world galvanized the South both in the process of getting it to locate to Nairobi and in its early and most difficult years: the 1970s into the mid-1980s.[48] Although they stood with UNEP largely out of a sense of Southern solidarity, the developing countries began buying into parts of the environmental agenda and, more important, demanding that the agenda be modified to incorporate their realities. Indeed, the call to set up the World Commission on Environment and Development (WCED) came out of a discussion at the UNEP Governing Council. While WCED might have come up with the term *sustainable development*, the stage for it had already been set by UNEP and its Governing Council at its tenth anniversary meeting in 1982.

Advancing the Global Environmental Agenda

Those who gathered in Stockholm in 1972 could scarcely have imagined the global environmental agenda becoming as advanced and as prominent in international affairs as it is today. UNEP played a significant part in this transformation.[49] Through its various activities, and especially training programs, it helped create an environmental constituency within and outside governments that has been at the forefront of moving this agenda forward. It played a pivotal role in putting desertification, ozone depletion, and organic pollutants on the global agenda.[50] Even for issues like climate change, biodiversity, and deforestation, UNEP's contribution has been more important than it is often given credit for.

International Environmental Law

International environmental law has probably been the single fastest growing subfield of international law; and UNEP has to be among the most active and productive UN agencies in terms of advancing international law. This is not an idle statement. Apart from the agenda-setting role it played on issues such as desertification, biodiversity, and climate change, it has been the principal negotiation manager for complex global regimes on ozone depletion, trade in endangered species, trade in hazardous wastes, persistent organic pollutants, regional seas, etc. For an organization as young and as resource strapped as UNEP, this is a remarkable achievement indeed. UNEP-managed treaty negotiations − such as those on ozone-depleting substances and, more recently, on persistent organic pollutants − are generally regarded to have been among the most efficient and successful global environmental negotiations.[51]

Legitimacy

By routinely suggesting that a new organizational architecture would lend legitimacy to global environmental governance, the proponents of GEO/WEO seem to imply that UNEP has less than sufficient legitimacy as an international organization. If they were not earnest, it would be funny that some proponents of a superorganization want to scrap UNEP and replace it with something that might look more like the World Trade Organization (WTO). Massive public demonstrations from Seattle to Prague and feelings of distrust and apprehension are what come to mind when one thinks of the WTO or the World Bank (another organization that is sometimes talked about as the model to follow). UNEP, on the other hand, does not have to place barriers or bring out riot police at its annual meetings and has a tradition of good relations with civil society. Indeed, in terms of general public legitimacy and honest efforts to involve civil society in its orbit, UNEP has fared much better than most international organizations, even though there remains room for improvement.[52]

In summary, while UNEP has its share of problems, they relate not to its mandate as much as to the resources it has been provided. The fact that some of its critics have never forgiven it for being located in a developing country does not help either. It is unfortunate that its leadership has sometimes been defensive about both its achievements and its potential, instead of building upon its rather rich legacy of performance. It is not a perfect organization, but it has been a rather good one. It would be sad if, in our zeal for organizational rearrangement, we made the allegedly perfect the enemy of the demonstrably good.

TOWARD BETTER GLOBAL ENVIRONMENTAL GOVERNANCE

It should be obvious that I am not persuaded by the need for an environmental superorganization. However, an argument against new organizational super-structures should not be confused with an argument for organizational inertia. All organizations should strive for improvement, and global environmental organizations – including UNEP – are no exception. There are a number of elements within the various proposals that do make sense – not as arguments for organizational overhaul, but as elements of an agenda to improve the existing organizational setup. Moreover, change that happens within the existing system is likely to be substantively less disruptive and politically more feasible. This final section highlights five key elements of a potential agenda for organizational improvement that can be pursued within the confines of the existing structures and would begin addressing the larger institutional challenges of global environmental governance discussed earlier.[53] It should he noted, however, that for all the reasons already discussed, some of these ideas are not going to be easy to implement. Yet, to the extent they can be implemented, they are likely to be easier to implement within UNEP's existing structure than within a new supraorganization of the GEO/WEO variety.

Enabling UNEP to Fulfill Its Mandate

There is no need to change UNEP's mandate. There is, however, an urgent need to provide it with the resources, staff, and authority it needs to fulfill its mandate. UNEP's shareholders – that is, the member states – need to invest in UNEP in proportion to the responsibilities they demand of it. One step in this direction might be to convert UNEP into a specialized agency (as opposed to a program) with the concomitant ability to raise and decide its own budget. Greater autonomy may not in itself be sufficient to translate to greater resources, but it could allow UNEP to be more innovative and even assertive in its resource mobilization strategies. However, given the political wrangling this would require, the UN General Assembly might consider maintaining UNEP's program status but providing it with greater autonomy in budgetary matters to ensure a sufficient and consistent resource base.

Indeed, UNEP was originally modeled on the United Nations Development Programme (UNDP) and should aspire to fulfill that original intent. While this would require more assertive leadership from UNEP, it would also obviously require the UN secretary-general and member states to give UNEP the budgetary and operational prominence that it has so often been promised, thereby giving it the respect it deserves. One step could be to invest in making its flagship *Global Environmental Outlook Reports* an environmental equivalent to the World Bank's *World Development Reports*, or UNDP's *Human Development Reports*.

Realizing Sustainable Development

Over the years, many have become quite fond of arguing that the problem with sustainable development is that it is very difficult to define. While defining it in precise terms is certainly not easy, it is also not entirely necessary. The real problem with sustainable development is that the governments of the world lack the commitment to realize it. The main culprit in this regard is governments in the North that have consistently reneged on their financial commitments. However, the governments of the South are also to blame for viewing sustainable development simply as an excuse to continue with development as usual without any regard to its environmental consequences.

From an institutional perspective, realizing sustainable development would imply streamlining mechanisms for financing sustainable development and monitoring and validating progress. Because of its problems of transparency and performance, many developing countries consider that the Global Environmental Facility (GEF) lacks legitimacy.[54] Other funding mechanisms are even more strapped for cash. There is a need to reconsider the operation of GEF, broaden the scope of activities that it can finance, replenish it to higher levels, and possibly place its management more firmly within UNEP, which enjoys more credibility with developing countries and routinely deals with issues of environment and sustainable development as its primary focus. The existing trilateral management structure involving UNEP, UNDP, and the World Bank can, in fact, be maintained while UNEP is given the role of lead agency in its actual management. Doing so would also allow UNEP to better fulfill its existing mandate.

Managing MEA Proliferation

Over the last decade, the great increase in negotiations pertaining to the new or existing multilateral environmental agreements (MEAs) has caused a serious problem of MEA proliferation and attendant pathologies of negotiation fatigue, particularly among developing country delegates.[55] This has placed an immense burden on most developing countries, which simply do not have the resources to keep up with the frantic pace of increasingly complex negotiations. Moreover, the frenzy to complete negotiation as quickly as possible has left behind a legacy of less-than-perfect agreements or resulted in too little attention being paid to questions of implementation.[56]

How do these various MEAs fit together? A certain clustering of independently negotiated treaties has begun to emerge organically as part of the evolution of international environmental law; it is timely to convert this into a deliberate schema.[57] Von Moltke, in particular, has outlined a useful list of possibilities for MEA clustering.[58] A co-location of MEA secretariats – which some WEO proponents also suggest – seems an equally pragmatic idea even though it is likely that some governments and secretariat staff might resist it. Yet it is an idea worth pursuing because it could provide efficiency gains, increase cross-treaty communication, and discourage MEA fiefdoms. Overlapping or joint meetings of related MEAs, possibly in permanent locations, would serve to ease the pressures on participating delegates and encourage more continuity in representation.

UNEP, with its good record of MEA management – both in terms of overseeing complex negotiations and of hosting MEA secretariats – again emerges as the best-suited candidate for this task. Hence, not only would this not require a new superorganization, it would also not require a major legal restructuring of UNEP's mandate. In fact, the task was already awarded to UNEP a decade ago by Agenda 21, which called upon UNEP to concentrate on (among other things) the "further development of international environmental law, in particular conventions and guidelines, promotion of its implementation, and coordinating functions arising from an increasing number of international legal agreements, inter alia, the functioning of the secretariats of the Conventions ... including possible co-location of secretariats established in the future."[59]

Coordination, Yes; Centralization, No

Echoing UNEP's original charter, Agenda 21 had also defined UNEP as the "principal body within the United Nations system in the field of environment" (Section 38.23). However, for good reason, the UNEP was never intended to be the only UN body with relevance to the environment. Centralization makes little conceptual sense for issues related to the environment and even less for sustainable development. The fabric of environmental concerns, and even more of sustainable development concerns, is a multivariate web of interlinked issues that do not have a clear center and are unlikely to respond to centralized policymaking. A reading of Agenda 21, or of the report of the World Commission on Environment and Development before it, would make it quite clear that if there is any body that has the authority to centrally devise all sustainable development policy – or to even coordinate all sustainable development policy – that body would be the United Nations as a whole rather than any subcomponent of it. Could one imagine creating a central entity that is responsible for all issues related to sustainable development, ranging from biodiversity to international debt, from climate change to education, from poverty alleviation to pollution? Should one imagine such a centralized entity, even if one could?

Given the fundamentally interlinked and cross-sectoral nature of these issues, UNEP's original mandate as a catalyst and coordinator was, in retrospect, well conceived. However, as already noted, UNEP has been less than successful in realizing its coordination mandate. At the same time, the coordination mandate is now spread out around the system: in addition to the Commission on Sustainable Development (CSD), the recently created Environmental Management Group (EMG) and the Global Ministerial Environment Forum (GMEF) both seem to have some elements of the coordination function in their mandates. This dilution of UNEP's coordination responsibility may not be a bad thing. Not only is coordination a thankless job but, as Mark Imber reminds us, "the primary responsibility for coordination rests with governments."[60] The agency heads that make up EMG and the senior government delegates that make up the CSD and GMEF seem far better positioned for UN-wide coordination than UNEP's secretariat staff could ever be expected to. Having multiple forums for coordination may also not be bad – there is enough cross-participation within these groups to keep duplication or contradiction manageable, while multiple forums could actually have the effect of reinforcing each other on the need for coordination.

Civilizing Global Environmental Governance

Providing the space and opportunity for meaningful participation of civil society networks in global environmental governance may well be the most important challenge from the institutional as well as the organizational standpoint.[61] Within the realm of global public policy, the environment is an issue on which civil society has been particularly active and influential.[62] However, there is a growing sense that international organizations are becoming increasingly introverted. Especially in the aftermath of recurrent civil protests arising from a deeply felt distrust of globalization – and of international organizations as the agents of globalization – both UNEP and CSD need to invest more attention to linking with civil society. In a recent report, Turiq Banuri and Erika Spanger-Siegfried lay out a detailed set of recommendations for establishing deeper linkages with civil society actors, particularly GPPNs, for leveraging the opportunities for policy innovation and cross-sectoral synergies that this would offer.[63] There is also the need to begin viewing civil society not just as stakeholders in but as motors of global environmental governance.[64] Following the tradition of human rights regimes, civil society networks could potentially become the real drivers of MEA implementation. Indeed, for political as well as logistic reasons, they may be more likely to play that role than governments or intergovernmental agencies.[65]

In conclusion, I have argued that not only is there no need for a new international environmental organization, but the discussions on this subject tend to distract attention from the actual reforms in the existing organizations that are needed. I outlined five elements of such an organizational reform agenda but recognize that these must be embedded in the larger challenge of institutional reform. In practical terms, this means that the key change has to come not in the structural details of existing or new organizations but in the support and political will that national governments are willing to invest in these organizations.

NOTES

1. Maurice Bertrand, *The Third Generation World Organization* (Dordrecht: Martinus Nijhoff, 1989).

2. For a particularly insightful discussion of global governance, see Oran R. Young, "Global Governance: Toward a Theory of Decentralized World Order," in Oran R. Young, ed., *Global Governance: Drawing Insights from the Environmental Experience* (Cambridge: MIT Press, 1997), pp. 273–299.

3. There have been a number of different proposals floating around. See, for example, Ford C. Runge, Francois Ortalo-Magne, and Philip Van de Kamp, *Freer Trade, Protected Environment: Balancing Trade Liberalization and Environmental Interests* (New York: Council on Foreign Relations Press, 1994); Daniel C. Esty, "The Case for a Global Environmental Organization," in Peter B. Kenen, ed., *Managing the World Economy: Fifty Years After Bretton Woods* (Washington, D.C.: Institute for International Economics, 1994), pp. 287–309; Steve Charnovitz, "Improving Environmental and Trade Governance," *International Environmental Affairs* 7, no. 1 (1995): 59–91; Frank Biermann, "The Case for a World Environmental Organization," *Environment* 42, no. 9 (2000): 22–31; David L. Downie and Marc A. Levy, "The UN Environment Programme at a Turning Point: Options for Change," in Pamela S. Chasek, ed., *The Global Environment in the Twenty-First Century: Prospects for International Cooperation* (Tokyo: United Nations University Press, 2000), pp. 355–377; and John Whalley and Ben Zissimos, "What Could a World Environmental Organization Do?" *Global Environmental Politics* 1, no. 1 (2001): 29–34.

4. See Anil Agarwal, Sunita Narain, and Anju Sharma, *Green Politics* (New Delhi: Centre for Science and Environment, 1999); Calestous Juma, "The Perils of Centralizing Global Environmental Governance," *Environment Matters: Annual Review* (July 1999–June 2000), (Washington, D.C.: World Bank, 2000), pp. 13–15; Calestous Juma, "Stunning Green Progress," *Financial Times*, 6 July 2000; Konrad Von Moltke, "The Organization of the Impossible," *Global Environmental Politics* 1, no. 1 (2000): 23–28;

Peter Newell, "New Environmental Architectures and the Search for Effectiveness," *Global Environmental Politics* 1, no. 1 (2001): 35–44. For a rebuttal of such critiques, see Frank Biermann, "The Emerging Debate on the Need for a World Environmental Organization," *Global Environmental Politics* 1, no. 1 (2001): 45–55.

5. Daniel C. Esty, "Stepping Up to the Global Environmental Challenge," *Fordham Environmental Law Journal* 8, no. 1 (1996): 103–113.

6. Biermann, "The Case for a World Environmental Organization."

7. Whalley and Zissimos, "What Could a World Environmental Organization Do?"

8. Downie and Levy, "The UN Environment Programme at a Turning Point."

9. See, as just one example, Frank Biermann, "Reform of International Environmental Institutions: Would a World Environment Organization Benefit the South?" paper presented at the annual meeting of the International Studies Association, New Orleans, March 2002.

10. See Oran R. Young, *International Governance: Protecting the Environment in a Stateless Society* (Ithaca: Cornell University Press, 1994).

11. Konrad Von Moltke, *Whither MEAs? The Role of International Environmental Management in the Trade and Environment Agenda* (Winnipeg: International Institute for Sustainable Development, 2001), p. 11.

12. Oran R. Young, *International Cooperation: Building Regimes for Natural Resources and the Environment* (Ithaca: Cornell University Press, 1989), p. 32.

13. Newell, "New Environmental Architectures."

14. See Von Moltke, *Whither MEAs?*

15. See Juma, "Stunning Green Progress."

16. Newell, "New Environmental Architectures," p. 40.

17. Agarwal, Narain, and Sharma, *Green Politics.*

18. Tariq Banuri, "Envisioning Sustainable Development," unpublished note (Boston: Stockholm Environmental Institute, 2001). Based on an original quotation from Samuel Johnson.

19. To get a sampling of views on what transpired, and why, see Tariq Banuri, *Noah's Ark or Jesus's Cross?* Working Paper WP/UNCED/1992/I (Islamabad: Sustainable Development Policy Institute, 1992); Adil Najam, "An Environmental Negotiation Strategy for the South," *International Environmental Affairs* 7, no. 3 (1995): 249–287; Richard Sandbrook, "UNGASS Has Run Out of Steam," *International Affairs* 73, no. 4 (1997): 641–654; Agarwal, Narain, and Sharma, *Green Politics.*

20. Adil Najam, "From Rio to Johannesburg: The State of Sustainable Development," paper presented at the annual meeting of the International Studies Association, New Orleans, March 2002.

21. See Agarwal, Narain, and Sharma, *Green Politics*; Juma, "Stunning Green Progress"; and Newell, "New Environmental Architectures."

22. Daniel C. Esty, "The Value of Creating a Global Environmental Organization," in *Environment Matters: Annual Review* (July 1999–June 2000), (Washington, D.C.: World Bank, 2000), pp. 13–14.

23. Biermann, "The Case for a World Environmental Organization," p. 29.

24. Biermann, "Reform of International Environmental Institutions," p. 16.

25. Agarwal, Narain, and Sharma, *Green Politics*, p. 372.

26. Ibid.

27. Tariq Banuri and Erika Spanger-Siegfried, *UNEP and Civil Society: Recommendations for a Coherent Framework of Engagement* (Boston: Stockholm Environmental Institute, 2000).

28. Wolfgang H. Reinicke, *Global Public Policy: Governing Without Government?* (Washington, D.C.: Brookings Institution, 1998).

29. See Wolfgang H. Reinicke and Francis M. Deng, *Critical Choices: The United Nations, Networks and the Future of Global Governance* (Ottawa: International Development Research Centre, 2000).

30. Banuri and Spanger-Siegfried, *UNEP and Civil Society*.

31. In this famous children's tale – one of the original Arabian Nights and the subject of a Disney animation film – the villain is able to steal the magic lamp from Aladdin's unsuspecting wife by making her an offer she cannot refuse: promising to replace old lamps for new.

32. Esty, "Stepping Up to the Global Environmental Challenge"; Biermann, "The Case for a World Environmental Organization."

33. Branislav Gosovic, *The Quest for Worm Environmental Cooperation: The Case of the UN Global Environment Monitoring System* (London: Routledge, 1992).

34. To again misquote Banuri ("Envisioning Sustainable Development") misquoting Mark Twain.

35. UN General Assembly, Res. 2997 (XXVII), adopted December 1972.

36. Richard Sandbrook, "The UK's Overseas Environmental Policy," in Brian D.G. Johnson, ed., *The Conservation and Development Programme for the UK: A Response to the World Conservation Strategy* (London: Kogan Page, 1983), p. 388.

37. Konrad Von Moltke, "Why UNEP Matters," *Green Globe Yearbook of International Co-operation on Environment and Development, 1996* (Oxford: Oxford University Press, 1996), pp. 55–64.

38. John McCormick, *The Global Environmental Movement* (New York: John Wiley, 1995), p. 152.

39. Mark Imber, *Environment, Security and UN Reform* (London: St. Martin's Press, 1994), p. 83.

40. Ken Conca, "Greening the UN: Environmental Organizations and the UN System," in Thomas G. Weiss and Leon Gordenker, eds., *NGOs, the UN, and Global Governance* (Boulder: Lynne Rienner, 1996), p. 108.

41. Indeed, no UN agency (including the UNDP or even the secretary-general's Secretariat) has been allowed to meaningfully fulfill the coordination function; moreover, there is no indication that any agency (current or future) will be allowed such a liberty.

42. McCormick, *The Global Environmental Movement*, p. 153.

43. Mark Imber, "Too Many Cooks? The Post-Rio Reform of the United Nations," *International Affairs* 69, no. 1 (1993): 56.

44. Conca, "Greening the UN," p. 112.

45. Von Moltke, "Why UNEP Matters," p. 58.

46. *Development and Environment: Report and Working Papers of Experts Convened by the Secretary-General of the United Nations Conference on the Human Environment,* held at Founex, Switzerland, June 1971 (Paris: Mouton, 1972).

47. Wade Rowland, *The Plot to Save the World* (Toronto: Clarke, Irwin, 1973).

48. See, especially, Gosovic, *The Quest for World Environmental Cooperation.* Note that this period also marks the height of Southern solidarity and the movement for a New International Economic Order (NIEO). During this period, the symbolism of UNEP being in Nairobi was of significant importance to the developing countries. This resulted in their very visibly and disproportionately supporting an organization that they had originally resented.

49. Lynton K. Caldwell, *International Environmental Policy: Emergence and Dimensions,* 3d ed. (Durham: Duke University Press, 1996).

50. Downie and Levy, "The UN Environment Programme at a Turning Point."

51. Richard Benedick, *Ozone Diplomacy: New Directions in Safeguarding the Planet* (Cambridge: Harvard University Press); Mustafa K. Tolba, *Global Environmental Diplomacy: Negotiating Environmental Agreements for the World, 1973–1992* (Cambridge: MIT Press).

52. Banuri and Spanger-Siegfried, *UNEP and Civil Society.*

53. Some of these ideas are informed by the author's participation at the "Expert Consultation on International Environmental Governance," organized by UNEP in Cambridge, England, on 28–29 May 2001. A report of the meeting is available online at www.unep.org/IEG/docs/.

54. Agarwal, Narain, and Sharma, *Green Politics.*

55. Adil Najam, "The Case for a Law of the Atmosphere," *Atmospheric Environment* 34, no. 23 (2000): 4047–049.

56. Adil Najam and Ambuj Sagar, "Avoiding a COP-out: Moving Towards Systematic Decision-Making Under the Climate Convention," *Climatic Change* 39, no. 4 (1998); Adil Najam, "Developing Countries and the Desertification Convention: Portrait of a Tortured Relationship," presented at the annual meeting of the International Studies Association, New Orleans, March 2002.

57. Najam, "The Case for a Law of the Atmosphere."

58. Von Moltke, "The Organization of the Impossible."

59. Agenda 21, Section 38.22[h].

60. Imber, "Too Many Cooks?" p. 66.

61. Banuri and Spanger-Siegfried, *UNEP and Civil Society.*

62. Leon Gordenker and Thomas G. Weiss, "NGO Participation in International Policy Processes," *Third World Quarterly* 16, no. 3 (1995): 543–555; Adil Najam, "Citizen Organizations as Policy Entrepreneurs," in David Lewis, ed., *International Perspectives on Voluntary Action: Reshaping the Third Sector* (London: Earthscan, 1999), pp. 142–181.

63. Banuri and Spanger-Siegfried, *UNEP and Civil Society.*

64. Tariq Banuri and Adil Najam, *Civic Entrepreneurship: Civil Society Perspectives on Sustainable Development,* vol. 1 (Islamabad: Gandhara Academy Press).

65. Adil Najam, "The Four C's of Third Sector-Government Relations: Cooperation, Confrontation, Complementarity, and Co-optation," *Nonprofit Management and Leadership* 10, no. 4 (2000): 375–396.

POSTSCRIPT

In his critique of arguments for a world environmental organization, Najam insists that attention should be focused on institutions rather than organizations. Preoccupation with creating new, more centralized organizational structures may not lead to significant improvements in the handling of environmental issues. Some participants in this debate seem to have been influenced by such arguments and have thus sought to find a different, "third way" of approaching this issue.

Daniel Esty and Maria Ivanova have written extensively on environmental issues and have been strong advocates of a new global environmental organization. Recently, however, they have modified their position, arguing for the creation of a "Global Environmental Mechanism" instead. While they argue that there is indeed a need for better coordinated "collective action" to address environmental issues, they no longer believe that this can be achieved through the creation of new organizations in the style of traditional international bureaucracies. Instead, they advocate using new communications technologies to build networks of cooperation between existing agencies. They suggest that rather than replacing organizations such as the UNEP, a Global Environmental Mechanism could act as a coordinating hub for facilitating cooperation, information sharing, and negotiation. Their new argument can be found in an article entitled "Revitalizing Global Environmental Governance: A Function-Driven Approach," available at www.yale.edu/forestry/publications/fespubfiles/geg/esty-ivanova.pdf.

Suggested Additional Readings

Charnovitz, S. "Improving Environmental and Trade Governance." *International Environmental Affairs* 7, no. 1 (Winter 1995): 59–91.

Conca, Ken. "Greening the UN: Environmental Organisations and the UN System." In Thomas G. Weiss and Leon Gordenker, eds., *NGOs, the UN, and Global Governance.* Boulder: Lynne Rienner, 1996: 103–19.

Doyle, W. Michael, and Rachel Massey. "Intergovernmental Organizations and the Environment: Introduction." In Pamela S. Chasek, ed., *The Global Environment in the Twenty-First Century.* New York: United Nations University Press, 2000: 411–26.

Esty, D.C. "The Case for a Global Environmental Organization." In P.B. Kenen, ed., *Managing the World Economy: Fifty Years after Bretton Woods.* Washington, D.C.: Institute for International Economics, 1994: 287–309.

Esty, Daniel, and Maria H. Ivanova, eds. *Global Environmental Governance: Options & Opportunities.* New Haven, Conn.: Yale School of Forestry & Environmental Studies, 2002. Available at www.yale.edu/environment/publications.

Haas, P.M., R.O. Keohane, and M.A. Levy, eds. *Institutions for the Earth: Sources of Effective International Environmental Protection.* Cambridge, Mass.: MIT Press, 1993.

Imber, Mark. 1993. "Too Many Cooks? The Post-Rio Reform of the United Nations." *International Affairs* 69, no. 1 (January 1993): 55–70.

Juma, Calestous. "The Perils of Centralizing Global Environmental Governance." *Environment Matters: Annual Review* (World Bank) (July 1999–June 2000): 13–15.

United Nations University. *International Environmental Governance. The Question of Reform: Key Issues and Proposals. Preliminary Findings.* Tokyo: United Nations University, Institute for Advanced Studies, 2002. Available at www.ias.unu.edu.

von Moltke, Konrad. "The Organization of the Impossible." *Global Environmental Politics* 1, no. 1 (February 2001): 23–28.

Whalley, John, and Ben Zissimos. "What Could a World Environmental Organisation Do?" *Global Environmental Politics* 1, no. 1 (February 2001): 29–34.

InfoTrac® College Edition

Search for the following articles in the InfoTrac® database:

Biermann, Frank. "The Case for a World Environment Organization." *Environment* 42, no. 9 (November 2000): 22–31.

Haas, Peter M. "International Institutions and Social Learning in the Management of Global Environmental Risks." *Policy Studies Journal* 28, no. 3 (Autumn 2000): 558.

For more articles, enter:

"global environment organization" or "environmental governance" in the keyword search.

Web Resources

For current URLs for the following websites, visit www.crosscurrents.nelson.com.

THE GLOBAL ENVIRONMENTAL GOVERNANCE (GEG) PROJECT

www.yale.edu/gegdialogue/

This research group based at Yale University has produced papers and books dealing with issues relating to global environmental governance that can be found at this website.

INTERNATIONAL INSTITUTE FOR ENVIRONMENT AND DEVELOPMENT

www.iied.org

This nonprofit environmental research institute provides extensive resources on a wide range of global environmental issues.

AGIR POUR L'EVIRONNEMENT

www.agirpourlenvironnement.org/campagnes/c16.htm

For those who read French, this NGO based in France has many resources available as part of its campaign for the creation of a global environmental organization.

GLOBAL ENVIRONMENTAL GOVERNANCE

www.worldsummit2002.org/issues/geg.htm

This web page, sponsored by the Heinrich Böll Foundation in Germany, contains many articles and position papers by various NGOs on the subject of a global environmental organization.

INTERNATIONAL ENVIRONMENTAL GOVERNANCE

www.unep.org/ieg/

The United Nations Environment Programme provides a website containing many documents and background papers on the topic of international environmental governance.

How to Write an Argumentative Essay

LUCILLE CHARLTON

Argumentative essays are written to convince or persuade readers of a particular point or opinion. Whether the point is to change the public's mind on a political issue or to convince a person to stop smoking, all argumentative essays have common elements: a well-defined, convincing argument, credible evidence, and a rebuttal of criticism. While most points of general essay writing apply to argumentative essays, there are several special guidelines the writer of a good persuasive essay must consider. The following sections introduce students to six basic steps in writing an argumentative or persuasive essay.

STEP 1: DEFINE THE ARGUMENT

It is easy to point out that there are two sides to every discussion; however, it is difficult to define precisely one's own opinion on a subject and write about it. First, the writer must be certain that there is, in fact, something to disagree about. For example, Castro is the president of Cuba: no one can dispute that fact. However, if I claim in my essay that Castro's policies have benefited the Cuban nation, many people would disagree with me. There must be room for disagreement with whatever position is taken, so an argumentative essay has to be more than an affirmation of acknowledged facts. In this way, argumentative writing differs from descriptive or journalistic writing. Also, the writer must state the argument in a precise thesis statement that will act as a controlling idea for the entire essay. All ideas expressed in the essay must relate to the thesis statement.

Second, an argumentative essay is more than a restatement of the two sides of the question. A simple recounting of opposing arguments does not give the reader any clear indication of how the writer feels about the subject, and is not really a persuasive statement. For example, a court transcript contains every word spoken by the witnesses at a trial. These statements are entered as evidence in the court, but it is up to the lawyers for both sides to interpret the evidence and present it in a persuasive manner to the jury, leaving no doubt about which side they are on. In the same way, the writer first carefully defines the subject, examines the evidence, and then interprets that evidence by writing a precise opinion. An argumentative essay takes one side of a controversial issue; there should be no doubt in the reader's mind where the writer stands on that issue.

STEP 2: GATHER THE EVIDENCE

Arguments need credible supporting evidence, and good persuasive writers assemble a variety of information from different sources. This evidence can be found in statements from authorities, statistics, or personal experience, or can be interpreted from research data. The authors in this book have chosen one or more of these types of evidence to support their positions. These four types of evidence can also be used by student writers in their argumentative essays.

When researching evidence to support a particular position, the writer needs to keep in mind the four *R's*: *reliable, relevant, recent,* and *referenced.*

First, all authorities used for supporting evidence need to be reliable – that means an acknowledged authority published in a recognized source. Evidence can be suspect if it is published only in unreliable sources, or if a researcher is unable to independently verify the statements. A good writer recognizes acceptable sources and is knowledgeable of the biases normally found in newspapers, magazines, journals, and Internet sources.

Because of the vast amount of material now available through electronic sources, writers must become skilled in evaluating the information presented. Newspaper and journal articles go through a process of editing and evaluation before publication. This acts as a check on information from unreliable sources. Electronic sources are not subjected to such scrutiny, so it is advisable to independently verify information from Internet sources. Consult the following web page from Cornell University for information on evaluating the reliability of electronic sources: www.library.cornell.edu/olinuris/ref/research/webcrit.html.

Reference librarians can assist students in finding a variety of trustworthy sources for essays. Using suspect information will damage the credibility of the writer. A variety of reliable sources adds credibility to the writer's arguments.

Second, sources need to be relevant; that is, they must have something to contribute on the immediate topic. The Economic Council of Canada has expertise in the area of the Canadian economy, but scholars know that it is an unlikely source for information on the status of Pakistan's nuclear weapons. Writers can easily lose unity in their essays by adding irrelevant quotes or paraphrases just to sound authoritative.

Third, a good writer looks for recent information on the topic. Using outdated information could affect the outcome of the argument. For example, if I were arguing for increased funding for AIDS victims in sub-Sahara Africa, I would not base my essay on statistics from 1995, when fewer cases of HIV were reported. The writer should be familiar with the effects of recent changes on the topic: politicians can reverse their positions, new statistics can change the writer's perspective, and new research can add to the evidence. Internet access greatly enhances a writer's ability to access updated statistics, and instructors expect student initiative in this area.

In addition, a writer must also know how much background research needs to be done to introduce the topic to the reader. Background information may be necessary to show how events have progressed over the last few years. For example, any serious discussion of the terrorist events of September 11, 2001, needs background information on the previous attack at the World Trade Center and the two United States embassy bombings.

Finally, all sources need to be carefully quoted and referenced in an acceptable citation form. There are a few basic rules to follow when using someone else's material:

1. Quotations are the exact words of the original author, and they must always be referenced. Consult one of the reference books or websites listed at the end of this article for correct formats. If you are unsure how to reference a particular source, consult with your instructor or a reference librarian.

2. Paraphrases are your restatement of the original author's ideas. Paraphrases keep the same idea, but are restated in your own words. All paraphrases must be referenced. Scholars and researchers frequently use both quotations and paraphrases from a variety of sources to make their arguments.

3. Be careful when using quotations. Do not take either quotations or paraphrases out of context, thereby misquoting a source. Make sure you do enough research to know the writer's position on a topic. Use quotations sparingly, only when you want to emphasize an important point. Double check all quotations to make sure you haven't missed anything in transcribing the words.

4. Give credit whenever using information that did not originate with you, except for general information or well-known facts. For example, you do not need to acknowledge that India became independent from Britain in 1947. However, you must acknowledge statistical data taken from census or research reports used to support your arguments. The contributors to this volume have acknowledged their sources at the end of their articles in notes or references.

In gathering the evidence, keep careful notes and records of all your sources. Make sure to acknowledge all of your sources. The reference manuals and websites listed at the end of this article have helpful information on how to cite your sources. Avoid plagiarism. If you are not certain what constitutes plagiarism, ask your instructor for assistance and consult your school's policy on plagiarism. All colleges and universities have serious penalties for plagiarism.

STEP 3: REFUTE THE OPPOSITION

In order to be convincing, writers have to support their argument while defusing criticism of the position taken. When researching the arguments, the writer also anticipates opposing viewpoints, researches them thoroughly, and is ready to refute them in the essay. Casting doubt on another writer's position or reasoning can clinch your support. This can be done in several ways. First, the writer can cite authorities that hold opposing views, then refute their arguments by quoting other sources or different statistics. Second, rebuttals of arguments can be constructed through differing personal experiences. A third method is to attack the opposition's interpretation of documents and facts.

Writers often concede some of the arguments an opponent makes, then challenge the opponent with a strong conclusion. Concessions should be included early in the argument. The strongest points should be left for the last, leaving no doubt in the reader's mind of the writer's intentions. Avoiding all mention of the opposing position is not a good strategy.

Whether building support for their own arguments or refuting criticism of their positions, writers must be careful to avoid argumentative fallacies, or mistakes in reasoning or argument. The most common fallacies that appear in essays are overgeneralization, faulty cause and effect, and misrepresentation of the opposition. Various writing manuals contain complete discussions of argumentative fallacies.

STEP 4: OUTLINE YOUR ESSAY

Good essay writers start with an outline that incorporates their key ideas into the body of the essay. All argumentative essays begin with an attention-getter: the writer quotes an interesting fact, makes a dramatic statement, or even illustrates with the opposite opinion. Once the reader is hooked into reading the essay, the writer continues with a thesis statement and proceeds with the arguments.

The body of an argumentative essay can be organized in two ways:

Pattern I

Introduction
Thesis statement
Background (if needed)
Listing of all your arguments with supporting evidence
A refutation of all your opponent's points
A reminder of your strongest arguments
Conclusion, including a strong opinion statement

Pattern II

Introduction
Thesis statement
Background (if needed)
Statement of your opponent's first argument, with concession or refutation

Statement of your opponent's second argument, with concession or refutation
Continued refutation of your opponent's arguments, in order
Conclusion, with a strong statement of your own opinion

Many of the contributors to this volume follow Pattern II, which is more effective for longer essays. Pattern I is acceptable for shorter essays with fewer points of supporting evidence, because the reader will not get lost following the train of thought from argument to refutation. In both patterns, concessions are made early in the argument, and a strong opinion statement concludes the essay.

STEP 5: DECIDE TONE AND STYLE

The tone and style of your essay will depend on your audience. Most writers assume that they are writing for intelligent people who have open minds on the topic. Therefore, the tone of the essay cannot be insulting or pejorative. Treat your opposition and your readers with respect.

Examples:

Wrong: As every intelligent person knows . . .
Better: Many people believe . . .

Wrong: Only children would assume that . . .
Better: I do not agree with this position . . .

The essay must also be readable. Using language that is either hard to understand or too casual for the audience will not win converts to your point of view. The language used in an essay must be clear, direct, understandable, and free of gender, racial, or other biases.

Examples:

Wrong: Legitimized concerns on this matter were postponed by the committee.
Better: The committee delayed discussion.

Wrong: Those guys really messed up on this one.
Better: The politicians made mistakes in their analysis.

Wrong: A cabinet minister is accountable for his decisions.
Better: Cabinet ministers are accountable for their decisions.

Most academic essays are written in a formal tone, making minimal use of the pronoun "I." However, be sure to know what your audience expects. Sometimes persuasive essays or speeches are directed at a particular group, and the writer can then use a less formal style of presentation.

STEP 6: CHECK AND DOUBLE CHECK

After writing a draft of an essay, follow this basic checklist of items. By working through the list, you can catch errors in your essay.

Argumentative essay checklist:

1. Have I defined the argument?

2. Do I have a well-stated opinion on the topic?

3. Is my thesis statement clear? Does it have sufficient support?

4. Is my essay unified? Do all parts of the essay relate to the thesis statement?

5. Have I avoided argumentative fallacies?

6. Are my tone and style consistent and appropriate?

7. Have I varied my sentence structure and vocabulary?

8. Have I concluded with a strong statement?

9. Does the opening paragraph grab the reader's attention?

10. Have I checked for spelling errors and misused words and expressions?

11. Have I cited all sources in an acceptable style?

12. Have I correctly punctuated my sentences?

SOURCES TO CONSULT ON ESSAY WRITING

Buckley, Joanne. *Checkmate: A Writing Reference for Canadians.* Toronto: Thomson Nelson, 2003.

Finnbogason, Jack, and Al Valleau. *A Canadian Writer's Guide.* 3rd ed. Toronto: Thomson Nelson, 2005.

Gibaldi, Joseph. *MLA Handbook for Writers of Research Papers.* 6th ed. New York: Modern Language Association, 2003.

Heckman, Grant. *The Nelson Guide to Essay Writing.* Toronto: Thomson Nelson, 2002.

For ESL Students

Hall, Ernest, and Carrie S.Y. Yung. *Reflecting on Writing: Composing in English for ESL Students in Canada.* Toronto: Harcourt Brace Canada, 1996.

Web Resources

The Internet has now become the best source for up-to-date information on essay writing. Listed below are several key sites that contain information useful for citation styles, evaluation of electronic sources, and general writing guidelines.

MODERN LANGUAGE ASSOCIATION (MLA) STYLE GUIDE
www.mla.org/style

AMERICAN PSYCHOLOGICAL ASSOCIATION (APA) STYLE GUIDE
www.apastyle.org/elecref.html

PURDUE UNIVERSITY'S ONLINE WRITING LAB (OWL)
owl.english.purdue.edu

THE RESEARCH AND WRITING PROCESS, FROM THE UNIVERSITY OF TORONTO
www.library.utoronto.ca/services/ilu/research.html

General Resources on Political Science

POLITICAL RESOURCES ON THE NET
www.politicalresources.net

ACADEMIC INFO: POLITICAL SCIENCE
www.blacknet.co.uk/education/polisci.html

INTERNET RESOURCES FOR POLITICAL SCIENCE, FROM THE MEMORIAL UNIVERSITY LIBRARIES
www.library.mun.ca/internet/subjects/polisci.php

Contributor Acknowledgments

The editors wish to thank the publishers and copyright holders for permission to reprint the selections in this book, which are listed below in order of appearance.

Issue 1

Robert Kagan, "The Benevolent Empire," *Foreign Policy* 111 (Summer 1998): 24–35. Reprinted with permission.

Richard Falk, "Will the Empire Be Fascist?" Transnational Foundation for Peace and Future Research. www.transnational.org (March 2003). Reprinted with permission.

Issue 2

Susan Strange, "The Erosion of the State," reprinted with permission from *Current History Magazine* 96, no. 613 (November 1997). © 1997, Current History, Inc.

Martin Wolf, "Will the Nation-State Survive Globalization?" Reprinted by permission of *Foreign Affairs* 80, no. 1 (January–February 2001). Copyright 2001 by The Council on Foreign Relations, Inc.

Issue 3

Samuel Huntington, "The Clash of Civilizations? The Next Pattern of Conflict" reprinted by permission of *Foreign Affairs* 72 no. 3 (Summer 1993). Copyright 1993 by the Council on Foreign Relations.

Douglas Alan Ross, "Ten Years After: The Inevitable Waning of Huntington's Civilizational Clash Theory?" © Nelson, a Thomson Company, 2003.

Issue 4

George W. Bush, *The National Security Strategy of the United States of America.* Found at www.whitehouse.gov/nsc/nss.pdf.

Neta C. Crawford, "The Slippery Slope to Preventive War," reprinted with permission from *Ethics and International Affairs* 17, no. 1 (March 2003): 30–36.

Issue 5

Jutta Brunnee, "The Use of Force against Iraq: A Legal Assessment," reprinted with permission from *Behind the Headlines* 59, no. 4 (Summer 2002): 1–8.

David Wingfield, "Why the Invasion of Iraq Was Lawful," reprinted with permission from *Behind the Headlines* 59, no. 4 (Summer 2002): 10–16.

Issue 6

Ernie Regehr, "Missile Proliferation, Globalized Insecurity, and Demand-Side Strategies," Waterloo: Project Ploughshares, *Ploughshares Monitor* (March 2001).

Frank P. Harvey, "The International Politics of National Missile Defence: A Response to the Critics," *International Journal* 55, no. 4 (Autumn 2000): 545–66.

Issue 7

Steven Meyer, "Carcass of Dead Policies: The Irrelevance of NATO," reprinted with permission of the author from *Parameters* (Winter 2003–2004): 83–97. The views expressed are personal ones and do not reflect the official policy or position of the National Defense University, the Department of Defense, or the U.S. government.

Rebecca Johnson and Micah Zenko, "All Dressed Up and No Place to Go: Why NATO Should Be on the Front Line in the War on Terror," reprinted with permission from *Parameters* (Winter 2002–2003): 48–63.

Issue 8

Francis Fukuyama, "Women and the Evolution of World Politics." Reprinted by permission of *Foreign Affairs* 77 (September–October 1998). Copyright 1998 by the Council on Foreign Relations, Inc.

J. Ann Tickner, "Why Women Can't Run the World: International Politics According to Francis Fukuyama," reprinted with permission from *International Studies Review* 1, no. 3 (Fall 1999).

Issue 9

Michael Chossudovsky, "Global Poverty in the Late 20th Century," reprinted with permission from *Journal of International Affairs* 52, no. 1 (Fall 1998): 293–312.

Gautam Sen, "Is Globalisation Cheating the World's Poor?" *Cambridge Review of International Affairs* 14, no. 1 (Autumn/Winter 2000): 86–106. Reprinted with permission.

Issue 10

Stephen Gill, "Toward a Postmodern Prince? The Battle of Seattle as a Moment in the New Politics of Globalization," reprinted with permission from *Millennium: Journal of International Studies* 29, no. 1 (2000): 131–40.

Jan Aart Scholte, "Cautionary Reflections on Seattle," reprinted with permission from *Millennium: Journal of International Studies* 29, no. 1 (2000): 115–21.

Issue 11

Thomas J. Courchene, "The Case for a North American Currency Union," reprinted with permission from *Policy Options* (April 2003): 20–25.

Andrew Jackson, "Why the 'Big Idea' Is a Bad Idea," reprinted with permission from *Policy Options* (April 2003): 26–28.

Issue 12

Kenneth Green, "Kyoto Krazy," and "Martin Joins the Kyoto Follies," reprinted with permission from www.fraserinstitute.ca/environment/index.asp?snav = en.

Désirée McGraw, "The Case for Kyoto: A Question of Competitiveness, Consultations, Credibility, Commitment and Consistency," reprinted with permission from *Policy Options* 24, no. 1 (December 2002–January 2003): 35–39.

Issue 13

Romilly Greenhill, "The Unbreakable Link—Debt Relief and the Millennium Development Goals," reprinted with permission from Jubliee Research @ nef (the new economics foundation) London. www.jubileeplus.org.

Denise Froning, "Will Debt Relief Really Help?" *The Washington Quarterly* 24, no. 3 (Summer 2001): 199–211. © 2001 by the Center for Strategic and International Studies (CSIS) and the Massachusetts Institute of Technology. Reprinted with permission.

Issue 14

Lloyd Axworthy, "Human Security: Safety for People in a Changing World," Ottawa: Department of Foreign Affairs and International Trade, 1999. Reproduced with the permission of the Minister of Public Works and Government Services, 2004.

William W. Bain, "Against Crusading: The Ethics of Human Security and Canadian Foreign Policy," reprinted with permission from *Canadian Foreign Policy* 6, no. 3 (Spring 1999): 85–98.

Issue 15

Douglas Cassel, "Why We Need the International Criminal Court," *Christian Century* 116, no. 15 (May 12, 1999). Copyright 1999 Christian Century Foundation. Reprinted with permission from the May 12, 1999, issue of the *Christian Century*. Subscriptions: $49/yr. from P.O. Box 378, Mt. Morris, IL 61054.

Alfred P. Rubin, "Some Objections to the International Criminal Court," *Peace Review* 12, no. 1 (2000), www.tandf.co.uk/journals/carfax/10402659.html. Reprinted with the permission of Taylor & Francis Ltd.

Issue 16

Joanna R. Quinn, "Truth Commissions and Restorative Justice." © Nelson, a Thomson Company, 2003.

Richard Ashby Wilson, "Challenging Human Rights as Restorative Justice." © Nelson, a Thomson Company, 2003.

Issue 17

Andrew Coyne, "The Case for Open Immigration: Why Opening Up Our Borders Would Be Good for the Country and Good for the Soul," reprinted from *The Next City* (Winter 1995), by permission of the author.

G.E. Dirks, "Why States Are Justified in Limiting Their Entry of Migrants." © Nelson, a Thomson Company,1998.

Issue 18

Frank Biermann, "Green Global Governance: The Case for a World Environment Organisation," reprinted with permission from *New Economy* 9, no. 2 (June 2002): 82–86.

Adil Najam, "The Case against a New International Environmental Organization," *Global Governance: A Review of Multilateral and International Organisations* 9, no. 3 (July–September 2003): 367–84. Copyright © 2003 by Lynne Rienner Publishers.